JAP

OKIN
& JAPAN'S SOUTHWEST ISLANDS

JO DAVEY

www.bradtguides.com

Bradt Guides Ltd, UK
The Globe Pequot Press Inc, USA

Bradt GUIDES
TRAVEL TAKEN SERIOUSLY

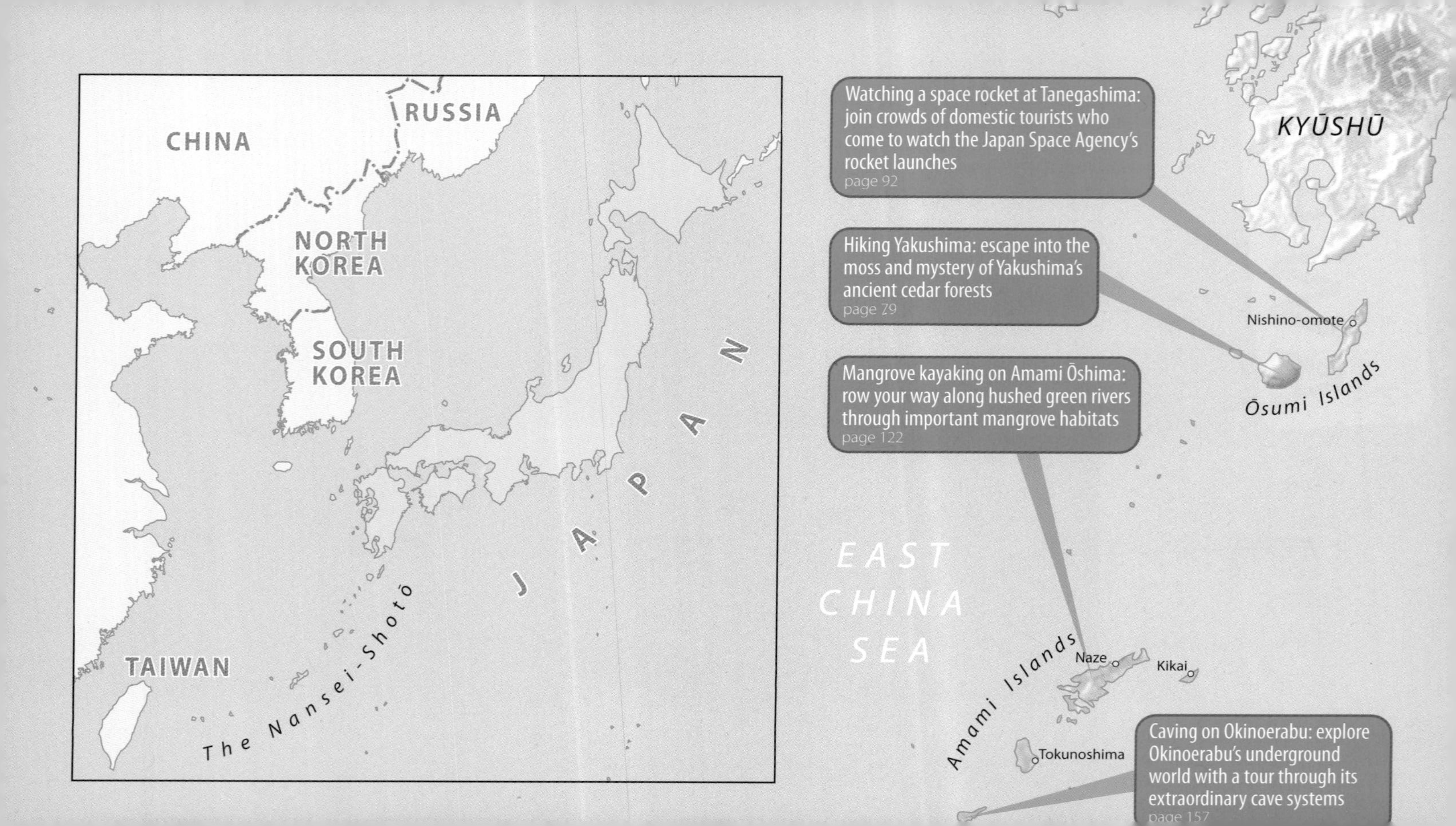
CHINA
RUSSIA
NORTH KOREA
SOUTH KOREA
TAIWAN
JAPAN
The Nansei-Shotō
EAST CHINA SEA
KYŪSHŪ
Nishino-omote
Ōsumi Islands
Amami Islands
Naze
Kikai
Tokunoshima
Watching a space rocket at Tanegashima: join crowds of domestic tourists who come to watch the Japan Space Agency's rocket launches
page 92
Hiking Yakushima: escape into the moss and mystery of Yakushima's ancient cedar forests
page 79
Mangrove kayaking on Amami Ōshima: row your way along hushed green rivers through important mangrove habitats
page 122
Caving on Okinoerabu: explore Okinoerabu's underground world with a tour through its extraordinary cave systems
page 157

Hiking Iriomote: disappear into Iriomote's wild, waterfall-filled jungle while hunting for the critically endangered yamaneko wild cat
page 330

Kabira Bay: enjoy the beauty of Ishigaki's Kabira Bay, with SUP tours, hidden beaches, mountain hiking and pearl shopping
page 302

Beaches on Yorontō: relax on blindingly white beaches that occasionally disappear beneath the glittering bright blue seas
page 168

History on Okinawa-hontō: discover the Ryūkyū culture through galleries and museums, and learn about the humbling horrors of World War II
page 173

Whales and turtles around Kerama: watch humpback whales raise their young in the waters around the Kerama and snorkel with sea turtles just off shore
page 233

Hammerhead diving from Yonaguni: sink into the rushing depths off Yonaguni's shore to sit among gathering hammerhead sharks
page 343

Taketomi Island: see old Ryūkyū life in Taketomi's preserved architecture, hunt for star sand on the beaches and go for a buffalo cart ride
page 306

Marine sports on Miyako: free dive, snorkel, scuba and surf on the archipelago's ultimate marine sports destination
page 264

Nago
Ishikawa
Koza (Okinawa City)
Naha
Kerama Islands
Okinawa Islands
Hirara
Yaeyama Islands
Miyako Islands
PACIFIC OCEAN

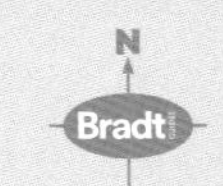

0 — 100km
0 — 50 miles

KEY
City
Town
International Airport

OKINAWA
& JAPAN'S SOUTHWEST ISLANDS
DON'T MISS...

TRADITIONAL CULTURE
Folk music is vital to island identity, with songs played on traditional instruments like the three-stringed sanshin PAGE 30
(PH/S)

WILDLIFE AND WILDERNESS
Yakushima's ancient forest is carpeted in hushed hiking trails and pillowy green moss; start exploring with the Shiratani Unsuikyō hike (pictured) PAGE 79
(GS/S)

MARINE SPORTS
The archipelago overflows with marine sports, including world-class snorkelling, scuba diving and whale watching PAGE 37
(tr/S)

HISTORY
Visit myriad museums and monuments on the Okinawan Islands, the battleground for the final stages of World War II; pictured here, Peace Memorial Park, Okinawa-hontō PAGE 191
(UA/S)

LOCAL CUISINE
Okinawan and Nansei-shotō cuisines are some of the healthiest in the world; tuck into classic dishes like *chanpuruu* stir fry PAGE 53
(Ko/S)

OKINAWA
& JAPAN'S SOUTHWEST ISLANDS
IN COLOUR

above (to/S) The symbol of the old Ryūkyū Kingdom, gorgeous Shuri Castle has been partly destroyed and reconstructed many times over PAGE 190

below left (SP/S) The kingdom's relationship with its oldest ally, China, is evidenced across Naha in architecture, arts, crafts, monuments and parks such as Fukushūen PAGE 190

below right (PH/S) Visit the World War II Japanese naval headquarters, a 450m-long tunnel complex where some 4,000 men were killed or committed suicide as the final battle ended PAGE 190

above (WS/D) The archipelago is covered in old castle ruins, including the well-preserved ramparts of Nakijin Castle on Okinawa-hontō PAGE 200

right (ml/S) Okinawa-hontō's north is given over to the deep green forests of Yanbaru PAGE 202

below (SB/S) The main thoroughfare of Okinawa's fun, sunlit capital, Naha, is Kokusai-dōri, where you can top up on trinkets and ice cream, browse markets and buy traditional crafts PAGE 189

AUTHOR

Jo Davey is a London-based freelance writer and photographer whose travels have taken her across six continents thus far. Her love for travel began and blossomed in Japan: within hours of landing in Tokyo, a naive 17-year-old proclaimed she would be back to live there one day. Eight years and several trips later, Jo found herself working in a restaurant outside Tokyo, training under a former Michelin-starred chef. She's usually found abroad, indulging one of her many interests: food, art, culture, language, nature, trekking, diving or festivals. When she's not scrambling her way around the world, she's writing about doing so or recreating the global dishes she comes across, with varying degrees of success.

AUTHOR'S STORY

Like every visitor to Japan, I had an image of the country compiled in my head and the Nansei-shotō wasn't it. Not once did visions of neon streets, anime fashion and scarlet temples morph into coral-rich seas, verdant untouched jungle or sand so white it shuts your eyes.

Then I visited the southwest islands in 2013 and my expectations of 'Japan' were blown out of their warm blue waters. The archipelago is a smorgasbord of colour and culture, food and folktales, and I was hooked. The Nansei-shotō has been surprising me ever since.

Unlike most first-timers to the islands, I hadn't actually come to see Okinawa-hontō. Instead, I was visiting a friend on Gerumajima, a tiny island in the Kerama to its west. I mostly ignored Okinawa-hontō as I headed straight from plane to ferry and on to a mini-island of impossible beauty, where my friend had been teaching for two years. It was his island life – idyllic, empyreal – that caught my attention. We laid on a jetty watching shooting stars, sang in a local restaurant while eating what I later discovered was shark pasta, and went squid fishing in the early morning off his pier. Who wouldn't come back for more?

Yet all this was merely scratching the surface. I visited again and again, and soon enough a banner of heart-rending history, myriad peoples, extraordinary geography and unique languages unravelled, fluttering from the mainland all the way down to Taiwan. Each of the archipelago's island groups feels, speaks, and looks wholly different; every island within them has its own character, tragedies, triumphs and history. The Nansei-shotō truly feels like Japan's final frontier, where English language only gets you so far and amenities open when the often ageing owners feel like it.

Adding to their mystery is the fact most Japan guidebooks dedicate minimal space to this archipelago, once an entirely separate kingdom in its own right. With no dedicated tourist guidebook, I needed little convincing to write one for Bradt. The world had other ideas: Covid hit in the middle of research, forcing me on the last flight out of Tokyo, and Japan's strict lockdowns kept me and the book at bay for years. Still, the excitement of setting foot on these islands once again kept me going, and will keep me going back for good.

First edition published July 2024
Bradt Travel Guides Ltd
31a High Street, Chesham, Buckinghamshire, HP5 1BW, England
www.bradtguides.com
Print edition published in the USA by The Globe Pequot Press Inc,
PO Box 480, Guilford, Connecticut 06437-0480

Project Manager: Elspeth Beidas
Cover research: Pepi Bluck, Perfect Picture

ISBN: 9781784776824

British Library Cataloguing in Publication Data
A catalogue record for this book is available from the British Library

Photographs Dreamstime.com: Jakub Michankow (JM/D), Nuvisage (N/D), Prayuth Gerabun (PG/D), Sean Pavone (SP/D), Watcharee Suphakitudomkarn (WS/D); Okinawa Convention & Visitors Bureau (OCVB); PIXTA: taku (t/P); Shutterstock.com: Beautifulblossom (B/S), Dan Giveon (DG/S), Dasian (D/S), EQRoy (EQR/S), Es75 (E/S), Feathercollector (F/S), Gary Saisangkagomon (GS/S), Gina Hsu (GH/S), Khun Ta (KT/S), Koenig_K (KK/S), Koi88 (Ko/S), machikophoto (ma/S), mmk_lab (ml/S), OTTO-FOTO (OF/S), PixHound (PH/S), Sean Pavone (SP/S), Shen Anwen (SA/S), shikema (sh/S), Songquan Deng (SD/S), Suchart Boonyavech (SB/S), tank200bar (ta/S), Tharuka Photographer (TP/S), torasun (to/S), tororo reaction (tr/S), Uwe Aranas (UA/S), Vlas Telino Studio (VTS/S), VTT Studio (VTTS/S), Yusuke Nishizawa (YN/S)

Front cover Looking over Shioya Bay from Ōgimi Village Observation Deck, Okinawa-hontō (t/P)
Back cover, clockwise from top left Shuri-jo, Okinawa-hontō (to/S); Yonaguni Atlas moth (VTS/S); Minna (SA/S); Shiratani Unsuikyō, Yakushima (GS/S)
Title page, clockwise from left Eisaa dancer (PG/D); Maehama Beach, Miyakojima (OCVB); hibiscus flower (E/S)
Part openers Page 67: Kabira Bay, Ishigakijima (sh/S); page 347: a busy street in Shinjuku, Tokyo (SD/S)

Maps David McCutcheon FBCart.S FRGS, assisted by Daniella Levin and Pearl Geo Solutions

Typeset by Ian Spick, Bradt Travel Guides Ltd
Production managed by Gutenberg Press Ltd; printed in Malta
Digital conversion by www.dataworks.co.in

Acknowledgements

The most important acknowledgement goes to my ever-patient and always generous family and friends, who may not have offered to hold my hand had they realised just how long they'd be required to do so. To my tirelessly supportive, funny and unstinting family Pat, Robin, Laura, CJ and Mark, for whom a sentence of thanks will never be enough; to all my friends, but particularly my cheerleading team of Sam Lewis, Amanda Smith, Heather McManus, Emma Citron and Sarah Chapman. Thanks also to those writer and editor friends, wherever they are in the world, who've made freelance life easier and more fun with their wit and occasional wisdom: particularly Neil Davey, Alex Mead, Jenny Linford and, of course, Jamie Lafferty.

Thanks to the entire Bradt team, especially Adrian Phillips for giving me this opportunity, and to Claire Strange and Elspeth Beidas for bearing with me for so long. Thanks also to Matt Joslin for all his help and humour. Special thanks to my comrade in the guidebook writing trenches, Tom Fay, who contributed the language appendix and helped keep me sane. Finally, I couldn't have done this book without the unstinting kindness and hospitality of friends and strangers in Japan, who passed me down the islands like an Olympic torch. There are too many to name – I hope you know who you are – but special thanks to Michael King, Shintaro Nagahara, Thomi Lee, Alex Bradshaw, Chuck Clenney, Tomo Morimoto, Hiroko Machida and Vivien Poon. イチャリバチョーデー。

FEEDBACK REQUEST

At Bradt Guides we're aware that guidebooks start to go out of date on the day they're published – and that you, our readers, are out there in the field doing research of your own. You'll find out before us when a fine new family-run hotel opens or a favourite restaurant changes hands and goes downhill. So why not tell us about your experiences? Contact us on 01753 893444 or e info@bradtguides.com. We will forward emails to the author who may post updates on the Bradt website at w bradtguides.com/updates. Alternatively, you can add a review of the book to Amazon, or share your adventures with us on social:

BradtGuides
BradtGuides & @Jo_davey
BradtGuides & @jodaveytravels

Contents

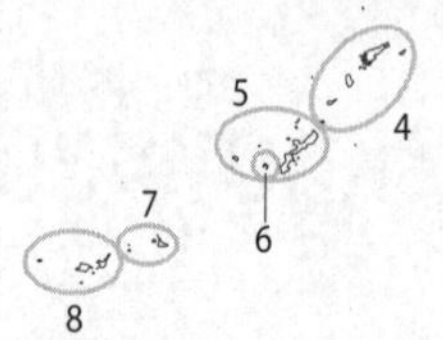

LIST OF MAPS

Introduction

If you've only been to or seen mainland Japan before, you can safely throw your expectations out the window when it comes to the Nansei-shotō. These southwest islands, as the name translates, are a huge surprise to everyone's image of Japan – which makes them a highly exciting exciting destination within an already immensely popular country.

For starters, the Nansei-shotō is geographically a world apart. Few people associate rainforests with Japan, yet the islands sit within the subtropical belt. Here you get not only rainforests but cloudforests, mangroves, wetlands, mountains, volcanoes, rivers, waterfalls and primeval forests, spread across myriad islands each with their own looks and personalities. And what's ubiquitous across the lot are beaches. Huge swathes of white and yellow and black sands that disappear into reef-rich waters of teal, cyan, navy, viridian; craggy coastlines with dramatic views that plunge into swirling currents. Each island comes with a slice of paradise and a piece of drama.

With such disparate habitats come remarkable flora and fauna. The archipelago has had five islands recognised by UNESCO for their biodiversity and import. Their isolated evolution has produced rare endemic species that form a huge part of island tourism, with treks and night hikes to spot creatures like the ancient Amami rabbit or the rare Iriomote cat.

Offshore, the islands really set themselves apart from Japan. While the mainland sits amid cooler oceans, the waters here are fed by warmer currents travelling up from dive spots like the Philippines and Taiwan. This results in migrations of great marine mammals like humpback whales, the presence of dolphins and dugongs, hammerhead sharks and manta ray collectives, large numbers of sea turtles and plentiful reefs full of tropical fish. The volcanic geology has created a playground of caves, stacks, arches and mysterious formations for divers to explore.

Culturally, the islands get even further from their neighbour – and coloniser. For centuries much of the archipelago was a separate and successful kingdom, only fully taken over by Japan in the late 19th century. This Ryūkyū Kingdom traded all across Asia, bringing in manifold influences not seen in the mainland. When Japan invaded, the islands were forced to assimilate, but laid-back Ryūkyū life could never fully integrate with traditional Japanese culture. Today the Nansei-shotō remains a different side of Japan, with its own quirks, culture and history.

One of these famous aspects is food. Okinawan cuisine is known worldwide as some of the healthiest on earth. The region is a Blue Zone, known for its longevity, which is to a great extent attributed to the cuisine. These islands are a gourmet treasure trove, combining aspects of different Asian foods and drinks from Japanese to Thai. Even between the northernmost and southernmost islands are large differences in dishes and ingredients – though the freshest seafood and sashimi can be found from top to bottom.

Undoubtedly there is a darker side to the Nansei-shotō. Those who have heard of Okinawa often associate it with war. When World War II's land invasion came to Japan, it came only to these islands. So recently annexed, its citizens should never have been part of the Imperial fight, yet they paid the ultimate price. History fans are inundated with memorials, museums, relics, ruins and untold stories across the island chain.

With such a wealth of interests, activities, nature and history, it's surprising the Nansei haven't garnered international tourist attention, outside of the main island of Okinawa-hontō. In some parts, tourism is essentially non-existent, giving a rare opportunity to experience unfettered Japanese life. Atop all this, the islands are remarkably safe, with a feeling of local community across the board. Whether visiting Japan for the first, second, third time or more, the Nansei-shotō more than earn their place on any itinerary. Few ever explore beyond their blue-green surface; those who do are privileged to know Japan in a wholly new light – prismatic, paradisiacal and overflowing with life.

KEY TO SYMBOLS

Symbol	Meaning	Symbol	Meaning
	Airport		Cave
	Tourist information		Golf course
	Museum/gallery		Waterfall
	Post office		Port
$	Bank		vLighthouse
	Hospital/clinic		Gardens
	Historic/important building		Mangrove
	Castle/fortifications		Tree/woodland feature
	Statue/monument		Beach
	Bar		Viewpoint/observatory
	Music venue		Summit (height in metres)
	Buddhist site		Other point of interest
	Shintō site		Monorail
	Cemetery/grave		Airport runway
	Tomb/mausoleum		Park
	Historic site/ruins		Built-up area
	Hot spring		

HOW TO USE THIS GUIDE

AUTHOR'S FAVOURITES Finding genuinely characterful accommodation or that unmissable off-the-beaten-track café can be difficult, so the author has chosen a few of her favourite places throughout the country to point you in the right direction. These 'author's favourites' are marked with a ✷.

PRICE CODES Throughout this guide we have used price codes to indicate the cost of those places to stay and eat listed in the guide.

Accommodation price codes Average price of a double room per night.

$$$$$	Over ¥18,400
$$$$	¥13,700–18,400
$$$	¥9,200–13,700
$$	¥4,600–9,200
$	Less than ¥4,600

Restaurant price codes Average price of a main course.

$$$$$	Over ¥3,800
$$$$	¥2,300–3,800
$$$	¥1,500–2,300
$$	¥800–1,500
$	Less than ¥800

JAPANESE NAMES There are multiple methods of Japanese to English romanisation. This book uses macron diacritics (eg: Ryūkyū) to indicate long vowels in Japanese words, as this will help with pronunciation. However, for ease of reading, these diacritics have been removed from words familiar to an English-speaking audience like tofu, sumo, Tokyo and Osaka. They have also not been used in Okinawan words (eg: *juushii*) or addresses, as major online map sources do not use them.

The majority of island businesses have Japanese (or local) language names. Where this is the case, the Japanese has been provided as many signs are in this original language and English will not be visible – the kanji is immensely useful for crosschecking. However, where the business only uses an English name, the Japanese has not been provided. See page 19 for further information on the Japanese language.

MAPS

Keys and symbols Maps include alphabetical keys covering the locations of those places to stay, eat or drink that are featured in the book. Note that regional maps may not show all hotels and restaurants in the area: other establishments may be located in towns shown on the map.

Part One

GENERAL INFORMATION

AT A GLANCE

Location West Pacific Ocean, southwest of Japan and northeast of Taiwan. The chain separates the East China Sea from the Philippine Sea.
Size 4,790km^2 (1,850 square miles)
Neighbouring countries No direct borders. Closest countries are Taiwan, China and South Korea.
Climate Humid subtropical and tropical rainforest
Status Republic
Capital and principal urban areas Naha, Ginowan, Ishigaki, Itoman, Hirara
Economy Agriculture, fishing and tourism
GDP ¥591.48 trillion (US$4.21 trillion; 2023)
Languages Japanese and 11 indigenous languages including Okinawan, Miyako and Yaeyama
Religion Ryūkyūan Shintōism, Shintōism, Buddhism
Currency Japanese Yen (¥)
Exchange Rate £1 = ¥197.65, US$1 = ¥155.64, €1 = ¥169.18 (May 2024)
International tel code +81
Time zone GMT/UTC +9 hours
Electricity and plugs 100V Type A socket
Weights and measures Metric
Flag The national flag of Japan is rectangular white with red circle in centre
National Anthem 'Kimigayo' ('His Imperial Majesty's Reign')

1

Background Information

GEOGRAPHY AND GEOLOGY

Comprising hundreds of islands, of which around 70 are inhabited, the Nansei-shotō curves from the southern tip of mainland Japan down towards the northeast coast of Taiwan. To its northwest, it's bordered by the East China Sea, to the southeast, the Pacific Ocean.

The highest point on the islands is Miyanouradake, a mountain on northerly Yakushima; covered in the island's dense forest, it reaches an altitude of 1,935m. Elsewhere, the archipelago's vast habitats include coastline, ocean, reefs, mangroves, wetlands, farmlands, forests, cloudforests, jungle and urban areas. It's famous for its beaches, translucent waters and wonderful marine life.

Despite the Nansei-shotō's 1,200km spread down the subtropics, its total area is really very little – and, of course, depends on who you ask. The generally accepted number is around 4,642–4,790km^2, a little smaller than Trinidad and Tobago, or a similar size to the city of Boston.

One of the reasons that size is hard to pin down is that no-one can actually agree on how many islands there are. The landscape itself doesn't help, every so often belching out a new little islet of volcanic grey. Arguments between Japan, South Korea and China over the ownership of tiny, uninhabited rocks also keep geographers (and international relations) on their toes. Nothing about this group of islands is set in stone.

NAMES The big hurdle in talking about the archipelago's geography is nomenclature: complex doesn't begin to cover it. There are over 15 different words in Japanese just to describe the varying island sections and subdivisions. Questions of politics, ownership and what even constitutes an island have combined to create a moniker minefield. Throw an unfamiliar language and script into the mix and unpicking the jumble is no easy feat – but it is rather necessary.

The name of the archipelago itself differs depending on where you're from. Americans usually opt for Okinawa, a broad name with no fewer than three definitions in the island chain. The British often go for the Ryūkyū Islands, a term coined from the original Ryūkyū Kingdom. This old-fashioned name can provoke amusement from Japanese people – like calling France 'Gaul'.

In Japanese, the archipelago is called the Nansei-shotō, 'the southwest island group', which is what this guide also uses. This incorporates the entire chain from the northeastern tip of Tanegashima to the southern and westernmost coasts of Hateruma and Yonaguni.

The islands within the Nansei-shotō are divided into myriad groupings, the simplest of which is the prefectural boundary across the middle. Japan has 47 prefectures (a jurisdiction similar to a county) known as *ken*, and the Nansei-shotō is made of two: Kagoshima-ken to the north and Okinawa-ken to the south.

Kagoshima-ken's section of the Nansei-shotō comprises the Ōsumi, Tokara and Amami island groups, collectively known as the Satsunan Islands. The Ōsumi islands are at the very top of the archipelago and contain Yakushima, one of its most famous islands. Despite this, the Satsunan are commonly overlooked or discounted from the chain because they don't belong to the better-known Okinawa Prefecture.

Okinawa-ken is Japan's southernmost prefecture and one of its poorest too. These lower islands are still referred to by geographers as the Ryūkyū Islands, named for the aforementioned kingdom that was eventually colonised by Japan. The Ryūkyū are subdivided into three groups: Okinawa, Miyako and the Yaeyama. In case that wasn't enough, Miyako and Yaeyama are collectively known as the Sakishima Islands.

Some smaller island groups, the Tokara, Senkaku and Daitō, do not feature in this book. This is due to their inaccessibility and remoteness, or their inability and disinclination to support tourism.

GEOLOGY The Nansei-shotō sits between two plates, on a boundary between the East China and Philippine seas. The archipelago was formed by tectonic deformation through subduction – the islands rising up as the Philippine Sea plate was pushed under the Eurasian plate, creating the massive submarine Ryūkyū Trench.

Under the turquoise it all gets a lot more complicated. The Nansei-shotō sits on a host of straits, troughs and trenches, dividing it further and changing the flora, fauna and geology as it goes. The islands are made of either coral reef limestone or metamorphic rock and, in general, get older the further south they spread.

The result of such complex tectonics is that the islands are a geographical miscellany. There are undulating, mountainous regions in Amami Ōshima, Iriomote and northern Okinawa-hontō. There are flat, low-lying sandy spits and coral islands, eroded over time to create cave systems, as well as beach islands so low they regularly disappear beneath the seas.

Naturally, where tectonic activity begins, earthquakes tend to follow. The largest earthquake recorded in the Ryūkyū Trench was a magnitude 7.5 in 1968. On average, the islands have about 60 tremors a year, but the majority pass without anyone even noticing, or only experiencing a small shudder. The last earthquake in the region to reach 7.0 on the Richter scale occurred just offshore of Okinawa-hontō in 2010. It collapsed some of the walls of Katsuren Castle, a UNESCO World Heritage Site, and injured two people.

Historically, the islands haven't always got off so lightly. The 1771 Great Meiwa earthquake caused rather weak ground shaking, but the resulting 30m-high tsunami killed around 12,000 people across Yaeyama and Miyako: a huge percentage of the population. The Nansei-shotō has suffered from other tsunamis, but not for many years.

CLIMATE

The Nansei-shotō is in the northern hemisphere, with cool winters peaking in January and hot summers around July, but it also falls in the subtropical belt. This means an inescapable mix of beautiful heat, close humidity, blistering sunshine and cooling rainfall.

Taking averages from Okinawa, the central-most group, August temperatures are around 30°C, with January's around 17°C. Overall, Okinawa's average annual temperature is 23°C.

SAKURA CHERRY BLOSSOMS

Think Japan and most people think cherry blossoms, or *sakura* – and despite their subtropical climes, the southwest islands are no exception. The stereotypical, pale-pink wild cherries grow north, in Kagoshima-ken, but Okinawa-ken is home to a darker pink species called the Taiwan cherry, or 'scarlet sakura'. The flowers are bolder and more bell-like, but some have mutated to be lighter and wider, mimicking the more traditional northern cherries.

The most important difference with these Taiwan cherry trees is that, unlike their wild mainland cousins, they bloom north to south – down the islands – rather than south to north. This is because they need some springtime cold in order to bloom, while the traditional cherry needs warmth. Consequently, the first place to see sakura isn't the warmer Yaeyama but northern Okinawa-hontō's Yanbaru area and the Amami Islands.

Okinawa announces the start of Japan's sakura season, when the sample tree in Naha's Sueyoshi Park first blooms. Okinawa-hontō also hosts the first cherry blossom festival, the Yaedake Sakura Matsuri, at Yaedake Sakuranomori Park in Motobu Town. This takes place from mid-January to early February. If you miss this one, there's another *sakura matsuri* in Nago, as well as others across the archipelago.

Though the islands aren't smothered in sakura like some of the mainland cities, there are plentiful places to have a *hanami* (flower viewing) party, which traditionally involves picnicking under the pink. Sueyoshi, Yogi, Yaedake and Nago Castle parks on Okinawa-hontō, and Suno Dam and Honcha Pass in Amami Ōshima, are great for catching the first blossoms. These initial flowers are called *kaika*, while full bloom – reached about a week later – is called *mankai*.

Temperatures are generally predictable in the archipelago; the weather, on the other hand, isn't so compliant. Confusingly, summers are both hot and wet, with the largest amount of sunshine, highest temperatures and greatest amount of rainfall. A very short rainy season (two to four weeks) starts in May–June, tapers off for July, then reappears around August–September. August is usually the hottest month and has the most rainfall, but these rains tend to be concentratedly brief. Yakushima, in the northernmost group, takes the rainfall crown as the wettest place in Japan – you'll want waterproofs here, just in case.

May–October is designated typhoon season, but the majority of storms take place towards September–October. November starts to cool off, though still has pleasant sunshine, while winters are nicely chilled, with increased cloud cover and wind but far less rain. Spring comes early here: thanks to the islands' southerly location, they're actually the first place in Japan to see sakura, with the pretty pink cherry blossoms flowering in late January instead of Tokyo's March–April time.

NATURAL HISTORY AND CONSERVATION

The natural history of these islands is remarkable for a few reasons. Firstly, when the Okinawa Trough formed in the late Miocene period, the island chain separated from mainland China and Japan, isolating species upon it. Some of these evolved uniquely, forging an independent evolutionary path that's led to large numbers of endemic species in a very small region. Indeed, the islands are Japan's most biodiverse biome.

The most notable examples are the five areas collectively recognised by UNESCO for their endemic biodiversity and high global value: Amami Ōshima, Tokunoshima (north and south), north Okinawa-hontō (Yanbaru) and Iriomote. Their combined uninhabited 42,698ha cover subtropical rainforests and contain a huge number of endemic species across plants, mammals, reptiles, amphibians, birds, inland fish and crustaceans, many of which are threatened or endangered. Two species in particular, the Amami rabbit and Ryūkyū long-haired rat, have ancient lineages, with no living relatives anywhere else on earth. Even each of the four islands has its own species not found on the others.

Further north, Yakushima was among the first of Japan's UNESCO World Heritage listings. Yaku has over 2,060 species and subspecies within its circular shore, including ancient specimens of Japanese cedar. Its ancient forest is unique to the region, partly because of where it sits in relation to the Watase Line or Tokara Gap, a major boundary between the Palearctic and Indomalayan biogeographic realms. The line's exact placement is a hot topic of biogeographic debate, but it essentially cuts the archipelago in half, affecting both fauna and flora. The species found in the Ōsumi and Yakushima differ greatly compared to elsewhere in the islands, thanks to this split.

On top of this, the Nansei-shotō is affected by the Kuroshio: a warm ocean current that flows northwards, bringing nutrients and warmth from the Philippines up past Taiwan to the archipelago. This mixing of oceans creates an incredibly rich marine ecosystem, home to a biodiverse array of mammals, reptiles, cephalopods, corals, fish and crustaceans. Interestingly, the coral reefs in the Kuroshio's path are also at a higher latitude than any other on the planet.

FLORA Plants rule supreme across the archipelago and the difference in species from mainland Japan is instantly noticeable. Here, the subtropics take over, with palm trees, bright pink bougainvillea, tortuous climbing figs, and enormous-leafed alocasia.

Yakushima is known for its primeval temperate rainforest, a rare ecosystem at this latitude. It's also one of the last vestiges of a habitat that used to cover Asia but has been greatly deforested elsewhere. Thanks to Yaku's steep ascendency from sea to high-reaching peaks, the island has a broad range of plant systems, from coastal and low-lying subtropical vegetation, along montane temperate rainforest, up to high moors and cold temperate bamboo grasslands. Its montane rainforest is particularly unique as its plants have adapted to excessively high rainfall and humidity.

Among Yaku's 1,900 species and subspecies of plants are the Japanese cedars known as Yakusugi, many of which are over 3,000 years old and have remarkable diameters. They also include the Yakushima rhododendron, the Yakushima gentian, and the Yakushima white pine tree, which is also found on neighbouring Tanegashima and was used for dugout canoes.

The archipelago's other UNESCO region, from Amami to Iriomote, has an incredibly rich floral biodiversity, with over 1,819 vascular plants. Here, subtropical rainforests give way to important mangroves, wetlands and coastlines. Native to these lower islands are sharp-fronded Sago palm cycads, tanibuta citrus (*citrus ryukyuensis*), the Okinawa pine, Ryūkyūan oak, Japanese banana, Easter lily, Ryūkyū juniper and plentiful orchids and flowering shrubs. Alongside these sit innumerable island-specific endemic plants, such as the Yaeyama palm (*satakentia liukiuensis*) and Amami violet.

FAUNA These islands never saw large predators, so their animals were left to evolve in isolation. The result is a wonderful mix of species across the archipelago. Birdlife is prolific, including the endemic Amami woodcock, Lidth's jay, Okinawa rail, Okinawa and Ryūkyū robins, Amami and Okinawa woodpeckers, Ryūkyū green pigeon and Amami thrush. The Ryūkyū minivet, a previously endemic species, has since spread its wings toward mainland Japan too.

Amphibians abound, with around half of all those found here endemic. The plentiful frog species include Hallowell's tree frog, Otton frog, Ishikawa's frog, Holst's frog, Ryūkyū brown frog, Ryūkyū tip-nosed frog and the rare Kampira Falls frog, found in the Yaeyama and Taiwan. Newts include the sword-tailed newt and Anderson's crocodile newt.

Reptiles are similarly numerous; endemic lizards include the Miyako and Sakishima grass lizards, Kuroiwa's ground gecko, and a wealth of skinks. Endemic species of the latter include Kishinoue's giant skink, Boettger's ground skink, Stimpson's skink, the Okinawa blue-tailed skink and the Ryūkyū short-legged skink. The Okinawa tree lizard is found here and in Taiwan.

Ophiologists can have a field day in the archipelago: endemic venomous snakes include four species of habu pit viper (three endemic to the islands, the fourth found in Kagoshima too), the Japan coral snake and Iwasaki's temperate Asian coral snake. Non-venomous endemic snakes include the Amami odd-scaled snake, Sakishima green snake, Ryūkyū green snake, Ryūkyū odd-tooth snake, a subspecies of red large-tooth snake, Yaeyama keelback, Pryer's keelback, and Pfeffer's reed snake. There are also Formosan odd-scaled snakes and different species of rat snakes, while black-banded sea kraits are prolific in the waters.

On land lives the endemic Ryūkyū black-breasted leaf turtle, while marine turtle species like loggerhead, green and hawksbill use the islands for nesting and breeding. Leatherback and olive ridley turtles inhabit the waters around the islands and supposedly don't breed here, though twice leatherback nests have been found on Amami Ōshima.

The seas also see whales, dolphins, porpoises, sharks and, most incredibly, dugongs. The subpopulation of Okinawa dugongs is incredibly rare and horrifically threatened: their extinction in the region is said to be inevitable. Also under threat is the Sekisei Lagoon – Japan's largest coral reef, between Ishigaki and Iriomote – which has seen 90% of its coral bleached due to pollution and climate change.

Endemic mammals include the Yakushika deer, Yaku macaque, the critically endangered Iriomote *yamaneko* cat (page 322), Amami black rabbit, Ryūkyū long-tailed giant rat, three types of Ryūkyū spiny rats and the Ryūkyū shrew. There's also the Ryūkyū or Erabu flying fox, which is native to the islands as well as Taiwan and northern Philippines. Insect species are abundant, with 1,607 endemic species in the UNESCO sites of Amami, Tokunoshima, Okinawa and Iriomote alone. Yakushima by itself is host to 1,900 insect species.

CONSERVATION One of the reasons UNESCO recognised Amami Ōshima, Tokunoshima, north Okinawa-hontō (Yanbaru) and Iriomote as a World Heritage Site is that they are in one of the 200 ecoregions considered most vital for global biodiversity conservation. Yakushima's conservation efforts, meanwhile, have been decades in the making. Once threatened by logging, the island is now more at risk from the impact of tourism, which it is taking steps to mitigate.

With large numbers of endangered and critically endangered species in the archipelago, as well as some that have already gone extinct, conservation is increasingly important. Challenges include protecting the Iriomote yamaneko cat, whose usual hunting grounds have been bisected by deadly roads, and the critically endangered and endangered Amami black rabbit and Ryūkyū spiny rats, which are at risk of predation, often from feral or house cats. Mongooses introduced in some islands to cull habu populations have also proven incredibly problematic for these species, but thankfully efforts to eradicate the invasive mongoose are proving largely successful.

US military The US military presence has undoubtedly been and continues to be harmful to conservation. Toxic environmental pollution including diesel and sewage spills that have contaminated waters, construction that has destroyed and threatened habitats, and ongoing expansion have done untold damage to Nansei-shotō ecology and wildlife.

Yanbaru, now a UNESCO-certified area of endangered wildlife, is host to the 7,500ha US Jungle Training Warfare Centre – an area expanded in 2016, leading to 24,000 trees being felled and loss of habitat for the rare Okinawa rail.

In the past 25 years there have been over 415 incidents of toxic spills or dumping from US military facilities. The result – disputed by some – is that Okinawa has found levels of PFAS (so-called 'forever chemicals') in waters surrounding US bases that are up to 42 times the safety standard. In April 2020, a barbecue at Futenma base saw 140,000 litres of PFAS firefighting foam accidentally released into the vicinity, which ran off into local streams.

The new Henoko base, being reclaimed atop a marine area, has been lambasted by marine experts. Sited on a fragile seabed that's vulnerable to earthquakes, the base will likely cause extensive damage to marine ecosystems and species. Sea turtles will lose egg-laying grounds, seabird nesting sites and feeding grounds are threatened, and endangered corals will be harmed in clearance.

Okinawa's small population of dugongs is particularly affected; their feeding grounds have already been decimated by development and runoff, while the species itself is threatened as bycatch, US military training activities and underwater disposal of undetonated explosives. Three of the critically endangered, rarely sighted dugongs have been spotted in the very bay where Henoko base is being built – it's one of their few remaining seagrass feeding sites.

ARCHAEOLOGY

PEOPLE The islands are usually separated into three prehistoric cultural sections: the Ōsumi in the north, the Amami and Okinawan groups in the centre, and the Miyako and Yaeyama (Sakishima) islands in the south.

It's uncertain when humans first appeared here and from where; archaeological finds suggest there were multiple methods of immigration into the Nansei-shotō. In Gushigami village on Okinawa-hontō, remains of the so-called Minatogawa people have been dated to around 17,000 years ago. It's believed these Palaeolithic humans crossed over on a land bridge from continental China. The Yamashita-chō Cave 1 in Naha, formed around 37,000 years ago, held deer and human bones, the latter dated to 32,000 years ago. These are the oldest human remains in Japan.

On Miyako, the Pinza-Abu Cave Man dates back to around 30,000 years ago, and is suspected to have been from a people who travelled from Malaysia or Java. In 2017, a full skeleton dating back 27,000 years was discovered in Ishigaki in the Yaeyama. Findings on the Yaeyama suggest they were fully settled some 3,900–4,500 years ago, with people most likely coming from Taiwan and neighbouring southern areas.

CULTURE The northern groups were influenced by the Jōmon and Yayoi cultures of the mainland, especially the Ōsumi, which were then still attached to the mainland. Their reach spread south to Okinawa, influencing the independent cultures already there: Jōmon pottery from Kyūshū has been found as far down as Okinawa-hontō but no further.

Prehistoric sites in the Sakishima have revealed no influence from mainland culture. Instead, there's evidence they were influenced by Indonesian, Taiwanese and Philippine cultures. Stone adzes (axes) are commonly excavated and differ across the Nansei-shotō, with those in the southernmost islands demonstrating a polishing style native to southeast Asia.

Shell adzes were typically made from huge clam shells and were used in the Sakishima 900–2,000 years ago. The only similar tools found are from the Philippines and Micronesia, further suggesting ties with these southerly nations. The abundant number of shells in the Nansei-shotō made for a booming trade in shell objects to the mainland, called 'The Shell Road', which lasted some 800 years. Recent digs on Hokkaidō have revealed shell decorations made in the Nansei-shotō, showing the extent of their reach.

Early Jōmon (8,000–10,000 years ago) remains are always found around coastlines and beaches, indicating a people reliant on fishing and the sea. Ruins from the middle to late Jōmon period (around 3,000–5,000 years ago) were larger and more numerous than earlier periods, with archaeological finds moving inland. Okinawan culture really bloomed during the late Jōmon period, with unique earthenware and

UNUSUAL FINDS

The islands aren't an internationally known site for archaeology, largely due to the language barrier as findings go untranslated. However, there have been some uniquely fascinating discoveries in the region. Artificial cranial deformation, which was common in surrounding countries, has also been found in a single instance in Japan: Tanegashima (page 91). This site was a continuous settlement of the Hirota people between the final Yayoi and the late Kofun periods (3rd–7th centuries CE). All of the skeletons excavated there were found to have artificial cranial deformations, with the skull flattened at the back. Given there was no evidence of this practice elsewhere in Japan, it appears particular to Hirota residents.

Korea, the Philippines and the Oceanic Islands were all known for their artificial cranial deformation at the time, but it seems most likely that the practice would have come from the Philippines, given Tanegashima's orientation and its southern trade. Hirota skeletons were also shorter than the continental and Kyūshū peoples of the period – none exceeded 154cm – and appear closer to Philippine peoples of the time.

The Hirota people also had a unique material culture different from any other Japanese island. Among their belongings were found almost 3,000 pieces of shell jewellery, imported from the southern Amami and Okinawan islands. They were interred in stone-covered graves atop coastal dunes, which contained multiple burials – the southernmost excavation site uncovered up to 157 individuals in an area of just 230m^2. These individuals were buried with glass beads and thousands of shell accessories unparalleled in the archipelago, including elaborate necklaces, engraved pendants, bracelets, spoons and vessels. Blocks of coral and cobbles had been lined up as grave markers.

butterfly-shaped bone products. These bones were typically dugong jaws that had geometric patterns carved on to them with holes for thread, suggesting they were accessories or charms. The late Jōmon period also showed signs of contact with mainland China.

The final Jōmon period (some 2,300–3,000 years ago) saw villages and rudimentary farming established, with increasing exchanges between the north and central groups and Kyūshū. In the Yayoi period, (1,700–2,300 years ago) copper tools started to arrive, believed to indicate overseas trading. Rice cultivation and production was made much easier by the introduction of foreign iron implements during this period. These tools also helped in the construction of castles, walls and weapons, playing an important role in cultural and economic development.

HISTORY

For such a small area, the Nansei-shotō has been through an astonishing, sometimes sickening amount. What became a massive Asian trading hub ended in the blasts and bombs of World War II's finale; today it's an oft-overlooked area in one of the world's most advanced countries.

Each island has its own history, noted in individual sections, but understanding their combined history largely comes down to colonisation. The northernmost Kagoshima islands are the simplest; little is known about the Ōsumi before their early colonisation by the mainland – from then on, they followed Japan's history. The three southernmost island groups, which form today's Okinawa Prefecture, eventually formed the Ryūkyū Kingdom. In between the two sit the Amami, colonised by both mainland and Ryūkyū powers.

EARLY CHRONICLES China makes first mention of the archipelago around 200BCE; it called the islands the Liuqiu, which would later become Ryūkyū. They pegged the place as a land of 'happy immortals' and sent repeated expeditions out to explore, setting off various social and cultural changes. A 610CE expedition demanded the islands submit to Chinese rule, but islanders are said to have fought them off.

Contemporaneous chronicles from Japan show contact with the islands, mentioning that they seemed to follow the Chinese emperor. When the Japanese emperor sent soldiers to explore the islands in 698CE, they are thought to have reached as far as Amami's Tokunoshima whose locals visited the mainland to pay tribute to the emperor. Tanegashima and Yakushima were brought under Japanese administration in the first years of the 8th century. The islands then became known in Japan as Nantō, the 'Southern Islands'.

Emissaries from Japan to China began stopping at the archipelago in the mid 700s, when it's first mentioned as a trade stop. It eventually became a massive intermediary seafaring trading kingdom, thanks to longstanding connections with China, Korea and Japan. Exposure to these countries would eventually influence Ryūkyū Kingdom culture.

MAINLAND CLANS The politically powerful Heike family, also known as the Taira, emerged on the mainland in the 9th century. Related to the Japanese emperor, they were eventually ousted by a rival family in 1186. The Heike fled to the islands, making the archipelago their exiled home – you'll see their name cropping up all over the Nansei.

In the mid 1100s, the Ōsumi region was subsumed by the Shimazu family's domain, known as Satsuma – yes, that Satsuma. The area (now part of modern-day

Kagoshima-ken) was where the small citrus was first exported to the west, lending the fruit its name. Unfortunately, this has had the unintended effect of rendering the once-fearsome Shimazu domain rather amusing in Western eyes.

By the 1200s, the Shimazu ruled some 12 islands including the Ōsumi and Tokara islands, but not Tanegashima, which was ruled by the Tanegashima clan. In 1300, the Shimazu reached further south and subdued the Amami Islands, bringing their conquered islands up to 18.

Tanegashima remained aloof and alone, alternatively clashing and colluding with the Shimazu. Eventually in 1415, the Shimazu handed over Yakushima and Kuchinoerabu to the Tanegashima family. The Tanegashima clan retained control of their eponymous island into the 1500s, as Portuguese traders introduced firearms to Japan, but eventually they became a vassal of the Shimazu, who then controlled the northern islands entirely.

OKINAWA'S UNIFICATION Prior to 1429, Okinawa was divided into three kingdoms known as the Sanzan (Three Mountains): Hokuzan, Chūzan and Nanzan. The kingdoms were unified when the central and economically strongest Chūzan, led by King Shō Hashi, conquered its neighbours. This was the birth of the Ryūkyū Kingdom.

By the middle of the 1400s, the kingdom appeared to rule parts of the Tokara Islands, as well as Kikaijima and Amami. The Shimazu tried to retake Amami but failed, while the locals rebelled against their conquerors. The end of the 1400s saw the kingdom head south, trading with Miyako and the Yaeyama. Miyako was next to be brought under Ryūkyū control.

The 1500s saw Yaeyama infighting and the Akahachi rebellion. Akahachi was a Yaeyama chieftain loved among the southern islands. He refused to pay tribute to the Ryūkyū Kingdom and is thought to have made moves to conquer Miyako. In turn, the kingdom asked the Miyako chief to quell Akahachi's forces; he did, finally bringing the Yaeyama under Ryūkyū control.

At this time, the kingdom's income was heavily based in trade, so its economy was tied to Japanese and Chinese markets. Not only did the kingdom make its own products, it acted as a go-between, selling Chinese products to Japan and Japanese products to China. To ease these relationships, the kingdom paid regular tribute to its neighbouring countries.

SATSUMA INVASION In 1609, the Shimazu invaded the Ryūkyū Kingdom on behalf of the Tokugawa shōgun, a de facto military dictator ruling Japan at the time. The Shimazu forced their way south, taking island after island from Amami down. The then Ryūkyū King, Shō Nei, tried to broker peace; the result was that he had to swear fealty to Satsuma, but could retain his position as monarch.

This was important to Satsuma too. China had refused to trade with Japan, so it was vital that Ryūkyū appeared to still be in control of its own trade. Ryūkyū's relationship with China remained strong; the seas were alive with boat traffic, trade and cultural exchange between the two nations.

Satsuma rule introduced staunch travel restrictions and the head tax: a harsh system whereby the amount of tax demanded was fixed per person, regardless of income. In the islands, once you reached a certain height, you were expected to contribute. The amount of tax demanded by Satsuma, often paid in materials, crafts and crops, was so high that it led to famine and death across the islands. Sugar production began in the 17th century, becoming a huge crop in the archipelago and a hefty part of tax payment.

In 1624, Tokugawa gave the Amami and Tokara islands to Satsuma, fixing their future prefectural boundary as part of Kagoshima.

MEIJI RESTORATION Relationships with the great powers of China and Japan helped keep it afloat, but the Ryūkyū Kingdom struggled. In the 1800s, farmers and villages were drowning under massive tax obligations, suffering famines and exhaustion, and finances began to fail. The kingdom incurred debt to meet its obligations, but this was not its biggest problem.

England's industrial revolution and expansion into Asia resulted in the 1842 Opium War and the defeat of China's Qing Dynasty. The loss of such a large Asian power and trading partner was felt throughout the Ryūkyūs and East Asia. Meanwhile, ships from Europe and America came to the floundering Ryūkyū Kingdom and began to demand trade rights and permission to send in Christian missionaries. The Ryūkyū refused; the closed-door policy of the shōgun forbade missionary work. Despite this, both France and Britain forcibly sent missionaries into Ryūkyū in 1844 and 1846, but the government prevented them from winning converts.

In 1874, long-standing tribute relations between China and Ryūkyū ended. Five years later, the new Meiji government – made up of politicians from Satsuma and Chōshū domain who governed under the newly restored power of the emperor – finally annexed and ended the Ryūkyū Kingdom. Its king moved to Tokyo and the islands became Okinawa Prefecture. China rejected the Japanese invasion of its long-term ally, but after being defeated in the First Sino-Japanese War by Japan in 1895, China was forced to hand over Taiwan and any claims to the Ryūkyū. To this day, there are disputes over ownership of some of the uninhabited islands.

The Meiji government initiated full-on erasure of Ryūkyū culture, including language, religion, and indigenous practices like tattooing (page 18). The Great Depression after World War I and the Great Kanto Earthquake of 1923 resulted in Japan's Shōwa Depression, which devastated Okinawa-ken. This era was known locally as the 'Cycad Hell', after the local poisonous palms islanders had to eat to stay alive (page 111). Taxes, typhoons and famine at this time forced many to leave Okinawa-ken and also spurred socialist movements.

WORLD WAR II One of the most important things to remember about the Nansei-shotō is that when World War II came to the islands, many of them had only recently been annexed by Japan. Locals still didn't see themselves as Japanese, and Japan didn't embrace them as their own either. Yet Japan's land war wasn't fought on the mainland but in Okinawa.

During Japan's colonial expansion, the empire conquered huge numbers of Pacific islands to use as defensive positions, keeping Allied troops far from the mainland. Throughout the war, America and its allies took those islands back at great human cost – tiny places made famous by bloodshed like Iwo Jima, Guadalcanal and Peleliu. Okinawa was the final hurdle, where Japan had formed its biggest defence hub of 100,000 army personnel. Okinawa-hontō was the keystone to Japan's collapse; if Allied troops could take the island, they would come within airstrike reach of the mainland.

Japan wanted to keep the US distracted with Okinawa while they scrambled together troops for a mainland invasion. By 1944, the war had grown close enough that Japan realised defeat was likely, but those in charge hoped to use the bloody battles of Okinawa as a bargaining chip. The harder and more costly the fighting in Okinawa, the more they could use for negotiating. In short, Okinawa was to be sacrificed for a better surrender.

Some 157,000 US Marines and 1,500 warships were stationed offshore. Warplanes made the first fast-carrier raid on Okinawa-hontō on 10 October 1944, a ferocious attack that effectively destroyed Naha. These airstrikes grew in strength and number, so much so that they became known as the 'regular run' on Okinawa-hontō. The destruction was so relentless that a reconnaissance flight leader stated he had 'never seen so many planes over one target at the same time'.

Between January and March 1945, the US navy sank more enemy craft than any navy in history, using submarines and ships to cut off vital supplies and reinforcements. The Kerama were the first to be taken by the US, and used as a base for the major Okinawa-hontō incursion. The fighting on Okinawa-hontō itself was some of the most vicious and violent, including famous battles like that of Hacksaw Ridge.

Civilians were regularly caught in the crosshairs, but they weren't just killed in active fighting. Japanese headquarters stated that anyone speaking a language other than Japanese – including the local languages – would be treated as a spy and killed. It was a death knell for many of the islanders, for whom Japanese still wasn't their spoken language. It's said that Japanese troops murdered civilians for food and water, as well as anyone who tried to surrender to the US. Japanese propaganda had already claimed that US soldiers would torture and rape captured civilians, leading many islanders to choose suicide.

POST-WAR US RULE The new Japanese constitution, created by Allied powers and reviewed by Japanese scholars, didn't come into affect until 1947. With no constitution from either the US or Japan to protect them, exploitation and cruelty was rife in the islands. Right after the Battle of Okinawa, local people were held in concentration camps, while land was taken for US military use – much of which was never returned. The military bulldozed battlefields, villages and farmlands to build over 80 bases across the islands.

After the dust had cleared, the US military was given governance of the islands from Amami down. They controlled the media in Okinawa, quashed resistance and rebellion, denied passports to those who criticised the government and elected officials on locals' behalf. The islands were used for US wars in both Korea and Vietnam, the latter making Kadena Air Base one of the busiest airports on the planet at the time.

More than 50,000 islanders were employed by the US military: doing dangerous and deadly work on bases, playing enemies in war games, working aboard naval ships, or being sent to Vietnam to drive buses. Locals died under US service in a war many of them opposed. Violent incidents also started to occur, with multiple instances of locals being robbed, raped, attacked and killed by American troops. Accidents happened too; famously, two children died after a crane ran over one and another was crushed by a parachuted vehicle.

Many locals did become friendly with the troops, whom they worked beside each day. Still, anti-base demonstrations grew fervent, and the US faced problems elsewhere with Russia. When the treaty came up for renewal in 1972, Okinawa was handed back to Japan. In the agreement, the US managed to keep their bases but hand over costs and upkeep to Japan. Japan promised to reduce the islands' base numbers to that of the mainland – but this never happened.

Okinawa-hontō still hosts over half the US forces in Japan. There remains consistent tension about the American presence in Okinawa, with accidents and a handful of brutalities still taking place. Furthermore, planned base expansions are set to destroy important marine ecosystems (page 8), adding ecological tensions to already strained socio-political ones.

GOVERNMENT AND POLITICS

THE GOVERNMENT Since 1947, the Japanese government has been split into three branches: judicial, legislative and executive. Legislative powers such as passing laws, controlling the budget and foreign treaties are controlled by the Diet, which is elected and consists of the House of Representatives and the House of Councillors. House of Representative members are elected for four years and councillors for six.

The Diet also elects the prime minister, usually the leader of the party with the most Diet seats. The cabinet, organised and run by the prime minister, holds executive power. The justice system is completely independent of the other branches of government and is headed by a Supreme Court.

Japanese citizens over the age of 20 can vote. Since 1955, the conservative Liberal Democratic Party (LDP) has overwhelmingly controlled the government. In 2009, however, the LDP lost its majority to the Democratic Party of Japan, who briefly appointed their own prime minister before losing to the LDP the following year.

THE IMPERIAL FAMILY As well as a prime minister-led government, Japan has an emperor. The Japanese imperial family is believed to be the longest direct descent monarchy in the world. The emperor is said to be a direct descendant of the sun goddess; in Japanese his title is Tennō, meaning 'heavenly sovereign'. Prior to World War II, the emperor held absolute power as a divine being; everything that occurred in the war was laid at then-Emperor Hirohito's feet. Only after Japan's defeat did Hirohito renounce imperial divinity, mostly at the demand of the US.

The post-war constitution redefined the emperor and gave sovereignty to the people, creating a democracy. The emperor became a symbol with no real political power. Succeeding emperors have shown no interest in restoring their power or divinity, particularly the humble Emperor Akihito, father of the current Emperor Naruhito.

The imperial family has been vehement about Japan's culpability in the war. It's believed there was friction between Emperor Akihito and recently assassinated Prime Minister Shinzo Abe, due to Abe's revisionist beliefs. After convicted war criminals were enshrined at Yasukuni (a Tokyo shrine to war dead), the imperial family ceased paying tribute there. Several prime ministers continued to go, including Abe.

Historically, women were allowed to be emperors and eight were. The post-Meiji era system changed the law to state that the succession had to be male to male. This law has caused real problems for the imperial family, and there are ongoing discussions about reverting back to the old system.

JAPANESE CALENDAR

Although Gregorian calendars are understood and used in Japan, Japanese years are based on the emperor. Each emperor is given an era title for the duration of their rule, which becomes their name after death. The current era, started in 2019, is Reiwa; before that it was Heisei for Akihito, Shōwa for Hirohito. The year is confusingly calculated from the date of the emperor's ascension to the throne. As Emperor Naruhito ascended in May 2019, May–December 2019 is known as Reiwa 1; the first part of 2019 was Heisei 31. Japan is the only country in the world to still use an era name system.

MILITARY The 1947 constitution stated Japan could never again maintain armed forces for aggression. Instead, national security would be achieved through international security arrangements with the US. However, after the outbreak of the Korean War in 1950, Allied occupation forces suggested that Japan gather a 'self-defence force'. In 1960 and 1970, a treaty between Japan and the US allowed the latter to operate military bases in Japan (page 13), the majority of which are on Okinawa-hontō.

ECONOMY

Farming was an important economy in the pre-modern Ryūkyū Kingdom. Between the 10th and 14th centuries, trade between East Asian countries boomed with the archipelago at its centre. Stretching between Japan and Taiwan, with China, Korea and the Philippines bordering, the islands competed with each other for trade.

When they were united as the Ryūkyū Kingdom, they became an incredibly successful trading hub, mostly through China with whom they had a great relationship. The kingdom swore allegiance to the Ming dynasty, allowing them to engage in trade. For a long time, the kingdom was an intermediary and a powerhouse in the Pacific, trading as far as the kingdoms of Palembang (Sumatra), Java (Indonesia), Siam (Thailand) and Malacca (Malaysia).

Goods included Ryūkyū products and sulphur, ceramics and silk from China, crafts from Japan, cotton and ginseng from Korea, and luxury products from southeast Asia such as dyes, spice, ivory and alcohol. The kingdom's vast trading network kept it from total colonisation for a while. Though it was invaded in the early 1600s, with northern islands Amami falling under Satsuma control, the southern islands were allowed some autonomy so Satsuma could make use of Ryūkyūan trade ties with China. Japan wasn't allowed to directly trade with China itself.

After the kingdom and its economy was fully colonised, Japan made a calculated effort to cut Okinawan ties to the old Ryūkyū Kingdom and China. To avoid local rebellion, Japan kept the old kingdom systems of land and taxation, gaining immense profit from taxes. The result of this stasis was that while the rest of Japan surged forward culturally, technologically and financially, Okinawa Prefecture got left behind.

Meanwhile, Japan had been to war with China and Russia, and entered an economic recession that lasted until the outbreak of World War I. This saw European powers in the region returning to Europe, creating a gap that allowed Japan to monopolise the Asian market. While Japan exported iron, medicine and munitions, Okinawa also profited from sugar exports.

However, the Shōwa Depression and several natural disasters after World War I hugely affected island economy. When World War II followed, the Japanese economy's production and growth was set back by nearly two decades. The Japanese people met disaster with dedication and diligence. New production and modernisation began a second period of economic development. During the occupation, the US invested almost $2 billion in food, industry and transport.

Japan's recovery seemed miraculous, and in some ways was. An economic bubble in the late 1980s sent the Japanese stock exchange sky high: financial speculation, risky bank loans and real estate prices also rocketed. The crash in the 1990s – known as the lost decade – hit the country incredibly hard and it still hasn't fully recovered. In regional terms, Okinawa has one of the lowest prefectural averages for per person income. According to 2022 statistics, of 47 prefectures Okinawa ranks 45th and Kagoshima 42nd.

Recent years have been focused on the role of women in the workforce. Japan has a traditional approach to family, with women raising children and running households and men working. This has created huge economic and social problems in the country. Women are a necessary, untapped workforce; those who do work, however, are paid remarkably less than their male counterparts (Japan has one of the largest gender pay gaps in 'developed' countries) and are rarely put in positions of power.

There's also an increase in the number of women who want careers. This is not only a result of Western influence and a growing awareness of gender equality, but also Japan's exceptional and rigorous schooling (page 24). Unfortunately, while women want to continue working – and many younger men resent providing for a family they barely see due to exhausting work hours – the social infrastructure isn't there to support them. As a result, birthrates have plummeted and the country is top-heavy with ageing citizens to look after.

Still, Japan has become known for its high-quality, efficient manufacturing, which is sought after worldwide. The country is one of the biggest ship and car makers, and relies on large exports of machinery, as well as chemicals and materials like steel, plastics, gems and precious metals. Notably, Japan's electronic and precision equipment such as cameras, computers and phones have become world-beating, with many travelling to the country to buy technology. Its largest export markets are the US and China.

NATURAL RESOURCES AND INDUSTRIES The Nansei-shotō is limited in its resources. For a long time, lumber, coal and sulphur were mined, particularly in the north of the archipelago. When reserves dried up, became protected or were simply sourced elsewhere, however, the islands became more reliant on their food production.

Okinawa Prefecture is a major sugarcane and tropical fruit producer, known for its pineapple and papaya. Local economy runs mostly on fishing, cattle, sugar and pineapple. The archipelago as a whole is reliant on seasonal tourism too.

Recent surveys of the submarine environment have revealed natural resources of gold, silver, lead, zinc and copper at the bottom of the sea along the archipelago. Scientists have also discovered submarine hydrothermal deposits northwest of Okinawa-hontō, near Iheya and Izena islands. The hydrothermal waters contain heavy metals, belched out by underground magma. It's believed the Izena cauldron, a depression near the island, contains 7.4 million tonnes of minerals and in 2019, Japan became the first country in the world to successfully mine ore at a depth of 1,600m below sea level.

Although these deposits represent huge potential for Japan, it may be a while before they become lucrative, feasible or environmentally sound. Disputes with China over ownership of the area and its resources make for a political minefield; the current cost and time of mining at such depths makes it a futile endeavour; and growing environmental concerns worldwide and the protection of the oceans mean it may never prove viable.

UNEMPLOYMENT According to estimates from the Ministry of Internal Affairs and Communications' 2023 Labour Force Survey, Japan has incredibly low unemployment rates of 2.6% nationally, but in Okinawa-ken it reaches 3.8% – the highest in the country. Kagoshima-ken sits lower than national at 2.1%.

The prefectures with the lowest unemployment rates have manufacturing industries, notably absent from these small islands. Okinawa also has various problems concerning US bases and long-term economic disparity compared to the mainland. Its late arrival to the mainland economy, coupled with being purposefully held back from modern reforms, means it has always faced economic and employment issues that other prefectures don't.

PEOPLE

Spread across two prefectures, some six island groups, and combining an entirely once-separate country, it's no surprise the islands have a hugely mixed culture.

The southern Ryūkyū people were seafarers, with extensive ties to their neighbours. Trade brought various cultures to these islands' shores, resulting in a unique blend of monuments, buildings, temples, decorations, and arts and crafts. Today, many islanders still rely on the sea for income and sustenance.

Descended from a separate and colonised kingdom, many Okinawans still don't feel fully Japanese, while others identify entirely as such – often the sentiment changes across generations. The introduction of US culture has definitely set Okinawa-hontō apart from its own neighbours, too.

In Kagoshima-ken, Amami has often been isolated, its people happy to be set apart from their southern and northern neighbours. Colonised and conquered by both repeatedly, it has a real mix of two cultures, while remaining wholly its own.

During mainland Japan's Nara period (710–94CE), the Ōsumi region was populated by the Hayato people (literally 'falcon people') who were believed to be of Austronesian descent. The Hayato culture and language was unique in Japan, famous in the region for its folk songs and dances. The Hayato resisted Japanese rule but were eventually defeated and many were made to emigrate to the mainland. Ever since, the Ōsumi have been largely culturally parallel to the mainland.

Today the people of the islands are seen as comparatively relaxed and chilled out compared with their mainland brethren. This is a result of island life, where everything has to be a little more fluid thanks to unpredictable weather, isolation, small populations, and a history full of fluctuations and change. While the mainlanders are famed for their timeliness, the islands are known for living on *shima-jikan* – 'island time'.

BLUE ZONE In recent years the archipelago has become famous as a so-called Blue Zone. This non-scientific term is used to describe areas where people are the most likely to live to 100 or older. There are currently five Blue Zone locations in the world, of which Okinawa is one.

It's thought people in these regions have fewer chronic health conditions thanks to nine common factors found within their environments and culture: natural movement in the day, cultural ways to dispel stress, an '80% full' approach to eating, a plant- and bean-heavy diet, moderate alcohol consumption, a sense of belonging, a sense of purpose, putting loved ones first and having a strong social network with healthy behaviours. Blue Zones have become popularised within dieting circles, but the reality is this longevity is a result of a holistic, localised environment that takes in diet, activity, outlook and community. The area included in the list is only ever described as Okinawa: it's unclear whether this refers to Okinawa Prefecture, the Okinawa Island group or simply the main island itself.

Okinawa's inclusion focuses on their long-living women. Okinawans have a strong sense of *ikigai* (the Japanese word for life purpose), lifelong friendship circles called *moai*, and tight familial relationships. They're known for the 80% full approach to eating, called '*hara hachi bu*', which reminds them not to overeat. They are keen gardeners, have plant-based diets and spend lots of time in sunshine, too. But Okinawa's place as a Blue Zone is at risk: while the oldest generation retains

TATTOOS

Tattoos are famously contentious in Japanese culture thanks to their association with criminality and the *yakuza* mafia. However, it wasn't always so on the islands – in fact, tattooing was common practice for women in the Ryūkyū Kingdom.

Ryūkyūan women would traditionally have the backs of their hands tattooed with simple, dark blue patterns. This little-known practice began at womanhood, and tattoos were added at major milestones such as marriage, first child and first grandchild. Styles and names differed in each island group; in Miyako they were often called *pizukki*, in Okinawa, *hajichi*.

These geometric tattoos served several purposes. They were thought both spiritual and beautiful, causing competition among women and admiration from men, who believed beautiful hands would cook beautiful food. It was also believed foreigners would find hajichi ugly, thereby protecting the wearer from kidnap – in particular from being taken away to *naichi*, the Japanese mainland.

One 14th-century folktale claims a young Okinawan priestess was sought after by a Japanese prince. He was determined to have her for his own, so the priestess's maid tattooed her hands. When the prince saw them he fled, believing them a bad omen. This tale gave rise to the idea that hajichi were symbols of a woman's morality and virtue.

Additionally, a woman's ability to endure the pain of tattoos proved her strength, including the ability to weather prospective mothers-in-law – the tattoos became a symbol that the woman hoped to impress and get on with her husband's mother. Lastly, it is said the tattoos helped women reach the next stage of life after death.

With so much meaning involved in the hajichi, the tattoos were incredibly important. Their patterns tended to differ socially. Lower classes tended to have arrowheads, circles and squares, while higher-class ornate, intricate tattoos could go up the arms.

In 1899, this centuries-old practice was banned by the Meiji government, though continued for years. The reasons were manifold, but one was to quash the authority of local priestesses in favour of their own, and hajichi represented female power. As part of these efforts to modernise and westernise Japan, tattoos became taboo and something to be ashamed of, and would eventually come to represent those who opposed authority – the yakuza. Taiwanese indigenous people also suffered the same fate when they were colonised.

Those with hajichi were punished and discriminated against. In extreme cases, women were forced to divorce their husbands or had their skin burned with hydrochloric acid. Hundreds were affected – a record covering only Yomitan village in the year 1982 reported 772 women with hajichi.

Efforts are now being made to revive the dead practice. A few tattoo artists in Okinawa and Japan now offer hajichi and women from the Okinawa have begun to have them inked.

its healthy lifestyle, this knowledge hasn't been passed on. Younger generations are facing increased financial strains and an Americanised diet full of fast food, imported with US forces. Today, Okinawa has some of the highest BMIs and obesity rates in Japan. Blue Zones founder Dan Buettner has publicly agreed that Okinawa should probably be removed from the list.

POPULATION Overall, the Nansei-shotō is a very small slice of Japan's total population of around 125 million. The population of Okinawa-ken is around 1.45 million, with around 90% of that living on Okinawa-hontō, and the Ōsumi and Amami islands around 46,500 and 121,000 respectively. As the principal city, Naha has the biggest population: the city centre has roughly 319,000 inhabitants while the greater area houses around 800,000. The estimated active-duty US military population in Okinawa is around 30,000, with another 25,000 family members.

LANGUAGE

Japanese is the official language of the islands. There are a number of local Ryūkyūan languages too, but these are largely spoken in the home by older residents. Unlike Indo-European languages, Japanese has a relatively short history of written records. It's thought to be part of the Altaic family of languages; it's not known when Japanese began to emerge, but it's likely Altaic speakers moved from Korea into Japan and the language merged with Austronesian languages.

Although Japanese seems to have evolved in isolation, it has been influenced by several languages over the centuries: indigenous Ainu and Ryūkyūan dialects, Portuguese and Dutch from trade, English after World War II and, of course, Chinese from its neighbours.

Chinese has had the most significant influence; in the 3rd or 4th century, Japan adopted the Chinese writing system and took with it a large number of Chinese words and morphemes. Today, many compound words are read with a Chinese reading. If you are familiar with Chinese script, it's likely you will be able to read the meaning of many Japanese *kanji* (characters).

There's zero expectation to learn any Japanese when visiting the country, but Japanese people are very impressed and very grateful if you try. Often, any attempts at Japanese are met with incredulous exclamations of '*Eeeeeh*?'. It's a familiar sound in Japan, a rather flattering one until it's followed by quick-fire Japanese. Sometimes if you speak one word, locals assume you speak them all.

With few English speakers, however, it's useful to get a basic idea of the language – learning even a few bits of vocabulary will make a big difference in rural Japan. English comprehension and use varies dramatically; in Okinawa-hontō, the long-term presence of the US military means English is a bit more common. Outside this, English is usually limited to large hotels, tour guides and visitors' centres, if they exist.

In most cases, the islands are so small that no English is spoken at all, so language apps can really help. The language guide at the end of this book will provide an overview of Japanese, as well as important phrases and words.

WRITING Japanese writing is where it gets truly complicated. Originally, Japan didn't have a writing system. They began to borrow logographs from China sometime after the 5th century, but this caused myriad problems. After all, Japan didn't have a script but it did have a language. Chinese characters already had both a meaning and a reading – which didn't match the spoken Japanese word at all. The result is that modern Japanese kanji have two readings: *kunyomi*, the native Japanese reading, and *onyomi*, the Chinese one.

To confuse things further, Japanese added in two syllabaries (alphabets, of a kind) on top. These represent the 46 main syllables used in Japanese. The first and most common is *hiragana*, a curvy script used to spell words without kanji, to indicate grammar and to spell out pronunciation. Hiragana was originally called 'women's writing' as it was created by women, who weren't taught kanji. After Japan's – some

OKINAWAN PHRASES

While there's no need to learn any Okinawan, the culture of the islands is delightfully reflected in its language and idioms.

Ichariba choodee	Once we meet and talk, we are brothers and sisters
Uya yushi kwa yushi	Parents and children teach one another
Nmarijima nu kutuba washii nee kuni n wasshiin	Forgetting your native tongue means forgetting your native country
Shinjichi nu ada nayumi	Kindness will never be wasted in any way
Shikinoo chui shiihii shiru kurasuru	Let's live helping each other in this world
Kamuru ussaa mii nayun	The more you eat, the more you gain
Kuu sa kana sa	Small things are lovable

say the world's – first novel was written by a woman, hiragana became popularised as an easier, uncomplicated script. The final script is *katakana*; it has the exact same syllabary as hiragana, but is an angular script used for foreign loan words, emphasis and onomatopoeia.

INDIGENOUS LANGUAGES Even before the Ryūkyū Kingdom, there were many indigenous languages across the archipelago. All of them fell under the Japonic language group and, much like Japanese, most were eventually written in Chinese.

They are often referred to as dialects (*hōgen*) of Japanese, but this is more of a political than linguistic debate. Although they may all be related, each developed separately, making them mutually unintelligible from Japanese and even unintelligible between islands. The languages are believed to be more different than Portuguese and Spanish are.

The local languages have been long under threat. After the islands were colonised by Japan, the Meiji government – in an effort to show a unified country and suppress dissent in the islands – banned indigenous languages in schools and public, and punished those speaking them. Many still used them behind closed doors and out of official hearing, however.

This suppression of indigenous languages was incredibly successful. Many of them are near extinction, with only a handful of elderly speakers left. Most people living on the islands now speak Japanese only, and UNESCO expects all Ryūkyūan languages to have disappeared by 2050. In recent years, there have been small local efforts to revive the indigenous languages, starting with Uchinaaguchi on Okinawa-hontō. Overall there are around six to ten languages on the islands, with hundreds of dialects between them.

Though not commonly used, you will see evidence of some of these languages as you travel the islands, particularly the Okinawan Uchinaaguchi language (see above). Okinawan words are often written in katakana, and the most common one you'll likely come across is *mensooree*: welcome.

RELIGION

RYŪKYŪAN RELIGION Though the islands didn't follow a major religion before annexation, they had their own indigenous one. It had roots in everyday customs like farming and fishing, with deeply natural and human elements. Over the centuries, it incorporated influences from Shintōism, Taoism and Buddhism – its similarity to the first means it's sometimes called Okinawa or Ryūkyū Shintō. It was both shamanistic, with a belief in spirits, and animistic, attributing souls to plants, inanimate objects and other natural bodies and phenomena.

Practices varied across the archipelago, but overall the Ryūkyūans shared a belief in ancestral spirits, demons and multiple gods who control natural areas like the sea, trees and rocks. (The line between gods and ancestors was fairly flexible, as both were considered spirits.) Throughout the year, these spirits were placated with rituals and blessings to ensure good harvest and safety. Today the Ryūkyū religion is little practised, but the belief in spirits endures.

Women One of the core principles of this religion was *unari-gami* – the spiritual superiority of women. Unari was a sister deity that had both the power to protect and curse her brother Ihiri, showing her as more powerful and spiritually superior. This brother–sister relationship became intrinsic to Ryūkyū religion and translated into everyday life, where sisters would protect their brothers and lead the household spiritually. It was even reflected linguistically: in Ryūkyūan languages, women were placed first – always 'women and men', 'female and male'.

Women's superior spirituality was also connected to the religion's value for nature and home: women were considered closer to nature than men, and ancestral worship took place in the home. The most important deity of the religion was also female: the islands' creator, goddess Amamikyu.

This female-centricity meant the Ryūkyū Kingdom gave women much higher status than its neighbours, Japan and China. Women had strong roles in the community, holding positions of guardians and shamans. All public festivals and rituals were conducted by women, and personal issues resolved by female shamans. In fact, the Ryūkyū Islands are said to be the only known example of an official national religion dominated, run and steered by women.

Originally, communities were matrilocal: after marriage, women would stay in the house of their mothers. Most women would marry within the community, creating a large family grouping in villages. One of the most famous Ryūkyū rituals is the tug-of-war (page 34), which began as a ritual representing two sides, male and female, and the idea was the female side would win to guarantee fertility. There's evidence that Okinawa-hontō once had a similar sumo wrestling ritual, between an adult man and an old woman. The old woman always won to ensure bountiful harvest.

Priestesses The religion was run by *noro* (high priestesses), *nigan* (village priestesses), and shaman figures called *yuta* – and there are still some of these figures practising today. Noro communicate with and channel ancestors and deities. They officiate events and divine the best days for agricultural/maritime practices. Each household was generally expected to send a girl to help the noro in her duties. On Kudakajima, all women were said to be part of the priesthood when between the ages of 31 and 70. Noro were also provided with land and had a measure of political power.

Despite noro remaining unwed and virginal, the position was often hereditary: a noro's eldest niece would inherit the position. There's evidence to suggest the islands saw menstruation as an expression of divinity – the idea of its 'pollution' only came after Buddhism's introduction – and noro and yuta were allowed to perform ceremonies and rituals while menstruating. In Hateruma, men are not allowed to enter shrines or see some rituals. When priestesses go into religious retreat, they often sew and darn, but before big events they aren't allowed to even touch male clothing. In instances where men had to enter sacred groves, they would need to dress up as women – regardless of their status.

Yuta were shaman who could communicate with the dead, and would deal with personal rather than community issues. Their job was to create harmony between the living and the dead and banish spirits: powers that were respected and often feared. Yuta also helped to solve daily issues between families, much like a counsellor.

King Shō Shin made massive changes to the priestess system in the 16th century. His sister was the Kikoe-ōgimi: the royal family's noro and the highest priestess in the kingdom. Shō Shin made it so the Kikoe-ōgimi appointed and presided over the kingdom's high-level priestesses, who in turn supervised local noro. This system was designed to centralise and control the religion through the government. After this, the Kikoe-ōgimi was usually the sister of the king.

Family and home Ancestors play a major role in the religion. Daily prayers and offerings are made at an altar in the home, and updates on each family member are spoken aloud for the benefit of departed loved ones. It's believed ancestral spirits are always observing their descendants; proper attendance to rituals ensures their benevolence, negligence their wrath.

The home's ancestral shrine is in one of the main rooms of the house, hidden in an alcove by sliding doors. Its three shelves hold flowers, memorial tablets in which the spirits reside, cups, an incense burner and food and offerings. In many Japanese religions, the spirits of the dead can only live on if the living are there to celebrate and remember them. This means regular prayers and offerings and makes continuing family lines vital.

The oldest and most powerful ancestors live in sacred natural places, such as caves, called *utaki*. The most sacred part of an utaki may only be entered by the noro. There are also household gods; one of the earliest is Hinukan, the hearth god, who is the messenger from the family to the other gods. Originally the hearth itself was worshipped, but now Hinukan is represented by three stones usually placed in the kitchen.

Furu-no-kami is one of the more unusual gods: the god of the toilet. This benevolent god resides in bathrooms, protecting them from becoming haunted places of evil and rejection. Bathrooms are therefore kept clean and treated respectfully.

Mabui *Mabui* is a kind of energy or life force unique to each individual: sort of like a soul, but more transferable. Mabui can be transferred through contact and objects – personal items regularly in contact with a loved one carry their mabui, and photos and paintings of them too. The older you get, the stronger your physical connection to your mabui is. Mabui can leave the body entirely because of poor relationships, shock, trauma, stress or loneliness. It's very much connected to depression, anxiety and illness, but rituals can be performed to restore it.

Spirits There are good, natural spirits that are worshipped through physical embodiments like trees, rocks and springs. There are also negative spirits, who dislike humans. If humans disturb their homes, negative spirits may cause harm or death, and so a yuta is called to appease the spirit. The belief in these negative spirits is so strong, even in recent decades, that development near supposedly haunted sites is avoided, with some building works even being abandoned mid-construction.

The most famous of these is the Nakagusuku Hotel on Okinawa-hontō. The story goes that locals warned against building on the site next to Nakagusuku Castle as it housed multiple graves. Construction began but was stopped after accidents and even deaths, and the hotel was left a half-finished ruin.

There are also visible, ghost-like spirits – often those who didn't receive a proper funeral or died in terrible circumstances. During the war, there were many sightings and stories of such ghosts. The islands also have multiple magical creatures such as dragons, *shiisaa* (often written as shisa) lion-dog guardians, and the *kijimunaa* – a banyan-dwelling sprite that likes to play pranks (page 203).

Sacred sites On the islands, shrines are known as utaki or *ontake*. Scholars suggest that the placement of these was a more important consideration than agricultural and fishing potential when choosing where to build villages. Many of these utaki are incredibly sacred, accessible only by female priests, while those in Yakushima (closer to mainland influence) are the realm of men. Although some of the better-known sites allow tourists past the *torii* gates, many do not, especially on smaller islands. As a general rule of thumb these paths are blocked off, but if you are uncertain whether or not to enter, err on the side of caution.

There are a handful of incredibly sacred places in the archipelago, including Seefa Utaki on Okinawa-hontō (page 192), Kudakajima (page 192) and Ōgamijima (page 270).

Tombs Tombs are incredibly important and differ greatly from mainland versions. The styles differ from island to island, era to era, but they usually resemble houses, with courtyards and porches, and contain the remains of multiple ancestors. They are often called turtleback tombs due to the doming of the roof, but are also said to resemble the womb.

Practices around the tombs also change between islands. A common shared ritual is regular gatherings at the tomb, where incense is lit, and food, drink and prayers are offered up. Many of these gatherings are almost party-like, with families enjoying picnics and local beverages. While ancestral shrines in the home are worshipped year-round, tomb worship is for special occasions.

A unique custom to many of these islands is *senkotsu*: bone washing. This practice involves leaving the body in a tomb for years until it has reduced to bone. The bones are then washed, usually in seawater, and placed in a box or urn, which is then returned to the tomb. This practice was once widespread but was inevitably stamped out by Japan. However, Yonaguni still practises bone washing (page 344).

OTHER RELIGIONS Buddhism was introduced around the 13th century and was protected by the royal government, which oversaw the construction of temples like Enkaku-ji. King Shō Taikyū had 23 Buddhist temple bells called *bonshō* made for temples and shrines, some of which remain today, including the Bell of the Bridge between Nations (Bankoku-shinryō-no-kane) in front of the state hall at Shuri Castle. The strong island association between women and religion meant that, even when Buddhism was introduced, sects with male-only clergy elsewhere had female clergy on Okinawa.

The Meiji government enforced Shintōism to replace other island religions, while their land reforms took land and power from the noro. The rise in psychiatry in the late 1900s might have put paid to the islands' shamanistic beliefs, but pro-Okinawan sentiment meant science and religion were able to coexist, and locals are likely to consult both when approaching mental health and life advice.

POWER SPOTS

Travelling around Japan, you'll likely hear the phrase 'power spot'. It is not, somewhat unfortunately, a place to charge your phone, but is instead a spiritual site of great spiritual energy. Power spots come from feng shui principles and are believed to give visitors a feeling of spiritual healing and refreshment. A more universal idea is that power spots are where you can feel in tune with nature and beautiful, meaningful surroundings.

Power spots often align with nature, places of worship or sites of historical significance, as they tend to relate to myths and gods – they're sometimes said to be where gods descended to earth. As these islands are home to some of Japan's most major creation myths, they are replete with these so-called power spots.

A lot of Japanese people identify as Buddhist or Shintō, but aren't always actively religious. Many Japanese mix and match their religions: some 80% of Japanese people get married under Shintō or Christian ceremonies, but 90% hold Buddhist funerals.

EDUCATION

Japan's education system plays a huge role in its national identity; many Japanese people are incredibly proud of their education and justifiably so. Internationally, Japan has one of the best education systems with exceptionally high literacy, science and numeracy rates.

The academic year begins in April and ends in March, with most schools adopting a three-term system. The education system is divided into five sections, with private and public options at each level: nursery, elementary, middle school, high school and university. Nursery begins at age three and largely focuses on moral, ethical and social teaching – learning how to clean up and to help others. Although science, maths, music and PE are included, there's time allocated to answering ethical dilemmas and moral conundrums. The practice encourages grey area thinking and social responsibility, aiming to create well-rounded, good citizens.

Although schoolchildren can leave education at 15, 99% of middle schoolers continue their studies. Those who do carry on must continue to study mathematics, English, and Japanese literature.

Japanese education involves an extraordinary number of examinations, which has garnered much criticism domestically and internationally. The Japanese term for these gruelling entrance exams is *shiken jigoku* – 'exam hell'. Schools often have half-days two Saturdays a month and cram schools are incredibly common. Selection to university is so rigorous that only around half pass on their first attempt. Competition is also rife and extracurricular activities are a large part of the school experience.

A huge amount of Japanese education is taken up learning kanji, the logographic writing system derived from Chinese (page 19). Learning kanji is difficult even for native speakers: by the time students leave primary school, they know 1,026, and learn a further 1,110 during secondary school. As you may notice, their foreign-language education is comparatively poor; this is often attributed to the rote learning approach favoured by Japan.

One of the most interesting differences in Japanese schools is the lack of cleaning and janitorial staff: students themselves are expected to keep the school clean. It's considered part of their education and is so instilled that it stays with them for life.

CULTURE

LITERATURE By limit of its small population, the Nansei-shotō has few celebrities born on its shores, and even fewer authors. However, the few it has are highly acclaimed, with four Okinawan writers earning Japan's prestigious Akutagawa Prize. Much of the literature being produced by island-born writers grapples with the darker sides of the islands and challenges the utopian image many Japanese people and foreigners have of these tropical climes.

War, oppression, violence, isolation and politics are common themes, particularly as so many of these writers were born in or lived through American occupation and Japanese homogenisation of the islands. One of the best places to start exploring Okinawan literature is the English-language book *Islands of Protest: Japanese Literature from Okinawa* (University of Hawaii Press, 2016), which brings together many stories from the following authors and more.

The prolific writer Tatsuhiro Ōshiro won the Akutagawa Prize for his 1967 novella *Kakuteru Pātī* (The Cocktail Party), which tells the story of an Okinawan man invited to a house party on a US military base, with Japanese, Chinese and American guests. The controversial but important book charts the political and social minefield of the party, and the disastrous events that follow.

Mineo Higashi's novel *Okinawa no Shōnen* (An Okinawan Boy) won in 1971. The novel is set in 1950s Okinawa, and centres on a protagonist who grows up in a family that arranges clandestine meetings in their apartment between American soldiers and Okinawan girls. Shun Medoruma won in 1997 for short story 'Suiteki' (A Drop of Water), which focuses on Okinawan cultural suppression, American and Japanese occupation, and the war. His short story 'Hope' is available to read in English online, and is a horrific tale of an Okinawan man seeking revenge for a local girl raped by US military men – based on the real rape of a 12-year-old Okinawan girl by US servicemen in 1995.

Eiki Matayoshi's 1995 novel *Buta no mukui* (The Pig's Retribution) is about a university student who returns to the islands in the company of three barmaids to get rid of a curse. Matayoshi's most famous work is *Jōji ga Shasatsu Shita Inoshishi* (The Wild Boar that George Shot), inspired by real life – a US soldier shot a local man and successfully argued his innocence at trial by claiming he thought the local was a wild boar.

Iriomote-born Sakiyama Tami is a tour de force, with stories that focus on ancestral voices, spirits and connections with nature. Her most famous is the novella *Yuratiku Yuritiku* (Swaying, Swinging), which takes place on an imaginary island, whose 80-year-old residents have been left alone by the rest of the world.

Norihiro Yagi is one of Okinawa's few *mangaka*, a manga writer and artist. His best-known works include *Angel Densetsu* and *Claymore*. There are also well-known poets from the islands, both modern and new. Male poets include Baku Yamanokuchi, Seiko Miyazato and Ben Takara but there's also a strong history of female poets including Tōma Hiroko, Onna Nabe and Chiru Yoshiya.

The Nansei-shotō is well known for its fables, often rooted in the Ryūkyūan religion (page 20). These stories range from cautionary and moralistic to utterly baffling. They are lighthearted and sweet, or cruel and downright creepy. Each island has a wealth of its own myths, described in chapters in *Parts 2 and 3* of this guide.

DRESS AND TEXTILES The islands are arguably home to Japan's richest textile traditions. Made with natural materials, both woven and dyed textiles are diverse and distinct, with each island having its own style, materials and techniques, still passed down today. Of the 17 officially designated traditional crafts of the islands, 14 are fabrics.

Silk and cotton were only introduced to the islands in the 16th century. Before this the upper classes wore ramie cloth (see below) and the lower classes banana fibre cloth (see opposite). In the Yaeyama, cloth was also made from flax and dyed with a yam-like kuru plant (see opposite). Other traditional fibres from the islands are linden (made from trees), kudzu, hemp, wisteria and mulberry.

These fabrics have a looser weave than others like cotton, making them breathable and light for wearing during a humid summer. The fabrics are highly valued by locals, as well as mainlanders and foreigners. Locals believe that cloth not only covers the physical body but the spirit too, helping it stay in the body.

Bingata The most famous type is Ryūkyū *bingata*, made using a traditional dyeing method. It originated in the 13th–14th century when trade from India, Indonesia and China was at its height and locals were exposed to their methods of creating fabrics. The word is often translated literally as 'red form', but it's believed that Ryūkyūan languages used *bin* to mean 'all colours'. 'Colour form' is a more accurate description of the remarkably detailed and beautifully bright cloth depicting island flora, fauna and landscapes.

Bingata kimonos are worn in traditional performances and you will see some of the most treasured hung in Okinawa's Prefectural Museum (page 190). Bingata was so in demand that it was used for tribute to Japan and China. Only royalty or the very wealthy could afford it; designs were strictly regulated by social status, which you could tell just from their pattern and colour. It was even rumoured that upper class women would keep the stencil pattern to their kimono so that no other woman would be able to replicate it.

Common people were only allowed to wear bingata for certain celebrations, and also only in darker colours. The nobility wore pale blue and yellow denoted royalty. The fabric is coloured using natural pigments – sulphur, arsenic, cochineal, indigo, vermilion, chalk and shells – rather than dyes. These colours are applied free-hand or using stencils, by resist dyeing: a process whereby *nori* (starch) is applied where no dye is desired. It would take a single person around nine days to paint a single kimono, though thankfully the artisans work in teams. The whole process involves ten steps and takes around one month to finish a single roll of cloth.

Ryūkyū kasuri *Kasuri* (also *gasuri*) is both a fabric and term for how patterns are blurred or 'splashed' in textiles; it comes from the Japanese verb 'to be misted'. Kasuri fabric uses pre-dyed fibres woven into specific patterns or images, also known as *ikat*. There are three ways to weave kasuri and it comes in three colours – dark blue (*kon*), white (*shiro*) and brown (*cha*). The colours, sizes and designs of kasuri reflected the wearer's status. Haebaru town on Okinawa-hontō has long been the home of Ryūkyū kasuri.

Ramie Ramie is made by weaving fibres created from indigenous nettles. The fibres are dyed with naturally occurring dyes from island trees and flowers. Reds and pinks are made from sappanwood and safflowers, yellow from fukugi trees, and blues from indigo, which was farmed prolifically in the islands. The material is then woven on a traditional loom. Yaeyama is said to weave the best ramie, which was prized by both China and Japan in trade and tax.

Miyako jōfu 'Miyako from west, Echigo from east' is a Japanese saying about the top two *jōfu* fabrics produced in the country. Miyako jōfu is a 100% handmade ramie fabric of exquisite quality – the word jōfu translates as 'superior cloth'.

The fabric supposedly originated in 1590, when the wife of a village official, who was generously rewarded by the king for heroism, wanted to gift the king something incredible in return. It took three years to produce the fabric but the king was so in awe that she continued to weave it for another 20 years. The fabric was taken to the shōgun in Japan and became a highly sought-after trade item. In 1978, Miyako jōfu was named an important Intangible Cultural Property of Japan.

The fibres are traditionally dyed dark blue or left white, then woven into fine splash patterns of white crosses, triangles and squares. The resulting fabric has a smooth, almost glossy finish. It's also one of the most expensive, as it takes so much time to create. A long-time weaver can produce around 20–30cm a day, and the 90 or so artisans on Miyako make around 20 rolls a year. A single roll of 37cm x 12m can cost around ¥1.2 million. Though exquisite, it's also durable.

Yaeyama jōfu Mainly woven on Ishigaki, Yaeyama jōfu is handmade using fine ramie (known locally as *boo*) thread. It usually has ikat or even double ikat patterning made with brown or indigo colours on white fabric. The brown dye is unique, made from the kuru plant native to the Yaeyama. Unlike many plant dyes, kuru doesn't discolour under sunlight but strengthens: it is left in the sun for ten days, then the colours are fastened using seawater.

Weaving skills are traditionally passed from mother to daughter, but World War II crippled the industry. As there was a steep reduction in the number of Yaeyama jōfu makers, the handmade thread used for the warp is often replaced with manufactured thread. A few artisans have been trying to bring it back and now a Yaeyama jōfu kimono by the best craftswoman costs around ¥2.8 million.

Bashōfu *Bashōfu* is created out of fibres from the leafstalks of a banana tree. As these grow wild and are easily cultivated, they were readily obtained by commoners and bashōfu became a cloth for poorer locals. In the Yaeyama, women traditionally wore bashōfu robes tied with twisted straw. The fibre is stripped from mature trees and sorted into fine, medium and coarse threads. These fibres are boiled with ash to soften them and are then further split and tied to form a continuous yarn.

The quality of the material is dependent on the fibres' thinness, how tightly they are woven together, and how silky they are. Bashōfu is somewhat crisp, very lightweight and doesn't cling, so is often used to create summer kimonos. It is often decorated with ikat patterns.

Yuntanza hanaori Made in Yomitan Village, this *hanaori* is a rare fabric made from colourful threads woven into geometric patterns on a plain background. The patterns represent money, longevity and family prosperity. The fabric was once given to the Ryūkyū government but nearly died out, until the village made an effort to keep it alive. The leader of the revival, Sada Yonamine who passed away in 2003, was designated a Living National Treasure in 1991.

Kumejima tsumugi This is the oldest type of *tsumugi* (cloth made from waste silk) in Japan and is an important Intangible Cultural Property of Japan. This cloth is dyed in the kasuri technique (see opposite), using indigenous plant and mud dyes. This creates a characteristic earthy colouring, and the resulting cloth is smooth and simple. Kumejima silk production started in the 15th century, when a Kume local studied Chinese methods of farming silk. The mulberry trees necessary to production grow very well on Kume.

Ōshima tsumugi Also known as silk pongee, this Amami cloth dates back to the 7th century – though silk fabric has been made in Amami since ancient times. The colouring is far more muted than the bolder Okinawa colours; the dyes are from native techigi trees, indigo and, more remarkably, mud. Ōshima tsumugi was worn by locals until 1720, when the Shimazu clan declared it only for government officials. The fabric was made into a tribute for the clan and became incredibly popular.

In the Meiji era, the wearing of it spread by those who could afford it and eventually people on the mainland created their own version. Now there are two types: authentic Amami *honba* and mainland *murayama*. Ironically, murayama was designed as an inexpensive, casual alternative to honba – which itself was always originally intended to be casual.

Yonaguni ori Believed to be at least 500 years old, Yonaguni ori is the name for the four handwoven and plant- and mud- dyed textiles in Yonaguni. Finer materials like cotton and silk are used for the warp, while hemp and *basho* are used for the weft. They are dyed in colours of yellow, brown, rust and green. At the Yonaguni Town Traditional Crafts Centre (page 342) you'll find fabric exhibits with looms for trainees. The centre provides them with raw materials, inspects their work and buys their products, helping continue the art form.

Kariyushi The only modern addition is an Okinawan shirt similar to the Hawaiian shirt. *Kariyushi* were designed to promote tourism to Okinawa, but were a complete failure. The excess of unsold shirts was given to hotel association members and staff, beginning their strange rise in popularity. They became internationally famous after the 26th G8 summit in Okinawa, where each head of state wore one. Usually floral, the most common layout is a pattern on only one side of the shirt.

CRAFTS Okinawan and Amami crafts are highly regarded in Japan, particularly glass, lacquerware, textiles and ceramics.

Ryūkyū glass It's thought Ryūkyū glassware began in the 17th century, when an envoy from Qing China brought over glassmaking techniques. Scholars believe glass manufacturing was widespread in Okinawa particularly, but didn't truly flourish until the beginning of the 20th century.

However, World War II curtailed the industry, as getting materials proved problematic. Glassmakers were forced to use waste and scrap – often soy and sake bottles, as well as Coca-Cola and whisky bottles brought by American troops. This not only determined the colours of the pieces (usually brown, blue and green), but the many impurities in the scrap glass created defects and bubbles when it was blown. The war also changed the types of products being made too. American demands meant that the common local products of fly catchers, oil containers, measuring cups, pickle and sweet jars became jugs, cups and decanters.

Today's iteration of the glassware makes for brilliant souvenirs. Thick, pointedly uneven, and still often full of those now archetypal and highly desired bubbles, each item is unique. The vivid colours, most often a cyan blue, are inspired by the tropical shades of the archipelago's sea, sky and flowers.

Lacquerware Known as Ryūkyū *shikki*, island lacquerware is distinct from the mainland. It uses inlaid seashell, local motifs and a contrast of black and brilliant vermilion that isn't found elsewhere. Thought to date back to the 1300s, the technique uses sap from the lacquer tree (originally a non-native species traded from China) to create the varnish. Originally, lacquerware was used for political and religious ceremonies. When Satsuma invaded in 1609, the lacquerware was confiscated and given to the Tokugawa shōgun.

The base hasn't much changed, made from indigenous woods like *deigo*, *shitamaki* (Japanese snowbell), *sendan* (Chinaberry) and white cedar. However, the styles have evolved over the centuries, ranging from plain to elaborate. The undercoat was once made of pig's blood, then mudstone powder and raw lacquer. The decoration style can be *raden*, using green turban or abalone shells; *chinkin*, which inlays gold leaf; or *haku-e*, with gold foil lacquering. The most famous and unique decoration is *tsuikin*, a raised lacquer overlay that produces a 3D appearance.

Yachimun and Tsuboya pottery Okinawan pottery, known locally as *yachimun*, first appeared over 6,500 years ago, but evolved over the centuries through trade and foreign influence. During the Satsuma era, Korean potters were brought to Okinawa-hontō and taught their trade to locals. Multiple kilns were opened in the capital but were eventually merged into a single workshop at Tsuboya (page 189), in Naha. This remains home to the finest island yachimun.

Production declined during World War II, but the Tsuboya district survived relatively unscathed and potters were the first people US troops allowed back to work. Their efforts are said to have started Naha's post-war economic recovery. (Thanks to its escape from war damage, the area is also one of the best places to see traditional housing; page 31.)

Tsuboya pottery comes in two forms: *arayachi* and *jōyachi*. Arayachi is simpler, using black and red clay from the south that's either left unglazed or glazed in black. Jōyachi is far more elaborate, using red and white clay from the north and multiple decorative enamels and glazes. The white clay used in jōyachi is peculiar to Okinawa, as are those designs done with red paint. Traditionally, the pottery was fired in stepped climbing kilns called *noborigama*, but these are no longer allowed. Fēnugama on Tsuboya Yachimun Street is the sole remaining noborigama in Tsuboya.

Zushigame bone boxes One of the most unique island objects are *zushigame*, or *jiishigaame*. These stone or ceramic storage boxes come in a variety of shapes and styles, and are used for bone storage. Traditionally, the dead were buried, then disinterred to have their bones washed (page 23). These bones were then stored in these zushigame. Their use has dwindled now, as cremation has become standard.

ART On the islands, there are 17 paintings designated cultural properties; the majority are housed on Okinawa-hontō. There are a handful of ancient painters from the islands, including the revered Ryūkyūan court painters Gusukuma Seiho (1614–44) and Genryō (1718–67).

Modern artists include Chuzo Tamotzu (1888–1975), a self-taught *sumi-e* ink painting artist born on Amami Ōshima. He moved to the US in 1920; his work is in multiple galleries, including The Met in New York. Contemporary Okinawan artist Yūken Teruya (b1973) exhibits his mixed media art worldwide, and is known for his intricate paper-cut work, depicting trees growing out of bags, currency and even toilet paper rolls. His pieces often look at the politics of Okinawa, such as a kimono featuring traditional motifs interspersed with American paratroopers.

Naka Bokunen (b1953) is famed for his bold, bright and colourful prints of Okinawan people and landscapes. Born on Izenajima, he features the island heavily in his works. He has also collaborated with Japanese novelist Banana Yoshimoto.

MUSIC The islands are a centre for music, with many traditional Japanese instruments and styles starting life in the archipelago. Music also plays an incredibly important part in preserving, teaching and spreading Ryūkyūan languages; for many locals, folk songs are one of the only times they get to speak and connect with indigenous language.

Ryūkyūan music can be split in two: classic and folk. Largely speaking, classical was the music performed in the royal government, and was heavily entrenched with dance and performance. Classical uses the *sanshin*, the zither-like *koto*, drums, bamboo flutes and the bowed lute *kokyū*.

Folk songs – referred to as *min'yō* – are the music of the people, often highly sentimental and representing the struggles of island life. They vary from island to island, though there are commonalities in terms of instrument, scales and style. The traditional singing style of most island folkloric songs is often nasal and involves extended notes. The scales used in Okinawan, Amami and mainland Japanese music not only differ from Western music but from each other; those familiar with the music can often tell a song's origins from its scale. The most famous folk songs are from Amami, called *shima uta* (page 118).

Sanshin This three-stringed instrument, called sanshin in Okinawa-ken and shamisen towards the mainland, is the backbone of Nansei-shotō music. Similar to a banjo, it is derived from the Chinese *sanxian*, which was introduced to the Ryūkyū Kingdom in the 16th century. Sanshin were played in the royal Ryūkyū court and at banquets to welcome envoys, but eventually the instrument became so integral to island culture that most homes in the archipelago owned one. It is brought out at events, gatherings and festivals, as well as some restaurants.

After World War II, when so many homes were destroyed, islanders would make *kankara sanshin*, with tin cans for the body. Today, sanshin music is experiencing a renaissance. With only three strings, it doesn't have the same chord capability of guitars and banjos: notes are largely played one at a time.

There are some differences between Okinawan and Amami sanshin construction and playing, leading to slightly altered sounds. Traditionally, the sanshin body is covered in snakeskin and treated as an heirloom, designed to be handed down over many generations. The instrument is revered in the Ryūkyūan culture, as it is said to be the sound of deities. (Many outsiders might argue this – sanshin can be an acquired taste.) In fact, the instrument is so special to islanders that there's a saying: if a fire broke out in a house, the first thing Okinawans would reach for is the sanshin.

Modern music There are many contemporary singers and songwriters from the islands. While some focus on traditional music, others have gone into mainstream pop and rock, often experimenting with traditional instruments and styles. Famous musicians and bands to check out are: The Hoptones, a male pop quartet from the 1960s; the critically acclaimed Rinken Band, who incorporate Eisaa dance and costumes into their live performances; Sadao China, famed for mixing Okinawan and Western music forms such as reggae; and 1970s folk-rock band Champloose, whose music focused on peace and activism in Okinawa. The band Ryukyu Underground is a British-American duo who met in Okinawa, and blend island folk songs with Western dubstep and dance music.

DANCE The islands have a plethora of performing arts, originally created for feasts and festivals where audiences often joined in. The most famous is the Kumiodori, a theatrical performance dating back to the 18th century, at a time when the kingdom had a government-appointed dance magistrate. Kumiodori is based on Ryūkyū legends, and combines traditional and ancient performing arts of the islands with influences from Japanese Noh and Kabuki. It has three parts: speech, dance, and classical music and singing. There is a huge amount of detail in the costumes and props, earning it a UNESCO Intangible Cultural Heritage accolade in 2010.

Other famous folk dances include the Eisaa (often seen as Eisa) and *shishimai* (lion dance), which are often performed at festivals and by local groups across the islands. Eisaa came to Okinawa in the 16th century and was originally a funerary ritual. Now it's performed at the end of the Obon festival as part of a parade to honour ancestral spirits. Three drums are used for the Eisaa: a large barrel drum, a medium drum and a tambourine-like drum.

Kachāshī is a folk dance that crops up regularly at celebrations and even just in local bars when someone's blasting local tunes. Kachāshī means 'mixing' in Okinawan, and involves flowing hand motions, usually above the head, that ebb and move like waves. Traditionally women have open hands, men closed fists.

FILM The islands have inspired and featured in many films, often as an exotic paradisiacal destination or as a scene of war. Notable island film stars are Brian Tee, who starred in *The Fast and the Furious: Tokyo Drift* (2006) and *Jurassic World* (2015), and Tamlyn Tomita, a Japanese-American actress who starred in *The Day After Tomorrow* (2004).

The most famous film about the islands is Studio Ghibli's animated classic, *Princess Mononoke* (1997). The forest-based film about the war between natural spirits and humans used the forests of Yakushima as inspiration, with some of the scenes drawn directly from known landmarks.

ARCHITECTURE The Ryūkyū Kingdom lives on in island architecture, with even new builds matching traditional styles. The traditional architectural style, known as *nuchijaa*, developed from family systems, religious beliefs and climate.

During the Ryūkyū Kingdom, common housing was legally restricted to certain sizes based on status. Only the elite could use roofing tiles, while common folk used grass thatch. These rules were lifted in 1889 during the Meiji restoration, allowing for the prolific red roofs seen today.

While larger structures use stonework or newer concrete for increased weather resistance, most houses are wood with stone outer walls. The red roof tiles are symbolic of the archipelago, made of Okinawan mud. Surprisingly, it's actually black mud from the south of Okinawa-hontō, but its high iron content oxidises during firing, producing the bright red colour. The tiles are uniquely useful: the ceramic is very breathable, allowing moisture to escape during the day, reducing humidity indoors. Frequent tropical storms and typhoons in the region mean tile replacement is a continual battle.

Traditional homes Houses are usually elevated by a single step to allow for air flow, but are otherwise one storey so they are low-lying and resistant against high winds. They're surrounded by stone or coral walls – and sometimes trees – for additional typhoon protection. The low, large eaves (*amahaji*) protect the roof from high winds and create shade for socialising and work. The main building is divided into different types of rooms: guest rooms (*ichibanza*), the altar room (*nibanza*), bedrooms and others, and the kitchen. In Amami, kitchens were traditionally built in separate buildings and linked by a small corridor. Floors are usually tatami, barring the earthen-floored kitchen, and rooms are separated by sliding *shōji* panels. Characteristically, houses are built in the centre of the plot, creating a sunnier area for allotments and a shaded area for play.

Traditional Okinawan houses are designed to suit the high-humidity climate of the tropics. The building shutters and shoji are left open to encourage cooling through-draughts, and there's no gate. This also allowed for house spirits to pass in and out freely. However, it was important only the right spirits got in and the bad ones were kept out. This resulted in the *hinpun*, a barrier between the opening and the house; there's a belief that negative spirits can only go in straight paths, thereby never reaching the house. Hinpuns also maintained privacy and weather protection. Traditionally, the sides of the hinpun were gendered, with men and guests of honour using the right and women the left.

One of the less-noticed details in Ryūkyū homes are their four corners – most houses have them after all. But on the islands, there are gods corresponding to the four corners, called Yushin. They each have their uses: north stops bad energy, south protects the family, east is the heavenly messenger and west brings luck to the home. It's therefore vital that each house has the four Yushin or it will bring bad luck.

You can see traditional architecture all over the islands. Taketomi (page 306) is the best-known and best-preserved island that is almost entirely traditional housing and villages, but there are plenty of examples elsewhere.

Castles Castles, or *gusuku*, crop up everywhere – usually as tumbling stone ruins, but there's also the grandiose halls of Shuri Castle (page 190). Shuri is a perfect example of how the larger Ryūkyūan architecture incorporated aspects of Chinese design and detailing. Both China and Japan had an influence on island architecture, thanks to their trading history. The Seiden at Shuri Castle is particularly distinct: its design features combine imperial Chinese elements as well as Japanese religious ones, creating a style entirely unique to the Ryūkyū Kingdom.

Feng shui Feng shui was introduced to the islands in the 14th century from China, and became a national policy of the kingdom in the 1730s. It fitted well with the island ideals of symbiosis between nature and people. Traditional Ryūkyūan houses coexist with nature and are designed to create harmony between inside and outside spaces.

Feng shui principles were brought into village and city planning and forest management. One of the classic principles is *hōgō*, which means 'embrace'. This meant trees were planted in a protective, hugging barrier around houses, villages and even coastlines, trapping positive living energy (*qi*) inside. Shuri Castle and the city that developed around it was positioned based on this principle. Villages were also set in grid patterns. Although many such settlements were destroyed in the war, there are still preserved feng shui villages: the best examples are Tonakijima (page 223) and Bise village (page 200) in northern Okinawa-hontō.

You may noticc seemingly random carved stones positioned at forked roads, intersections, or outside houses. They're not directions or signs but spiritual feng shui stones called *ishigantō*. They're meant to tackle those straight-walking evil spirits, preventing them from accidentally entering houses.

SPORTS AND ACTIVITIES

KARATE Karate is the most famous of the Nansei-shotō sports. It's believed karate began life on the battlefield back in the 7th century. When Satsuma invaded, they banned the manufacture and carrying of all weapons for locals. This ban wasn't of short duration: it was reinforced in the late 1800s when Japan fully took over the archipelago. The weapons ban is one of the reasons why karate became so important to Okinawan people.

Though it may have originally been used for attack too, karate's primary goal is defence. It's designed to subdue an opponent in the least harmful way possible, generally using an understanding of the opponent's anatomy, nerves and weak points to control and quell them. Karate became incredibly popular across Japan, then internationally; there are now 50 million practitioners, known as *karateka*, across the globe.

The name karate, meaning 'empty hand', is actually a relatively recent moniker. Originally it was just called *te*, meaning 'hand', then became Uchinaa-de (Okinawa-te) in the local language. Three distinct forms were eventually developed: Shuri-te, Naha-te and Tomari-te. Shuri-te is now known as Okinawa Shōrin-ryū, Naha-te by Gōjū-ryū. Tomari-te was often seen as a hybrid of the other two, so gradually disappeared. Its modern replacement is Uechi-Ryū.

KOBUDŌ Karate's lesser-known cousin is *kobudō*, an Okinawan martial art using weapons. As expected, its history is debated; some believe it is older even than karate and was developed by the Pectin warrior clan. Others believe it developed in response to the 17th-century Satsuma invasion as a way for farmers to protect themselves against Satsuma samurai. This theory is largely down to the fact that the weapons used are farm tools. It's possible that both hold truth, that kobudō was developed by warriors early on, but became popularised when traditional weapons were taken away and farm implements were substituted.

Kobudō literally translates as 'old martial art' and uses several types of weapons. The most common is the *bo* staff, but there is also the three-pronged *sai*, the infamous *nunchaku*, *tonfa* batons, and *kama* sickles.

TEGUMI Tegumi is also known as Okinawa sumo, and while it's easy to see the similarities when watching a match, the aim of the game and its rules are different. There is no specific ring for a match and the object is to get your opponent on their back with both shoulders connected to the ground. To make matters more complicated, your hands are wrapped around your opponent's belt, essentially tying you together. (The 'te' part of its name is the same as in karate – 'hand'.) It's also known as *mutō*, and its origins are entirely unknown. Nowadays it isn't so popular, but it was often practised and watched in the early 1900s.

TŌGYŪ BULLFIGHTING Bullfighting is a popular pastime in Okinawa, Tokunoshima and some of the other islands, but this isn't Iberian-style bullfighting. *Tōgyū* is also known as *ushi-zumō*: 'bull sumo'. Here, bulls aren't pitted against humans but each other, and much like in human sumo, injuries aren't welcomed.

As with sumo wrestlers, animals have ranks with the top being *yokozuna*, and matches can last anywhere from seconds to a quarter of an hour. However, unlike human sumo, animals are divided into weight classes. The fight isn't usually bloody: bulls bash heads and lock horns, pushing against each other and forcing the other to get tired and give up.

The animals even have coaches who are there to prevent them from getting seriously hurt – if there's anything more than a flesh wound, matches are stopped. Coaches prepare the bulls for fights by getting them to walk through sand to strengthen their legs and push against tyres on trees, like punching bags, to strengthen their necks. It's hardly animal-friendly, but it's a far cry from the gore and death of the more famous European bullfights. Tōgyū is so popular and culturally important that the animals are considered status symbols for their owners.

There's evidence that tōgyū has been practised since at least the 1100s. At one point the sport was banned because farmers spent so much time training bulls and watching games that they forgot to actually farm. It didn't get widely popular until the Meiji period, though, becoming such a part of island life that bullfighting was back up and running just a few months after the war ended. Post-war, official rules were put in place for tōgyū tournaments.

TUG-OF-WAR Tug-of-war seems a surprising sport to find on the islands, but it's an incredibly common activity in harvest and thanksgiving festivals across the Nansei-shotō. Tug-of-wars can represent two sides, for example male and female, or simply opposing villages. Although there are opposing teams, tug-of-wars might also be a ceremonial activity towards a common goal; the outcome often determines the year's fortune for an island's crop or health.

Tug-of-wars crop up from north to south, with slight tweaks across villages and groups. The most famous is in Naha, Okinawa-hontō (page 189). This giant tug-of-war is a huge crowd-pleaser, where you can see participants trying to distract their opponents, going so far as to use sticks as weapons.

2

Practical Information

WHEN TO VISIT

There's often conflicting advice about when to visit the Nansei-shotō. The summer is remarkably sunny, but also has the rainy season. Autumn is the ideal temperature for hiking, but then there may be typhoons. Winter is relatively temperate, but lots of things close. Spring is great, but cooler, busier and more expensive.

In short, nothing is predictable: such is the nature of subtropical weather. You'll get large amounts of sunshine from March to October, but you're also likely to get rain too. Some of the best and most beautiful islands, like Yakushima, get rain regardless of the season; it's part and parcel of their attraction.

During the winter and typhoon seasons, some of the smaller accommodations and tour operators close and don't open again until February–March time. Typhoons can occur at any time if the conditions are right, but the season is said to be May–October. In general, they hit around September and October.

The islands are an outdoor destination, so weather is vital to making plans. Spring and late autumn are perfect for hiking, when humidity and rainfall aren't

PEAK SEASONS FOR WILDLIFE AND FLORA

Dashes represent lower seasons, crosses high.

Animal	Jan	Feb	Mar	Apr	May	Jun	Jul	Aug	Sep	Oct	Nov	Dec
Coral spawning					-	-	-	-	-			
Hammerhead	x	x	x									
Hawksbill		-	-	-	-	-	-	-	-	-	-	
Loggerhead			-	-	-	-	-	-	-	-	-	
Manta						-	-x	x	x	x	x-	
Stonefish	-	-	-	-								-
Whale		x	x-	-								

Plant	Jan	Feb	Mar	Apr	May	Jun	Jul	Aug	Sep	Oct	Nov	Dec
Azalea			x									
Bougainvillea		x	x									
Cherry	-x	x	x-									
Cosmos	x	x										
Hibiscus											x	x
Iris			-x	x-								
Lily				-x	x-							
Sunflower	-	x	-									

unbearable. Marine sports are particularly affected in poor weather, as seas become choppy and too dangerous to navigate by boat, never mind diving, snorkelling and swimming. The ideal season for these depends on what you hope to see; the tables on page 35 show a rough guide for both wildlife and floral peak seasons. As most of the islands are accessed via ferries, high winds and storms can see your travel plans cancelled last minute. Although ferry cancellations happen throughout the year, they are more likely off-season.

HIGHLIGHTS

With such a large number of islands, picking highlights feels near impossible. On the Ōsumi, Yakushima is a well-known, well-deserved highlight with its trails through ancient moss-covered forests, ethereal ambience and natural beach hot springs. Elsewhere on the Ōsumi, you can watch space rockets take off from Tanegashima, or bathe in the lauded hot springs of Iōjima.

On Amami, the main island is a must for remarkable UNESCO-listed scenery, with mangroves, winding rivers, waterfalls and stunning island viewpoints, as well as interesting local cuisine. On its neighbours, explore music and cultural heritage on lively Kikai, watch whales play off Tokunoshima's coast, go caving on Okinoerabu and find paradise on the phantom beaches of Yoron.

Okinawa offers city life, youth and beauty with everything from shopping and tug-of-war festivals to deep forests and sacred shrines. Off its coast, the stunning Kerama-shotō are a must, with incredible diving, turtle grounds and migrating humpback whales. Miyako's highlights include small mangroves, natural caves, white-sand beaches, surfing and some of the archipelago's best diving sites.

On the Yaeyama, Iriomote rules supreme, with wildlife, dripping jungle, Amazon-like rivers, ancient nature worship and its own endemic cat. Taketomi holds insights into ancient ways of life, with its preserved villages and stars and beaches, while Ishigaki is a land of pearls, manta rays and mountain hikes.

ACTIVITIES

Canoeing and kayaking Sea kayaking is a popular pastime on many of the islands, excellent for seeing hidden coastal landscapes like pouring waterfalls and secret beaches. Canoeing is best done in the archipelago's mangroves: the biggest and best are on Iriomote and Amami Ōshima, where you can peacefully work your way up deep green rivers to see thriving ecosystems.

Caving Coral islands offer up excellent caving opportunities, none more so than Okinoerabujima. Here you can find some of Japan's longest cave systems, only reachable by guided tour. Tours range from beginner to intermediate, with the biggest attraction, Ginsuidō, taking a good 6 hours. Smaller caves, often used as hideouts during World War II, are littered throughout the archipelago and can be visited solo. Many of them – even the smallest – have sad or sacred histories, making each worthy of a detour. Check out Kumejima's Yaajaa, a burial cave, and Okinawa-hontō's underwater Blue Cave.

Hiking With extraordinary scenery, these islands offer phenomenal hiking and trekking. Yakushima in the north is particularly well known throughout Japan for trails through its ancient forest, but southerly Iriomote has an amazing number of short and longer treks hidden in its rich jungle. Amami Ōshima has wonderful hiking too, but to make best use of its protected sacred forests you'll need to take a local guide. Okinawa-hontō, Ishigaki and Tokunoshima also have their fair share of routes, many with shorter hikes to gorgeous waterfalls, mountains and nature spots.

Scuba-diving and snorkelling The Nansei-Shotō is Japan's marine destination. You'll find diving and snorkelling opportunities on every single island, though some are easily better than others. If you are looking for a diving holiday, head to the brilliant Yaeyama for manta scrambles and hammerhead dives, the Kerama for turtles, corals and whales, or Okinawa and Miyako for cave systems. The Kerama and Miyako are arguably the best spots for snorkelling, with teeming reefs close to the beaches.

SUGGESTED ITINERARIES

A LONG WEEKEND If you are popping to the islands for a long weekend out of a longer Japan itinerary, you'll want to fly. Okinawa-hontō is a great option for those looking for a mix of modern city culture or shopping with some history and tradition thrown in. Spend a day exploring Naha, another seeing the aquarium to its north, and the last driving south to see war memorials and the Seefa-Utaki, or Sēfa-Utaki, shrine. Alternatively, fly to Yakushima and pick up a rental car for a weekend of hiking mountain forests and hot springs, or Miyakojima for embracing the beach bum life and topping up the tan.

A WEEK If you have a week to play with, pick an island group and stick with it. A week gives you ample opportunity to explore some of the Yaeyama, with a couple of days exploring Ishigaki, a day trip to Taketomi traditional village, and four days hiking, kayaking or river cruising in Iriomote. A week-long Okinawa trip allows for exploring Okinawa-hontō's wild Yanbaru north for waterfalls and wildlife, as well as at least an overnight trip to the Kerama.

If heading to Amami, explore the entirety of Amami Ōshima by car and pick another of the islands to explore depending on whether you prefer caving, culture, beaches or wildlife. For Miyako, you can make the most of its connected bridges and see the majority of the island group, bouncing from pristine sands to surf to scuba and snorkel spots.

TWO WEEKS With two weeks you can start to incorporate multiple island groups or, alternatively, go deeper into a group and explore its outer islands. Some offer truly unique experiences, like Yonaguni's hammerhead shark diving, Kumejima's cave burial ground, Tarama's rural isolation, Kuroshima's cow festival and more. You can also spend longer on the groups' larger central islands, discovering rarely used hiking trails, alternate dive sites and secret beaches.

TOUR OPERATORS AND TOURIST INFORMATION

All island-specific tour operators and tourist offices are noted under individual sections. Larger Japan tour operators may include some of the islands in their itineraries, but will rarely go to the smaller, more obscure ones. Your best bet is to look to tour operators with experts in the region who can adapt to your needs, like those listed on page 38. For those travelling in Okinawa Prefecture, there is a very handy multilingual tourist contact centre (☎ 0570 07 7201; w okinawa-mcc.jp) which includes a 24-hour contact form on their website. Kagoshima Prefecture has an English tourist website too (w kagoshima-yokanavi.jp/en).

Fabulicious Travels Harrow Manorway, London; m 07907 746090; e Denise@fabulicioustravels.com; w fabulicioustravels.com. Independent travel agency, offering unrivalled personal service, unbiased & professional advice & able to access some of the best choices of travel products worldwide.

Inside Japan 0117 244 3380; e info@insidejapantours.com; w insidejapantours.com. UK-based Japan specialist who does tailor-made tours around Japan, hand-picking the most knowledgeable guides for each region. Led by passionate expert James Mundy, Inside Japan aims to 'get beneath' the country's surface – ideal for these outlying islands. Stellar accreditation, sustainability & reputation.

Travel Local w travellocal.com. A UK-based website where you can book direct with selected local travel companies, allowing you to communicate with an expert ground operator without having to go through a 3rd party travel operator or agent. Your booking with the local company has full financial protection, but note that travel to the destination is not included. Member of ABTA, ASTA.

RED TAPE

VISAS AND PASSPORTS Visa allowances depend on your nationality. Tourists travelling on a UK passport are allowed 90 days travel visa-free. If you are travelling to Japan on this visa, you will not have to do anything in advance to enter the country, but must fill out a customs declaration and immigration form on the plane.

A little-known quirk also allows for the citizens of eight countries to extend their tourist visa for a further 90 days without having to leave the country; the UK is one of these. If you are planning to extend your visa this way, you will need to go to the closest local government office that performs these extensions (see opposite). Be aware that these extended visas are not common knowledge, even for border staff, who usually expect you to have a return flight within 90 days. It is best to bring proof of this exception in Japanese, just in case. Note that these extensions are granted at the government's discretion, and you may for whatever reason be denied.

Tourist visas do not allow you to work in the country. Japan does offer working holiday visas, as well as business visas and more (see w uk.emb-japan.go.jp/itpr_en). Your passport should have at least six months' validity left to enter the country. When travelling in Japan, you are expected to keep your passport on you at all times. Police officers are allowed to randomly demand identification, and can stop you in the street and search you.

CUSTOMS Japan prohibits any import and use of narcotic drugs, ammunition and firearms and punishment is strict for anyone caught breaking these laws. It isn't just illegal drugs that are strictly prohibited: some medications and even non-medicated items that are readily available over-the-counter in Western countries are also prohibited (page 40).

Currency in excess of ¥1 million has to be declared at customs. Foreign tourists can buy electronics tax-free if they are purchased in licensed shops – most commonly large chain department stores. Duty-free allowance only extends to items under ¥200,000. You can bring in 400 cigarettes, 100 cigars, three 760ml bottles of spirits and 60ml of perfume. Always check the current allowances on the Japanese customs website (w customs.go.jp) before you fly.

EMBASSIES AND CONSULATES

All consulate services are provided to the British Embassy in Tokyo (1 Ichiban-chō, Chiyoda-ku, Tokyo; 0352 11 1100; w gov.uk/contact-consulate-tokyo; ⌚ 09.30–16.30 Mon–Fri). If you are looking for immigration services, like extending your

90-day tourist visa as a UK national, you can use regional immigration bureaus within the islands.

REGIONAL IMMIGRATION BUREAUS

Ishigaki Port Branch Office Ishigaki Port Joint Government Bldg 1-1-8 Hamasaki-chō; 0980 82 2333; 09.00–12.00 & 13.00–16.00 Mon–Fri
Kadena Branch Office Rotary Bldg 1-290-9 Kadena; 0989 57 5252; 09.00–12.00 & 13.00–16.00 Mon–Fri
Kagoshima Branch Office Kagoshima Port Joint Government Bldg 18-2-40 Izumi-chō; 0992 22 5658; 09.00–12.00 & 13.00–16.00 Mon–Fri
Miyakojima Branch Office Hirara Port Joint Government Bldg 7-21 Aza Nishizato; 0980 72 3440; 09.00–12.00 & 13.00–16.00 Mon–Fri
Naha Airport Branch Office Naha Airport Terminal, 174 Kagamizu; 0988 57 0053; 09.00–12.00 & 13.00–16.00 Mon–Fri

GETTING THERE AND AWAY

All flights from the UK to the islands require at least one stopover, usually on the Japanese mainland. The most common route is through Tokyo (via either Haneda or Narita airport), offering a great option for those wanting to combine a trip of mainland city and island life. For the Ōsumi, the northernmost island group, you can fly into Kagoshima and get a ferry down from there.

Multiple airlines serve the myriad airports across the island chain. The most common access point is Naha International Airport on Okinawa-hontō, which is connected to the city nearby by monorail. The majority of the islands are reached by ferries or jetfoils, run by a plethora of companies. For further information about access, see individual island sections.

HEALTH *with Dr Daniel Campion*

Health care in Japan is of a very high standard. In general patients pay 30% of fees and the government the remaining 70%, but there are universal health-care insurance systems and health insurance programs to help fund those who cannot pay. For travellers, you or your insurance will be required to fund the entirety, which can be expensive if you're not covered. Delays in treatment can occur while medical facilities check your coverage and you may need to cover the cost in advance and be reimbursed by your insurance. Some insurance companies have specific medical facilities they work with to avoid this, so check in advance.

PREPARATIONS It's vital to buy travel insurance that covers all of your activities and pre-existing conditions. For guidance on English-speaking doctors and medical access, look to the Japan National Tourism Organisation website (w jnto.go.jp/emergency).

When packing for a trip to Japan, make sure to bring an emergency medical kit just in case. It's difficult to find medication when faced with a language you don't speak or read, so it's worth bringing basic painkillers, insect repellent, antihistamines and any other medications you might commonly need. Check, however, that they are legal to bring into the country (page 40).

Prolonged immobility on long-haul flights can result in **deep-vein thrombosis (DVT)**, which can be dangerous if the clot travels to the lungs to cause a pulmonary embolism. The risk increases with age, and is higher in obese or pregnant travellers, heavy smokers, those taller than 6ft/1.8m, and anybody with a history of blood clots, recent major operation or varicose veins surgery, cancer, a stroke or heart disease. If any of these criteria apply, consult a doctor before you travel.

Prescriptions and medicines Japan has strict rules about certain medications and medical items you are allowed to bring into the country, many of which are surprising – contact lenses being one. Drugs are set into five categories in Japan, each with their own rules. Check your medication in advance to ensure you can travel with the amounts you need. You can get a medical import certificate called a Yakkan Shoumei (薬監証明) allowing some in the country. This can take around a week to receive. If your application is urgent, indicate this in the email subject line of your application. If you need the certificate in paper format, this adds a couple of weeks to the timeline.

To apply for a Yakkan Shoumei, download the form from your country's Japanese embassy website and follow their instructions. Email this and any necessary supporting documentation to the pharmaceutical inspector in Japan at your destination port, as found on the embassy website. You'll need a Yakkan Shoumei if you are bringing: more than two-month's supply of over-the-counter drugs such as ibuprofen, vitamins and disposable contact lenses; more than one-month's supply of prescription drugs; more than one home medical device per person, such as epi-pens or insulin pens, or if the device must be used under doctor's orders.

To bring narcotic medications into Japan you will need a narcotics certificate, which differs from a Yakkan Shoumei. 'Narcotics' include codeine, morphine, sufentanil and oxycodone. These applications require an import/export form, a doctor's letter and flight details to be sent to the Narcotic Control Department of the area you are arriving in. Be warned – these may be outright forbidden.

The only completely banned category are stimulants: these are illegal to bring into Japan. Stimulants also aren't limited to recreational drugs – some over-the-counter and prescription drugs are included. Phenylephrine found in decongestants such as nasal spray and cold and flu treatments is included, and some inhalers, allergy and sinus medications contain banned stimulant substances and are strictly prohibited without exception.

Vaccinations There are no mandatory vaccinations for travelling to the Nansei-shotō but you should confirm your primary courses and boosters, such as tetanus vaccine, are up to date. Seasonal influenza and COVID-19 boosters are recommended for those at increased risk. Vaccines should ideally be checked at least six to eight weeks before you travel, but don't panic if time is short: many can be given shortly before departure. You'll find up-to-date information on the required vaccines at **w** travelhealthpro.org.uk.

Depending on pre-existing conditions and your planned activities, you may wish to get other vaccines. Hepatitis B vaccine is essential for health workers and should be considered for people working with children or participating in contact sports. This virus is transmitted through blood and body fluids (including sexual transmission). For prolonged travel in rural locations Japanese encephalitis vaccine may be recommended (see opposite). Rabies has not been reported in pets or terrestrial wild animals in Japan, but bats may carry rabies-like viruses. Rabies post-exposure treatment is available in Japan. Vaccination before travel is only recommended for travellers at highest risk, such as those working directly with wildlife.

Travel clinics and health information A full list of current travel clinic websites worldwide is available on **w** istm.org. For other journey preparation information, consult w travelhealthpro.org.uk (UK) or w wwwnc.cdc.gov/travel (USA). All advice found online should be used in conjunction with expert advice received prior to or during travel.

MEDICAL PROBLEMS Many health problems abroad can't be vaccinated against, such as sun exposure, animal bites, good hygiene, accident prevention and food and water safety, and require preventative measures.

Make sure to have travel insurance that covers all the activities you expect to partake in as well as repatriation in an emergency. For current disease outbreaks, see the websites listed above.

Mosquitoes and ticks Japan is free of malaria. **Japanese encephalitis** is a viral infection which causes inflammation of the brain. It can be fatal, although most infections are asymptomatic. It is transmitted by mosquitoes which usually feed between dusk and dawn. These mosquitoes are found throughout Japan except Hokkaidō. They usually feed on wading birds and pigs which are the natural hosts of the virus, so human cases are commonest in rural areas where there are rice fields, swamps or pig farms. The disease is rare in travellers, but vaccination should be considered if you are spending time in high-risk areas. It's always sensible to make sure your accommodation is insect-proof, wear long sleeves and trousers, and to cover exposed skin with a repellent such as DEET or icaridin. **Ticks** carrying tick-borne encephalitis or Lyme disease are more commonly found further north in Japan. However, they are present throughout the country and may harbour other infections. Avoiding tick bites is the best way to mitigate the risk, so if walking in forests or grasslands, try to cover exposed areas of skin and check your body for ticks after any hike or outdoor activity. If found, ticks should be removed as soon as possible – see below for advice.

Leptospirosis This bacterial infection is caught by swimming in rivers contaminated with the urine of infected animals. Cases have been reported in Okinawa, usually during summer, but are uncommon. Symptoms include a sudden fever, headache, jaundice and muscle aches, between two and 26 days after exposure. If you get these symptoms, seek medical advice. Leptospirosis can be treated with antibiotics, ideally at an early stage.

TICK REMOVAL

Ticks should ideally be removed complete, and as soon as possible, to reduce the chance of infection. You can use special tick tweezers, which can be bought in good travel shops; or failing this, with your fingernails, grasp the tick as close to your body as possible, and pull it away steadily and firmly at right angles to your skin without jerking or twisting. Applying irritants (eg: Olbas oil) or lit cigarettes is to be discouraged as a means of removal since they can cause the ticks to regurgitate and therefore increase the risk of disease. Once the tick is removed, if possible douse the wound with alcohol (any spirit will do), soap and water, or iodine. If you are travelling with small children, remember to check their heads, and particularly behind the ears, for ticks. Spreading redness around the bite and/or fever and/or aching joints after a tick bite imply that you have an infection that requires antibiotic treatment. In this case seek medical advice.

Rabies Rabies is a deadly disease but most travellers are at very low risk: terrestrial rabies was eliminated from Japan 60 years ago. Bats, however, can potentially still carry rabies-like viruses. Bites or scratches from bats can usually be felt, but the small wounds may be hard to see. Rabies is preventable with timely post-exposure treatment. After any contact with a bat (even if a bite or scratch was uncertain) wash the wound thoroughly and seek medical advice.

Heat illness and sunburn Island weather is very changeable – sweltering sunny days can soon turn to downpours and vice versa, so it's important to be prepared. Heat illness can occur when exposure to the sun and/or humidity cause an imbalance of water and sodium and you're unable to effectively regulate temperature. It's easily preventable but its most severe form (heatstroke) can be fatal.

Drink water and sports drinks frequently and limit time spent in the heat. Wear breathable loose clothing, use a hat or parasol, wear sunglasses and use fans or air conditioning. Certain medications (including various blood pressure tablets, antidepressants and antihistamines) may increase your risk of heat illness, so extra caution is advised. Symptoms of **heat exhaustion** include profuse sweating, pale clammy skin, fast shallow breathing, nausea, headaches, rapid weak pulse and stomach cramps. In this case you should move to a cool place immediately, loosen/remove clothing and apply cold water to the neck, armpits and groin. Drink plenty of fluids – if there's a nearby vending machine, Pocari Sweat or a similar sports drink containing electrolytes may be helpful to replace losses from sweat. **Heatstroke** occurs when the body's cooling system has broken down completely. The skin becomes hot and red, breathing slows and confusion and dizziness lead to unconsciousness. Cooling the body down is paramount and immediate medical assistance is essential.

The sun is more intense in this subtropical archipelago compared to other regions of Japan. Sunburn can be at best uncomfortable, and at worst can lead to fever, blistering, severe pain and hospitalisation. A broad-brimmed hat, UV-blocking sunglasses and broad spectrum, high protection factor sunscreens (30 SPF-plus with UVA rating of 4/5 stars) are recommended, even on cloudy days.

Food poisoning from fish or shellfish Japanese food hygiene standards are excellent, but occasional cases of seafood poisoning have been reported in subtropical regions. Marine toxins such as ciguatera (which can contaminate reef fish including grouper and red snapper) are not destroyed by cooking: take local advice on which seafood is safe to eat. Seek medical advice if you feel unwell after eating; the DAN book linked on page 46 provides more detail. It is safest to avoid pufferfish (fugu), a popular local delicacy. Meticulous preparation is required to remove its poisonous parts, which contain a lethal nerve toxin.

SAFETY

Japan is a remarkably safe country to travel in, arguably even more so on the islands than the mainland. The small community feel on the most remote islands means that everyone is acquainted and looks out for one another. Theft is usually limited to borrowing an umbrella in a moment of need.

Islands like Taketomi are famed for not having keys to their houses: doors are simply left open. On Miyakojima, keys are left in motorbikes; on Ishigaki, bicycles are unchained. Leaving bags of valuables on the beach while you surf, snorkel or swim is not unheard of – it's really quite common.

EMERGENCY NUMBERS

110 Police (on mobiles, m 112 & 911 redirect to 110)
118 Maritime emergencies
119 Ambulance & fire brigade
171 Earthquake assistance

However, this open community attitude doesn't necessarily extend to the largest islands, especially Okinawa-hontō where there's a big-city feel and a lot more foreign tourism. While it's lovely to rely on the kindness of strangers and communal protection, always exercise caution when travelling. Look out for your wallet and valuables, keep bags in safe spaces and don't flash large amounts of cash around.

Most Japanese ports, as well as bus, tram and train stations, have lockers large enough to fit suitcases in. These are a great option if you're doing a day trip between islands and haven't checked into the next hotel, but be aware these can fill up quickly. Most accommodations will happily take your bag for free, though don't expect it to be locked up in a safe room.

Crime is so low on these islands that many of them don't actually have any police. On some, the entire police force has been replaced with a slightly eerie statue called Mamoru-kun, designed to remind drivers to slow down at junctions. You will find a police presence elsewhere, though the stations on sleepier islands aren't open 24 hours a day.

The most common concern on these islands isn't crime but nature. The archipelago's beauty comes with a sting in its tail – sometimes literally. The islands are surrounded by glorious oceans, flora and fauna, a fair number of which can kill if you don't take precautions.

SEA SAFETY The blue, crystalline waters are siren-like in their allure, and it's easy to heed their call without considering safety first. Many islands have strong reef currents, which flow out through the gaps in reefs: this means a beach may look shallow and safe but can hide hazardous currents that can drag you to deeper waters. If you feel yourself being carried out by a current, do not swim against it: swim parallel to the shore, across the current.

Swim in designated areas – if it's a non-swimming beach follow the guidelines – and avoid swimming alone. Take regular breaks and drink enough water, especially as the sun is strong and the cooler sea masks its heat. Don't drink alcohol before swimming and make sure to be in good physical condition. If uncertain, get guidance from an instructor or join a tour.

For scuba-diving, make sure the companies you dive with are licensed. Even if you are a licensed dive master, contact local dive companies to learn the area and its hazards from those in the know. Also check the requirements in advance if you have a specific dive in mind – the hammerhead dive in Yonaguni, for example, needs not only a licence but an extensive history of dives. Keep your knowledge up to date, and make sure diving is covered by your insurance. Always remember to leave 24 hours between flying and diving.

WILDLIFE Where there's virgin jungle and endless seas, there's a whole host of exotic brilliant animals – and Okinawa's can inflict deadly damage. Respect animals and never get too close, regardless of whether the species is considered 'safe'. Even the most poisonous creatures rarely attack unless provoked.

Habu pit viper The archipelagic poster child for dangerous creatures, this arrow-headed snake can be seen on posters all over the islands. Even if you don't read Japanese, the liberal use of exclamation marks should give you an idea of just how deadly it can be.

Simply put, its venom can kill you. You're lucky if you happen to be near a hospital when bitten but habu bites often occur on remote trails. It's important to be cautious and look out for these snakes in the undergrowth. There are different habu species and other, non-deadly snakes on the islands, making immediate identification tricky. Make sure you look up the three most common (habu, hime habu and sakishima habu) so you know what to look for. These three all have black in their patterning – while this is common for a few snakes in this area, it's an easy measure of which to avoid. Habu also have the telltale arrow-shaped head of vipers and grow to an average 1.5m, but remember the ones you come across may be juveniles. All of them have small scales on their heads – but if you can identify these, you're already too close. Habu do not hibernate but they're more active between April and November. They are nocturnal and during daytime will often sleep in walls, caves and thickets. They don't jump but are good at climbing and swimming. They tend to be irritable and aggressive, so if you do see one, stay well out of its way. Striking distance is over a metre.

If you get bitten, keep calm and first check if it was a habu. If you cannot identify or see it, look at the bite mark. Habu leave two fang marks and may bite one to four times. A minority of habu bites are 'dry' and do not contain venom, but you should seek medical advice in any case. With venomous bites, the area will become very painful and swell up within 30 minutes. If you think it's a habu, stay as still as possible as running circulates the venom faster. Call loudly for help and ask to be taken to hospital – the words 'habu' and '*byōin*' and the wound should be enough. If there's no-one around, use your phone to call an ambulance and ask for an English speaker. If this is unsuccessful, call your accommodation and get them to send help. If you can easily reach your car or transport, get to the hospital, and if you must walk, go slowly. Remove any jewellery or tight-fitting clothes from the affected area. Severe swelling is common after habu bites: tight binding and tourniquets must be avoided. A splint can help prevent movement of the bitten limb. The bite can be covered with a clean dry dressing or local pressure pad. Treatment with antivenom is effective.

Black-banded sea krait (*Irabu umihebi*) This sea snake is beautiful to watch gently whipping through the reefs. It's a gorgeous creature, with yellow and blue-black bands along its body, which grows up to 80cm. Unfortunately, it's a pretty but deadly diving buddy. Its venom is more toxic than the habu's and can cause muscle and nerve damage including paralysis. Luckily these animals are wonderfully docile and are quite happy for divers to watch their journey from afar. They will only bite if provoked, so make sure to keep your distance and look out for any coiled on the ocean floor or between rocks. If you do get bitten, clean the wound and get to a hospital as quickly as possible.

Blue-ringed octopus (*Ōmarumondako*) Size can be deceiving. These tiny octopuses are incredibly beautiful – their pale yellow bodies are dotted with deep lapis-coloured rings. If you see one of these, your best bet is to go in the opposite direction. At some 12cm, these are some of the deadliest sea creatures in the world. They carry a tetrodotoxin and are capable of injecting enough in a single bite to kill a human. Again, seek emergency medical treatment – CPR may be required.

Geography cone snail (*Imo-gai*) These clams are prized for their orange and white patterned shells, making them tempting to pick up while they go along the ocean floor: don't. They are one of the deadliest animals on these islands. They use a harpoon-like stinger filled with venom to immobilise their prey and will quite happily use it on you too. If untreated, their venom can easily kill a human. There is no specific antivenom and treatment is supportive. It's likely only scuba-divers and snorkellers will encounter these as they prefer the sea floor, but be cautious nonetheless when picking shells up on the beach. If you get stung, clean the wound and get to the hospital as quickly as possible.

Box jellyfish (*Chironex*) The box jellyfish season is May to October. It is found in any waters above 50cm deep and can cause paralysis, cardiac arrest, and extremely painful stings. In many busy swimming areas, jellyfish nets are used to keep jellyfish at bay, but smaller ones can still sneak through. If stung, get out of the sea and don't rub the affected area. Pour vinegar on the area – a technique only effective with box jellyfish stings. Restaurants, hotels or nearby shops will likely have vinegar (*binegā*, or *su*) you can use. Avoid applying alcoholic solutions or suncream. A photo of the injury may help non-English speakers understand. If tentacles remain on the skin, gently scrape them off with a bank card or use tweezers – gentle is key. Immersion in hot water (up to 45°C) may help the pain. Larger stings can be fatal. Make sure to monitor breathing and heart rate until the ambulance arrives: basic life support including CPR may be required.

Portuguese man o'war These blue, balloon-like creatures bob along the sea – not a single organism but a colony of them – with tentacles filled with venom. They are not often deadly, but can be to children if stings aren't removed quickly. Get out of the water and remove any tentacles with tweezers or a bank card. Do not use vinegar on the wound, but rinse it with seawater or hot (not scalding) water for about 20 minutes. Apply a hot compress and seek medical attention if it gets worse, you have difficulty breathing, pains or if it covers a large area. Do not bind the affected area tightly.

Fire coral These coral-like animals are actually closer relatives of jellyfish and sea anemones than coral, and they carry the family sting. If you brush against one, it triggers millions of microscopic stingers which are likened to a flame being held to your skin. This pain can last a while but is thankfully not deadly. Rinse with seawater, apply vinegar and expect a rash. Applying hydrocortisone cream to the affected area may provide some relief. Antibiotics and a tetanus booster may be necessary; seek medical advice.

Stonefish The sting of the well-camouflaged stonefish is excruciating and can be deadly if left untreated. Stonefish sit in the sand – and can survive out of the sea in low tide – and are most often trodden on. Immediately seek medical treatment and pour hot water into the wound (around 45°C). Nausea, vomiting and weakness may occur. Antivenom can neutralise the toxic effects but should be administered in hospital because serious allergic reactions are possible.

Other hazardous marine life The following first aid is applicable to these sea creatures: crown-of-thorns starfish, sea urchin, flower urchin, striped catfish eel and lionfish. Remove any large visible spines as gently as possible and bathe the area in hot water (around 45°C). Avoid rubbing the area. Over-the-counter pain medications may be sufficient in mild cases. If there are any signs of toxicity, an allergic reaction, infection, or if spines can still be seen or felt in the wound, seek medical aid. Check if you need a tetanus booster. The Divers' Alert Network (DAN) has a good online resource with detailed information on hazardous sea life: **w** dan.org/health-medicine/health-resource/dive-medical-reference-books/hazardous-marine-life.

NATURAL DISASTERS The islands are prone to typhoons, which are seasonal and thereby predictable, as well as earthquakes, tsunamis and volcanic activity. Earthquakes are regular and happen most days in Japan, the majority too small to ever notice. The islands rarely see any major earthquakes or resulting tsunamis, but it's vital you know what to do should there ever be an alert.

For further safety information while travelling the Nansei-shotō, download the Safety Tips app (**w** jnto.go.jp/safety-tips/eng/app.html) that gives push alerts about earthquake, tsunami and weather early warnings. For all weather and disaster-related information, look to Japan's Meteorological Agency (**w** jma.go.jp).

Typhoon If there is a typhoon, stay inside as strong winds can pick up and propel dangerous objects. Keep away from glass windows. A prediction of the duration will be available from Japan's Meteorological Agency. Transport is usually affected – check services and if you are due to fly back during the typhoon, consult your airline or travel agent for information. It is best to contact them as soon as a typhoon is forecast. If you are on the islands after a typhoon, stay away from beaches until they are declared safe – waves can remain choppy and high.

Earthquakes Many earthquakes pass unnoticed or are a short rumble that is unsettling but not dangerous – they're often over before you've had a chance to think. Japan has an early warning system in place for quakes of magnitude 6 and above, but the advance notice is usually seconds at most. Alerts will scroll across most TV channels and a text is sent to all phones connected to Japan's major mobile networks. While you may not be connected yourself, most people around you will be: if you're in a public place and every phone suddenly buzzes, be alert.

If you're inside, do not rush out but open the door to your room so that you can clear an evacuation route. Stay away from glass, windows and furniture and try to keep yourself low while protecting your head. Stay inside until the shakes are over. Japan's buildings are designed to withstand earthquakes; in doing so, they intentionally wobble which feels scary but actually helps protect you.

If outside, get to an open space like a park or square as quickly as possible. Stay away from walls, narrow roads, cliffs, the coast and rivers. Crouch on the ground and protect your head. If in a car, slow down, park on the shoulder and turn off the car. Wait inside until the shakes are over. Do not lock the doors. Once you leave the car, make sure to take the key with you.

Tsunami Tsunamis may follow a major earthquake – once the tremors have finished, it's best to be overly cautious. If you are near a river, beach or coastal area, head inland and await information.

If there is a tsunami alert, immediately run to high ground – this may be a natural landmark or a building. If you are in a car, drive there. If you do not know where to evacuate, ask those around you or follow locals. Islanders will know the nearest evacuation points for this eventuality and your accommodation can tell you in advance.

Tourist sites and coastal areas will have signs showing the elevation from sea level. Please take note of these and reach a shelter above sea level when evacuated –

head for as high as you possibly can. Many of the small islands are very flat and will have a known, single point to head towards.

Safe evacuation requires co-operation and help. Act promptly and calmly, follow the advice of locals or hotel staff, and if you see anyone in need of assistance, help them or ask others to. If there is an alert and you are near the beach, encourage and warn others to evacuate. Never approach the beach or sea until the tsunami alert has been completely lifted.

Volcanoes Volcanic activity is relatively common in Japan, particularly in Kagoshima Prefecture, but major eruptions are rare. There are five volcanic alert levels escalating from 1 to 5: 1 is potential for increased activity; 2, do not approach crater; 3, do not approach the volcano; 4, prepare to evacuate; and 5, evacuate. Not following these guidelines can result in a threat to life.

No action is required for Level 1 forecasts. Level 2 only affects climbers, who should refrain from approaching the crater in line with current determined areas. For Level 3, climbers should refrain from entering the determined danger zones and those residing in nearby areas should stand by. At Level 4, possible eruptions could cause serious damage to residential and non-residential areas nearer the crater and people should be prepared to evacuate from alert areas. Those with limited mobility or dependents should prepare to evacuate at Level 3 and evacuate at Level 4.

Level 5 indicates that an eruption is likely imminent and will cause serious damage: everyone should evacuate from the determined danger zone. In an evacuation, follow instructions from police, fire brigade or hotel staff.

WOMEN TRAVELLERS

Thanks to its remarkable safety record, Japan is a wonderful place to travel as a woman. Even in bigger cities, violent crime is low and it is unusual for locals to engage with strangers on the street. Catcalling is notably absent. There is a healthy drinks culture, particularly for office workers, but groups keep to themselves and don't bother foreigners. Spiking of drinks is rare but can still happen.

However, the two crimes Japan is renowned for are sexually driven: the taking of up-skirt photos and groping on trains. These are generally limited to big cities on the mainland and rarely happen to foreign-looking women. Still, be vigilant on escalators and stairs and be aware of those around you in train carriages. Many trains operate a female-only carriage during rush-hour.

On the islands, communities are generally tight-knit and friendly, and all tourists are looked after well. However, there are always exceptions, both from local and foreign offenders. In recent years there have been allegations of multiple sexual assaults on solo female travellers on Yakushima, most of which go unreported. A deeply problematic side to the close local community is the unwillingness to report – or even punish – neighbours, friends or family. These allegations have been little spoken of in newspapers, but have been leaked by local whistleblowers living on the island. Statistically these alleged crimes are few and uncommon but once is enough: if travelling to Yakushima as a solo female traveller, avoid staying in guesthouses run by lone men.

Okinawa-hontō sees a lot of foreign tourists and settlers due to the presence of the US military, and there have been multiple incidents of sexual crimes, violence and rape committed by military men against local girls and women. As with any travel, err on the side of caution: avoid walking alone at night, stick to well-lit paths and don't leave drinks unattended. Still, it's hard not to enjoy the sense of safety in Japan as a solo female traveller – a rare thing.

There are no clothing regulations in Japan, but Japanese women tend to dress on the modest side. Low-cut tops and short shorts aren't very popular, so don't be surprised if you garner a few stares. Beachwear is limited to the beaches, so always bring something to change into before heading elsewhere.

LGBTQIA+ TRAVELLERS

Japanese society is incredibly private when it comes to relationships, regardless of orientation or identity. Public displays of affection are rarely seen – even heterosexual couples are generally limited to hand-holding. Occasionally you might see young teens being more openly affectionate, but this is usually only in big cities. Out of respect for the Japanese culture, travellers should keep overt gestures of affection or romance out of the public eye regardless of gender or sexual orientation.

Japanese society is slow to change and accept people considered outside of the status quo, but people are very rarely aggressive. Differences – from tattoos to blonde hair – usually earn a stare from the older generation but little more. This relative welcome means Japan is a country of thriving subcultures, of which the LGBTQIA+ community is one. However, Japan's subculture clubs, groups and gatherings are mostly found in bigger cities rather than remote areas. Finding any kind of club or bar on some of these islands is difficult enough.

That said, you'll find gay bars and clubs in the gateway cities and the larger towns and cities on the islands, particularly Naha, Miyako and Ishigaki. The majority of these are aimed more at men. A list of establishments, events and community spaces can be found at Stonewall Japan (w stonewalljapan.org), along with a Trans* Guide to Japan, with resources and medical information for transgender people.

TRAVELLING WITH KIDS

The archipelago is a wonderful place to bring children. It's safe, clean and there are plentiful child-friendly activities such as rocket launches, boat rides, museums, the world's second largest aquarium, caves, zoos, snorkelling, beaches and easy hikes. Temples and shrines offer a great introduction to the culture, though even adults can tire of the endless supply of them.

Japan's baby and child accoutrements like nappies and food are similar to the West, and some larger hotels offer babysitting services. There are lots of public parks with play facilities and though there aren't always public toilets, most big shops will have them. The majority of paid activities and transport systems (including domestic flights) offer a range of children's discounts based on their school age, with the youngest often going free.

INFORMATION ON TRAVELLING WITH A DISABILITY

The UK's **gov.uk** website (w gov.uk/government/publications/disabled-travellers/disability-and-travel-abroad) has a downloadable guide giving general advice and practical information for travellers with a disability (and their companions) preparing for overseas travel.The **Society for Accessible Travel and Hospitality** (w sath.org) also provides some general information.

For Japan-specific advice, the **Accessible Japan** (w accessible-japan.com) and **Barrier Free Japan** (w barrierfreejapan.com) websites offer lots of good information for travellers with a disability.

Though children can be fussy eaters and Japanese food very different from Western, there are lots of options available. Many places have set meals for children, and if they're not keen on local dishes there are plenty of other options, especially on Okinawa-hontō. Italian and American food are both popular, and you can pick up lots of exciting snacks at convenience stores to keep even the fussiest eaters topped up. Department store food courts are prevalent, and also offer great value and variety.

There are pitfalls, however. You may need to check in advance that restaurants accept younger children, particularly more high-end, traditional ones. There is often an ambience to dining and respect for food in these kinds of restaurants that a messy toddler doesn't exactly uphold: it's an experience best left to older children.

Breastfeeding is highly encouraged in Japan, but the reserved culture means it is rarely done in the open. However, breastfeeding and family rooms are common in big shops and museums, and are usually immaculate. If you hope to breastfeed in public, it is recommended to bring a cover with you. You won't get awful responses without, but it's likely to make people feel awkward.

Japan, particularly the Nansei-shotō, isn't pram-friendly. If you are taking children on public transport, it's best to avoid rush-hour. There are designated seats for those with small children, pregnant women and the elderly, but even getting to these on packed trains isn't easy.

If you're heading to more remote islands with younger children, be aware that prams will not make it around many of the walkways: even tourist-heavy Taketomi is entirely paved with large gravel and stones and only has cars on the main road.

As with adults, be careful in the sea. There are currents in some areas so make sure to keep children supervised and only swim in designated safe spaces. There are also plenty of dangerous critters (page 43), so make sure children do not touch animals or go searching for shells without an adult present.

WHAT TO TAKE

With so many activities available, those with their own equipment will want to pack accordingly whether it be wetsuits, dive gear, hiking boots and poles, snorkels, camping gear, golf clubs or surfboards. It's also worth packing an emergency medical kit (page 39) just in case you fall foul of scratches, bites and jellyfish stings, or even humdrum colds. There aren't many dedicated pharmacies on the islands and it can be incredibly complicated trying to get what you need with minimal Japanese – just make sure to abide by customs regulations (page 38).

If you're keen to spot animals while on the islands, you'll find a pair of binoculars incredibly useful. These aren't just for ornithologists: whale watching from the island coastline is possible, and a pair of binoculars gets you a close-up of their frolicking.

The voltage in Japan is 100V and plugs are a type A or B, typically with two flat prongs. These are similar to North American plugs, but due to the difference in voltage you will still likely need an adapter for American items.

Clothing-wise, your wardrobe should reflect a variety of weathers. Definitely bring a waterproof if you are going to some of the lusher islands like Yakushima and Iriomote, as well as appropriate clothing for hiking or water activities – but don't bring thong-back swimwear. Japan dresses conservatively and it won't be welcomed.

MONEY AND BUDGETING

All the islands use Japanese yen (JPY), represented by the symbol ¥ internationally and 円 in Japan. Yen is easy to get from most bureaux de change and travel agencies, but may need to be ordered in advance. Airport currency exchange outlets usually carry yen but often offer very poor rates.

Yen is divided into notes of ¥1,000, ¥2,000, ¥5,000 and ¥10,000, as well as coins of ¥1, ¥5, ¥10, ¥50, ¥100 and ¥500. In Japanese, the currency is pronounced *en*. At the time of going to print, ¥100 is equivalent to £0.50 GBP, €0.63 EUR and $0.70 USD (January 2024). Yen is an important currency internationally, as the third most traded currency on the foreign exchange market and the third most widely used reserve currency.

One of the most surprising things about tech-savvy Japan is just how old-fashioned it can be, and money is no exception. Using a PIN number at checkout is becoming more common, but you'll likely also face MAG-strip payments and signatures – that's if there's card facilities in the first place.

Many rural areas won't accept anything but cash. Smaller islands are particularly problematic as some don't even have a bank. Post offices will often have ATMs, but it's not guaranteed, and they will regularly reject certain bankcards, such as American Express. Irregular hours also mean banks and post offices won't always be available when you need them. Bring enough cash to cover trips to these islands and pay with card where you can.

Despite enduring claims otherwise, you can have a budget-conscious trip to Japan. Food can be remarkably cheap, budget accommodations are available, and transport is rarely painfully expensive. Outside some sports, many activities don't need tours or guides, and you can self-drive. In general shoestring accommodations run below ¥5,000 while seriously budget meals would cost under ¥2,000 for three. There are also ways to minimise unnecessary overspend by shopping at discount stores like Daiso or Don Quixote, where many items can be bought for much cheaper. (There is, of course, a luxury option for travelling the islands too.) Some average prices include:

1.5l bottle water	¥127 (£0.67)
½ litre beer	¥350 (£1.85)
loaf of bread	¥280 (£1.48)
street snack	¥100–200 (£0.53–1.06)
T-shirt	¥1,000–5,000 (£5.29–26.44)
litre of petrol	¥175 (£0.93)

BARGAINING AND TIPPING Japan is not a country of bargaining or haggling. It's so unheard of that they're more likely to be totally confused than offended. And this exactitude works both ways: tips are also a no-no. Even telling a shop to 'keep the change' will earn you some odd looks, and you'll end up leaving with the exact change anyway. Some shops have charity pots by the registers if you're keen to get rid of those pesky ¥1 coins. Similarly, if you pay the bill at a restaurant and walk out without your change, you may find yourself being chased down the street for the sake of a few yen. This money culture also means overcharging isn't much of a problem in Japan.

GETTING AROUND

BY AIR Unsurprisingly, the archipelago is quite reliant on air travel. Each island group is served by at least two airports, if not more. They aren't very popular routes, which means they can be expensive, but there are low-cost carriers operating too. The relevant airlines are listed in individual island sections in *Part Two*.

BY SEA Ferries are a non-negotiable for travelling the islands, but they're not as reliable as flights. Changeable weather often affects boats, especially the smaller crafts, and ferries are subject to sudden changes and cancellations.

Many islands are only accessed by ferry. Make sure to check timetables, which ships are fast or slow (and therefore more or less expensive) and when planned holidays or works are happening. Always consider your schedule when booking a ferry; try to avoid the last ferry for popular day-trip islands like Taketomi, and don't rely on a ferry the day before an all-important flight.

Be sure to check the ferry company website the day before and morning of your ferry. Port changes are possible, particularly on the Amami Islands where ferries are highly susceptible to weather. Alterations usually drop you at another port on the same island, but if you're catching a connecting ferry this may result in missing the boat. And occasionally, some islands have to be missed altogether due to weather.

Ferries require you to fill out a passenger application/embarkation form, which usually includes English-language translations. It's used to contact you and keep track of your whereabouts should anything happen. You need to be at the boarding point half an hour before departure time and it's expected that you carry your own luggage on to the ship, though occasionally they do have porters. You will need to show your ticket as you get on and off – don't lose the ticket in-between as staff are sticklers for seeing it both times.

BY ROAD As the islands don't have trains (aside from the Naha monorail), they are entirely reliant on road transport. Road infrastructure varies wildly. On the larger islands there are plenty of tarmacked large, urban and rural roads. However, many have limited road networks, the quality and quantity of which diminish the further you get from main ring roads. Occasionally roads and bridges may be damaged by natural disasters but this is unusual. Despite the limited road networks, most of them are well maintained and passable. Although there are many unpaved or gravel roads, it's rare that you will need to use or drive them.

Buses exist on some islands and run to excellent schedule. Unfortunately, that schedule is very limited. They often begin late and finish early, making it hard to rely on them for exploring an entire island. Unless you have a day or multi-day pass, buses work on a system where you pay as you get off. Some are flat fares, but more often than not it depends on where you join the bus. Sometimes you can take a paper ticket with this information as you get on via the rear doors of the bus (if they have them). If there is no paper ticket, just look at the front of the bus where an LED screen will show the up-to-date fares for each stop; take note of your stop, which will have a number and maybe kanji. On exiting the bus, don't hand money to the driver but put it in the slot at the front, along with any paper ticket. Most buses also come with a change machine where you can get the exact change from smaller note denominations (under ¥2,000). Buses on small islands work out very cheap, but those on the larger and more touristed islands can rack up.

Rental cars are a necessity on some of the islands and there are plenty of domestic and international options available at ports and airports. It's always best to book in advance though, especially on popular islands like Yakushima. Cars are usually small and automatic, and are driven on the left side of the road. **Moped and motorbike rentals** are a good option too. On small islands cars are either unnecessary or non-existent.

CYCLING AND WALKING Not every island is ideal for cycling or walking, but there are plenty of options for doing both. On many of the small islands it's the most pleasant way of travelling, especially when the weather is excellent and there are plenty of stops along the way. Cycle rental is prolific, arguably the most common transport available.

ACCOMMODATION

There are myriad accommodations in the archipelago. Larger islands and towns have familiar international hotels, and a good number are home to luxury high-end resorts or whole villa rentals.

Outside of these you will largely find guesthouses called *minshuku*, which are cheaper, more local versions of traditional Japanese *ryōkan* (ryōkan themselves are rare on these islands). Minshuku are typically family run and often offer full or half board, especially on those islands without restaurant or supermarket options. These guesthouses come in a range of styles, from supremely basic and rather run-down to highly elegant. Naturally, the price is reflected in each. A large majority of minshuku are converted homes, so often feature shared bathrooms. They are one of the most welcoming and delightful ways to experience the southwest islands.

There are also budget options, including multiple hostels. Better yet, there are many campsites with facilities that either charge very little or are entirely free. For the free ones, it's best to contact the local town office in advance to let them know you will be staying. Often these sites are on beaches and give you incredible views, but take care to note incoming weather systems.

Due to the size of some of the islands and the popularity of others, it's hard to just turn up and assume you will get accommodation. Some minshuku demand advance warning so they can also get food in. It's worth booking ahead or at least having a list of options to hand just in case.

EATING AND DRINKING

FOOD One cannot visit Japan without talking about the food. Japanese cuisine is one of the most acclaimed in the world: Tokyo has the largest number of Michelin-starred restaurants of any city in the world by far, with Kyoto coming joint second. Abroad, Japanese food is often synonymous with haute cuisine, but it's far more than that; its cheapest restaurants offer a better quality and variety of home-cooked or fast food than most other countries.

The long, 3,500km stretch of the country means that cuisine is regional, with local ingredients and styles creating a massive national menu. Okinawan cuisine is known worldwide for its health benefits, helping to earn Okinawa a 'Blue Zone' designation (page 17). Although the food of the islands differs from the mainland, there are common elements intrinsic to Japanese cuisine that are worth noting.

Japanese staples Japanese food (known as *washoku*) is mostly based around rice. It's believed that rice cultivation was brought to Japan from Korea some time around 900BCE, and began in southern Kyūshū. Rice has been such a consistent ingredient and industry that the entire country's economy revolved around rice for centuries and there are even festivals and rituals dedicated to rice. Although rice came over from mainland Asia to Japan, Japanese mythology says that it was bestowed by the sun goddess Amaterasu.

When rice was scarce and heavily taxed, meals were bulked out with other ingredients in a peasant dish called *takikomi gohan*, which is still eaten today. In Okinawa – where rice was often scarce due to non-arable land – this dish is called *juushii* (see opposite and page 195). Today, rice is at its lowest consumption (60kg per person annually) thanks to imports of bread and pasta, but is still vital in most meals, like *donburi* (topped rice bowls).

Alongside rice, noodles have been a key staple since the arrival of soba buckwheat noodles from China, posited around 400BCE. Thicker wheat udon noodles came later, in the 700s. Noodles are particularly popular in the Nansei-shotō, which struggles to farm rice, and some islands have developed their own version of soba: Okinawa, Miyako and Yaeyama.

Some of the most common elements of Japanese dishes are dashi, *shōyu* (soy sauce) or mirin. Together, these make up the base for many dishes like *katsudon* and *nikujaga*. Sometimes *sake* (alcohol) is added too. These ingredients are so prevalent that it's important to note for those with allergies to soy or vegetarian/vegan diets, as dashi is made from bonito fish flakes. On the islands, dashi is commonly made with pork or chicken bones too.

Nansei-shotō cuisine Archipelago cuisine has been influenced by old trading partners, incorporating elements of Chinese, Korean, Thai and Pacific Island cuisine. For example, many of the pork dishes have Taiwanese equivalents, and the use of taro and papaya is mirrored in Pacific and Filipino cuisines. Since annexation, there's been an inevitable gastronomic exchange between mainland Japan and the islands, but there are still many things you won't find outside the archipelago that are symbols of island cuisine.

Most of the dishes still eaten today came from peasant cuisine rather than court dishes. Local fare was made with ingredients gathered from the sea and fields, and based on the idea food is medicine – an idea that prevails today. The islands have a strong connection between health, wellbeing, family and food.

It's this cuisine that is credited for islanders' longevity. They have some of the longest life spans in the world and many put this down to their diet. Ironically, statistics suggest that Okinawa Prefecture has some of the higher BMI rates in Japan. This likely comes down to the hefty American influence in Okinawa-hontō: the US military brought with it many fattier, Western foods that became incredibly popular: tacos, fried chicken, hamburgers and, oddly enough, Spam. There are now efforts to protect the local cuisine, by encouraging new farmers and producers to carry on the Ryūkyūan food culture.

Nansei-shotō specialities Ingredients and dishes naturally vary from island to island. ***Chanpuruu*** is the archipelago's best-known dish – a kind of stir fry usually including tofu, vegetables and meat or fish. The name is Okinawan for 'something mixed', and has been used to describe Okinawan culture as well as just this dish. The most popular version is ***gooya chanpuruu*** (often seen as *gōya chanpurū*). *Gooya* looks like a knobbly cucumber, but is actually a bitter melon gourd rich in vitamin C. Gooya crops up quite a lot in island cuisine as tempura, in salads or pickled, and it has even been used in beers in place of bitter hops, but it can be an acquired taste.

Another local favourite is **Okinawa soba**, made using wheat flour rather than Japanese buckwheat. The chewy noodles are served in a broth made from pork and dashi and are often topped with *sooki* (page 54) or tofu, egg, fish cakes, spring onions and pickled ginger.

Unlike these dishes, **juushii** – the one traditional island rice dish – began in the royal court. Legend has it that the recipe was kept secret by servants for three centuries. It's made of seasoned rice cooked with various ingredients, commonly konbu seaweed, carrot, shiitake mushrooms and pork, but recipes vary across the islands and from family to family. For many, it is a much-loved family dish, vital to celebrations and Buddhist religious services. You can order it in restaurants, but you are most likely to find it in convenience stores as *onigiri* rice balls.

The dish of Amami is ***keihan* rice**, a donburi bowl topped with strips of chicken breast, omelette and shiitake, which takes a tropical turn with finely chopped papaya and dried peel of the *shima mikan* (cherry orange). The bowl is topped off with steaming chicken broth. Other toppings can include egg, pickles and nori, and sake is occasionally added to the broth. Another Amami regular is ***abura sōmen***: a fried noodle dish that came to the islands during the Meiji era. Noodles are boiled until al dente then fried in oil with leeks, meat and vegetables. Over the years, each household and restaurant has developed its own way of doing abura sōmen.

The ultimate Okinawan–American meal, meanwhile, is **taco rice**: a somewhat unsettling mix of spiced minced beef, salsa and cheese atop Japanese white rice. Incredibly popular with locals, American military and tourists, taco rice might not be haute cuisine but it is in high demand.

Much like China, Okinawa is known for using as much of the pig as possible in its cooking. In ***mimigaa***, the cartilaginous ears are sliced thinly and prepared either by boiling or pickling. Served with sliced cucumber and a dressing of either peanut-miso or ponzu citrus, mimigaa has a crunchy texture that's not for the squeamish. For **sooki** (often sōki), pork spare ribs are stewed with their cartilage in a mix of *awamori* (page 57), *kokutō*, shōyu and dashi for 3–4 hours. The sooki become soft and tender, melting in the mouth, and are usually served atop soba in soup.

Rafutee is a stew of succulent pork belly simmered in shōyu and glazed with kokutō brown sugar that absolutely melts in your mouth. It originated in China but has become wholly Okinawan; it was once part of royal Ryūkyū cuisine. Believed to increase longevity, it's often served atop Okinawa soba. For ***ashitebichi***, pigs' feet are simmered until they practically fall apart, before being served up on a bed of soba noodles, daikon, konbu and broth – sometimes made from the self-same trotter. Pigs' trotters contain huge amounts of collagen, which is good for the skin.

Tempura may have come from the mainland, but the Nansei have made it their own. Island tempura is richer, with more seasoning, which is why it doesn't always come with the traditional dipping sauce. Tempura here is more a snack than main meal. Many of the ingredients are unique: *mozuku* and *aosa* (or *aasa*) seaweed, *nigana* and *handama* greens, *beni-imo*, gooya, Spam, sausages, and *sunui* (pickled konbu).

Another unique find is the delightfully named ***inoshishi-sashimi*** (wild boar sashimi), a speciality of the Yaeyama Islands. Although it's available across Japan, Ryūkyū wild boars (*kamai*) taste a little different. Their meat is slightly sweet and, despite the thick rind of umami-filled fat, it's lower in calories and cholesterol than pork and beef. The boar feast on acorns and chestnuts, producing a rich flavour similar to Iberian pork. As the meat is often served raw or as *tataki* (lightly seared), it's only available fresh in the November–February hunting season. Be aware there's a risk with eating raw, wild meat, although the isolated animals on Iriomote are generally safe.

From the warm seas, meanwhile, comes ***irabujiru***: sea snake soup. Made from the beautifully striped sea krait, this soup is eaten in Ishigaki, Miyako and Kudaka. Originally a court delicacy for the king, the soup is incredibly healthy thanks to being high in collagen, minerals and protein. The snake is smoked and dried, becoming incredibly hard and rich in umami. It's then rendered gelatinous by being cooked in dashi alongside pigs trotters, taro and seaweed.

Meat The islands are known for beef, goat, pork and chicken. In the West, *wagyū* is synonymous with the best beef money can buy, but the term literally means

'Japanese cow' and denotes any of the four Japanese cattle breeds. ***Kuroge***, the Japanese black cow, has been farmed on the islands for centuries. Kuroshima in the Yaeyama even has a yearly cow festival, and the cows bred there often get sent on elsewhere to become world-famous beef.

Goat (*yagi* or *hija*) is rarely eaten elsewhere in Japan but is hugely popular on the islands. It's often eaten raw as sashimi, a regional speciality, but can also be found in soups and stir fries. Yagi is commonly eaten at celebrations and as a remedy against fatigue.

Aguu is the native Okinawan pig, and is one of the most sought-after meats and breeds in Japan: think the wagyū of the pork world. Aguu is high in protein and vitamin B1 and low in cholesterol. Despite having less fat than other pig breeds, it's incredibly rich in flavour. Aguu can be used from tail to snout, resulting in the Okinawan saying 'everything is eaten except the oink'.

Fruits and vegetables The islands are the key producer of Japan's fruits. The climate means **tropical fruits** grow easily, including citrus, pineapple, mango, papaya, dragon fruit, starfruit, banana and passionfruit. There are also some rare fruits like the inimitable ***atemoya***, also known as the 'pineapple sugar apple'. These bumpy-skinned green lumps look incredibly unappetising, but the price tag should clue you in to their real worth: utterly sensational and worth every extortionate penny.

Shiikwaasaa (literally 'sour food') is the native citrus of the islands, with innumerable spellings that seem to increase in vowels with every iteration. It's known for its extremely sour but refreshing flavour and as an island superfood. Shiikwaasaa are packed full of vitamins and minerals that are believed to ease rheumatism and flavonoids that supposedly inhibit cancer. Locals also say they fight fatigue, though that might be down to their potent lip-puckering abilities. Yanbaru, where they are traditionally grown, is known for its longevity. The unripe fruits are green, harvested in July–October, while the ripe ones from November to January are golden and milder. Shiikwaasaa is used in foods but mostly as a drink. You'll find it in bars served with awamori and in shops as a canned fizzy drink.

Gourds are a massive part of Okinawan cuisine: there's *moui* (pickling melon), gooya (bitter melon), *shibui* (winter melon), *nabera* (luffa), cucumbers and more. Other **local vegetables** include *shima rakkyō*, an onion much like spring onion but with a stronger smell and saltier flavour; winged beans; turmeric; vibrant purple handama spinach; bitter nigana greens; *chomei gusa*, a herb known as 'longevity grass'; shell ginger; mugwort; and Okinawa chillies.

The king of the Nansei table, however, is the purple, sweet beni-imo potato. Beni-imo was the staple crop, not rice, so has long supported island people – in terrible typhoon seasons, it was often the only crop left, making it vital to survival. It has a starchy, sticky texture and sweetness that makes it perfect for desserts and as a filling, but it's also steamed and fried. *Kandaba*, the leafy part of the potato plant, also found its way on to the menu in poorer times.

For something fun, try ***umibudō***, a seaweed that looks like a string of green pearls. Literally called 'sea grapes', these caviar-like beads burst in your mouth and are incredibly popular with tourists. High-mineral, low-calorie, they're not all that common in local restaurants, but you may see them served as side dishes and toppings.

Seafood There are so many different fish in the island waters that even Japanese people struggle to know what sashimi they're ordering. The most commonly eaten fish are also farmed: grouper (*mibai*), double-lined fusilier (*gurukun*), tuna, bonito (skipjack tuna) and tiger prawns. *Tobiuo*, flying fish, are incredibly popular in Yakushima, despite their prolific bones, while *kibinago* (silver herring) is a Kagoshima Prefecture speciality served as sashimi or tempura. ***Ikasumi***, squid ink, is also a commonly used ingredient – its most traditional dish is *ikasumi jiru*, a thick squid ink soup served with leafy greens and three pieces of either chicken or pork. The pitch-black soup looks quite unnerving in the bowl, and even worse on your teeth. Ikasumi is so associated with health benefits and flushing toxins that soup made with it used to be the first meal given to babies.

Bonito or skipjack tuna is essential to cuisine as part of dried *katsuoboshi*. The annual arrival of the fish is such a vital part of Japanese life that it has a specific name: *hatsugatsuo*. Hatsugatsuo heralds summer and Okinawa is the first to see this fish in April, catching it exclusively by line. In fact, Okinawa is a little obsessed with the fish: it consumes the highest amount of bonito of any prefecture and when the rest of the country flies koi carp flags on Children's Day, Motobu town (the main bonito fishery port on Okinawa-hontō) flies bonito banners instead. A traditional Okinawan way of eating bonito is to dip the raw fish in miso, shiikwaasaa or red pepper, with a glass of awamori.

Tiger prawns are farmed across Okinawa Prefecture, though Kumejima is the main producer. Kume's mineral-rich, high-nutrient seawater – famed throughout Japan – is used to produce massive, healthy organic prawns. The prawns are eaten as sashimi, tempura and toppings – they're also commonly consumed whole, shell and all, as the relatively soft shell is high in calcium.

Tofu Tofu, often written tōfu, is prolific here, with a host of variations. There's *shima-dōfu*, which is traditionally made with island seawater; Okinawan speciality *jiimaami tōfu*, which is made of peanuts; and finally, *tōfuyō*. A bit like marmite, tōfuyō divides its audience. It's made by fermenting tofu in red *kōji* rice mould and awamori to create a substance remarkably similar to a strong, rich cheese: imagine a creamy stilton with a hint of sweetness to it. Served as a pink-red cube with a small utensil to slice off little amounts, tōfuyō is a must-try on the islands.

Sweets The best sweets and souvenirs come with *kokutō*. Whether it's Amami Ōshima's *kokutō awamori*, *kokutō chinsuko* shortbread, or kokutō-basted succulent pork, this brown sugar makes everything better. One of the largest agricultural products of the islands, it's produced from north to south. It comes as no surprise that even the sugar here is relatively healthy – kokutō is made by boiling unrefined sugar, keeping the minerals and flavour intact.

Literally translated as 'deep-fried sugar', ***saataa andagii*** are a kind of island doughnut. The style and size differ depending on maker and island; they can come as dense, purple, tennis-ball-sized heavyweights, or smaller, sugar-sprinkled puffs. Made with simple flour, sugar and eggs, they often include additional ingredients like purple sweet potato or brown sugar. The inside is usually more cake-like than traditional doughnuts, but the outside is crispy and dark brown. One of the best things about saataa andagii is that they don't keep very well – you simply must eat them immediately.

Essentially the same as mainland *mochi*, ***muchi*** (sometimes *onimuchi*) is made of pounded gluttonous rice, sugar and water. Ingredients like brown sugar, purple yam and mugwort are added to some, while others are wrapped and infused with things like ginger leaves. Onimuchi means 'devil mochi', and comes from a folktale where a brother-turned-demon began attacking humans and animals, so his sister made his favourite muchi filled with nails. When he ate the spiked muchi he became ill, and she used the opportunity to push him off a cliff. Given this charming tale, it seems surprising that muchi is often consumed with the family. The coldest season of Okinawa (end of January to early February in the Gregorian calendar) is called *muchibusa*, and is a time when families make and consume muchi in a variety of forms.

DRINKS The islands' most famous drink is *awamori*, also known as *amui* or *shimazake* (island sake). No visit to the archipelago is complete without trying some of this unique firewater, which is Japan's oldest distilled spirit, dating back over 600 years. The drink was brought to the islands from Thailand and was highly prized – in the 15th century, only royals were allowed to drink aged *awamori kosu*.

Awamori is brewed across multiple islands, even some of the smallest, and comes in a wide variety of types, flavours and strengths. The typical range is 30–40 proof, but Yonagunijima is known for its *hanashu*, a 60 proof awamori that's the only alcohol in Japan legally allowed to be brewed that strength. It's made using Thai long-grain rice and kōji, a black mould that's commonly used in Japanese food and drink preparation including soy sauce and miso. Unlike sake, awamori is distilled rather than fermented, which produces the high alcohol content. It's often paired with traditional Okinawan foods and there's also an awamori chilli sauce called *koregusu*, which you'll notice throughout the archipelago's restaurants and bars.

Awamori is essential to socialisation and ritual on the islands, including religious and memorial events. It's traditionally drunk neat from small clay cups (*chibuguwa*) that are very small, meaning it quite literally brings people together when making a toast and clinking cups. The cups also encourage drinkers to take wee, slow sips while listening to everyone's conversation. That said, there's no right or wrong way to enjoy it. Common mixers include hot water, oolong tea, tonic, herbal liquor, shiikwaasaa juice (page 55) or Okinawa turmeric (*ukon/ucchin*) soda. The latter is believed to prevent hangovers. You can also buy flavoured awamori, such as fruit, coffee-milk and black sugar, and cocktails such as Okinawan sangria. One of the most popular souvenirs is *habushu*, an awamori with a poisonous habu snake in the bottle (think tequila worms but way bigger).

Other local spirits include the unique, brown sugar ***kokutō shōchū***, only produced on the Amami Islands. It has a little more of a rum-like taste with a touch of sweetness and fruitiness. It also has the wonderful ability to leave you less hungover than many other spirits. Some even say it helps increase good cholesterol and encourage enzyme production that reduces blood clots. There are 25 distilleries across five islands in the Amami group, producing some 170 varieties. Make sure to also try Okinawa Gin, made with botanicals found on the islands: shiikwaasaa, juniper berries, guava leaves, gooya, roselle and long peppers.

The local beer of Okinawa-hontō, **Orion**, is an island icon served absolutely everywhere. It is brewed using fresh mountain spring water from just behind the brewery. It has a light taste, making it popular to sip on the beach in hot, humid summers.

EATING OUT The most common type of restaurant is a *shokudō* (食堂), essentially an eating hole. It often has plastic food displays in the window and is relatively inexpensive, usually serving mainly Japanese cuisine with some Western options. The easiest and best meal to order is a set course called *teishoku*. This normally includes some manifestation of main dish, bowl of rice, miso soup, salad and pickles and is generally around ¥1,000–1,400. It's incredibly filling and excellent value. Otherwise, there is usually a standard selection of rice dishes (donburi) and noodles like ramen, soba or udon.

Izakaya are a sort of pub-bar equivalent that are ideal for a casual meal and a drink. They usually have a great atmosphere, alcohol and locally made snacks and full dinners, and offer counter seats, table seats or tatami floor seats, depending on size. It's typical to order a few dishes at a time, like *yakitori* (chicken skewers), sashimi, grilled fish and Western snacks like chips.

Yakitori restaurants are popular after-work spots, offering everything from picky bits designed to accompany alcohol or larger selections for full meals. Sit round the counter and watch the chef grill your choice – order several then reorder your favourites. Note that prices are usually per single skewer.

Vegetarianism, veganism and other dietary requirements Despite regular claims to the contrary, there is an ancient vegetarian/vegan scene in Japan, begun many moons ago when Buddhists brought *shojin-ryōri* vegetarian cuisine to the country. It is, after all, a country dedicated to tofu and soy. There are plenty of dishes on most menus, but it is important to always check their contents.

Pescatarians have no trouble dining in Japan, but vegetarians and vegans may need to exercise more caution. Fish stock, known as dashi (page 53), is a major base for soups, noodles, rice bowls and marinades – a lot of miso soups can be made with dashi. Some people don't even consider dashi when it comes to vegetarianism, so it's worth making sure each dish is fish and dashi free.

Those with restrictive diets can certainly navigate their way through, but it's worth learning or writing down the phrase explaining your needs in advance. On the bigger islands you'll always find more familiar Western foods like burgers and pizza if desired.

Restaurant etiquette It's understandable to baulk upon entering a restaurant where both the language and menu seem incomprehensible. In many ways, it's best to come to Japan's table with an open mind.

On entering a restaurant you'll likely be greeted with a hearty welcoming '*irasshaimase!*'. Next comes the number of your party, '*nan-mei sama?*', which you can answer with your fingers as many Japanese do. You might be presented with a hot towel (*oshibori*), which is used to wipe the hands. If there is no English menu and you're feeling adventurous, simply ask for whatever they recommend. If you would understandably prefer a little more control, pointing and simply asking a single-word question for fish, beef, pork, chicken, or vegetable is a good start (page 361). It's worth saving the kanji or writing for different major ingredients and dishes, so you can cross reference.

Before tucking in you will often hear people say '*itadakimasu*', the Japanese form of 'bon appétit'. Chopsticks (*o-hashi* or *hashi*) are generally used, but you can ask for Western cutlery. There are many little foibles about chopstick use, but the two main ones are to never pass food between chopsticks, and to never leave your chopsticks sticking up in a bowl of rice – the latter is a symbol associated with the dead. Place your chopsticks on the chopstick rest, or across the top of your plate or bowl. In general, over-ordering and leaving leftover food isn't polite, nor is taking home leftovers. When eating with groups, don't start eating until everyone has their food and ask before taking the last bite from communal dishes.

When you finish eating, you can ask for the bill by crossing one index finger over the other to form an X. Often you will be given a bill that you take to the cashier at the front of the restaurant. You don't usually leave cash on the table by way of payment and there is no tipping in Japan. Only the larger, more international restaurants take credit cards so cash is a must. If you're feeling brave, upon leaving you can call out '*gochisōsama deshita*' – a 'thank you for the meal' phrase that you'll hear others say.

The islands are so full of fish that sushi and sashimi is everywhere, making it a fairly casual dish rather than a high-end experience. You can eat sushi with chopsticks or hands, and it's the fish side of sushi that should be dipped in soy, not the rice. Generally the chef will pre-wasabi your sushi to his recommended amount; if you want more, don't mix it into the soy but have it on your plate. The pickled ginger is a palette cleanser.

Japan has an abundance of delicious noodle dishes. At most shops, patrons will slurp the noodles as they eat them. This is an accepted practice, particularly among men, as it cools the boiling hot noodles off.

PUBLIC HOLIDAYS AND FESTIVALS

Japan's calendar is chock-full of holidays and festivals, both national and locally. They are one of the country's true highlights: if there's a possibility of catching a celebration, prioritise it above all else.

The national holidays of Japan are listed below; important local festivals are noted in individual island sections. As well as the regular national holidays, there are three times of the year where Japanese people travel en masse across the country, either to family homes or for a holiday. These are the period around New Year (27 Dec–4 Jan); the so-called Golden Week, a run of four national holidays falling between 29 April and 5 May; and Obon or Bon, which is celebrated in mid-August on the mainland and mid-July on the islands due to the lunar calendar. These week-long holidays are hellish for bookings and prices, and at New Years in particular, sites and shops are closed. If you're planning to visit during these times, you'll need to book everything well in advance – the moment bookings are possible in some cases. Sakura (cherry blossom) season can also be very busy in the mainland cities, but island blooms arrive earlier (page 5) and aren't as famous. Note that if a national holiday falls on a weekend, the following working day will be a substitute holiday.

JAPANESE NATIONAL HOLIDAYS

1 January	New Year's Day (Shōgatsu)
January, second Monday	Coming of Age (Seijin no hi)
11 February	National Foundation Day (Kenkoku Kinen no hi)
23 February	The Emperor's Birthday (Tennō no Tanjobi)
Around 21 March	Vernal Equinox (Shunbun no Hi)
29 April	Showa Day (Shōwa no hi)
3 May	Constitution Day (Kenpō Kinenbi)
4 May	Greenery Day (Midori no hi)
5 May	Children's Day (Kodomo no hi)
July, third Monday	Ocean Day (Umi no hi)
11 August	Mountain Day (Yama no hi)
September, third Monday	Respect for the Aged Day (Keiro no hi)
Around 23 September	Autumnal Equinox (Shūbun no hi)
October, second Monday	Health and Sports Day (Taiiku no hi)
3 November	Culture Day (Bunka no hi)
23 November	Labour Thanksgiving Day (Kinrō Kansha no hi)
31 December	New Year's Eve (Omisoka)

NANSEI-SHOTŌ FESTIVALS Many of the traditional festivals on the islands are decided by the old lunar calendar, imported from China. To Westerners, this calendar can be a bit of a nightmare to fathom and so it's wise to double-check dates nearer the time.

The New Year is celebrated on the islands with traditional foods, shrine visits and a big cleaning called *osoji*, which purifies a space ready for the gods to visit. New Year's Eve in Japan is much like Christmas in the West – many travel back to their hometown for family celebrations of food, games and TV. Islanders tend to ring in the new year with a cup of awamori, and Okinawans may visit Shuri Castle for *chohai-okishiki*, a New Year's celebration of dancing. It's also tradition to wake up to see the first sunrise of the year, so beauty spots are often filled with people. Around February, you can also experience the more low-key Lunar New Year, called Soguwachi.

Spring sees the women's Hamauri festival, where women purify themselves by submerging their hands and feet in the sea. They also bring special dishes in colourful bentō-style boxes: seafood, rice and adzuki beans, and *sangwachi-gwaashi*, a traditional sweet. Hamauri coincides with the opening of the beaches, so it has become a more family-oriented event. In mid-March, for the Shimi lunar festival, people visit the graves of ancestors, cleaning them, making offerings, praying and eating. It's thought important that ancestors see continued affection between relatives and that they have been honoured.

Summer brings *haaree* or *haarii* (dragon boat races), a Shintō ritual that prays for safe and plentiful fishing while honouring the sea gods. There are also multiple tug-of-war events (page 34) that take place across the summer and autumn seasons.

Lunar Obon is a busy time on the islands, when people return to hometowns to commune with relatives, living and dead. On the islands Obon lasts three days: *unke* is the first day, when people greet their ancestral spirits, *nakanuhi* is the most important day, when families gather round altars and spend time together, and *ukui* is when spirits are sent back to the afterlife. Island Obon features traditional dancing: Eisaa, Bon Odori, and shishimai dances (page 31).

In autumn, the islands celebrate Kajimayaa Day, an event honouring the idea that when elders turn 97, they return to their youth. (The name comes from little windmills children play with.) There's a parade where elders ride in decorated cars and visit their communities, with people shaking their hands for luck.

Winter has the muchi festival, dedicated to the hearth god Hinukan. Steamed rice cakes are offered to the fire altars, wrapped in shell ginger or palm leaves. Those wrapped in ginger are said to stave off colds, and ward off negative spirits; families with children often hang muchi (page 56) around the house to pray against hunger. At the end of the year, Hinukan (who watches over the house and hearth) returns to the land of the gods to report all the earthly events of the last year. Families pray that Hinukan will only pass on the good events, and that he will have a peaceful rest before the new year begins.

SHOPPING

Okinawa-hontō is the only place with real shopping opportunities (page 186). The rest of the islands fall into varying categories of having a collection of shops, a single supermarket, a few local markets, a single establishment or nothing at all. It's therefore important that you plan in advance.

On these islands, business hours go beyond flexible and enter the realm of nebulousness. Naha and bigger towns will keep regular times, but local shops called *kyōdō-baiten* – especially on the more remote islands – will have advertised times but open when they feel like it; they'll often have signs saying just that. With such small communities, many shop owners know when to open and close, and customers to buy what they need.

It's best never to rely on a shop being open: random closures can happen at any time and an ageing population means permanent closures are possible. Your best bet for shops being open is usually the morning and afternoon; don't go too early, in the middle of lunchtime, or too late, just to be on the safe side. Many shops don't get regular deliveries from bigger islands, meaning if you find food it's best to take advantage. Supplies can also be delayed by weather.

Travelling around the islands you may also see honesty stalls, called *mujinbaiten* or *mujinhanbai*. These are often filled with vegetables and fruits farmed from someone's house and are unmanned. They're great to use, especially for a passing snack – leave the right change or more if you don't have it.

SOUVENIRS Japan might be known as one of the world's best shopping destinations, but the Nansei-shotō are far from it. And while Naha does have electronic and luxury goods shops, you're better off leaving your bigger purchases for mainland cities like Tokyo and Osaka. Where the city does excel, however, is souvenir shops – from beautiful authentic wares to cheap touristy tat.

Japanese people are expected to bring back edible souvenirs for family, friends and colleagues from their travels, and you'll see boxes of these sweets and crackers piled high in shops, airports and ferry terminals. If you're visiting a Japanese family or colleague, it's polite to bring something like this with you. They make excellent gifts for home, too, as they're designed to travel.

The islands have some incredible indigenous crafts, such as pottery, lacquerware and textiles (page 25). Some of these can be costly, thanks to their handmade craftsmanship, but they're unique and long-lasting, and there are smaller items for the budget-conscious.

ARTS AND ENTERTAINMENT

The Nansei-shotō is incredibly rich in traditional arts, performing arts and crafts (page 25), and their centre is Okinawa-hontō. There are plentiful **cinemas** all over this main island, though you may struggle if films have been dubbed. The archipelago is speckled with tiny **museums and galleries** detailed in individual chapters; the national ones are in Naha and are truly excellent. Okinawa-hontō also has the **National Theatre Okinawa** (w nt-okinawa.or.jp/english), where you can catch performances of traditional dances, plays and music. **Music** is an incredibly vital part of Nansei-shotō culture, particularly in the Amami and Okinawa groups. Locals love to perform and can often be found in restaurants or izakaya with a sanshin and a song.

OPENING HOURS

In general, most businesses open between the hours of 09.00 and 17.00, with occasional lunch breaks. Weekends, particularly Sundays, are not good bets for banks or post offices, but these change between each individual office. For galleries and museums, Monday is the most common day to close. Restaurants often open for lunch hours (11.30–14.00) and then dinner hours (17.00 on), but always check in advance of your visit. For shops, see opposite.

MEDIA AND COMMUNICATIONS

INTERNET The majority of accommodations will provide Wi-Fi, but this isn't always reliable on the islands. When out and about you can usually find Wi-Fi in shops such as FamilyMart or Starbucks, but these are absent on smaller islands. On these, the best bet is the port building.

The easiest way to make sure you're not stuck without a form of contact or online maps is to get pocket Wi-Fi, a portable router that you connect to on the go. These can seem a minefield for visitors, as there are many companies offering multiple packages, some of which can be incredibly expensive. It's important on these remote islands to look at coverage options – you'll be fine on Okinawa but may be a bit stuck in the Iriomote jungle. Always make sure to ask.

You can shop around in advance online, collecting your pocket Wi-Fi at the airport or having it sent to your accommodation. Alternatively, you can pick a deal up on arrival at the airport. Popular providers include Ninja (w ninjawifi.com), Sakura Mobile (w sakuramobile.jp), Japan Wireless (w japan-wireless.com/en) and Rental Wifi (w rentalwifi.com), but there are plenty to choose from.

You can certainly manage in Japan without data, but it's not always easy. Either way, apps that allow you to pre-download maps and translation services to use offline, such as Google Translate and Maps.me, are incredibly useful.

PHONES Japan is surprisingly unfriendly when it comes to using foreign phones. You will be charged a small fortune to use your mobile on a Japanese network, making Wi-Fi (see above) invaluable. The most commonly used communication app is Line, not WhatsApp. You'll regularly see individuals and companies offering their Line number via QR codes, and it's a good way to chat with smaller tours and accommodations. Line also has a payment facility.

Japanese telephone numbers are 10–11 digits long and come in a variety of formats. They commonly begin with a 0 followed by an area code; in Okinawa this is 98-8 or 98-9, in Kagoshima 99. The international dialling code of Japan is +81, which you will have to add in place of the first 0 if calling from a non-Japanese phone. Emergency numbers (page 43) are three digits long.

POST One of Japan's most brilliant inventions is *takuhaibin*, a cheap domestic delivery service run by Yamato Transport (w kuronekoyamato.co.jp/en). It can sometimes be cheaper to send your luggage across the country this way than pay for the allowance on your flight. It's especially useful if you have liquid souvenirs, large sporting equipment or perishables. On the mainland delivery is usually next day, but from Okinawa it can take two. The service is so ubiquitous that you can use it from your hotel, post offices, convenience stores, airports and major railway stations, with deliveries to private homes and more. (Always check in advance that your accommodation will take delivery.) You can usually specify a delivery date, with the company holding on to your luggage for a few days if needed. Price depends on the size, but a 25kg or under suitcase from Tokyo to Okinawa would generally cost under ¥5,000.

Post offices are also a bit of a lifesaver on these islands: they're often the only place with an ATM. The ATMs are kept in a separate glassed-off section, and usually have longer opening hours than the post offices themselves. Sending post is easy in Japan, but packages abroad require a fair number of forms in Japanese – this is where translation apps come in handy. Sending postcards (*hagaki*) and buying stamps (*kitte*) is easy to do with minimal gesturing at the window. Post is generally quick and cheap, with small letters to Europe costing around ¥110. Red postboxes can be found outside post offices and around towns and villages.

PRINT MEDIA Japan's biggest newspapers are the *Yomiuri Shimbun*, a conservative-leaning publication, and the *Asahi Shimbun*, which is liberal. For English speakers, the website of the large, more centrist *Mainichi Shimbun* (w mainichi.jp/english) is excellent, as is the English newspaper the *Japan Times* (w japantimes.co.jp). In Okinawa, the main newspapers are the *Okinawa Times* and *Ryūkyū Shimpo*, the latter offering an English-language website (w ryukyushimpo.jp/tag/RyukyushimpoEnglishNEWS).

TELEVISION AND RADIO Japan has multiple television networks but the most important is NHK, which stands for Nippon Hōsō Kyōkai. This is Japan's public broadcasting corporation, equivalent to the UK's BBC, and has regular news updates, variety and panel shows. There are multiple radio stations, again the most major run by NHK.

CULTURAL ETIQUETTE

Japan is a nation bound by etiquette, with myriad societal rules, regulations and idiosyncrasies to navigate. However, no-one expects foreigners to know everything. As with any travel, just do your best to respect the local culture and customs – luckily in Japan the big taboos are easy enough to remember.

Firstly, **taking off shoes inside** is important, though this does not apply to larger hotels and most restaurants. The general rule of thumb is to look in the entrance on arrival; if you spot shoes or a shoe rack, switch your footwear for the slippers provided. Another rule is that if there are tatami mats, shoes off. There will often be a separate pair of slippers for the toilet, and you will inevitably forget to switch them back at some point – think of it as a rite of passage. All of this means slip-on, slip-off shoes are useful.

Naturally, **littering** is internationally awful, but Japan is exceptionally strict on it. You'll notice there are no signs of litter, even though public bins are generally absent (a common and frustrating feature across Japan). Most Japanese people carry their rubbish back home with them, even cigarette butts – you should do the same. Collecting natural objects, particularly star sand, is prohibited.

On **public transport**, phones should be on quiet mode and conversations kept low – these are shared spaces and the Japanese respect that highly. The Japanese beat the British hands down for **queueing**, too; make sure to line up at stations and terminals.

Japan is not a country for **public displays of affection**. You won't be punished for them, but you will be making everyone else uncomfortable – stick to hand holding only. **Bowing** is customary as a greeting and goodbye, but don't overdo it. A very low bow is rather subservient, generally reserved for those serving others, and it would be strange to see a foreigner doing it. No-one expects you to learn Japanese words, but they truly go a long way in making your trip easier and your interactions better.

Clothing on the islands is a little more relaxed than mainland Japan thanks to the heat and American influence, but people still dress relatively conservatively. Villages ask that you don't walk around in swimwear or half clothed. In places like Taketomijima, where the village itself is a sight, remember that people live there and you cannot walk into their houses or land; respect the walls.

In general, Japanese people don't blow their noses in public, walk while eating or smoking, or cross the road without using pedestrian crossings, and will always ask for photos and never, ever tip. Food etiquette can be found on page 58.

Visiting **shrines** is a must. Those on the islands are usually less grand and are called utaki or ontake; outside of cities, they're normally found in sacred natural places. The shrines hold great importance to local people and should be treated with utmost respect like any other religious space. Some sacred places aren't obvious shrines; they might be natural areas, wells, stones, ruins or hidden in the forests. In general, those closed to visitors will have a small wooden fence across the torii, but if in doubt, stay out. In any sacred space, keep noise and activity low, and don't move or remove natural elements, climb on rocks or go beyond fenced areas.

In general, Japan is very **camera friendly**, but there are exceptions – particularly in religious spaces on the lower islands. There are secret festivals too, such as the three Komi celebrations on Iriomote, where cameras and recordings are prohibited. These rules must be followed. Always make sure to ask if you can photograph, especially portraiture as many aren't comfortable with it.

ONSEN AND SENTŌ Japanese public baths come in two forms: *onsen* and *sentō*. The difference technically lies in the water, with onsen using natural hot springs and sentō formed from tap or well water. However, sentō are also in general more basic – they are cheaper, everyday baths designed for local people to use if they didn't have their own. They're a brilliantly local experience, but don't often come with the beautiful views and scope of onsen, which have waters rich in minerals and can be outdoor (*rotenburo*) or indoor (*notenburo*). The northern islands are littered with natural onsen, one of the most culturally important and glorious experiences of Japan, but they're not always easy to navigate, especially if you don't speak or read Japanese.

Both sentō and onsen are worth a visit and luckily the rules of bathing are the same at both. You'll notice hot baths on maps, signs or entrances from the steam symbol ♨ or the character 湯/ゆ. When entering larger, gender-segregated baths, follow the cliché of blue curtains for men (男), red for women (女).

The most obvious point – and usually the one Westerners struggle with – is that you must be nude. This includes outdoor and mixed gender onsen, unless there is a sign clearly stating otherwise. Most onsen will have a shared changing room and various facilities for your needs, but natural outdoor ones will just have a place to put your clothes in the open. For those with changing rooms, make sure to take off your shoes or slippers and place them in the baskets, lockers or shelving provided. Then disrobe and place your things in a locker or one of the larger baskets. For small outdoor onsen, find a rock.

The best approach to an onsen is to not fret and enjoy it. Japanese people are often curious about foreigners and can stare on the odd occasion, but this curiosity doesn't usually translate over into the onsen – not for long, anyway. Bathing with family and friends is an everyday activity done from birth in Japan.

Once you're unbound and hopefully unbothered, it's time to wash. It might be tempting to run straight into the hot water, for modesty or warmth, but you have to wash your body fully before entering the bathtub. This may be a short swift splash outside with a small, handled pot used to take water from the main bath, or a longer rinse sat inside at a row of showers with a plethora of free lotions and potions. If you have long hair, tie it up, and generally avoid extensive grooming like shaving. It's normal in Japan to sit while showering, as standing is somewhat inconsiderate to others – make sure anything you use, such as stools, are washed down and replaced where you found them. Showering and cleaning yourself isn't just for other's sake – it's part of the onsen ritual that somehow feels far more indulgent than the usual process at home.

The actual baths aren't for washing: nothing should enter the onsen water except you and perhaps a wristband locker key if you have one. Towels, soaps and shampoos shouldn't go near the water and are best kept in a locker where available. The only exception is a small onsen flannel that people use for washing, but they too don't enter the water. Put them on the side away from the pool or do as the Japanese do and place them folded on your head.

In small onsen, such as the ones you find on Kuchinoerabu and Iōjima, it's important to remember to share: some may have shifts or time limits. Try not to hog individual one-person baths in hotels either. Onsen and sentō are generally quiet, meditative places so keep chatting to a low volume and don't let children splash. Phones are not allowed anywhere in bath houses.

The final consideration is tattoos. Technically, they're not allowed, but if you inform them in advance, some onsen will be okay with you displaying them if your artwork is small. Some will ask you to cover them, so it's wise to bring some bandages/plasters with you in case of this. Expect stares if you have any larger art: tattoos (especially full-body ones) have long been associated with yakuza mafia (page 18). In general, tattoos aren't welcome, but the idea is starting to change, so don't give up hope until you check. If all else fails, you can try the 24-hour outdoor coastal onsen of Yakushima and Iōjima, where if you go at late/early hours you may have the place to yourself.

TRAVELLING POSITIVELY

Alongside adhering to local etiquette and culture, the most important thing in this archipelago is protecting wildlife. Though only parts of the archipelago fall under UNESCO protection, many of the islands have endemic species and protected habitats.

Almost everyone visiting these islands interacts with the sea. This means being aware of animals like sea turtles, who lay on beaches and mustn't be startled. In particular, using reef-friendly sunscreen is an absolute must. The chemicals in normal sunscreen can do untold damage to already fragile ecosystems. Please make sure to pick up reef-friendly options, which are sold in the UK but can also be found in Japan.

Also make sure you pick up and take home all of your rubbish – difficult as that can be in a country like Japan, which uses plastic wrapping like it's going out of fashion. The islands have volunteer groups of locals who clean up beaches; though Japan is an incredibly clean country, rubbish from neighbouring countries and boats floats in off the sea, and has become increasingly problematic. Many once-beautiful beaches are being ruined by plastic waste. If you are happy to do your bit, pick up whatever you find; if nothing else, prioritise netting and plastic bags, which animals can confuse for food and/or become trapped in.

Part Two

THE ISLANDS

3

The Ōsumi Islands

A stamen-like spray of ship routes and scattered islands hangs off the southern coast of Kyūshū. This mapped-out flower of ferries leads to the Ōsumi Islands (Ōsumi-shotō; 大隅諸島): the first island group of the Nansei-shotō and the first hint that there's another, more tropical, side to Japan.

The Ōsumi are a stepping stone between Kyūshū's glorious green and Okinawa's sun-kissed, palm-freckled tropics; a group of ethereal forests, belching volcanoes and the occasional beach. The Ōsumi comprises six inhabited islands, four of which are small, sparsely populated and rarely visited. The two big hitters – the real reason anyone visits – are Yakushima and Tanegashima. While Tanegashima is known

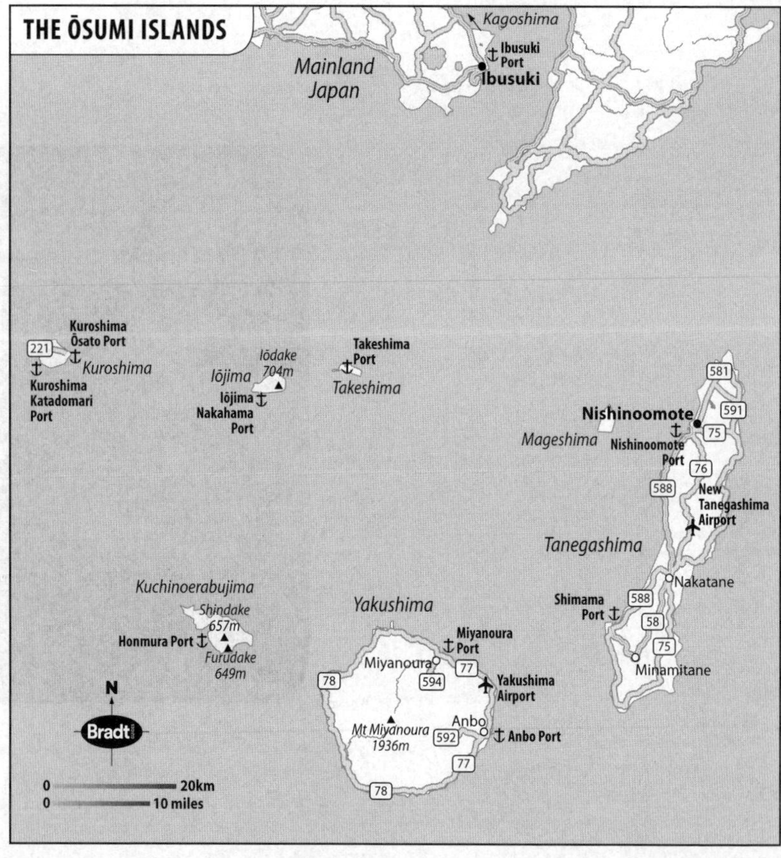

domestically as the home of the Japanese Space Agency, Yakushima is internationally renowned for its nature. Here, visitors come to hike deep into primeval forest, immersing themselves in ancient trees and hushed, mist-mottled folklore.

The remaining four islands are so overlooked as to be called entirely forgotten. A world away from tourism, Kuchinoerabujima and the three Mishima islands offer some unique landscapes and experiences – but are so far off the beaten track that visitors may struggle to slash their way through the logistics of visiting hyper-local, tight-knit communities with no tourist support.

The island group's proximity to Kyūshū means it has far more in common culturally with mainland Japan than Okinawa, and even to next-door neighbour Amami. It also means that this island group is one of the most visited of the archipelago, easily accessed by boat from Kagoshima.

YAKUSHIMA

Japan's Nansei-shotō starts off with a resounding, UNESCO-recognised bang. Yakushima (屋久島) is not only one of the most idyllic of all Japan's islands, but one of the most beautiful places in the entire country. It permanently hovers in best-of lists for landscapes, waterfalls, mountains, trees and island treasures. Indeed, thanks to its awesome ancient mountain forests, biodiversity and great millennia-old cryptomeria trees, Yakushima was also among the first places in Japan to be UNESCO inscribed in 1993.

Yakushima's primeval forests are, after all, sacred places, and have been for centuries. The 39 inner mountains in particular – including Miyanouradake (宮之浦岳), the highest mountain in Kyūshū at 1,936m – with their thick mantle of meandering branches and roots, were revered, and each village worshipped at a mountain shrine (into which women weren't allowed). Yakushima has been called the realm of the gods, and was said to be the first place on earth the gods touch down before moving on to their own shrines.

It's not a stretch of the imagination. Outside the forest (which covers around 90% of the island's 505km^2), Yakushima feels like many other low-population islands, with pottering locals and small-town spirit. Under the cover of the canopy, however, the island develops an unearthly, otherworldly feel: the primitive quiet broken by bird calls and the drip from wet leaves; cedar trees standing sentinel over a soft cloak of moss; the flick of a deer's fluffy white ear. After just 5 minutes in the forest you can understand why Yakushima was the inspiration for Studio Ghibli's film *Princess Mononoke*, full of forest spirits and prehistoric gods.

Humans aren't the only ones enjoying the island's nature, though. Alongside the endemic *yakushika* deer, thought to be messengers of the gods, Yaku is home to *tanuki* (Japanese raccoon dogs), the Erabu flying fox, Ryūkyū green pigeons, Ryūkyū robins and the endemic Yakushima macaque. Found only here, these monkeys are smaller and heavier than their mainland cousins. Though once near-endangered, their numbers have bounced back thanks to efforts from locals to co-exist with the often cheeky creatures. Occasionally, especially around the less-inhabited western coast, you can see the Yakushima deer and macaques playing together, but don't be fooled: the monkeys can become aggressive so keep your distance.

One of the reasons the island has such an exceptional landscape is down to its rainfall. A telling description of Yakushima is that it's the wettest place in Japan and rates pretty highly in the world too. The local saying is that it rains '35 days a month' on Yaku, with almost 5m of rain a year and in some mountainous areas up to 10m. Never let that put you off though: it's the reason Yakushima is so remarkably lush.

As well as rain and subtropical sun, Yakushima is the southernmost point in Japan to see snow.

The waters around Yakushima are home to an exceptional number of fish species, plus occasional dolphins and whales around February–March. The island is also one of the world's leading sea turtle spawning sites. You can see them across beaches in the summer, coming to lay their eggs.

Alongside Okinawa-hontō and the Kerama Islands, Yakushima is one of the most touristed places in the archipelago, its population of around 13,500 utterly outnumbered by the 300,000 visitors a year. Tourism is now one of the island's main industries, alongside orange and tea farming.

HISTORY When Chinese emperors heard of a land of 'happy immortals' off their empire's eastern shore, myriad expeditions were sent to find it. In 608CE, one of these expeditions was successful – but the explorers didn't find immortals, treasures, nor a permanently happy people. What they found instead were potential prisoners, who were brought back to China despite being unable to communicate with their captors. Though no-one knows for certain which island they came from, it is presumed the expedition landed north of Okinawa-hontō, because when the captives were presented to the Chinese Imperial Court, they met a Japanese envoy who declared they were speaking the language from the island of Yaku. If true, the Chinese court seems to have had more interest in Yakushima than the Japanese one did.

Fishing implements uncovered in the south date back some 17,000 years, but the first signs of settled human habitation come around 6,000–7,000 years ago. The existence of 'southern islanders' was recorded in the early 600s CE, but the first Japanese mention of Yaku itself came later. The Nihonshoki chronicles, published in 702CE, references courtiers being sent to the island with a small armed force around 698CE.

Little else is known of Yaku's early history. In the 16th century it saw battle and was ruled by neighbouring Tanegashima, before falling to the hands of the Shimazu clan. In 1708, during Japan's era of isolation from the West, an Italian missionary found his way to the island, causing the Shimazu clan to set up monitoring stations for foreign vessels across Yaku.

What put Yakushima on Japan's map was its forest – not for its beauty but timber. Yakushima cedars, known as *yakusugi*, were used in the construction of Hokoji Temple's Great Buddha Hall in Kyoto completed in 1586, propelling the island's resources into the spotlight. With the Shimazu clan strictly controlling the supply of timber, forestry became Yakushima's biggest industry, with tracks and logging developing the island. Some of these old logging cart tracks remain in the forest, cutting through the trees on the way to Jōmon-sugi – Japan's biggest and best cedar, calculated to be anywhere between 3,000 and 7,200 years old. (Happily, Jōmon-sugi and several other huge, ancient trees – Kigen-sugi, Yayoi-sugi, Daiō-sugi, Yamato-sugi and Bandai-sugi – escaped logging as up until the Edo period, locals saw yakusugi as holy and rarely cut them down.)

In 1881, the forests that had been deemed common and used by locals for centuries were declared government owned, leaving islanders without enough fuel. Locals and the government fought for ownership for over a century, and today most of the Yaku forests are still owned by the government.

Thankfully the war over the forests came to an end with the discovery of Jōmon-sugi in 1968 and the UNESCO inscription. Today, Yakushima is far more protected and logging halted.

GETTING THERE AND AWAY Yakushima has an airport, with flights run by JAL's Japan Air Commuter (w jal.co.jp/jp/en). Multiple flights a day operate from Kagoshima (40mins) and once daily from both Osaka Itami (1hr 40mins) and Fukuoka (1hr). When weighing up the cost–time benefit, flights aren't always the most useful option. However, you can occasionally get discounts on the Kagoshima flights that make them only a few thousand yen more than Yakushima's expensive jetfoil.

Yakushima has two ports, Miyanoura and Anbō, on the north and west coasts respectively. They're serviced by two types of ferry from Kagoshima. The high-speed Tane-Yaku jetfoils (☏ 0570 00 4015; w tykousoku.jp) named *Toppy* and *Rocket* leave from Kagoshima's high-speed ship ferry terminal for Miyanoura four times a day (1hr 50mins) and Anbō six times a day (2hrs 40mins). These jetfoils also operate from Ibusuki Port in the south of Kagoshima Prefecture to Miyanoura thrice daily, taking 1 hour 15 minutes. You can also book these services online at Direct Ferry (w directferries.co.uk) and Yakushima Travel (w yakushimatravel.com/ticket-english).

The main issue with the speedy jetfoil is the price: a one-way ticket on the jetfoil is about the same price as a return on the car ferry, *Ferry Yakushima 2* (☏ 0992 26 0731; w ferryyakusima2.com). This ferry operates from Kagoshima's Minami-futō Port (South Passenger Terminal) to Miyanoura and back once a day. It takes 4 hours, double the duration of the jetfoil, but if you have the time and a tighter budget it works out well. The overnight ferry, *Ferry Hibiscus*, is incredibly basic and is used mostly as a cargo ship and as a budget option for workers and locals. The 13-hour journey is understandably not very popular with tourists, but it's the cheapest way to get around, saves on accommodation costs and is an adventure in itself. This ferry departs from Kagoshima Taniyama Port.

You can also travel between Yakushima and Tanegashima on the Tane-Yaku jetfoils, from both Miyanoura (45mins) and Anbō (50mins) to Nishinoomote. There are cheaper options for this journey – notably the above-mentioned *Ferry Hibiscus* – but they aren't very regular and usually operate at unpleasant hours. However, given the extraordinary price difference it's worth considering as an alternative.

GETTING AROUND Far and away the best option for getting around Yakushima is **rental car**, or **moped** should you want to risk the wet weather. Be aware, though, that vehicles book up well in advance, some forest roads are very narrow, and petrol is expensive compared to the mainland. It can be worth checking with your accommodation to see if they also offer car rentals.

A ring road covers Yakushima's round 132km circumference, with a few offshoots into the island's mountainous interior. Two **buses** operate on Yakushima, Tanegashima-Yakushima Kotsu (0992 59 2888; w iwasaki-corp.com) and Matsubanda Kotsu (0997 43 5000; w yakushima.co.jp), but both are slow, sporadic and really quite expensive. Routes cover the majority of the ring road, from Nagata in the northwest around the north, east and south to Oko-no-Taki in the southwest, taking in both ports and airport. They also go towards the trailheads of Shiratani Unsuikyō, Kigen-sugi/Yakusugi Land and Arakawa, though the latter only operates March–November. The main issue with these trailhead buses is that they operate in such a small window that you cannot do the Jōmon-sugi hike in time to use them. Bus leaflets, including timetables and maps, can be picked up from any entry points on Yakushima.

In addition to buses (and rental cars), Mastubanda also operate **taxis** and sightseeing taxis (0997 43 5555). Other firms include Yakushima Taxi (Anbo: 0997 46 2321, Miyanoura: 0997 42 0611) and Anbo Taxi (0997 46 2311). Taxis are useful for early/late hikes but expensive.

Vehicle rental

Matsubanda Rent-a-Car まつばんだレンタカー; Yakushima Airport 719-37 Koseda; 0997 43 5000; w yakushima.co.jp/car_rental

Nippon Rent-a-Car ニッポンレンタカー屋久島空港営業所; Yakushima Airport 719-37 Koseda; 0997 49 4189; w nrgroup-global.com

Orix Rent-a-Car オリックスレンタカー 屋久島空港店; Yakushima Airport 773-6 Koseda; 0997 43 5888; w car.orix.co.jp

Times Car Rental タイムズカー屋久島空港店; Yakushima Airport 815-27 Koseda, 0997 43 5700; 1200-1 Miyanoura (port), 0997 42 2401; w timescar-rental.com

Toyota Rentals Airport Shop トヨタレンタカー屋久島空港; 812-40 Koseda; 0997 43 5180; w rent.toyota.co.jp/eng

YES! Yakushima 797-21 Koseda; w yesyakushima.com. Extensive English support for car, scooter, bicycle & hiking equipment rental.

TOURIST INFORMATION As a popular island, there's plenty of information online from English-speaking tour operators, as well as the Yakushima Tourism Association (w yakushimatourism.com). They operate offices in Anbō (屋久島観光協会安房案内所; 187-1 Anbo; 0997 46 2333; 08.30–18.00 daily) and Miyanoura (屋久島観光協会宮之浦案内所; 823-1 Miyanoura; 0997 42 1019; 09.00–17.00 Tue–Sun).

WHERE TO STAY

Miyanoura

Ocean View Guest House (2 cottages) オーシャンビューゲストハウス屋久島; 1458-3 Kusugawa; 0808 917 8937; w oceanviewyakushima.com. 2-bedroom modern wood guesthouse with fully fitted kitchen, bathroom, large living room & sea-view veranda, or smaller twin bedroom with bathroom, kettle, crockery, toaster & fridge. **$$$$$**

Cottage Yakusugi House (whole house) コテージ屋久杉の家; 2478-74 Miyanoura; 0908 910 8940; w yakusugihouse.com. Charming & homely wooden house for 5 guests with packed kitchen-diner, tatami rooms & futons, & Western room. Laundry available, TV, free bike rental & pretty grounds. Also operates another annexe building. **$$$**

Yaedake Sanso Lodge (8 cottages) ロッジ 八重岳山荘; 2191 Miyanoura; 0997 42 1551; w yaedake.jp. Set in the forest & lantern lit, Yaedake is beautifully immersive – & therefore popular. Cottage rooms are modern wooden lodge & Western, sleeping 2–5, some en suite. HB available & car necessary. Laundry, hiking rentals, free canoes. **$$$**

Anbō

Guesthouse Manmaru (8 rooms) 旅人の宿まんまる; 540-19 Anbo; 0997 49 7107; w manmaru-yakushima.com. Boutique guesthouse with gorgeous onsen bathroom overlooking the ocean & nicely renovated Western/tatami en-suite rooms. Guest kitchen well equipped, laundry, BBQ, snorkel rental, b/fast & lunchboxes available. **$$$**

Suimeiso Minshuku (9 rooms) 水明荘; 1 Anbo; 0997 46 2078; w suimeisou-yakushima.com. Budget accommodation by riverside in centre of village, with small to large tatami rooms & 2 Western-style rooms. Some have en suite, many have river views. Shared bathroom, lovely shared lounge area, HB available. Basic but brill & good enough for Ghibli director Hayao Miyazaki. **$$**

Elsewhere

Sankara Hotel Resort & Spa [map, page 70] (31 rooms) 0800 800 6007; w sankarahotel-spa.com/en. Yakushima's ultra lux hotel with full-service spa, outdoor pool with bar, a 24hr gym, rental cycles & 2 restaurants including French Ayana. Rooms are warm, welcoming & fully equipped with deep bathtubs in en suite & designer toiletries. B/fast inc. **$$$$**

✷ **Yakusugirou Shichifuku** (6 rooms) 屋久杉郎七福; 2287-4 Isso; w yakusugiroushichifuku.com. Run by incredibly kind, English-speaking local artist Baba Kimika, this 1933 guesthouse in Isso is a stunning yakusugi-made traditional home with shared kitchen/lounge/bathroom, beautiful river view tatami rooms & café opposite. Kimika may offer lifts & even host guest parties. **$$$**

WHERE TO EAT AND DRINK

Yakushima is known for its prolific citrus fruits, including ponkan and *tankan* mandarins, as well as its exceptional flying fish, which feature on many local menus. It's also known for its naturally growing medicinal herbs – the original kanji used in Yaku's name meant 'medicine island' – such as turmeric.

Restaurants aren't in short supply; there's everything from fast-food chains to local eateries. There are also shops offering early bentō box lunches for you to take on hikes, but you'll need to reserve one the day before pick-up. Try Shimamusubi (島むすび; 2452-54 Miyanoura; 0997 42 0770; 04.00–08.00 daily) in Miyanoura or Asahi Bento (あさひ弁当; 2353-320 Anbo; 0997 46 4007; 04.00–08.00 daily) in Anbō.

Kotobuki 古都蕗; 1482-20 Koseda; 0997 43 5317; noon–21.00 Fri–Sat. Only open 2 days a week & off a hard-to-find side road, Kotobuki's gorgeous grounds, traditional wood house & excellent daily changed set menu make the effort worthwhile. **$$$**

Anei Maru 安永丸; 2400-120 Anbo; 0997 46 3055; w aneimaru.co.jp; 17.30–22.30 daily. English-friendly family fish restaurant doing a great set meal straight from their fishing boat of the same name. Sushi, flying fish & sashimi. **$$**

Hiyoriya ヒヨリヤ; 1436-35 Koseda; 0801 893 8043; 11.00–14.30 Wed–Sun. Exceptional vegan/vegetarian restaurant serving healthy set meals that taste as good as they look, with drinks to match. $$

Restaurant Ju お食事処 樹; 2478-181 Miyanoura; 0997 42 1839; 11.30–13.30 & 17.30–20.30 Tue–Sun. Cheap, fab family restaurant that often earns a queue of hungry locals; grab a kitchen bar seat & order something fishy, like flying fish teishoku. $$

Wakadaisho 若大将; 79 Miyanoura; 0997 42 0161; 18.00–23.00 Mon–Sat. A Miyanoura must, this fisherman's restaurant serves its own catch in a cosy, late night-looking spot. Wooden bars, sake, the best sashimi & English menus. $$

Banshaku 晩酌; 277-20 Hirauchi; 0997 47 2383; 18.00–22.30 Tue–Sun. Locally loved izakaya with English menus, beautiful garden setting & cheap hearty meals. Ideal for after a day hiking. $

Shiba Tofu Shop 柴とうふ店; 1377-2 Nagata; 0997 45 2048; 08.00–17.00 Tue–Sat. Wonderfully friendly owners who make their own shima-dōfu by hand twice a day (which you can sometimes watch). Western & Japanese meals are tofu-heavy – try the stacked burgers. $

SHOPPING You won't lack for food shops in the towns: there's an A Co-op in Onoaida, Anbō and Miyanoura, as well as other large supermarkets. Most of these offer pre-cooked bentōs and meals that can be taken on hikes. The most 'Yakushima' souvenir is cedar – there's no end to shops selling wood crafts straight from the forest – as well as island tea.

Arts and crafts

Ariga-to 2401-10 Miyanoura; 0805 309 5213; w ariga-to.shop; 10.00–18.00 Thu–Mon. Deerskin items & accessories.

Pukaridō ぷかり堂; 719-39 Koseda; 0997 43 5623; w pukarido.com; 08.30–18.00 Thu–Tue. Jewellery, crafts & handmade island souvenirs.

Sugisho 杉匠; 650-113 Anbo; 0997 46 2123; w sugisyou.com; 08.00–18.00 daily. Yakusugi items.

Takashi Kawamura 650-90 Koseda; 0704 475 2310; w tkawamura.work. Artist depicting Yakushima in intricate ink line drawings.

Clothing and jewellery

Ru Gajumaru ル・ガジュマル; 413-74 Koseda; 0997 43 5011; 10.00–18.00 daily. T-shirts, jewellery, clothing.

Yakushima Messenger 屋久島メッセンジャー; 413-76 Koseda; 0997 43 5630; w yakushima-messenger.com; 10.00–18.00 Sat–Thu. Stylish shop with clothing & trinkets.

Food and drink

Honbo Shuzo 屋久島伝承蔵本坊酒造; 2384 Anbo; 0997 46 2511; w hombo.co.jp; 09.00–16.00 Mon–Sat. Shōchū distillery with shop, tasting & tours.

Yakushima Roaster やくしまロースター; 2670-16 Anbo; 0997 46 3377; w yakushimaroaster.com. Roasted & unroasted coffee beans.

Yakushima Ukon-no-Sato 屋久島ウコンの里; 2476-20 Miyanoura; 0997 42 0723; w yakushima-ukon.com; 09.00–11.30 & 13.00–16.00 Mon–Fri, 09.00–11.00 Sat. Turmeric products.

Souvenirs

Yakushima Kanko Centre 屋久島観光センター; 799 Miyanoura; 0997 42 0091; w yksm.com; 09.00–18.00 daily. Souvenirs, café & bike rentals.

SPORTS AND ACTIVITIES With loads of activities on the island, including marine sports and hiking, there are a good number of operators with the following all English speaking.

Green Mount 0997 47 1080; e info@greenmount.jp; w greenmount.jp/english. Offers SUP tours, as well as a variety of camping & trekking tours.

One Drop 0709 038 1081; e onedropyakushima@gmail.com; w onedrop-yakushima.com/english. Ocean & river kayaking, trekking & complete island tours.

Yakushima Geographic Tours w yakugeo.com. Private tours with local guide taking in hiking, kayaking, river trekking & custom sightseeing.

Yakushima Marine Club Kaiolohia 屋久島マリンクラブカイオロヒア; e kaiolohia@po4.synapse.ne.jp; w yakushima-marine-club.kaiolohia.com. River kayaking, diving & snorkelling.

YES! Yakushima w yesyakushima.com. 'Yakushima English Service' offers rentals & tours covering trekking, tea plantations, night turtle watching, overnight stays, kayaking, scuba, snorkelling & SUP.

OTHER PRACTICALITIES

Banks and post offices

Anbo Post Office 安房郵便局; 187-67 Anbo; 0997 46 2072; 09.00–17.00 Mon–Fri, ATM: 08.00–19.00 Mon–Fri, 09.00–19.00 Sat, 09.00–18.00 Sun

Kamiyaki Post Office 上屋久郵便局; 126 Miyanoura; 0997 42 0042; 09.00–17.00 Mon–Sat, 09.00–12.30 Sun, ATM: 08.45–18.00 Mon–Fri, 09.00–17.00 Sat–Sun

Minami Nippon Bank 南日本銀行; 93 Miyanoura; 0997 42 0511; w nangin.jp; ATM: 08.45–11.30 & 12.30–18.00 Mon–Fri, 09.00–11.30 & 12.30–17.00 Sat–Sun

Medical

Yakushima-mori Hospital やくしま森の診療所; 2395-1 Anbo; 0997 47 1010; 08.30–12.00 & 14.30–17.30 Mon–Tue & Thu–Fri, 08.30–noon Wed & Sat

Yakushima Tokushukai Hospital 屋久島徳洲会病院; 2467 Miyanoura; 0997 42 2200; w yakushimatokushukai.com

Police

Yakushima Kurio Substation 屋久島警察署栗生駐在所; 1165-3 Kurio; 0997 48 2032

Yakushima Miyanoura Police Box 屋久島警察署 宮之浦交番; 288-6 Miyanoura; 0997 42 0002

Yakushima Police Station 鹿児島県 屋久島警察署; 304-42 Anbo; 0997 46 2110

WHAT TO SEE AND DO The first thing most people do in Yakushima is find their accommodation and don some hiking boots. Yaku's towns are nice to wander but not necessarily packed with activities.

Miyanoura The first stop in Miyanoura (宮之浦) is usually the **Yakushima Environmental Culture Village Centre** (屋久島環境文化村センター; 823-1 Miyanoura; 0997 42 2900; w yakushima.or.jp; 09.00–17.00 Tue–Sun; exhibition hall: adult/child ¥530/270–370). Right at Miyanoura Port, this centre has tourist information, as well as safety guidance and displays about the nature, culture and landscape of Yakushima – plus a souvenir shop and café. The **memorial park** (名残の松原) just across from the centre holds Yakushima's UNESCO World Heritage registration monument and is a much nicer place than the port to sit and wait for your ferry.

Heading east into town, you'll meet the fine **Yakujinja** (益救神社; 277 Miyanoura; 0997 42 0907; w yakujinja.com), which sits near the mouth of the Miyanoura River. This shrine has acted as guardian of the Yaku and Tanega people since ancient times. Along the river is the rather obscure and uninspiring-looking **Yakushima Town and Folk Museum** (屋久島町歴史民俗資料館; 1593 Miyanoura; 0997 42 1900; 09.00–17.00 Tue–Sun; ¥100), which shows bits of island life and history, and has an English information folder at reception.

Across the river and into the hills is the stunning **Ushidokomoisho** (牛床詣所), a forest shrine of towering trees and moss-coated stone torii. Found on the road to Shiratani Unsuikyō (page 79), it's a sacred space where families greeted and waved off men who went to the mountains to pray during the Dake-mairi festival, as women and children could not participate. Further up is the **Yakushima Comprehensive Nature Park** (屋久島総合自然公園; 2077 Miyanoura; 0997 42 2727; 08.30–17.00 daily; adult/child ¥300/100), an 8ha botanical garden on the Miyanoura River with a lush open lawn and Yakushima rhododendrons.

Just south of Miyanoura, off the main road, is the local **Kusugawa onsen** (楠川温泉; 1364-5 Kusugawa; 0997 42 1173; 09.00–20.30 daily; ¥300, towel rental available). Adorably small and hidden in the trees, this onsen has been used for centuries by locals, who appreciate soaking in the 27°C water with the sound of the river running alongside. From May to June, bathers can watch fireflies around the Yunogawa from the pools, which accommodate around ten people at a time. It's as local as they come and more sentō than onsen; you'll likely be alone or sharing the two small baths with an octogenarian local.

The east and Anbō Just beside the airport is a fascinating coastal area, known as the Crystal Cape (クリスタル岬) or the **Nitahayasaki Mine Ruins** (仁田早崎鉱山跡). The path to this strange peach landscape, once a tungsten mine, is quite overgrown and not maintained, but the colour of the rocks against the vivid sea is worth the short detour. The east's **Makurajō Yōgan** (枕状溶岩) and the **Tashiro Coast** (田代海岸) it sits on are similarly nice spots to escape. This unknown area is made of rock formations, basalt lava and a small beach.

Heading south, pass the lovely **Funayuki Shrine** (船行神社; 9-2 Funayuki; w kagojinjacho.or.jp) before hitting **Anbō** (安房). This town has three bridges crossing the river, but the **Matsumine Bridge** (松峯大橋) furthest up has the best views over the valley's leafy forests. In summer, you can occasionally see turtles in the water below. Across the bridge and on a path up the road is **Takinogawa Monolith** (滝之川の一枚岩), a calming spot where the river runs over a massive sedimentary rock. Perfect for dipping toes during a picnic.

On the road to the Arakawa trailhead and Yakusugi Land (page 80) is the **Myōjōdake Observatory** (明星岳展望台), which overlooks the valley and the Anbō River slicing through the mountains. To its south is the **Yakushima World Heritage Conservation Centre** (屋久島世界遺産センター; 2739-434 Anbo; 0997 46 2992; w env.go.jp; 09.00–17.00 daily, closed Sat Dec–Feb) which introduces Yakushima's national parks and UNESCO practices. Next door is the **Yakusugi Museum** (屋久杉自然館; 2739-343 Anbo; 0997 46 3113; w yakusugi-museum.com; 09.00–17.00 daily, closed first Tue each month Dec–Jul; ¥600), dedicated to the island's cedar trees. The museum has an English audio guide and exhibits on forestry and the culture around yakusugi.

Stop in at **Sarukawa Banyan Tree** (猿川のガジュマル), taking a short walk along a forest trail to see the huge aerial roots of a vast *gajumaru*, and **Haruta Beach** (春田浜海水浴場). Harutahama is on Yakushima's largest uplifted coral reef, so it's one of the best places on Yaku to snorkel and swim with colourful flora and fauna.

Mugio's **Ōyama Shrine** (大山神社; 728-23 Mugio) is a glorious woodland Shintō shrine with a wooden torii that blends into the trees and a carpeted path leading up mossy lime-green steps. The shrine at the top is small and sturdy – it's definitely the journey, not the destination, that makes this visit worthwhile.

The Taino River is where the island of water comes alive. Before emptying into the sea, the Taino tumbles down three sets of falls. First is **Senpiro-no-taki** (千尋の滝): a tumult of water that spreads over a great granite shelf before dropping 60m into a 200m-wide gorge. Fed by Yaku's voluminous rains, Senpiro has an observation deck (千尋の滝 展望所) just downstream. Its name means '1,000 fathoms', referencing an old unit of measurement the size of open hands – said to be the width of its fall. Visible from the first bridge south of Senpiro is **Ryūjin Falls** (竜神の滝), the second cascade of the trio.

Last but not least is the extraordinarily picturesque **Torooki Falls** (トローキの滝), which sits at the mouth of the Taino. Unusually, Torooki pours straight into the sea from 6m up, just in front of a classic Japanese scarlet bridge that briefly flashes in and out from the forest. From the observatory here, you can see the waterfall, bridge and Mount Mocchom.

The south **Hara** (原) in the southeast has the family-friendly **Canopy Treetop Walk** (梢回廊キャノッピ; 677-44 Hara; 0997 49 3232; w canoppi.com; 09.00–17.00 Thu–Tue; from ¥1,000), where you can walk 300m through the Yaku forest canopy. It also has the pretty **Yakujinja** (益救神社; 721 Hara), a small vermilion shrine that stands bright in the green.

Heading west, check out Onoaida's tropical-looking **Hoshoku Shrine** (保食神社; 977-1 Onoaida) and the views from **Onoaida Lighthouse** (尾之間灯台) on the cape before hitting the Onoaida Onsen.

Built by village locals, **Onoaida Onsen** (尾之間温泉; 1291 Onoaida; 0997 47 2872; noon–21.00 Mon, 07.00–21.00 Tue–Sun; adult/child ¥200/100) is a scorching bath supposed to have cured a shot deer 350 years ago. It remains a local haunt, with many using it daily, and is a great stop after hiking – the footbath outside is wonderful for sore feet. It's not for the faint-hearted though: the water runs up to 49°C.

Moving inland up the Suzu River reveals the brilliant **Janokuchi Falls** (蛇之口滝). Despite being 30m high and 100m wide, Janokuchi glides rather than thunders its way down over a smooth granite surface. The 3.5km walk to the falls takes you through subtropical jungle, starting from the Onoaida Trail or Janokuchi hiking course entrance, near the Onoaida Onsen car park. Close to the river's mouth is the noble-looking **Kojima Shrine** (小島神社).

The centre of the south coast has two big-hitters: the natural coastal onsen of Hirauchi Kaichu and Yudomari. **Hirauchi Kaichū** (平内海中温泉; 7-2 Hirauchi; 0997 47 2953; ¥200 donation) is a 400-year-old open-air tidal onsen, accessible for 2 hours before and after low tide – the longer you wait after low tide, the hotter the two pools here are. It's a particularly good spot for stargazing at night, sunk in the warm sulphuric waters. There's no dressing room, swimwear/underwear is prohibited and it's also unisex; if you're feeling shy then use a sarong or towel to cover yourself up till the final moment. Otherwise, there's a footbath you can use, clothes on.

Yudomari Onsen (湯泊温泉; 1714-28 Yudomari; 0997 48 2806; ¥200 donation) is another blissful beachside open-air bath: listen to the waves and watch sunrise or sunset as you steep in near-24°C water. Slightly larger and less warm than Hirauchi, Yudomari has a bamboo divider for gendered pools but there still isn't much left to the imagination once outside the water. Onsen towels can be used to protect your modesty, or you can don swimwear in the remote baths 30m away. Thankfully, the baths are open 24 hours so if you aren't comfortable, you can hopefully find a quieter time to use them. Like Hirauchi, it has a clothed footbath available and is an enjoyable sunset spot. The dressing room is next to the car park.

Round to the southwest is **Yakushima Fruit Garden** (屋久島フルーツガーデン; 629-16 Nakama; 0997 48 2468; 08.30–16.30 daily), also known as Papaya Village. This garden houses nearly 2,000 species of tropical plants and fruits. Bananas, papayas, mangoes, guava, pineapples, plums and tankan (a subtropical mandarin) are grown and made into products and popular souvenirs. Down the road (or indeed across it) is the **Nakama Gajumaru** (中間ガジュマル), a massive banyan tree on the north side of Nakama Bridge believed to be around 500 years old. String-like aerial roots spread out over the road to form a tunnel you can walk and drive through.

The west The west opens up with **Kurio Beach** (栗生海水浴場), its cyan shallows famous for sea turtles who spawn here in the beautiful white sands. Up from the beach is the **Kurio Shrine** (栗生神社; 1698 Kurio) and the **Shakunage-no-mori Park** (石楠花の森公園), which sits along the river and blooms bright with rhododendrons in April. On the splurge of sea-smoothed rock that is Kurio's **Kamezono headland** (カマゼノ鼻), the **Tsukasaki Tide Pool** (塚崎タイドプール) offers amazing sunset photos across the filled rock pools.

Heading north brings you to **Ōko** or **Ohko Waterfall** (大川の滝). One of the 100 best waterfalls in Japan as chosen by the Ministry of the Environment, Ohko is the tallest fall on Yakushima at 88m and one of the largest by volume. The spray is a perfect way to cool off; you can walk right up to the basin, though swimming in the pool is prohibited. It's believed that drinking the fall water is good for your health, as the water picks up minerals from the rocks and forest.

This western road is also known as **Seibu Rindō Forest Path** (西部林道), a narrow and winding World Heritage-listed coastal road. Driving along you meet a huge variety of plants and, more importantly, Yaku deer and macaques.

The north Nagata is best known for its two extraordinary beaches: **Maehama** (永田前浜) and **Inakahama** (永田いなか浜). These long sprawls of cream sands are some of Japan's most important loggerhead turtle spawning grounds. They're said to see the highest number of laying turtles in the North Pacific – between May and July, there can be more than 20 turtles nesting in one night. During summer when they lay and hatch, overnight access to the beach is prohibited between 19.30 and 05.00, but you can join a tour with local companies (page 74) and the Yakushima Sea Turtle Hall (屋久島うみがめ館; 805-1 Miyanoura; 0997 47 1800; w umigame-kan.org; 09.00–18.00 Tue–Sun; ¥500) in Miyanoura, which also has more information about the turtles and their conservation.

Upstream of the Nagata River is the **Yokogawa Valley** (横河渓谷), where the **Emerald Pool** (エメラルドグリーンのプール) resides. The valley is carved through granite, and this natural swell of water in the river has become a popular spot. Be aware, however, that though the surface of the river looks calm there is a fast current near the riverbed. Flash floods are also possible when it rains, so take care.

The road north holds two observatories on the way to Isso: **Sunset Hill Observation Deck** (夕日の丘展望所) and **East China Sea Observatory** (東シナ海展望所). The little fishing port of Isso itself has the **Nunobiki Falls** (布引の滝) just off the roadside and **Isso Beach** (一湊海水浴場), a great curve in a natural bay that's a favourite for swimmers. The end of the beach moulds into a small jutting peninsula, largely overlooked but home to the picturesque and sacred **Yahazudake Shrine** (八筈嶽神社). This amazing shrine, fronted by the eye-catching red of a torii and the rushing froth of the sea, disappears into a cave where you can find hanging votive tablets and seashells.

Shitogo Gajumaru Park (志戸子ガジュマル公園; 133-1 Shitogo; 0997 42 0079; 08.30–17.00 daily; adult/child ¥240/180) is a magical place to wander the aerial roots and green canopies. There's a huge banyan tree said to be over 500 years old and it's easily accessible compared to many of the forest trails. In the village you'll find the **Sumiyoshi Shrine** (住吉神社; 576 Shitogo), a wonderfully green glade with a moss-coated shrine.

Hiking Yakushima's hikes are marked with pink tape, tied about trees and branches. The trails are usually clearly signed, but the island's forest is dense – people have gotten lost in Yakushima, and some haven't returned. With disappearances as recently as 2023, it's important to plan in advance and prepare, but more importantly to always let someone know where you are going and the time you expect to be back. More often than not this can just be your accommodation owner, who can raise an alarm. Be careful if it has rained heavily: there's a lot of moss, foliage and slippy rocks about.

Some trailheads and forests require you to pay an entrance fee (though often not in the earliest of hours), but all are worth the price. These fees go towards protection and upkeep, particularly of waste disposal, which has proven a big problem in the past: they ask you not to use trails as toilets and use only the facilities provided. Otherwise, bring everything back with you – everything.

Those treks listed below are the most common, but Yakushima is filled with trails, peaks and rivers. Returning visitors or those with extra time should look into the Sanshin-sugi Three Cedar Trek, Ishizuka and Kosugidani villages, or the mountains of Nagata, Eboshi, Shichigo and Aiko.

Shiratani Unsuikyō Shiratani Unsuikyō (白谷雲水峡) is Yaku's most popular hike, a tranquil 1-hour upward valley trek alongside the cherry blossom-flanked waterfalls of the Shiratani River. The trail is comprised of maintained walkways, paths, bridges and steps that wind between cedars, laurels and moss-coated granite as waterfalls thunder nearby. It's easily combined with other routes, including Bugyō-sugi, Taiko-iwa, the Moss Forest and particularly the Yayoi-sugi (弥生杉) course, which follows Shiratani then loops into the forest past the ancient Yayoi cedar.

Bugyō-sugi Course The easy 3-hour Bugyō-sugi Course (奉行杉コース) follows Shiratani then loops on, covering a number of natural sights along the way. Rich foliage takes you past six giant cedars, including the three-legged (三本足杉), three-branched (三本槍杉) and split gate (二代くぐり杉) specimens, crossing multiple clear babbling streams en route.

Moss Forest This leisurely, ethereal trek through the Moss Forest (苔むす森) takes around 4 hours. Often called the Princess Mononoke Forest, the woodland unsurprisingly acquired its nickname after the release of the hit animation based on the area. Though this fame has rather eclipsed the real deal, reality is far better. The forest life, including decaying leaves, stumps and trees, is covered in hundreds of moss species, painting it a quilted kaleidoscope of green. Reach the forest by crossing the bridge from the Shiratani's left bank and following halfway up the Taiko-iwa trail.

Taiko-iwa Meaning 'drum rock', Taiko-iwa (太鼓岩) is a large granite boulder that looks over a large sweep of Yakushima's great interior – its rivers, valleys, pillowy emerald forest and the oft-obscured Okudake mountain range. (The setting was immortalised in Ghibli's *Princess Mononoke* as the wolf clan's home.) Although a beginner's trail, the round trip takes around 5–6 hours, and involves a fair schlep up steep stairs and ascents.

Getting up to Taiko-iwa and its unbeatable view for sunrise is wholly worthwhile – though getting here in the dark requires your own car/a taxi and some serious torches. Sunrise hits to your left, coursing over the sea and the skeleton of an old sugi tree; in low season, you'll likely get this morning view all to yourself.

Jōmon-sugi This is the big daddy of Yaku treks. Jōmon-sugi (縄文杉) is the oldest and biggest yakusugi on the island, the king and heart of the Yakushima forest. There are two approaches to it. The main one leaves from the Arakawa trailhead taking some 8–11 hours over 22km; the trailhead is open to buses from March to November only, and you'll need to start early. The alternative is a rather hardcore possibility, combining Jōmon-sugi with the Shiratani Unsuikyō in a single day, but you'll need good weather, quieter, less-crowded days and determination. This trek joins the Arakawa one at the Kusugawa split (楠川分かれ) and takes around 12 hours, though can be done in far less if you're really blitzing it: 6 hours is a personal best. You can also do Arakawa–Jōmon–Shiratani, using the first bus to Arakawa, or flip it and take an early taxi to Shiratani. Just make sure to keep an eye on timings if reliant on last buses.

The extraordinary trek itself isn't arduous, just long. It covers Wilson's stump, the old Daiō-sugi and the old logging rail track that wends through the forest. Better still, it immerses you deep into Yaku forest and in low season you may get a good amount of the trail to yourself. The only downside to the trek is unfortunately Jōmon-sugi itself. In an understandable effort to protect the tree from increasing tourism, the surrounding area is littered with wooden walkways apparently installed by a devotee of MC Escher. The tree now has a wooden observatory, too – it's all rather jarring after a day of walking through unblemished, primitive forest. Jōmon-sugi itself remains impressive and awesome, reaching 25.3m up and 16.4m around.

Yakusugi Land Yakusugi Land (ヤクスギランド; **w** y-rekumori.com) may sound like an ill-advised theme park but this is actually one of the most incredible sections of forest in Yakushima. Here, five trails and walkways tiptoe about a 270ha forest of moss, cedars, laurels and streams. Yakusugi is an enchanting must, its courses taking anywhere from 30 minutes to 3½ hours. There isn't much elevation to tackle, but some trails aren't often used so can be rough.

The longest trail within Yakusugi Land is to the so-called Astronomy Forest (天分の森), where you can find logging ruins from the Edo period. Astronomy Forest is moss on steroids: it's comparably unvisited and feels entirely otherworldly.

From Yakusugi Land, you can branch off for much longer, harder hikes: to Yamato-sugi (大和杉), one of the oldest cedars on Yaku at 3,000–4,000 years old, and Tachūdake (太忠岳). Yamato-sugi is well into the forest, far from the beaten path; from Yakusugi Land entrance and back it takes around 8 hours. The Mount Tachū, or Tachūdake, trail leaves Yakusugi Land and climbs through beautiful forest, across bridges, round boulders and through rhododendrons to reach the Tenchūseki monolith (literally 'heavenly pillar') at the summit. It's another 8-hour trip, reaching 1,497m elevation – take the requisite kit and supplies.

Mount Miyanoura It may be one of the most popular hikes on Yaku, but Mount Miyanoura (宮之浦岳) is no simple walk. Reaching 1,936m high, this is one of Japan's famous mountains and takes 10–11 hours to complete. The hike begins at the Yodogawa Trail (淀川登山口) entrance, along the river's clear waters, past the Hananoe wetlands and granite landscapes, until you reach the peak. From here

MYTHS AND FOLKTALES: THE MOUNTAIN SPIRITS

The indigenous Yakushima religion centres around mountain worship. There are a variety of legends about the gods of the mountains, one of which is their procession. In October, it's said that the gods gather and travel from Mount Mocchom northward to Wariishidake. Their procession passes by a place called Miyakata, and it's said if you're there you can hear the sounds of beating drums and flutes and see the lights of lanterns.

However, people should be careful. Further stories of these processions say they take place every month on the 15th, so those who work in the mountain should take a day off and not enter as the gods will punish them. It's said that anyone who disobeys will meet a god on a white deer, and its wild deer will attack with their antlers. Some people are said to be *kamikakushi* (神隠し) – quite literally 'spirited away'. If a god does pass in front of you, you should squat with your head down and wait for it to pass.

Another spirit said to descend the mountain on the days of the mountain god festival is Yamahime, the mountain princess. This long-haired tree spirit is said to be stunningly beautiful, but many legends warn she is dangerous: if you return her smile and laughter, she will suck your blood. Some say you must laugh before she does, in order to avoid such a fate. The terrifying folktale is said to have been created to stop children from wandering off into unsafe mountains, but many claim to have seen Yamahime themselves.

there's a 360-degree panorama which takes in the clouds and phenomenal ridges, including the Okudake range's hidden peaks. Though long, the climb itself is straightforward. On the way to the trailhead, sightseeing buses will often stop at the grand Kigen-sugi (紀元杉), 19.5m high and 8.1m around, the largest 3,000-year-old cedar accessible by car.

The journey to Kuromidake follows almost the exact same route, branching off some 2 hours before Miyanoura's peak at the Kuromi split (黒味分かれ), from where Kuromi's peak is only another 30 minutes away.

Mount Mocchom In the south of Yakushima sits Mount Mocchom (モッチョム岳), one of the hardest climbs on the island. It's only 940m but the ascent is never-endingly steep and involves some crawling and ropes to help you up. Mocchom's granite peak sits rather alone, nearer the coastline, giving you an excellent view of the seascape below. Taking around 6 hours, the hike includes the great 3,000-year-old Bandai-sugi (万代杉)

TANEGASHIMA

Many visitors to the Ōsumi come for Yakushima and Yakushima only. Few eyes ever wander beyond, to the thyme-coloured cambers on the blue horizon. Those who peer east, however, will spot Tanegashima (種子島), a spindly island stretching 57km from north to south.

A laid-back, somewhat weather-beaten place, Tanegashima has a population of around 27,000 that's spread across three areas: northern Nishinoomote, home to Tanegashima's only city, central Nakatane and southern Minamitane. Most of the island is given over to agriculture, but it is also home to caves, unique fauna and serene scenery. Its forests are an important bird habitat, its mangroves ecologically

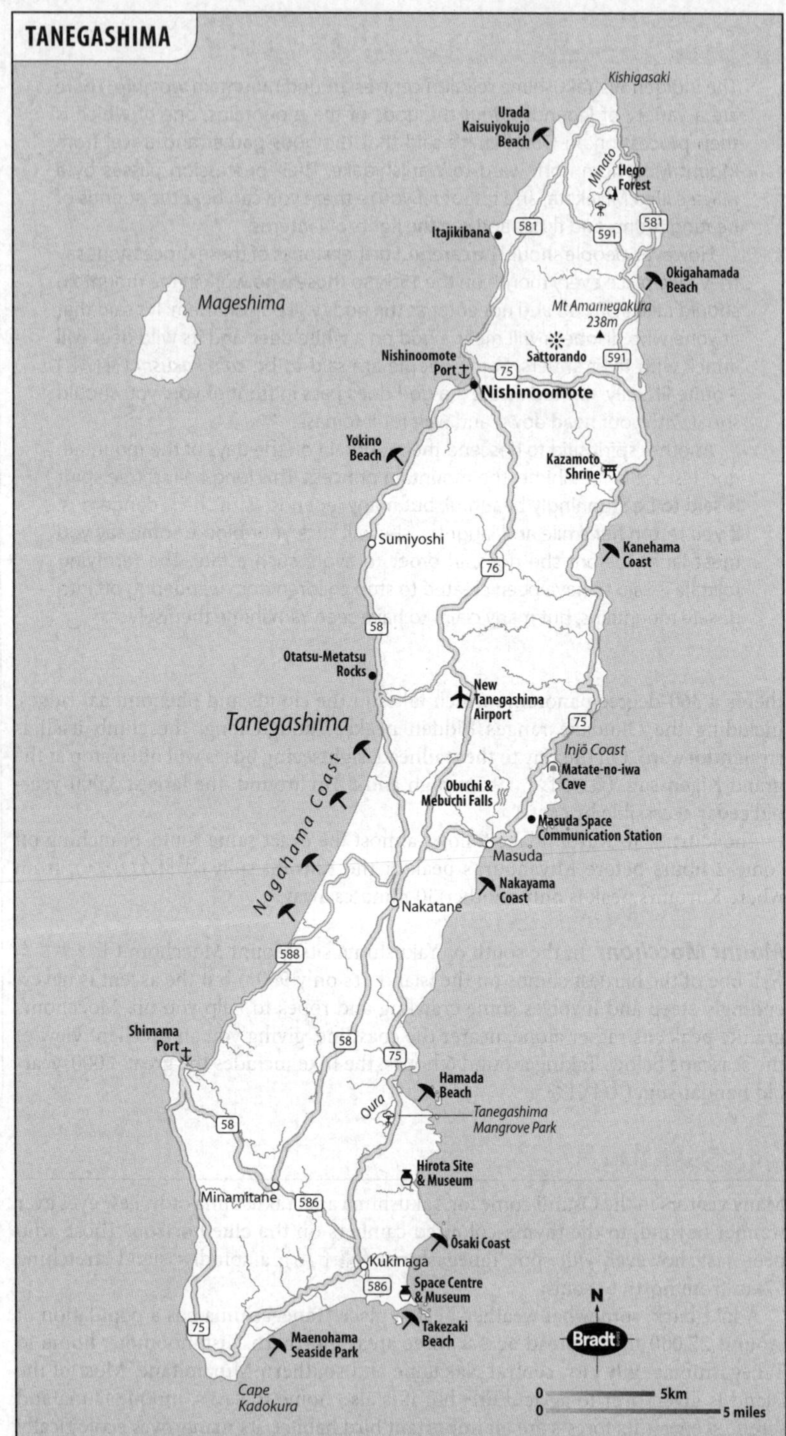
TANEGASHIMA
Kishigasaki
Urada Kaisuiyokujo Beach
Minato
Hego Forest
581
591
Itajikibana
Okigahamada Beach
Mageshima
Mt Amamegakura 238m
Sattorando
Nishinoomote Port
75
Nishinoomote
Yokino Beach
Kazamoto Shrine
Sumiyoshi
Kanehama Coast
76
58
Otatsu-Metatsu Rocks
New Tanegashima Airport
Tanegashima
Injō Coast
Matate-no-iwa Cave
Nagahama Coast
Obuchi & Mebuchi Falls
Masuda Space Communication Station
Masuda
Nakayama Coast
Nakatane
588
Shimama Port
Hamada Beach
Oura
Tanegashima Mangrove Park
Hirota Site & Museum
Minamitane
586
Ōsaki Coast
Kukinaga
Space Centre & Museum
Takezaki Beach
Maenohama Seaside Park
Cape Kadokura
N
Bradt
0
5km
5 miles

TANEGASHIMA FESTIVALS

The island has a great line-up of festivals, particularly modern ones. The Tanegashima Rocket Marathon takes place in March, and the April Tanegashima Cups sailing event brings people from across Japan to race from Nishinoomote Port to Yamakawa Port on the Kagoshima Peninsula.

The summer Teppō Matsuri is the largest event, celebrating the island's history (see below): it's a gun festival with a Portuguese-inspired parade where traditional matchlock guns are fired by locals in traditional clothing. There are colourful floats, a small portable shrine (*mikoshi*), fancy dress, dancing, drumming and singing, as well as an 8,000-strong firework display in the evening.

More traditionally, Annō hosts a Stick Dance in October, a thrilling spectacle incorporating sickles and sticks, while the Hōman Shrine rice-planting festival in April prays for good harvest. To celebrate the new year, 36 arrows are shot into a large target at the Seirin Shrine as part of Ōmato Hajimeshiki, aka 'the great opening ceremony'; this 500-year-old tradition came from a master archer in the 1500s. The festival prays for peace and protection from disease, and is said to take place on the coldest day of the year as locals believe being battered by cold winds protects you for the year.

vital, and its coasts filled with rugged beauty and unique formations. Tanegashima is especially picturesque in springtime, when it becomes carpeted in various blooms.

The beaches here are also excellent: even the rockier ones can sometimes have fossils littered about. Most of the island's sand beaches are white, but those on the west have black iron ore deposits – perfect for keeping kids (and adults) entertained with magnets. Many of them are used by turtles for laying eggs from May to July. They're also often populated by surfers; Tanegashima is known as Japan's best surf spot – one of the few in the country – getting good-sized waves most of the year.

HISTORY For such an overlooked island, Tanegashima has played some big roles in Japan's history. It first came to Japanese notice around the late 600s, when the court sent surveillance missions out. In 1140, it was given to the Shimazu clan, beginning a long period of turmoil and warfare. In the Kamakura period (1185–1333) ownership fell to a Shimazu retainer, the eponymous Tanegashima clan, who ruled it (and occasionally Yakushima) until the Meiji restoration.

The Tanegashima claimed descent from the Heike clan, who were exiled to Tanegashima in 1185. They brought with them metal-workers and craftsmen who had unique techniques for forging metal. Combined with Tanegashima's unusual iron sand deposits, this led the island to become renowned for its sharp-edge tools – a reputation that remains to this day, with *Tanegashima hōchō* (knives) particularly popular with chefs and *tane-basami* (scissors) with bonsai cultivators. (Interestingly, when the Heike clan arrived on the island, they brought more than craftsmen: their Kyoto accent influenced Tanegashima Japanese, and islanders are said to still retain a Kyoto twang today.)

With this history of toolmaking, it's perhaps unsurprising that Tanegashima was the birthplace of Japanese firearms. In 1543, shipwrecked Portuguese sailors brought arquebus rifles to Tanega – the then-lord of the island, Tanegashima Tokitaka, saw the power of the weapons and immediately paid a princely sum for two of them. He ordered a Tanegashima blacksmith to painstakingly disassemble and recreate the rifles, helped by Portuguese sailors who returned the following year. The resulting matchlock guns soon came to be known as 'Tanegashima' around Japan and became instrumental in the unification of the country, changing its course for good.

Tanegashima also formed part of the trading route between Ningbo (western China) and Sakai (south of Osaka), so was often at the heart of international commerce. This made it a hotspot for not only merchants, but also regular shipwrecks. In 1885, the US merchant bark *Cashmere* wrecked off the Masuda coast – the locals saved the sailors they could and cared for them until they could return to America, earning them a medal of honour from the US. The British *Dramerton* ship similarly ran ashore in 1894 on its way to Hong Kong, bringing with it an unfamiliar breed of chicken that the islanders named after the English – Ingee – which is now a speciality of Tanegashima. (A monument to the *Dramerton* and its crew is at Maenohama Seaside Park.)

During World War II, Nishinoomote was garrisoned by the Imperial Japanese army, bringing bombing attacks from the US navy in 1945. In 1969, Tanegashima rocketed to the scientific forefront as the base for Japan's Space Agency, JAXA. It was chosen as rockets are best launched closer to the equator, and Okinawa had yet to be returned to Japanese governance at the time. The island sees multiple launches through the year, which tourists can watch from viewpoints.

GETTING THERE AND AWAY Access to Tanegashima is by ferry, or flight to New Tanegashima Airport in the centre of the island. JAL's commuter group (w jal.co.jp/jp/en) runs around four flights a day from Kagoshima to New Tanegashima Airport, taking 40 minutes.

Ferries to Tanegashima depart from Kagoshima and Yakushima. Yakushima is the much shorter and cheaper journey, and as it's unlikely you'll miss Yakushima from your itinerary, it's recommended to travel between the two islands directly. Many of the same ships and companies that go to Yakushima also access Tanegashima.

From Kagoshima, you can catch the high-speed jetfoils (☎ 0570 00 4015; w tykousoku.jp) taking 1 hour 35 minutes with seven departures daily. Be warned, though, that one of these departures goes via Ibusuki in Kagoshima-ken's south, taking 3½ hours. The jetfoils are offensively expensive compared to other options but are reliable and quick. Four of the seven jetfoil services from Kagoshima operate between Yaku and Tanega – these take 50 minutes and are triple the cost of other, slower options.

Those slower options include Cosmoline's (w cosmoline.jp) *Princess Wakasa* ferry, which takes 3½ hours and is far cheaper. It operates one return journey a day, starting at Kagoshima's Minami-futō Port in the morning and leaving Tanegashima in the afternoon. There's also the Yakushima *Hibiscus* ferry (w yakushimaferry.com), which has rather more inconvenient timings. The outbound leaves Kagoshima Taniyama Port in the early evening, arriving late into Tanegashima. It then continues on to Yaku at an ungodly 05.00, bringing you into Yakushima 2 hours later, before anything is open. The ferry returns to Kagoshima Taniyama via Tanegashima, leaving Nishinoomote in the late morning.

Finally, the *Ferry Taiyou* (☎ 0997 42 0100; w town.yakushima.kagoshima.jp/ferry-taiyou) operates between Tanegashima's southern Shimama Port, Yakushima Miyanoura and Kuchinoerabu. It leaves once daily, the departure times, weirdly, depending on whether the date is an odd or even number. It's the cheapest option but is very little known, even on Tanegashima – it's the kind of ship that has a price list for livestock tickets.

GETTING AROUND Tanegashima's 445km^2 is spread vertically, making it a long way between north and south. Though volcanic, it's comparatively flat compared to Yakushima, with a highest point of 282m. Still, it has some serious lumps and bumps, meaning bicycles are a no-go for longer distances.

Cars are easily the best way forward. There are a few to choose from so shop around or try hiring one through your accommodation/guide as they may get good deals. The majority of car rental places operate an office from both the airport and Nishinoomote.

There are three major bus lines, which aren't always reliable but are delightfully cheap. There's a single bus loop around Nishinoomote, with services operating in both directions six times a day (📞0997 22 1111). The route begins at the port, and takes in Hanazatohama Park, Yoshiminagayama Park and Wakasa Park.

It's vital to note that other bus services don't run on Sundays. This includes two buses serving the airport (📞0997 22 9600) – one from Nishinoomote and another from Minamitane – both running four return journeys a day; prices are based on length of journey, so keep an eye on your destination and fare. There's also the Yamato bus, which travels from Nishinoomote to Minamitane, via Nakatane. The full journey takes around 1 hour 20 minutes and there are five buses a day each way.

Taxis are available from Nishinoomote: Ichimaru (📞0997 22 1010) and Hayashi (📞0997 22 1411). Reservations will likely be in Japanese only though you may get lucky.

Vehicle rental

Niko Niko Rent-a-Car Tanegashima Airport ニコニコレンタカー 鹿児島種子島空港店; 4952-26 Nokan; 📞0997 26 2566; w 2525r.com

Nippon Rent-a-Car Nishinoomote ニッポンレンタカー 種子島西之表営業所; 220-4 Kamomecho; 📞0997 23 5050; w nrgroup-global.com

Nissan Rent-a-Car Tanegashima Airport 日産レンタカー 種子島空港店; 2692-61 Masuda; 📞0997 27 5523; w nissan-rentacar.com

Orix Rent-a-Car オリックスレンタカー 種子島店; 49-1 Nishinoomote; 📞0997 23 4152; w car.orix.co.jp

Rental Bike Tanegashima レンタルバイク種子島; 7253-15 Nishinoomote; 📞0997 28 3660; w www7b.biglobe.ne.jp/~rentalbike-tane. Rental bicycles & mopeds with helpful owner.

Seeds Car Rental シーズレンタカー; 126 Kamomecho; 📞0997 23 6477; w seedsrentacar.com

Toyota Rental Tanegashima Airport トヨタレンタカー種子島空港; 4952-25 Nokan; 📞0997 27 7077; w rent.toyota.co.jp/eng

TOURIST INFORMATION Tanegashima Sightseeing Information Centre (種子島観光協会; 49-1 Nishimachi; 📞0997 23 0111; w tanekan.jp; 🕘 08.00–17.00 daily) in Nishinoomote Port has maps and pamphlets as well as a souvenir shop, free Wi-Fi and toilet. The Machikado Information Centre (まちかどインフォメーションセンター; 191 Nishimachi, Nishinoomote; 📞0997 22 9220; 🕘 10.00–17.30 Tue–Sun) has a small amount of tourist information and free Wi-Fi. There's not a huge amount of English spoken on Tanegashima – some might say zero, even occasionally in tourist offices.

WHERE TO STAY

North

Tanegashima Araki Hotel (36 rooms) 種子島あらきホテル; 78 Nishimachi, Nishinoomote; 📞0997 22 1555; w araki-hotel.co.jp. Opened in 1848, Tanega's oldest hotel, complete with free-flowing hot spring onsen, is popular with all & close to port. Rooms are Western & Japanese, with plush beds & amenities. Beer garden, sauna, terrace, rental cycle, laundry & dinner option too. **$$$$**

Miharuso (14 rooms) 旅館美春荘; 7486-6 Nishinoomote; 0997 22 1393; w miharusou.jp. Refurbished in 2019, this minshuku serves excellent food & has traditional tatami rooms & 1 Western one with en suites. It also runs a surf shop called Origin. HB & b/fast options. $$

Centre

Island Inn Hope (14 rooms) 島宿HOPE; 500-130 Hirayama, Minamitane; 0997 26 7235; w shimayado-hope.com. Pleasant guesthouse near mangroves & Chikura Grotto, with en-suite Western dbls & river or garden views. Rooms are bright & broad with private terraces; grounds have kids' playground & beautiful shared spaces. Dishes are excellent traditional Tanega fare. B/fast available. $$$

Challenge Base YOKANA (1 room, 1 dorm) チャレンジ拠点YOKANA; 5184-25 Noma, Nakatane; 0804 949 5157; w challengebase-yokana.com. Hostel with private & dorm rooms, & downstairs open area where locals hang out. All bathrooms & showers shared. Rooms are clean & neat, dorms wooden, & there's a co-working space, laundry, playroom & kitchen. $$

South

The Beach Club Sandalwood (1 villa) ザ・ビーチクラブ・サンダルウッド; 7288 Nishino, Minamitane; 0997 26 0015; w beachclub.hotel-sandalwood.com. Jaw-dropping private villa resort with huge ocean-view windows, high ceilings, modern wood & concrete décor. Fully equipped, with private chef HB available. $$$$$

Hotel Sandalwood (16 rooms) ホテル サンダルウッド; 525 Nakanokami, Minamitane; 0997 26 0015; w hotel-sandalwood.com. Lovely hotel with open, bright tatami & Western rooms & rare hot-spring baths in every room. Food is homegrown vegetables & local Ingee chicken, carefully selected by chef. Garden with terrace. HB options. $$$$$

Tanegashima Iwasaki Hotel (57 rooms) いわさきホテル; 3367 Kukinaga, Minamitane; w tanegashima.iwasakihotels.com/en. What this bright baby-pink hotel lacks in subtle décor, it makes up for in activities. South of the space station, it's right on the area's best surf beach – kayaking, surfing, diving & snorkelling are all available. It's relatively quiet, with nice bedrooms, & well equipped. $$$$

WHERE TO EAT AND DRINK

Inomoto 味処井元; 189-1 Nishimachi, Nishinoomote; 0997 22 1218; w aji-inomoto.jp; 11.30–14.00 & 17.00–22.00 daily. Handsome wooden restaurant with tatami dining. Excellent bar menu & delicious set menus featuring spiny lobster, crab, sashimi & Japanese donburi. $$$

Shōchū Bar Tanegashima 焼酎BAR種子島; 110 Higashimachi, Nishinoomote; 0801 797 1996; w tanegashima-shochu.business.site; 19.00–midnight Mon–Sat. One of the few late-night spots: home cooking & local shōchū in a small, welcoming bar. $$$

Okonomiyaki Yasubei お好み焼安兵衛; 2769 Nakanokami, Minamitane; 0997 26 1401; w r.goope.jp/yasu-bei; 11.00–22.30 daily. You may have to fight for a seat in this Minamitane stalwart. Food is cheap, delicious & huge, courtesy of some friendly Osakan grandmothers. $$

Uosho Ichijo 魚匠 一条; 23 Higashimachi, Nishinoomote; 0997 23 1838; 17.00–22.00 Tue–Sat. Big portions & exquisite seafood in this popular, if entirely cluttered, spot. The sashimi is a highlight. $$

Kashi Watanabe 菓子処渡辺; 5105 Noma, Nakatane; 0997 27 0062; w kashi-watanabe.com; 08.00–19.00 daily. Nakatane patisserie great for snacks & souvenirs, including fresh cheesecakes & annō/purple potato pies. $

Sakaiya 酒井屋; 7121 Nishimachi, Nishinoomote; 0997 22 0187; w t-sakaiya.com; 09.00–17.30 daily. Amazing menu of Japanese sweets & Tanegashima treats. The Western-style cakes are superb, but make sure to try something traditional & potato-based. $

Steppin' Lion ステッピンライオン; 5293-1 Noma, Nakatane; 0997 27 0502; 11.30–18.00 Mon & Wed–Sat, 11.30–17.00 Sun. A Jamaican-Japanese hybrid, this colourful wooden shack regularly sells out. The jerk chicken burgers are brill, but there's also rice & chicken bowls, jerk plates & beers. $

SHOPPING Tanegashima has a good number of convenience stores and food shops. There are supermarkets in Nakatane and Minamitane, plus several in Nishinoomote,

TANEGASHIMA'S LOCAL DELICACIES

Annō-imo is a sweet potato produced only on Tanegashima. Legend has it that the island was the first place in Japan to successfully grow sweet potatoes – hence their Japanese name, *Satsuma-imo*, after the domain. These annō-imo are fed to the *kurobuta* pigs, giving their flesh a sweet flavour, and are also used in local shōchū. There are a few shōchū worth seeking out: Kouzuma Shuzo makes the Hayabusa II sweet potato shōchū, created with yeast that has travelled in space, Yotsumoto Shuzo creates a shōchū using purple sweet potato and another with red rice, and the Shimanoizumi shōchū is made using traditional rice polishing techniques from the Meiji era.

Thanks to the marine climate, tea grown in Tanegashima is the earliest tea harvested in Japan. One of the green tea cultivars (shōju) thrives exclusively on Tanegashima, making it a popular and unusual brew. The island is also thought to have the fastest rice harvest in Japan, with seedlings planted in March and ready for harvest in July. Tanega's name actually means 'seed island', which some attribute to the idea that Tanegashima was where rice was first imported on to the islands.

Tanega is also known for its large, sweet peanuts (*rakkasei*), still often farmed by hand. After being harvested in July, they were traditionally boiled with salt but today they're hugely popular as *rinkake*: a snack of peanuts and Tanega brown sugar (page 90).

including Sunpia (サンピア食品館; 7459-1 Nishinoomote; 0997 23 3511; 09.00–21.00 daily) and A Co-op (Aコープ 中種子店; 5137-8 Noma; 0997 27 3131; w acoop-ks.co.jp; 09.00–20.00 daily). The convenience stores aren't major chains like Lawson or 7-11, but are well stocked and dotted all over the island.

Tanegashima has great souvenir shops where you can pick up souvenirs, scissors, weaponry, space memorabilia and more.

Arts and crafts

Ikenami Workshop 池浪刃物製作所; 9881 Ikeda, Nishinoomote; 0997 22 0513; w park10.wakwak.com/~ikenamihamono; 09.00–17.00 Mon–Sat. Scissors made using traditional Tanegashima techniques.

Yokinoyaki Pottery 能野焼; 710 Sumiyoshi, Nishinoomote; 0997 23 1410; w yokinoyaki.jp; 08.30–18.00 daily. Hand-making pottery experience & shop.

Souvenirs

Aoyasu Souvenir Centre 青安商店みやげ品センター; 49-1 Nishimachi, Nishinoomote; 0997 22 0224; 07.00–17.00 daily. Souvenirs at Nishinoomote Port.

Space Museum 宇宙科学技術館; 9999-7 Kukinaga, Minamitane; 0997 26 9244; w fanfun.jaxa.jp; 09.30–16.30 Tue–Sun. Gift shop selling everything space & rocket related, such as space food & water.

Takasaki Brewery 髙﨑酒造; 6993-1 Nishimachi, Nishinoomote; 0997 22 0707; w takasakishuzo.online; 09.00–18.00 Mon–Sat. Shōchū & sake shop attached to brewery.

SPORTS AND ACTIVITIES

Blue Peace 3365-2 Kukinaga, Minamitane; 0997 26 7155; w bluepeace.tanegashima-info.com. Sea kayak courses.

GT Life Fishing Guide Service 種子島GTフィッシングガイド; 3355 Kukinaga, Minamitane; 0805 261 5462; w life-fishing.com. Fishing tours.

Jah-la-sora 12 Nakanokami, Minamitane; 0908 660 5868; w jahlasora.com. Canoe & kayak tours.

Lulu Sun ルルサン; 741 Hirayama, Minamitane; 0997 27 3110; w lulu-sun.com. Adventure kayaks.

Ocean Guides オーシャンガイズ; 11477-1 Nishinoomote; 0997 22 0880; w oceanguides.main.jp. Kayak, canoe, SUP.

Sea-Mail シーメール種子島; 7253-15 Nishinoomote; 0997 24 3960; w sea-mail.sakura.ne.jp. Diving school.

OTHER PRACTICALITIES

Banks and post offices

JA Minamitane JA種子南種子支所; 2450 Nakanokami; 0997 26 1211; 08.30–17.00 Mon–Fri

JA Nakatane JA種子中種子支所; 5281 Noma; 0997 27 1211; ATM: 08.30–20.00 Mon–Fri, 09.00–19.00 Sat–Sun

JA Nishinoomote JA種子西之表支所; 694 Nishimachi; 0997 22 1212; ATM: 8.30–20.00 Mon–Fri, 09.00–19.00 Sat–Sun

Minamitane Post Office 南種子郵便局; 2753-39 Nakanokami; 0997 26 0042; 09.00–17.00 Mon–Fri, ATM: 08.45–18.00 Mon–Fri, 09.00–17.00 Sat, 09.00–12.30 Sun

Tanegashima Post Office 種子島郵便局; 61-1 Nishimachi, Nishinoomote; 0570 94 3490; 09.00–18.00 Mon–Fri, 09.00–17.00 Sat, 09.00–12.30 Sun, ATM: 08.45–19.00 Mon–Fri, 09.00–17.00 Sat–Sun

Medical

Tanegashima Medical Centre 種子島医療センター; 7463 Nishinoomote; 0997 22 0960; w tanegashima-mc.jp; 09.00–12.30 & 14.00–17.00 Mon–Sat

Tanegashima Public Hospital 公立種子島病院; 1700-22 Nakanokami, Minamitane; 0997 26 1230; w tanegashima-hospital.com; 09.00–12.00 & 14.00–17.00 Mon–Sat

Police

Minamitane Police Box 種子島警察署南種子交番; 2790 Nakanokami; 0997 26 0282

Nakatane Police Box 種子島警察署中種子交番; 5122-30 Noma; 0997 27 0110

Tanegashima Police Station 種子島警察署; 16381-9 Nishinoomote; 0997 22 0110

WHAT TO SEE AND DO Almost all sights on Tanegashima are at the whims of a rocket launch: most places close during launch days.

Nishinoomote Nishinoomote (西之表) starts with a bang as the home of the **Teppōkan Gun Museum** (鉄砲館; 7585 Nishinoomote; 0997 23 3215; 08.30–17.00 daily, closed on the 25th of the month Sep–Jun; adult/child ¥400/140–280). Dedicated to historic guns from around the world, the exhibits contain some of the first guns made on Tanegashima, as well as displays on local culture and folklore. The building itself is also interesting: its design was inspired by the ship that brought the guns to Tanegashima.

You can buy a combination Gun Museum ticket (¥550) that includes entrance to **Gessōtei Samurai Residence** (月窓亭; 7528 Nishinoomote; 0997 22 2101; w gessoutei.blogspot.com; 09.00–16.30 daily, closed on the 25th of the month Sep–Jun; adult/child ¥200/100–150). This lovely 220-year-old building is a well-preserved samurai house – home to one of the most remote samurai in Japan – with small displays, an English-language video and beautiful garden. The entry fee covers tea and cake on arrival and the staff can teach you some basic *kyūdō* (Japanese archery).

By the museum is the **Seirin Shrine and Tanegashima Tomb** (栖林神社・種子島家墓地; 7597 Nishinoomote), dedicated to Hisamoto Tanegashima, the 19th lord. Each year it hosts the Ōmato Hajimeshiki festival (page 83). Behind the shrine is the Tanegashima clan cemetery, where the island leaders were buried. The larger building next door is the **Hongen Temple** (本源寺;

7602 Nishinoomote), a grand hall built in 1468. In the south of the city is another handsome temple, **Nittenji** (日典寺; 15189 Nishinoomote), and the rather more dilapidated, but arguably more charming, **Onoyama Shrine** (王之山神社; 16174 Nishinoomote).

To the port's north is the **Yasaka Shrine** (八坂神社) and the **Jienji Ruins** (慈遠寺跡; both 6973 Nishinoomote). Jienji, built in 809, was once a focal temple for the Satsunan Islands. When the Portuguese ship drifted ashore in 1543, crew members lived in the temple inn for half a year and it became an important cultural exchange point. The temple was demolished in 1868, and a monument was built in place on the now Yasaka Shrine site, the marble for which was donated by Portugal.

At the very back of the city is **Yuukigaoka** (夕暉が丘; 10059 Nishinoomote), a sunset viewpoint overlooking Nishinoomote and Mageshima on the horizon, with a memorial and a tower of peace.

The north On the road north, if you're not templed out, pop into the elegant **Ise Shrine** (伊勢神社; 935 Nishinoomote) and the **Sunset Hill Observatory** (夕陽が丘展望広場), before hitting **Itajikibana** (板敷鼻; 3886 Kunigami), an unusual, flat rock formation. On a clear day, you can see the Ōsumi Peninsula, Kaimondake, Iōjima, Takeshima and Yakushima. It's also a fishing spot for big catches such as parrotfish and black sea bream. The sea is often clear enough to see the coral and it's a good sunset spot.

Heading to the northernmost cape, pass by Kunigami's beautiful moss-covered **Nakame Shrine** (中目神社), then continue on to **Urada Kaisuiyokujo Beach** (浦田海水浴場; 123-1 Kunigami). This long stretch of white sand is perfect for a proper beach day. The protective cove makes it a good option for families as well as snorkellers, anglers, kayakers and divers, and the water quality has earned it a place on Japan's list of the top 88 beaches. There's also a pastel pink swing seat popular with posers. The **Urada Shrine** (浦田神社; 345 Kunigami), just north of here, is a pretty place dedicated to white rice; legend says the enshrined god of Urada sprinkled rice seeds from the shrine's stones, bringing white rice to Tanegashima. It's coupled with the southern Hōman Shrine (page 92). Further inland is the **Oku Shrine** (奥神社), which has a gigantic ficus with incredible roots.

At the northernmost tip stands a lighthouse marking the end of the Nansei-shotō. A rather cool fact about **Kishigasaki** (喜志鹿崎) is that the East China and Kuroshio currents collide with each other here: the force is so powerful that it often creates unusual triangular waves. Travelling down the east coast brings you to the Minato River. Its mouth has two shrines worth visiting: the mysterious coastal **Minato Ebisu** (湊のエビス) and the picturesque **Minato Shrine** (湊神社). The river itself has a small mangrove area (メヒルギ自生地) too.

To the south is a stunning sight: **Hego Forest** (ヘゴ自生群落). Hego are subtropical tree ferns and this uniquely large, naturally grown group stretches about 1km across into the north's depths. With some of the ferns reaching up to 4m in height, there's a truly prehistoric forest feel. The road past this forest makes a stunning drive or cycle route. Further south is **Kiorizaka** (木折坂), an observatory overlooking the coast, and the delightfully un-manicured **Iseki Shrine** (伊関神社; 1085 Iseki), at the top of a huge flight of forest steps. Heading to the coast, you'll find **Okigahamada Beach** (沖ヶ浜田海岸), a peaceful spot hemmed in by unsightly concrete piers.

One of the highest points on the island, at 238m, is **Mount Amamegakura** and its park (天女ケ倉・天女ヶ倉公園). From the top, you can get a great view of the coastline and nearby sugarcane farmland. There is also a viewing platform that is perfect for stargazing – you can see the Milky Way on clear nights and shooting stars during meteor showers. The park itself is nothing special but the view over the Pacific is brilliant. There is also a nearby shrine, certified as one of Japan's 'sacred places of yoga' in 2020.

Awkwardly slap bang in the centre of the north is **Sattōrando** (さっとーらんど; 2111 Nishinoomote), an observation point and worthwhile stop in summer when the surrounding hydrangeas are in cool, colourful bloom.

Central east The **Kazamoto Shrine** (風本神社; 5962 Genma) has a beautiful approach, flanked by aerial roots and jungle. The shrine itself features a large wooden room with beautiful ceilings that has a real Japanese aesthetic; the Tanegashima family prayed here for safe voyages. Kazemoto is dedicated to many gods, including those of the wind, marriage, learning and girls. It's said a woman will have a girl if she offers a girl's kimono to the shrine.

The huge beach of **Kanehama Coast** (鉄浜海岸) is nationally known for its surf and black iron sand, which was harvested here years ago. Named after this iron ore, the beach is framed by dramatic rocks. Just south of Kanehama is the incredible **Akō Arch** (アコウのアーチ), a natural archway over the road, formed by a fallen Japanese sea fig tree. The tree fell due to a typhoon but rooted in horizontal place.

Driving down the east coast, over the towering **Cashmere Bridge** (カシミヤ橋), eventually brings you to **Matate-no-iwa Cave** (馬立の岩屋). According to legend, the tenth lord of Tanegashima suddenly disappeared, leaving his horse standing at this cave's entrance – *matate* means 'standing horse'. The cave was said to be connected to Hōman Pond in Minamitane (page 92). You can't enter the cave anymore due to falling rocks and cave-ins. It stands at the north end of the **Injō Coast** (犬城海岸), which is known for its strange but beautiful landscape of boulders, caves and rocks formed by wave erosion.

Inland is the **Obuchi and Mebuchi Falls** (男淵女淵の滝). This pretty, brightly coloured waterfall is split in two – the Obuchi upper falls and the Mebuchi lower falls. It's unusual to have waterfalls on Tanegashima as it has little to no highlands,

LOCAL RECIPE: RINKAKE

Rinkake is a hugely popular sweet peanut snack on Tanegashima. There's a factory on the island that makes them – they're great souvenirs – but you can make your own easily at home.

500g peanuts, skin removed
250g brown sugar
100ml water
1 inch ginger, grated (optional)

1. If the peanuts have skins on, fry them in a pan to remove the skin.
2. Boil the brown sugar and water together. When it starts to boil, add the grated ginger if using and simmer for a minute.
3. Mix the peanuts into the sugar quickly.
4. Carefully spread the peanuts over a baking tray with greaseproof paper over and allow to cool.

and this one flows even through dry season. The walk to the falls can be confusing, so make sure to keep an eye out for foliage-covered signs and have a map to hand.

Back on the west coast road, check out the **Injō Observatory** (犬城展望所) for views across the landscape, coast and farmlands. Further south, off the winding road before coming into Masuda town, is the **Tobata Chimney** (戸畑の煙突). This tall chimney stack rises in the middle of sugarcane farmland and is a remnant of the Pacific War, when the Japanese navy built a base on Tanegashima. Construction began in 1942, but it was never used as much of it was destroyed in air raids. The chimney is believed to have belonged to the baths.

Nearby is the **Masuda Space Communication Station** (増田宇宙通信所; 1887-1 Masuda; ☎ 0997 27 1990; w track.sfo.jaxa.jp/facilities/masuda.html; ⌚ 10.00–17.00 daily), a facility monitoring the satellites and rocket flights. You can tour the station for free, though signs and information in English is limited. Masuda is also home to the ethereal wooden **Imahime Shrine** (今姫神社).

From here you can head to Nakatane town, or continue on the very quiet west road. This gives over to the pretty curve of the long **Nakayama Coast** (中山海岸) – a very popular surfing spot. Eventually it reaches the **Kumano Shrine** (熊野神社; 6029 Sakai). Just north of the beach, this shrine lies at the top of a steep flight of steps. It's visited by many locals praying to the married deities enshrined there for good marriage and easy childbirth.

In Nakatane itself, you can visit the **Nakatane Town Historical and Folklore Museum** (5173-2 Noma; ☎ 0997 27 2233; w tanekan.jp/nakaminzoku; ⌚ 09.00–17.00 Tue–Sun; adult/child ¥160/50–80), which houses various Nakatane cultural properties, and the **Kumano Onsen** (熊野温泉; 5542 Sakai; ☎ 0997 27 9211; ⌚ 11.00–21.00 Fri–Wed, to 20.00 Oct–Mar; adult/child ¥300–400/200). This onsen overlooks the gorgeous Kumano Coast and has saunas, jacuzzis, and free Wi-Fi.

South of town, see the **Furuichi House** (古市家住宅; 3353 Sakai; ☎ 0997 27 1111) and **Sakai Shrine Big Cycad** (坂井神社の大ソテツ). Built in 1846 by the samurai and village head Gensuke Furuichi, Furuichiya is Tanega's oldest surviving building – an example of true Tanegashima architecture. It has a tatami room, stunning tea room with sunken hearth (*ro*) and lovely grounds. It was carefully renovated in 2001–02, when the whole house was dismantled and restored. The surrounding area is home to Japan's largest cycad palm tree, a 600-year-old giant that stands next to the Sakai Shrine, up the stairs to the left. At 7m high and 10m across, the tree's alien-like limbs have wandered so far that they need support from struts and scaffold.

The south The southwest opens with the **Tanegashima Mangrove Park** (種子島マングローブパーク; 419 Hirayama; ☎ 0997 26 1111), an area overlaid with vibrant green mangrove trees and boardwalks that seem to float over the foliage. Visitors can kayak down the Oura River through the mangroves, which are the northernmost in Japan.

South of the Oura's estuary is **Hamada Beach** (浜田海水浴場), a long bank of bright sands with a beautifully half-buried stone torii and a gorgeous tangerine-coloured coastline that includes **Chikura Grotto** (千座の岩屋) and **Arch Rock** (アーチ岩). Chikura is a family-friendly web of caverns that can be explored 2 hours before and after low tide. The main cave area is huge: it's said to fit 1,000 people at a time and stretches for around 100m. The striated Arch Rock, with its jade-coloured waters below, is the area's best photo spot. Kayaking tours go to the reefs some 500m offshore here, where you can snorkel.

Further south is the **Hirota Site and Museum** (広田遺跡ミュージアム; 2571 Hirayama; ☎ 0997 24 4811; ⌚ 09.00–17.00 Tue–Sun; ¥300), a must for archaeology lovers. Tanegashima is the only Japanese island to show archaeological evidence of head-binding, as practised by the Hirota people (page 9). The museum explains the history behind the nearby coastal Hirota Site, a mass grave from the Yayoi/Kofun periods. Some 113 bones were found dressed and decorated with shell accessories and products, a unique custom to Tanegashima. The shells used are native not to Kyūshū but seas to the south, suggesting they were brought through trade with other countries, like the Philippines. One of the most important objects excavated is a shell engraved with the kanji for mountain – it's believed to be the oldest written character in Japan.

Below this lies the ultimate Tanegashima site: the space station. The rocket launch pad area is first, followed by the best launch viewpoint, Rocket Hill Observatory (ロケットの丘展望所). Passing the beautiful **Ōsaki Coast** (大崎海岸) with its fine sand and **Tōdai-shita surf point** (灯台下さーふぽいんと), you come to the **Space Centre and Museum** (JAXA 種子島宇宙センター 宇宙科学技術館; 9999-7 Kukinaga; 0997 26 9244; w fanfun.jaxa.jp/visit/tanegashima; 09.30–16.30 Tue–Sun). Not only is it Japan's biggest space station, but, perched on the tropical coast, it's the most beautiful too. If you're lucky, you may see a takeoff, but even if you don't it's a remarkable sight: sitting on a southerly bay surrounded by turquoise waters, white sand and red cliffs.

The free museum runs three 75-minute bus tours (also free) of the facility daily, which include off-limits areas, including the launch sites. These tours are usually in Japanese, but the museum will happily organise an English guide for free if you book in advance. In the museum itself are games, interactive exhibits and a cafeteria, making it perfect for families.

The area is closed on rocket launch days, so if that's the case then head to one of the many observatories to watch: **Spacegaoka Park** (宇宙ヶ丘公園), **Hasetenbō Park** (長谷展望公園), **Ebinoue** (恵美之江展望公園), **Kamori Peak Deck** (カーモリの峯展望台) or **Nanairozaka Observatory** (七色坂展望公). The last two are particularly pretty, regardless of any launches. At Kamori, you can enjoy cape views with the addition of Drinking Elephant Rock (象の水飲み岩) – a geologic delight but a rather questionable elephant – and the somewhat unfortunate baby pink Iwasaki Hotel in the back. The observatory also overlooks **Takezaki Beach** (竹崎海岸), a brilliant surfing spot. Nanairozaka is furthest from the launches, but offers a pretty palette of rice fields and coastline – the name *nanairo* means 'seven colours'.

Kukinaga village (茎永) is home to Tanegashima red rice. This local crop is celebrated at the **Tanegashima Red Rice Museum** (たねがしま赤米館; 4058-1 Kukinaga; 0997 26 7444; 09.00–17.00 Thu–Tue), an obscure museum and shop which also has videos showcasing the performing arts and events of Minamitane Town. Just next door is the **Hōmanjinja** (宝満神社), a picturesque, popular shrine that deifies Tamayori-hime (see opposite). It's paired with Urada Shrine in the north: according to legend, when Urada's white rice runs out, you can bring the red rice from Hōman and it will turn white, and vice versa. In April, the shrine hosts a rice planting ritual, with songs, drums and prayers for harvest. The legendary **Hōman Pond** (宝満の池) nearby attracts waterfowl and has pretty viewpoints.

Cape Kadokura (門倉岬) is the southernmost tip of the island and is where the Portuguese vessel carrying firearms crashed, so you'll see statues and memorials commemorating this. The cape is also home to **Maenohama Seaside Park** (前之浜海浜公園), an 8km white sand beach that's a spawning ground for sea turtles: it's peaceful, pure and perfect. Also at Kadokura is the **Misaki Shrine** (御崎神社),

MYTHS AND FOLKTALES: MINAMITANE'S RED RICE

Long ago, a beautiful princess named Tamayori-hime arrived in Kukinaga, carrying rice on her horse's back. The villagers had to hunt daily for their food, so she offered them her rice to cultivate. Saved from hunger, they made rice paddies out of the wastelands. But one year the sun was relentless, and the water in the fields dried up. Desperate, the villagers tried to draw water from the pond in the mountains where the gods lived. Tamayori-hime told them not to, but the villagers dug ditches to drain the pond anyway.

No sooner had they done so than there were huge cracks of thunder and the water flowing from the pond was dyed the colour of blood – the gods' wrath had been awoken. Tamayori-hime, afraid for the village's suffering, went to the pond alone as a sacrifice. The sound of thunder subsided, heavy rain began to fall, and the rice fields were replenished. Ever since that day, the rice harvested in Kukinaga has been red. The villagers named the pond Hōman-no-Ike and built the Hōman Shrine to worship Tamayori-hime.

which has beautiful hibiscus and a vermilion torii. If you're staying in Minamitane during summer, pop to the **Hikari Field** (ひかりの郷; 330 Nishino) where you can often spot fireflies at night.

In the town itself you'll find the free **Minamitane Town Local Museum** (南種子町郷土館; 2420-2 Nakanokami; ☎ 0997 26 1111; ⌚ 09.00–17.00 Tue–Sun, closed 4th Fri of month) which holds folk tools, crafts and festival paraphernalia. There's also the **Buried Cultural Property Centre** (南種子町埋蔵文化財センター; ⌚ 09.00–17.00 Tue–Fri), which shows archaeological finds. Just outside town is the lovely **Kawachi Onsen Centre** (河内温泉センター; 341 Nakanokami; ☎ 0997 26 2510; ⌚ 10.00–21.00 Wed–Mon; adult/child ¥250–350/150), with extensive facilities including a forest bath generator, swimming pool, ultrasonic bath, infrared sauna and restaurant.

Central west At 12km, **Nagahama Coast** (長浜海岸) is the longest sandy beach on the island, with a mix of black and white sand. It's famous for the sea turtles that land in its white sands to spawn every year from May to August, as well as sunsets and surf. In fact, the entire quiet west coast is one elongated sunset spot that looks towards Yakushima's great bulk.

Sights along its length include the **Otatsu-Metatsu Rocks** (雄龍雌龍の岩) – two boulders tied together and lapped by the sea. The rope between them symbolises marriage: legend has it that a couple who died here after being thrown into the sea by a storm landslide were reincarnated as these rocks. The name means 'male and female dragon rocks' – the male is on the right, the female on the left.

If you drive the coast in summer, look for the sunflowers at **Himawari Field** (ひまわり畑; 7887 Sumiyoshi) south of Sumiyoshi. In **Sumiyoshi** (住吉) itself is the pleasant Sumiyoshi Shrine (住吉神社; 5199 Sumiyoshi) and the Sumiyoshi Banyan Tree (住吉のカジュマル). This huge, tangled banyan grows on the corner of a road and was supposedly transplanted from Okinawa in the first year of the Meiji era, to protect from wind and tides. The rest of the transplanted banyans form a barrier along Sumiyoshi's coastal road. Just before coming full circle to Nishinoomote is windswept **Yokino Beach** (能野海水浴場), a lovely spot flanked with large trees that's popular with surfers and families for swimming, sunbathing and sunsets.

KUCHINOERABUJIMA

What brings people to little-known, little-visited Kuchinoerabujima (口永良部島) is simple: volcanoes. This wild, comet-shaped island just west of Yakushima is a hotspot of volcanic activity thanks to Shindake and Furudake – literally 'new' and 'old' peaks. Shindake is the larger and more active of the two at 657m, with a 200m crater, while Furudake is close behind at 649m.

The island's rugged shores of igneous rock give life to thick forests when the lava fields aren't flowing – which happen less often than you might think. Shindake is one of the most active Japanese volcanoes, with eruptions in 2015 and 2020. The oldest recorded eruption was in 1841, when lives and villages were lost. Although eruptions haven't claimed lives for a long time, the terrain around the peaks is dangerous and not for the inexperienced – in 2009 an American author and volcano enthusiast climbed the volcanoes for research and never returned.

Shindake was mined for sulphur in the Meiji era. A vibrant village called Nanakama – named for the seven pots used in sulphur refinement – grew up around this industry, and at its height reached 40 households. However, a Shindake eruption in 1955 killed eight people, injured 26, and burned 38 houses, resulting in the village's abandonment and eventual destruction in a later 1977 eruption. The ruins are at one of the trailheads for the Furudake climb.

Outside of volcanoes – and the onsen that are warmed by them – Kuchinoerabujima attracts visitors looking to experience local island life through homestays. The ageing demographic gives a real feel of old world Japan and you'll likely be the only tourist on the island. The seas around Kuchinoerabujima are known for their rich marine life and fishing is another big draw here, with lobster and shellfish particularly popular on the island.

In 2012, the island's 35.77km² was designated part of the Kirishima-Yaku National Park. It's home to turtles, freshwater crabs, wild deer, mountain goats and endangered Erabu flying foxes. The latter can be seen taking to the skies after sunset (though they also hang out in forest trees in the day) and have been

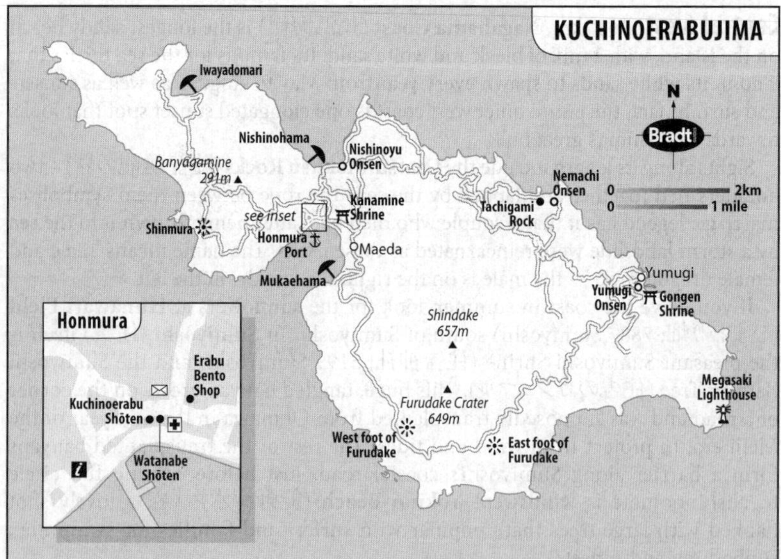

designated a national monument of Kuchinoerabu. The best sight on the island, though, is the seasonal blooming of *maruba-satsuki,* a type of azalea that has found a curious home only on the mountainsides affected by volcanic gases – the strange juxtaposition of baby pink carpeting the rugged, steaming volcanoes is spectacular. There are also large numbers of bootlace orchids (*Erythrorchis altissima*), more than on the other islands, which you can spot living on trees in the forest.

Kuchinoerabu is a long, narrow island, pinched in the west where the main village of Honmura lies. Honmura sits in a bay that provided a natural shelter from the strong currents around the islands, so was often used on trading routes between China, Satsuma and the Ryūkyū Kingdom. The smaller section of land to the northwest is the remains of the old Banyagamine volcano, while the southeast has the newer, active Shindake and Furudake volcanoes. To the north, you can see the Mishima and on clear days you can even see the southern tip of Kyūshū and Mount Kaimon. To the south, you can see the beginning of the Tokara Islands.

The main industry for the 90 locals here is fishing, with a small amount of beef agriculture and tourism. As islanders left for bigger cities, abandoned farmland was planted over with cedars or *daimyō* bamboo, which the islanders compete to harvest during rainy season.

Both Yakushima Town government and islanders are hoping to encourage people to relocate to Kuchinoerabujima and revitalise the island. Part of their efforts include the Kuchinoerabujima Activation Cooperative, where islanders join together to cultivate sweet potatoes for shōchū and medicinal plants. There is also a preservation society for island arts.

GETTING THERE AND AWAY The island can only be reached by boat from Yakushima, so makes an ideal one- or two-day trip from there.

Ferry Taiyou (page 84) skips between Yakushima Miyanoura, Tanegashima Shimama and Kuchinoerabu Honmura daily; on even dates it goes in the morning from Yaku to Kuchinoerabu and back, on odd dates it leaves in the afternoon. Tickets can be bought through to/from Tanegashima too, where the boat continues on to on even days and arrives from on odd ones. There are also private ferries operating between Kuchinoerabujima and Yakushima with Fumimaru (☎ 0904 517 2715).

There is no working airport on the island, though there is a helipad for emergencies.

GETTING AROUND Kuchinoerabujima has a ring road that skirts around the island's volcanoes, making travel easy – as long as you can find transport. There are no buses or taxis and there's about one rental car and a single scooter – if you can get it, take it. You can try renting a car from your accommodation, but otherwise the only official rental is at the ENEOS petrol station (ENEOS 畠豊二口永良部; SS 588 Kuchinoerabu; ☎ 0997 49 2281; ⏰ 09.00–12.00 & 13.00–17.00 Mon–Fri). The bumpy roads and big hills of Kuchinoerabu make cycling unpleasant. You can always bring a rental car, moped or cycle on the ferry over from Yakushima, however, should your rental company allow it.

From Honmura, it's about 1km to Maeda, a tiny town of six households. Yumugi, a tiny but beautiful settlement in the east that grew up around an onsen, is about half an hour by car. Onsen are dotted around the island but the nicest are at Yumugi. Some accommodations may be willing to drop you at the various onsen if your transport is limited.

TOURIST INFORMATION There really isn't much in the way of information here. There's a Kuchinoerabujima Tourism Information Centre (口永良部島 観光案内所; 372 Kuchinoerabu; w kuchinoerabujima.com; ⌚ 09.00–11.00 even dates, 14.00–16.00 odd dates) timed to open with the ferry, which remains closed when the ferry is cancelled. The website is in Japanese but can be online translated.

This island's volcanoes are active: Shindake erupts regularly, with villagers having to be evacuated. Although the eruptions are generally not violent or dangerous, stay alert and listen out. Even when not erupting, the volcanoes can still prove deadly; make sure to check the current warnings and arrange through your accommodation or the tourist centre to take a local guide – people have died on this volcano while walking without one. There are a few concrete volcano shelters around that face away from the caldera: these can be used for protection in extreme circumstances.

WHERE TO STAY There are a few minshuku in Honmura, plus one in Yumugi. All the minshuku cost a similar amount and have half board included.

Minshuku Banya (4 rooms) 民宿番屋; 1469-8 Kuchinoerabu, Maeda; 0997 49 2202; w kukiyamaunsou.co.jp/bannya. Hotel up from the harbour; its wooden interior has 4 rooms over 2 floors, with a toilet on each & a shared bathroom & café. Each room has a TV, AC, fridge-freezer, kettle & laundry. Locally sourced food is available at the restaurant. **$$$$**

Minshuku Kanagatake (6 rooms) 民宿金岳; 1465-3 Kuchinoerabu, Maeda; 0997 49 2605; w stay-kanagatake.jimdofree.com. Mix of Japanese/Western style rooms, with Western toilets, baths & TV. 2 meals a day made from local sea & mountain ingredients. It's about 20mins on foot & about 5mins by car from Honmura Port: ask for a pick-up service at reservation. Option for bed only. **$$–$$$$**

WHERE TO EAT AND DRINK There are no restaurants on the island so your accommodation is your best bet for food. The minshukus use fresh island ingredients that include catches of the day – locally caught lobster if you're lucky.

If you come for a day trip, there are two small stores in Honmura. Kuchinoerabu Shōten (雑貨品店くちのえらぶ商店; 527 Kuchinoerabu; 0997 49 2211; ⌚ 09.00–noon & 13.00–18.00 Mon–Fri, 13.00–17.00 Sat) is for minor groceries, while Watanabe Shōten (渡辺商店; 527 Kuchinorabu; 0997 49 2244; ⌚ 09.00–noon & 13.00–17.00 Mon–Fri) sells alcohol. For lunches you can usually pick up bentōs from accommodations, or try Erabu Bentō Shop (エラブの弁当屋; 0806 568 0395; ⌚ 09.00–noon & 13.00–17.00 daily) for the same.

Kuchinoerabu is known for its Japanese lobster, daimyō bamboo, *horoku* strawberries, *shima* bananas, sea bilberries, Indo-Pacific sergeant fish and great turban shells.

SPORTS AND ACTIVITIES The island has a few marine tours, including diving and fishing tours: the most comprehensive is Diving Service SeaKISS (513 Kuchinoerabu; 0997 49 2170), which operates diving, snorkelling, cruising and fishing tours from its guesthouse. A popular dive spot is at the Sensuigahana Cape, near the Nemachi Hot Spring, where there's a rock shaped like an eagle (supposedly); if you dive into the sea here you will notice bubbles welling up from the hot spring 10m below.

OTHER PRACTICALITIES Kuchinoerabu has no police or fire service, but it does have a clinic: Kuchinoerabu Island Clinic (口永良部島へき地出張診療所; 533-1 Kuchinoerabu; 0997 49 2119; ⌚ 08.30–noon & 13.00–17.00 Mon–Fri). There is a post office too (口永良部簡易郵便局;516 Kuchinoerabu; ☎0997 49 2007; ⏰ 09.00–17.00 Mon–Fri), but there is no ATM – you would have to use the savings window, which cannot be relied upon, so make sure to bring enough cash.

WHAT TO SEE AND DO Kuchinoerabu is more about nature and onsen than traditional sights. Though look out for the designated 'Eight Views of Kuchinoerabujima' on your way round: Shinmura, Iwayadomari, Nagasako, Furudake Crater, Banyagamine, Furudake Western and Furudake Eastern feet, and Tachigami Rock.

The onsen in Honmura (本村) is closed as of 2023, but it's worth walking to the somewhat hidden **Kanamine Shrine** (金峯神社; 1224 Kuchinoerabu) nearby. It features picturesque stone torii gates overlooking the blue waters of the bay and is a beautiful spot in the sunshine for taking a break or having a picnic. The beach on the eastern side of the port is **Mukaehama** (向江浜), used in May–September as a nesting site for green turtles. It's possible to see turtles spawning, or see baby turtle footprints – if you do spot the latter, don't damage them as they are used for research purposes by the local turtle protection group. During the summer, you might be able to spot a few turtles that live just offshore from the Miura fishing port – one is a bit of a celebrity with the locals as it is missing a front flipper.

On the road north of Honmura is an offshoot trail that goes towards **Nishinohama** (西之浜), a beach with shallow areas to laze in and snorkelling. This same road north of Honmura brings you to **Nishinoyu Onsen** (西之湯温泉; 825-2 Kuchinoerabu; ☎0997 43 5900; ¥200). It looks like a coastal fisherman's shack, but don't be fooled: inside, hot springs bubble up during high tide. Iron and salts turn the water brown; it's around 22.5°C, though locals adjust the temperature after 17.00. This onsen isn't segregated by gender, but priority for the indoor bath is given to women and the outdoor to men. If you want to enter a bath that isn't your gender's prioritised area, check with people before doing so.

The road west of Honmura takes you to two of the eight views, **Shinmura** (口永良部島八景新村), a nice ocean sunset spot if out exploring, and **Banyagamine** (番屋ヶ峰). This comparatively dormant volcano is covered in bamboo and in itself isn't picturesque – mostly taken up by antennae and communications buildings. But the view across Kuchinoerabu towards Shindake is good – you might just need to hike up a little off the road to see it, thanks to the prolific bamboo.

The western road ends on the north coast with another of the eight views, the bay at **Iwayadomari** (口永良部島八景岩屋泊). Once a settlement, this beach is now a great snorkelling spot with reef fish such as puffer and Moorish idols aplenty, and is usually deserted. There are a few caves in this area, which are believed to have once been inhabited, and on clear days, you can spot Iōjima puffing away in the distance.

Heading clockwise from Honmura and the Nishinoyu Onsen, the road covers the north of the island towards the 'standing god' **Tachigami Rock** (立神岩), another of the eight views. This isolated giant erupts from the shoreline, with an archway at its base that strong and daring swimmers go through; it's thought to be one of the oldest rocks on the island. The coast around Tachigami changed colour thanks to the hot spring activity, which also brings fish to the area.

Facing Tachigami Rock is **Nemachi Onsen** (寝待温泉; 1714-28 Kuchinoerabu; ⏰ 24hrs; ¥200 donation) in the northwest. This long-standing onsen has milky-white waters that are warmed by hot water boiling up through the sea – the temperature is a refreshing 21.4°C, having been near 50°C at source. There is only one bathtub, so groups may need to take turns in shifts.

MYTHS AND FOLKTALES: THE GONGEN CHICKEN

A long time ago, two deer hunters came across a fine, white chicken standing in the rain. Instead of running away, the chicken raised and lowered its head at them. As they approached it, their feet grew hot, and when they arrived at the place it stood the chicken disappeared and white water boiled up from the ground.

This hot spring was so soothing that they built a small onsen around it, without telling the other villagers. However, the secret couldn't be kept for long, so they made it into a communal onsen. The chicken gongen (incarnation), believed to be an embodiment of Buddha, was enshrined and worshipped.

The road continues on to **Yumugi Onsen** (湯向温泉; 1739-2 Kuchinoerabu; ⌚ 24hrs; ¥200 donation), another long-established onsen and the most popular on the island. Its mineral-rich water is said to be effective against skin problems and muscular/joint pain. The waters are cooler in winter, around 21.3°C, though are 46°C at the source. Beside the onsen is **Gongen Shrine** (権現神社), dedicated to a temporary manifestation of a Buddha who apparently appeared in the form of a chicken (see above). Though small, Gongen is one of the most exceptionally picturesque shrines on the Ōsumi. It has been beautifully overtaken by a gigantic banyan tree, the roots and boughs slowly creeping across the roof and breaking through the shrine.

The southeast of the island ends in **Megasaki Lighthouse** (メガ崎灯台), a small lighthouse without much of a view considering the longer walk to get to it. After this the island turns to Furudake, and along the main road you'll see signs indicating the viewpoints of its **East** (古岳東麓) and **West** (古岳西麓) feet. They offer vistas of the island: the west towards Honmura and the bay, the east across the vegetation and forest to the tail-end of the island.

You can climb the **Furudake Crater** (古岳火口) in about an hour from the trail entrance on the main road. As an active volcano, Furudake has its dangers including steam vents and toxic gas, though it's generally easier to climb than Shindake. Always keep to the paths and don't go off track. There are two trail entrances: Nanakama (七釜登山道入口), after the original mining village, in the east, and Hatake (畠登山道入口) just south. The latter is about a 3-minute bike ride from the other, and is a shorter walking route. Even the sign at the top has steam rising out from its legs, and there's quite the view from the crater.

Just next to Furudake is **Shindake** (新岳). It's possible to hike the mountain, but it's highly recommended to take a guide – just ask at your accommodation either on the island or on Yakushima. The volcano is incredibly active so always check before attempting to climb as it is often closed off to all hikers.

THE MISHIMA

Before the ferry hits Yakushima, you'll pass a spattering of islands on your right; some distant hazy lumps upon the horizon, over 100km from Kagoshima. These are the Mishima – Iōjima, Takeshima and Kuroshima – little visited by anyone except those who live there.

Two of the three sit on the rim of the Kikai Caldera, a mammoth underwater volcanic crater that changed the planet when it exploded 8,000 years ago. It was the last explosion of such a size in earth's history, and the crater it left behind could fit Mount Fuji inside. (The caldera is still active: in 1934–35, it created a small island

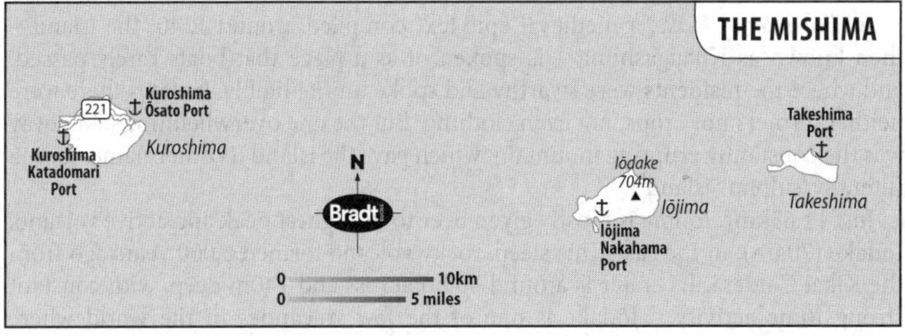

called Shōwa-Iōjima, off Iōjima's coast.) The islands were kept relatively separate until 1412, when the leader of the Shimazu clan gave them to the Tanegashima family head. This began their grouping together as the Mishima, which has continued on, out of the limelight, ever since.

Comprising three small islands with barely any shops, restaurants or accommodation, they'll never be a tourist destination – and the locals seem more than content with that. Visiting the Mishima without any Japanese language skills isn't easy, but they're worth a stop if you're looking for something remote, local and occasionally unusual. Just bear in mind that accommodation is limited, especially in low seasons, and you absolutely must reserve in advance – don't just turn up. Most minshuku are a similar price, which includes two meals unless stated otherwise, as there are few or no restaurants. Hardly any minshuku offer port pick-up as everything is walkable. Usually there are free camping options, but you should check with the Mishima Information Centre (page 101) in advance of your stay. This will likely require a Japanese speaker.

GETTING THERE AND AWAY Even getting there takes some effort. The Mishima ferry schedule (w mishimamura.com/ferry) requires a doctorate to decode and it changes every month, just when you think you've got the hang of it. You'll need to check the website for up-to-date timings and days. There are four ferries a week, some of which are day loops, others two-day loops.

All ferries leave Kagoshima in the morning and stop at Takeshima first (3hrs), then Iōjima (40mins), Kuroshima Ōsato (1hr 10mins), and finally Kuroshima Katadomari (30mins), with a 15-minute wait at each. The day ferry then returns straight to Kagoshima (4hrs), while the two-day loop ferry stops overnight at Kuroshima Katadomari. The next morning, this does the journey in reverse, stopping at each island before arriving back into Kagoshima in the afternoon.

This means no Mishima island can be done as a day trip: you'll have to allow at least one overnight here. If your return ferry to Kagoshima lands on a two-day loop, you're in for a longer journey back. You can buy a ticket that covers each island from the Mishima departure area at Kagoshima's New Port some 1½ hours before departure.

There is a possibility to charter a Cessna plane (w mishimamura.com/gaiyoukankou/access), which takes about 50 minutes from Kagoshima to Iōjima and runs twice a week. If you're so inclined, it will cost around ¥20,000 per person and there's only space for about three passengers.

IŌJIMA Not to be mistaken for the infamous Iōjima of World War II (anglicised as Iwo Jima), Iōjima (硫黄島) is an island backwater with some surprises up its kaleidoscopic sleeves.

In *The Tales of Heike*, a medieval epic text compiled around 1240, the island – then known as Kikaigashima – is spoken of as a place that boats rarely passed, and where the residents were swarthy and spoke unintelligibly. It states there were neither farmers nor crops, not even clothing. But the one overwhelming take-away was the constantly erupting mountain, which gave the island its other name: Iōjima (literally 'sulphur island').

Just 11.65km^2, Iōjima is mostly given over to its highest peak and active volcano, Iōdake (704m), in the east. This steep, rocky volcano formed 6,000 years ago from the Kikai Caldera. Its crater is around 400m across and 140m deep, with constant strong fume activity – Iōdake is one of the few volcanoes in the world where volcanologists can collect gases at very high temperatures of 800–900°C.

In fact, Iōdake has been regularly belching out sulphur dioxide and ash since 1998, including recent discharges in November 2019 and April and October 2020. This sulphur dioxide eats away at metals and can damage the respiratory system

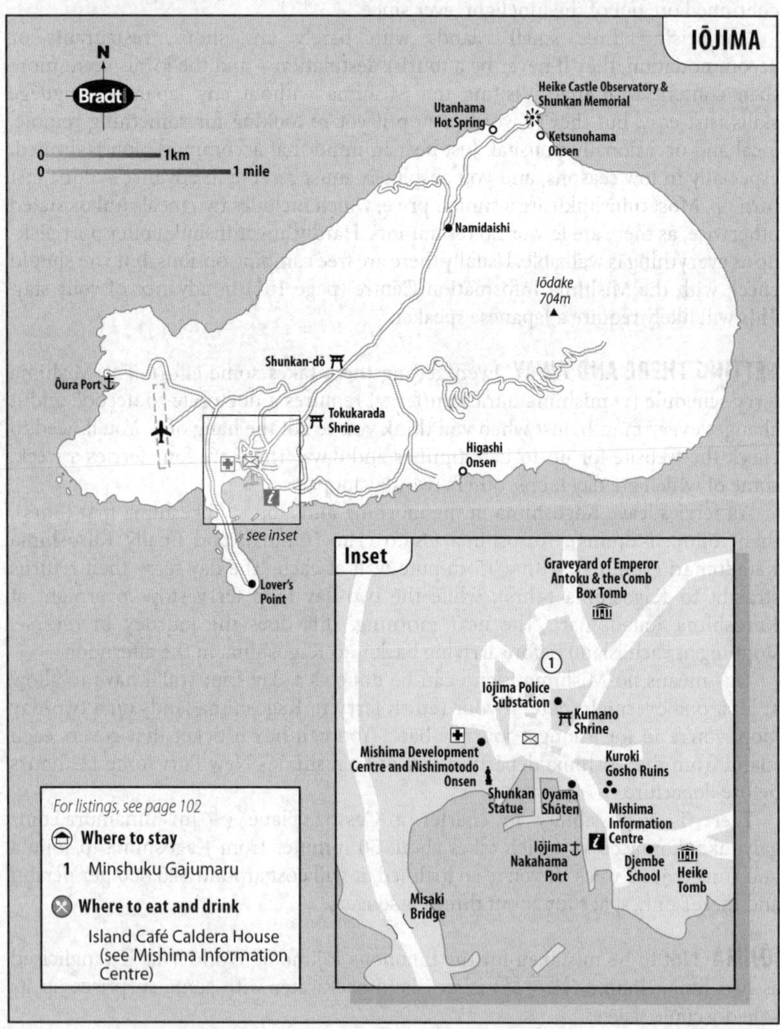

THE MENDON FESTIVAL

Iōjima is known for its masked Mendon deity, which appears in the ancient Hassaku Taiko dance that takes place around August. This festival both comforts the spirits of the dead and drives out evil. The dance involves a singer and ten others, who carry flags, dance and beat drums. At the end of the dance, young men disguised as the god Mendon (メンドン), with large masks made by island teenagers, appear and exterminate evil spirits by hitting festival-goers with a branch. After the dancing is done, the Mendon run around and enter local houses to scare children and generally be a nuisance – crying kids with amused parents is a common scene.

and trigger asthma even at low concentrations. Luckily, the high-altitude volcano's gases are blown in the opposite direction to the village. And while Iōdake regularly vents ash and smoke, it hasn't spilled lava for 1,200 years.

Sulphur dioxide is no friend to agriculture either, making growing crops difficult. Despite this, the mineral-rich volcanic soil has created a verdant landscape, lush with forests of camellias, azaleas, bamboo, leopard plants and plum blossoms. The most remarkable effect of this mineral mix isn't on the land but in the water: the port, as you'll notice on arrival, is a deep terracotta red thanks to iron and oxygen deposits. Further out, the sulphur gives the sea around Iōjima a yellow hue. This red-blue-yellow mix makes for unbelievable diving, with rainbows swirling in the sunlit waters – you might even spot the odd turtle, known to use the island for egg-laying.

These minerals also make for fantastic natural onsen, which litter the island's coastline and are some of the best in the country. Higashi Onsen in particular regularly makes bucket lists across the world, with few realising just where it is.

Perhaps an even more astonishing find on Iōjima is its white and blue peacocks. Once belonging to a hotel resort, they became a wild flock that reproduced and now roam the island. You can often spot them on the school lawns and hear their cries through the forests.

History Previously called Kikaigashima, Iōjima is supposedly where the high priest Shunkan, a Buddhist monk, was exiled in 1177 after plotting against the Heike clan. After two years of despair, Shunkan committed suicide by refusing to eat. The site of his exile and grave are hotly debated but Iōjima has leaned into the legend heavily, with a worship hall, statue and memorial.

During the Meiji period, the local economy was based around sulphur then silica mining. A road to the summit crater was constructed for sulphur mining, but this has since been deemed unsafe. The final mine closed in 1997, dropping the population dramatically. Now the islanders number just over 100, with the economy reliant on fishing, beef, bamboo shoots and camellia products. There was once an airport, opened in 1973 with a tiny 600m runway, but it now only runs chartered flights.

Getting around This is where it gets rural: there is no bus service, car, or moped rental on Iōjima. This isn't as disastrous as it might sound – even the furthest places from the port are around an hour's walk away – but it's time-consuming and hot. Rental bicycles (including electric) are occasionally available at the Mishima Information Centre (三島村観光案内所; 87 Iōjima; 0991 32 2370; w mishimamura.com; 09.00–noon & 13.00–17.00 Tue–Wed & Fri–Sat, 09.00–10.00 Sun), at the port and main village, but ask in advance.

If you can't face that much walking or cycling, check to see if your accommodation owner has a car and is willing to either play chauffeur or rent it to you. The islanders generally expect this, but availability isn't guaranteed.

Rather delightfully, there are no ferry staff on Iōjima – the villagers are happy to help the ferry dock for free.

Where to stay *Map, page 100*

Minshuku Gajumaru (5 rooms) 民宿ガジュマル; 88 Iōjima; 0991 32 2105. The largest minshuku on Iōjima, commonly used for return visitors & workers. Shared bathrooms, common room & a chatty landlady who catches all the fish herself. **$$$$**

Where to eat and drink *Map, page 100*

Iōjima is so rural that islanders have to order their food online and have it delivered by boat – their rubbish collection and gasoline deliveries happen the same way. In short, you're not going to be picking up a bite here and a meal there: what you see is what you get, and even that is lucky. Nearly all accommodation except camping provide food in their rates. If not, you can bring food with you as long as you don't need refrigeration. There's a single café, Island Café Caldera House (島café カルデラハウス; 11 Iōjima; 0991 32 2370), a communal kitchen space with tourist information. There's also a single shop, Oyama Shōten (大山商店; Iōjima; 0991 32 2107), by the port. It's relatively pricey, unreliable at best and stocks only basics. It also sells out fast.

Other practicalities Due to volcanic activity on Iōdake, it's important to keep abreast of the latest warnings (page 46).

For other essentials, there's the Iōjima Police Substation (警察署硫黄島駐在所; 80 Iōjima; 0991 32 2111), a remote clinic (硫黄島へき地診療所; 90 Iōjima; 0991 32 2110) and the Iōjima Post Office (硫黄島郵便局; 89-14 Iōjima; 0991 32 2200; 09.00–16.00 Mon–Fri), but there is no ATM. Bring enough cash with you.

What to see and do A port doesn't seem like your typical sightseeing spot, but with its unearthly orange waters, **Nakahama Port** (長浜湾) is one of Iōjima's top sights. Though it's said to be dyed seven colours by the constantly emitted minerals and gases from the volcano, the waters usually range from a deep rust red to vibrant orange.

The **Mishima Development Centre** (三島開発総合センター; 90-61 Iōjima; 0991 32 2257; 14.00–19.30 Tue, Thu & Sat) is the large pink building just northwest of the port. It has islander facilities like a library and remote clinic, but more importantly a communal onsen, where you can join locals.

The **Shunkan Statue** (俊寛の像) at the port, over the small red bridge in front of the Development Centre, is the first of two statues to Shunkan. It commemorates the moment the two conspirators exiled with Shunkan were pardoned and sailed back to the mainland. Shunkan tried to follow the ship, wading into the water and begging to be taken back too.

On the jutting southern branch of the bay, **Lover's Point and Misaki Bridge** (恋人岬・岬橋) are said to bring couples good luck. There are two bells to ring three times: the **Bell of Hope** (希望の鐘) is in the middle of the peninsula near the bridge, the **Bell of Happiness** (しあわせの鐘) is at the very end of the path. More prosaically, the point affords one of the best views of the island's looming peaks and is great for sunsets. On a clear day you can see all the way to Yakushima, Kuchinoerabujima and a faint shadow of Tanegashima.

The **Kuroki Gosho Ruins** (黒木御所; 25 Iōjima) site near the harbour is said to be where Emperor Antoku lived. Antoku was the 81st emperor of Japan, who

MYTHS AND FOLKTALES: TŌDAIKI, THE LIGHTHOUSE DEMON

The old legend behind the Tokukarada Shrine tells of a cursed father and his son. Minister Kurano was sent as an envoy to the Tang Emperor in China, but never returned. His son Hitsuno began to worry, and made his way after his father to look for him.

He was welcomed to the emperor's palace with a big feast, but while eating he came across an unusual piece of furniture: a candlestick known as a *tōdaiki*, or 'lighthouse demon', made from a living human being who has been cursed to be unable to speak. The figure was covered in tattoos, stood on a plinth and had a huge candle balanced on his head.

As Hitsuno gazed at the grotesque sight, the candle figure began to weep. It slowly moved, biting off the tip of a finger to write his identity in blood. To his horror, Hitsuno realised the man was in fact his father, cursed by the angry emperor. Hitsuno fled with his cursed father back to Japan, but their ship met a storm on the journey back and his father died at sea. The son buried his father at the Tokukarada Shrine.

rose to the throne at the age of one during a time of extreme clan conflict in the 12th century. In a great sea battle, his grandmother flung herself and six-year-old Antoku into the sea, choosing to die rather than be captured. Legend has it that Antoku actually survived and came to Iōjima, with Taira Sukemori's daughter who became his wife. His descendants are said to be still alive today as the Nagahama family – on whose land the stone walls of the original residence remain.

The lovely **Kumano Shrine** (熊野神社; 80 Iōjima) is in the middle of the village, marked by torii on two sides. It was supposedly built by Shunkan's exiled co-conspirators, who thought the view from the port towards Mount Yahazu looked similar to that of the Kumano Sanzan shrines in Wakayama, where they used to pray. They held a festival to worship the Kumano Sanzan god, hoping to be returned home. It worked – the two of them, minus Shunkan, were welcomed back. Later, this shrine was apparently designated the Imperial Palace of Emperor Antoku, before being used to house sacred treasures. Today it is the location of the Hassaku festival dance.

The north of the village has the **Graveyard of Emperor Antoku and the Comb Box Tomb** (安徳帝墓所/櫛匣局墓). This small graveyard is one of multiple places in Japan that claim to be Antoku's legendary burial place. Nestled in among camellia trees, a wooden signpost points out the moss-covered path to the grave, which is on the road to the right of the school. A little further into the forest is the magical Comb Box Tomb, apparently the tomb of Antoku's wife. Despite his son and vassals being buried next to him, she is buried 10m behind. The strange name comes from her own – Kushibuki – which translates as 'comb box'.

Iōjima is covered in around 46ha of camellia forest. In spring, when the forest is in full bloom, the bushes and their carpet of red-pink petals on the moss-covered floor is a sight to behold. The fruit is used to create oil, soaps, shampoos and conditioners. One of the better places to see the plants is at the camellia garden and road. This begins near the **Tokukarada Shrine** (徳躰神社) – you'll see a handy painted signpost with a camellia flower showing the way.

The Tokukarada Shrine itself is a very small stone shrine up a pathway off Tsubaki Road, about 1km out of the village. It commemorates a strange old legend, as explained on the tourist information sign, about a father sent to China and turned into a candlestick, and the son who comes to retrieve him (see above).

The hall of **Shunkan-dō** (俊寛堂), at the northern tip of the village ring road, where the northernmost road branches off, was built where Shunkan supposedly lived during his exile. It was constructed so that islanders could worship him and his remains, which are said to be buried here (as well as in southern Kikaijima).

From here the road carries on to the northeast coast. On the way, on a right-hand gravel slip road, are the **Namidaishi** (涙石). These 'tear stones' are where the exiled Shunkan stood looking out to sea, hoping for rescue. When none came, he cried bitterly, earning the stones their name. At the end of this road, 4km from port, is the **Heike Castle Observatory and Shunkan Memorial** (平家城展望台・俊寛上演記念碑). The castle, said to have been built by the Heike family after the Battle of Dannoura in 1185, is no longer there, but the views of Iōdake and Iōjima, where the volcano erupts from the roaring blue seas, are outstanding. The lava-moulded mountainside is draped in quilted greenery and the ever-present cloud coming from the caldera sits white against bright skies. You may even see vents coming out the volcano's side.

From here, you can take a walk to **Ketsunohama Onsen** (穴之浜温泉): the entrance to the trail is just in front of the castle observatory car park. It's a 10-minute walk, with the path getting increasingly narrow and overgrown and passing a volcano observation station, but it quickly emerges on the coast – you'll likely smell the sulphur. The creamy blue sea here is about 25°C, but even if you don't take a dip, it's worth wandering just to see the cliffs and colours. There's a similar spot called **Utanhama Onsen** (ウタン浜温泉) to the west of the castle ruins. It's accessed by a small path (overgrown, naturally) off the northern road, 5 minutes' walk from the car park. Keep an eye out for a white stone shaped a bit like a buoy.

The road west out of the village goes past the old airport to **Ōura Port** (大浦港).The port is no longer used, unsurprisingly given its small size, but it has a beautiful bay view with a rocky landscape and deep-tinted seas. On calmer days, islanders come here to fish and even swim, though the latter isn't recommended as the sea is often rough and the rocks incredibly dangerous.

On the right of the village is the **Djembe School** (みしまジャンベスクール; 218 Iōjima; 0991 32 5001; w ttmjp.net). This unexpected school for West African drumming was founded by master drummer Mamady Keita, who brought djembe music to the world stage through a documentary film and was afterwards invited on Japanese TV. Keita wanted to work in small communities like the Guinean one he grew up in and chose Iōjima for the site of an Asia-based school, as his student Tokuda-san – who now runs it – was born there. Thus began a cultural exchange between Mishima and Guinea, with the djembe becoming a sort of local instrument and musical symbol for the people of the islands. The school runs weekly lessons for locals, but there is a 2-hour tourist experience too (book on their website). Just past the school is the small **Heike Tomb** (平家墓), hidden away in a bamboo grove, which commemorates the descendants of Heike and the supposed Emperor Antoku. It was built in the late 1300s to early 1400s. You will see the entrance by the white information board.

The final stop on Iōjima is the most important: **Higashi Onsen** (東温泉). There's a reason it tops lists of the best onsen in Japan. The colours of the water and rocks are gorgeous, and sunset here, looking towards Takeshima, is unbeatable. Taking photos at a hot spring isn't allowed in Japan – with people bathing nude, it's an absolute no-no – but there is often leeway with remote natural onsen as they are frequently deserted. Don't go expecting to take a photo, but take quick advantage if you're the only bather.

TAKESHIMA This quiet island keeps itself to itself, with locals relying on agriculture and fishing. It's not built for tourists, but if you're willing to brave being out of your depth it's a nice place to spend a day exploring, seeing Mishima life and snorkelling.

Takeshima (竹島) is the smallest Mishima, measuring 4.2km^2. Notably flat – the highest point, Magomeyama, is only 220m – it's covered almost entirely with *ryūkyūchiku* (daimyō bamboo). Bamboo forms not only the landscape but the agriculture too: bamboo shoots, eaten raw or cooked, are harvested each May. Much of the island's dark soil pastureland is for black cows, which outnumber inhabitants: Sataura Ranch alone keeps some 100 cows while there are just 70 people. Most of these live collected in the only village, near the port on the northwest side of the island.

Throughout Takeshima are Jōmon archaeological sites that suggest it's been occupied for at least 3,000 years. As with its fellow Mishima, Takeshima was often used as a place of exile, in particular for the Heike clan. In the 1700s, smallpox ripped through the Mishima and Takeshima was hit hard multiple times: in 1726, 25% of residents died, and in 1793, 32% died and others fled the island. This brought about the Makata Odori, a women's dance supposed to ward off smallpox and relieve the island's plight of both dying and fleeing villagers. It happens at the Seidaimyō Shrine on 21 and 22 January. Takeshima also has a Hassaku dance where a masked demon called Takamen hits people with a stick to dispel evil.

Practicalities Quiet doesn't fully cover it: there's no tourism office, no restaurants, no transport, no police, no bank and hardly any Wi-Fi. The only tourist information available is from Iōjima's Mishima Tourism Centre (page 101). There's a single clinic (竹島へき地診療所; 7 Takeshima; ☎ 0991 32 2054), and electric cycle rental through NPO Mishima (NPO法人みしま; ☎ 0503 713 3404; w mishimamura.org/about), which it's best to reserve. Luckily, the furthest walk from the port is under an hour and most sites are in the village. Everything relies on your accommodation, which will feed you three meals a day and may offer vehicle rentals or rides.

There's a single shop with supplies (竹のいえ; 2 Takeshima; ☎ 0991 32 2053; w takenoie.net). Run by a young Japanese man who moved here, it's the first Takeshima shop for over 20 years and acts as a local meeting spot. There's a barbecue area and a chance to sit with a beer and watch locals pass by. It sells some snorkelling gear, gifts and T-shirts and is next to the post office (竹島簡易郵便局; 7 Takeshima; ⏲ 09.00–12.20 & 12.50–17.00 Tue–Wed & Fri, 09.00–17.00 Mon & Thu), which has no ATM.

What to see and do Sights on Takeshima are minimal. For centuries part of the collapsed caldera edge at Komori Port, a volcanic pyroclastic rock known as Takeshima stone, has been used for making monuments on the island. You can see this at **Seidaimyō Shrine** (聖大明神社), a rare 'downhill shrine' that is below the stairs rather than above it. It's guarded by equally rare *komaneko* cat sculptures made from Takeshima stone, instead of the usual *komainu* lion dogs. Inside the shrine are several objects of worship; legend states it was built to honour the dragon god.

Beside Seidaimyō is a cemetery of carved stone pagodas. Great trees have started growing through and over it, earning it the nickname of Takeshima Angkor-wat. The pagodas are also of Takeshima stone and are unique to the island. You'll also find the six buddha statues, *rokujizō* (六地蔵), created to pray for peace on the island. In Buddhism, when a human dies they're said to be reincarnated into one of six worlds: those of heavenly beings, humans, struggles, animals, hungry ghosts or hell. The rokujizō are said to help guide you wherever you end up.

Gajumaru Gate (ガジュマル門) is a large 200-year-old banyan tree that forms a tunnel across the road. It's become a sacred symbol of the island, as its dense foliage is said to be the home of a god. It's also believed to help you find love or marriage.

Most of the coastline is cliffs, but Takeshima is the only Mishima with an actual swimming beach, at **Komorikō** (籠港). Located on the south coast, roughly 15 minutes' walk from the village, it is completely isolated. The bay here is also used as a fishing boat harbour in harsh weather, and is full of silver stripe herring. Its mineral-rich, archetypal aquamarine waters are ideal for snorkelling and fishing and you may even spot dolphins. To check out a shipwreck, look to Yakushima dive shops operating in Takeshima (page 74).

The road south, past vistas of bamboo and the sweeping curves of the road along the isthmus, brings you to the little **Ōyama Shrine** (大山神社) and eventually the **East Coast Red Cliffs** (赤壁). Here the pebble beach gives way to terracotta-coloured cliffs that were pressed together during the island's formation. (Though impressive in colour, don't be fooled by some of the unnaturally red photos that are floating about.) You'll also spot **Eeme Standing Rock** (エーメ立神).

In the west you can see **Onbo Cape** (オンボ崎). Legend says that this was where those who were washed ashore in the nearby shipwreck were mourned. It is now a scenic spot where on clear days you can see Iōjima belching away on the horizon, the small uninhabited island Shōwa-Iōjima, and sometimes Yakushima too. It's particularly good for sunset shots, as the sun haloes Iōjima.

If you stay on Takeshima, look to full-board guesthouses Minshuku Hamayuri (民宿はまゆり; 7 rooms; 1 Takeshima; ☎ 0991 32 2150; w minsyukuhamayuri.wixsite.com/website) or Minshuku Kubota (民宿くぼた; 6 rooms; 8 Takeshima; ☎ 0991 32 2171; w superliner.com/kubota). There's also a Onbozaki Campsite (オンボ崎キャンプ場; ☎ 0991 32 2225) but reserve in advance.

KUROSHIMA The oldest and largest of the Mishima, 15.37km^2 Kuroshima (黒島) is known as 'Little Yakushima' thanks to its dense forest and moody mountains. The name Kuroshima itself means 'black island', in reference to this dark terrain looming from the sea. It's an unkempt reserve for wild birds, rare plants and flowers – here you can spot Japanese weasels, hoopoes and swallows. The island's highest peak, Yaguradake (622m), and its clifftop waterfalls and hidden little shrines make for some interesting sights, but Kuroshima is very much a rural backwater.

The most westerly and remote of the Mishima, Kuroshima is the only one of the three not formed by the Kikai Caldera. The strong currents around the island helped isolate it, making early travel difficult and keeping the island out of Japan's reach and interest.

Today there are just under 200 people living on Kuroshima, split across two settlements: Ōsato and Katadomari. It's said the islanders are descendants of the Heike clan, who were exiled here. The main industry is beef, with ranches dotted all over the island – yet another name for the island is Satsuma Kuroshima, to differentiate from its Yaeyama namesake, which is similarly known for its cows (page 315). It's said that the cattle here have 'strong legs', thanks to the island's steep, rugged slopes.

Culturally, Kuroshima has a strong tradition of dance. The island is home to the 400-year-old Ōsato Hassaku dance, in which performers – wearing elaborate costumes featuring masks, grass/beaded skirts and gourds tied about the waste – beat mortars and rice scoops together to symbolise production and prosperity. The Katadomari Bon Odori involves a *taiko* drumming dance, the *kasa* (hat) dance and the memorial dance *kuyō odori*. This last is said to calm and comfort the spirits of

MISHIMAMURA BREWERY

In 2018, Kuroshima managed the near-impossible feat of establishing a new shōchū distillery. Licensing laws make starting new distilleries incredibly difficult, but the benefit to the island overrode the red tape. Mishimamura Brewery Muku-no-Kura (みしま焼酎無垢の蔵; 204 -1 Kuroshima; 0991 33 2345; w mishima-shochu.jp/en; 09.00–17.00 daily) is a rare public shōchū brewery that began back in 2005 but was only officially certified 14 years later. The project is run by a co-operative of Mishima residents, Mishima Village Office and well-established shōchū companies. The shōchū is made using local mountain water and sweet potatoes, cultivated primarily by senior citizens and potato farmers. In 2017, their new shōchū Mendon was created. You can apply online through the extensive English website for an excellent free small brewery tour; they may even pick you up from your ferry. Please note it's considered good manners to buy some of this one-of-a-kind shōchū if you're taking the free tour – never mind if they pick you up too.

those who have died due to illness or disaster, and acts as a memorial service for their families. In Ōsato, there is a bow and arrow dance (*yumiya odori*), where the dancer wears a *tenugui* (decorative towel) wrapped around his head and becomes the spirit of the deceased.

Practicalities Kuroshima is roughly round, the majority of its 15.37km² forested and mountainous. There are two settlements with ports, uphill Katadomari in the southwest and Ōsato in the northeast. The south is largely left to nature, though there is a road covering the entire perimeter and a few travelling through the centre. Otherwise, Kuroshima is the familiar story: no police, no shops, no restaurants, no transport, and they even recently stopped their rental bike scheme. The journey between Katadomari and Ōsato is around 1 hour 35 minutes on foot, but the island is hard-going to walk so you wouldn't necessarily want to attempt it. There's a medical centre (大里診療所; 67-4 Kuroshima; 0991 33 2003) and a whopping two post offices: Ōsato (大里簡易郵便局; 15-15 Kuroshima; 0991 33 2055; 09.00–17.00 Mon–Fri) and Katadomari (片泊簡易郵便局; 135 Katadomari; 0991 33 2030; 09.00–17.00 Mon–Fri). Neither have ATMs.You are essentially reliant on accommodations, who do full board with lovely local ingredients, for all. Minshuku are very local; more often than not they are used by Japanese civil engineers and geologists coming to the island for work. Check out Ōsato's Minshuku Satoshin (民宿里心; 3 rooms; 2 Kuroshima; 0991 33 2033) run by maternal Sayoko or Katadomari's long-standing Minshuku Ichigogawa (民宿一五川; 4 rooms; 777 Kuroshima; 0991 33 2067); bookings are over the phone in Japanese only.

What to see and do The only real sight in Katadomari is the forested **Sugao Daimyō Shrine** (菅尾大名神社), dating to 1629, which contains two mirrors of worship and 16 natural stones.

The road out of Katadomari splits, with the main road heading north over the island and the other south. This southern road leads to the **Shiotebana White Cliffs** (塩手鼻), a unique white cape with clear plate joints in the rock – if you're not into rocks it's still a pretty cool landscape with a superb view for watching sunset over the East China Sea. Shiotehana is also a great fishing spot, full of striped beakfish. Both fishing and spearfishing are popular on Kuroshima.

KAMIKAZE ON KUROSHIMA

Kuroshima played an unwitting role in the Pacific War, when it was cut off from its mainland supply route, leaving islanders without food and experiencing starvation. During this time of famine, an unusual relationship grew between the islanders and the kamikaze special attack forces.

As war drew to a close and kamikaze attacks increased, pilots started crash-landing near or on Kuroshima. One was 24-year-old Ensign Shibata, who suffered severe burns all over his body but was taken care of by the islanders. Treated as a military hero, the islanders fed Shibata from the small amounts of white rice they had carefully stored, despite facing starvation themselves.

Not long after Shibata, another crash occurred, from which 21-year-old Ensign Abe was rescued unharmed and was amazed to find his colleague on the island. Abe wanted to return to his mission, but weather and boat availability made it impossible. They were soon joined by Ensign Ena, and by the end of the war multiple kamikaze had been found dead on Kuroshima, with six saved by the islanders.

There's now a statue to commemorate the pilots and a memorial service takes place there each year. After the war, the island escaped US administration and remained Japanese territory.

Beside Shiotebana is the **Kuroshima Shiroi Kannon** (黒島白衣観音), which commemorates a maritime accident in 1895 where mainland fishermen tried to shelter from a storm at Kuroshima, but were wrecked off the coast. Their bodies washed up at Shiotebana, where this statue was built in memory of 411 victims. Nearby is **Ibadon's Tomb** (イバドンの墓), a Kamakura-era tomb belonging to a warrior who features in Kuroshima folktales. Every year on 23 June, Katadomari women clean his tomb and offer flowers, dumplings and dances. This road here leads all the way round to Ōsato, via the **charcoal pot trace** (炭釜跡), the ruins of a charcoal kiln in a field off the road. Charcoal was a huge source of income for the island during the Meiji era. Be warned this road isn't well maintained but is also devoid of any real sights: don't bother if you're walking. The road north between Katadomari and Ōsato has a few little oddments along the way. There's the **Kuroshima Heike Castle Ruins** (黒島平家城遺跡), a barely there overgrown viewpoint over a ridge below, where the ruins of a Heike family castle revealed pottery and celadon traded from China. Further along is the all-important Mishimamura Brewery (page 107), which sits before the road to **Akahana** (赤鼻), a picturesque cape located at the northernmost tip of Kuroshima, with great fishing and a large ranch. While Akahana is on the left, to the right are the mountains. Climbing Yaguradake and its surrounding peaks is about all the excitement to be had on Kuroshima. There are hiking paths to the summit, the shortest of which takes 30–40 minutes, but from the towns it can be a 4–6-hour round trip. The paths are rarely used so the conditions aren't great – make sure to have a map and take care. In Ōsato is the little **Kuroo Daimyō Shrine** (黒尾大名神社), believed to be built in 1598, and the unusually named **Equality Daikeikai Myōtō** (平等大慧会妙塔). Even more unusual than this red-and-white Ryūkyū-style building's name is its purpose: it was built to commemorate the sins islanders committed by eating and killing animals and plants in order to live. To the east is the **Kuroshima Peace Park** (黒島平和公園), which commemorates the kamikaze who crash-landed on Kuroshima (see above) as well as those who died in the war.

4

The Amami Islands

There's something unknowable about the Amami Islands (Amami-guntō; 奄美群島). The dark, forested undulations of the mainland, the far-flung scattering of barely known, rarely visited offshoot islands – all seem to render the group mysterious. And in many ways, this suits Amami.

The islands sit in a cultural trench, caught in a divide between the mainland and northern Ōsumi and southern Okinawa Prefecture. Although the group are historically, geologically and culturally spoken of as a unit, Amami Ōshima is some 150km from the group's southernmost island Yorontō. Meanwhile, Yorontō is just 22km from Okinawa-hontō. It's only natural, therefore, that the strength of influence from both the south and north are felt differently across the group.

This latitudinal spread shows up in language. There are several dialects of the Amami language, which are spoken on Amami Ōshima, Tokunoshima and Kikaijima. The southernmost islands, Okinoerabujima and Yorontō, speak dialects of the Kunigami language, which is concentrated on northern Okinawa-hontō.

Amami has a tumultuous past with its neighbours to the south. Culturally, the islands share a huge amount with Okinawa and the Ryūkyū: for example, the Amami languages are closer to the Okinawan ones (some shared entirely) than to those of Kyūshū. Politically and historically, however, Amami shares much more history with the mainland and Ōsumi Islands.

HISTORY

Charting the jumbled history of swapping one Amami subjugator for the next is PhD-worthy. Limited written history suggests Amami began as an independent trading nation which fell under the rule of the mainland shōgunate until the 15th century. This is when the Ryūkyū Kingdom invaded and by 1450, all but Kikaijima had fallen under their reign. In 1466, Kikai was conquered too. The Amami people certainly didn't concede willingly – there were uprisings in 1536, 1537 and 1571 against the kingdom, all of which were quashed, leaving Amami under Ryūkyū control for 170 years.

This all changed again in 1609, when the Shimazu clan landed on Amami Ōshima and travelled down the group until they reached Okinawa. Within three years the clan conquered the Ryūkyū Kingdom and put Amami back under mainland control. The Satsuma years began easily enough for Amami, but as the domain lost money it imposed impossible sugar taxes on the island group; the amount expected was so great that the islanders couldn't afford to farm anything but sugarcane, leading to starvation and famine. Sugar became such a major factor in Amami life that it snuck its way into many foods and drink: today brown sugar awamori is one of its finest exports, only allowed to be made on Amami.

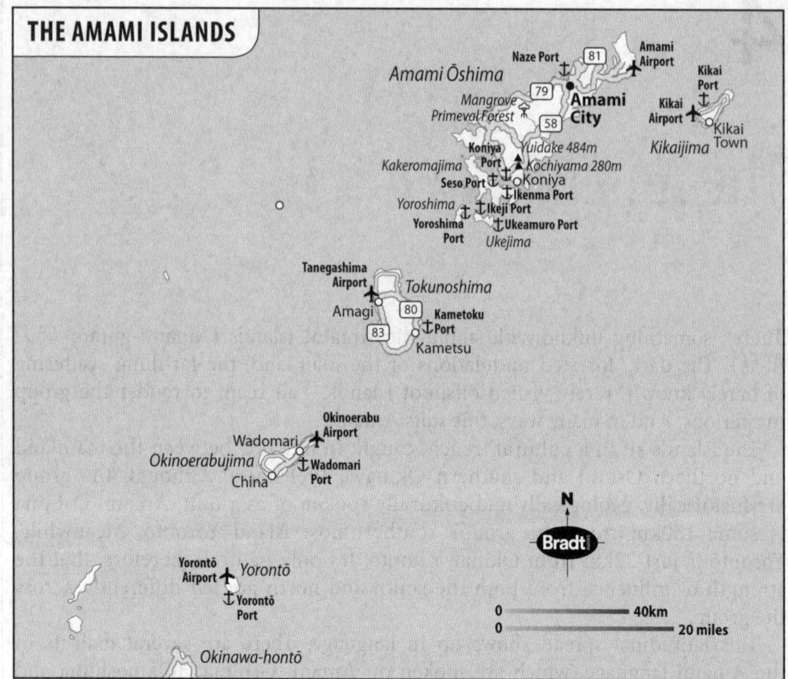

After the Meiji restoration, Amami was put under the governance of the Kagoshima Prefecture. Several almost peaceable decades passed until World War II. Over 20,000 Japanese soldiers were stationed on the Amami Islands during the conflict, but they never experienced ground combat. Instead, they found themselves under attack from sporadic US aerial and submarine bombardments.

At this time, the US often called the Amami group the 'northern Ryūkyūs', annoying the Japanese and Amami people, who had long considered the islands part of Japan. After Japan lost, the Amami Islands were taken by the US military, along with their southern Ryūkyū neighbours. The US military ceased all interaction between Amami and the rest of Japan – including their close Ōsumi Island neighbours just north.

For the people of Amami, this was yet another drastic change to their lives and culture. Most of them had only ever known life under Japan, and their history under the Ryūkyū Kingdom was tempestuous and temporary. Most Amami people identified as Japanese, and insisted on being called Northern Nansei, rather than the loaded moniker of Ryūkyū.

As peace treaties began to surface in 1947, the Amami islanders collectively asked to be returned to Japan. In response, the then-military governor abolished islanders' rights to free speech, publication, beliefs, unions and assembly. His successor, realising the abolition of these rights reeked of dictatorship, reinstated some – but still banned public gatherings, statements and anything critical of US military occupation. Ironically, these rights had been forcibly enshrined in Japan's post-war constitution by the same forces denying them on the islands.

Amami's economy tanked under the US, as it had relied heavily on mainland trade and connections. The US focused on Okinawa, leaving Amami to sit unsupported, separated and often starving as food prices rocketed. In 1949, the US military government that distributed food enacted a threefold price hike to island-wide protest.

To alleviate starvation, municipal governments decided to distribute goods at the old prices regardless and people continued to protest. These protests resulted in the US military expanding a spy network into Amami, and the municipal government's actions were discovered. The military made the municipalities pay back the revenue loss and removed their purchasing power.

By 1949–50, suggestions of a peace treaty had Amami islanders hopeful of being returned to Japan. There were mass rallies and petitions, one of which pointed out the distinction and great differences between Amami and Okinawa Prefecture. In 1951, 99.8% of Amami and Tokara islanders over 14 signed a petition stating their wish to return to Japan. This unanimous verdict was presented to the UN, Allied Councils and Japanese government, but the peace treaty concluded in September 1951 gave continued governance of Amami and the islands to its south to the US. Only the Tokara returned to mainland control.

In 1952, the US ambassador to Japan apparently considered Amami reversion to Japan favourably, but only of some of the group: the southernmost islands of Yorontō and Okinoerabujima would be wrenched from Amami and kept under US control. This caused uproar across the Amami group.

At the end of 1952, the representatives of Amami's reversion movement met with the US ambassador and Japanese prime minister and presented the signatures of now 99.9% of the Amami population asking for return. Finally, in 1953, the US

AMAMI FOODS

Amami may not have the international renown of Okinawa when it comes to food, but it has a great cuisine known as *shima juuri* that's incredibly healthy, far less Westernised, and relies on seasonal, local produce.

Pork is arguably Amami's favourite meat; until the late 1900s, each household would raise black pigs as a source of protein. At New Year, pork and vegetables were eaten while the remainder of the pig was preserved in miso and salt. Today's favourite Amami pork dish is arguably abura sōmen (pages 54 and 120).

Amami's signature dish keihan, however, uses chicken, while seafood is naturally popular. Seafood dishes include *aosa* seaweed tempura and *mada jiru*, an ink soup made from bigfin reef squid – an Amami speciality. Two lobster species (*kanoko* and shima) are caught off the islands at night by skin divers, and are commonly served in miso soup or as sashimi.

Today fresh food and ingredients are plentiful, but Amami cuisine was long affected by the islands' colonisers. Satsuma forced islanders to replace precious rice crops with sugarcane, which was then traded with Kyūshū. Starvation became common, leading to Amami becoming reliant on *sotetsu*. These poisonous cycad palms were commonly used as windbreaks and boundary markers, but during famine they became an unexpected food source. If not prepared correctly (and laboriously), sotestu is deadly.

The palm returned to plates during and after World War II, when crops were once again scarce. Amami is one of the only places left that still eats sotetsu today. Locally called *nari*, one of its popular products is nari miso, often used in salads and soups, as well as nari flour. Nari is really high in protein, vegetable fats and iron, but low in sugar, and is said to help prevent disease.

announced it would relinquish hold of Amami and return it to Japan in full and did so on Christmas Day.

The result of the brutal US occupation ignited both a nationalist Japanese sentiment among Amami people, accelerating the adoption and use of Japanese language, and a new pride in their own Amami heritage. Conversely, the gap between Amami and the southern islands, particularly Okinawa-hontō, widened. The decimated Amami economy meant many islanders still had to work on Okinawa, but after the Amami reversion they faced anti-Amami action, leading to many of them being fired.

The actions of the US military and US-occupied Okinawa left Amami with great bitterness towards Okinawa. Some people on Amami still resent being grouped in with the Ryūkyū Islands, a sentiment that recently came up when applying for UNESCO status. The original 2003 nomination labelled the mix of Amami, Okinawa and Yaeyama islands simply as 'Ryūkyū-shotō', resulting in huge opposition that got it changed in 2017 to Amami-Ryūkyū.

AMAMI ŌSHIMA

Amami Ōshima (奄美大島) – literally 'Amami Big Island' – is not only the heart of the island group, it's also the only one with any sort of international acclaim. Not many people visit Amami Ōshima; even fewer visit its outlying siblings. Skipping the island, the second largest in the entire archipelago at 712.35km^2, is a common mistake.

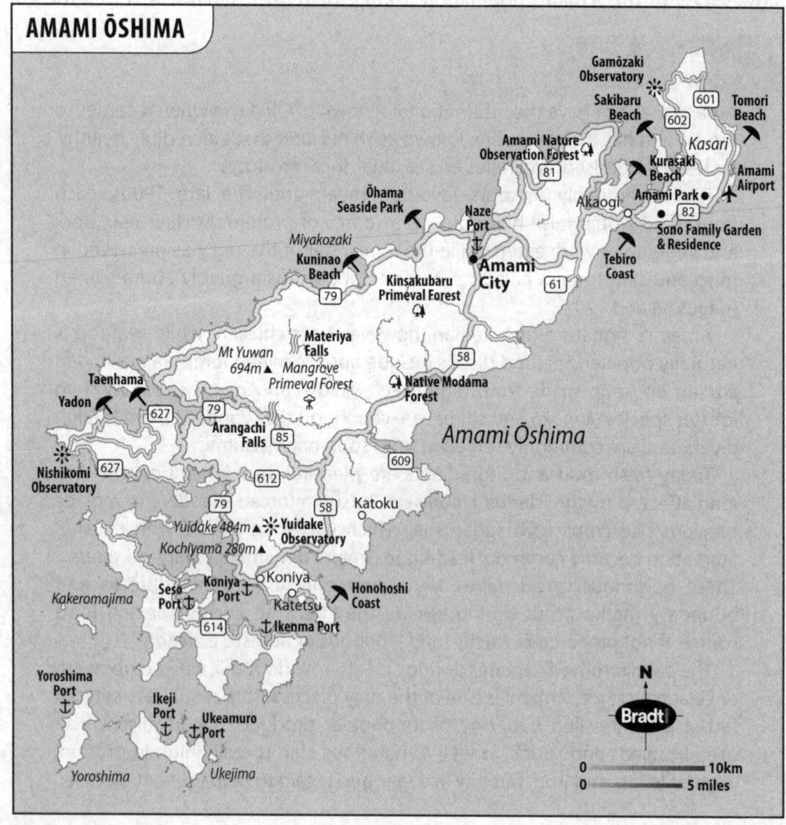

RELIGION ON AMAMI ŌSHIMA

Amami Ōshima's table-tennis back and forth between colonisers (see below) resulted in a mixed religion on the island. The Ryūkyū Kingdom brought the influential noro and yuta (page 21), who designated the Amami wilderness as Kamiyama (God's Mountain). It was believed this was where Teruko, god of the mountains, and Naruko, god of the seas, descended upon the island, and no-one was allowed to clear the land, build on it or use it for cultivation without noro permission. This caused conflict with the Shimazu, who brought not only Zen Buddhism but brown sugar, which they hoped to cultivate across the island.

Satsuma efforts to increase sugar production in the dying days of the shōgunate forced islanders into gruelling work and harsh living conditions. This didn't encourage the Amami people to take up the oppressors' religion. When the Meiji government tried to eradicate Zen Buddhism from Japan in the 1870s, the Amami islanders were only too happy to see it go, and Buddhist temples and priests were wiped from Amami. When Buddhism returned, it was in the form of Shin Buddhism.

Noro continued to exist, despite mainland oppression, until after World War II, when they died out. Yuta have remained however, and there are new and active yuta on Amami today, who offer fortunes, life and health advice.

Catholicism, introduced in 1892, also found a relatively strong hold here. The poverty-stricken islanders were still making offerings of both labour and money to priestesses, but Catholic missionaries offered a far easier life. Catholic churches offered stipends to students, employed local residents and looked after the people – particularly those with leprosy, which ran rampant through the islands after the war.

On Amami today, Kamiyama is still believed sacred, and during festivals it's believed that the gods descend from the mountain and travel celestial paths on the island, down to the beaches. Locals will greet gods, welcoming them to their villages, and send them off at the end of the festivals.

Amami Ōshima's most interesting aspect is its individualism: it proliferates with endemic species and unique customs. The island's culture was influenced by both the mainland and the Ryūkyū Kingdom (the latter most of all); as it got passed to one, it got cut off from the other, in a repeated pattern of influence and isolation. This means that although its craft and folk culture may have originated elsewhere, it developed in a way entirely unique to Amami.

Amami Ōshima also has its own linguistic quirks. Although locals speak standard Japanese today, they often converse in Amami Japanese, a hybrid dialect bafflingly known as *ton-futsūgo* – 'potato common language'. Ton-futsūgo is primarily Japanese, with influences from Kagoshima and accents, words and phrases from Amami. Amami surnames also differ from Ryūkyū ones: the Shimazu clan bestowed surnames (a privilege of the samurai) on wealthy islanders in exchange for financial backing. To differentiate islanders from mainland people, they were given single character surnames – a rarity in Japan. (It's been suggested that this was to keep the islands looking Ryūkyūan, so that China would continue to trade with them.)

Folk beliefs in nature are very strong on Amami. The islanders have long lived according to the cycles and rhythms of nature: the tides, the seasons, bird migrations, star movements and the phases of the moon guided everyday life. A unique belief of Amami is that butterflies and moths, known as *hapura*, are said to

AMAMI ŌSHIMA FESTIVALS

Festivals are a large part of Amami life, particularly the summer *hōnensai*. This harvest festival is held in villages in lunar August and is much anticipated. Men and boys take part in sumo, dedicating their victories to village gods. Historically, the villages on Amami Ōshima had limited interaction with each other, thanks to the mountainous forest interior, meaning many areas developed their own customs. In the southern Setouchi district, the Yui hōnensai has a traditional tug-of-war made from harvested rice straw. After the battle, the rope is used for the sumo ring.

The lunar August Arasetsu is a unique festival from Akina in Tatsugō, marking summer harvest. It's comprised of two main rituals, the most famous being the wonderfully weird divining event, Shochogama, which determines the harvest for the year. It involves about 40 men atop a thatched-platform, erected overlooking the village rice paddies in the morning. They rock and shake the construction until it collapses, with the direction it falls determining the harvest: a southerly direction bodes well for a good one. The local *hachigatsu odori* is then danced on top of the collapsed roof.

be the spirits of the dead. This is based not only on the insects' regenerative abilities, but the fact triangles have long been associated with the soul. Since butterfly wings are roughly triangular, they were said to hold protective power. Triangles also pop up in beautiful Amami cloth called *Ōshima tsumugi* and celebratory muchi is cut into triangles for the Sangachi festival.

Nature still plays a part on Amami Ōshima, today as much as ever. The island's wild expanse of thick forests, winding rivers and rich mangroves forms part of the Nansei-shotō's protected UNESCO World Heritage Site, designated in 2021. Together, these habitats play host to extraordinary biodiversity and multiple endemic species (a result of the island being isolated by rising sea levels). The primary example is the Amami rabbit, found only here and on Tokunoshima, which is deemed a living fossil due to its clear lineage from an ancestral hare species. There's also Lidth's jay, a rare thrush called *otora-tsugumi*, the world's largest tree fern *hikage-hego*, the Otton frog, the Amami spiny rat, and the colourful Amami Ōshima frog. Its coral-rich waters are also home to the amazing white-spotted pufferfish, famous for the male's elaborate circular sand designs, which was discovered here as recently as 2014.

GETTING THERE AND AWAY Multiple cities across Japan fly to Amami Ōshima, including Tokyo, Osaka, Naha, Fukuoka and Kagoshima. Flights from Tokyo take around 2½ hours, from Naha 1 hour. Operators include JAL (**w** jal.co.jp/jp/en), Skymark (**w** skymark.co.jp/en) and Peach Aviation (**w** flypeach.com), with the latter operating some low-cost options. Amami Airport is in the very northeast of the island, around 45 minutes' drive or an hour bus from Amami City.

Alternatively, you can reach Amami by ferry, operated by either Marix Line (**w** marix-line.co.jp) or A-Line ferries (**w** aline-ferry.com), sometimes called Marue Ferry. A-Line and Marix helpfully alternate travel dates of their ferries – which company you use will depend on what day you hope to travel.

There are two routes from Kagoshima: the so-called Kagoshima route and the Amami Kaiun route. The Kagoshima route travels from Kagoshima Shinkō (New Port) terminal on A-Line's *Akebono* and *Naminoue* ferries, and Marix Line's *Queen Coral Cross* and *Queen Coral Plus*. It travels down the archipelago, calling at Amami

Ōshima (Naze Port), Tokunoshima (Kametoku Port), Okinoerabujima (Wadomari Port), Yorontō, and Okinawa-hontō (Motobu and Naha ports). Through A-Line you can buy a multi-stop ticket that allows you 21 days unlimited ferry travel along the Kagoshima–Amami–Okinawa route. Tickets are interchangeable between the two companies. The journey from Kagoshima to Amami Ōshima is very long at 11 hours, so best overnighted.

The second route is the Amami Kaiun, only operated by A-Line's *Ferry Amami* and *Ferry Kikai*, departing from Kagoshima's Kita-futō Port (North Passenger Terminal). This ferry travels the Amami Islands, up to Okinoerabu: Kikai–Amami Naze–Amami Koniya–Tokunoshima Hetono and, on *Ferry Kikai*, on to Okinoerabujima China.

The ferries are by and large well maintained, though some are older than others. Generally you have shared tatami rooms for sleeping or private options, spotty Wi-Fi, 24-hour vending machines and a café/shop. Naze Port is in the north of the island and Koniya Port in the very south. If you're in Koniya and looking to access parts of Amami Ōshima, Kakeroma, Ukejima or Yoroshima by sea outside the normal ferry routes, you'll need to charter a boat with one of Amami Sea Taxi (0997 72 4760), Setouchi Charter Ship Cooperative (0997 72 0377) or Koniya Chartered Boat Association (0997 72 0332).

GETTING AROUND Amami Ōshima is not only big but cumbersome: a remarkably ragged bit of rock whose natural attractions make it hard to traverse. The island is roughly split into three: the north where there are beaches, the main city and resorts; the jungled centre with mangroves and rivers; and the more parochial south with island-filled vistas and local life.

The most advisable way to get around all this is **rental car**; there's a main road connecting the north and south, with offshoots around the perimeter. There are rental companies at the airport and Amami City and reservations are highly recommended.

There's also the public **Shimabus** (0997 52 0509; w shimabus.co.jp). These buses operate across ten routes but are infrequent, can be expensive and don't access large parts of the island. They can, however, get you between the major areas: the airport, Amami City, Setouchi in the south and the mangroves. Buses between the airport and Amami City leave every 30 minutes; every 90 minutes between Amami City and Setouchi. Bus fares increase with distance; be aware that buses have machines to change smaller notes, but are unable to do ¥5,000 notes or larger. Definitely make sure to have lower denominations on hand. There are also one-, two- and three-day passes available from the airport or at the Shimabus counter in Amami City or port.

If you are sticking to a single area of Amami Ōshima, you can get around by **bicycle** using accommodation rentals, but you will be cycling for large parts of the day – pleasant but challenging.

Vehicle rental

Amami Rent-a-Car 奄美レンタカー; Amami Airport: 2231-8 Kazaricho Oaza Manya; 0997 55 2633; w amami-rentacar.com; Naze Office: 10-15 Nazeirifunecho; 0997 54 1421

Nippon Rent-a-Car ニッポンレンタカー奄美空港営業所; 2221-4 Kazaricho Oaza Manya; 0997 55 2400; w nipponrentacar.co.jp

ORIX Rent-a-Car オリックスレンタカー 奄美空港前店; Amami Airport, 2176 Kazaricho Oaza Manya; 0997 63 1201

Times Car タイムズカー奄美空港店; Amami Airport, 467 Kasaricho Oaza Wano; 0997 63 0240; w rental.timescar.jp

TOYOTA Rent-a-Car トヨタレンタカー奄美空港; Amami Airport: 473 Kazaricho Oaza Manya; 0997 63 0100; w rent.toyota.co.jp; Naze Office: 6-12 Nazeminatomachi; 0997 54 0100

TOURIST INFORMATION The airport has a useful tourist information counter with an extraordinary number of leaflets and displays for guides, tours and access information. There's also the Amami Ōshima Tourism and Products Association in Amami City (一般社団法人あまみ大島観光物産連盟; 1F AiAi Hiroba, 14-10 Nazesuehirocho; 0997 53 3240; w amami-tourism.org) and in the south, Setouchi Town Sightseeing Information Centre (せとうち海の駅; 2F Umi-no-eki 26-14 Ominato; 0997 72 1001; w setouchi-welcome.com).

WHERE TO STAY

North

✷ **Denpaku & MIJORA Beachfront** (8 houses, 28 rooms) 伝泊; 50-2 Kasaricho Oaza Sato, Amami; 0997 63 1910; w den-paku.com. 3 stunning accommodations: luxury hotel, cheaper guesthouse & fantastic project renting & revitalising local houses. Recommended traditional wooden houses for larger families, luxe MIJORA beachfront suites with infinity pool for couples & singles. MIJORA operates phenomenal restaurant & b/fast. Cooking experiences, tours, bike rentals. **$$$–$$$$$**

Hotel New Amami (174 rooms) ホテルニュー奄美; 9-2 Nazeirifunecho, Amami; 0997 52 2000; w newamami.com. Standard, inoffensive budget hotel with clean rooms on the smaller side, complimentary touches, sauna, public baths, laundry, b/fast. **$$$**

En- Hostel & Café Bar (6 rooms) enゲストハウスフェバー; 10-1 Nazeirifunecho, Amami; 0997 69 3773; w en-amami.com. Sweet modern hostel in town centre with café, shared lounge, parking, terrace & bar. Private rooms & dorms available. **$$**

South

The Scene Amami Spa & Resort (21 rooms) ザ・シーン; 970 Sokaru, Setouchi; 0997 72 0111; w hotelthescene.com. Modern sea-view rooms at this luxury wellness resort on the island's southernmost spit. Restaurant bar & lounge; activities including kayaking, hot springs & yoga on the sea-facing terrace. **$$$$$**

Tanpopoya (3 rooms) たんぽぽやぁ; 18-6 Koniya, Setouchi; 0997 76 3302; w tanpopoyaa-amami.com. Gorgeous fun guesthouse of wood & knick-knacks, ideal for families & long-term stays. Shared kitchen, lounge, baths. Can be rented as whole house. Transfers available. **$$$**

Seiwa Sakai Guesthouse (2 dormitories) 堺ゲストハウス奄美; 1-5 Matsue Koniya, Setouchi; 0901 917 3968; w sakaigh-amami.seiwa-sakai.co.jp. Dorm-style rooms that can be booked as privates for couples or families. Recently renovated shared facilities, luggage storage & lockers. Rental bikes, fishing equipment & snorkels. **$$**

WHERE TO EAT AND DRINK

North

✷ **2 Waters** 986-1 Kamesaki, Amami; 0997 57 1988; w den-paku.com/eat_amami; 18.00–21.00 Tue–Sun. Beautiful beach-facing counter restaurant showcasing local ingredients; creative dishes, Japanese wines, cocktail pairings. Based at Denpaku's MIJORA hotel (see above). Exclusive & small, reservation recommended. **$$$$**

Keihan Hisakura けいはんひさ倉; 516 Yanyu, Tatsugo; 0997 62 2988; w www4.synapse.ne.jp/hisakura; 11.00–20.00 Fri–Tue, 11.00–16.00 Wed–Thu. Named after the island dish, Keihan serves up the perfect Amami meal made with chickens raised by the owner. Sunlit, welcoming & ridiculously popular. Wheelchair friendly. **$$**

Muchakana むちゃかなな; 4-18 Nazekanekucho, Amami; 0997 52 8505; w muchakana.com; 17.30–midnight daily. Chic izakaya with plentiful island food, & a wall of alcohols. Try the aasa tempura, salt-grilled boar & rare awamori. High-end traditional *kaiseki* meal available. Proudly LGBTQIA+ friendly. **$$**

✷ **Yurai Tokoro** ゆらい処; 18-28 Nazeirifunecho, Amami; 0997 52 7008; 18.00–23.00 daily. Amazing little restaurant serving old Amami specialities including sotetsu miso, *taaman* potatoes and abura sōmen. Sweet owner makes her own flavoured shōchū too. **$$**

La Fonte ラフォンテ; 1325-3 Akaogi, Tatsugo; 0997 62 3935; w lafonte-amami.com; 11.00–17.00 Wed–Mon. Prettily decorated female-owned farm-to-cone gelateria. Local flavours include brown sugar, yoghurt tart, island banana, salt, or Japanese plum sorbet. **$**

South

Tazuki たづき; 12-3 Koniyakasuga, Setouchi; 0704 321 9556; 11.30–14.00 & 18.00–23.00 Mon–Sat. Cosy izakaya that serves up excellent local fare with flair. Sushi, sashimi & noodles, but the squid-ink pasta is best. $$

Amami Yakuzen Tsumugi-an 奄美薬膳 つむぎ庵; 87 Sumiyocho Oaza Yakugachi, Amami; 0997 69 2390; 11.30–15.30 daily. Lunchtime soba restaurant on Rd 58. Puts local ingredients known for health properties into homemade soba. Black pork *nankotsu* bowls are best. Cheap, filling & utterly delicious. $

Ōshiro Mochi Shop 大城もちや; 23-2 Funatsu, Koniya, Setouchi; 0997 72 0328; w r.goope.jp/amami-ooshiro. Running over 60 years, this is the place for *yomogi mochi* (mugwort rice cake), known locally as *fuchimochi*. Buy it freshly made, wrapped in leaves: it's the ultimate mochi (page 56) experience. $

KOKUTŌ SHŌCHŪ

Amami's best product by far is kokutō shōchū. From the early 1600s, the islands were made to pay taxes in brown sugar and tribute in homemade distilled spirits. When Satsuma took control, distillation was banned or highly regulated, but in the Meiji era a method of home-distilling awamori was brought over from Okinawa. Though home brewing was still illegal, Amami people continued in secret.

Under American administration after World War II, rice was rationed, leaving brewers to turn to potatoes and barley to make their spirits. Such spirits proved unpopular, so leftover brown sugar was used instead. This ingenious method was recognised by the Japanese government after the island group was returned to Japan, and the Amami Islands became the only place allowed to produce brown sugar spirits.

Now, there are over 25 distilleries on five of the Amami Islands. Together they produce over 150 brands of shōchū. Each distillery and island has its own method and local ingredients, creating a wide variation of the same product. Water is particularly important: the main island of Amami Ōshima has wonderfully clear soft mountain water, which is low in minerals, while Yoron, Okinoerabu and Kikai all have mineral-rich waters thanks to their coral origins. Tokunoshima has a mix of both soft and hard.

The basic production of brown sugar shōchū involves soaking, washing then steaming rice. Black kōji mould is then spread over it and allowed to form malted rice. Water is added and it's left to ferment for up to a week. A brown sugar solution is then added to the resulting mash, which goes into the distiller. Impurities are removed, the spirit is diluted with water, then bottled.

Kokutō shōchū is drunk in multiple ways. The recommended way according to brewers is on the rocks, believed to bring out the aroma and depth of flavour. The most popular way is with water in a ratio of 2:3 or 1:1 – preparing it in advance is supposed to mellow the spirit. It can also be drunk with hot 40°C water, or served straight and chilled.

Brown sugar shōchū is surprisingly versatile. It can be added to coffee, milk and even tomato juice as a brown sugar Bloody Mary. Herbs like basil, ginger and shiso are more modern additions, as well as slices of pepper and cucumber. Amami Ōshima's Nishihira Distillery has a real claim to fame, in that its *tōji* (master distiller) and CEO is a woman. Selena Nishihira inherited the distillery from her father and grandfather to become one of Japan's few female tōji.

SHIMA UTA

Music is a huge part of Amami life. Folk songs here are called *shima uta:* in the local language, *shima* doesn't mean 'island' as it does in Japanese, but 'community'. Nowadays the term is often misapplied to folk music from Okinawa, much to Amami chagrin, but shima uta use different scales, the thinner-stringed Amami sanshin, and singers commonly use falsetto. Songs also occasionally have small chijin drums and whistling.

It's believed shima uta developed during the colonial years under Satsuma – essentially songs of slavery. Forced to work sugar plantations, the songs expressed the villagers' struggles, history and hopes, with themes covering morals, religion, humour, pain and longing. The songs varied wildly across Ōshima, thanks to the naturally isolating mountainous landscape, as well as across the group – but improvisation is also common, leading to an ever-changing, popular format. People still sit around the family table, singing and riffing on old songs together: a form of 'song play' called *uta ashibi*. Shima uta has even entered the modern charts, with young singers selling out gigs and being broadcast on national radio.

ENTERTAINMENT AND NIGHTLIFE The majority of Amami's nightlife is in the northern city's western flank, but there are drinking spots all over – hardly surprising for an island famous for brown sugar kokutō shōchū. If you head to Setouchi, make sure to pop into the Koniya shōchū shop and do a daytime tasting (see below). If you look hard enough, you may even find Koniya's secret izakaya, worthy of an elite Tokyo bar.

Ponopono 11-13 Nazekanekucho, Amami; ☎0997 69 3008; w cafeandbarponopono.wixsite.com/mysite; ⌚ 20.00–03.00 Mon–Sat. Warm & welcoming wood-lined drinking spot that turns into a music venue until the wee hours.

Roadhouse ASIVI アシビ; 4-3 Nazekanekucho, Amami; ☎0997 53 2223; w a-mp.co.jp; ⌚ 20.00–03.00 Wed–Mon. Over 40 brands of kokutō shōchū served up in a great live music venue that's a favourite with locals.

SHOPPING There are enough big shops in both towns that you don't have to worry about stocking up on supplies, especially if packing food for hiking. Koniya has plenty of traditional sweet shops, including the famous Ōshiro Mochi Shop (page 117), but if buying as souvenirs, check they will last the journey.

Amami Beer Shop 奄美のおみやげ店なら; 1–2 Nazeminatomachi, Amami; ☎0997 58 8100; w amamibrewpub.jp. Raw beer hall with souvenir shop selling local beers & more.

Amami Bussan Souvenir Shop 奄美物産; 7-7 Ominato Koniya, Setouchi; ☎0997 72 0204; w amamibussan.jp. Souvenir shop selling Amami goods including bags, food, trinkets & alcohol.

Amami Pearl 奄美パール; 1054-6 Koniya, Setouchi; ☎0997 76 3303; w amamipearl.com. Setouchi jewellery shop selling local pearls.

Isao Hayashi Art Studio 1693 Tehiro, Akaogi; ☎0803 207 1817; w isaohayashi.com. Artist Isao Hayashi paints colourful landscapes inspired by Amami nature.

Setouchi Shuhan Liquor Shop 瀬戸内酒販; 3-3-8 Ominato Koniya, Setouchi; ☎0997 72 0818; w setouchisyuhan.com. Some of the most knowledgable people in shōchū on Amami. Come to buy souvenirs & do tastings.

SPORTS AND ACTIVITIES If you want to head into the true wilderness you'll need a certified eco guide to do so, best booked through the Amami guiding website (w amami.or.jp/guide_en). One of the best areas to explore with your guide is Kinsakubaru Primeval Forest (金作原原生林): mountainous jungle where indigenous animals and subtropical broad-leafed plants thrive. These include the huge Alocasia odora, a Totoro-worthy leaf used as umbrellas; a giant 150-year-old oak; and the tall, flying spider-monkey tree ferns, considered living fossils as they date back to the Triassic period. Animal-lovers may spot Lidth's jays and the Ryūkyū tree lizard.

Amami Tours w amamitours.com. Brilliant English-speaking tours led by Aussie Amami resident John Cantu. Nature, animal, culture, food & night tours with hotel transfers.

Aqua Dive Kohollo アクアダイブコホロ; 820-3 Kunetsu, Setouchi; 0997 72 4969; w en.kohollo.jp. Organises whale-watching & whale swim tours.

Happy Sky ハッピースカイ; 0905 749 9413; w happysky.flier.jp. Paragliding on Amami.

Mangrove Park マングローブパーク; 478 Ishihara, Sumiyocho; 0997 56 3355; w mangrovepark.com. Central hub in mangroves offering kayak tours.

Santarō no Sato 三太郎の里; 555-13 Surigachi, Sumiyocho; 0997 69 5077. Tourism exchange with souvenir shop, bike rental, café & weaving experience.

Unimare w unimare.jp. Wide range of activities including snorkelling, diving & massage.

Zero Gravity ゼログラヴィティ; 122 Seisui, Setouchi; 0997 76 3901; w zerogravity.jp. Company specialising in disabled access marine activities.

OTHER PRACTICALITIES Amami has plenty of ATMs dotted about, including one at the airport and multiple banks in the Amami City area. In Setouchi the best bet is Koniya Post Office (古仁屋郵便局; 8 Matsue; 0997 72 0042; 09.00–17.00 Mon–Fri, ATM: 08.00–20.00 Mon–Sat, 09.00–20.00 Sun). There are a couple of hospitals, clinics and a wealth of police boxes.

Amami Chūō Hospital 奄美中央病院; 16-5 Nazenagahamacho, Amami; 0997 52 6565; 08.45–19.00 Mon–Sat

Amami Police Station 奄美警察署; 5-2 Nazenagahamacho, Amami; 0997 53 0110

Minami Ōshima Clinic 南大島診療所; 16-4 Koniya, Setouchi; 0997 72 0107; 09.00–12.00 & 17.00–18.00 Mon–Fri

Setouchi Police Station 瀬戸内警察署; 1283 155 Koniya, Setouchi; 0997 72 0110

WHAT TO SEE AND DO

North The north of Amami Ōshima is a squiggly peninsula of peninsulas, full of beaches, quiet communities, viewpoints and sights. Tempting as it is to scoot straight from the airport to the main city, the best of the north is between the two. Eye-catching, well-equipped white sand beaches like **Yōan** (用安ビーチ), **Tsuchihama** (土浜海岸) and **Tomori** (土盛海岸) pepper the east coast not far from the airport.

The region to the airport's north is quiet **Kasari** (笠利), a pretty cape where **Ayamaru Misaki Kankō Park** (あやまる岬観光公園; 0997 63 8885; w ayamaru.amamin.jp) has tourist information, a café, beach playground and an observation deck. This overlooks one of the ten scenic views of Amami, across the reefs, rocks and sotetsu to Kikaijima.

On Kasari's east is **Gamōzaki Observatory** (蒲生崎公園展望台) and shrine, dedicated to one of the Heike family samurai. Heike samurai are said to have fled to Amami Ōshima after losing the Battle of Dannoura (1185), and formed bases here and elsewhere on Kasari Bay to watch for enemies. Today it's a far less perilous, pretty sunset spot. Below this sits a small town, Akakina (赤木名), of little restaurants and a couple of intimate resorts.

West of the town, across the bay of newly planted mangroves that's popular with seabirds, is a little peninsula. It's the perfect place to cycle: you can spend a day wending your way to the impossible blues of **Sakibaru** (崎原ビーチ), a near-empty picture-perfect beach, or **Uttabaru Beach** (打田原ビーチ), a calm inlet with shower facilities. The peninsula is also home to **Amami's largest banyan tree** (奄美一の巨大ガジュマルの木), an incredible specimen of sprawling aerial roots.

To the west of the airport are two of the island's biggest attractions, both housed within **Amami Park** (奄美パーク; 1834 Kasaricho Oaza Setta; ☎0997 55 2333; w amamipark.com; ⏲ 09.00–18.00 daily, Jul–Aug 09.00–19.00, closed 1st & 3rd Wed every month). **Amami-no-Sato** (奄美の里; adult/child ¥310/150–220), or Amami Village, is where visitors can learn about the islands' history, nature and culture. There are areas dedicated to each island and English descriptions. **Tanaka Isson Memorial Art Museum** (田中一村記念美術館; ☎0997 55 2635; adult/child ¥520/260–370) is dedicated to the life and work of Tochigi-born Tanaka Isson, who moved to Amami at age 50 and painted the island prolifically. The 80-plus works chart his entire career and there's a 'forest' made up of the native plants that he painted.

Travelling further west brings you to **Myōjinzaki Observatory** (明神崎 展望台), a short trek with views that take in the entire coastline and deep blue seas – particularly rewarding at sunrise. This area is also home to a small village with the little-visited but pretty **Sono Family Garden and Residence** (薗家住宅主屋・庭園; 85 Kasaricho Oaza Yoan) and the **Ataewandaishin Shrine** (与湾大親神社), which overlooks the coast; both are worth a visit if travelling the road connecting north and south.

LOCAL RECIPE: ABURA SŌMEN

Abura sōmen changes depending on who makes it, so if you find yourself without ingredients make intelligent swaps, whether it's noodles, fish, meat or vegetables. Serves two.

200g sōmen noodles
100g pork belly
50g Chinese leeks/spring onion/chives
30g carrot
20g dried sardines/sardines
2 tbsp vegetable oil
2 tbsp dashi fish stock
White sesame seeds

1. Julienne the carrot, chop the Chinese leeks into inch-long pieces and cut the pork into 0.5cm slices.
2. Sprinkle the noodles into simmering water making sure they're not in one lump. Stir for a minute, then turn off the heat, let sit with lid on for 30 seconds, before washing with cold water.
3. Fry the sardines in the oil, then add pork, then carrot, then leek.
4. Add the dashi (if you don't have dashi, use salt or half a stock cube) then fry up the noodles. Serve hot, sprinkled with white sesame seeds.

Nearby, **Kenmun Village** (ケンムン村; 1246 Kasaricho Yoan; 0997 63 1178; w basyayama-mura.com/activity; 10.00–17.00 daily) run by Bashayama-mura Resort offers a variety of hands-on Amami experiences, including shima uta singing lessons and ceramic-, kokutō candy- and salt-making.

From here, Amami's north gets squeezed between the East China Sea and Pacific Ocean. You can see this rather beautiful phenomenon at the **Two Ocean Hill View** (2つの海が見える丘), also known as the Kashiken Pass, which overlooks the two. It's not only a popular observatory but a great jumping point for paragliders. The town within this narrow belt is Akaogi (赤尾木), known for **Heart Rock** (ハートロック). This heart-shaped rock pool is popular with social media snappers. Is it the best looking thing on this stunning island? Of course not, but its shallows do show off the prettiest of Amami blues, and the **Tebiro Coast** (手広海岸) and beach itself is worth walking.

The west of Akaogi holds the excellent **Ōshima Tsumugi Village** (大島紬村; 1945 Akaogi; 0997 62 3100; w tumugi.co.jp; 09.00–17.00 daily; adult/child ¥500/200), dedicated to Amami Ōshima's tsumugi cloth (page 28). Ideal for kids and adults, here you can take a production tour and have a go at mud dyeing, weaving and dressing up (reservation required). You can even bring your own items to dye. It's not all about the tsumugi, though – there is a large, natural subtropical garden to get lost in, too.

The remaining quiet peninsulas to the north offer nice drives and a few beaches. Ashitoku (芦徳) holds **Kurasaki Beach** (倉崎海岸), a long calm coastline with crystal-clear waters ideal for snorkelling, and a freckling of great beachside cafés. In the Nagakumo mountains, the **Amami Nature Observation Forest** (奄美自然観察の森) has various walking paths, brilliant observatories and a centre with exhibitions and tours.

The north coast here is home to a cycad (sotetsu) grove (ソテツ群落) where you can see a rare forest of the poisonous palms. They take centuries to grow and hearken back to the Jurassic period, when they were so abundant the era has been called the Age of Cycads. Further along the coastal road is the **Kaganbana Tunnel** (かがんばなトンネル). At first glance, this ridiculously short 29m tunnel is hardly photogenic. But after its completion in 1998, locals noticed that in the days around the spring and autumn equinoxes, the tunnel perfectly lines up with the bright, burning orange sunset. If you happen to be around at the right time, set up your camera on the bay to its east – there will be a sign to guide you.

On the way to **Amami City** (奄美市), also known as Naze, go via the **Daikuma Viewpoint** (大熊展望広場) to see the town and bay cosseted by mountains. Another excellent view is in the southwest of the city, at the spiritual **Ogamiyama Park** (おがみ山公園).

The city itself is a rather sleepy town made of hotels, restaurants and nightlife – the best of which is on **Yanigawa Street** (屋仁川通り). During the day, pop into the **Amami City Amami Museum** (奄美市立奄美博物館; 517 Nazenagahamacho; 0997 54 1210; 09.00–17.00 daily), which has impressive displays on traditional Amami life, with English translations too. Traditional boats, houses, instruments and animal exhibits abound.

West Amami's west is mostly beaches and capes, with a few waterfalls and walks dotted around. **Ōhama Seaside Park** (大浜海浜公園) has been selected as one of the best beaches in Japan, and also hosts turtle spawning. As such, its straight length of bright sand can get crowded in the busy season but stick around once people disperse to watch an East China Sea sunset. There's a short trail and garden of great banyan trees, hibiscus and palms. It's also home to the **Amami Ocean Exhibition Hall** (奄美海洋展示館; 701-1 Naze Oaza Koshuku, Amami; 0997 55 6000; w ohama.marutani-amami.com; 09.30–18.00 daily; adult/child ¥500/100–300) – a small aquarium – and a water park. Parking, toilets and showers are available.

Miyakozaki (宮古崎) further along is a bamboo-covered cape with amazing panoramas of sea, cliffs and the rolling green of Amami's north coast. It's a perfect spot for watching sunset. The lookout point is a 20-minute walk from the parking area. Further south is the coral-rich snorkelling spot **Kuninao Beach** (国直海岸), and the beautiful row of fukugi trees that line the village road. The neighbouring **Amami Wildlife Conservation Centre** (奄美野生生物保護センター; 551 Ongachi; 0997 55 8620; 09.30–16.30 Tue–Sun) has a mammoth array of taxidermied Amami wildlife to go along with their exhibits. Across the river is **Boregura** (群倉): an open air museum on Road 79 where you can see a traditional Amami *takakura*, where harvested rice was stored.

It's rare anyone takes this west coastal road (it bypasses the main mangrove attraction), but if you're driving to Setouchi you can loop back west and visit two falls. **Karuigyo Falls** (カルイギョの滝) emerges from the forest and is visible from the road – there's nowhere to pull over, but there's not exactly traffic to contend with. **Materiya Falls** (マテリヤの滝) is in Amami Forestpolis Park (奄美フォレストポリス) along narrow, winding forest roads. Small but powerful, Materiya tumbles into a teal-green pool that then flows into the mangrove. The name comes from the local language, meaning 'basin where the sun shines'; a natural break in the tree canopy meant sunlight hit only the waterfall, which you can still see around noon. It was used as a Ryūkyū journey post station where travellers would heal their fatigue; today it's a perfect spot for picnicking, watching dragonflies and bathing in bird calls and the rush of water.

Central The real star of the island's centre and Amami Ōshima itself is the **Mangrove Primeval Forest** (マングローブ原生林), also called **Kuroshio-no-Mori Mangrove Park** (黒潮の森 マングローブパーク; 478 Ishihara, Sumiyocho; 0997 56 3355; w mangrovepark.com; 09.30–18.00 daily; adult/child ¥500/100–300). This pristine mangrove sits in the area of Sumiyochō, which is nearly 95% forest. It's the second largest mangrove in the archipelago after the one on Iriomote (page 321), and you can get an idea of its scale from lookout points that take in the vibrant mattress of green. At high tide, the mangroves fill with water and you can continue on SUP or canoe under the arches of its trees. At low tide, the mangrove comes alive with crabs and critters scuttling between the mangrove roots.

One of the oddest attractions on Amami is the oft-overlooked **Native Modama Forest** (モダマ自生地) off Road 58. It isn't easy to spot – until you start looking up. This forest is made from the world's largest bean: a giant pea pod that hangs from branches, reaching up to 1m in length. Called *modama* in Japanese (Latin: *Entada rheedii*), these trees are believed to have been brought here on the ocean from Africa. You can see the big beans from the road, but there's also a little forested clamber to a waterfall where you can see the swirling, twirled modama tree trunks.

Although you need a guide to enter the forest here, you can visit multiple falls just a short walk from the road. Route 85, connecting Uken to the east coast, houses **Arangachi Falls** (アランガチの滝), a 30m cascade that drops into a pool full of freshwater tanaga prawns and Japanese mitten crabs, often used in local cuisine. The falls come from **Mount Yuwan** (湯湾岳), the highest point of Amami Ōshima at 694.4m. You can drive the majority of the way to the peak, parking at a lot on a mountain road and walking the 15 minutes along a good path through the bird-thick forest for excellent views.

Further along Route 85, via a giant banyan, is **Akatsuchiyama Viewpoint** (赤土山展望台), one of the best central panoramas showing Ōshima's broad swathe of trees.

South The south is largely mountainous, with truly stunning views across the islands dotted around Ōshima's south sea. Its heart is Koniya, a little town with a mix of run-down and surprisingly chic charm.

On the eastern side, before hitting the town, is **Katoku** (嘉徳), a tiny little village with the **Katoku Museum** (嘉徳美術館; 422 Katoku), a small, remote art space in the local school grounds. It's unmanned and free to see the 30 or so artworks. Katoku's coast and black-sand beach is rough, making it popular with surfers. There's also the lovely **Yoshikawa Indigo Dyeing Workshop** (よしかわ工房; 0997 78 0017), run by a Japanese grandmother. You may want an English-speaking guide (page 119) but the experience is hands-on, not verbal.

Koniya (古仁屋) town has brilliant local produce shops, nice casual restaurants, and a smattering of cool spots. It's also home to the **Coral Bridge** (コーラル橋), a bit of a romantic meeting point for local teens. The bridge was shaped after the semicircular Mabe pearl farmed in the town and is good viewpoint. Koniya is also the port for the southern islands, and its terminal is the great **Setouchi Umi-no-eki** (瀬戸内海の駅), an information point, shop, restaurant and market.

To the town's east is **Manenzaki Observatory** (マネン崎展望台), a spot overlooking the ocean on the way to **Katetsu** (嘉鉄). This chilled village has **Katetsu Beach** (嘉鉄ビーチ) and the rather dubitably named **Heart-shape Lake Viewpoint** (ハートが見える風景), a place where you can look back at Katetsu's bay and squint very hard to see a heart in the water.

The very east of Setouchi is attached to Ōshima by a thin isthmus, the **Honohoshi Coast** (ホノホシ海岸), a meditative, scenic spot made up of smooth stones, winding walks and dramatic cliffs. It's prized for the rattling, drumming sound the rounded pebbles make as the waves wash over and pull back on them – a sound that's amplified in some of the area's low caves and tunnels. The unusual rock formations and landscapes are great to explore with kids, and there's also shore and boat fishing, where you can catch bonito, octopus and lobster. In October–

MYTHS AND FOLKTALES: AMORONAGU

The *amoronagu* of Amami Ōshima are a kind of *tenyō* – a spirit found in Japanese Buddhism similar to nymphs or angels. These 'celestial maidens' wear beautiful coloured kimonos, which are often said to be the source of their flight. Their name translates literally as 'girl who fell from heaven'.

As with all folktales, there are many variations and supposed sightings. Said to inhabit the Ashiken area, amoronagu generally bathe in pools and waterfalls, appearing as people come down mountain paths. In some versions, however, an amoronagu comes to earth to find a man, descending in a gentle rain. Upon finding one, she tries to seduce him with a smile and if he gives in to her temptation he dies and is taken back to heaven with her. Some amoronagu are said to offer a ladle of water – if you drink from it, you will perish.

December, the area is dotted with *isonogiku* daisies. Across the isthmus is an island with pretty beaches and outlooks – and a great sunset spot at **Yadori Beach** (ヤドリ浜) and campground.

There are two great viewpoints overlooking the entirety of Amami Ōshima's corrugated southern coast – you can take a long walk from Koniya or drive to both. **Kochiyama Observatory** (高知山展望台) comes first, after about 90 minutes' walk up 280m: a curlicue tower that shows off the superb forested fingers of Setouchi, reaching into the cyan sea, and the islands beyond. On clear days you can see as far as Tokunoshima, 46km away, and the pearl cultivation and bluefin tuna farms in the sea. In January, the park is painted pink with cherry trees – one of the earliest places to see sakura (page 5) in Japan – and is a stunning sunset spot.

Further along, **Yuidake Observatory** (油井岳展望台) has a broader, though not necessarily better, view of the same scattered islands. It's more accessible than the staired Kochiyama viewpoint, but both areas have habu snakes so take care. If walking, you can continue on the road away from Koniya and down the mountain towards the west, ambling your way back to town along the coast. It's not the most tantalising walk but you will pass the old and impressive **Tean Ammunition Bunker** (手安弾薬本庫跡) – a big underground storage hanger left over from the war, now filled with bats.

Wartime relics continue in the southwest with **Nishikomi Observatory** (西古見観測所跡), a pretty lookout that was dug into the headland by the Japanese army in 1945. It was used for surveillance and measuring the direction and distance of targets. The structure was revamped in 2004, when the extensive vegetation was removed, and you can now go in to the building. This area is also where you'll find the gorgeous, and often empty, **Yadon** (屋鈍海水浴場) and **Taenhama** (タエン浜) beaches.

KAKEROMAJIMA

If you're looking to keep a kaleidoscope of blue, green and sun-bright white beaches all to yourself, look no further than quaint Kakeromajima (加計呂麻島). Said to be one of the most beautiful of the Amami Islands, Kakeroma is only around 77km^2 but its long, circuitous coastline runs 147km, surrounded by coral reef. Its lush hills

KAKEROMA FESTIVALS

Kakeroma's festival calendar is packed with events. One of the biggest is Shodon-Shibaya, which takes place at the Ōchon Shrine (大屯神社) in lunar September. This festival began some 800 years ago and involves 11 different performances. According to legend, this festival began as part of a theatrical cultural exchange between Sukemori Taira – a member of the Heike clan who escaped to Amami and built his house in Shodon – and the islanders. It also incorporates influences from both Japanese (Yamato) and Ryūkyū cultures, since Shodon was on an ancient sea route between the two.

The Mushi Okuri takes place at the beginning of lunar April, with each village having its own unique celebration. The Arahobana noro ceremony in lunar June celebrates Kakeroma's first harvest, while Funme in lunar June celebrates the first millet.

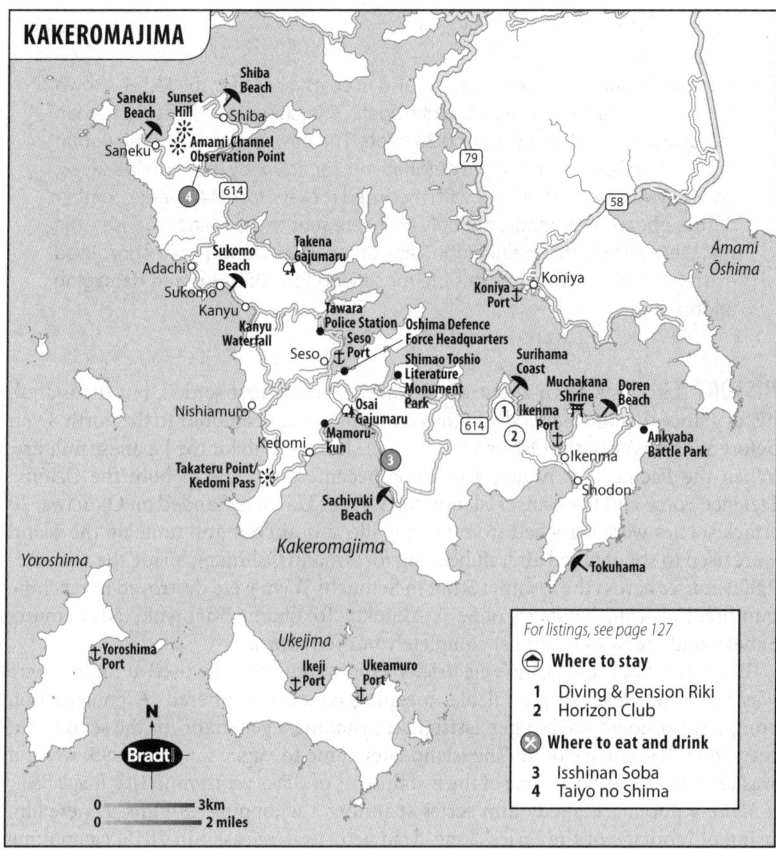

and sun-kissed inlets sit almost entirely within the Amami Guntō National Park. Running parallel to Amami Ōshima's southern coast, the island is as serrated and scraggly as it comes, with so many capes, promontories and peninsulas that it's easy to get lost looking at a map. Luckily, the whole place is circumnavigated by a single road.

There are 30 small villages on the island, with a combined population of under 1,600, but no single main town. Although it's a lot smaller and less developed than Amami Ōshima, its lack of tourists and conveniences is definitely in its favour. You'll get nature to yourself, a touch of true Amami island life and original archipelago scenery. Life here is not only beautiful but healthy too: Kakeromajima was rewarded for these qualities by being named among the 100 Japanese villages, as chosen by the Asahi Shimbun and Forest Culture Association, that are considered healthy, beautiful and nurture local life.

Kakeroma is known for its millet vinegar, naturally fermented using yeast and acetic acid bacteria found on the island – the only natural brewed vinegar in Japan. It's also recognised for its dive spots, which largely sit in the Ōshima Strait between itself and the main island. The most unexpected aspect to Kakeroma is the unfounded but seemingly unkillable rumour of its underground marijuana scene, with plants supposedly grown secretly on hillsides, undiscovered by the minimal police force.

SHINYŌ

During World War II, Kakeroma was also used as a base for the lesser-known *shinyō*, the Japanese navy's suicide boats. The shinyō were fast, one-man motorboats that reached around 30 knots. The bow was stuffed with around 300kg of explosives that would detonate on impact, or by the captain's say so, and they were also equipped with mounted rockets. In 1944, a large number of these boats were made, but only 400 were sent to the islands for use – the rest were left on the mainland in case of invasion. During their short-lived existence, shinyō were responsible for sinking four US ships and damaging another four.

HISTORY Little is known about when Kakeroma was first settled, but the island's history since then has generally followed that of its big neighbour to the north. Even before World War II, the Ōshima Strait was a strategic hub for the Japanese military. When the Pacific War began, Kakeroma became the home of both the Ōshima Defence Force and the Nansei Islands Navy. After US forces landed on Okinawa, 20 attack sorties were launched from here, while anti-aircraft gun units on the island were used to shoot allied aircraft heading for Amami Ōshima. During the war, over 2,000 houses across the Ōshima Strait in Setouchi Town were destroyed in machine gun fire. Kakeroma's villages of Sesō, Akitoku, Tokuhama, Sachiyuki, Nishiamuro, Saneku and Shiba were almost completely burned down.

Until the 1960s, the island's electricity supply could only be used at night. There was no national subsidy available, meaning education suffered. A construction company president offered her assistance, installing a generator for the school, but the school has since closed. The island later came to vague fame in 1995, when it was used as a location for one of the instalments of *Otoko wa Tsuraiyo* (*It's Tough Being a Man*), a popular comedy film series spanning a whopping 48 films. A new film using old footage of the series' long-dead actor was released in 2019, catapulting Kakeromajima back into the limelight for a second time.

GETTING THERE AND AWAY Kakeromajima is about 15–20 minutes from Amami Ōshima's Koniya Port. There are three options: a small sea taxi (☎ 0997 72 4760), the *Ferry Kakeroma* (☎ 0997 72 3771) or a private charter (☎ 0997 72 0377). Koniya Port isn't big, but the boats leave from different places on the marina – make sure to check in advance where to wait. Both tickets can be bought at the Umi-no-eki port building.

Ferry Kakeroma takes cars and alternates between the two ports on Kakeroma's northern coast – Ikenma in the east and Sesō in the west – so make sure to check which port you're coming into when planning car or bike rental. Sesō is closer to Saneku Beach and has a souvenir and produce shop, rentals and petrol stations. Ikenma is closer to Shodon and Ankyaba Battle Park.

GETTING AROUND Kakeroma is a long island with a fair number of hills. If you are willing to brave its ups and downs, you can rent **electric bikes** at each port – bus and rental car are much easier on the thighs.

You can hire a **car** on-island for about half the price it costs to bring one from Amami Ōshima on the ferry. However, since there are such a small number of rental cars and shops available, make sure to reserve early. There are four main places to rent cars: their fleet are generally small vehicles.

Kakeroma **buses** (w kakeroma-bus.com) are the definition of local: sometimes if you tell the driver exactly where you're going he will drop you right outside rather than waiting for the bus stop. Each of their routes operates about four times a day and covers a fair amount of the island: from Saneku, Shiba and Adachi in the northwest, through central Sesō, Nishiamuro and Kedomi, to Ikenma, Shodon and Tokuhama in the southeast.

Vehicle rental

Kakeroma Rent-a-Car 加計呂麻レンタカー; 122 Seso; 0997 75 0427

Kakeroman Service カケロマンサービス; 282 Shodon; 0909 729 3654; w kakeromanservice.mystrikingly.com

Shima Rent-a-Car Kakeroma 加計呂麻レンタカー; 191 Seso; 0808 038 1409; w shima-ren.com

TOURIST INFORMATION Kakeroma falls under Setouchi Town, so information is best sourced from the Umi-no-eki port hub in Koniya (page 123) before getting on the boat.

WHERE TO STAY *Map, page 125*

More often than not, Kakeroma is made into a day trip but overnighting is an excellent choice. If you do decide to stay, there are plenty of options to choose from.

✷ **Denpaku Lily-no-Ie** (whole house) 伝泊 リリーの家; 394 Shodon; 0997 63 1910; w denpaku.com. Once a film set, this stunning, spacious house was renovated & is now run by Denpaku. Up to 6 guests live like locals with sprawling tatami rooms & old-style bathtub, but also Wi-Fi & comprehensive kitchenette. **$$$$**

Diving & Pension Riki (4 rooms) ダイビング&ペンション Riki; 527-1 Shokazu; 0997 76 0069; w rikikakeroma.net. Cheerful & simple pension comes with a communal fridge, Wi-Fi, AC, TV & table tennis. All rooms have ocean views & there's a dive shop for rentals & tours. Best of all, it has HB for spectacular meals with locally caught seafood. **$$$**

Horizon Club (4 cottages) ホライゾンクラブ; 518 Shokazu; 0997 73 2024; w horizonclub-kakeroma.strikingly.com. Little wooden cottages built by owner, who also cooks homemade dishes with fresh seafood & shima vegetables. All cottages have sea views. HB available. **$$$**

✷ **Guesthouse Kawa** (whole house) ゲストハウス川; 60 Nishiamuro; 0997 75 0555; w guesthouse-kawa.com. Unbelievably cheap, utterly charming & run by a local monk. If the local restaurant is closed, the owner will cook & guests decide the fee. Accommodates up to 8, & there are some free kayak & life jacket rentals too. **$$**

WHERE TO EAT AND DRINK *Map, page 125*

Many places on Kakeroma are seasonal or weekend only, so make sure to check in advance rather than rely on advertised opening hours.

Isshinan Soba 一心庵蕎麦屋さん; 1200 Osai; 0907 982 8722; Apr–Oct 11.00–14.00 Sat–Sun. Only open on high season w/ends, this traditional soba restaurant serves its own noodle mix influenced by Kakeroma & Aso in Kyūshū. Make sure to try the duck zaru-soba. $$

Restaurant Mocca お食事処もっか; 8 Nishiamuro; 0702 829 9984; w mock.amebaownd.com; 11.00–14.00 daily, 18.30–23.00 Mon & Wed–Sat. Popular restaurant & mini gallery serving island dishes, set meals & sake. Try the eel bowl or island udon & check out art by local illustrator Chazu. $$

Taiyo no Shima 太陽の島カフェ; 197-1 Satsukawa; 0806 595 5143; 11.30–15.00 Fri–Tue. Handsome seaside café specialising in seasonal vegetable curry, exceptional cakes & herbal fruit teas. $$

67 Shokudo 67食堂; 306-3 Shodon; 0997 76 0667; 11.30–16.00 Wed–Mon. Simple udon &

chicken rice restaurant with a counter overlooking the beach. $

Kaname-chan かなめちゃん; 344 Shodon; 0997 76 0132; 11.30–13.30 & 18.00–late Sat–Sun. Great value w/end izakaya serves set meals of *yaki soba*, curry & *takoyaki* octopus balls & drinks in the evening. There's a pretty outside area where you can eat under the deigo tree overlooking the bay. $

Tiki Café ティキカフェ; 121 Sukumo; 0905 686 1058; noon–16.00 Sat–Sun. Cheery w/end café known for its shaved ice using seasonal flavours, including millet vinegar from Nishida factory – unusual but popular. If you try one thing, make it the *makkuro* (pitch black) cheesecake. $

SHOPPING Kakeroma isn't overrun with shops. By the port behind the Icchamun Market there's Misaki Shōten Shop (咲商店; 743-2 Seso; 0997 75 0002; 08.00–18.00 daily), but its opening hours aren't guaranteed. In Nishiamuro, there's the Shigeoka Shōten (茂岡売店; 5 Nishiamuro; 0997 75 0265; 09.00–20.00 Mon–Tue & Thu–Sat) and in Shodon there's Hayashi Shōten (林商店; 348 Shodon; 09.00–17.00 daily).

asivigocoro 25 Kanyū; 0909 570 2646; w asivigocoro.com. Arts & handicraft shop at Guesthouse Kamudy with a focus on jewellery. Workshop experiences available.

Icchamun Market いっちゃむん市場; 742-39 Seso; 0997 75 0290; 08.30–18.00 daily. By Sesō Port, this market & visitor base has plentiful fresh fruit, vegetables & food, as well as ice cream, brown sugar & souvenirs like traditional woven teru baskets & seashell & cycad nut accessories.

Kakeroma-no-mori Marsa かけろまの森marsa; 231 Kanyū; 0704 405 6203; w marsa-jam.com; 11.00–14.00 daily. Shop & café creating island cheesecakes, additive-free jams made with Kakeroma fruits & local honey products such as Kakeroma honey cider & honey ices. Café needs reservation.

SPORTS AND ACTIVITIES The island has some great activities, with a surprising number of tour companies offering boat rides, diving, island drives and more.

Cross Island Tours 512 Doren; 0902 013 5228; w crossisland-kakeroma.com. Eco-tours that cover nature, reiki, trekking or marine sports.

Diving & Pension Riki ダイビング&ペンションRiki; Page 127. Diving & whale experiences on both Amami Ōshima & Kakeroma.

Gori Marine ゴリマリン; 587-1 Shokazu; 0806 966 6313; w gorimarine.jp. Whale watching & swimming, diving, fishing, banana boats, SUP, kayaks, wakeboarding & snorkelling.

Grand Blue Kakeroma グランブルーカケロマ; 518 Shokazu; 0806 448 2024; w grandbluekakeroma.mystrikingly.com. Yacht sailing & snorkelling/SUP tours from a catamaran in the Ōshima Strait take you to beaches only accessible by boat.

Kakeroma Island Resort Hare Hare カケロマアイランドリトリートハレハレ; 0505 329 8955; w halehare.com. SUP, snorkelling, yoga, photography sessions & boat cruises.

OTHER PRACTICALITIES There are post offices with ATMs in Nishiamuro and Shodon (as well as in remoter Saneku and Oshikaku). There's a clinic at Sesō, Kakeroma Tokushukai Clinic (加計呂麻徳洲会診療所; 747-1 Seso; 0997 75 0116; 09.00–17.00 Mon–Sat), but it's primarily a care centre for the elderly – for medical problems you're better off going back to Koniya. There are two police stations.

Nishiamuro Post Office 西阿室郵便局; 2-1 Nishiamuro; 0997 75 0056; 09.00–16.00 Mon–Fri, ATM: 08.45–18.00 Mon–Fri, 09.00–12.30 Sat

Seikan Police Station 瀬戸内警察署生間駐在所; 79 Ikenma; 0997 76 0143

Shodon Post Office 諸鈍郵便局; 345-6 Shodon; 0997 76 0006; 09.00–16.00 Mon–Fri, ATM: 08.45–18.00 Mon–Fri, 09.00–12.30 Sat

Tawara Police Station 瀬戸内警察署俵駐
在所; 141 Tawara; 0997 75 0772

WHAT TO SEE AND DO The first port of call after the actual Sesō Port is the small **Ōshima Defence Force Headquarters** (大島防備隊本部跡). Instead of turning right out of the town, take the little left road along the bay where you'll likely see construction-like gravel work. Walk along the water and you'll come to the old headquarters of the wartime navy, which includes a concrete trench, cenotaph and an ammunitions store that you can still half enter – just be careful of habu.

Continuing the island's loop road brings you to the little peninsula of Oshitaku, where you can find the **Shimao Toshio Literature Monument Park** (島尾敏雄文学碑公園). Shimao was both a writer and wartime naval commander, stationed at Kakeroma. He was due to be a Shintō kamikaze, but instead met his wife and became an author. Shimao is famed for his post-war literature, which covers themes of women's mental illness – his wife was institutionalised and he chose to live with her in the institution. While the park has limited interest for those who haven't read his work, you can walk along the bay (which is often filled with aasa seaweed) to see shinyō boat hangars from the **18th Shinyō Squad Base Ruins** (第18震洋隊基地跡), one of which has a restored shinyō boat (page 126).

Surihama Coast (スリ浜海岸) was picturesque enough to be used in the Japanese film *Otoko wa Tsurai yo*. It's a quiet, sweet stretch of sand on the north coast that offers a lot of marine activities like swimming, snorkelling, windsurfing, diving, jet skiing and fishing. Surihama is known for its marine life, including turtles that swim just offshore, and there are shower/toilet facilities.

Past Ikenma Port is **Muchakana Shrine** (むちゃ加那神社), named for a beautiful girl who was supposedly lured to her death by a group of jealous island women. Her mother, who was also legendary for her beauty, threw herself into the ocean in her grief. Miserable as the shrine's history is, it has a fine prospect across the strait. After the shrine is **Doren Beach** (渡連ビーチ), a calm white-sand space with impossibly blue shallow seas and useful facilities. It's popular for swimmers, campers and beach volleyball players.

The eastern end of Kakeroma is host to the extensive **Ankyaba Battle Park** (安脚場戦跡公園), one of the best remaining war sites on the island. Ankyaba was used to monitor and defend Japan's naval fleets, as well as to keep gunpowder and munitions. It's now a park where you can wander the concrete ammunition hangar, guard station, small reservoirs and depot – and admire the stunning views.

Shodon (諸鈍) is one of the island's larger communities, known for its 800-year-old Shodon-Shibaya festival. The village itself has a row of **deigo trees** (諸鈍デイゴ並木) along Shodon's beach, **Nagahama** (諸鈍長浜), one of which is thought to be over 300 years old. These trees spring into stunning crimson flowers in May, but don't dawdle as they can bloom for just one week. Shodon is also home to the **Kakeroma Exhibition Exchange Centre** (加計呂麻島展示・体験交流館; 316 Shodon; 0997 76 0676; 09.00–17.00 daily; adult/child ¥300/100–200), which has exhibits about the history and performing arts of Kakeroma. Unfortunately the information is in Japanese only, but the exhibits are mostly photos, crafts and ritual costumes. There is a small café and souvenir shop and a place to rent snorkels and fins, too. At Shodon's southernmost tip is **Tokuhama** (徳浜), a wide beach with shallow reefs. Opening out on to the Pacific, this gentle lagoon is a spot for sea turtle laying and star sand (page 312). There are toilets, showers and excellent stargazing.

Kakeroma's southern coast is largely given over to peninsulas thick with adan and sotetsu, small quiet communities and beaches. **Sachiyuki Beach** (佐知克海岸)

has shallow vibrant waters ideal for swimming and sits in front of the Nishida brown sugar and millet vinegar factory. Here you can buy freshly made kokutō and even see it made once every three days in the December–April season.

Curving around Ikomo Bay brings you to **Osai** (於斉) – which quickly connects back to northern Sesō – where you can find the **Osai Gajumaru** (於斉のガジュマル). This massive banyan tree draws lots of people with its gnarled branches and walking, splaying roots, where you can swing on a Tarzan rope overlooking the beach. Behind it is a pretty shrine that's worth popping into. A short hop along is an oddity: Ikomo's **Mamoru-kun** (伊子茂まもる君). There are few traffic or street lights on Kakeroma, so this fake policeman was erected to stop cars crashing into the sea barrier. Despite being pretty alarming when walking back late from the izakaya, he's a much beloved local character and one of the many Mamoru-kun police officers around the archipelago.

Drive along the narrow road to **Takateru Point**, also known as the **Kedomi Pass** (タカテルポイント・花富峠), a lookout on the winding way between Nishiamuro and Kedomi. There's a gorgeous view over the green coves and gradating blue seas, and it's excellent for sunsets too. The little village of **Nishiamuro** (西阿室) has its own **giant banyan** (ガジュマルの巨木) but has a much more important and excellent claim to fame. It is home to the **Eel River** (うなぎの川), a little stream that runs through the village which is filled with giant eels. Not only are these eels huge, but they've been recorded doing remarkable things. In the drier months, these eels up and leave the stream and walk – yes, walk – into the mountains. So baffling was this behaviour that Japanese TV station NHK came to film the process. You can feed this eels by buying eel snacks from the nearby shop. In the west of the village, there's a little lookout point at a small shrine, which overlooks the great bay.

Heading north to **Kanyū village** (嘉入), you'll find a road connecting back to the opposite coast. Here you can see the sacred **Kanyū Waterfall** (嘉入の滝), the only one on the island. Known locally as Utirimizunu, it's just 15m high but it has been a sanctuary for noro priestesses since ancient times, who bathed in its supposed cleansing waters.

Sukomo (須子茂) is a traditional village with preserved religious buildings. Rather than large shrines or temples, these smaller Amami Islands tend to have two places of worship: *ashage* and *toneya*. Ashage are where you pray for a good harvest, toneya are for rituals. They're usually small covered platforms, and you'll often find sacred *ibiganashi* rocks nearby. Sukomo has one of the more distinct ibiganashi – a large stone that stands on a mound next to its ashage – as well as a toneya and a narrow pathway called 'Gods Road'. From its quiet and calm **Sukomo Beach** (須子茂海岸) you can swim and sea kayak, and spot outlying islands. **Adachi** (阿多地), another sleepy traditional village with old ashage, has a **giant deigo tree** (巨大デイゴ) which blooms red around May–June. It is said this deigo was planted as a landmark for the trading port with the Ryūkyū Kingdom, sometime between 1266 and 1609, before Amami was invaded by the Satsuma domain. Beside it are the twin 'husband and wife' trees, the **Fūfu Deigo** (夫婦デイゴ).

Saneku (実久) on the island's north coast is a parochial spot with a beach so beautiful it also made it on to NHK's TV drama *Shima no Sensei*. It's easy to see why: **Saneku Beach** (実久ビーチ) is one of the most idyllic beaches on Kakeroma, the stunning sea turning aqua to ultramarine as it leaves the coast. The colour is so special that it is known locally as 'Saneku blue'. The beach allows for barbecues, has amazing stargazing, and there's a small shop, Hama no Oten (はまのお店; 88 Saneku; 0801 767 0075; lunch Wed–Mon), with rentals, snacks and small meals. Off the beach is the Blue Cave, a popular snorkelling site.

Saneku has traditional stone walls – the sticks you may see placed against them are there to repel habu snakes. The village also houses the **Saneku Sanjiro Shrine** (実久三次郎神社), a red-and-cream shrine to the cousin of the first Kamakura shōgun. It hosts an annual festival with sumo wrestling, songs and dance, the blowing of conch shells and purification with salt.

On the way across the north coast, the road brings you past the **Amami Channel Observation Point** (大島海峡展望所) and **Sunset Hill** (夕日の丘), which overlook the East China Sea and the Ōshima Strait, as well as Saneku Beach. It's beautiful in the daytime, but it made its name as the best place on the island for watching spectacular Kakeroma sunsets. **Shiba village** (芝) has yet another gorgeous little beach, **Shiba Beach** (芝海岸), and **traditional coral walls** (サンゴの石垣).

On the road back to Sesō, stop at the **Takena Gajumaru** (武名のガジュマル), a stunning, huge banyan tree that stretches out in the forest alongside a pleasant path. There's also a local ashage building and stream along the way – just make sure not to wander off the beaten track as there are habu.

UKEJIMA AND YOROSHIMA

Hidden from Amami Ōshima's gaze by Kakeroma, Uke (請島) and Yoro (与路島) are little-populated, quiet outposts that make for escapist day trips, ideal for anglers and hikers. However, the beauty comes with a bite: both islands are known for their high-density populations of habu. Anyone hiking the trails must take serious precautions and in some cases need permission and guides.

Ukejima is the first and largest of the two at 13.34km^2, and its rapidly declining population of 77 is reliant on tourism and the fishing industry. The island's dense, untouched nature is home to protected plants and animals like the *ukeyuri* lily, designated as a natural monument, and the *rubane* stag beetle. Its highest point, **Miyochondake** (ミヨチョン岳), reaches 398m, offering amazing views over Uke and the neighbouring islands. The 30-minute hike from the trail entrance (2hrs from Ikeji) is a little hazardous, with occasional thick fog and narrow rocky paths, and you are required by the town to fill out a form and take a local volunteer guide with you. It's recommended you ask your accommodation on Amami Ōshima, Kakeroma or Uke to do this form for you, two weeks in advance.

If you don't fancy the hassle and habu of Miyochon, there are two settlements on Ukejima's north coast – Ukeamuro and Ikeji – connected by a single road where you'll find a small shrine and heliport. The villages and roads are grown over with deigo trees, hibiscus, cycads and flowers. Off land, the healthy seas are filled with coral reefs, making for good snorkelling. The **Kunma Coast** (クンマ海岸) on the east side of Ikeji is a near-private swathe of butter-yellow sands and island-dotted seas with calm waves ideal for swimming.

Yoroshima, or Yorojima, is the smallest inhabited island of the Amami group, with around 70 people in its 9.35km^2. It's known for its old traditional paths lined with coral walls: an insight into how Amami Ōshima used to look. Yoro's highest point is Okachiyama, at 297m, and it has just a single settlement on its east coast; the rest is wilderness, beach and extensive fishing grounds. The latter includes *izari* – a traditional type of nighttime clam hunting, reliant on the receding tides. In summer, Yoro sees the rare and intricate *sagaribana* flowers, which bloom for a single night.

Small roads crisscross the island beyond the settlement to the other coasts, which are made up entirely of beaches. The best of these are **Kobama** (コバマ), **Adetsu** (アデツ) and **Sakiyakinya** (サキアキニャ) in the north, **Koashini** (コアシニ) and **Takahara Beach** (高原海岸) in the west and the **Onawa Coast** (大縄海岸) in the south. These beaches are as private as you can get in the archipelago. North of the village on an outcrop facing Ukejima are the **Yoroshima Defence Base Ruins** (与路島砲台跡), left over from the war. Take care when reaching any of these remote areas; not only are there prolific habu but wild boar too. It's recommended you let people know before you go exploring.

Between Yoro and Uke is **Hamiya** (ハミヤ島), or Hanmya, Island (ハンミャ島), an uninhabited island of sand dunes. Its name means 'interval' in the local dialect, in recognition of how it sits between its neighbours. You can charter a boat to take you to Hamiya, with permission from Yoroshima's mayor (0908 761 7128; e yoroshima.kanko@gmail.com). Make sure to protect the sand dunes: don't slide down them. For years the sand remained untouched and in place, but recently due to increased visitors it has begun to slip and decrease.

PRACTICALITIES Both islands are accessed by the Setonami boat from Koniya Port. There's a single round trip per day and an extra one-way Mondays and Fridays. The journey takes 45 minutes to Ukeamuro, another 10 minutes to Ikeji, and then a further 25 minutes to Yoro. Tickets are bought at the waiting room of Umi-no-eki (26-14 Ominato; 099 77 2377). You can also charter a sea taxi (pages 115 and 126) from Koniya or Kakeroma's Ikomo Port, but they unsurprisingly cost much more. Getting around either island is done on foot.

With so little to do except relax, Uke works best as a day trip from Amami. If you do decide to stay, however, Minshuku Minami (民宿みなみ; 678 Ikeji; 0997 76 1233) is a great bet. Uke has a single reliable shop, Ukeamuro Shōten (請阿室商店; 523 Ukeamuro; 0997 76 1055), and a post office with ATM (池地郵便局; 551-1 Ikeji; 0997 76 1148; 09.00–16.00 Mon–Fri, ATM: 08.45–18.00 Mon–Fri, 09.00–12.30 Sat). It's best, however, to bring supplies and money with you.

Surprisingly, Yoro has a tourism association with an excellent website, though most of it is Japanese only (w yorojima.jp). On the island, there are no shops or vending machines. There is, however, a post office (与路郵便局; 370 Yoro; 0997 76 1350; 09.00–16.00 Mon–Fri, ATM: 08.45–18.00 Mon–Fri, 09.00–12.30 Sat). If you want to stay on Yoro try Minshuku Mandikashavera (民宿マンディカシャヴェラ; 427-2 Yoro; 0997 76 1372).

KIKAIJIMA

Kikai (喜界島) is a sort of rough-and-tumble, overlooked sibling of Amami Ōshima, best described in its own island word *yonyōri* – 'slow and relaxing'. It's not the place to come for five-star refinement, but you'll find laid-back people, secluded beaches and local watering holes full of kokutō shōchū and Kikai's main currency: food.

The easternmost Amami island, flung some 23.5km off the east coast of Amami Ōshima, has gone by many names: Kikaigashima, Kyaa in the Kikai language, and Kikiya in northern Ryūkyūan. During the Satsuma reign, it had a far more sinister name, Satokibijigoku – 'sugarcane hell'.

Today, Kikai adds 'the island of corals' to its nicknames. The 48km-round island is the result of an elevating coral reef that rose from the teal seas some 100,000 years ago and hasn't stopped since – it rises 2mm a year, making it the second-fastest coral uplift on the planet. The island even has its own reef institute, where visitors can learn about this ecosystem.

Largely agricultural and flat, reaching only 214m at its highest point, Kikai doesn't have the animal life of Amami. However, it is a paradise for butterflies.

In May–June and more so in October–November, the island comes alive with migrating butterflies that have travelled up to 2,000km, bringing researchers from across Japan to study them. Lepidopterists are unusually common in Japan – it's a hobby that really took off in the 1980s – and you may spot them wandering around with old-fashioned nets looking like they've stepped straight out of a Pokémon game. Even if you're not a butterfly lover, it's wonderful to spot these beautiful insects, like the blue-brown chestnut tiger butterfly or *asagimadara*, known for its long-distance migration. The *oogomadara* is also found on Kikai. It's

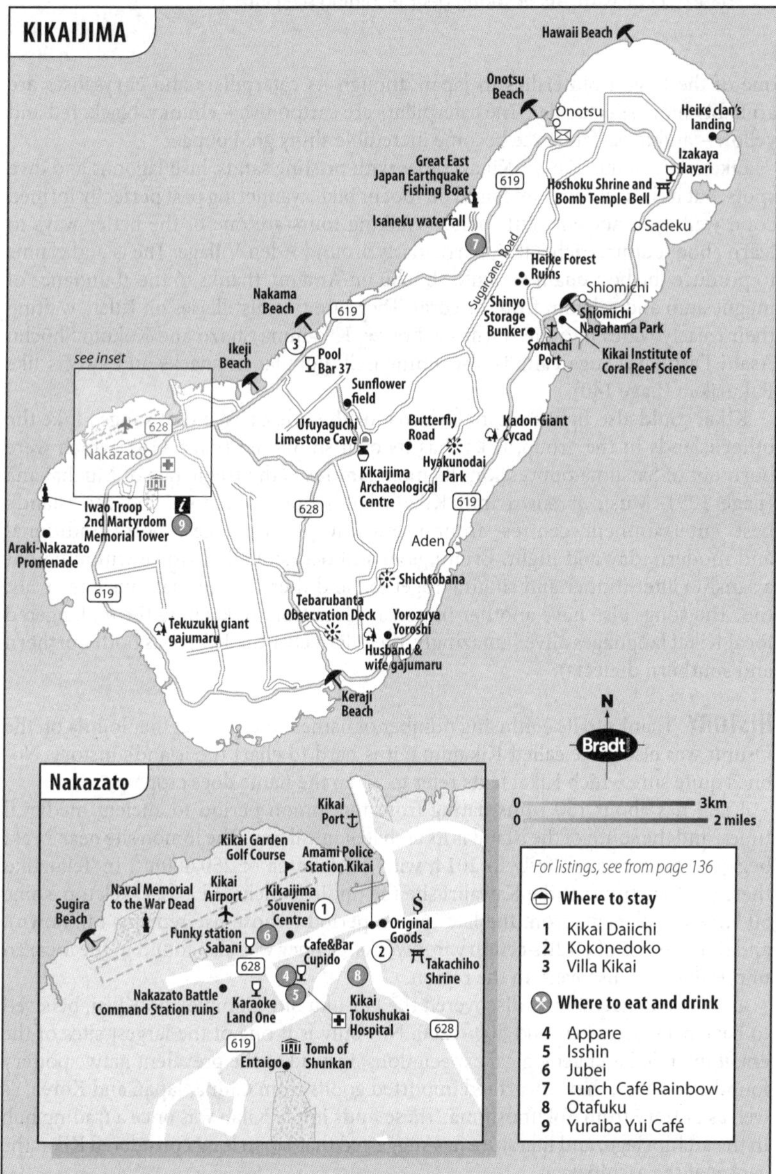

KIKAI FESTIVALS

Kikaijima's August dance for a good harvest consists of a singer, drummer, flautists and dancers. Women are the principal dancers, though everyone gets involved. The dance is done in a circle, often around a *dohyō* (a raised sumo ring made from earth), and each village has its own variation. Kikai also has an unusual connection to Okinawa in Eisaa: the Okinawan dance was brought back to Kikai and proliferated among locals. Now there is a big Eisaa dance scene with lots of young people joining the club.

one of the largest butterflies in Japan, though its caterpillars and chrysalises are arguably more spectacular. The caterpillars are cartoonish – chunky, black, red and yellow – and these fat larvae become incredible shiny gold pupae.

Like many of the islands, Kikai comes with pristine sands, lush lagoons and dive spots, but its best charms are found on foot or bike, wandering past perfectly formed coral walls and ancient settlements. Walking tours are one of the better ways to learn about culture-rich Kikai, particularly around Aden Village. The island claims to produce the best quality kokutō shōchū on Amami, thanks to the abundance of magnesium and calcium from its coral. There are two distilleries on Kikai, wafting their treacly wares into the warm sea breeze: Kikaijima Shuzo and Kokutō Shōchū Asahi Distillery. Sugarcane is also immensely popular in snacks and sweets like Fukurikan (page 140).

Kikai could also fight Amami Ōshima for the title of 'island of songs'. Like the other islands in the group, Kikai has its own shima uta (page 118), which were born out of Satsuma oppression. Its most famous is the tragic tale of Muchakana (page 129). Music is sown into Kikai's landscape even now, and the island's best entertainment centres around musical performances, both traditional and modern, day and night. Evenings in still occasionally involve whipping out a sanshin after dinner and singing together, and there are annual music festivals, too. The songs also have another important function, of keeping the endangered local Kikai languages alive (amazingly, the relatively little Kikai has both northern and southern dialects).

HISTORY Thanks to its confusing number of names, and the fact that Iōjima on the Ōsumi was also once called Kikaijima, it is hard to chart the island's history. No-one's quite sure which Kikai texts refer to when the name does crop up.

Kikai has about 150 ruins dating from the Jōmon period to ancient medieval times, and the south of the island is its archaeological hub. The Jōmon site near Araki began to be excavated fully in 2014, with a total area of 250,000m^2. In Tekuzuku there are four ruins: at the Kawajiri site the findings included a foal skeleton, some 50 large circular pits from the late Jōmon period (whose use remains unknown), and the remains of a 12th-century ironworks. Amber was also found in the area: an unprecedented discovery in the region.

In 2006, archaeologists discovered the Gusuku Site Complex on Kikai, believed to have been active around 800–1200. Not only is it one of the largest sites of the era, it upended archaeological expectations; instead of the prevalent native pottery found elsewhere, they unearthed imported goods from China, Japan and Korea, as well as pottery from Tokunoshima. These finds imply Kikai was once a trading hub in the archipelago, and literature has suggested that Japan long considered Kikai the centre of the archipelago.

The rest of the island's early history can only be guessed at through documents. An 11th-century text states that Kikaijima was ordered by Dazaifu – now a major religious site outside Fukuoka but then the administrative centre of Kyūshū – to arrest the Nanban, a name for the Amami islanders, in 998. Nothing more is said about the order, or indeed what a small population might do against mighty Amami Ōshima. However, historians have taken this to mean that the island was under some Kyūshū influence at the time – if, of course, it's the correct Kikai.

The island featured in the 1306 will of a member of the Hōjō clan, which had ties to the shōgunate and supposedly the Heike family too. Elsewhere, a Korean man who ended up on the islands in the 1450s states that Kikai was beset by regular Ryūkyū invasions. By the 1460s, Kikai was the only remaining Amami island to not pledge loyalty to the Ryūkyū Kingdom. Forces of 2,000 soldiers and 50 warships were sent from Okinawa, led by King Shō Toku himself, to invade.

There is little evidence as to why he wanted Kikai. Though Ryūkyū traders regularly stopped at the island, Kikai had a small population, minimal value and provided neither useful harbours nor resources. Nonetheless, after several days of battle the king conquered it, beheaded the island chief and placed an officer in charge, returning to Shuri triumphant at having expanded the kingdom's reach.

In 1609, Kikai, along with the rest of the Amami, fell to Satsuma, who imposed sugar taxes. In 1862, a member of the imperial household, Murata Shinpachi, was exiled to Kikai on the order of the Shimazu clan. It's said that Murata brought a variety of advances to the island, from toilets to literacy.

During World War II, Kikai's airport was used as a naval air base, serving the kamikaze Special Attack Forces. More than 50 bunkers were built on the island to protect from bombs – after American forces landed on Okinawa, Kikai's airport was bombed relentlessly, as it was seen as one of the most important bases for Japanese forces. Almost 2,000 of Kikai's near 4,000 houses were destroyed in military air raids.

GETTING THERE AND AWAY As Kikai has an airport, located on the west coast, it's accessible from more than just Amami Ōshima. It takes just over an hour from Kagoshima Airport to Kikai, and there's also a transfer flight via Kagoshima from Osaka's Itami Airport. There are two return flights a day from Kagoshima to Kikai. Flying to Kikai from Amami Airport takes about 15 minutes, and there are three return flights a day. All flights are operated by JAL's Air Commuter group (w jal.co.jp/jp/en).

Kikai is accessed by two ferries: *Ferry Amami* from Naze Port on Amami Ōshima and *Ferry Kikai* from Kagoshima, both operated by A-Line (w aline-ferry.com). For the former, services there and back operate Tuesday–Saturday, taking 2½ hours, with departure times depending on the day of the week. Ferries from Kagoshima take 11 hours so unless you're travelling overnight it can be a real time hog. *Ferry Kikai* departs Kagoshima every weekday, stopping at Kikai on the way to either Okinoerabujima or Tokunoshima. Ferries back to Kagoshima leave every day except Sunday and Monday.

Although ferries are much cheaper than flights, they are more affected by bad weather and will often be cancelled earlier and remain out of action for longer. Port changes can also occur in sudden bad weather; if this happens, you'll be dropped at Sōmachi Port in the northwest. Frustratingly, you won't find this out until the ferry tries to dock and has to announce the change. Contact your accommodation and keep an eye on your map location – the ferries have patchy Wi-Fi, best found near the information desk.

GETTING AROUND Kikai is a long island stretching from southeast to northwest, made up of over 30 settlements. The island is relatively flat; should you want to **cycle** around you could, but with a 48km circumference it's worth considering a vehicle. Getting around some of the smaller villages is best with a bike or **moped**, as lanes can be narrow.

The main town of Nakazato is beside the airport and primary port in Kikai's southwest. Nakazato has the largest collection of restaurants and accommodations on Kikai, as well as **taxis**, though they are limited.

There is a Kikai **bus** (62-1 Wan; ☎ 0997 65 0061) with three lines: the north clockwise route, the south counterclockwise route, and the central route that crosses the island. Buses meet up with plane departures and arrivals too. They run about every hour and are wonderfully cheap; there's also a one-day ticket for ¥800 that means you can hop on and off.

Taxis

Hinode Taxis 日の出タクシー; 187-1 Wan; ☎ 0120 93 0208

Kikaijima Sightseeing Charter Bus 喜界島観光貸切バス; 2966-12 Akaren; ☎ 0997 65 1811. Charter for larger sightseeing groups.

Vehicle rental

Airport Shop Rental Bikes 空港売店レンタバイク・レンタサイクル; 201-9 Nakazato; ☎ 0997 65 4388. Rental motorbikes & bicycles from the airport.

Fukami Rent-a-Car 深水レンタカー; 197-14 Nakazato; ☎ 0997 65 1070; w fukamizu-m.net

Kikai Airport Rental 喜界空港前レンタカー; 200 Nakazato; ☎ 0997 65 4355; w kikai-rental.net. Offers port transfers.

Kikai Daiichi Rent-a-Car 喜界第一レンタカー; 142-4 Kikai; ☎ 0997 65 2111; e htl@kikai1.com. Run by Kikai Daiichi Hotel; has car & cycle rental.

Kikai Rent-a-Car 喜界レンタカー; 197-14 Nakazato; ☎ 0997 65 3618 (airport office), 0997 65 1551 (headquarters); w kikai-rentacar.com. 1min walk from the airport & has online booking.

TOURIST INFORMATION Kikai has the Kikaijima Tourist Information Centre (喜界島観光物産協会; 1298 Wan; ☎ 0997 65 1202; w kikaijimanavi.com) that's strangely far out of the main town – a 30-minute walk from the harbour. It's a good centre though, with a shop and café. Kikai Joyful Travel Centre (喜界ジョイフル旅行センター; 2967 Akaren; ☎ 0997 65 3422) handles flights, ferries and hotel bookings and can recommend tours on the island. Locals on Kikai, known as Shimachu, are some of the friendliest in the archipelago: they make any island visit.

WHERE TO STAY *Map, page 133*

Kikai is slim on the ground when it comes to hotels. The majority are near the port, largely uninspiring business establishments, but there's a villa hotel to the north that's well worth leaving town for.

✷ **Villa Kikai** (5 rooms, 1 villa) 1036 Nakama; ☎ 0808 808 1573; w villa-kikai.com. Oceanfront villas immaculately laid out, with excellent living & kitchen areas, comfy beds, laundry, picture windows & more. 2 maisonette suites, 1 large family villa & 3 dbl/twin rooms available. Modern, gorgeous place & friendly, helpful owner. **$$$$–$$$$$**

Kikai Daiichi Hotel (27 rooms) 喜界第一ホテル; 142-4 Wan; ☎ 0997 65 2111; w kikai1.com. A little outdated but clean & welcoming. Daiichi has rental cars/bicycles, Japanese restaurant & the only large public bath/sauna on Kikai. B/fast available. **$$$**

Kokonedoko (2 dorms) ココネドコ喜界島; 62-1 Wan; ☎ 0997 58 8885; w coconedoco.com. Hostel with compact & female-only dorms. Friendly, cheap & excellent for getting into the Kikai community spirit. Free lockers, shared bathrooms & large kitchen/eating space; HB option. **$**

WHERE TO EAT AND DRINK *Map, page 133*

It's no surprise that an island that likes to eat has a great number of restaurants in which to do so. There are cafés and restaurants aplenty, but make sure to also check out izakaya and bars like Funky Station SABANI and Izakaya Hayari (page 138), which offer cheap eats and excellent local entertainment.

Isshin 一心; 325 Wan; 0997 65 0091; 18.30–22.00 Tue–Sat. Cosy yakitori spot with Kagoshima chicken, Kikai fish & veggies over charcoals, served alongside Kagoshima sake. Take the daily recommendation. $$$

✷ **Jubei** 喰い処十兵衛; 445-7 Wan; 0997 65 3520; 11.30–14.00 & 18.00–23.00 Wed–Mon. This restaurant that becomes an izakaya is the best for local *shima gozen* cuisine. Try aosa tempura, yagi sashimi, *yakōgai* giant conch & *karajuuri*. Also has an excellent shōchū selection. Private tatami rooms available. $$$

Appare 和食厨房 天晴; 302-5 Wan; 0997 65 3188; 17.00–23.00 Tue–Sun. Popular, often crowded, izakaya with Osaka-trained owner. Specifically serves island ingredients on an à la carte menu with goat & shōchū. $$

Lunch Café Rainbow ランチカフェ 虹; 1467 Isaneku; 0997 66 1104; 07.00–16.00 Wed–Fri & Sun–Mon, 07.00–10.00 Sat. Adorable café in lovely rural setting with cheap, hearty set meals & supremely friendly staff. $$

Yuraiba Yui Café ゆいカフェ; 1298 Wan; 0997 65 0958; w kikaijima-yui.com/cafe.php. Tourist association farm shop & café, selling & using local ingredients in delicious pastas, cakes & salads. Try the *mikan* cream pasta and *soramame* tea, made with beans. $$

Otafuku おたふく; 193 Wan; 0997 65 0330; noon–14.00 & 18.00–20.00 daily. Hearty Hiroshima-style *okonomiyaki* (a delicious savoury pancake) in a cool little restaurant. Owner also has own brand of spicy seasoning, featured in his spicy soba & udon. $

KIKAI'S LOCAL FOODS

The roughly 6,400 Kikai islanders are pretty mad about their food, namely yakitori and yagi (goat). Goat is easy to farm and raise, is healthy and has little smell. The meat is eaten in *yagijiru* soup, as chilled sashimi with pungent garlic sauce, as *sukiyaki*, and *karajuuri*: a Chinese-origin dish of goat liver marinated in shōchū and slowly cooked in its own blood. Karajuuri doesn't exactly look or sound appetising, but if you can get over the ingredients and aesthetic it's well worth a try. Goat is particularly popular in izakaya, where you can sample most of the yagi menu.

Other popular dishes include tempura made with *sakunaa* (an island plant that looks like a giant parsley) and *yakougai*, the largest shellfish on Kikai. *Icchaashii* (a dish named after the Kikai for 'stir fry') is a mix of shima-dōfu, seasonal vegetables and pork stir-fried together. *Shimun* is Kikai's most traditional food, a celebratory stew that changes depending on the season and festival. One of the most surprising local products is sesame seeds: Kikai produces 60% of Japan's sesame seeds. It has cultivated sesame for over a century; the seeds are sold as is, but also used to make dressings, a kind of sugar and sesame oil. From summer to autumn, the roads are filled with sun-dried sesame seeds -- a quite literal 'sesame street'. They're traditionally dried in the sun at Araki Beach.

Aside from kokutō shōchū, Kikai is famous for a rather surprising drink: its own version of Coca-Cola. *Tobatoba* cola is made from mikan oranges by a local couple and bogglingly tastes like the real deal, but somehow healthy and better. Order it at Funky Station Sabani (page 138) and see for yourself.

ENTERTAINMENT AND NIGHTLIFE

Cupido 302-3 Wan; 0905 286 1524; 18.00–midnight Mon–Sat. Sleek female-owned café-bar serving fried chicken *kara-age*, pizza, original cocktails & sweets. Attracts a good number of women, so excellent for solo female travellers.

✷ **Funky Station Sabani** 500-8 Wan; 0997 65 0930; 18.00–02.00 Tue–Sun. The major, unmissable player on Kikai's nightlife scene, this is where locals & visitors come to eat, drink, perform & be merry. Food is cheap (the parrotfish burger is brill), owner Sakai-san is lovely & the drink is plentiful. Watch locals join shima uta, Eisaa dancing, classic & modern performances – and have a go too.

Izakaya Hayari 居酒屋はやり; 1615-1 Shitooke; 0997 66 0006; 17.30–23.00 Fri–Wed. Found in the northeast, this tiny, basic izakaya doesn't lack for size in portions, arguably serving up the best yagi in Kikai. Try traditional meals of yagijiru or *tonsoku* (pig's foot).

Karaoke Land One カラオケランド ワン; 445-7 Wan; 0997 65 0919; 12.00–02:00 Wed–Mon. Kikai's only karaoke box – small, but does exactly what you need.

Pool Bar 37 323 Nakama; 0805 200 0037; 20.00–midnight Tue–Sun. As cool as hangouts get: driftwood, shoji screens, dim lights & inviting buttoned leather sofas. Beers, cocktails, spirits, pool & handmade food.

SHOPPING There are a healthy number of supermarkets and shōten shops in the main town, the biggest of which is Shopping Centre Fukuri (ショッピングセンターふくり; 78 Nakazato; 0997 65 1234; 07.00–23.00 daily) by the airport if you need to stock up. There's also a farmers' market at the tourist office (page 136) selling food products and more.

Kikaijima Souvenir Centre 喜界島おみやげセンター; 446-13 Wan; 0997 65 3211; 08.30–22.00 daily. Best souvenir selection on Kikai where you can also ship souvenirs nationally.

Original Goods オリジナル工房; 37 Wan; 0997 65 0605; 08.30–18.00 Mon–Sat. Store selling souvenirs & operating workshops where you can make T-shirts, caps, bags, stickers, postcards & more.

Yorozuya Yoroshi よろず屋宜; 464-1 Keraji; 0997 66 4303; w kikai-yoroshi.jp; 07.30–19.00 daily. Community shop selling Kikai products such as souvenirs, food & toys.

SPORTS AND ACTIVITIES Kikai has diving and marine sports, as well as locally run walking tours.

Amami Eco Tour Guides 奄美群島認定エコツアーガイド; 0997 52 6032; w amami.or.jp/guide_en. Tours of Kikai with English-speaking locals who are Amami certified eco guides.

Diving Shop BeGlad ダイビングショップビーグラッド; 2725 Akaren; 0997 65 2525; w divingshop-beglad.jimdofree.com. Diving shop offering fun, experience & licence dives; primarily Japanese language.

Fishing Chrysanthemum 遊漁船 天人菊; Araki; 0806 429 5840. W/end recreational fishing boat. W/days need to be reserved in advance.

Kikai Island Service 喜界アイランドサービス; 2685-2 Sakiku; 0997 66 4300. SUP, kayak & snorkelling tours.

South Beats サウスビーツ; 555-15 Wan; w south-beats.com. SUP, snorkel, kayak; equipment & camping rental.

Yonemori Diving Service ヨネモリダイビングサービス; 8 Hayamachi; 0997 66 1166. Dive shop also catering for snorkelling & sea & land guiding.

Yonyōri Kikaijima よんよーり喜界島; 0997 65 1202. Local volunteer guides. English can be limited but tours are an unfathomable ¥500. Multiple themes.

OTHER PRACTICALITIES There's a post office with ATM in town, as well as multiple banks such as the Amami Ōshima Shinyōkinko Bank (奄美大島信用金庫喜界

支店; 2759-3 Akaren; ☎0997 65 1311; ⏰ ATM: 09.00–18.00 daily). Outside of the main town there's the Onotsu Post Office (小野津郵便局; 1033-1 Onotsu; ☎0997 66 4522; ⏰ 09.00–16.00 Mon–Fri).

There's a single police station, Amami Police Station Kikai (奄美警察署喜界幹部派出所; 46 Wan; ☎0997 65 4309), and a general hospital, Kikai Tokushukai Hospital (35 Wan; ☎0997 65 1100; ⏰ 09.00–17.30 Mon–Sat).

WHAT TO SEE AND DO Kikai begins in the southwest, with the airport, port and main town. This is also where you'll find Kikai's finest beach, **Sugira** (スギラビーチ), which sits in the coast behind the airport. Also known as Nakazato Beach, it's a natural inlet of pure sands surrounded by reefs, making it quiet and safe for swimming. It's popular for snorkelling, barbecuing and camping, too – and for exceptional sunsets. Look out for sea turtles and hermit crabs, as well as planes taking off and landing on the runway behind, screened only by a wire fence.

Beside Sugira is the **Naval Memorial to the War Dead** (海軍航空基地戦没者慰霊碑). In itself it's a rather grey cenotaph, but around the memorial and airport you may spot *gaillardia pulchella*, the beautiful yellow-and-coral flowers that were presented to special attack pilots by Kikai girls before their farewell. It's said these flowers are a result of the seeds dropped during that time. To the beach's south is a secret little cove, hidden from the road, and to its north is the fun **Kikai Garden Golf Course** (喜界ガーデンゴルフ; 451-1 Wan; ☎0997 65 1855; ⏰ Apr–Sep 08.00–17.00 daily, Oct–Mar 08.00–15.30 daily; ¥2,000 w/day, ¥2,500 w/end).

This bay and the nearby Nakazato area were heavily attacked during the war, as they were the site of military sorties and commands. There are multiple war ruins and memorials left, including the **Nakazato Battle Command Station ruins** (中里戦闘指揮所跡; 200 Nakazato), which sit just in front of the airport. It's believed this is where kamikaze pilots were given their final briefing before their last flight. Further inland is the **Entaigo** (掩体壕), one of some 50 bunkers built on the island to protect kamikaze planes. This great hangar was the only one made from concrete so survived, and was likely used as a maintenance site.

Nearby is a **Tomb of Shunkan** (俊寛の墓), the priest who was exiled to the archipelago in the 1100s (page 101). Iōjima on the Mishima has, if not more claim, at least more monuments to Shunkan, than Kikai – but the tomb here was investigated and human bones consistent with an outsider of high status with a small sword wound were found.

If you pop by the Kikai Tourist Information Centre, ask if there are any *oogomadera* (オオゴマダラ) butterflies about. This area is deemed an appreciation point for them, where you can often find the glittering golden pupae and newly hatched adults – season and weather depending.

On the port's north is the **Takachiho Shrine** (高千穂神社), a pretty wooden hilltop shrine overlooking the bay village. It was built in 1870 after Buddhism was abolished, to replace the lost places of worship. Its deity is named Ninigi no Mikoto and the shrine is very popular on New Year's Day.

To the north of the town, the coast makes way for **Ikeji Beach** (池治海水浴場), a shallow stretch that isn't just popular with humans – there are plentiful hermit crabs in summer, and turtles come here to lay their eggs. Ikeji's extended coral reef is rich with marine life and ideal for snorkellers, but this is also a popular spot with surfers, too. The surf isn't big, but you'll occasionally catch a wave worth the board wax. Further along the coast is **Nakama Beach** (中間ビーチ) – a hidden wonder behind Villa Kikai. Entered on the hotel's left, Nakama is a shallow and pretty stretch framed by adan trees.

From Nakama it's best to head inland, where the island begins to rise towards the eastern coral terraces. On your way, you can take in the **sunflower field** (ひまわり畑) if it's in bloom, the artefacts on display at **Kikaijima Archaeological Centre** (喜界島埋蔵文化センター; 1203 Takigawa; 0997 55 3308; 09.00–17.00 daily) and the 30m-long **Ufuyaguchi Limestone Cave** (ウフヤグチ鍾乳洞).

Ufuyaguchi once had stalactites and stalagmites, but during the war it was used as an air defence position for the nearby garrison, resulting in the stalactites being destroyed and some of the stalagmites being removed. Further along is the **Butterfly Road** (蝶の道), an appreciation point for the rare chestnut tiger butterflies, or asagimadara (アサギマダラ), seen here April–May and October–November. You'll notice yellow road signs with butterflies on, warning travellers to take care in the area.

There are a few observation points along the ridge line. The southernmost is **Tebarubanta Observation Deck** (テーバルバンタ), ideal for those interested in Kikai's geology with views across the fast-rising coral reef terraces. Covered in trees, fields and communities, these terraces aren't just simply pretty, they're also remarkably rare. On the road down from Tebarubanta is a marvellous pair of towering banyan trees: the **husband and wife gajumaru** (夫婦ガジュマル), estimated to be around 850 years old.

The next viewpoint is **Shichtōbana** (七島鼻), the highest point on Kikai. Also known as Point 211 due to its height, this was used as a radar base during the war, built partially by a women's voluntary corps; you can see remnants on the hill. Today it's used as a takeoff spot for paragliders and hang gliders. **Hyakunodai Park** (百之台国立公園) is the final lookout: from here you get clear views down the east coast, across the sugarcane farmland and on into the endless horizon.

LOCAL RECIPE: FUKURIKAN

Fukurikan is a Kikai soft, brown sugar cake originally offered to ancestors at Obon, but today is regularly found at supermarkets and bakeries.

200g soft brown sugar
200ml water
200g plain flour
2 eggs, beaten
5g bicarbonate of soda
5ml white vinegar

1. Sift flour and bicarbonate of soda together.
2. Put the water and sugar in a saucepan over medium heat. Skim any impurities (scum) that comes off the top as you melt the sugar into the water.
3. Once dissolved, add vinegar to the mix and let it cool.
4. Once cold, add the beaten eggs and stir.
5. Add the liquid into the flour mix a third at a time.
6. Pour the dough into a 7-inch cake tin.
6. To cook, use a steamer or steam oven. If you have neither, place a baking tray in your oven and fill with water just before cooking. For steamers, put the tin in the pan, cover with a cloth and lid, and set on a low heat for 40 minutes. For ovens, set the heat to 180°C and steam for 30 minutes.

Heading back to the west coast, take in the small **Isaneku waterfall** (伊実久の滝) on the drive to the oft-overlooked **Great East Japan Earthquake Fishing Boat** (東日本大震災漂流漁船). This hard-hitting memorial in blue and white is a 0.4-tonne fishing boat from Kesennuma in Miyagi, which washed ashore here after the Tohoku earthquake and tsunami in 2011, having been swept 1,600km down Japan's coastline.

Nearby is the **Sugarcane Road** (サトウキビの一本道), a 3.5km-long hill of tarmac that splits Kikai's sugarcane fields in two and disappears into the horizon. It's a popular spot for photographers, particularly if the weather is being co-operative.

The northern village of **Onotsu** (小野津) has traditional coral walls, a legendary spring (雁股の泉) and the small, delightfully secluded **Onotsu Beach** (小野津海岸). It's ideal for swimming and fishing as the waters are wonderfully clear, though the picturesque setting is rather impaired by the surrounding grey of concrete and paving stones. Still, it doesn't stop sea turtles from visiting, as they use the beach for spawning and hatching in the summer.

The northern coast doesn't hold huge interest. In the northwest is **Hawaii Beach** (ハワイビーチ), once known as Annyadumari. Its new moniker is rather questionable – much of its sand is washed away – but its blue seas have corals close to shore, protected by the rocks, so it's good for inexperienced snorkellers. On the east side is the supposed site of the exiled **Heike clan's landing** (平家上陸之地), which sits on a beach in front of a handsome shrine.

If you pass through Sadeku (佐手久), check out the **Bomb Temple Bell** (爆弾釣鐘) hanging inconspicuously on the approach to the **Hoshoku Shrine** (保食神社). After the war, during US occupation, metal was in short supply, and so wartime objects were turned into everyday items. Bombs were dismantled and their gunpowder used for dynamite fishing, and their bodies used for temple bells like this one.

Coming into **Shiomichi village** (塩道) you can explore the **Heike Forest Ruins** (平家森), where some 200 members of the Heike clan set up a castle to defend themselves against pursuers. On the coast is **Shiomichi Nagahama Park** (塩道長浜公園) – a perfect place for a picnic and enjoying the cool Kikai breeze under the warm sun. The beach is incredibly shallow; the entire area was once underwater and used as a kindergarten pool. It's also the setting for another pitiful Amami shima-uta, 'Shiomichi Nagahama Bushi', in which a young man dies by being dragged by a runaway horse, in an effort to please a beautiful woman.

Shiomichi is also home to the **Kikai Institute of Coral Reef Science** (喜界島サンゴ礁科学研究所; 1508 Shiomichi; 0997 66 0200; w kikaireefs.org; 11.00–15.00 daily) where research is conducted on the unique reef. If you pop in, you'll find an exhibition room of coral specimens and, if you're lucky, an English-speaking researcher may be free to give you a quick rundown of their work.

To the right of Shiomichi's small Kannondo cemetery, under the road veering off into the trees, is the remains of a hidden **Shinyō Storage Bunker** (震洋格納壕跡) where suicide boats were stored. It's believed around 50 of the shinyō boats were kept here, but the war on Okinawa ended before they were ever deployed. Further down the coast you pass the **Kadon Giant Cycad** (嘉鈍の巨大ソテツ), a massive sotetsu thought to be 300 years old.

The east coast's historical treat is **Aden** (阿伝集落), a well-preserved traditional village and one of the island's oldest. A particularly unusual feature of the village is that the homes and buildings are made of exposed coral walls. They may seem rudimentary, but they were designed so that the breeze could flow through the walls in the summer months to keep the village cooler. This airflow system also means that the outer walls are less affected by typhoons, while still sheltering the

MYTHS AND FOLKTALES: THE SUN AND THE MOON

The late folklore scholar Ichiro Iwakura was born in Aden, so it should be no surprise that Kikai is full of myths and legends. One such is the story of how the sun became the sun, and the moon became the moon.

Today, the sun rises in the day and the moon at night, but in reality it should have been the other way round. Long ago, the sun and the moon were talking in the sky. They made a bet that if a legendary *siyakanaro* flower blossomed on one of their bellies in the night, the one on which it bloomed would govern the daytime. The other would become the light at night.

They fell asleep, and overnight a siyakanaro flower bloomed on the belly of the moon. The sun, however, woke up first and saw his friend's belly. Wanting to be the daytime light, he secretly took the flower and replanted it on himself. When they awoke, the moon agreed that his friend had won. Now the sun comes out in the daytime and the moon at night – but the sun's punishment for tricking his friend is that no-one can ever look at him again. Meanwhile, the moon's beautiful face shines for all to see forever.

houses behind them. The village itself is picturesque to walk through, with bright green foliage bursting over the top of the moody grey walls, especially as part of a tour. To Aden's south is **Keraji Beach** (花良治ビーチ), where you can see sea turtles swimming in the clear turquoise waters from April to May.

Following the coast round further brings you to **Araki** (荒木) and **Tekuzuku** (手久津久), two coastal settlements that have been made a national park. Here you'll find the extraordinary **Tekuzuku giant gajumaru** (手久津久の巨大ガジュマル). Over a century old, this tree's 16m trunk circumference and sky of leaves isn't just a spectacle but a rarity. Usually, when they reach this size, banyan branches tend to break from the weight. In this one's case, however, the aerial roots are so concentrated around the trunk that they support it well.

The southwest offers up a wonderful seaside walk, the **Araki-Nakazato Promenade** (荒木中里遊歩道). This stroll between coral and flora stretches from Nakazato towards Araki Port. Some 300m from the information board is a beach where thousands of hermit crabs collect together, while further along is **Iwao Force 2nd Battalion Martyrdom Memorial** (厳部隊二番機殉難供養塔) for an entire battalion that died in a single night battle over Kikai on 16 May 1945. Offshore, you may be able to catch sight of dolphins or even whales. (This is also one of the better fishing spots for big catch on Kikai.) For the best views, head here at sunset, when the pathway is bathed in gold.

TOKUNOSHIMA

Tokunoshima (徳之島) is a treasure trove of traditions and natural beauty slap bang between Amami Ōshima and Okinoerabu. Its subtropical wonderland is full of endemic indigenous species and unique landscapes, whipped into shape by the rough seas and carpeted in dense, primeval forest. Some 42km southwest of Amami Ōshima, Tokunoshima is often overlooked in favour of its larger neighbours to the north, despite sharing the same ancient ecology. But Tokunoshima has lots to offer anyone that escapes to its welcoming shores.

Called Tukunushima in the local language, it's the second largest island in the Amami group at some 248km². The island is volcanic, but has rare instances of granite and limestone too, creating underwater rivers and varied dramatic scenery. Its mountainous areas are in the centre and to the north, reaching their highest point at Inokawadake: a tree-covered 645m peak in the middle of the eastern coast. The flatter south has long been used for agriculture.

Tokunoshima's plentiful rainfall makes its laurel forests lush with rare animals and plants. The endangered Tokunoshima spiny rat – a big rodent without a Y chromosome – and banded ground gecko are endemic here, and the Amami black rabbit, Ryūkyū robin and Lidth's jay also call Tokuno (and Amami) home. The beautiful red-eyed Kuroiwa ground gecko, an endangered species, is found on both Tokunoshima and Okinawa-hontō. Orchids thrive here, too, their gentle beauty bright in the dark canopy. However, Tokunoshima's habu population renders its forests more dangerous and less explored.

Offshore, the island's seas contain caves and coral reefs, and, from December to April, humpback whales who come to raise their young here. You can even see them from the island's coastline, frolicking and frothing up blows. Many of Tokuno's beaches are vital nesting sites for green and loggerhead turtles, who lay and hatch over the summer, joined between June and July by innumerable *okayado* crabs laying eggs too.

Aside from wildlife, Tokuno is also known for its high number of world record supercentenarians, leading it to be dubbed the 'island of longevity'. It also has a claim to fame on the opposite side of the age range: as the rest of the country struggles with a diminishing birth rate, Tokunoshima has one of the highest in Japan. Unfortunately, this doesn't mean the island's population is on the rise: large swathes of young people are moving to find work elsewhere, meaning the population is still declining.

Tokunoshima has been influenced from north and south, its culture a mix of Amami, Okinawa and Japan. The indigenous language, a form of Ryūkyūan known locally as *sïmagucï*, has nearly died out and been replaced by Japanese. Certain indigenous words, like those for thank you (*oboradaren* or *oboradaani*), are however still in everyday use.

HISTORY There's little by way of historical information on Tokunoshima. Records from 698CE show that a Japanese courtier was sent to the north of the archipelago

TOKUNO FESTIVALS

There are plenty of interesting festivals on the island. The Inokawa Natsume *odori* is a dance with drums that goes on all night and into the following morning, with people visiting houses throughout. Akimuchi in Omo town is a harvest festival involving a scarecrow called Issanbō, who represents the god of fortune. This scarecrow leads children around the village to bless houses.

Each village on Tokunoshima holds a harvest festival, and each seems determined to outdo the other. The large Dondon-matsuri in Tokunoshima town has a miscellany of events – sumo, boats and parades – to celebrate summer. The Amagi festival is similar, with fireworks to finish it off, while Isen Town's summer festival adds a laser show on top.

The kokutō (brown sugar) festival at Aze Prince Beach Kaihin Park is a smaller celebration on Children's Day in Golden Week. Sugarcane is squeezed using the traditional method, where a cow attached to a corkscrew machine that squashes the cane is led in a circle. The day is awash with free sugarcane juice and kokutō, as well as performances.

TOKUNOSHIMA

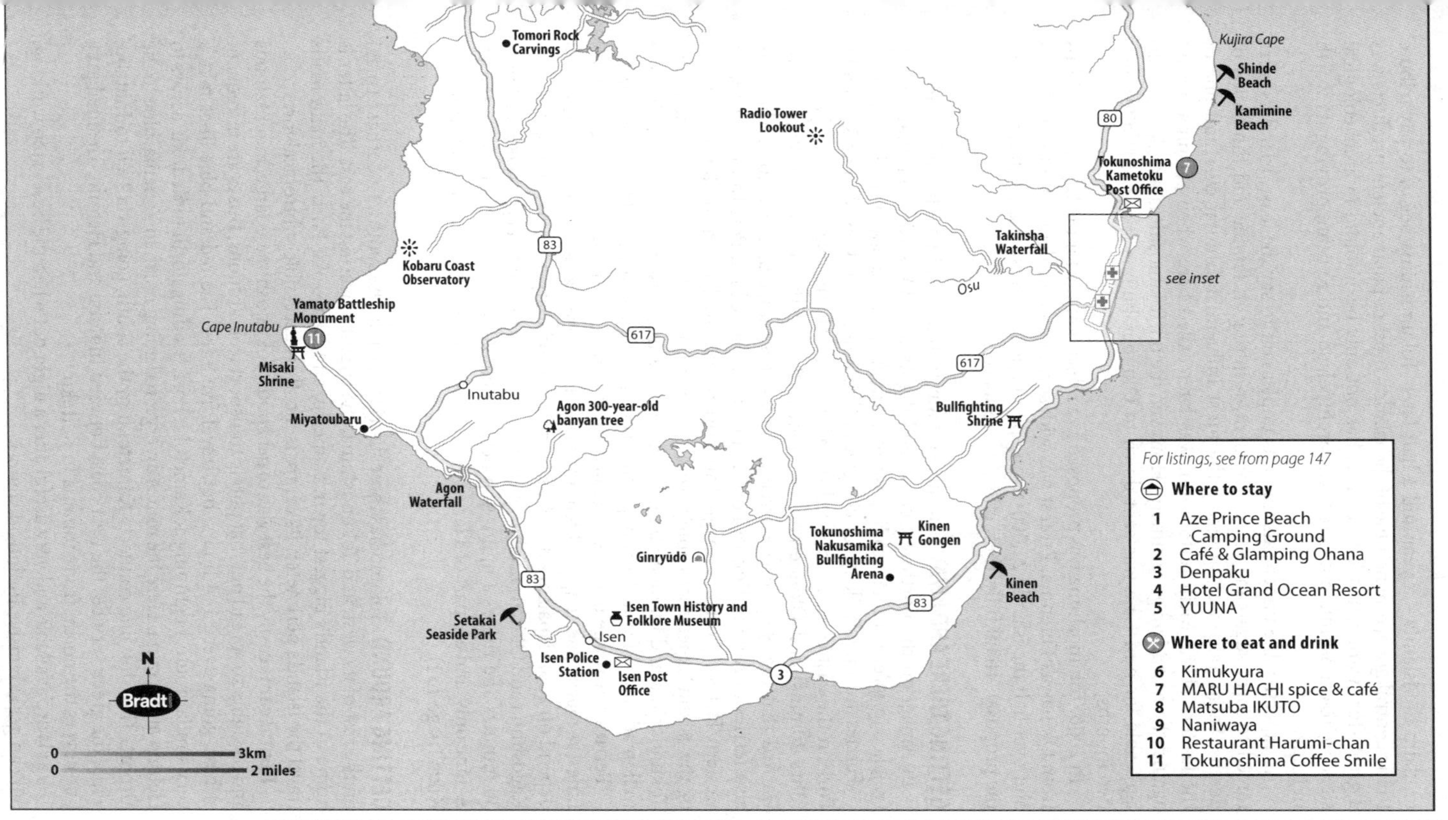
Kujira Cape
Shinde Beach
Kamimine Beach
Tomori Rock Carvings
Radio Tower Lookout
Tokunoshima Kametoku Post Office
7
80
83
617
Takinsha Waterfall
Osu
see inset
Kobaru Coast Observatory
Yamato Battleship Monument
Cape Inutabu
11
Misaki Shrine
Inutabu
Agon 300-year-old banyan tree
Miyatoubaru
Bullfighting Shrine
Agon Waterfall
Tokunoshima Nakusamika Bullfighting Arena
Kinen Gongen
Ginryūdō
Kinen Beach
Isen Town History and Folklore Museum
Setakai Seaside Park
Isen
Isen Police Station
Isen Post Office
3
N
Bradt
0 3km
0 2 miles
For listings, see from page 147
Where to stay
1 Aze Prince Beach Camping Ground
2 Café & Glamping Ohana
3 Denpaku
4 Hotel Grand Ocean Resort
5 YUUNA
Where to eat and drink
6 Kimukyura
7 MARU HACHI spice & café
8 Matsuba IKUTO
9 Naniwaya
10 Restaurant Harumi-chan
11 Tokunoshima Coffee Smile

to claim the islands – a year and a half later, Tokunoshima began to pay tribute to the central government. One of the island's most popular ancient products was a great stoneware called kamui. This has not only been found in archaeological sites on Tokunoshima but across the archipelago and Kyūshū, proving its worth in trade.

As expected, life under Satsuma was unpleasant to say the least. Islanders were forced to farm sugarcane as tax payment, resulting in famine and thousands of deaths. Saigo Takamori, arguably the most influential samurai ever and one of the leaders of the Meiji restoration, was later exiled here when Satsuma turned against the new Meiji government. However, life on Tokunoshima was deemed too agreeable for him – he was sent down to Okinoerabujima (page 151) after only two months.

In 2006, Tokunoshima was proposed as a relocation site for the US Marine Corps from Okinawa's Futenma. Protest was widespread and virulent, with local officials and over half the island's 22,000-strong population expressing their disapproval of the proposal. Thankfully, their efforts were successful.

GETTING THERE AND AWAY The quickest way to Tokunoshima is by air. The airport is in Amagi on the northwest coast, and flights with JAL's Air Commuter group (w jal.co.jp/jp/en) connect to Kagoshima, Amami and Okinawa via Okinoerabu.

Ferries are a more likely, far cheaper option however. Tokunoshima's Kametoku Port on the east coast is accessed from Amami Ōshima's Naze Port to the north (3hrs 20mins) and Okinoerabu's Wadomari Port to the south (1hr 50mins). Be warned that the Naze ferry currently leaves at a rather ungodly hour. There are also ferries to Amami Koniya Port and Okinoerabu China Port from the smaller, western Hetono Port in Amagi. This port is also used when the Kametoku side of the island experiences rough seas – something that occurs more often with Tokunoshima and Okinoerabu than the other Amami islands. Check the website well in advance of your ferry departure time in case you need to transfer across.

Ferries via Kametoku are operated by A-Line (w aline-ferry.com) and Marix Line (w marix-line.co.jp), which alternate departure dates – your company will depend on your departure day. This ferry is part of a larger route running between Kagoshima and Okinawa Naha. The full cruise from first to final port takes 25 hours 30 minutes and there's a multi-stop ticket available. Ferries via Hetono are run by A-Line only, and are part of a larger route between Kagoshima and Okinoerabu via Kikai (page 132).

GETTING AROUND Tokuno has three districts: Isen in the southwest corner, Amagi on the rest of its west, and Tokunoshima, the largest, covering the east. The latter is home to the island's biggest town, Kametsu, and Kametoku Port. The main roads travel the island's perimeter: its centre is mostly inaccessible subtropical forest.

Rental car is easily the best way to get about. Tokunoshima is large, mountainous and its sights so spread out that public transport feels arduous. **Buses** are infrequent at best, going every 1–4 hours, but travel five lines. The red and blue lines take a very similar route, beginning at Kametoku Port, heading north to Kedoku, across to Hetono and Asama. Here the routes diverge: red going north to Yonama, blue to the airport. The pink line connects Kametoku to the south, going via Isen to Inutabu, while the green services the west coast between Inutabu and Hetono. The final grey line covers the north, from Yonama to Kedoku.

Taxis are available and very useful after a night out when the buses stop working, but can get expensive for long distances.

Taxis

Akimaru Taxis 秋丸タクシー; 998 Kametsu; 0120 21 3889

Hotel New Nishida Taxis ホテルニューにしだタクシー; 7380 Kametsu; 0120 33 0300; w new-nishida.com/company.html

Isen Taxis 伊仙タクシー; 2124 Isen; 0997 86 2104

Vehicle rental

ORIX Rent-a-Car オリックスレンタカー; 185-1 Asama (airport), 2184-99 Kametoku (port); 0997 81 2300 (airport), 0997 83 3500 (port); w car.orix.co.jp

Shirama Motors 白間モータース; 31-9 Hetono; 0997 85 4154. Motorbike/moped rental.

Times Car Rental タイムズカー; 174-1 Asama (airport), Hotel Grand Ocean 7510 Kametsu (port); 0997 85 5656 (airport), 0997 82 0777 (port); w rental.timescar.jp

Tokunoshima Car Rental 徳之島レンタカー; 7734 Kametoku; 0997 82 0900

Toyota Rent-a-Car Tokunoshima Airport トヨタレンタカー徳之島空港; 143-1 Amagi; 0997 85 5500; w rent.toyota.co.jp

TOURIST INFORMATION There are limited spots for information – essentially, the only option is the Tokunoshima Tourism Organisation (徳之島観光連盟; 1-1 Asama; 0997 81 2010; w tokunoshima-kanko.com) within the airport.

WHERE TO STAY *Map, page 144*

✷ **YUUNA** (5 villas) 結那; 47 Kedoku; 0997 81 6006; w ui-yuuna.com. Mind-blowingly beautiful luxury villas overlooking the beach, 2 with pools, 3 with saunas. 2-wall panoramic windows on each. Wooden, modern, & overflowing with perks & extras. The owner is incredibly helpful too. **$$$$$**

✷ **Denpaku** (6 houses) 伝泊; 1-2 Furusato; 0997 63 1910; w den-paku.com. One of 6 beautiful, fully equipped villas across Tokunoshima, ranging from north to south. Denpaku rents, buys & revitalises traditional local houses. Perfect for couples, families & larger groups. **$$$$**

Café & Glamping Ohana (2 rooms, 1 villa) 1434-17 San; 0805 314 4075; w tokunoshima-ohana.com. Auberge with excellent café, glamping & modern pleasant rooms, plus rentals & seaside views. **$$$**

Hotel Grand Ocean Resort (80 rooms) ホテルグランドオーシャンリゾート; 7510 Kametsu; 0997 83 3333; w hpdsp.jp/oceanresort. A fine hotel, if rather dated, overlooking the beach at Kametsu. Japanese & Western restaurant, b/fast available. Extra facilities include karaoke, golf & massages. **$$$**

Aze Prince Beach Camping Ground (campsite) 畦プリンスビーチキャンプ場; Aze Prince Beach, Aze; 0997 83 4111. Basic but well-kept free campground with cooking facilities – ring the town office in advance. **$**

WHERE TO EAT AND DRINK *Map, page 144*

Tokunoshima is no shopping centre, but there's no shortage of supermarkets and convenience stores in Kametsu, Amagi and even Isen if you want to self-cater or picnic.

Kimukyura きむきゅら; 1132-1 Shimokushi; 0997 84 1186; w kimukyura.com; 11.00–14.00 & 18.00–22.00 Thu–Tue. Restaurant attached to a hotel that does a roaring trade in much-loved set meals like chicken *nanban* and kara-age. Perfect place to refuel on a drive round the island. $$

MARU HACHI spice & café 1933-3 Tokuwase; 0909 196 1210; 11.00–17.00 & 18.00–21.00 daily. Cool restaurant serving slap-up Indian curry set meals – hearty & cheap. $$

Matsuba IKUTO まつ葉; 7356 Kametsu; 0997 82 1229; 18.00–23.00 daily. Classy izakaya with island specialities, including excellent sashimi. $$

Naniwaya なにわ屋; 7698 Kametsu; 10.00–13.00 & 14.00–19.00 Mon–Sat. Takoyaki octopus balls & *oden* stew in a wonderfully local setting by the port. $

Restaurant Harumi-chan 御食事処 はるみちゃん; 972 Kametsu; 0997 82 1661; 11.00–midnight daily. Tokuno specialities found only at

TOKUNO'S LOCAL FOODS

Tokuno's cuisine is heavily Okinawan, but it has its own local dishes. One local speciality is goat, and during the March Sangatsu Sanchi festival, islanders take part in mudskipper fishing and clamming. This was traditionally done by mildly poisoning rock pools with indigenous grasses, waiting for the creatures to come to the surface – occasionally they would catch even bigger prey like octopuses. The clams and mudskippers are used in soup and porridge. Another of the festival's traditional foods is mugwort dumplings, called *fuchidagu*.

Harumi. Try goat soup, goat sashimi & shellfish in the island/*banshaku* set meals. $

Tokunoshima Coffee Smile とくのしまコーヒーの店喫茶コーヒースマイル; 1642-4 Inutabu; 0997 86 8277; w rito-guide.com/coffeesmile; 10.00–18.00 Thu–Sun. The only place selling Tokunoshima-made coffee, with a Battleship Yamato museum attached. $

ENTERTAINMENT AND NIGHTLIFE

Bar&KaraokeRoom A-HOUSE 7315 Kametsu; 0997 83 2981; w jazzbarahouse.amamin.jp; 18.00–midnight daily. Jazz bar & karaoke place with live music.

Izakaya Yoi-yoi 居酒屋良酔; 7422-1 Kametsu; 0997 82 0841; 18.00–midnight Wed–Mon. Very lively izakaya with plentiful food & drink & live shamisen on Sat.

Kimitarou Bar きみたろう酒場; 7349 Kametsu; 0997 83 2170; 18.00–03.00 Tue–Sun. By no means the finest establishment in Kametsu, but it stays open latest & has good food & a great bar selection.

LocoMoco ロコモコ; 944-5 Kametsu; 0702 157 3599; w japanese-izakaya-restaurant-9483.business.site; 18.00–midnight Fri–Mon, 18.00–23.30 Tue–Thu. Modern izakaya with great Westernised food & dim-lit vibes.

SPORTS AND ACTIVITIES

Tōgyū bullfighting is incredibly popular here – so much so that the island's mascot is a tōgyū bull. Tōgyū has been practised on the island for over 500 years, featuring in 300-year-old island songs. Tournaments are held in January, May and October, taking place at Matsubara bullring in the north and Nakusamikan bullring in the south.

The island is enough off the beaten track to make English tours nigh on non-existent; this makes diving difficult but whale watching should be easy. Ask your accommodation to book for you.

Marine Service Kamui マリンサービス海夢居; 532-1 Shoda; 0997 82 1514; w ms-kamui.com. Diving, whale watching & whale swimming (through subsidiary Whale Adventure).

Musubiya Tokunoshima 結や; 421 Shimokushi; 0803 903 2704; w musubiya-tokunoshima.com. Cycle tours taking in culture & nature.

Sea Divers Navi シー・ダイバーズ・ナビ; 7578 Kametsu; 0997 83 0170; w sea-divers-navi.com. Licensing, experience & fun dives.

OTHER PRACTICALITIES

There are plentiful banks, post offices, police stations and medical facilities across Tokunoshima.

Banks and post offices

Amamishinyō Kumiai Tokunoshima Bank 奄美信用組合徳之島支店; 7262 Kametsu; 0997 82 1241; 09.00–15.00 Mon–Fri

Isen Post Office 伊仙郵便局; 2087-11 Isen; 0997 86 2042; 09.00–17.00 Mon–Fri, ATM: 08.45–18.00 Mon–Fri, 09.00–17.00 Sat–Sun

Kedoku Post Office 花徳郵便局; 2935-6 Kedoku; 0997 84 0043; 09.00–17.00 Mon–Fri, ATM: 08.45–18.00 Mon–Fri, 09.00–12.30 Sat
Tokunoshima Kametoku Post Office 徳之島亀徳郵便局; 2054-3 Kametoku; 0997 82 1041; 09.00–16.00 Mon–Fri, ATM: 09.00–17.30 Mon–Fri, 09.00–12.30 Sat

Medical

Miyagami Hospital 宮上病院; 7268 Kametsu; 0997 82 0002; 09.00–noon & 14.00–18.00 Mon–Sat
Tokunoshima Tokushukai Hospital 徳之島徳洲会病院; 7588 Kametsu; 0997 83 1100; 09.00–noon & 17.00–19.30 Mon–Fri, 09.00–noon Sat

Police

Hetono Police Station 平土野駐在所; 533-1 Amagi; 0997 85 2002
Isen Police Station 伊仙駐在所; 2589-8 Isen; 0997 86 2339
Kedoku Police Station 花徳駐在所; 780-22 Kedoku; 0997 84 0075
Tokunoshima Police Box 徳之島警察署徳之島交番; 7770 Kametsu; 0997 82 1616

WHAT TO SEE AND DO The first thing to do on arrival in the sleepy town of Kametsu (亀津) is to head out of it. The road leading directly inland, along the Ose River, takes you to the first little hike of Tokunoshima: **Takinsha Waterfall** (タキンシャ). You'll see yellow-headed signboards directing you to the Takinsha new entrance (タキンシャ新入口) , which takes a quick and easy path to this pretty, gladed cascade.

On the 80 road south from the port, towards the town of **Kinen** (喜念), is the **Bullfighting Shrine** (闘牛神社). Full of bellowing, wrestling bronze bull statues, it's a unique and relatively elaborate homage to the island's bullfighting history. Further into town is the **Tokunoshima Nakusamikan Bullfighting Arena** (徳之島なくさみ館), which you can peek into even if an event isn't on. On the coast, **Kinen Beach's** (喜念浜) 20km of sand dunes and shore is wonderfully scenic.

Kinen itself is home to another, very different shrine: **Kinen Gongen** (喜念権現). Hidden away at the end of a forest path overrun with roots and trees, this small cave utaki has a delightful wildness, its stone torii standing amid toppled woodland ruins. The cave has been worshipped as a guardian deity for centuries, prayed to for rain and harvest. The shrine is said to have been the hiding place of a stunning Kinen girl, who tried to conceal her beauty from the village men by living in the cave. Another legend says a Satsuma deputy heard of her beauty and demanded she marry him, threatening her parents when she refused. She took her own life in this cave to protect them and her chastity – the villagers both pitied and praised her, afterwards worshipping her spirit as Gongen-sama.

West from Kinen Gongen is **Ginryūdō** (銀竜洞), an ancient utaki once known as Anahachiman, where people worship the female deity of the surrounding villages. Translated as 'silver dragon cave', Ginryūdō was once a popular tourist destination, but now it's become rather charmingly left to the forest. The entrance is framed by a stone torii, and the cave has flowing water, stalactites and rocks seemingly dripping in silver. Beware of habu.

Further round the coast, the **Isen Town History and Folklore Museum** (伊仙町歴史民俗資料館; 2945-3 Isen; 0997 86 4183; w rekimin.wixsite.com/home; 09.00–16.30 Tue–Sun; adult/child ¥200/50–100) doesn't exactly overflow with English information. However, its exceptionally cheap entrance fee and simple exhibits make it worth popping in. The museum covers nature and archaeological artefacts such as earthenware, animal skeletons and human bones excavated from the Tokunoshima Kamuiyaki Pottery Kiln ruins. Towards the western coast is **Setakai Seaside Park** (瀬田海海浜公園), with clear fish-filled waters, paddling shallows, facilities and excellent sunsets.

Agon (阿権) on the east coast has a **300-year-old banyan tree** (300年ガジュマル), the oldest and largest tree on Tokunoshima. Located in an old samurai neighbourhood, the gajumaru is set off by the traditional coral walls alongside it. Amami's folkloric *kenmun* tree spirits are said to live in the banyan, which is also a symbol of health. **Agon Waterfall** (阿権の滝) can be seen from the coastal road by Agon Bridge – the one running parallel to Highway 83's bridge – but you can also head to the sandy beach alongside the bridge to get a closer look.

This west coast is where Tokunoshima's diverse landscapes begin to shine. **Miyatōbaru** (みやとーばる) is an unusual coastal rock formation where you can see mélange rocks and the reef zone which is still used for salt collection. It carries on up to **Cape Inutabu** (犬田布岬), one of Tokuno's most beautiful places. The ocean scenery here is stunning; not just for the unearthly blue and cragged coast, but for the animals in it. In February–April, you can stand on the rocks and spot whales, their erupting mist dotting the horizon. At sunset, the endless sea and cape light up, the sun setting into the tip of the somewhat ugly **Yamato Battleship Monument** (戦艦大和慰霊塔). The *Yamato* was one of the Japanese navy's greatest ships and one of the most powerfully armed ships ever made. Despite this, it was sent on a desperate one-way mission to hold off allied forces in World War II, knowing it wouldn't come back. It was sunk in April 1945, a few nautical miles out to sea.

To the left of the cape is **Misaki Shrine** (御崎神社), its pathway marked by a large red torii. Misaki's lonely torii gate stands overlooking the ocean, fronds of cycads and rock framing it on the horizon. At a clear sunset, you can catch the light perfectly between the two stone lanterns. North of the cape is another observatory, the **Kobaru Coast Observatory** (小原海岸展望台).

Northwest, further inland, are the **Tomori Rock Carvings** (戸森の線刻画). These engravings have sailing ships and arrow motifs and are the most detailed of Tokunoshima's carvings – the only place these have been found on Amami. Their age and purpose are unknown, but they're thought to have been painted in the early Edo period (1603–1867), perhaps as a diary of island events. Into the mountains you'll find the **Amami Black Rabbit Observation Hut** (アマミノクロウサギ観察小屋), one of the best places to see the rare black creatures. The area around has plenty of the plants they prefer; visit at twilight, stay quiet, and you should spot them.

Central west is **Senma Coast** (千間海岸), one of the better spots for diving and off-the-beach snorkelling. Senma has a drop-off close to shore where so many turtles like to hang out they're said to be a guaranteed sighting. North of Senma is **Innojōfuta** (犬の門蓋), a breathtaking seaside site of eroded coral rock. Formed by years of erosion and rising reefs, the landscape includes cliffs, caves and strangely shaped rocks. The best known of these are two arches called **Megane-Iwa** (めがね岩) – literally 'glasses rock'.

Certainly don't go out of your way to view the **Yamato Castle Ruins** (大和城), which were destroyed in World War II after the stronghold became a battle command post. Instead come for the valley views overlooking Amagi on the west coast. There's a similar view from the other side of the valley, **Maeno Observatory** (前野展望台) – do one, not both.

Beside the airport is **Unbuki** (ウンブキ), a submarine cave of uplifted coral that connects to the ocean 400m away. The ebb and flow of the sea leaves a unique brackish habitat, and the area around Unbuki is wild with gnarled roots, wrenched rocks and resonating caves. Above the airport is Matsubara (松原), where you can find the **Matsubara Shrine** (松原神社), the **Bullfighting Arena** (松原闘牛場; 57 Matsubara) and the **Amagidake Matsubara mountain trail**. The trail winds

MYTHS AND FOLKTALES: KUIKIRIUSHI

Naturally, an island obsessed with cows should have a cow monster. The legend of the headless horseman is renowned in the US, but Japan has its own spin on the idea. There are many myths about 'cut neck horses', known as *kubikireuma*, all over the country. These headless horses are sometimes ridden by fallen warriors, but it's always the animal missing a head.

On Tokunoshima, there's the legend of the *kuikiriushi* – a headless cow. Sporting a severed bloody neck where its head should be, this decapitated cow is said to have come down from a hill in today's Amagi region called Shirushinshira – 'White Cow Hill'.

through subtropical forest and takes in three waterfalls, ending in an astonishing 360-degree panorama over the forest and island.

Mushiroze (ムシロ瀬) on the north coast is one of the few examples of granite found on a volcanic and coral island – a fact perhaps appreciated only by geologists. However, these huge stone slabs, set against the backdrop of the sea, are also a climbing playground for the intrepid, or a chilled viewpoint to fish or watch sunset to the sound of the waves. You may even see turtles in the water, or whales during the winter–spring season. The area's name comes from *mushiro,* a woven straw mat the rocks are said to resemble.

The northeast holds the 200m-long **Kanamizaki Cycad Tunnel** (金見崎ソテツトンネル), made up of 400-year-old giant cycad trees. They lead to **Kanamizaki** (金見崎), a cape with an ocean panorama taking in both north and west coasts and the looming mountains behind. On the beach below is **Tukka** (トゥッカ), a picturesque rock arch in the sand.

The east coast isn't quite as littered with sites as the west. **Todoroki Shrine** (轟木神社) sits on the road between Kedoku (花徳) and Amagi (天城町), and while the neat little shrine is small and arguably forgettable, the view from it is spectacular, showing off the island's stunning greenery and rolling mountains that grow blue into the horizon. **Boma** (母間) is home to rock carvings both old and new: the **Boma Heart** (母間ハート), an Instagram-friendly carving in an otherwise ugly concrete divider, and the **Boma Rock Carvings** (母間の線刻画). These ship and arrow line drawings are engraved into four megaliths on Mount Inokawa's eastern slope. It's thought that noro used to pray here for good harvests.

The road south passes by **Kujira Cape** (クジラ岬), aka Whale Cape, beautiful **Kamimine Beach** (神嶺浜) and **Shinde Beach** (シンデ浜). The cape is named and known for the whales regularly spotted here, while Shinde is an excellent lagoon full of soft corals and sea creatures. Just beyond the lagoon, where the ground drops away, is a haven for sea turtles, who nest on the beach.

Before returning to port, head up a winding, very narrow and rather overgrown road to the old **Radio Tower Lookout** (電波塔). It's not one for big cars, but if you reach the top you'll get views out over the south of the island.

OKINOERABUJIMA

Just under 100km away from Amami Ōshima's southern tip and 60km north of Okinawa-hontō, blooms Okinoerabujima (沖永良部島), one of the most passed over islands in the archipelago. Isolated and distant, it often loses out to its neighbours for their paradisiacal beaches, nature and food. Okinoerabu has its own

OKINOERABU FESTIVALS

Erabu has a few festivals, outside its famous lily one. The *Kamihirakawa no taija odori* – more easily called the Giant Snake Dance of Kamihirakawa – comes from China village, and features a blend of themes from both Ryūkyū and mainland performing arts. The story behind the dance is that a giant snake disguised itself as a stunning woman to gain entrance to a temple, whereupon he started destroying the temple and hurting people. A monk killed the snake, prompting a celebratory dance. The dance takes place on an outdoor stage, where a spectacular fire-breathing snake appears at the end. The Yakko odori (Young People's Dance) is held across the island and though it originally came from the Satsuma region, on Okinoerabu it is set to Ryūkyū music.

crown jewels, however, that eclipse all others. Known as 'the flower island' or 'the island of lilies', Okinoerabu is mantled in beautiful Erabu Easter lilies from April to May. These flowers, named for the island, came to the notice of the mainland around a century ago and became so sought after that the prized bulbs were traded for ridiculous sums. Okinoerabu was the go-to place to get flowers during the Meiji era and they've been cultivated here since 1899. Today the island is a huge producer of cut flowers, as well as being responsible for some 90% of Erabu lily bulbs in Japan. Every year when the lilies bloom, there's a flower festival that crowds the island with domestic tourists.

Beautiful blooms aside, the island's real draw is caving: Okinoerabujima is home to around 300 caves. Like Kikai, Okinoerabu is a rising coral island, but here this has resulted in a mammoth underground network of hollowed-out coral and limestone that's been washed through with ground and seawater. The most spectacular is easily Ginsuidō, a stunning show cave of white and turquoise. The island has more geological diversity than Kikai, with karst landscapes and subtropical forest, but due to being a coral island, it doesn't have half as much biodiversity as Tokunoshima and Amami Ōshima. Nonetheless, you'll be able to see humpback whales in winter and dogtooth tuna in spring, and Erabu is an important spawning site for multiple sea turtle species, which come to lay eggs between April and October. On land, Okinoerabu is the northern limit for the *konohachō* – a butterfly known for mimicking a dead leaf with its wings closed.

Okinoerabu's approximately 13,000 citizens are spread across its 93.8km^2 between two towns: Wadomari in the northeast and the rather frustratingly named China (pronounced Chee-na) in the southwest – a nightmare for searching online maps. Its highest point is Ōyama (大山), only about 240m high. Though the islanders largely speak Japanese, some also speak Shumunni, a version of the Kunigami dialect from northern Okinawa-hontō.

Like many of these islands, Okinoerabujima's tongue-twisting name hasn't always been set in stone. It was once called Okiyerabushima, when the Amami group first became part of Kagoshima Prefecture, and even as recently as 2012 there were suggestions it should be Okierabujima instead. You'll still hear the latter, but more commonly it's mercifully shortened simply to Erabu.

HISTORY During the 14th century Three Mountain Kingdom period, Okinoerabu was under the control of Okinawa-hontō's northern kingdom, Hokuzan. Much of Erabu's culture, including its cuisine and festivals, derives from this region. After Okinawa's unification, Erabu belonged to the Ryūkyū Kingdom. It's said that when

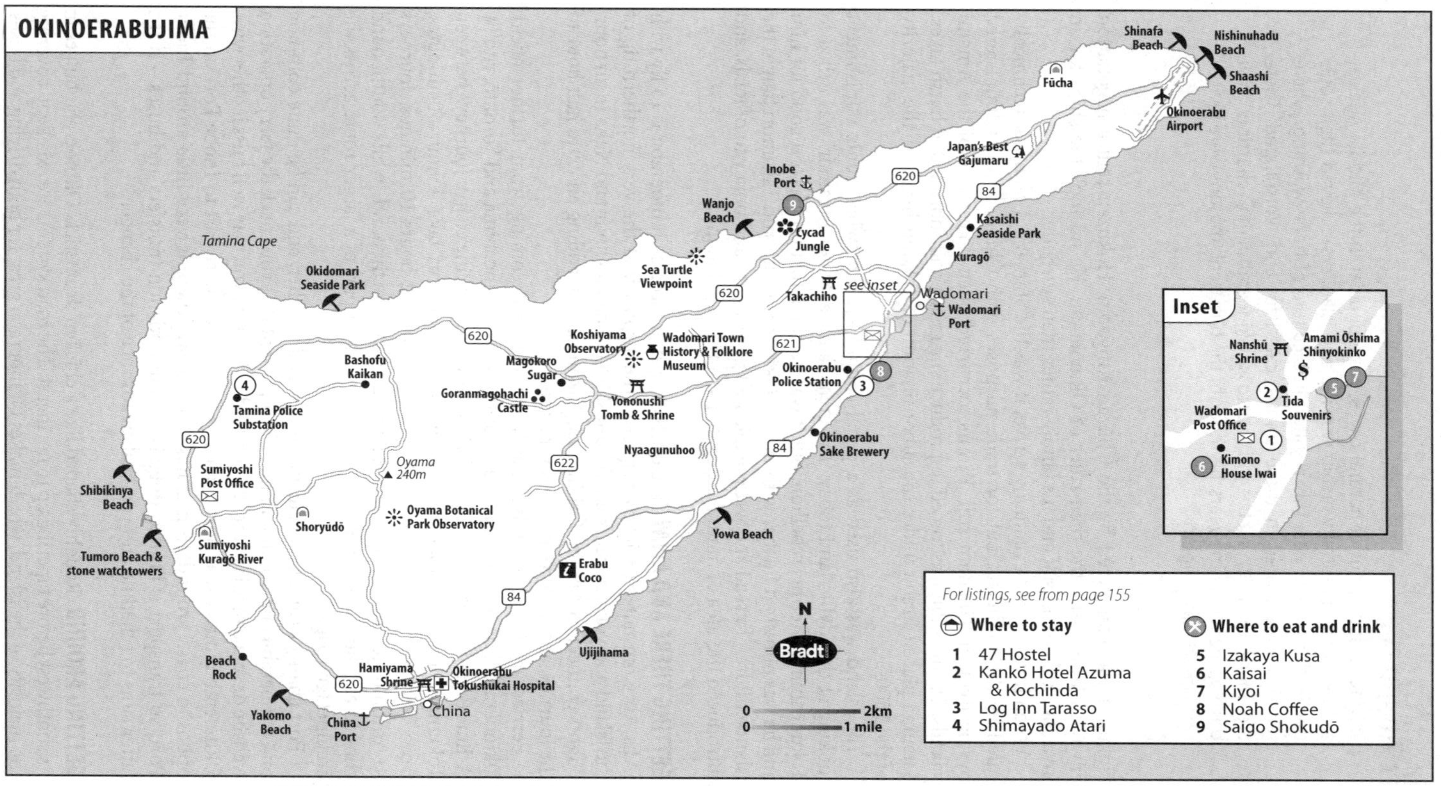
OKINOERABUJIMA
Shinafa Beach
Nishinuhadu Beach
Shaashi Beach
Fūcha
Okinoerabu Airport
Japan's Best Gajumaru
Inobe Port
Wanjo Beach
Cycad Jungle
Kasaishi Seaside Park
Kuragō
Tamina Cape
Sea Turtle Viewpoint
Takachiho
see inset
Wadomari
Wadomari Port
Okidomari Seaside Park
Koshiyama Observatory
Wadomari Town History & Folklore Museum
Bashofu Kaikan
Magokoro Sugar
Okinoerabu Police Station
Goranmagohachi Castle
Yononushi Tomb & Shrine
Tamina Police Substation
Nyaagunuhoo
Okinoerabu Sake Brewery
Oyama 240m
Sumiyoshi Post Office
Shibikinya Beach
Oyama Botanical Park Observatory
Shoryūdō
Yowa Beach
Tumoro Beach & stone watchtowers
Sumiyoshi Kuragō River
Erabu Coco
Ujijihama
Beach Rock
Hamiyama Shrine
Okinoerabu Tokushukai Hospital
China
Yakomo Beach
China Port
Inset
Nanshū Shrine
Amami Ōshima Shinyokinko
Tida Souvenirs
Wadomari Post Office
Kimono House Iwai
N
Bradt
0 2km
0 1 mile
For listings, see from page 155
Where to stay
1 47 Hostel
2 Kankō Hotel Azuma & Kochinda
3 Log Inn Tarasso
4 Shimayado Atari
Where to eat and drink
5 Izakaya Kusa
6 Kaisai
7 Kiyoi
8 Noah Coffee
9 Saigo Shokudō

TŪRU TOMBS

Tūru tombs, dug out of natural caves, were popular in the Middle Ages at a time when ancestral worship was rife and islanders believed their souls dwelled in their bones. This resulted in a culture of bone washing, where remains were stored in these tombs, cared for and worshipped. There are more than 50 such tombs across Okinoerabujima, charting their development over the years. It's thought the tūru tomb masons were invited up from Okinawa-hontō.

Hokuzan was conquered by the Chūzan Kingdom, Hokuzan sent a negotiation envoy to Yononushi, the then-ruler of Okinoerabu. He mistook the ships for an invasion, killing himself and his family rather than surrender.

When invasion did eventually arrive, it was the Shimazu. Erabu was technically ruled by their officials, but for trade purposes with China, it was administered by the Ryūkyū Kingdom still. Famine occurred often; like many of the Amami islands, Okinoerabu was forced to produce sugarcane and subjected to harsh taxes. Satsuma placed Erabu under the subordination of Tokunoshima for the majority of the 1600s.

The island was also used as a penal colony – a somewhat ironic punishment looking at the idyllic land today. The great samurai Saigo Takamori was exiled to Tokunoshima after his rebellion, but it was decided Tokuno was too good for him and he was punished further with exile to Okinoerabu. It's said Takamori taught the island children to read and write, explained governance and policy to officials, and introduced the idea of mutual aid systems in times of famine.

GETTING THERE AND AWAY The quickest way to access Okinoerabu is to fly with JAL's Air Commuter (w jal.co.jp/jp/en). The airport is at the very northern tip of the island and you can get from Tokunoshima in half an hour and Naha in an hour. Flights connect to Amami Ōshima via Tokunoshima, adding an extra half hour to the journey, and also go to Kagoshima too.

Ferries are far cheaper but inevitably slower if coming from further afield. Okinoerabujima ferries are the same as those to Tokunoshima and Yorontō, run by A-Line (w aline-ferry.com) and Marix Line (w marix-line.co.jp). Journeys between Tokuonoshima Kametoku and Okinoerabu Wadomari take 1 hour 50 minutes, from Tokunoshima Hetono to Okinoerabu China 2 hours 10 minutes. Journeys to Yorontō go from Wadomari, taking 2 hours northbound, while southbound clips in at 1 hour 40 minutes. These ferries travel part of a larger route across the archipelago (page 114).

Port changes can also occur in sudden bad weather, and can be quite common on Okinoerabu and Tokunoshima. It's important that you check the ferry operation website or social media at the start of the day, because you may well miss it otherwise. Okinoerabujima's usual port change is from Wadomari Port to Inobe Port on the opposite coast, around 15 minutes' drive away. There is very little around Inobe Port, so transport is limited to taxis, accommodation transfers and buses – if the latter runs to schedule and you hear in advance of the change.

GETTING AROUND Roughly shaped like a chicken drumstick, Okinoerabu bulges in its southwest before tapering up to northeast. The road systems are excellent, covering the majority of the island, which makes Okinoerabu great for both driving and buses.

Okinoerabu **buses** (☎ 0997 93 2054; w okinoerabubus.org) have five lines, covering the entire island. The blue and red lines follow almost the exact same path from China up the south/east coast, with the red going one stop further to the airport. Green and purple travel different routes north from China, over the coast and to Wadomari, while orange goes from China across the island and up the north coast to Inobe. One-day tickets are available for ¥1,200, while a single costs from ¥140. The blue and red lines are most regular, with just under ten journeys a day, while green and purple go down to six and orange four.

Accommodations will generally pick you up from the port or airport, but having your own **car** is a great way to see Okinoerabu's sites, which are scattered about.

The good news is that there are no habu on Okinoerabu, so you can wander without fear.

Vehicle rental

Atelier Rent-a-Car アトリエレンタカー; 584-6 Wadomari; ☎ 0907 290 9452

Menshori Rent-a-Car めんしょりレンタカー; 1048 Wadomari; ☎ 0997 92 2756; w hayashi-auto.com/okinoerabu-island

Taniyama Motors 谷山モータース; 1207 Wadomari; ☎ 0997 92 9180. Cycles & mopeds.

Teru Rent-a-Car Teruレンタカー; 147-6 Wadomari; ☎ 0906 639 8466; w k-teru.com

Toyota Rent-a-Car Okinoerabu Airport トヨタレンタカー沖永良部空港; 1720 Kunigami; ☎ 0997 92 2100; w rent.toyota.co.jp

TOURIST INFORMATION Okinoerabujima's tourist information office is casually named Erabu Coco (エラブココ; 1029-3 China; ☎ 0997 84 3540; w okinoerabujima.info; ⌚ 10.00–17.00 daily). It's a sightseeing base that provides information, sells souvenirs, has rental equipment and helps plan your stay. You can download an English pamphlet in advance from their website. Erabu Coco also offers experiences and tours, like *churatama* (a miniature glass buoy) souvenir making, sanshin playing and cycling days. The office has working spaces for anyone who needs an office on the go and showers too.

WHERE TO STAY *Map, page 153*

Shimayado Atari (whole house) しまやど當; 2270 Tamana; ☎ 0997 84 3807; w shimayado-atari.com. Beautiful renovated wooden house; study & book room, tatami rooms, courtyard, terrace, bath & secluded garden full of subtropical plants. HB island dishes available. **$$$$$**

✷ **Kankō Hotel Azuma & Kochinda Hotel** (Kankō, 15 rooms; Kochinda, 12 rooms) 観光ホテル東&コチンダホテル; 568 Wadomari; ☎ 0997 92 1283; w azumahotels.com. Kochinda is a beautiful boutique hotel on a relative budget, run by Kankō Hotel, with plush, dark wood, Western en-suite rooms surrounding a traditional garden. Kankō Hotel offers a more traditional hotel experience, with friendly owners. B/fast & cycle rental available. **$$$**

Log Inn Tarasso (8 rooms) ログインタラソ; 147-6 Wadomari; ☎ 0997 85 1239; w yuilog.info. Port or ocean view rooms in simple but chic wood building with terraces. Restaurant, café & shop; Japanese b/fast option. Luggage storage, parking & laundry available. Thalasso spa next door. **$$$**

47 Hostel (5 rooms, 1 dorm) 47ホステル; 576-5 Wadomari; ☎ 0909 025 5285. Warm, welcoming hostel with private tatami rooms & dorms. Small shared lounge & bathrooms, free drinks, bike hire & free parking. Great value & clean, with spacious rooms. **$–$$**

WHERE TO EAT AND DRINK *Map, page 153*

✷ **Saigo Shokudō** 西郷食堂; 1169-2 Inobe; ☎ 0997 92 1103; ⌚ 11.30–14.00 & 18.00–22.00 Mon–Fri. One of the best restaurants on the island, Saigo is run by a multigenerational fishing family, with the day's catch on full display in the tank by reception. The freshest fish on the island presented

OKINOERABU'S LOCAL FOODS

Agriculture is a large part of the island's income. Its red-earth fields are rich in minerals so perfect for farming. This makes it home to the *harunosasayaki*, the earliest harvested potato crop in Japan. These potatoes are native to Erabu, and are picked from the ground between February and April. Mangoes also grow on the island and are made into mango jam that can be picked up at stores and souvenir shops.

After the spring potatoes, Okinoerabu's best-known speciality is *sodeika*, or diamond squid. This dish of squid is served either raw as sashimi or fired, atop a bed of salad. More modern takes on the traditional dish include a whole range of squid products: squid ham, squid sausages and squid with soy beans. The sodeika sausage in particular has won awards.

Shimaguwa is the Okinoerabu mulberry, a leaf that's believed to control blood glucose levels. It's found tucked into everything from teas, sweets and cakes to soba. *Kikurage*, also known as the cloud ear mushroom, is a crazy-looking fungus that's rare, delicious and good for you, being high in iron and fibre. On Okinoerabu, kikurage is cultivated on the remains of processed sugarcane. Naturally, the island also proudly produces its own kokutō shōchū (page 117), and the locals' favourite sweets are simple lumps of brown sugar. Finally, Okinoerabu has another, rather unexpected crop for this area of the world: coffee.

in myriad, lip-smacking ways, from sashimi to whole spiny lobster donburi, with set meal options. $$$–$$$$

Kaisai 海幸; 493-3 Wadomari; 0997 92 3826; noon–14.00 & 18.30–22.00 Mon–Sat. Largely fish & shellfish restaurant with friendly & knowledgeable owner, private rooms & plenty of sake. Check out the seafood set meal for the daily recommendation. $$$

Izakaya Kusa 居酒屋草; 512-7 Tedechina; 0997 92 1202; 18.00–midnight daily. Welcoming tatami izakaya using seasonal local ingredients, veggies from kitchen garden & seafood just offshore. Also offers all you can drink (*nomihodai*) for groups. Try local brown sugar shōchū, beef tongue & *yachimuchi* brown sugar pancakes. $$

Kiyoi きよい; 537 Wadomari; 0997 92 2327; 11.30–13.30 & 18.00–22.00 Mon–Sat. Hugely popular local spot for katsudon, as well as classic Japanese dishes & fresh island fish. $$

Noah Coffee ノアコーヒー; 123-3 Wadomari; 0809 097 7456; 09.00–18.00 Fri–Wed. Noah operates a coffee farm on the island, making its brews 100% local. Home-roasted coffees & coffee snacks, products & souvenirs. A must on your drive round. $

SHOPPING There are lots of shops, including a 24-hour convenience store, co-ops and Nishimuta FCs. Despite also being home improvement stores, the latter actually sell a lot of food and delightfully cheap take-away meals. The biggest supermarkets tend to be on the outskirts of the small towns. A Co-op is the largest, with one in Wadomari (Aコープ 和泊店; 1769-1 Tamashiro; 0997 92 3518; 09.00–19.30 daily) and one in China (Aコープ 知名店; 2095 Serikaku; 0997 93 4120; 09.00–19.30 daily).

Erabu Coco Page 155. Shop here is excellent, selling jewellery made from island seashells.

Kimono House Iwai きもの家 いわい; 555 Wadomari; 0997 92 0212; 08.00–18.00 Mon–Sat. Ōshima tsumugi shop selling various clothes & woven items.

Magokoro Sugar まごころ製糖; 611-1 Goran; 0997 92 2857; 09.00–17.00 Mon–Sat.

Magokoro's always-smiling owner produces & sells amazing brown sugar products made the traditional way without additives or sweeteners. Perfect for gifts.

Okinoerabu Sake Brewery 沖永良部酒造; 1999-1 Hanatori, Tamaki; 0997 92 0185; 08.30–17.00 Mon–Sat. Brewery shop selling their own local alcohols & offering tasters too.

Tida Souvenirs 物産処ていだ; 584-21 Wadomari; 0997 85 1633; 08.00–noon & 13.00–18.00 Mon–Fri, 08.00–17.00 Sat–Sun. Classic souvenirs in Wadomari.

SPORTS AND ACTIVITIES

Craft workshops

Bashōfu Kaikan 沖永良部芭蕉布会館; 1270 Shimojiro; 0997 93 4753; w okinoerabu-bashofu.jp. Workshop making bashōfu cloth, a native Amami cloth made from banana fibres, with expert Chiyoko Nasegawa. Reservations required for experience – Japanese only but hands-on teaching. English tour videos available.

Farmhouse Inn Blue Ocean 農家民宿ブルーオーシャン; 475-1 China; 0997 93 2811. Farmhouse run by an older couple who offer fun farming experiences, like vegetable planting, cutting flowers & harvesting, followed by BBQs with locals.

Outdoor activities

Great Nature Okinoerabu 1089-7 Azefu, Wadomari; 0801 898 3882; w greatnatureoke.com. Snorkelling, diving, caving & spear fishing.

GT Divers GTダイバーズ; 471-3 Wadomari; 0997 92 4566; w gtdivers.net. Diving & whale watching.

Okierabu Caving Association 沖永良部島ケイビング協会; 678-3 China; 0903 815

CAVING ON OKINOERABU

This is what puts Okinoerabu on the map. The ever-moving, ever-shifting coral and tectonic plates have created a playground underneath the island's red soil skin. Though there are hundreds of caves, only four are accessible by tour. You'll need a guide and reservations to explore them as they involve proper caving gear, being immersed in water and narrow crawl spaces: in short, excellent fun.

Okinoerabujima's tallest cave is Ginsuidō (銀水洞), meaning 'Silver Water Cave'. With a total length of 3km, Ginsuidō has a huge domed room and a wall of stalactites over 5m long, but its prettiest aspect is the room of tiered pools. These white mallow-like formations are filled with water, which guides light with torches to show off its bright blue. Their beauty has put Okinoerabu on the map, as they've featured in several TV programmes. Ginsuidō takes around 5 hours and involves crawling through narrow spaces between water and stalactites, earning it an advanced level.

Suirendō (水連洞) was once a tourist cave that has since been abandoned. It's now a great exploration cave with waterfalls and pools, swimming and narrow holes to climb through. At 3 hours, it's marketed as an intermediate cave. At 2 hours, Daijadō (大蛇洞) is the recommended beginner's cave involving water, clambering, and stunning stalactites and formations. Shoryūdō (page 159) is the easiest cave, designed to be walked into without guide or special gear.

Needless to say, don't embark on a tour if you're claustrophobic or afraid of small, tight spaces. You should be in good physical health and able to swim, and bear in mind that body shape and size will be taken into account for safety in the narrow passes. With that said, caving is the thing to do on Okinoerabujima: it's a non-negotiable must for those who are willing and able.

8281; w okierabucave.com. The ultimate caving company on Erabu. English-speaking guide Kobayashi will take you through Erabu's 4 caves, providing coffee, clothing, equipment, a history of Okinoerabu's caves & great conversation.

OTHER PRACTICALITIES Erabu isn't large, but it has all the amenities you need: banks, post offices, police stations and medical facilities. Be aware that many banks and ATMs don't open at the weekend.

Banks and post offices

Amami Ōshima Shinyōkinko 奄美大島信用金庫; 581 Wadomari; 0997 92 1331; 09.00–11.30 & 12.30–15.00 Mon–Fri; 312-1 China; 0997 93 2033; 06.00–15.00 Mon–Fri

China Post Office 知名郵便局; 312-10 China; 0997 93 2042; 09.00–17.00 Mon–Fri, ATM: 08.45–18.00 Mon–Fri, 09.00–18.00 Sat

Sumiyoshi Post Office 住吉簡易郵便局; 2550-1 Sumiyoshi; 0997 93 2284; 09.00–16.00 Mon–Fri

Wadomari Post Office 和泊郵便局; 548-1 Wadomari; 0997 92 0042; 09.00–17.00 Mon–Fri, ATM: 08.00–19.00 Mon–Fri, 09.00–19.00 Sat–Sun

Medical

Okinoerabu Tokushukai Hospital 沖永良部徳洲会病院; 2208 Serikaku, China; 0997 93 3000; 09.00–11.30, 14.00–16.00 & 17.00–19.00 Mon–Fri, 09.00–11.30 Sat

Police

China Police Box 沖永良部警察署知名交番; 498-1 China; 0997 93 2003

Okinoerabu Police Station 沖永良部警察署; 120 Wadomari; 0997 92 0110

Tamina Police Substation 沖永良部警察署田皆駐在所; 2373-4 Tamina; 0997 93 4952

WHAT TO SEE AND DO At the top of Wadomari's quiet warren is the handsome **Nanshū Shrine** (南洲神社), built in memory of the samurai Saigo Takamori (page 154), also known as Saigo Nanshū. You'll see a bronze statue of the man himself and his dog – a replica of the famous one in Tokyo's Ueno Park. Further inland is another shrine, **Takachiho** (高千穂神社), which has a traditional island sumo ring.

Heading into the centre of the island, you'll find the **Yononushi Tomb and Shrine** (世之主の墓・世之主神社). This tūru tomb dug out of a natural cave is where the 15th-century island ruler Yononoushi, who killed himself and his family at the prospect of being conquered, is enshrined with his wife and his son. The castle ruins are the remains of a mansion built by the Hokuzan lord from Okinawa, who travelled to Okinoerabujima. The shrine itself isn't spectacular, but the view from the torii gates – when the vegetation is cleared – is quite something, with the island stretching out and away from the hilltop.

On the way back to the coast, go via **Nyaagunuhoo** (ニャーグヌホー), a pretty, low-lying waterfall that trickles through the trees. **Yowa Beach** (与和の浜) was once rife with trade ships in the Ryūkyū period; down the coast is another beach, **Ujijihama** (ウジジ浜), which is known for its unusually shaped rocks that stick out of the sea. It's particularly pretty when the sun rises between its standing rocks, light scattered in the waves. Ujiji is also the site of an 1890 Canadian shipwreck, destroyed in a typhoon with 22 people aboard. The ten survivors were cared for by locals for 17 days before safely returning home, thus beginning a relationship between Okinoerabu and Canada.

In the very centre of the island, at its highest point, is the **Ōyama Botanical Park Observatory** (大山植物公園 展望台). This spiral tower overlooks the entire island, as well as Tokunoshima, Yorontō and northern Okinawa-hontō. In late January–early February, the park fills with cherry blossoms. Between here and the island's southernmost coast is **Ginsuidō**, Erabu's most astonishing cave (page 157).

MYTHS AND FOLKTALES: THE MAKING OF OKINOERABU

Originally, Okinoerabu was made like a see-saw: if you stood on one side of the island, the opposite side would lift up from the sea. This annoyed the gods Shimakouda and Kunikouda, so they sought out the king of the gods to fix it. 'Place black rocks on the east coast, white ones on the west', he said. They did as he told and the island stopped moving. They then sought his advice on how to make humans. 'Draw the shape of a person in the dirt, then blow on it', he replied. They did so and populated Okinoerabu with people.

But the people could not have children – so they went back to the king. 'Build the man's house on the windward side, the woman's on the leeward side', was the advice. The winds combined, and they were blessed with children. To make food, he told them to collect seeds from Niragashima, the palace of the Dragon King. But the Dragon King refused to give them any, because the first harvest festival was not yet finished. Shimakouda and Kunikouda tried to steal the rice instead and were killed.

The king of the gods, concerned that they had not returned, sent a messenger to see what had happened. The messenger revived the pair with a magic potion, and they told the God King their story. He sent them back to Nirai to return the stolen rice. Once they had done so, they finished the festival and were given a sheaf of rice. From that day on Okinoerabujima had a rich rice harvest and plentiful children.

Passing through China (知名), pop to the **Hamiyama Shrine** (はみやま神社) with its short row of scarlet torii gates, before heading to **Yakomo Beach** (屋子母ビーチ). Popular for its coral reef, it also has views to Yorontō and Okinawa-hontō, and is a brilliant sunset spot. North along the coast is **Beach Rock** (ビーチロック), a low-tide geological formation of stratified limestone rocks.

This western coast holds two more brilliant beaches, thoroughly off the tourist map. The lesser-known is **Tumoro Beach** (トゥモロ浜), south of Sumiyoshi Port and accessed by a tiny farm slip road. It's an amazing sand hideaway backed by thick, Ghibli-esque gajumaru trees and forest. Near the slip road is another of the archipelago's **stone watchtowers** (志喜屋武当のウブス), built during Yononushi's reign. North of the port is stunning **Shibikinya Beach** (シニキニャ浜), similarly secluded and backed by forests and gnarled roots.

In Sumiyoshi town (住吉) itself is the **Sumiyoshi Kuragō River** (住吉暗川), hidden in a small dark cavern surrounded by lush trees and thick moss atop cragged rocks. The river, which used to be an important water source for the town, is at the bottom of the stairs. The way down is almost pitch black and slippery, but there is a switch for lighting.

Shoryūdō (昇竜洞; 1520 Oazasumiyoshi; ☎0997 93 4536; w chinatyo-syoryudo.com; 🕘 09.00–16.30 daily; adult/child ¥1,100/200–500) in Oyama's foothills is an Erabu caving highlight. This extensive coral limestone cave is filled with remarkable formations with grandiose names, such as the Pillar of Enthusiasm and the Gate of Longevity. Discovered in 1936, Shoryūdō is the longest flowstone cave in Japan, with a total length of 3,500m. Only 600m of that is accessible to tourists, but it's abundant with over 25 types of stalactites, some of which look as if they are dappled with silver and gold. It takes about an hour to go round the cave, which is the only one on the island that doesn't require a guide.

Okinoerabu's northwest point is **Tamina Cape** (田皆岬), a 51m-high clifftop that's one of Amami's ten views. It overlooks the sea and the coastal landscape, a stunning panorama of craggy green and gradated blue that stretches into the horizon. Below, you can see the reef, the occasional turtle and even humpback whales. The area is also home to a travertine marble quarry, whose stones were used in the National Diet Building in Tokyo.

To the east you'll find the **Okidomari Seaside Park** (沖泊海浜公園), a long, 400m strip of creamy sand that's a popular swimming beach with rock pools, camping and sunset views. Make sure to call at **Bashōfu Kaikan** (芭蕉布会館; page 157), where you can try making Okinoerabu's amazing banana fibre cloth. Even if you don't book an experience, pop by anyway to see the cloth being made by one of the few remaining experts on the island.

The ruins of **Goranmagohachi Castle** (後蘭孫八城跡) are some of the best in the archipelago – not because they're almost complete, but because they're excellently overgrown, the forest doing its best to improve the castle's dilapidation. Giant gajumaru, dangling roots and piled rocks surround enclosed graves, outer stone walls and even holes believed to have been used for escape.

If you can face a museum without English descriptions, **Wadomari Town History and Folklore Museum** (和泊歴史民俗資料館; 1313-1 Neori; 0997 92 0911; 09.00–17.00 Thu–Tue; adult/child ¥200/100) displays the town's cultural assets and folk materials. If that's not your cup of tea, go next door to the **Koshiyama Observatory** (越山展望所) for broad views and an excellent cherry blossom garden when in bright pink and red bloom. At night, the observatory is spectacular for stargazing.

LOCAL RECIPE: KOKUTŌ SHŌCHŪ COCKTAILS

Although Amami Ōshima is better known for its kokutō shōchū, Okinoerabujima is a big fan of the drink and is proud of its kokutō – some claim its kokutō is the archipelago's best. Often related to rum, the alcohol packs a punch with a sweetness.

PASSION FRUIT AND KOKUTŌ SHŌCHŪ DAQUIRI

1 large passion fruit or 2 small
20ml fresh lemon juice
10ml of sugar syrup
60ml Kokutō shōchū

Remove the passion fruit seeds and shake them well with the lemon and a drizzle of sugar syrup. Strain into a glass before adding kokutō shōchū and stir.

KOKUTŌ SHŌCHŪ MOJITO

60ml Kokutō shōchū
½ lime
10 mint leaves
1 tsp sugar
crushed ice
soda water

Muddle the mint, sugar, lime and soda water in a glass. Add crushed ice and pour shōchū on top.

Erabu's north is a crinkled coast of quiet beaches and ocean views. **Sea Turtle Viewpoint** (ウミガメビューポイント) lives up to its name – it overlooks the shallows where sea turtles regularly hang out, and there are free mounted binoculars to help you spot them. **Wanjo Beach** (ワンジョビーチ) just alongside is one of the best and most eye-catching beaches, being used multiple times as a film location. It's ideal for swimming, with calm shallows, a snorkelling reef, white sand and well-maintained facilities. Just behind Wanjo is Okinoerabu's small **cycad Jungle** (ソテツジャングル), a wandering 500m garden of butterflies, cycads and other tropical flora.

In the northern region of Kunigami is the so-called '**Japan's Best Gajumaru**' (日本一のガジュマル; 2904 Kunigami). In 1898, the very first graduates of Kunigami Elementary School planted this banyan tree. Now, the 125-year-old giant is 8m tall and branches out 22m, supported by poles. It's a natural monument of the town and one of Japan's 100 famous trees. Naturally, it still sits in the school grounds, but you can happily ask to take a look – often a wave and a point will do.

The northernmost point is where you'll find **Fuucha** (フーチャ), a dynamic coastal cave partially eroded by the tide. High tide still plays a role in Fuucha's spectacle; on windy days, the full sea erupts up through the cave towards onlookers above. This geyser-like whoosh reaches around 10m high when the waters are rough – in typhoons, it can get up to 70m. Heading round the coastline brings you to three beaches: **Shinafa** (シナファ浜), a quiet spot where white spider lilies grow; the crystal clear waters of **Nishinuhadu** (ニシヌハドゥ); and the picture-perfect, stack-sprinkled **Shaashi** (シャーシビーチ).

Past the airport back towards Wadomari brings you to a famous – if seasonal – Okinoerabu sight. **Kasaishi Seaside Park** (笠石海浜公園) is where 16,000 Erabu lily trumpets burst into bloom from April to May. They're planted every year by the islanders, who in October 2020 earned the Guinness World Record for 'largest number of flower bulbs planted in an hour' – 15,690. Though the lilies are temporary, the park is home to a beach, observation tower, barbecue and camping spots.

The final, subtle roadside stop before hitting Wadomari is **Kuragō** (暗川), marked by a white signboard to the right of the Wadamatsu Shop (和田マツ商店). Descend down the steps into the darkness to find Okinoerabu's 'dark river'. This underground waterway was used by locals in the past for both washing and drinking. Women and girls were expected to transport the water; this was heavy labour, as they had to work with candle lamps on their heads and buckets on their backs. Water supplies were installed in 1957, and so the well fell into disuse.

YORONTŌ

The final piece of Kagoshima Prefecture, the end of the wild and forested Amami group, comes as quite the surprise. Yorontō (与論島) has few animals to speak of, no deep dark woods to explore, no great cavern systems to lose yourself in. It just about scrapes together a hill. But what Yorontō does have – what Yorontō does best – is beaches.

The island is only 23.7km around but has 60 beaches, the majority of which are made of tooth-white sands and sweet-wrapper seas. Made up of coral reef, surrounded by coral reefs, Yorontō is all about the blinding beauty of its rich ocean. Scuba diving, snorkelling, sunbathing, sandcastles and bobbing turtles – which use some 300 locations on the island for laying eggs from May to August, hatching in August–September – have earned Kagoshima's southernmost island two nicknames: 'therapy island' and 'the pearl floating in the East'.

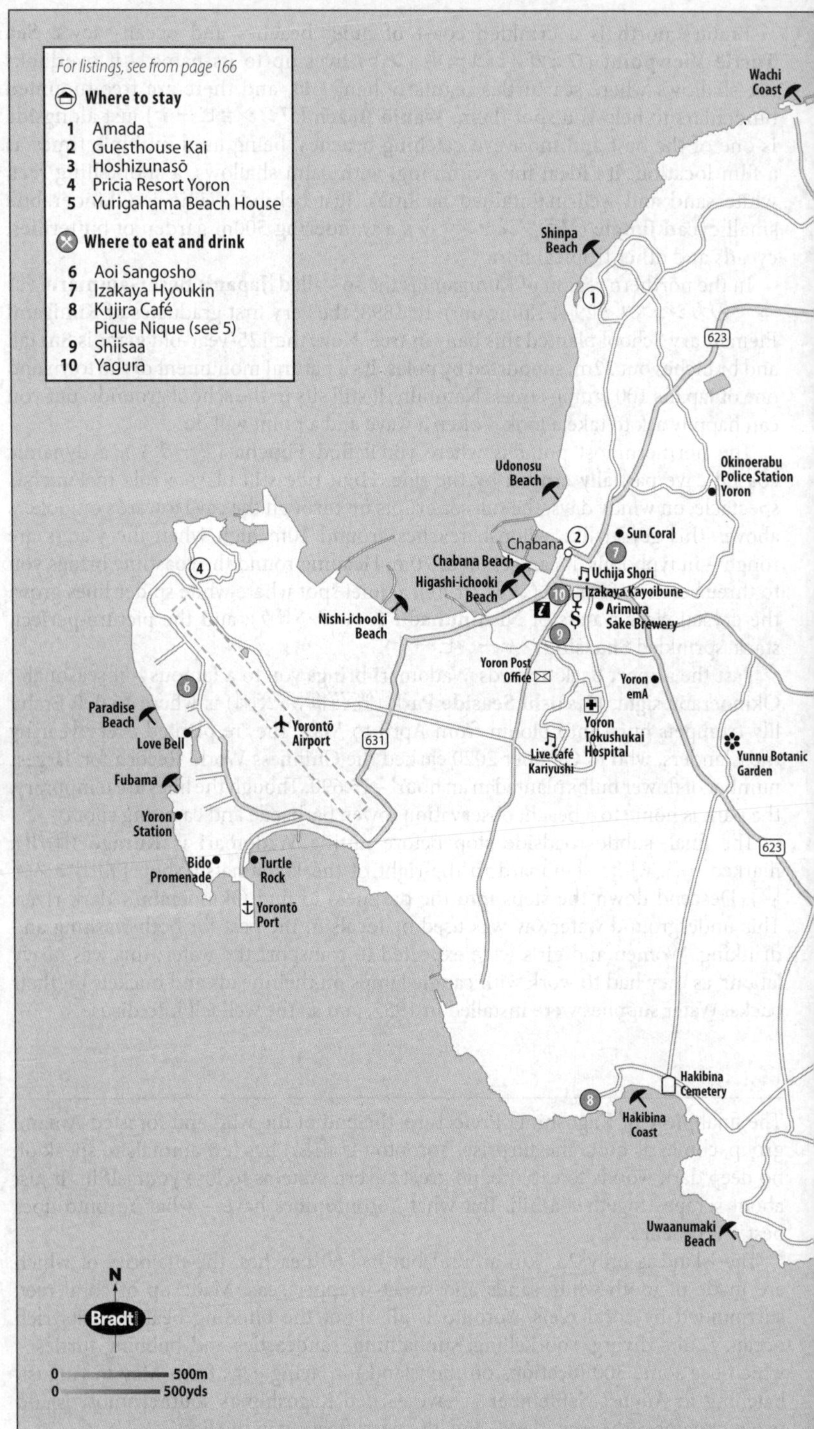
For listings, see from page 166
Where to stay
1 Amada
2 Guesthouse Kai
3 Hoshizunasō
4 Pricia Resort Yoron
5 Yurigahama Beach House
Where to eat and drink
6 Aoi Sangosho
7 Izakaya Hyoukin
8 Kujira Café
Pique Nique (see 5)
9 Shiisaa
10 Yagura
Wachi Coast
Shinpa Beach
623
Okinoerabu Police Station
Yoron
Udonosu Beach
Sun Coral
Chabana
Chabana Beach
Uchija Shori
Higashi-ichooki Beach
Izakaya Kayoibune
Arimura Sake Brewery
Nishi-ichooki Beach
Yoron Post Office
Yoron emA
Paradise Beach
Yorontō Airport
631
Love Bell
Yoron Tokushukai Hospital
Live Café Kariyushi
Yunnu Botanic Garden
Fubama
Yoron Station
623
Bido Promenade
Turtle Rock
Yorontō Port
Hakibina Cemetery
Hakibina Coast
Uwaanumaki Beach
N
Bradt
0 500m
0 500yds

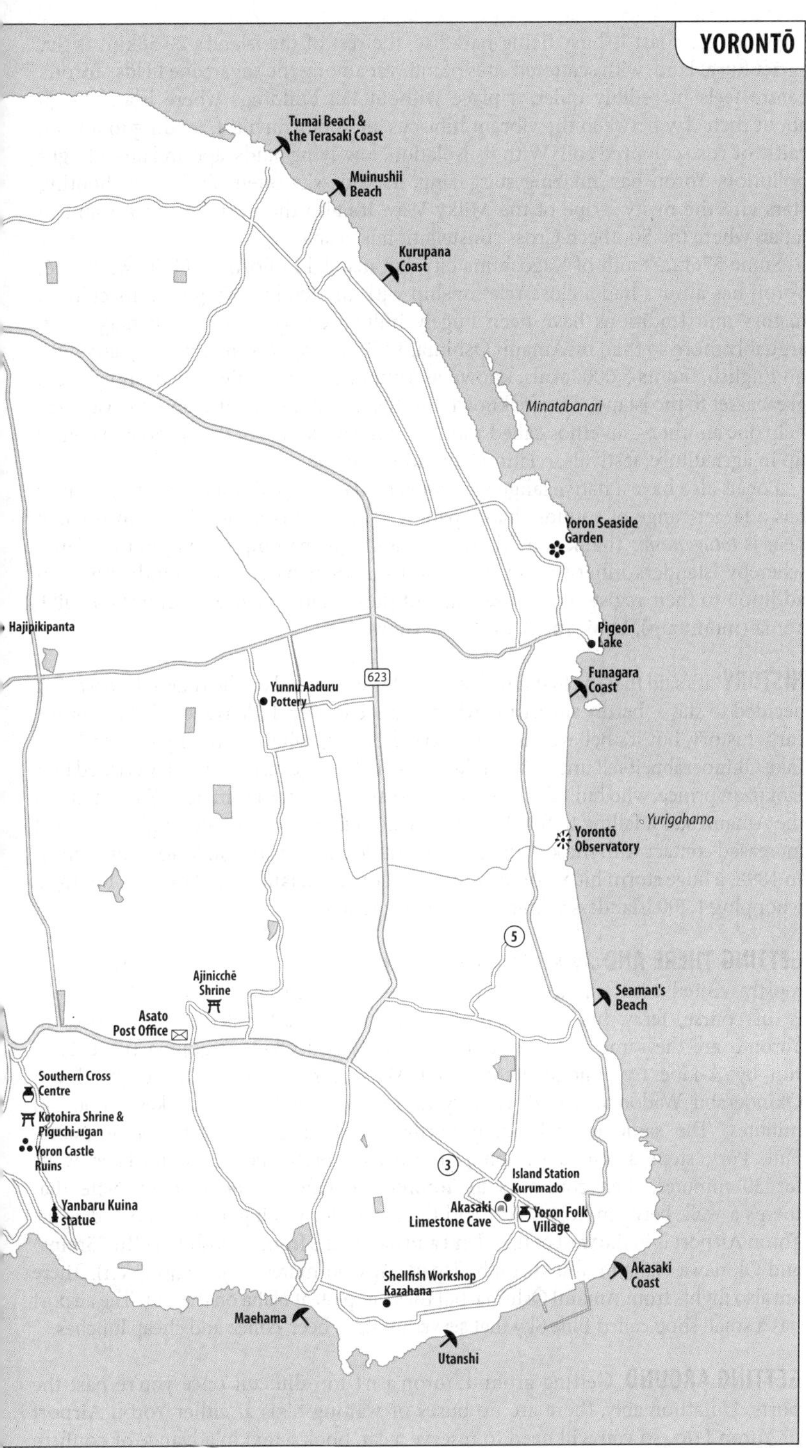
YORONTŌ
Tumai Beach & the Terasaki Coast
Muinushii Beach
Kurupana Coast
Minatabanari
Yoron Seaside Garden
Hajipikipanta
Pigeon Lake
Funagara Coast
623
Yunnu Aaduru Pottery
Yurigahama
Yorontō Observatory
5
Seaman's Beach
Ajinicchē Shrine
Asato Post Office
Southern Cross Centre
Kotohira Shrine & Piguchi-ugan
Yoron Castle Ruins
Yanbaru Kuina statue
3
Island Station Kurumado
Akasaki Limestone Cave
Yoron Folk Village
Akasaki Coast
Shellfish Workshop Kazahana
Maehama
Utanshi

While the coast is busy being paradise, the rest of the island's 20.58km² is flat agricultural land, with scattered sites of interest among the sugarcane fields. Yoron's centre feels incredibly quiet, a place without tall buildings where islanders go about their day between the vibrant hibiscus and bougainvillea, tending to lowing cattle or rust-coloured soil. With its isolation, low-lying landscape and absent light pollution, Yoron has amazing stargazing, its wide sky often filled with shooting stars and the misty stripe of the Milky Way. It's also the northernmost island in Japan where the Southern Cross constellation is visible.

Some 576km south of Kagoshima city, but just 23km north of Okinawa-hontō, Yoron has always had a close relationship with the Ryūkyū Kingdom. Its culture, history and traditions have been hugely influenced by its southern neighbour, arguably more so than by Amami Ōshima, 147km away. Yoron remains pretty light on English, but its 5,000 locals, known as Yunnunchu, are brilliantly friendly and a great asset to the island. They're known for their community spirit and the way they help one another – an ethos called '*yui*'. Yui is the backbone of the island and comes up in agriculture, festivals, relationships and daily life.

Locals also have a native language, *yunnu futuba*, which despite sounding similar has a larger range of sounds than Japanese. The most common local word you'll hear is *totuganashi*: 'thank you'. There's also a unique naming system on the island, whereby islanders inherit an extra name from their parents or grandparents, in addition to their registered name. Many of these names have a natural theme like Yama (mountain), Ushi (rock) and Hana (flower).

HISTORY It's said that the first humans to settle here landed on the Akasaki Coast, and decided to stay – hardly surprising when you see it. Very little is recorded of Yoron's early history, but it's believed to have started paying tribute to the Ryūkyū in 1266. Like Okinoerabu, it fell under the Hokuzan Kingdom's governance and was ruled by a Hokuzan prince, who built the never-finished Yoron Castle. From here, Yoron follows the Amami story, falling to the Ryūkyū Kingdom then Satsuma, although Yoron had increased contact with the kingdom in both trade and culture thanks to its proximity. In 1898, a huge storm hit Yorontō, resulting in drought, famine and disease, forcing a whopping 1,200 islanders to migrate en masse to Kyūshū.

GETTING THERE AND AWAY Despite being part of the Amami group, Yorontō is mostly visited as a trip from Okinawa-hontō. The cheapest means of transport is, of course, ferry, but as always these are very weather-dependent. Ferries to Yorontō are the same as those to Tokunoshima and Okinoerabujima (page 114), run by A-Line (w aline-ferry.com) and Marix Line (w marix-line.co.jp). From Okinoerabu Wadomari the daily ferry to Yorontō's westerly port takes 1 hour 40 minutes. The same ferry heading northward starts at Okinawa-hontō's Naha-Futo Port, stops at Okinawa-hontō's northern Motobu Port 2 hours later, waits for 30 minutes, then continues to Yorontō, arriving 2½ hours later. Note that there's a walk between Yoron Port and the passenger waiting area, so don't dawdle. Yoron Airport is in the west of the island and has flights from Kagoshima (1hr 25mins) and Okinawa Naha (40mins) run by Japan Air Commuter (w jal.co.jp/jp/en). There are also flights from Amami Ōshima, but these stop off at Naha on the way. The airport has a small shop called Blue Sky that serves up sake, beer, coffee and cheap lunches.

GETTING AROUND Getting around Yoron isn't too difficult once you're past the ports. Unfathomably, there are no buses or waiting taxis at either Yoron Airport or Yoron Port, so you will need to reserve a car, book a taxi in advance or confirm

YORON FESTIVALS

Yoron has a wealth of annual celebrations. The Sangachi-sanchi noro festival welcomes gods from Nirai Kanai and drives pests off the fields and back to the legendary home of the gods. There are warnings for not taking part: legends say if you don't go to the sea and play on this day, a disaster may occur or, perhaps worse, you might become an owl. Another superstition says that seafood must be added to the dinner on this day or you will become deaf or unable to catch any fish for the remaining year. Children born since the last Sangachi-sanchi, particularly girls, are dipped into the sea. Mugwort muchi is made and eaten at this event.

The island is known for its 15th Night Dances (与論十五夜踊り), which take place on the 15th of lunar March, August and October at the Kotohira Shrine. These ancient dances pray for rain, harvest, peace and prosperity from the dragon god and give thanks. Legend says that Yononushi, who ruled the island in the 16th century, sent his sons across Amami, Ryūkyū and Japan to research dances, and the blended *jyūgoya odori* was the result. The dances are separated into two groups: the first is mainland Satsuma *kyogen* dances, the second Ryūkyū-style dances. The dances alternate, demonstrating the influence from the island's north and south.

There is also the August Yoron Coral festival, the largest summer festival with boat races and shows, and the Umibiraki which prays for sea safety and where newborns are soaked in seawater.

Yoron is also a big fan of island sumo: students from across the island and its neighbours come to wrestle here, often at the end of the harvest festival.

a pick-up/drop-off with your accommodation (which most offer). Once at your accommodation, the nicest way to travel is by **bicycle**. The island is small and relatively flat, with only one main hill that you can always dismount for and walk up. Mostly you're dotting from beach to beach, making cycling a pleasure. If you haven't got the time to cycle you can use the public bus or rent a vehicle. It only takes an hour to drive round Yoron by **car**. There are plenty of car hire places, but you can also check with your accommodation to see if they offer car rental. There are two **taxi** companies, both offering sightseeing hire, but each only has a fleet of two cars so may take some time – reserve in advance. **Bus Minamirikun** (☎0997 97 3331) runs a bus service with adorably small vehicles closer to minivans. The routes are very simple northbound and southbound loops from Chabana, each leaving about five times a day. Board at bus stops or hail like a taxi; you can purchase a two-day unlimited ticket on board that costs only ¥500 for adults, ¥300 for kids.

Taxis

Minami Taxi 南タクシー; 1581-2 Chabana; ☎0997 97 3331

Vehicle rental

Coro Rent-a-Car コロレンタカー; 173-3 Riccho; ☎0997 97 2533; w cororentaka.com

Nangoku Rent-a-Car 南国レンタカー; 253-1 Chabana; ☎0997 97 2141; w yoron-nangoku.com. Cars, motorbikes & bicycles (electric available).

Yoron Ocean Rental Car ヨロンオーシャンレンタカー; 1F, 238 Chabana; ☎0997 85 1666; w yoron-ocean.com. Cars & motorbikes.

Yoron Rental Car ヨロンレンタカー; 48-7 Chabana; ☎0997 97 3633; w yoron-rentalcars.sakura.ne.jp. Cars, motorbikes & cycles (electric available).

TOURIST INFORMATION The Yoron Tourism Association (ヨロン島観光協会; 33 Chabana; 0997 97 5151; w yorontou.info; 09.00–17.00 daily) has a lot of information to hand and can help you on your travels round the island. Their website is excellent and you can download pamphlets in advance. They also organise tours, including eco-tours, nature and history walks. While on Yorontō, you can also pick up the so-called Kingdom of Panauri Passport – a cultural initiative where you pay ¥400 for the passport, which gives you discounts at participating stores and sights, and enables you to collect stamps for a free gift.

WHERE TO STAY *Map, page 162*

Amada (whole villa) 2483-7 Chabana; 0120 07 0300; w amada-yoron.com. Architecturally stunning, Amada is luxury accommodation for 4 people with private pool, sommelier-chosen wine cellar, cypress barrel sauna, private BBQ, laundry, kitchen. As good as it gets. **$$$$$**

Pricia Resort Yoron (97 rooms) プリシアリゾートヨロン; 358-1 Riccho; 0997 97 5060; w pricia.co.jp. Santorini-inspired resort by Kanebo Sunset Beach, with outdoor pool, restaurant, shop & laundry. Rooms range from large dbls to villas with living room, private pool, sauna, & rooftop dining area. Offers tours & diving. **$$$$$**

✷ **Yurigahama Beach House** (2 rooms) 百合ヶ浜ビーチハウス; 79-1 Furusato; 0997 85 1000; w yurigahama.com. Beautiful guesthouse run by Pique Nique (see below) owners & local English-speaking guide. 4-bed Western rooms with modern take on traditional décor, there's laundry, gorgeous shared area with sunken *kotatsu* table, TV & shared bathroom. Guided tours recommended; b/fast & e-scooters available. **$$$$**

Hoshizunasō (6 rooms) 星砂荘; 616-3 Yoron; 0997 97 3710; w yoronhoshizunaso.com. Very laid-back pension-style, family-run accommodation, used as a set in a Japanese movie. Tatami & Western rooms with sink, shared bathrooms, huge kitchen-diner space with self-catering amenities. HB, rental bikes & tours available. **$$$**

Guesthouse Kai (6 rooms) ゲストハウスKAI; 2309 Chabana; 0705 503 6971. Pretty accommodation with super basic Western-style rooms. Operates an eco-tour & diving company, a souvenir shop, a separate site dormitory & rental cars. There's a large kitchen, patio-garden & welcoming feel. **$$**

WHERE TO EAT AND DRINK *Map, page 162*

Yoron is known for its own wagyū beef and Amami black guinea fowl, local fish, spiny lobster and an extraordinary range of crops. These include island banana, dragon fruit, passionfruit, mango, atemoya, papaya, bitter melon, brown sugar, mozuku seaweed and *moringa* – the latter two made into speciality noodles. Yoron also has a wealth of medicinal herbs, which have been used for centuries to treat patients – you can taste some of them at Pique Nique.

Kujira Café くじらカフェ; 1622-3 Riccho; 10.00–16.00 Wed & Fri–Sat. Cutesie café and shop with comfy seats & beach view. Menu of fancy drinks & simple dishes: dutch pancakes, curry & noodles, & island muffins, or shima'ffins. **$$**

✷ **Pique Nique** 薬草カフェピクニック; 79-1 Furusato; 0907 208 8295; w pique-nique-snack-bar.business.site; 11.00–17.00 Fri–Tue. Café at Yurigahama Beach House (see above) using Yoron medicinal herbs in dishes such as tofu taco rice, spicy curry & excellent burgers. Husband & wife team – Nobuyuki-san offers English-language guided tours too. **$$**

Shiisaa Restaurant シーサー屋ヨロン店; 20-15 Chabana; 0903 328 0508; w 438yoron.com; 17.00–midnight daily. Menus including Yoron & Okinawan cuisine, fresh seafood, & over 500 types of island shōchū & awamori. Try Yoron's gooya (bitter gourd) chips, liver sashimi or island tuna. **$$**

Yagura やぐら; 175 Chabana; 0997 97 2290; 17.00–midnight daily. Brilliant izakaya run by a grandmother who makes a different buffet menu of island specialities each night. **$$**

Aoi Sangosho あおいさんごしょう; 637-1 Riccho; 0997 97 3599; w yorontoh.wixsite.com/website; 11.00–16.00 daily. Known for its

THE YORON DEDICATION

Brown sugar shōchū produced on the island, known locally as *shimayūsen* (島有泉), is involved in a delightful island custom called the 'Yoron dedication' (Yoron-kenpō), which you may find yourself part of in izakaya or restaurants. This ceremony, meant to demonstrate hospitality and entertain guests, depends on the number of people taking part. First the host puts however much shōchū they decide into a cup. After introducing themselves, they drink the cup, leaving a few drops that they then put on their head – 'returning it to god' (the Japanese words for 'hair' and 'god' are the same).

They turn the cup over to show they have nothing left and then it's the next person's go. The host pours their drink while the guest holds the cup, and this continues for as many people as necessary. You're never forced to drink, though – you can opt out and return it to the host if needs be.

mozuku soba, black pig gyoza & unlimited refills of rice & pickles. $

Izakaya Hyoukin 酒屋ひょうきん; 2297-1 Chabana; 0997 97 3557; 17.00–midnight daily. Serving up local Yoron sake, sashimi, sooki and tempura dishes from its small countertop, this Chabana bar does cheap drinks & hearty sides. $

ENTERTAINMENT AND NIGHTLIFE There's a surprising number of bars and izakaya on Yorontō. The majority are filled with locals and welcoming – take your pick.

Dining & Music Uchijashori dining&musicうちじゃしょり; 2F 242-1 Chabana; 0802 757 4683; 19.00–23.00 Tue–Sun. Cute & colourful live music venue, owned by Yoron tourism ambassador & musician.

Izakaya Kayoibune 居酒屋かよいぶね; 35-1 Chabana; 0997 97 3189; 17.00–midnight daily. Great snacks, unique Yoron meals & great atmosphere that pulls in islanders.

Live Café Kariyushi らいぶcafe かりゆし; 130 Chabana; 0997 97 4432; w kariyushibandyoron.com; 19.30–23.00 Tue–Sun. Shop of Kariyushi, a band that performs internationally. Enjoy their original music as well as Yorontō & Okinawan folk songs.

SHOPPING The majority of shops are in the Chabana area, including the largest store on the island, A Co-op Yoron (Aコープ よろん店; 64 Chabana; 0997 97 2004; 09.00–19.30 daily). There are plenty of other little stores about Yoron for you to pick up bits and pieces.

Arimura Sake Brewery 有村酒造; 226-1 Chabana; 0997 97 2302; w shimayusen.jp; 08.00–17.00 Mon–Sat. Brewery where you can do tours & buy sake.

Island Station Kurumado 島の駅 くるまどう; 688 Mugiya; 0997 97 5124; w onizuka.ocnk.net; 09.00–17.00 Tue–Sun. Shop manufacturing & selling pure brown sugar & sweets from Yoron.

Shellfish Workshop Kazahana 貝工房かざはな; 1294 Mugiya; 0997 97 3032; w yoronkazahana.stores.jp; 09.30–18.30 daily. Handmade accessories incorporating local shells.

Sun Coral サンコーラル; 2300-1 Chabana; 0997 97 4339; w sun-coral.shop; 09.00–19.00 daily, closes 18.00 Oct–Jun. Largest souvenir shop on Yoron, also sells famed moringa noodles.

Yoron emA ヨロン・エマ; 309-5 Chabana; 0905 777 9683; w retreat.yoronema.com; 09.00–16.00 Mon–Sat. Yoron-designed T-shirts & art by local artists.

Yunnu Aaduru Pottery ゆんぬあーどぅる焼窯元; 909 Furusato; 0997 97 5155; 09.30–16.00 Sat–Thu. Workshop where you can buy Yoron-style pottery.

SPORTS AND ACTIVITIES Yoron is all about the sea, so it's no surprise that it is replete with marine activities and operators. Everything from diving and snorkelling to windsurfing and jet skiing is available. Diving spots include a shipwreck, arches, sinkholes, towers, a tuna migration area and Chabana's 'Underwater Palace' where you can get married.

Gallery Kai ギャラリーかい; 2309 Chabana; 0705 50 3697. 2hr coastal hike tours.
Pricia Resort Yoron プリシアリゾートヨロン; 358-1 Riccho; 0997 97 3939; w pricia.co.jp/activity. Huge array of marine activities, including diving. Run by hotel (page 166), which means better English access.
Seaman's Club シーマンズクラブ; 10-1 Mugiya; 0997 97 3207; w seamans.iku4.com. Glass boats, wakeboards, kayaks, reef fishing.
Skin Dive Yoron スキンダイブヨロン; 229-12 Chabana; 0908 058 4810; w select-type.com/s/skindive-yoron. Skin diving tours & blue cave marine trekking.
TANDY Marine TANDYマリン; Oganeku Beach, 16 Furusato; w yoron-love.com. Vast selection of marine tours, including sea turtle tours, banana boats, SUP, jet ski, snorkelling, boat charters, rentals & sunset cruises. Also stargazing & firefly tours.
Turamarin トゥラマリン; Udonosu Beach, Chabana; 0909 585 4970; w twuramarin.crayonsite.com. Windsurfing, wakeboarding, SUP, snorkel.
Yoron Diving Service ヨロンダイビングサービス; 1466-4 Riccho; 0997 97 3940; w yoron-diving.com. Fun, experience & C-Card licence diving as well as hire.
Yunnu Experience Centre ゆんぬ体験館; 3313 Riccho; 0997 84 3661; ⏲ 09.30–17.30 Thu–Tue. Excellent centre where you can do multiple crafting, sanshin, coffee roasting & historical experiences.

OTHER PRACTICALITIES

Banks and post offices

Amami Ōshima Shinyōkinko Yoron 奄美大島信用金庫与論支店; 37-6 Chabana; 0997 97 3181; ⏲ 09.00–15.00 Mon–Fri
Asato Post Office 朝戸郵便局; 1575 Asato; 0997 97 2016; ⏲ 09.00–16.00 Mon–Fri, ATM: 09.00–17.30 Mon–Fri, 09.00–12.00 Sat
Yoron Post Office 与論郵便局; 68-6 Chabana; 0997 97 2042; ⏲ 09.00–17.00 Mon–Fri, 09.00–12.30 Sat–Sun, ATM: 08.00–19.00 Mon–Fri, 09.00–19.00 Sat, 09.00–18.00 Sun

Medical

Yoron Tokushukai Hospital 与論徳洲会病院; 403-1 Chabana; 0997 97 2511; w yorontokushukai.jp; ⏲ 09.00–12.00 & 15.30–17.00 Mon–Fri, 09.00–12.00 Sat

Police

Okinoerabu Police Station Yoron 沖永良部警察署与論幹部派出所; 2092-1 Chabana; 0997 97 2803

WHAT TO SEE AND DO Yoron's what to see and do is a tick list of Elysian beaches. The entire coast is covered in them: some long, popular stretches, others sheltered, hidden little coves. Taking your time around the coastline allows you to stop and pick your personal favourite – there are enough to make sure you don't have to share.

Between the port and airport is the **Bidō Promenade** (ビドウ遊歩道), a refreshing, rocky headland walk along the coast. (It's perfect if you're waiting for or getting off the ferry.) Only 500m, it begins at the port's supposed **Turtle Rock** (ウェルカメ) and finishes at **Yoron Station** (ヨロン駅) – an unusual faux train station built in 1979, despite there being no railway on the island. Just north of the promenade is **Fubama** (フバマ), a pretty, deserted stretch of buttery sands, blue waves and caves.

Fubama quickly turns into **Paradise Beach** (パラダイスビーチ), the first of Yoron's blissful stretches of ivory sand and pellucid waves. Overlooking the beach is the **Love Bell** (愛の鐘), a typically Japanese tourist spot where you ring the bell

WHAT'S IN A NAME?

One of Yoron's more noticeable differences is its name: Yoron is the only island in the archipelago that doesn't usually end in '-jima' or '-shima'. This came from a 1970s tourism campaign, after Okinawa's reversion to Japan, when Yoron wanted to makeover its image and differentiate itself from the other islands. The change stuck around. It can happily be called Yoronjima – no-one will be confused – but its more common name is Yorontō. The -tō ending is just another way of pronouncing the same 'island' kanji.

with your partner and seal your romance. Perhaps more importantly, for both romance and sightseeing, is the fact this spot is amazing for stargazing. By day, you can see Okinawa-hontō, Izenajima and Iheyajima from here.

The coast north of the airport is, as expected, full of beaches – so full, in fact, that you'll notice the piles of sand pouring out on to the pavements. **Nishi-ichooki Beach** (西イチョーキ長浜), **Higashi-ichooki Beach** (東イチョーキ長浜) and **Chabana Beach** (茶花海岸) almost blend into one long arc, leading towards the main town of **Chabana** (茶花). The town itself isn't much more than a quiet thoroughfare for restaurants, bars and shops; beyond it to the north is **Udonosu Beach** (ウドノスビーチ). This beach is hidden behind adan and foliage, and scattered with rock formations. Its astonishingly clear calm waters host a coral colony offshore, where you may spot turtles. Popular with islanders, there's also a little path to the right that appears only when the tide is out.

Shinpa Beach (シナパ) in the northwest is a small, quiet little section where you can guarantee a picnic to yourself and a stunning sunset. The **Wachi Coast** (宇勝海岸), which curves around the northwest and north, is full of blissful beaches with overhanging rocks, soft sand and lapping waves. Towards the northeast is **Tumai Beach** (トゥマイ) and the **Terasaki Coast** (寺崎海岸) – both places where dragons are said to live, thanks to the dragon-shaped rocks on each. The male is on Tumai, the female Terasaki, but it may take a long day of squinting in the blistering sun to see them.

Tumai gives way to **Muinushii Beach** (ムイヌシー浜), a tiny little rocky cove of white sand and azure, then on to **Kurupana Coast** (黒花海岸), entered through a somewhat traditional tunnel of adan. Below Kurupana is the **Minatabanari** (皆田離), an islet off the coast formed of tortuous rock formations, which you can walk to at low tide.

One of the first non-beach sights is **Yoron Seaside Garden** (ヨロンシーサイドガーデン; 2019 Furusato; w amebaownd.com; ⌚ 10.30–17.30 daily; ¥500), a tropical garden/café space often used for weddings. The entrance fee actually covers a drink, so it's an ideal place to refresh after a cycle. To its south is a rocky outcrop oddly named **Pigeon Lake** (鳩の湖); you'll see a sign boulder at the top of the **Funagara Coast** (船倉海岸). More of a puddle in the rock, it's said this 'lake' never dries up, and was used as a watering hole by the pigeons of a local lord. The puddle resides next to a small shrine and monument to Ajinicchee, a local hero whose major shrine lies inland.

Funagara and **Seaman's Beach** (シーマンズビーチ) form part of the **Ōganeku Coast** (大金久海岸): a great 2km swipe of white sand down the east of the island and the most famous area of Yorontō. It is divided by the **Yorontō Observatory** (ヨロン島展望所), another rocky overlook that takes in the beaches and bay. At the southern end of Ōganeku is the best lookout for **Yurigahama** (百合ヶ浜), the star of

Yoron's show. Some 1.5km off Ōganeku, this island of sand seems to morph, moving depending on the tide and time of day. In some seasons, Yurigahama disappears entirely, earning it the nickname 'Phantom Beach'. Mostly accessible from spring to summer, and a few weeks in autumn, Yurigahama is pure paradise, with sparkling waters filled with fish and blinding bright sand. Legend has it that if you pick up as many pieces of star sand (page 312) as your age here, you will live a happy life. To get to the island, you will need to take a quick glass-bottom-boat tour or private craft from the Ōganeku Coast. Make sure to check the tourist association's website or office (page 166) for the yearly schedule of Yurigahama's appearance.

The **Akasaki Coast** (赤崎海岸) makes up Yorontō's southeast, its beach all white sands and stunning bright seas. It's quiet, full of coral and a beautiful spot to chill, with beach shops and stall cafés just beside it. Inland is the little **Yoron Folk Village** (与論民俗村; 693-2 Mugiya; ☎ 0997 97 2934; w yoronminzokumura.com; 🕘 09.00–18.00 daily; adult/child ¥500/300), a private, outdoor folk museum where you try your hand at traditional crafts and see old houses and displays. Get creative with bashōfu cloth workshops, *kusakizome* (plant dyeing), toy making, and extracting brown sugar from sugarcane. Guides and workshops here are currently Japanese-language only, but it has a great souvenir shop too.

A short hop from the folk village is **Akasaki Limestone Cave** (赤崎鍾乳洞; 678 Mugiya; ☎ 0997 97 2069; 🕘 09.30–18.00 daily; adult/child ¥500/200). Eroded from Yoron's coral reef over many years, and discovered by students in 1965, Akasaki is a humid cavern where you can see cool geological formations, including stalactites, formed by the ocean. It only takes about 20 minutes to investigate.

Heading on to the south coast, past **Utanshi** (ワタンジ海岸) and **Maehama** (前浜海岸) beaches, Yorontō begins to build to a little cliffside crescendo – a relative blip but enough to get you panting on the bicycle. This ridge leads you away from the coast towards the town of **Asato** (朝戸), or you can cycle down its hill towards the port, passing the somewhat random statue of a Yanbaru kuina bird, commemorating the 40th anniversary of Okinawa's reversion (沖縄復帰40周年ヤンバルクイナ像). This route down passes the little-visited **Uwaanumaki Beach** (ウワーヌマキ海岸) and the **Hakibina Coast** (ハキビナ海岸), where you'll pass **Hakibina Cemetery** (ハキビナ墓地霊園). The latter is perhaps a strange inclusion in a sightseeing guide, but it's a perfect example of the different burial styles of Okinawa, Yoron and Ryūkyū Kingdom graves.

Carrying on along the ridge you'll find a collection of sights, starting with the **Southern Cross Centre** (サザンクロスセンター; 3313 Riccho; ☎ 0997 97 3396; w southerncrosscenter.wixsite.com/mysite; 🕘 09.30–17.30 Thu–Tue; adult/child ¥400/200). Yorontō's museum, it shows off the island's history, culture, nature and daily life – in Japanese. However, there's a nice observatory on the fifth floor that overlooks the island and its neighbours.

The centre shares its hill with the **Yoron Castle Ruins** (与論城), which are less ruins these days and more a lookout point: all that's left are fortified walls. The castle was built in the early 1400s by Ōshan, the third son of the King of Hokuzan, Okinawa-hontō's northernmost kingdom. When that kingdom fell, construction stopped and the castle was never finished. The 200m of stonework left is said to be in the shape of a dragon.

The castle grounds are great to walk, being overgrown and given to roots and ruin, but the clearing at the top holds a host of shrines and monuments, including the **Kotohira Shrine** (琴平神社). Three gods are enshrined here, who are prayed to for maritime and travel safety. First built in the 1820s, the original shrine was burned down in 1945 air raids, but was rebuilt in 1950 using donations from islanders.

MYTHS AND FOLKTALES: AJINICCHEE

Centuries ago, there was a young man called Ajinicchee from Yorontō, who excelled at martial arts, swordsmanship and archery. When he turned 26, he went to Okinawa-hontō to have an audience with the Ryūkyū king, who promised him the earth if he served beside him. After years of faithful service, Ajinicchee asked to go back home; after being refused many times, the king asked him to leave behind a keepsake. Ajinicchee didn't have anything to offer, so was forced to leave his bow that he borrowed from his younger sister, Injuruki.

Upon returning home empty-handed, Ajinicchee saw how upset his sister was, and went back to Shuri to retrieve the bow. He succeeded in stealing it back, but the angered king sent soldiers to Yorontō after him. The young warrior fought them all and won, sending back a message to the king: don't send soldiers here again.

On hearing this, the king sent 1,000 more soldiers, but Ajinicchee was waiting for them, his fierce silhouette watching from atop the hill as the warships sailed toward his island. The highly trained Ryūkyū soldiers didn't stand a chance. Hundreds were wiped out, but Ajinicchee also perished in the battle. Although satisfied, the king was concerned the warrior's family would fight in his honour, so he sent 1,000 more soldiers to attack Ajinicchee's clan.

Injuruki took the lead: she was a brave archer and killed many, but she, too, eventually died. She was beheaded, but her head was said to have soared high into the sky, singing a spell, shaking from left to right. The Ryūkyūan soldiers fled to their boats in horror, only to meet a big storm that sank every last ship. No-one returned to Shuri.

It's here that Yoron's Jugoya Odori is held. Opposite the shrine, right at the back, is a very different place of worship: **Piguchi-ugan** (辺後地拝所). This is a more traditional shrine, an ancient site of worship from Yorontō's original island religion.

Meeting Yoron's ring road, which sits strangely far inland, head east to the **Ajinicchee Shrine** (按司根津栄神社; 522 Asato; 0801 149 8516; w ajinicchee.jimdofree.com). It's dedicated to Yoron's hero, the brave Ajinicchee (see above). Here you can make a wish by writing on one of the votive horse prayer plaques and tying it on the nearby strings.

Heading clockwise around the ring road, you'll find the **Yunnu Botanic Garden** (ユンヌ楽園; 1393 Chabana; 0997 97 2105; 09.00–17.00 daily; ¥300), a gorgeous subtropical garden that's far more wild than most Japanese gardens – fittingly Nansei. It has a pretty arched bridge, over 300 species of wild tropical plants and fruits, plenty of bright blooming flowers and the odd goat. Its ever-blossoming seasonal flowers bring in rare butterflies, making Yunnu seem like an ethereal slice of Eden.

Yorontō's final stop is **Hajipikipanta** (舵引き丘). This central hill's enjoyable mouthful of a name means 'Hill Where the Rudder of the Boat was Caught' – a baffling moniker with a legendary back story. It's said that this hill is the birthplace of the island: Yoron's origin myth is that when the two gods Shiniguku and Amamiku went fishing, the rudder of their boat got caught on something in the shallow water. When they stepped out of the boat, here at Hajipikipanta, the reef swelled up and Yorontō was created. While the gods and boats are long gone, the view on a clear day shows Okinawa's Kunigami to the south, Iheya and Izena islands in the west, and Okinoerabu and Tokunoshima to the north.

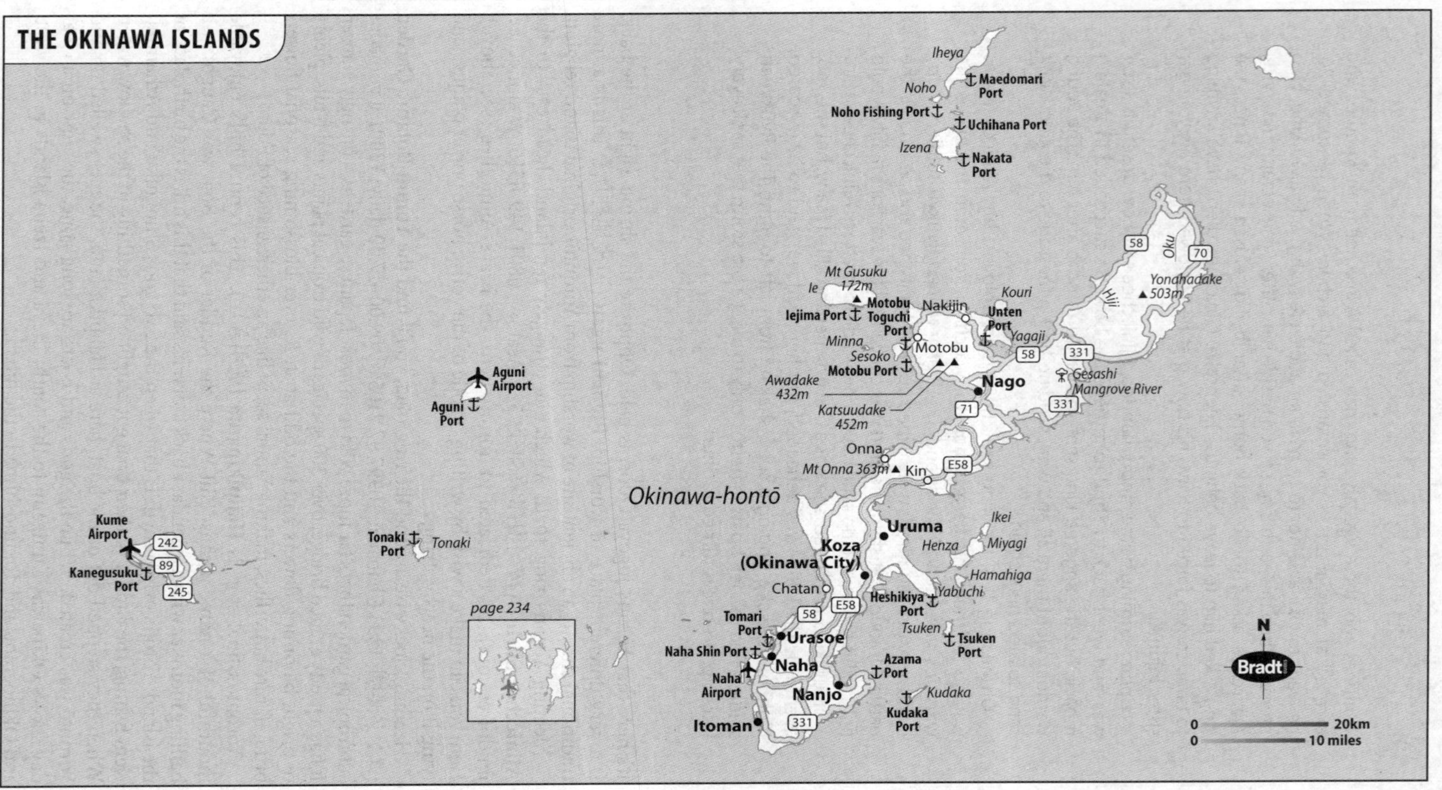

THE OKINAWA ISLANDS
Iheya
Noho
Maedomari Port
Noho Fishing Port
Uchihana Port
Izena
Nakata Port
58
70
Oku
Yonahadake 503m
Hiji
Mt Gusuku 172m
Ie
Motobu Toguchi Port
Iejima Port
Nakijin
Kouri
Unten Port
Yagaji
Minna
Sesoko
Motobu
Motobu Port
58
331
Gesashi Mangrove River
Awadake 432m
Katsuudake 452m
Nago
331
71
Aguni Airport
Aguni Port
Onna
Mt Onna 363m
Kin
E58
Okinawa-hontō
Uruma
Ikei
Henza
Miyagi
Koza (Okinawa City)
Hamahiga
Chatan
Heshikiya Port
Yabuchi
Kume Airport
242
89
Kanegusuku Port
245
Tonaki Port
Tonaki
page 234
58
E58
Tomari Port
Urasoe
Tsuken
Tsuken Port
Naha Shin Port
Naha
Azama Port
Naha Airport
Nanjo
Kudaka
Kudaka Port
Itoman
331
N
Bradt
0 20km
0 10 miles

5

The Okinawa Islands

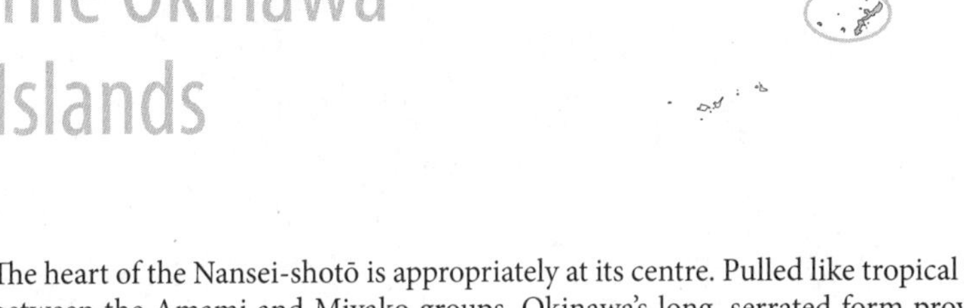

The heart of the Nansei-shotō is appropriately at its centre. Pulled like tropical taffy between the Amami and Miyako groups, Okinawa's long, serrated form provides the archipelago's backbone. The Okinawa group (Okinawa-shotō; 沖縄諸島), with its main island orbited by a satellite of smaller, somewhat forgotten ones, is a fair representation of the whole island chain.

To its western limits are Kume, Aguni and Tonaki, overlooked but perfect little snapshots of parochial Okinawan life. Scattered about the main island, as if dropped from a great height, are myriad fragments that make up some of the Nansei-shotō's most important religious and mythic spaces: islands like Iheya, Izena and Kudaka. The Okinawa-shotō also includes the Kerama: a neon-watered group to the west with such a wealth at its sand-dusted feet that it has a separate chapter (page 233).

Where the Okinawa group breaks away from archipelago embodiment is, ironically, its defining central island. Alongside the wildlife-packed jungles, sprinkled beaches, and troubled history found elsewhere, Okinawa-hontō has cities. It thrums and bustles with urban life: with suburbs and towns that spiderweb out from it southeast. Where the rest of the Nansei has quiet villages and workaday port towns, Okinawa-hontō has both the prefectural and old kingdom capitals, Naha and Shuri. It bursts open with museums and galleries, great shrines and castles, shopping streets and malls. You'll find tourists, English, extensive roads, public transport, even nightlife. This is where the unique influences that created the Nansei-shotō culture – Okinawan, Japanese, American, Chinese and more – amalgamate under flashing lights and untouched forests.

OKINAWA-HONTŌ

If you've heard nothing else about the archipelago, you've probably heard of Okinawa. Okinawa-hontō (*hontō* meaning 'main island') is the largest island of the Nansei-shotō and the heart of the archipelago.

Located in the centre of the island chain, Okinawa-hontō (沖縄本島) was the Ryūkyū Kingdom's seat of power. The original capital was Shuri in the southwest, where the royal family was based and where Shuri Castle remains, despite nature and humanity's continued efforts to destroy it. Not only the heart of power, Okinawa-hontō is the hub of the prefecture's unique culinary, artistic and musical traditions. Today, the island and prefectural capital is Naha, just south of Shuri: a small capital city with a big heart. The total population of Okinawa-hontō sits at around 1,384,700, including US personnel and families, with 800,000 people living in Greater Naha. Naha is the archipelago's transport hub, where most visitors fly to before heading on elsewhere.

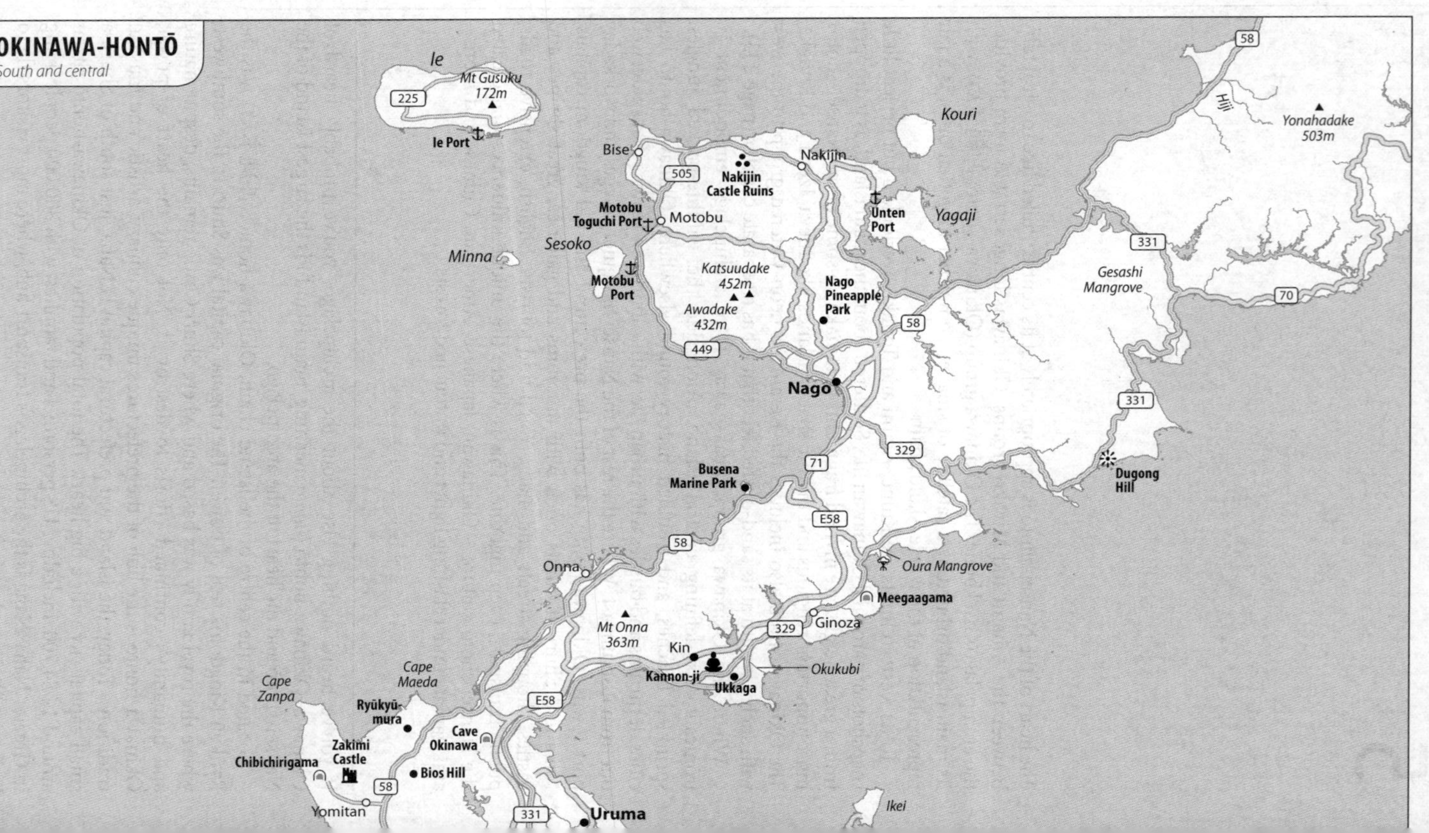
OKINAWA-HONTŌ
South and central
Ie
Mt Gusuku
172m
225
Ie Port
Kouri
Hiji
Yonahadake
503m
58
Bise
505
Nakijin
Castle Ruins
Nakijin
Unten
Port
Yagaji
Motobu
Toguchi Port
Motobu
Sesoko
Minna
Motobu
Port
Katsuudake
452m
Awadake
432m
Nago
Pineapple
Park
331
Gesashi
Mangrove
70
58
449
Nago
331
329
71
Busena
Marine Park
Dugong
Hill
E58
58
Onna
Oura Mangrove
Meegaagama
Mt Onna
363m
329
Ginoza
Kin
Kannon-ji
Ukkaga
Okukubi
Cape
Zanpa
Cape
Maeda
Ryūkyū-
mura
E58
Cave
Okinawa
Zakimi
Castle
Chibichirigama
Bios Hill
58
Yomitan
331
Uruma
Ikei

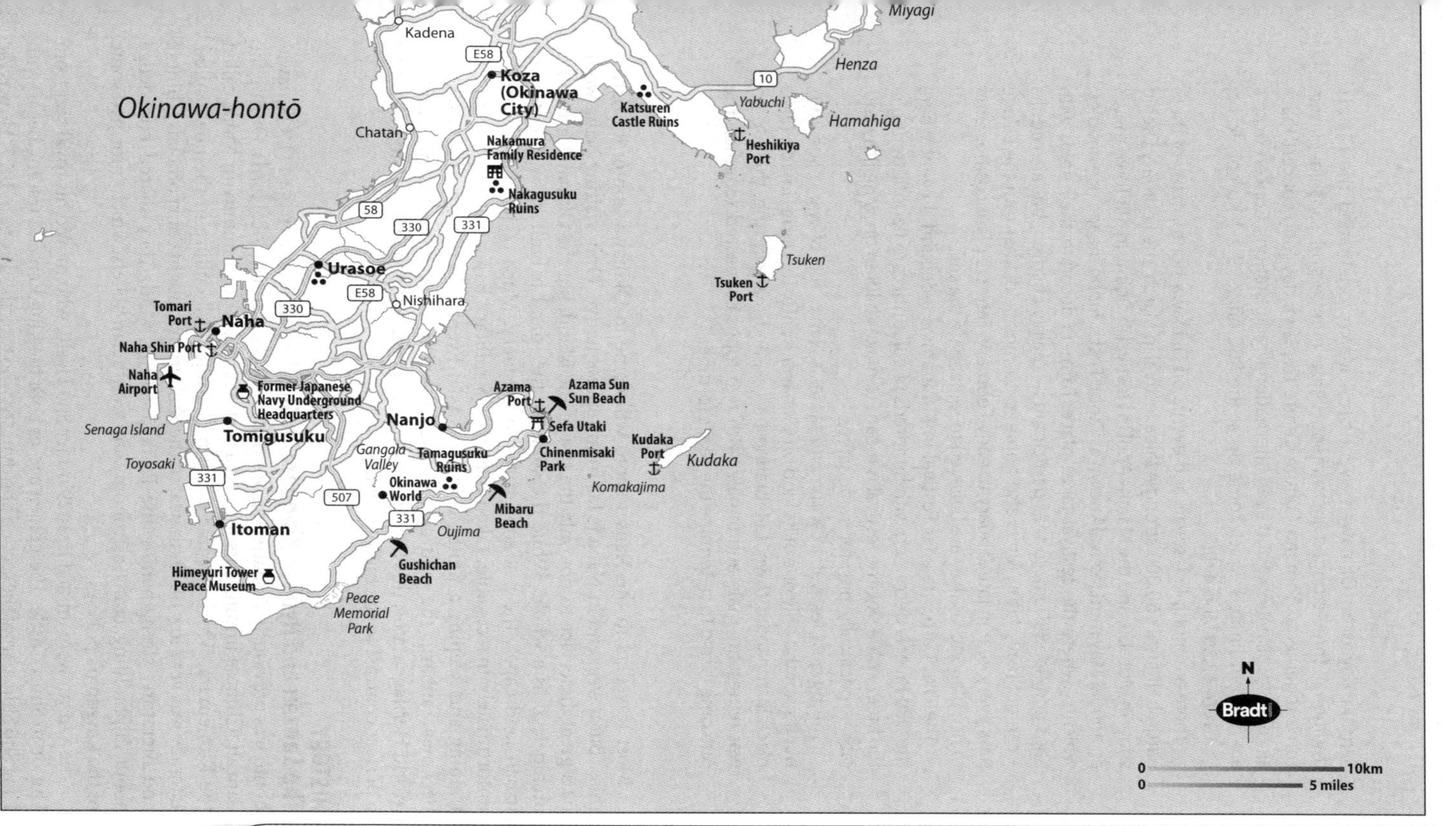
Okinawa-hontō
Kadena
E58
Koza (Okinawa City)
Chatan
Nakamura Family Residence
Nakagusuku Ruins
Katsuren Castle Ruins
10
Yabuchi
Henza
Miyagi
Hamahiga
Heshikiya Port
58
330
331
Urasoe
E58
Nishihara
Tsuken
Tsuken Port
Tomari Port
Naha
330
Naha Shin Port
Naha Airport
Former Japanese Navy Underground Headquarters
Senaga Island
Tomigusuku
Nanjo
Azama Port
Azama Sun Sun Beach
Sefa Utaki
Chinenmisaki Park
Kudaka Port
Kudaka
Komakajima
Gangala Valley
Tamagusuku Ruins
Toyosaki
331
Okinawa World
507
331
Mibaru Beach
Oujima
Itoman
Gushichan Beach
Himeyuri Tower Peace Museum
Peace Memorial Park
N
Bradt
0
10km
0
5 miles

OKINAWA-HONTŌ FESTIVALS

Sanshin day is an Okinawan event on 4 March, celebrating the island's traditional three-stringed instrument. Large numbers of sanshin players come together at Yomitan Culture Centre to play a day-long concert that's aired on local, national and even international radio stations. Concert tickets are free but limited – pick some up at the RBC office (3-2-1 Kumoji, Naha; ⌚ 10.00–17.30 Mon–Fri).

There are multiple festivals and events on Okinawa-hontō, many of them natural: Higashi's 50,000-strong Azalea festival in March, the February Orchid show in Motobu, and the March–April Iris festival in Ōgimi. In Kin Town there's an annual May mud festival known as Tanbo Festa. *Tanbo* means 'rice paddies', which is where the festival takes place. Farmers decorate their fields with flags and flood them, so that participants – mainly children, but also adults – can get really filthy. Kin is also home to cosmos fields that turn the village pink every year in late January to early February. Farmers plant cosmos prior to rice planting, as they are believed to rejuvenate the soil.

The Oku Carp Streamer Festival in Kunigami is a delightful event where the Oku River is decorated with hundreds of colourful carp flags fluttering in the breezy blue sky. The festival is meant to make children grow healthy and, rather specifically, pray for traffic safety.

The biggest festival, in scope and fame, is Naha's tug-of-war (page 189), but it's not the only one of its kind on Okinawa-hontō. The June Umachi takes place in Yonabaru town. Celebrating harvest and thanksgiving, this tug-of-war represents male and female, with two ropes connected together. The outcome is said to determine the year's fortune.

Most travellers to the Nansei-shotō will come to Okinawa-hontō: it's hard to miss. But a weekend in Naha is far from representative. Only visiting Naha would be a great disservice to not only the rest of the island, but the Okinawa group and archipelago as a whole. While the south of the island is built up with cities and urban landscapes, the rest soon turns to greenery. Much of its central forest is unfortunately inaccessible, taken over by US military bases that use the land for training and keeping a foothold in East Asia. Eventually though, this landscape becomes Yanbaru: the wild and wonderful north. Now protected by UNESCO World Heritage status, this land is relatively underdeveloped for tourism, making it a perfect contrast to the built-up south.

HISTORY

The Sanzan and Ryūkyū Kingdom Before the Sanzan era (page 11), Okinawa-hontō was previously a smattering of smaller domains run by local lords. During the Sanzan, Chinese immigrants formed a sort of scholar's community in Naha, called the Kumemura, which became a seat of learning and culture in the now capital. Literacy was very low on Okinawa, so the Kumemura taught court officials Chinese and literature, strengthening the Ryūkyū–China bond. They shared knowledge about shipbuilding, crafts, astronomy and Confucian beliefs, which informed some of the kingdom's policies.

The Sanzan were unified in 1429 under Shō Hashi, who moved his royal seat from Urasoe to Shuri Castle. The 'golden age' of both the kingdom and trading began with King Shō Shin, part of the second Shō dynasty, who took the throne in 1477. He was the most influential Ryūkyū ruler, whose half-century reign was filled with reformation, creation and prosperity. He began construction on many of the kingdom's most prestigious buildings and cultural projects, and expanded the kingdom's territory.

This was when the kingdom became an international trade hub: the age of *bankoku shinryo,* 'the bridge to 10,000 nations'. For centuries, Okinawa-hontō thrived with influence and allies across the Pacific – until one of those allies, Satsuma, invaded. Satsuma soldiers used firearms when Okinawans had spears and swords; the castles at Urasoe, Nakijin and even Shuri were captured, and in a mere month the independent kingdom ceased to be. Despite this, the kingdom carried on much as it ever had. It even had a 'second golden age', where the dance, music, martial arts, crafts and cloth of Okinawa developed into today's recognisable forms.

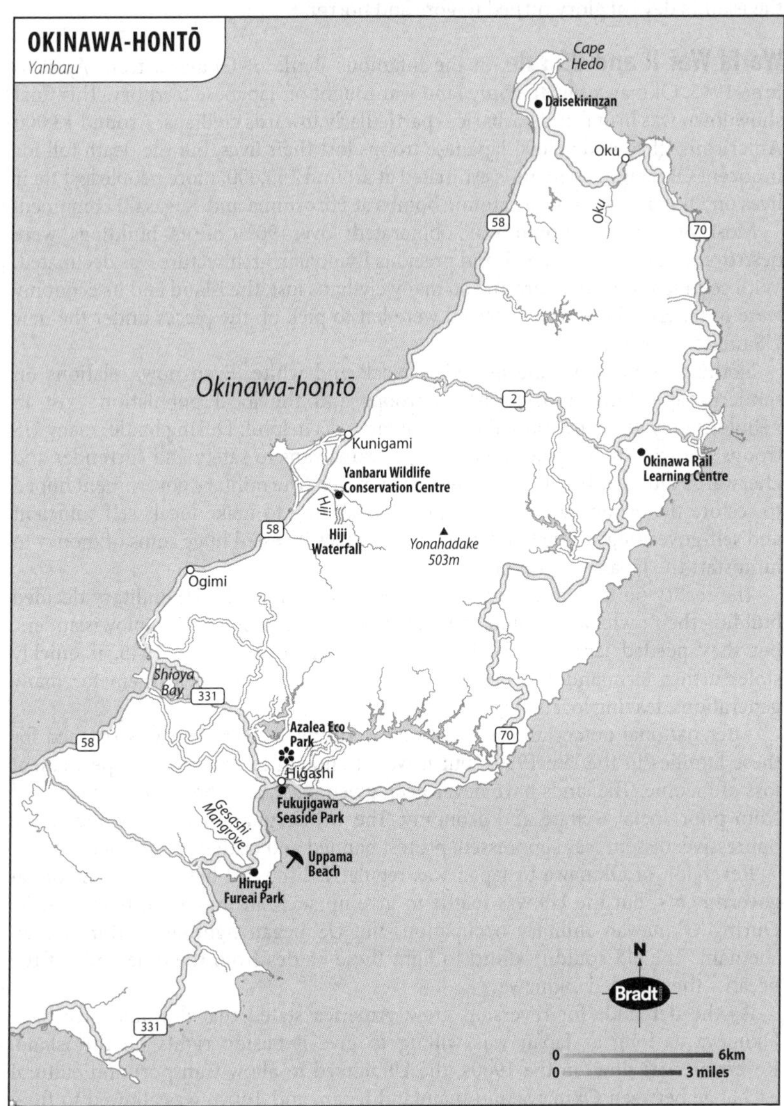

The 19th-century arrival of the US Black Ships, a fleet that forcibly prised open closed-off Japan, is well documented. What's lesser known is they first made landfall on Okinawa-hontō; Commodore Matthew Perry arrived in Ryūkyū on 17 May 1853, ignored Satsuma's claims to the kingdom, and made a show of demanding an audience with King Shō Tai.

When the world came knocking, Japan realised its behind-times place on an increasingly powerful international stage. It modernised at an incredible pace and fully annexed the Ryūkyū Kingdom (page 12). On Okinawa-hontō, poor economic conditions forced many to leave and work elsewhere in the ever-growing empire. Okinawans were expected to enlist for wars against their one-time allies, Korea and China, until eventually the Pacific Theatre of World War II came to Okinawa, and the island's days of glory turned to gore and horror.

World War II and US rule In the infamous Battle of Okinawa from April to June 1945, Okinawa saw the only land war fought on Japanese territory. This final showdown was brutal and barbaric – particularly towards civilians. Around 13,000 American-Allied and 90,000 Japanese troops lost their lives, but the death toll for innocent Okinawan civilians is estimated at around 150,000; more people lost their lives on Okinawa than in the atomic bombs at Hiroshima and Nagasaki combined.

Most of Okinawa-hontō was obliterated: over 90% of its buildings were destroyed, Naha was flattened, and precious Ryūkyūan architecture was decimated. With so much infrastructure and so many civilians lost, the island and its economy were in tatters. Those who survived were left to pick up the pieces under the new US military governance.

Nothing about this time period is black and white. Even now, relations on modern-day Okinawa between US troops and the local population exist in nebulous grey. In many ways, the US military was helpful. During battle, many US troops did what they could to encourage Okinawans to safety and surrender and afterwards did their best to clear the seas of mines. The military government hoped to restore the economy as soon as possible, aiming to make locals self-sufficient and self-governing. To that end, the US and Allies invested huge sums of money to jumpstart the Japanese economy.

The reality on the ground wasn't always so altruistic. The US military decided building their own bases would stimulate the local economy and employ islanders, but they needed land. Although it had seized lots of land in 1945, it quickly stole further farmland and homes from families who had held them for many generations, leaving locals without income.

After national outcry and international scrutiny, a settlement was reached for these families in the late 1950s, but it wasn't enough to recover their permanent loss of income. The lands have never been given back, and the prefecture suffered from poor social welfare and economy. The US occupation was also incredibly oppressive: dissent was suppressed, protest banned and criticism punished.

Reversion of Okinawa to Japan was regularly discussed between international governments, but the US was loathe to give up such an important base in Asia. During Okinawan military occupation, the US began fighting in Korea, then Vietnam. The US couldn't afford to fight these battles from the other side of the ocean – they needed Okinawa.

As the demands for reversion grew, America stated that it would give back Okinawa as long as Japan was willing to give it basing rights on the island. Reversion was slow: in the 1960s, the US agreed to allow transport and cultural exchange between Okinawa and mainland Japan, and Tokyo was allowed to fund

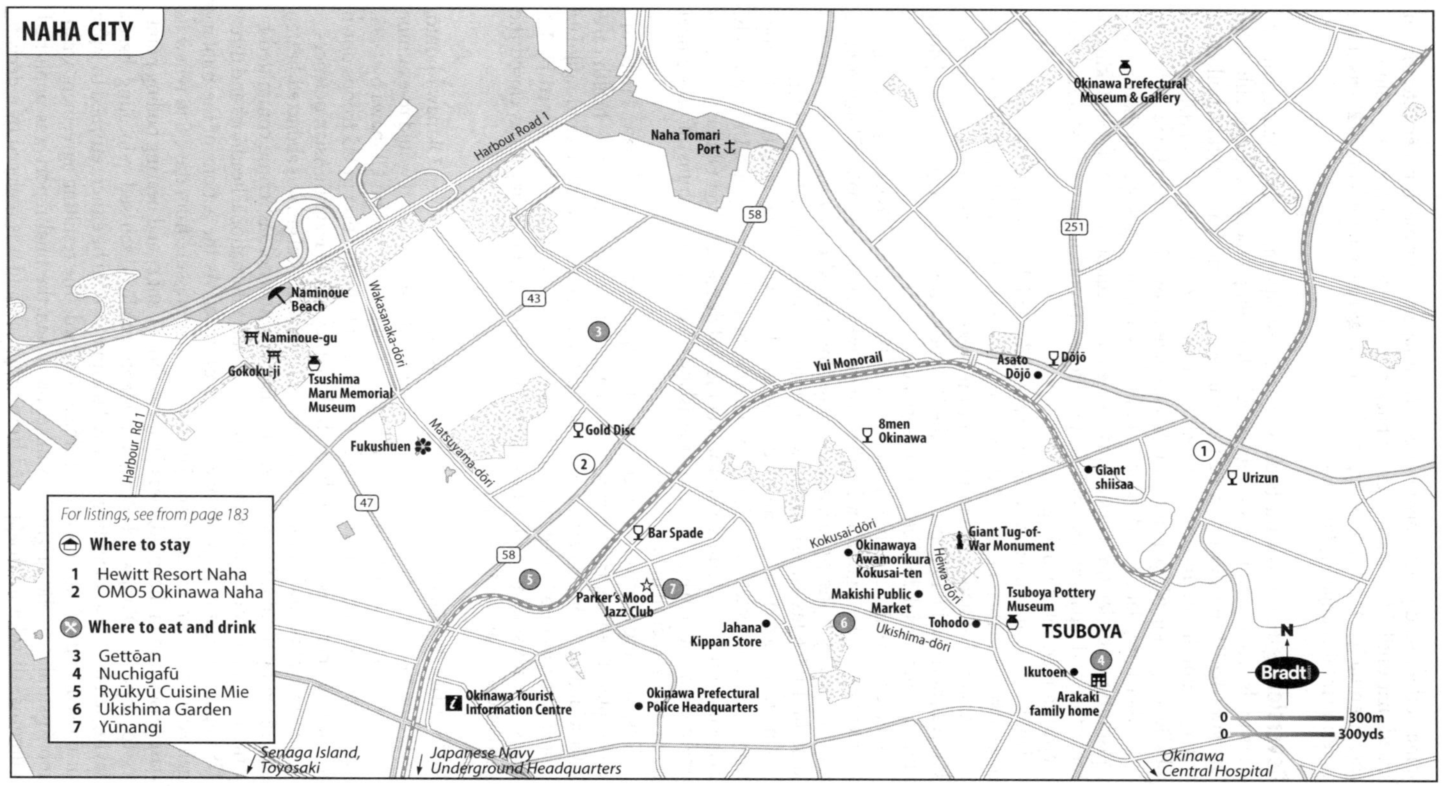
NAHA CITY
Harbour Road 1
Naha Tomari Port
58
Okinawa Prefectural Museum & Gallery
251
Naminoue Beach
Naminoue-gu
Gokoku-ji
Tsushima Maru Memorial Museum
Wakasanaka-dōri
43
Yui Monorail
Asato Dōjō
Dōjō
Harbour Rd 1
Gold Disc
8men Okinawa
Fukushuen
Matsuyama-dōri
Giant shiisaa
Urizun
47
Bar Spade
Kokusai-dōri
Giant Tug-of-War Monument
Okinawaya Awamorikura Kokusai-ten
Heiwa-dōri
Parker's Mood Jazz Club
Makishi Public Market
Tsuboya Pottery Museum
Jahana Kippan Store
Tohodo
TSUBOYA
Ukishima-dōri
Ikutoen
Arakaki family home
Okinawa Tourist Information Centre
Okinawa Prefectural Police Headquarters
N
Bradt
0 300m
0 300yds
Senaga Island, Toyosaki
Japanese Navy Underground Headquarters
Okinawa Central Hospital
For listings, see from page 183
Where to stay
1 Hewitt Resort Naha
2 OMO5 Okinawa Naha
Where to eat and drink
3 Gettōan
4 Nuchigafū
5 Ryūkyū Cuisine Mie
6 Ukishima Garden
7 Yūnangi

some of the island government budget. Then Japanese prime minister Sato Eisaku stated that until Okinawa was given back to Japan, the post-war era would never end. Eventually, Okinawa was returned to its original colonisers in 1972 – its third governmental change in 100 years.

Reversion Fitting Okinawa back to a Japanese system of governance after 27 years under American rule was remarkably difficult: politically, socially, culturally. Okinawa had been destroyed in the war, so the American military built new systems from the ground up. Okinawa's economy also relied heavily on US military jobs, leaving Okinawa permanently differentiated from the rest of Japan.

Furthermore, Japan had been rebuilt in Okinawa's absence: it had a new constitution, new laws. The result was a huge socio-economic gap between Okinawa Prefecture and Japan, and though Japan believed it could improve these disparities, many islanders felt it would get worse.

Unlike the Amami Islands, Okinawans didn't hold the unanimous belief that reversion was to their benefit. Okinawa had suffered mainland discrimination since it was annexed; it had been sacrificed by the Japanese government for the country's survival, both in the 1945 defeat and the 1951 peace treaty. The vagueness and delay of reversion plans didn't help reassure islanders.

Still, a ten-year development plan was initiated for the Ryūkyū Islands to try to overcome these significant hurdles. There were efforts to make Okinawa more tourist friendly – the right-hand drive system insisted on by the Americans was kept until 1978, tax-free shopping was rife and US dollars were legal tender.

American decisions still affected Okinawa, however – the retraction of troops from Vietnam created over 15,300 civilian redundancies in six years. Unfortunately, many other forms of primary sector income had disappeared on Okinawa, causing unemployment to rise. In short, the islands were at the whims of two global economies rather than one.

Despite being relatively poor compared to Japan and the US, Okinawa Prefecture wasn't objectively so. However, it lagged behind in many other ways – health care, infrastructure, welfare, parks and housing. Today, Okinawa continues to rank last in many prefectural categories, including space per resident: not helped by US bases. Yet investment in Okinawa is less of a problem and today it has closed the gap between itself and the mainland.

Anti-military tensions The US still has several bases on Okinawa-hontō, including Kadena Air Base. At the end of the 1980s, the US said it would re-examine its position in Asia, including a withdrawal of all US Marines on Okinawa by 1995. This obviously didn't happen. While there was a big reduction in US troops down to 100,000, there was concern about the hole they would leave in Asian defences.

Tensions came to a head in 1995, when a 12-year-old local girl was abducted, beaten and raped by three US servicemen. It wasn't the first nor last crime committed by American military on Okinawa-hontō, but it made international headlines and threw US–Japanese relations on Okinawa into stark relief. As the actions of the military gained more and more criticism, Japan was under pressure from the US to renew its base leases: and in the middle was Okinawa-hontō, angry and nearing boiling point.

To appease Okinawa, both governments finally discussed relocating bases, saying ten facilities (including massive Futenma) would be either returned to Japan or moved, and various military exercises stopped. The resulting agreement wasn't too dissimilar to the original promise, but when the final report was published, Futenma's dissolution disappeared from proposals and was replaced by a decision

OKINAWAN LANGUAGES

The mainland spent the years between the restoration and war forcing Okinawa to conform to Japanese standards – be it language, religion, education or tattooing (page 18). In many ways they succeeded, but despite Japan's best efforts, Okinawan identity has remained strong.

Okinawa-hontō has two local languages: Okinawan and Kunigami. Okinawan, known locally as Uchinaaguchi, is spoken in the south. Kunigami (also Northern Ryūkyūan) starts in the north and stretches up into the Amami Islands; it largely correlates to the former northern Hokuzan kingdom. The Japanese spoken on Okinawa-hontō is actually called Uchinaa-Yamatuguchi: Okinawan Japanese. This dialect has formed as Japanese has been adapted and changed by traditional local languages, as well as some American English thanks to the US presence. It's perfectly intelligible to Japanese speakers, though some words have a different meaning or grammar, and new vocabulary has also been added. It's not known how many people still speak the Okinawan languages, but there's an increased interest in revitalising and regenerating them, particularly Uchinaaguchi.

to make a huge sea-based facility. A 1996 prefectural referendum showed 89% of voters supported base reductions and a revision of the forces agreement, which included handing over any US military personnel suspected in off-base crimes. However, only 59% of voters turned out.

To this day, Okinawa seeks resolution to the US bases issue, described as the island's biggest problem. US bases cover 25% of Okinawa-hontō's landmass, and the large majority of islanders want to be rid of them – but they are not naive to the repercussions. With issues brewing on mainland Asia with North Korea, China, Taiwan and Russia, the US presence is a major national security factor. Additionally, the island is still economically reliant on their existence, and it doesn't look set to change any time soon.

However, with bigger environmental awareness worldwide, the presence of the bases in protected regions may encourage international intervention: the recent UNESCO designation may prove fruitful. In 2016, the US returned 40km^2 of the north-based training area, a major milestone in Okinawan history. This return reduced the US footprint on Okinawa-hontō by 20%, and there are hopes that many of the bases south of Kadena will also be returned.

GETTING THERE AND AWAY Okinawa-hontō is the main port for all travel in and out of the prefecture. Naha Airport has international flights to Seoul, Taipei, Hong Kong and Shanghai with a large variety of carriers, and domestic flights across Japan. The airport is easily accessible by private and public transport, being in the city outskirts.

Okinawa has multiple ferry ports across the island, each servicing different outer islands. Naha has three: Tomari (to the western Okinawan islands like Kume and the Kerama), Naha (Kagoshima and Amami) and Naha Shin (Tokyo/Osaka/Kobe). In the southeast, Azama Port serves Kudaka Island and Heshikaya Port Tsuken Island. The northwest has Unten Port for Izena and Iheya, Motobu Toguchi Port for Minna, and the major Motobu Port serving Iejima and all the Kagoshima islands to the north, as well as mainland Kagoshima itself. For details on each ferry, see individual island pages.

OKINAWAN SUPERSTITIONS

The island comes with some great idioms and superstitions. While the rest of Japan has no equivalent to 'bless you' after sneezing, Okinawa has quite the unique approach. There's a belief that sneezing leaves people vulnerable to their mabui (page 22) being taken by negative spirits. To prevent this, Okinawans sometimes say '*kusukee*' – which literally translates as 'eat shit' – to ward them off.

There's also an unusual folk belief that you become younger in your later years, eventually returning to the womb in death. This is supposedly why tombs on the islands are shaped like a womb. On elders' day on the islands, older people are handed a child's pinwheel, representing this supposed return to youth.

Salt plays a part in keeping residents protected from negative spirits, much like throwing salt over your shoulder in the West. In the olden days, every room in the house would have a spoon of salt to keep them away. You may even see it in the front of shops to this day: it allegedly keeps out not only bad spirits but bad customers.

If you're sailing down from Kagoshima, via other islands, A-Line's (0992 24 2121; w aline-ferry.com) little-advertised Yui kippu (結いきっぷ) ticket means you can get on and off the ferries freely within 21 days – but you will need someone who speaks Japanese to book on your behalf.

GETTING AROUND How you get around on Okinawa-hontō depends on how far flung you'd like to go. If you only have a couple of days in Naha, the public transport system is ideal with monorail, trains and buses reaching the capital's major sites. The **Yui monorail** (w yui-rail.co.jp/en) runs from Shuri to the airport in just 40 minutes across 19 stations and offers handy day passes with attraction discounts.

Local Okinawa **buses** (w okinawabus.com/en) operate across the island, paid for with cash or rechargeable IC cards which can be bought at some FamilyMarts and monorail and bus stations. Okinawa passes (w okinawapass.com) allow for unlimited bus and monorail travel. Airport and limousine buses are operated by a few companies, like Kosoku Bus (w kosokubus.com/en) and Japan Bus Online (w japanbusonline.com/en). Taxis are also an option, though expensive.

There is also the Churachari **cycle** rental scheme (w docomo-cycle.jp/okinawa), which uses an app to rent bicycles around Naha and between southwest Itoman and Chatan.

If you plan to travel south or north, there are buses, but for full and easy access to the entire island, get a car. **Car rental** here is incredibly simple, especially if picking up from the airport. If you can't locate your car hire office, the tourist information desk will phone them for you. Alongside the larger ferries which stop at Motobu en route north, there's also a high-speed Daiichi Marine Ferry (w daiichi-marine.com) between Naha and Motobu, taking 75 minutes.

Taxis

Daiichi Kotsu Taxi 第一交通のタクシー; 1190 Ameku, Naha; 0120 78 0124; w okinawa-taxi.0152.jp

Okinawa Kotsu 沖縄交通; 192 Aja, Naha; 0988 61 2224; w okinawa-kotsu-grp.co.jp

Vehicle rental

Nippon Rent-a-Car Kencho-Mae ニッポンレンタカー県庁前; 1-1-1 Kumoji, Naha; 0988 67 4554; w nipponrentacar.co.jp

Nissan Rent-a-Car 日産レンタカー那覇空港第; Naha Airport, 2-13-13 Akamine; ☎ 0988 58 0023; w nissan-rentacar.com
Orix Rent-a-Car オリックスレンタカー 那覇空港店; 1-1174 Toyosaki, Tomigusuku; ☎ 0988 51 0543; w car.orix.co.jp/eng
OTS Rent-a-Car OTSレンタカー 那覇空港店; Naha Airport, 3-37 Toyosaki; ☎ 0988 56 8877; w otsinternational.jp/otsrentacar/en
Times Car Rental タイムズカー 那覇空港店; Naha Airport, 457-1 Kagamizu; ☎ 0988 58 1536; w timescar-rental.com
Toyota Rent-a-Car トヨタレンタカー那覇空港店; Naha Airport, 2-15-11 Akamine; ☎ 0988 57 0100; w rent.toyota.co.jp/eng

TOURIST INFORMATION Okinawa isn't short of tourist information: ports, airports and all major villages have a tourism centre where you can find maps, information and help.

Kunigami Village Tourism Association 国頭村観光協会; 1569-1 Okuma; ☎ 0980 41 2420; w kunigami-kanko.com
Nago City Tourism Association 名護市観光協会; 1F 1-20-24 Onaka; ☎ 0980 53 7755; w nagomun.or.jp
Naha Airport Information Centre 那覇空港観光案内所; 1F Naha Airport; ☎ 0988 57 6884; w otic.okinawa
Nanjō City Tourism Association 南城市観光協会; 541 Kudeken; ☎ 0989 48 4611; w okinawa-nanjo.jp
Okinawa Tourist Information Centre 沖縄観光情報センター; 2F 1-20-6 Izumizaki, Naha; ☎ 0989 53 8271; w otic.okinawa. Tickets, wheelchair & pram rental, baggage storage & package delivery.
Yomitan Tourism Association 読谷村観光協会; 2346-11 Kina; ☎ 0989 58 6494; w yomitan-kankou.jp

WHERE TO STAY

Naha *Map, page 179*

Map, page 179

Hewitt Resort Naha (355 rooms) ヒューイットリゾート那覇; 2-5-16 Asato; ☎ 0989 43 8325; w hewitt-resort.com/naha. Steps from Kokusai-dōri, a gorgeous hotel with infinity pool, rooftop terrace, 2 restaurants & bar lounge. Bath-shower en suite alongside soft beds & clean, classy rooms. **$$$$**
OMO5 Okinawa Naha (190 rooms) OMO5沖縄那覇; 1-3-16 Matsuyama; ☎ 0503 134 8095; w hoshinoresorts.com. Part of the Hoshino group, OMO5 are modern, fun apt-like suites, designed around each city. Beautifully done with bar/lounge, café, shop & tours. **$$$**

South

Asahinoyado Shidakaji (3 rooms) 朝陽の宿 涼風; 189-1 Kakinohama, Nanjo; ☎ 0806 481 4747; w shidakajiokinawa.com. Large, beautiful rooms with wood floors, minimalist feel, en suite & verandas. Small library, dining room & courtyard. **$$$$**
Villa Sachibaru (4 rooms) ヴィラさちばる; 18-1 Tamagusuku, Nanjo; ☎ 0702 322 8023; w sachibaru.jp/villa. Garden & sea views, 500m from Mibaru Beach. Magnificent picture window suites have washing machine, equipped kitchen & en suite, with b/fast available. Restaurant, spa & terrace. **$$$$**
Goyukkuri (2 rooms) ごゆっくり; 255-29 Odo, Itoman; ☎ 0803 956 7025; w goyukkuri.jp/english. Homely Japanese guesthouse with 1 tatami & 1 Western room, with shared kitchen, dining room, lounge, bathrooms & laundry. **$$$**

Central

MB Gallery Chatan (88 rooms) MBギャラリーチャタン; 38-1 Mihama, Chatan; ☎ 0989 21 7111; w mb-gallery.jp. Gym, bar, restaurant & glorious rooftop pool; MB's shared spaces are tasteful & stylish. Broad suites have large windows, balconies, lounges, en suites & complimentary touches. **$$$$$**
K's Fun Garden Inn (whole house with tent) ケーズファンガーデン; 306-3 Serikyaku, Nakijin; ☎ 0980 56 1115; w ksfungarden.com. There's room for up to 6 people in this heavenly retreat with garden & camping. Overlooks Nakijin Bay with

fully equipped kitchen, clean white interiors & terrace. $$$$

Guesthouse Machiya Koza (3 rooms) 町家Koza; 1-2-8 Misato, Koza; ☎ 0989 23 3799; w machiya-koza.com. Fun guesthouse in keeping with chilled Koza vibe. Japanese & Western rooms ideal for longer stays with kitchen, bathroom & laundry shared. $$

North

Matayoshi Coffee farm (3 villas & camping) 又吉コーヒー園; 718-28 Gesashi, Higashi; ☎ 098 043 2838; w matayoshicoffee.jp. 2 standard villas & 1 deluxe villa, each with kitchen, terrace & jacuzzi. Deluxe also has wood stove & sofa bed. Free & designated areas for camping ($–$$). $$$$$

Oku Yanbaru no Sato (8 rooms) 奥ヤンバルの里; 1280-1 Oku, Kunigami; ☎ 0980 50 4141; w okuyanbarunosato.net. Old-style cottages in the middle of blissful nowhere. Kitchenettes, bathrooms, laundry with garden setting. BBQ meal included with most bookings. $$$

Hundred Days Hotel (12 rooms) 100日間のホテル; 940-1 Arume, Higashi; ☎ 0980 43 7480; w 100dayshotel.com. Unmanned hotel with all the plentiful amenities of a higher-end resort like memory foam beds. On the picturesque mouth of the Gesashi Mangrove River, rooms are huge & feature jacuzzi en suites & balconies. $$

WHERE TO EAT AND DRINK Naha has just about everything: Kokusai-dōri offers casual restaurants and bars, as well as *omoromachi* upscale restaurants; there's also izakaya, craft breweries, and traditional and international cuisine. In the resort towns, hotel restaurants reign supreme, while the quieter south and north rely on more local cafés and eateries. Motobu is known for its soba: some 70 noodle restaurants are collected around Route 84, near the town. The best places to check out are often the roadside stations, which serve cheap, fresh local food from stalls. Known as *michi-no-eki*, the best – including Kyoda (17-1 Kyoda, Nago), Onna-no-Eki Nakayukui Market (1656-9 Nakadomari, Onna) and Yui Yui Kunigami (1605 Okuma, Kunigami) – are in Yanbaru.

Naha *Map, page 179*

Ryūkyū Cuisine Mie 美栄; 1-8-8 Kumoji; ☎ 0988 67 1356; w ryukyu-mie.com; ⏰ 11.30–15.00 & 18.00–22.00 Mon–Sat. Brilliant (but pricey) Ryūkyūan cuisine in traditional setting – make sure to try the tōfuyō. $$$$$

Gettōan 月桃庵; 2-21-17 Matsuyama; ☎ 0989 17 2785; w gettou-an.owst.jp; ⏰ 18.00–23.00 daily. This traditional family restaurant might not look like an oasis in central Naha, but inside you'll find a beautiful garden & proper Okinawan food. $$$$

Nuchigafū ぬちがふう; 1-28-32 Tsuboya; ☎ 0988 61 2952; w bukubuku.okinawa; ⏰ 11.00–14.30 & 17.30–21.00 daily. Food at this restaurant in the Tsuboya district is perfectly paired with old ceramic tableware. Small plates of traditional dishes including tempura, jiimaami tofu, gooya & more. $$$$

Ukishima Garden 沖縄県那覇市松尾; 2-12-3 Matsuo; ☎ 0989 43 2100; w ukishima-garden.com; ⏰ 11.30–18.00 Fri–Sun. Vegan organic restaurant. Lunches are American & Japanese classics with beers or *amazake* banana shake – a cup of thick island sunshine. Dinner tasting menu. $$$

Yūnangi ゆうなんぎい; 3-3-3 Kumoji; ☎ 0988 67 3765; ⏰ noon–15.00 & 17.30–22.30 Mon–Sat. You'll be lucky to get a seat at this simple izakaya as it serves up great food: try the Okinawa soba. $$

South

Café Curcuma カフェくるくま; 1190 Chinen, Nanjo; ☎ 0989 49 1189; w curcuma.cafe; ⏰ 10.00–17.00 Mon–Fri, 10.00–18.00 Sat–Sun. Hilltop café serving healthy Thai dishes with a superb view over the sea. $$

Forest Terrace 森のテラス; 143-3 Chinen, Nanjo; ☎ 0989 49 1666; ⏰ 11.00–17.30 Wed–Mon. Pasta, cake & drinks nestled in exquisite forest setting. $$

Kunnatu Mozuku Soba もずくそばの店くんなとぅ; 460-2 Shikenbaru, Nanjo; ☎ 0989 49 1066; w mozuku-soba.com; ⏰ 11.00–15.00 Mon–Fri, 11.00–17.00 Sat–Sun. Shop & eatery dedicated to all things mozuku seaweed: set meals with tempura & noodles. $$

Japan forced the islands to grow *kokutō* (brown sugar), which has since become a beloved crop – most famously it is used to create Amami's *kokutō shōchū* PAGE 117

above left (KT/S)

Fishing and seafood are the lifeblood of island tables PAGE 55

above right (EQR/S)

A vast array of tropical fruits grow on the archipelago, including the unbeatable atemoya – a sugary, creamy local treat PAGE 55

right (KK/S)

Try local noodles, island vegetables, special tofu, wild boar, seafood, goat and more in great-value *teishoku* set meals PAGE 57

below (OCVB)

above (SP/D) Unusual natural structures like Kumejima's strange 'Tatami Stones' can be found the length of the archipelago PAGE 231

left (JM/D) The Miyako Islands rely heavily on super-long bridges to join them together, creating spectacular modern structures that stretch across the turquoise sea PAGE 255

below (ma/S) Tanegashima is home to Japan's space agency JAXA and one of the most beautiful launch pads on the planet PAGE 92

Japan's best beaches are found in the archipelago; the most famous is Miyako's Maehama, a stunning stretch of pure white sand PAGE 269

above (OCVB)

Scuba rules supreme here, with plentiful wildlife and underwater structures to see PAGE 37

right (ta/S)

The best whale watching is in the Kerama Islands, where you can spot humpbacks off shore or get closer on boat tours PAGE 235

below (OCVB)

above (DG/S) The most famous Nansei-shotō festival is Naha's giant tug-of-war, but this old tradition takes place in villages across the archipelago, usually to celebrate harvest PAGE 34

below (PG/D) The islands are awash with traditional dances like Eisaa, which is performed at festivals and celebrations, accompanied by drums, colourful parades and singing PAGE 31

below right (N/D) Step back in time on Taketomi, where its pretty village full of traditional Ryūkyū architecture is proudly preserved by locals PAGE 306

Shrines dot the islands, including Japanese-style Naminoue-gū in Naha PAGE 190

above (PH/S)

Spot *shiisaa* – lion-dog guardians – on roofs and walls throughout the archipelago PAGE 23

right (VTTS/S)

The islands are home to Japan's most famous textiles; you can still see many of these fabrics being made by hand and even have a go yourself PAGE 25

below (KT/S)

above (OCVB) Haterumajima is said to have some of the best stargazing in Japan, with 84 of the 88 constellations visible PAGE 332

below (YN/S) Kayaking through mangroves on Iriomotejima, which is sometimes called 'the Galapagos of the East' PAGE 321

Westernmost Yonaguni is home to the rare Yonaguni Atlas moth, with a wingspan of up to 24cm PAGE 345

above left (VTS/S)

Endemic Easter lilies blanket certain islands like Iejima from April to May, bringing festivals as they bloom PAGE 204

above right (GH/S)

Birdwatchers will uncover a treasure trove of endemic species that includes Amami's handsome Lidth's jay PAGE 7

right (F/S)

Yakushima is famed for its precocious macaques PAGE 69

below left (B/S)

The elegant little *yamaneko*, a critically endangered wildcat, is found only on Iriomote PAGE 322

below right (TP/S)

above (SP/S) Sakurajima is a constantly erupting volcano that sputters ash across the great southern city of Kagoshima PAGE 358

below (D/S) Tokyo is like nowhere else; explore a lesser-known side of the world's biggest city at places like the azalea-strewn Nezu Shrine PAGE 352

Nakamoto Sengyo Tempura 中本鮮魚てんぷら店; 9 Ou Tamagusuku, Oujima; 0989 48 3583; w nakamotosengyoten.com; 10.30–18.00 Fri–Wed. One of Oujima's many tempura shops, Nakamoto is 3 generations strong at making Ou's best deep-fried seafood. $

Central

Wine & Dining The Orange 246-1 Maeganeku, Onna; 0989 64 7711; w kafuu-okinawa.jp; 06.30–10.00, 11.30–15.00 & 18.00–22.00 daily. Kafuu resort seafood restaurant serves perfectly plated low-calorie seafood dishes, with meat & vegetable options. Fine dining in beautiful setting. $$$$

Ufuyaa うふやー; 90 Nakayama, Nago; 0980 53 0280; w ufuya.com; 11.00–16.00 & 18.00–22.00 daily. Traditional wood house soba restaurant with awesome jungle views & cheap delicious meals. Dinner reservations required. $$$

Café Gallery Doka Doka カフェギャラリー土花土花; 243-1 Maeganeku, Onna; 0989 65 1666; w dokadoka.jp/cafe. Attached to the workshop Seikagama, this flower-covered café with incredible sea views serves pizzas & sweets in the owner's ceramics. $$

Café Ichara カフェイチャラ; 2416-1 Izumi, Motobu; 0980 47 6372; w ichara-okinawa.com; 11.30–17.00 Thu–Mon. Gorgeous hideaway terrace café in primeval forest serving set menus & pizza using handmade miso. $$

Charlie's Tacos チャーリー多幸寿 本店; 4-11-5 Central, Koza; 0989 37 4627; 11.00–21.00 Fri–Thu. Famous tacos in Koza & one of the few remaining 'A-sign' US military-approved restaurants from 1956. Retro atmosphere with 3 taco types. $$

Urumarché うるマルシェ; 183-2 Maehara, Uruma; 0989 23 3911; w urumarche.com; 09.00–20.00 daily. Fresh, local food at a farmers' market & food court, with restaurants serving up meals made from the produce on sale. $$

Kishimoto Shokudo きしもと食堂; 5 Toguchi, Motobu; 0980 47 2887; 11.00–17.00 Thu–Tue. Ageing delightfully, this restaurant is part of Motobu's soba road & serves up perfect noodle bowl sets. $

North

Emi no Mise 笑味の店; 61 Oganeku, Ogimi; 0980 44 3220; w eminomise.com; 11.30–16.00 Fri–Mon. Adorable café-restaurant serving Okinawa classics & set meals. $$

Hiro Coffee Farm ヒロ コーヒー ファーム; 85-20 Takae, Higashi; 0980 43 2126; noon–17.30 Thu–Mon. One of the first coffee farms on Okinawa, this colourful café in a baby-pink building sells coffee & coffee-flavoured foods, such as buns, jellies & even sausages. $

ENTERTAINMENT AND NIGHTLIFE Most resort hotels have their own glamorous bars with drink prices to match the décor, but if you're looking for something more casual and into the wee hours, you'll likely want to visit Naha and Koza.

8men Okinawa エイトメン 沖縄; 6F Hachino's 2-17-46 Makishi, Naha; 0989 88 9585; w 8menokinawa.com; 19.00–03.00 Tue–Sun. Welcoming Naha LGBTQIA+ bar run by international gay couple, with outdoor terrace, karaoke machine & happy hour.

Bar Spade バー・スペード; 202 Yonaha Bldg 3-23-10 Kumoji, Naha; 0989 88 8005; w barspade.com; 21.00–05.00 daily. Neon colours this narrow early-hours bar peddling shots & table football.

Bobby's ボビーズ; 1-5-18 Central, Koza; 0989 55 5816; w bar-783.business.site; 21.00–01.00 Tue–Sun. Found in an alley off Ichibangai arcade, this classy Koza cocktail joint offers incredible, creative cocktails in a chilled-out atmosphere.

Gate 2 Garage 1-9 Central, Koza; 0989 34 9199; 21.30–01.00 Fri–Sat. Beloved live music venue in Koza with worthwhile 50s rock & blues acts & license plate decoration.

Gold Disc B1F 1-14-19 Matsuyama, Naha; 0988 68 1268; w golddisc-okinawa.com; 18.00–01.00 Tue–Sat, 18.00–midnight Sun. Live rockabilly bar with good food, good drinks & good dancing.

Parker's Mood Jazz Club 5F Urban Bldg 1-9-11 Kumoji, Naha; 0988 61 2565; w parkersmood.com; 20.30–midnight Thu–Sat. Moody live jazz spot with hefty spirit menu.

Poco a Poco Chatan ポコアポコ 北谷店; 2F 2-16-7 Chatan, Chatan; 0989 89 0058; w f387107.gorp.jp; 18.00–01.00 daily. Izakaya by Araha beach serving Okinawan & Western dishes. All-you-can-eat-or-drink options make it popular with young Okinawans.

Urizun うりずん; 388-5 Asato, Naha; 0988 85 2178; w urizun.okinawa/index.html; 17.30–midnight. Featured in Anthony Bourdain's *Part's Unknown*, this excellent izakaya celebrates Okinawan cuisine & is a great drinking spot.

SHOPPING Okinawa-hontō is a breath of fresh shopping air compared to the rest of the archipelago. Here you'll find abundant farmers' markets and JA supermarkets, spilling over with fresh local produce; you can pop into any number of convenience stores to stock up on snacks and quick bites. Better still, you can find actual souvenir shops, from the tackiest of tat to forever pieces of Okinawan art and crafting. For cheaper trinkets, Kokusai-dōri, airport shops and the large number of shopping centres have it all (though Kokusai is often pricier).

Arts and crafts

Akara Gallery – Bokunen Museum 9-20 Mihama, Chatan; 0989 26 2764; w gallery.akara.asia; 11.00–20.00 daily. Gallery where you can buy nature-inspired art by Bokunen, a printmaker from Kumejima.

Aragaki Kawara Factory 1F American Village 9-19 Mihama, Chatan; 0989 45 2617; 11.30–20.00 daily. Traditional Ryūkyū red tiles made into coasters & aroma stones.

Ikutoen 育陶園; 1-22-33 Tsuboya, Naha; 0988 66 1635; w ikutouen.com; 09.00–18.30 daily. Modern Tsuboya pottery.

Kakuman Ryūkyū Shikki 株式会社 角萬漆器; 1-54-1 Shuriyamagawacho, Naha; 0989 43 3810; w kakuman.jp; 10.00–18.00 Mon–Sat. Supposedly the oldest surviving Kadena lacquerware shop, founded over 120 years ago.

Ryūkyū Glass Village 琉球ガラス村; 169 Fukuchi, Itoman; 0989 97 4784; w ryukyu-glass.co.jp; 09.30–17.30 daily. Ryūkyū glass workshop with on-site shop.

Shuri Ryuzen 首里琉染; 1-54 Shuriyamagawacho, Naha; 0988 86 1131; w shuri-ryusen.com; 09.00–18.00 daily. Bingata studio where you can buy traditional cloth.

Tohodo 陶宝堂; 1-7-9 Tsuboya, Naha; 0904 353 5933; 10.00–18.30 daily. Sells wide selection of old & new pottery from Tsuboya, including Jiro Kinjo works.

Food and drink

Jahana Kippan Store 謝花きっぱん店; 1-5-14 Matsuo, Naha; 0988 67 3687; w jahanakippan.com; 10.00–17.00 Mon–Fri, 10.00–16.00 Sat. 120-year-old traditional confectioners, patronised by royalty.

Okinawaya Awamorikura Kokusai-ten おきなわ屋泡盛蔵国際店; 2-8-5 Matsuo, Naha; 0988 68 5252; 10.00–22.00 daily. Awamori store – look out for Tsukayama Distillery's Kokuka & Zuisen Distillery's Seiryū.

SPORTS AND ACTIVITIES As the seat of Ryūkyū culture, Okinawa-hontō is the home of many traditional sports (page 33). Some are practised daily, others sporadically and some just at annual festivals, but all have a fascinating history and a cultural insight into Okinawa-hontō.

Birdwatching and nature Yanbaru in the north is the place to go for birdwatching. The birds endemic to Okinawa-hontō are naturally the big-hitters: the beloved Okinawa rail and Okinawa woodpecker. The Okinawa rail is most likely found at night or twilight hours around the Oku River Valley, the Benoki Dam area and around Ada village, but you may just spot some crossing roads in Yanbaru – drive carefully. The Okinawa woodpecker is a rare bird found in mature forests; the best place to search for it is on the small tracks off Route 2, which crosses Kunigami's mountainous spine.

You'll also find Nansei-shotō endemics, such as the Ryūkyū robin and Ryūkyū green pigeon. The robin is often seen around Hiji Falls and is regularly around at dawn. The scarce Amami woodcock is sometimes spotted at night, as is the more common Ryūkyū scops owl and the Japanese scops owl. Yanbaru's forests also hosts the handsome Ryūkyū minivet.

In Kijoka's flooded fields, you'll be able to spot plentiful wading birds. Alongside egrets, you'll get the long-toed stint, cinnamon bitter, white-breasted waterhen and common, green and wood sandpipers. Occasionally spotted are Temminck's stint and the greater painted snipe come winter.

Naha also sees some birdlife: by Senaga Island is an enclosed lagoon where you can occasionally find black-faced spoonbills, and Manko is popular for spotting waterbirds: look from the two bridges (Toyomio and Haryū) that cross it and visit the waterbird and wetland centre nearby.

Alongside birds, Okinawa-hontō is home to the rare Okinawa sekkoku orchid and the remarkable irukanda, a vine that hangs with large, grape-like flower bunches.

Golf Okinawa's climate means you get lush fairways, beautiful views and temperate games year-round. The island has several stunning courses and clubs – the challenging Atta Terrace Resort (1079 Afuso, Onna; 0989 67 8554; w terrace.co.jp/en/atta), newly renovated PGM Golf Resort Okinawa (1043 Aza-Fuchaku, Onna; 0989 65 1100) and well-established Chura Orchard Golf Club (1577 Afuso, Onna; 0989 67 8711; w churaorchard.co.jp) are particular favourites with locals and visitors alike.

Karate The most famous Japanese sport, karate actually comes from Okinawa-hontō. You can experience Okinawan karate classes in English language on the island. There's Asato Dōjō (1-8-18 Asato, Naha; 0803 908 1712; w asatodojo.com; 16.00–21.30 Mon–Fri, 09.00–20.30 Sat) run by Brit James Pankiewicz, which welcomes all levels and ages. Asato also conducts online classes to continue your practice at home.

There's also Yomitan's International Karate Study Centre (1020-1 Takashiho; 0803 200 5471; 09.00–17.00 Mon–Fri) – a picturesque dōjō run by Englishman Kevin Chaplin, where individuals or groups can learn from masters. Guests are also welcome to use the dōjō for training and there are dormitories for those studying for longer.

If you're not a karateka but want to enjoy some martial arts fun, head to Naha's Dōjō Bar (101 Asato; 0989 11 3601; w dojobarnaha.com; 19.00–midnight Wed–Mon), a karate-themed restaurant and bar. For those wanting to learn more about the art rather than practise it, you can visit the Karate Museum (2-17-6 Uehara, Nishihara; 0989 45 6148; w tetsuhirohokama.net; 11.00–16.30 Mon, Wed & Fri, 14.00–16.00 Sat), run by Hokama Tetsuhiro-sensei, one of the foremost karate masters. The Karate Kaikan (854-1 Tomigusuku, Tomigusuku; 0988 51 1088; w okic.okinawa; 09.00–17.00 Thu–Tue) is a beautiful school and a must-see for enthusiasts, where staff can help you arrange training.

Tōgyū bullfighting There are about 20 bullfighting tournaments on Okinawa each year in Uruma's Ishikawa multipurpose dome. The bulls aren't just from Okinawa – they come from across Japan to compete. The All-Island Bullfighting Tournament happens three times a year in May, August and November. Seeing one of the tournaments is a day's activity with ringside seats, snacks and drinks.

Tickets can be purchased at the entrance for around ¥2,000 and you'll want to bring a cushion or something padded to sit on the concrete seats.

Tours

Craft workshops

Aikaze 藍風; 3417-6 Izumi, Motobu; 0980 47 5583; w aikaze.okinawa. Traditional indigo dyeing workshop.

Naha City Traditional Arts & Crafts Centre 工芸品販売 那覇市伝統工芸館; 2F Tenbusu Naha, 3-2-10 Makishi; 10.00–19.00 daily. Workshops in glass blowing, bingata, *shuri-ori*, *tsuboyaki* & tsuikin lacquerware.

Uminchi 海ん道; 1931 Maezato, Itoman; 0989 94 0016; w uminchi.com. Café, sea grape picking & salt making.

Outdoor activities

Aloha Divers 41-9 Toguchi, Yomitan; 0809 168 0902; w alohadiversokinawa.com. Diving, certification & snorkelling.

Bokenjima 冒険島; 149 Maeganeku, Onna; 0989 89 3511; w bokenjima.jp. Diving, snorkelling, SUP, kayaking & trekking tours.

Marine Life マリンライフ; 29-72 Tanacha, Motobu; 0980 47 5349; w marine-life.jp. Fishing experiences on raft, boat & shore.

Okinawa Kayak Ease 沖縄カヤックイーズ; 566-15 Mizugama, Kadena; 0989 23 5871; w okinawa-kayak.jp. Day, night & sunset kayaking.

Reef Encounters 1-493 Miyagi, Chatan; 0989 95 9414; e info@reefencounters.org; w reefencounters.org. Shore, boat & night diving.

Spitz Trekking 2382 Maeda, Onna; 0989 65 0012; w spitz-trecking.com. Experienced Taataki Falls treks.

Yanbaru Club やんばるクラブ; 730-4 Gesashi, Higashi; 0980 43 6085; e yanbaru_kayak@yahoo.co.jp. English-language tours of the Gesashi mangrove lasting 1½ or 2½ hours.

OTHER PRACTICALITIES Unlike most islands, getting hold of cash is no problem on Okinawa-hontō. The majority of convenience stores – FamilyMart, 7-11 and Lawson – have ATMs, as well as banks, larger supermarkets and post offices. The only region lacking in cashpoints is northernmost Kunigami: get money before you go. There are multiple police stations (w police.pref.okinawa.jp) and hospitals across the island.

Medical

Motobu Memorial Hospital もとぶ記念病院; 972 Ishikawa; 0980 51 7007; 08.30–12.30 Mon–Fri

Ōgimi Village Clinic 大宜味村立診療所; 1306-62 Shioya; 0980 50 5450; 08.30–noon & 13.30–17.30 Mon–Fri (morning only Thu), 08.30–12.30 Sat

Okinawa Central Hospital 沖縄セントラル病院; 1-26-6 Yogi, Naha; 0988 54 5511; 09.00–17.30 Mon–Sat

Onna Clinic 恩納クリニック; 6329 Onna; 0989 66 8115; 08.30–noon & 13.30–17.30 Mon–Sat (morning only Tue & Thu)

Police

Motobu Police Station 本部警察署; 850-1 Ohama; 0980 47 4110

Nago Police Station Ada Substation 名護警察署安田駐在所; 66 Ada; 0980 41 7125

Okinawa Police Station 沖縄警察署; 2-4-20 Yamazato, Koza; 0989 32 0110

Okinawa Prefectural Police Headquarters 沖縄県警察本部; 1-2-2 Izumizaki, Naha; 0988 62 0110

WHAT TO SEE AND DO

The south The south is Okinawa's cultural capital, the chosen site of the Ryūkyū Kingdom capital, Shuri. It's home to elaborate limestone caves and the vine-laced seat of island religion Seefa Utaki, and was the scene of the worst fighting during the Battle of Okinawa. Today it is dominated by Naha: the prefectural capital and the only true city (and shopping destination) of the islands.

Naha Naha (那覇) is the first port of call for most who visit these islands, which is in some ways a shame – a number of people never go any further and believe this is the sum of Okinawa. Naha is undoubtedly fun, but in some places is almost theme park in its feel. Nearly entirely new and born from a Japanese–US–island mix, it at times feels like the most touristy parts of Tokyo have been dropped in the tropics, then sprinkled with a little bit of Texas. However, it's easy, it's friendly and there's a lot to see by just walking around, including great shops, food, nightlife and history.

Kokusai-dōri (国際通り) is the long, bustling main drag of lights, a neon-filled 1.6km of souvenir shops, restaurants and tourists that spill across the pavements. Tacky? Yes. Fun? Absolutely. This street is the closest the islands ever get to the big city life of Japan, with rainbow-bright signs, inane jingles and market sellers.

At the north end of Kokusai sits the **giant shiisaa** (さいおんうふシーサー) – a symbol of Okinawa that wards off evil spirits and brings good fortune, which can be seen across the prefecture. Presumably this particular 3.4m-high ceramic statue is doing great things for Naha residents. Nearby, in Kokusai's centre, is a **rope monument** (那覇大綱モニュメント; 3-12 Makishi) from Naha's Giant Tug-of-War (see below).

Off Kokusai, the streets scuttle off into short, angular warrens. **Ukishima-dōri** (浮島通り) is a mix of old and new, excellent for secondhand clothes and couture boutiques, traditional sweet shops and stalls selling kariyushi, Okinawa's Hawaiian shirt, while **Heiwa-dōri** (平和通り) is overrun with island ingredients, dishes and restaurants. Markets proliferate – **Makishi Public Market** (牧志公設市場) in particular is ideal for foodies.

Makishi leads on to the old **Tsuboya** (壺屋) architectural district, home of Ryūkyū pottery and a highlight of Naha. The neighbourhood has been actively making ceramics since 1617, with many still family run, making it the best and most authentic place to buy pottery (including your own shiisaa if you wish). It's also one of the lone areas that survived the war, making it a beautiful place to wander and see traditional Okinawan houses, including the kiln at the **Arakaki family home**

NAHA TUG-OF-WAR

Just behind Kokusai-dōri is a wonderfully strange monument: a mammoth coil of knotted rope, used in Naha's annual Giant Tug-of-War. This October event started life as a religious community event that pitched whole villages against each other, and still happens across the archipelago. Naha was originally four towns, divided into east and west, which is how the tug-of-war rivalry was set up. Each of the four towns was represented, with the rope originally being called the 'Yumachi' (four towns).

As Naha grew, the tug-of-war grew alongside it. It took place during national celebrations and festivals until 1935, when it was discontinued. War and occupation meant it wasn't revived until 1971, in celebration of modern Naha's 50th anniversary. It then became an annual event and an international symbol of both the city and Okinawa.

Today, a conjoined 200m, some 40-tonne rope is pulled between symbolic east and west by 15,000 people, earning a Guinness World Record in 1995 and bringing in around 250,000 spectators. Taking place at Kumoji Crossing, this festival is a huge three-day spectacle; alongside the tug-of-war there are parades of traditional Eisaa and Hatagashira dances, drummers, sanshin and conch shells, and even karate displays.

(新垣家住宅; 1-28-32 Tsuboya). For more information on the ceramics made here, head to the **Tsuboya Pottery Museum** (那覇市立壺屋焼物博物館; 1-9-32 Tsuboya; 0988 62 3761; w edu.city.naha.okinawa.jp/tsuboya; 10.00–18.00 Tue–Sun; adult ¥350).

Towards the coast is **Fukushūen** (福州園; 2-29-19 Kume; 0988 69 5384; 09.00–21.00 daily; adult/child ¥300/150, daytime discounts), a garden commemorating the friendship between Naha and Fuzhou, China, after people from there immigrated to Okinawa some 600 years ago. Designed in grand Chinese style, the park lights up spectacularly at night.

Naha's coast itself is a row of parks, home to the **Gokoku-ji** (護国寺; 1-25-5 Wakasa; w w1.nirai.ne.jp/njm; 09.00–18.00 daily) and **Naminoue-gū** (波上宮; 1-25-11 Wakasa; w naminouegu.jp; 09.00–17.00 daily): picturesque clifftop shrines and temples that provide a beautiful vista beside **Naminoue Beach** (波上ビーチ), the only swimming beach in Naha. Asahigaoka Park (旭ヶ丘公園) also has the **Tsushima Maru Memorial Museum** (対馬丸記念会; 1-25-37 Wakasa; 0989 41 3515; w tsushimamaru.or.jp; 09.00–17.00 Fri–Wed; adult/child ¥500/100–300); in 1944, the ship evacuating people from across Okinawa Prefecture was torpedoed by the US navy. Among the 1,418 dead were 775 schoolchildren.

Some 4km south of Naha, dug into a hillside, is the **Former Japanese Navy Underground Headquarters** (旧海軍司令部壕; 236 Tomigusuku; 0988 50 4055; w kaigungou.ocvb.or.jp; 09.00–17.00 daily). This 450m-long tunnel complex formed the Japanese naval headquarters and ended up as their grave: a combined 4,000 men committed suicide or were killed in these tunnels. The site, a remarkable if haunting place, features a small museum with some signage in English.

Further south is **Senaga Island** (瀬長島), a modern hotspot for young Okinawans and tourists alike. With cutesie cafés, modern boutiques and hot springs, little Senaga packs a lot in its resort. It overlooks the sea and Naha Airport, so many come to watch the sunset and planes land. There's also an unusual crab park for kids.

Below Senaga sits shopper's heaven **Toyosaki** (豊崎), an island with huge malls full of luxury brands and electronics, a seaside park with beach, courts and playgrounds and the AI-utilising DMM Kariyushi aquarium (DMMかりゆし水族館; 3-35 Toyosaki; 0989 96 4844; w kariyushi-aquarium.com; 09.00–20.00 daily; adult/child ¥2,400/1,500–2,000).

Shuri The original capital from 1429 to 1879, Shuri was once full of temples, shrines, tombs and of course, the castle. Everything was razed in the war, but places like Shuri Castle were painstakingly rebuilt in the 1990s and Shuri still holds the key to understanding Ryūkyū history.

The **Okinawa Prefectural Museum and Gallery** (沖縄県立博物館・美術館; 3-1-1 Omoromachi; 0989 41 8200; w okimu.jp/en; 09.00–18.00 Tue–Thu & Sun, 09.00–20.00 Fri–Sat; museum: adult/child ¥530/150–270, gallery: adult/child ¥400/120–220) is unmissable. The museum charts the entirety of Okinawa's history with interactive exhibits and extensive English-language information including free audio guides. Meanwhile the gallery houses some of the prefecture's most beautiful artworks and crafts.

The largely reconstructed castle, or **Shuri-jō** (首里城; 1-2 Shurikinjocho; 0988 86 2020; w oki-park.jp/shurijo; 08.00–18.30 daily; adult/child ¥400/free), is Naha's greatest treasure, though it's worse for wear after a devastating 2019 fire. Now under reconstruction that's expected to finish in 2026, this 5ha site is known for its unique use of Chinese and Japanese architectural styles in its Seiden hall. The original castle, built in 1237 and expanded in 1469, was said to match the grandiosity of Kyoto and Nara. It was the headquarters for Japanese troops in World War II and was mostly destroyed. **Shuri Park** (首里城公園) contains important stone gates, ponds and temples, including the Kannondō Jigen-in, which survived the war.

The **Tamaudun** (玉陵; 1-3 Shuri; 0988 85 2861; 09.00–18.00 daily), a Ryūkyū royal mausoleum built in 1501 by Shō Shin for his dynasty, is a rare architectural leftover. A limestone tomb of multiple rooms built into the cliff, it's made to look like a wooden building and features stone shiisaa and a gabled red-tile roof. To its south is the Kinjo Town 16th-century cobble road, known as the Pearl Road. This was the 10km historic thoroughfare between Shuri and Naha Port: the remaining 300m is still flanked by traditional houses.

The **Shikinaen** (識名園; 421-7 Shinji; 0989 17 3501; 09.00–18.00 Thu–Tue (until 17.30 Oct–Mar), to Shuri-jō south is the garden of the royal family's 1799 villa, incorporating Chinese, Japanese and Ryūkyū elements. Used for hospitality for Chinese envoys, its highlights are the heart-shaped pond, observation deck and Chinese-style house.

North of Shuri are the **Urasoe Castle Ruins** (浦添城跡; 2-53-1 Urasoe), the original seat of the Ryūkyū Kingdom before Shuri. Overlooking the sea, the area is now a great park home to the castle's remaining large stone walls. This park is better known as the infamous Hacksaw Ridge, an area of battle where American forces suffered huge loss of life due to the escarpment terrain. There are monuments and wartime artefacts throughout the park.

Itoman and Nanjō These two areas in the south are places of war, peace and religion. **Itoman** (糸満市) is the unenviable home to war. The **Peace Memorial Park** (平和祈念公園; Mabuni; 0989 97 2765; w heiwa-irei-okinawa.jp; 08.00–22.00 daily) was the final battleground of World War II and scene of the worst fighting on Okinawa. Now a 40ha park overlooking the ocean, its huge tree-lined expanse is freckled with sombre memorials, tombs and museums that mourn while advocating peace. This includes the Cornerstone of Peace (平和の礎), where row upon row of black granite cenotaphs name all those who died across each nation, and the Okinawa Peace Hall, home to a large Buddha and an impactful series of artworks. The park is also the location of the **Okinawa Peace Memorial Museum** (沖縄県平和祈念資料館; 614-1 Mabuni; 0989 97 3844; w peace-museum.okinawa.jp; 09.00–17.00 daily; adult/child ¥300/150), which introduces the history and conditions of the battle, and traces the subsequent reconstruction of the prefecture.

Some 10 minutes' west, **Himeyuri Tower and Peace Museum** (ひめゆりの塔・ひめゆり平和祈念資料館; 671-1 Ihara; 0989 97 2100; w himeyuri.or.jp/en; 09.00–17.25 daily; adult/child ¥400/110–200) tells the story of how female high school students and their teachers were forced into being nurses on the frontline. The tower sits above the cave that acted as their emergency field hospital, and the remains of 227 girls who died doing this work are laid to rest here. There is English signage throughout, and video accounts with English subtitles from some of the surviving students.

The best of Okinawa's caves are in **Nanjō** (南城). Tour the mysterious and exquisite **Gangalaa Valley** (ガンガラーの谷; 202 Maekawa; 0989 48 4192; w gangala.com/en; 09.00–17.30 daily; adult ¥2,500). The collapsed limestone valley is home to lush subtropical forest peppered with caves and shrines. **Okinawa World** (おきなわワールド; 1336 Maekawa; 0989 49 7421; w gyokusendo.co.jp; 09.00–17.30 daily; adult/child ¥2,000/1,000) next door is home to animal displays, orchards and the amazing Gyokusendo. This great 5km cave system is Okinawa's largest, and has more than a million stalactites and stalagmites formed over centuries.

Off the south coast lies **Ōjima** (奥武島), a quaint island connected to Okinawa-hontō by bridge that's known for its fish. It's home to ancient boat racing and fishermen festivals, and some of the best squid, seaweed and tempura on Okinawa. Make sure to try the sushi bowls and the mozuku and aosa tempura from the multiple stalls at Imaiyu Market. Ōjima's **Kannondō** (奥武島観音堂) has a golden Kannon (Buddhist bodhisattva) statue given as thanks to the islanders for rescuing a 17th-century Chinese ship.

Either side of Ōjima are beaches. The westerly 2km-long **Miibaru Beach** (みーばるビーチ) has white coral and quiet sands ripe for glass-bottom boat rides and marine sports. Westerly **Gushichan Beach** (ぐしちゃん浜) has shallow waters with a calm coral reef pond. The beach has interesting rock formations used for bouldering.

When driving east, make sure to pass over the Niraikanai Bridge (ニライカナイ橋), where there's an observation deck overlooking the bridge's dramatic 80m-high curve across the landscape. This bridge heads to the most sacred place in the Ryūkyū Kingdom: **Seefa Utaki** (also Sēfa Utaki; 斎場御嶽; 270-1 Nanjo; 0989 49 1899; w okinawa-nanjo.jp/sefa; 09.00–18.00 daily (until 17.30 Nov–Feb), closed 1–3 May & 1–3 Oct). This UNESCO site overlooks Kudakajima, the Island of the Gods (see below), and an hour-long trail winds through the southern greenery to a shrine used by the chief noro priestess. On the coast nearby, the bafflingly named **Azama Sun Sun Beach** (あざまサンサンビーチ) is popular with families for its shallow waters and grassy banks, plus facilities like showers, lockers, rentals and a beach house where you can get barbecues.

Another sacred spot in this area is the **Tamagusuku Ruins** (玉城城跡), a pilgrimage stop for the Ryūkyūan royal family. Reaching 180m high, it shows off views of the surrounding landscape, the sea and Kudakajima. At the tip of a cape surrounded by coral reef sits **Chinenmisaki Park** (知念岬公園), a promenaded green space overlooking Kudaka's blue beauty.

Tiny, uninhabited **Komakajima** (コマカ島) is a day-trip islet 15 minutes' boat ride from Chinen Marine Leisure Centre. Komaka is mostly white sand and coral reef; join a snorkelling or diving tour (page 188) to see the vibrant marine life.

Kudaka Just 5km off the main island's southeast coast is Kudaka (久高島), a small island that is one of the holiest places on Okinawa. Known as the island of the gods, it's said to be the first island made by the Ryūkyūan creation goddess Amamikyo. She is believed to have first landed at Habyaan (ハビャーン) on Cape Kabeeru and also to have brought five fruits and grains to Ishiki Beach (伊敷浜), enabling Okinawan life and agriculture to advance – the archipelago's harvest and festivals originate from this legend.

Ryūkyūan kings and officials used to annually pilgrimage to Kudaka and sacred rituals are performed here to this day. (On event days, you may not be able to access the north of the island.) The island's 260 residents view the area outside the village as a shared sanctuary belonging to no-one, but take care to preserve it as they believe the entire of Kudaka is sacred and borrowed from the gods.

A high-speed ferry from Azama Port takes 15 minutes to reach Kudaka's southeast settlement, while the normal ferry takes 50 minutes; both run three times a day and are operated by Kudaka Kaiun (w kudakakaiun.jimdofree.com). Once there, the best way to explore Kudaka's unspoilt green and white landscape is by bicycle or walking, though make sure to take water with you. At just 1.3km^2, you can easily make your way about its beautiful beaches, traditional housing and sacred shrines. Make sure to see the holy **Fuboo Utaki** (クボー御嶽) and **Cape Kabeeru** (カベール岬), two of the Seven Sacred Sites of the Ryūkyū. While these are accessible to visitors, take care to respect island rules as some of its holy places are off-limits.

Elsewhere there are many pretty beaches and viewpoints to explore. There's a **giant gajumaru** (巨大なガジュマルの樹) in the south and sensational sea views from the northerly **Romance Road** (久高島ロマンスロード). In the main village, the preserved **Upuratu House** (大里家; 151 Kudaka) supposedly played a part in Ryūkyūan politics; it was the home of Kudaka's chief priestess, who Shō Toku, the unpopular final king of the First Shō Dynasty, fell in love with while on a pilgrimage here. While he was busy romancing her, he was ousted from his throne.

Kudaka is known for its sea salt, its seasonal mozuku seaweed and irabujiru – sea snake soup. If you're willing to try it, smoked irabu soup is known for being highly nutritional. The northeastern edge of the island, Kabeeru, is designated a natural treasure for its flora.

Most people don't stay, but if you do, try camping at the very basic Kudakajima Beach Camping Ground (久高島ビーチキャンプ場; 0808 378 8435; w kudaka.hp.peraichi.com) overlooking Meegi Beach (メーギ浜).

Central Okinawa-hontō's centre has a good number of villages, filled with traditional crafts, beaches and a proliferation of islands. Western Yomitan has pottery workshops, Chatan resorts and shopping, and Koza bars and music. On the quieter east side is Uruma, US-influenced Kin Town and the Yokatsu Islands. The spine of Okinawa is mostly given over to both forest and US bases: the most famous of these, Kadena, lies between the central coasts.

West coast **Chatan** (北谷) is a town of trendy restaurants and shopping – not one to necessarily dedicate your time to if you're limited. It offers a melting pot of modern US and Japanese culture, best summarised by the American Village mall (アメリカンビレッジ; 9-1 Mihama; w okinawa-americanvillage.com; ⏲ 10.00–22.00 daily): a theme park of shopping and American food.

The mall is on the coast, which is again full of further restaurants. Depot Island (デポアイランド) is a colourful complex with a sunset promenade while the Chatan Fisharina area has great seafront fish restaurants serving American classics like seafood chowder. The beachfront walk continues north up the Miyagi coast, where you'll find hip café districts like Sunabe. Miyagi is also popular with divers and surfers, ideal for those wanting a guarantee of English instructors.

The very south of Chatan's coast is Araha Beach (アラハビーチ), a popular, crowded stretch of white sand with a full-scale sailing-ship playground and barbecue spot nearby. The north is home to Toguchi Beach (渡具知ビーチ), where American forces landed.

An hour from Naha, **Yomitan** (読谷) is a central highlight: there's Ryūkyū food, brilliant beaches, castle ruins and traditional crafts. Yomitan is the centre of modern Okinawan pottery, with around 20 workshops still making their own unique style of ceramics. Pop into the traditional Yachimun-no-Sato pottery co-operative (やちむんの里; 2653-1 Zakimi; 0989 58 6488) where you can see firing kilns and galleries.

Alongside pottery, Yomitan's Traditional Crafts Centre (読谷山花織事業協同組合; 2974-2 Zakimi; 0989 58 4674; w yomitanhanaori.com; ⏲ 09.00–17.00 Mon–Fri, 10.00–17.00 Sat–Sun) demonstrates and teaches the techniques behind the local hanaori fabric, for which threads are naturally dyed then woven on a wooden loom to create handsome geometric patterns. There are three traditional designs: a coin representing money, a pinwheel for longevity and a fan for future generations.

Inland, make sure to stop at **Chibichirigama** (チビチリガマ; 1136-1 Namihira), a humbling but picturesque hidden cave off a small road where 83 residents committed mass suicide for fear of being captured and tortured by US soldiers. To Chibichirigama's west sits **Zakimi Castle**'s (座喜味城跡) undulating 15th-century ramparts – some of the best preserved on Okinawa. Standing proud on a 127m-high hill, the castle ruins have great views across the sea to the Kerama and house a small museum about the area, the castle and its history.

The village is lined by multiple beaches and untouched coastline, including the 30m-high cliffs of **Cape Zanpa** (残波岬). Plant-carpeted Zanpa is known for its sunsets, lighthouse and Okinawa's largest shiisaa (残波大獅子) at 8.75m, but it also has an activity park for keeping kids entertained, a barbecue area and access to **Zanpa Beach** (残波ビーチ). The cape is also popular with fishermen: you'll spot them dotting the cliff, patiently awaiting dinner. Yomitan's food scene features much fish but also *beni-imo*, a gorgeously sweet and startling purple sweet potato. Make sure to pick up beni-imo-themed snacks and meals.

East coast The **Nakagusuku Ruins** (中城城跡; 1258 Tomari Nakagusuku; 0989 35 5719; w nakagusuku-jo.jp; 08.30–18.00 daily, to 17.00 Oct–Apr; adult/child ¥400/200–300), a 30-minute drive from Naha, are the restored remains of multiple mountaintop castles dating back to the 1440s. Overlooking Nakagusuku Bay, the strong Ryūkyū limestone walls still stand and are one of the best castle sites of Okinawa.

The ornate **Nakamura family residence** (中村家住宅; 106 Ogusuku; 0989 35 3500; w nakamurahouse.jp; 09.00–17.00 Fri–Tue; adult/child ¥500/200–300) is a traditional 18th-century house of wood and tile. The family are believed to have been overseers (*jitōdai*) of the region, and the mansion has all the beautiful archetypes of Ryūkyū architecture: a hemp fence and fukugi trees surrounding outer buildings like an *ashagi* (annexe), takakura (stilted storehouse), *meenuya* (livestock barn) and a well.

Koza (コザ), also known as Okinawa City, is a phenomenally fun town 20km north of Naha with a strong musical connection and vibrant nightlife. It's famed for its cosmopolitan feel that really captures the US–Okinawan mix, known as '*chanpuruu*' after the Okinawan mixed-up dish (page 53). There are so many American influences, shops and clubs that you know a base must lurk nearby – and indeed one does, in the form of Kadena.

Koza has been heaven for music lovers since the 60s and 70s, embracing both traditional and modern genres. Jazz, blues, rock, Latin and Okinawan folk music pour from the pubs, bars and festivals; enter any bar on **Gate Street** (コザゲート通り), often called Kadena Gate 2 Street as it leads from Kadena base, and you're guaranteed a great evening.

Koza Music Town (コザ・ミュージックタウン; 1-1-1 Uechi; 0989 95 9104; w kozamusictown.com) is a landmark music venue with concerts, restaurants, a tourist office and the fun Eisaa Hall museum for learning about local music and festivals. Koza also hosts a traditional Obon festival with colourful dancing and costumes, the three-day Zento Eisaa festival and the Peaceful Love Rock summer festival.

Gate Street also houses **HiStreet**, aka Okinawa City Postwar Cultural Materials Exhibition Hall (沖縄市戦後文化資料展示館 ヒストリート; 1F 2F Tasato Building 2-2-1 Chuo Okinawa; 0989 29 2922; w histreet.okinawa.jp/histreet). This museum examines life in Koza after the war and the blending of cultures that resulted.

Aside from music, Koza has the **Okinawa Zoo and Museum** (沖縄こどもの国; 5-7-1 Goya; 0989 33 4190; w okzm.jp; 09.30–17.30 Wed–Mon), ideal for children, with floral displays in summer, Christmas lights in winter, and of course a whole menagerie of animals. There's also the spectacular **Southeast Botanical Gardens** (東南植物楽園; 2146 Chibana; 0989 39 2555; w southeast-botanical.jp; 09.30–22.00 daily; adult/child ¥1,540/600–1,050 daytime), one of Japan's largest outdoor botanical gardens. Explore over 50,000 plants across 1,300 species, such as baobab and dragon's blood trees, and some 50 animals like capybara and exotic birds.

On the road north, look out for the kaleidoscopic murals by Ginten Arcade and Koza crossroads. Done by local artists, they depict the history of Koza town.

The central east coast finishes with Uruma (うるま), an agricultural area that isn't overwhelmed with sites but has a few worthwhile stops on your way to the Katsuren Peninsula and the Yokatsu Islands.

Katsuren Castle Ruins (勝連城跡; 3908 Katsuren; w katsuren-jo.jp; 09.00–18.00 daily; adult/child ¥600/400) make up an informative outdoor museum. The castle was once home to a famous *aji* lord called Amawari, a former peasant who was one of the last hold-outs against the Ryūkyū king. Built on an isolated hill in the 15th century, the castle had strategic views over the centre and north of Okinawa, as well as Kin Bay and the Yokatsu Islands. To the north of Katsuren is

LOCAL RECIPE: JUUSHII

The ultimate and only Okinawa rice dish, juushii is simple and lipsmackingly good. You can make it in a saucepan as long as it's non-stick, but the easiest way is with a rice cooker, as it tells you the exact water needed. Japanese rice is needed for the stickiness, but you can use alternatives. Burdock is hard to come by, but the whole point of juushii is to use what you have.

180ml Japanese rice, soaked for 20mins
100g pork mince or sausage meat, broken up
2 tbsp soy sauce
1 tbsp sake
1 tbsp mirin or sugar
1 tbsp sesame oil
1 tsp dashi or fish stock cube
½ tsp salt
carrot, julienned
burdock, julienned
mushrooms, chopped

1. If using a rice cooker, add enough rice and water according to one portion measurements. Then add the rest of the ingredients, switch on and sit back.
2. For saucepan, place soaked and drained rice in the pot and add a ratio of rice to water 1:1.2. If using 180ml rice, add around 200ml water.
3. Add the rest of the ingredients, bring to boil then cook on low, with lid, for about 12–15 minutes. Check water is absorbed by gently tipping the saucepan, lid on, over the sink.
4. Remove from heat and let steam, lid on, for 10 minutes. Mix together with rice scoop and eat.

pretty **Uken Beach** (宇堅ビーチ), a favourite among both humans and turtles, with safe swimming for young ones, barbecue areas and camping.

The north of Uruma, where Okinawa's waist gets really cinched, is home to **Cave Okinawa** (479-1 Ishikawa Kadekaru; w cave-okinawa.com; ⏲ 09.00–17.30 daily; adult/child ¥500/300), which mixes ancient stalactite formations with colourful illuminations, and **Bios Hill** (ビオスの丘; 961-30 Ishikawa; w bios-hill.co.jp; ⏲ 09.00–18.00 daily; adult/child ¥2,200/1,000) – a rich subtropical park with walking paths and a lake boat cruise (included with entry). Filled with wild birds, orchids, botanical gardens and forest ferns, it also offers myriad experiences like buffalo cart rides, canoeing and dressing up in traditional clothing.

Yokatsu Islands A small group of islands off the Katsuren Peninsula, the four easiest Yokatsu (与勝諸島) are connected to the mainland by bridge drive known as the Underwater Road (海中道路; Kaichūdōro): Henza, Miyagi, Ikei and Hamahiga. The rest are a short boat trip away, while the uninhabited Ukibara and Minamiukibara are stop-offs on snorkelling tours. The Yokatsu aren't more than a quick day trip, and can easily be incorporated into your schedule.

Henza Known for its rich seafood culture, Henza (平安座島) is a small island just 7km around. It's the first of the islands you meet coming from Okinawa-hontō over the 5km Kaichū-dōro. The Henza Kaichū bridge is so long that it has its own beach (海中道路ビーチ) and Umi-no-Eki Ayahashikan rest stop (海の駅あやはし館; ☎ 0989 78 8830; w r.goope.jp/uminoekiayahashi; ⏲ 09.00–17.00 daily), which also houses the Sea Culture Museum (文化資料館) dedicated to Henza seafaring heritage.

Walk or cycle through Henza's quiet streets and along its painted seawall (平宮護岸アートコンクール), a 300m mural by students, portraying Henza culture. Along the wall is a small torii gate (竜宮門) looking towards little Nanzajima (ナンザ岩・亀島), aka 'Turtle Island' due to its shape – a popular place to watch sunrise at New Year. A modern myth is that if you set a photo of the torii as your phone background, you'll have good luck.

The local fishing port (与那城町漁業協同組合) is the busiest part of calming Henza, where fish is still unloaded and sold daily – check out the morning fish market. At the Sangwachaa fisherman festival in spring (lunar March), people wade into the shallows and pray to the sea gods for a good catch and family safety before enjoying a giant fish parade.

Miyagi A teeny bridge connects Henza's east to Miyagi's (宮城島) west. With its beautiful coastline, untouched beaches and relative elevation (120m), Miyagi is ideal for a scenic drive or cycle, giving you views across the Yokatsu and Katsuren Peninsula.

The gorgeous wild east-coast beaches are the draw here: Tobaru Beach (桃原ビーチ), Akuna Beach (アクナ浜), Ukuno Beach (ウクノ浜) and Ndakachina Beach (ンダカチナ浜). Tobaru is the easiest to access, but the others like Ndakachina require varying levels of steep pot-holed drives, delicate manoeuvring and a walk. However, Ndakachina is arguably the best view due to Kahou Banta (果報バンタ). This cliff and observatory is the island's highest point, and overlooks the beach's magnificent blue-white-green bay, sheltered by sheer coastline. Kahou Banta is also home to the Nuchimaasu Salt Factory (ぬちまーす観光製塩ファクトリー; 2768 Yonashiromiyagi; w nuchima-su.co.jp; ⏲ 09.00–17.30 daily) where you can pick up souvenirs and delicious salt ice cream.

Through the little northern village you'll pass the Nangusuku ruins (南グスク), which requires a very wild walk to reach its small cave and old stone castle steps, before coming to Tonnaha Beach (トンナハビーチ), an easily reached recreational beach.

Ikei A hop over the Ikei Bridge (伊計大橋) brings you to the easternmost Yokatsu. Ikei (伊計島) is a low-lying quiet island with a surprising amount to offer for its size: history, sugarcane agriculture and swimming beaches.

Immediately to the right of the bridge are the ruins of Ikeigusuku (伊計グスク), a sacred place from ancient Ryūkyū times. There's a trail from the car park that's barely maintained, but gets you nice views across the bridge and hidden beaches. Be warned, though, that parts of the trail get wet during higher tide.

Noro used to conduct ceremonies and rituals north of Ikeigusuku, which is now Ikei Beach (伊計ビーチ; w ikei-beach.com; ⌚ 09.00–17.00 daily; adult/child ¥400/300). These long gentle shallows in a small cove are perfect for little ones and have plenty of fish to see, though you have to pay for the pleasure. There are lifeguards, barbecue rental and plentiful marine activities like glass boats, jet skis and kayaks. Similarly, Ōdomari Beach (大泊ビーチ) charges and the northernmost beach is private for resort guests, but Higashi Beach (東の浜) is as yet un-monetised.

Passing by the sunflower fields, a picturesque golden spread when in summer bloom, brings you to the Nakabaru ruins (仲原遺跡). This prehistoric pit-dwelling site was inhabited some 2,000–2,500 years ago and is the largest on Okinawa. Human bones, earthenware pots and stone axes have all been excavated here and some of the thatched, dug-in dwellings have been recreated for visitors.

Hamahiga To the south of Henza is old-fashioned Hamahiga (浜比嘉), a sacred and stunning island of nature and spirituality. A popular fishing spot, the island also has traditional architecture, resort hotels and near-empty beaches.

Across the 900m bridge and to the west is a small village home to the fine white sands of Hamahiga Beach (浜比嘉ビーチ) and the family-friendly Butterfly House greenhouse (ちょうちょうハウス; 384-1 Katusrenhama; ☎ 0907 397 2779; ⌚ 10.00–17.30 Tue–Sun).

Hamahiga's east is sprinkled with religious sites. First comes Norohaka (ノロ墓), a priestess's grave in the forest, then the rather overgrown Higagusuku ruins (比嘉グスク), and finally Amamikyu's grave (アマミチューの墓) on Amanji Island. This is where the creation gods from Ryūkyū myth, Amamikyu (also Amamichuu) and Shinerikyu, are said to be entombed.

The southeast coast starts with the sacred rock formations of Hamahigaryūgū (浜比嘉竜宮), off the concrete path, and heads down to Muruku Beach (ムルク浜) and Shirumichuu Beach (シルミチューの浜).

Hamahiga's highlight, however, is Shirumichuu (シルミチュー): a stunningly vine-twisted shrine with torii and 108 stone steps leading up to a cave. This cave is where Amamikyu, Shinerikyu and their children are said to have lived. As such, many couples come here to pray for fertility. Every New Year, the Higa noro picks up a pebble from the beach and places it in a pot inside the cave.

Yabuchi Yabuchi (藪地島), sitting just below the Henza Kaichū bridge, is remarkably tiny and as such isn't much of a destination. It's mostly given over to an extremely bumpy single main road, agriculture and broad tidal flat beaches that don't quite have the lure of their white-sand cousins elsewhere on Okinawa.

At its southern tip, however, is Janee Cave (ジャネー洞, also Janeh), also known as Yabuchi Cave Ruins, a huge sacred limestone cave and archaeological site, which locals believe is the birthplace of our ancestors. Shell arrowheads have been excavated here, indicating cultural exchange and trade with southern China. Reaching the cave is via an ethereal forest walk full of gigantic banyans with thick sprawling roots. The cave itself is sacred to locals and has a shrine and altar for praying, as well as a narrow entrance that takes you to a karst cavern of stalactites. The beach nearby is worth a visit and make sure to say hello to the many stray cats.

Tsuken Tsuken (津堅島) is famed for one thing and one perplexing thing only: carrots. Lying 6km south of the Katsuren Peninsula, Tsuken's mineral rich soil has long been helping to grow plump, unbeatable carrots that are said to be the sweetest in Japan. Naturally, mascot and theme-loving Japan has prolifically capitalised on this unique detail, and Tsuken is more commonly known as Carrot Island. (Tsuken is also known for its sweet *chikin-dekuni* radish, which is prized for pickling, but it rarely gets a look-in.)

Tsukenjima is accessed from Uruma's Heshikiya Port via the 15-minute high-speed ferry, leaving twice daily, or the slower 30-minute Ferry Kugani, leaving thrice; both are run by Kamiya Kankō (**w** tsuken.shimatabi.jp). Just 2km long, 1km wide and almost entirely flat, Tsuken is easily walkable, but you can rent a bicycle from the port too.

With 80% of the island farmland, and 60% of that entirely carrots, Tsuken uses the vegetable in a variety of products: cakes, juices, salad dressings and even cider make for good souvenirs. There's also a carrot-shaped observatory (ニンジン展望台) in the southwest, though it's looking a little dilapidated.

Exploring Tsuken's coast is a wonderful way to work off the carrots. The island is hemmed in by glorious sandy beaches on all sides, meaning you can pick and choose your own private little patch of white sand from which to swim and snorkel. Tumai Beach (トゥマイ浜) reaches over a kilometre down the west coast, making it one of the largest natural beaches on Okinawa. Its sheltered calm sea makes it popular with families from Okinawa-hontō, who come here during summer to play and barbecue on the beach. There are also cafés and rental shops. Across from Yajiri Beach (ヤジリ浜) in the north lies Afu, a tiny islet you can walk to in high tide.

By the port is Hootugaa (ホートゥガー), a well set in jagged rocks and cliffs that was said to be discovered by a pigeon. The views here are beautiful, with green adan trees looming over the extraordinary bright seas. Beside this is the Makaa (マカー), a shrine for those hoping to have children. On the southern tip of Tsuken are the ruins of its red brick lighthouse (津堅島灯台跡) – the first modern lighthouse to be built on Okinawa in 1896.

Onna, Kin and Ginoza Okinawa-hontō's waistline is largely given over to long scenic drives, beginning with Onna's 30km northwest coastline, best known for the Blue Cave off **Cape Maeda** (真栄田岬) – the most popular dive point on Okinawa. From atop the cape there are observatories overlooking the ombré waters of the East China Sea. Below is a submarine cave famed for its extraordinary and entirely natural blue illumination; it can only be accessed by swimming underwater, but the length is short enough to use snorkels.

For more experienced divers, the oddly named Manza Dream Hole is a cave that descends 30m and is full of garden eels and fan coral. In addition to snorkelling, diving and swimming, you can catch sight of dolphins or, come February–March, humpbacks.

Near Maeda is **Ryūkyū-mura** (琉球村; 1130 Yamada; ☎ 0989 65 1234; w ryukyumura.co.jp/en; ⏲ 09.30–17.00 daily; adult/child ¥1,500/600), a theme park reproducing a traditional village with shows, craft classes, dancing and a sugar factory. Excellent for kids and adults alike, Ryūkyū-mura is a hands-on experience of old Okinawa.

Onna (恩納) overflows with beaches, but also hotels – it's the island's premier resort destination. This means the beaches are well maintained but often busier and some require payment. Manza Beach (万座ビーチ), under the watchful white pyramid of the ANA Continental, and northerly Sun Marina (サンマリーナビーチ) are arguably the best of these preened beaches. Meanwhile, Seaside Park Nabii Beach (恩納村海浜公園ナビービーチ) is managed by Onna Village itself and has good facilities, and relaxing Hamabaru Beach (ハマバルビーチ) is quieter than most.

The 20m-high Cape Manzamo (万座毛) in Onna's northwest has a craggy coastline with crashing waves, battered rocks and protected plant communities. From here you get views across Nago Bay up to the northern mountains and to Mount Onna to the east, as well as of Manzamo's own unique 'elephant trunk' shape. Further north is the **Busena Marine Park** (ブセナ海中公園; 1744-1 Kise; ☎ 0980 52 3379; w busena-marinepark.com; adult/child ¥1,050/530), which features an underwater observatory, allowing any age and ability to see the diverse Okinawan sea life.

On the east coast are Kinchō, commonly called Kin Town (金武) in English, and Ginoza (宜野座). Over 50% of these rural, rich green regions are occupied by the US Marine Corps, including Camps Hansen and Schwab, leaving mostly coastline open to visitors. Most people stick to Onna's coast on the drive, but there are a handful of stop-offs here.

Ukkagaa (ウッカガー; 640 Kin) is a historic well with a gorgeously overgrown banyan tree overtaking its torii gate and spring waters ideal for kids to play in. These waters help to grow Kin's local speciality *taimu*, a type of taro. A short walk from Ukkaga is the handsome wooden architecture of **Kannonji** (観音寺; 222 Kin), a temple with a huge old tree and sacred cave.

The Shinkaichi district in **Kin Town** is known for its Americana bars and diners that are wonderfully English-friendly – some menus even have prices in US dollars. Shinkaichi has a feel of Okinawa under US administration, and indeed Kin's biggest export – taco rice – dates back to that time. Created by a local restaurant, taco meat on rice has become a staple and symbol of modern Okinawan cuisine.

Kin's north is given over to the mangrove river **Okukubigawa** (億首川), which features four mangrove tree species and is brilliant for kayaking and ecotours. The area around the Okukubi is full of observatories and boardwalks, so you can experience the river even if you don't fancy getting on the water.

Ginoza is mostly quiet, narrow beaches and little else. If driving the east coast, stop at Matsuda (松田) for one of the guided (some arguably expensive) tours of the relatively untouched 230m-long cave **Meegaagama** (メーガー洞; 78 Matsuda; w matsuda-kucha.jimdofree.com; ⏲ 09.00–17.00 daily; adult/child from ¥1,500/500). Further north into Nago are the pretty **Kushi Kannondō** (久志観音堂) temple and **Ryūkyū Sedona** (琉球セドナ), a coastal geological formation said to resemble those surrounding the US city of Sedona.

The Motobu Peninsula and Nago The main reason any traveller to this island leaves Naha is **Motobu** (本部): home to **Churaumi Aquarium** (沖縄美ら海水族館; 424 Ishikawa; ☎ 0980 48 3748; ⏲ 08.30–18.30 daily, to 20.00 & 21.00 in mid-July–August). An international powerhouse emblazoned across Instagram,

Churaumi is the world's second largest aquarium. Covering touch pools and coral reefs to the deepest ocean, the aquarium holds multiple world-first breeding records, including coral using sunlight and seawater and whale sharks. Its major draw is the huge viewing tunnel that reveals massive tiger sharks, meditative whale sharks and beautiful manta rays.

The aquarium sits within the 70ha **Ocean Expo Park** (海洋博公園; 424 Ishikawa; 0980 48 2741; w oki-park.jp/kaiyohaku/en), which includes Okinawan village reconstructions and a botanical garden. Also inside is **Emerald Beach** (エメラルドビーチ), a magnificently bright stretch of coral sand beside a lagoon, handily divided into 'play' and 'relax' areas. In fact the entire coastline of Motobu and Nakijin (今帰仁) is overrun with beautiful beaches, private and public; it's hard to go wrong by picking the closest when you need a top-up of sand and sun. Similarly, there are plentiful viewpoints, but make sure to visit **Arashiyama Observatory** (嵐山展望台; 1460-2 Goga) with its green-and-blue views across the nearby islands and the inland sea.

Nearby, the traditional seaside village of **Bise** (備瀬) has 250 houses embedded in a forest of 20,000 fukugi trees, planted as natural windbreaks from the region's prolific typhoons. A sign of old Okinawa, Bise's fukugi are the island's best: one is estimated to be 300 years old. Explore Bise on foot, wandering around its little sun-dappled lanes and immersing yourself in the village landscape, or take a bicycle or buffalo cart ride.

The peaks of **Katsuudake** (嘉津宇岳) and **Awadake** (安和岳) overlook the Motobu Peninsula and come spring have wonderful cherry blossoms. Climbing these mountains is a little tough but relatively short. Awadake has a looping trail (1hr 40mins) across some steep and rocky sections, with amazing views of conical karst terrains, lush subtropical forest and the peninsula. The trailhead begins on Awadake's southeast – park nearby. The views from Katsuudake beside it are similar, but the trail is a more manageable and shorter there-and-back one. The two hikes can easily be combined.

Nakijin Castle Ruins (今帰仁城跡; 5101 Imadomari; 0980 56 4400; w nakijinjoseki-osi.jp; 08.00–18.00 daily, to 19.00 May–Aug; adult/child ¥600/450) was the main castle of the old northern kingdom and once one of the largest fortresses on Okinawa. The sinuous ramparts and walls are still impressive, sitting 90–100m above sea level. The panoramic views reach to Izena and Iheya on good days, but Nakijin is at its best in January–February, when the Taiwan cherry trees bloom a deep pink in the day and are uplit at night.

Nago's (名護) south is predominantly taken up by US bases and training grounds, but its centre and north have a selection of sights. The beloved **Nago Pineapple Park** (ナゴパイナップルパーク; 1195 Biimata; 0980 53 3659; w nagopain.com; 10.00–18.00 daily; adult/child ¥1,200/600) is a fun little theme park based on fruit that's been grown here for a century. See how they're cultivated, learn the varieties, pet animals and, of course, eat pineapple products.

Across Nago's forested, plum tree-filled centre to the east coast, you'll find the **Ōura Mangrove** (大浦マングローブ) and the **Dugong Hill viewpoint** (ジュゴンの見える丘).

Motobu Islands

Sesoko Sesoko (瀬底島) sits off Motobu's west coast near Churaumi Aquarium (page 199), connected by the 762m Sesoko Bridge. A little jaunt from the mainland, Sesoko hasn't got a whole lot to offer on land, but beneath its calm cyan seas it has a sprawling reef with a maze of caves, arches and tunnels suited to all diving levels.

The island's 8km coast is known for **Sesoko Beach** (瀬底ビーチ), an 800m broad carpet of fine sand that has excellent sunsets, translucent waters filled with tropical fish and views out to Minna and Ie islands. Below Sesoko Bridge is the smaller **Anchihama** (アンチ浜), a beach often used by locals and tourists alike for barbecues. **Sesoko's Tail** (瀬底のしっぽ) to the south is a wild and craggy lookout point with views to Okinawa-hontō.

Due to its good diving, Sesoko has a surprising number of resorts in its north – not quite in keeping with the island's original secluded village life. Still, the low level of light pollution makes for great stargazing, and there are some independent little cafés and eateries like Fuu Café (557 Sesoko; 0980 47 4885; 11.00–17.30 Fri–Tue) where you can sit back with home-roasted coffee and do absolutely nothing. Within the main village is the **Sesoko Toteikun** (瀬底土帝君), a little walled-in shrine, and **Sesoko pottery studio** (瀬底島ポタリー; 30 Sesoko; 0708 508 3266; 10.00–17.30 Tue–Sun), ideal for souvenirs.

Minna This croissant-shaped island 7km off the northwest mainland is known for swimming, snorkelling and spreading yourself out on the sands for some much-needed sunshine. Less than 0.5km^2 in area, Minna (水納島) is a cluster of trees enveloped in white sand, which slides under shades of teal into fish-filled coral reefs and glittering sea. Choose from eastern **Todaishita** (灯台下のビーチ), southern **Kamomeiwa** (カモメ岩のビーチ), northern **Minna** (水納ビーチ) and western **Nishinohama** (西の浜).

Water visibility here is up to 30m and dive sites are filled with tropical fish; two of the most popular locations are Kujiraiwa reef, said to resemble a whale, and a massive submarine cable which has become a coral ecosystem. Marine tours and ferries to Minna depart from Motobu Toguchi Port, in the central area of the city and north of the major Motobu Port. The ferry takes 15 minutes and leaves three times a day, returning half an hour later.

Minna was uninhabited until the 1900s, when people from Sesoko came to settle here. The island is considered sacred and, having been left to nature's devices for so long, is a great, isolated getaway free from development.

Yagaji Off the north of the Motobu Peninsula in Nago are three islands connected by bridges: mini Ōjima, Yagaji and Kouri. You can reach Yagaji (屋我地島) two ways from the mainland: over Ōjima (奥武島), home only to a northern beach, or direct from the peninsula over Warumi Bridge (ワルミ大橋).

Yagaji is a laid-back island of gentle outdoor activities – it's not big on sights. People come here to camp and set up a beach barbecue, fish for their dinner and kayak the calm waters of the small inland sea. Yagaji's interior is a mix of sugarcane fields and forest, while its coast is lined with nice **beaches** like Yagaji (屋我地ビーチ) in the south, long Sumuide (済井出の浜) and Airakuen (愛楽園の浜) in the north. Yagaji Beach is notable for a low-tide sandbar known as 'the pure road', which leads to little islets, and as a place to fish for Japanese whiting. Airakuen has a remarkable and horrendous history as a leper colony, where sufferers of the disease were exiled to live in caves before a still-going sanatorium was built in the 1960s.

There are also protected mangroves and mudflats ripe for kayaking and wildlife spotting. The bark of the black mangroves here was used to naturally dye materials made on the island. To the north by Untenbaru Fishing Port is the **Dutch Graveyard** (ウランダー墓), a misnamed cenotaph to two French sailors who died in 1846 during trade negotiations. The 'Dutch' part comes from the fact Ryūkyūans called all Westerners 'Ulanders', aka 'Hollanders', thanks to their exposure to Dutch sailors. Nearby, Yagaji is connected to Kourijima by an enormous bridge with a must-visit **observatory** (古宇利大橋南詰展望所) overlooking its expanse.

Kouri Attached to Yagaji by the stunning 2km Kouri Ōhashi (古宇利大橋) bridge, little Kouri (古宇利島) is a white-sand haven known locally as 'Love Island'. With a radius of just 1km, Kouri's interior can be explored in only 15 minutes, though you'll want to tarry a while on some of its sun-kissed beaches.

Folklore has it that at the beginning of mankind, Kouri was home to Okinawa's 'Adam and Eve': two lovers who lived in a cave by the sea. Conveniently, nature saw fit to sculpt two **heart-shaped rocks** (ハートロック) out to sea at pretty **Tiinu Beach** (ティーヌ浜), which have become symbolic of the tale and of Kouri.

The coast has a few gorgeous **beaches** much quieter than Tiinu, like Tokeihama (トケイ浜), secret Soopaihama (そーばい浜) and tiny Chigunuhama (チグヌ浜). Kouri Beach (古宇利ビーチ), just beside the bridge, is the island's most popular and often sees many Motobu tourists. It has clear waters, marine activities and a handful of cafés nearby.

The island's second star sight is **Kouri Ocean Tower** (古宇利オーシャンタワー; 538 Kouri; 0980 56 1616; w kouri-oceantower.com; 10.00–18.00 daily; adult/child ¥1,000/500), a bullet-shaped 82m-high observatory and centre that has the best views on Kouri. You can see the island itself, the breathtaking inland sea and Okinawa-hontō. Inside the tower is a seashell museum that houses over 10,000 shells from around the world. Pick up a shell-based souvenir or some Kabony pumpkin sweets, a Kouri speciality.

Yanbaru Some 3 hours north and a far cry from the busy streets of Naha, Yanbaru (山原) is the deep, forested and mountainous north of Okinawa-hontō. Recently designated a UNESCO natural heritage site, Yanbaru's 174km² is where the island goes wild with waterfall hiking, wildlife spotting and mangrove kayaking. The area is home to several endemic flora and fauna species, making it a must for nature-lovers.

Yanbaru is made up of multiple regions. On the northeast side is Higashi (東), the smallest village on the island. It's enveloped by nature, comprising mostly forests run through with yellow-green rivers. The Gesashi River (慶佐次川) here is home to the largest mangrove on Okinawa – a 10ha playground of treks and kayaks. **Hirugi Fureai Park** (ヒルギふれあい公園; 54-1 Gesashi; 0980 51 2433) has boardwalks and observatories throughout the mangrove where you can get up close to the protected habitat.

Near the estuary is **Uppama Beach** (ウッパマビーチ), a quiet beach perfect for sunset and year-round swimming. Further north, **Fukujigawa Seaside Park** (福地川海浜公園; 334 Kawata; 0980 51 2301; 09.00–18.00 daily, to 17.00 Nov–Mar) is a perfect beach for families: it has kayaking, stand-up paddle boarding and safe swimming with jellyfish nets.

Higashi is known for its azaleas, which bloom in March. The village hosts a three-week azalea festival, Tsutsuji Matsuri, in the **Azalea Eco Park** (東村村民の森つつじエコパーク; 766-1 Hirara; 0980 43 3300; w tsutsuji-ecopark.com; 08.30–17.30 daily). Higashi is also a farming community and the home of Okinawan pineapples: it has the largest production in the whole of Japan. Recently, coffee farms have become popular, with places like **Matayoshi Coffee Farm** (又吉コーヒー園; 718-28 Gesashi; 0980 43 2838; w matayoshicoffee.jp; 10.00–16.30 daily, tours Nov–Apr) offering tours and roasting experiences.

Ōgimi (大宜味) is a highly forested area known for bashōfu textiles, irises and longevity. The iris flower festival takes place in March–April at Kijoka iris fields (喜

MYTHS AND FOLKTALES: KIJIMUNAA

The *kijimunaa* (キジムナー) or *bunagaya* are the best-known creatures in Okinawan folklore. These mischievous childlike spirits live in large banyan trees and love to fish. Small-bodied with red hair that can sometimes cover their bodies, they also have oversized heads – the meaning of bunagaya.

The trouble-making kijimunaa love to play pranks on humans. Like many Japanese mythological creatures they are linked to fire – there are many stories of kijimunaa stealing fire from paper lanterns and wandering about with ghostly flames. Locals may occasionally claim to have spotted one walking through the mountains, forests, beaches or riverbanks holding a flame. One of the naughty kijimunaa's favourite pranks is to sit on sleeping people's chests, rendering them immobile and unable to sleep. The feeling even has a name in Japanese – *kanashibari*. Naturally, any islander facing kanashibari wants to get rid of it quickly. Luckily, there are two things kijimunaa hate: octopuses and flatulence. Only one of them tends to be at hand in the middle of the night. Thus people from the islands will suggest if you can't fall asleep, try farting as hard as you can. The kijimunaa will quickly disappear.

如嘉ターブク), turning it into a sea of purple. The village is beside gorgeous **Shioya Bay** (塩屋湾), which you can see from Ōgimi Village Observation Deck (六田原展望台) and from Boujimui (ボウジムイ・坊主森) if you fancy a hike. There are plenty of further hikes to be had in Ōgimi, but the most famous is Taataki (ター滝) in the south; the trail to this waterfall is relatively easy, taking about 30 minutes one way, and there's a walk behind the falls too.

In Kunigami (国頭), the **Hiji Waterfall and suspension bridge** (比地大滝・比地大滝の吊り橋; 781-1 Hiji; ⌚ 09.00–18.00 daily, to 17.30 Nov–Mar; ¥500) takes you through Yanbaru's green heart of tree ferns and flowering plants. The walk itself is easy: about 40 minutes up with the odd stair and steep section. The trail is well maintained, ending in the pretty, 26m-high falls. Keep an eye out for the endemic forest tortoise and for birds like Pryer's woodpecker, Ryūkyū robins, Japanese paradise flycatchers and, in winter, grey-faced buzzards. You can also camp overnight at the entrance.

Near Hiji's entrance is the **Yanbaru Wildlife Conservation Centre** (やんばる野生生物保護センター; 263-1 Hiji; ☎ 0980 50 1025; w ufugi-yambaru.com; ⌚ 10.00–16.30 Tue–Sun), also known as the Ufugii Nature Museum. It's an excellent museum and information point where you can learn all about Yanbaru, get maps and hiking advice.

Not far from Hiji is **Yonahadake** (与那覇岳), the highest point on Okinawa. Its near-6km there-and-back hike is sometimes closed for environmental protections, but otherwise takes you through rich forest – be warned you're walking for the pleasure and wildlife spotting as there isn't a pay-off view at the end.

Past beaches, lookouts, monuments and forest, Kunigami – and Okinawa-hontō – ends in **Cape Hedo** (辺戸岬; w hedomisaki.com). This cape has a café and panoramas over dramatic limestone cliffs to the East China Sea and Pacific, and on to Yorontō. A bonfire festival was once held on the cape to pray for safe return, and you'll find viewpoints around its perimeter, from Kayauchi Banta (茅打バンタ) in the west to the amusing bird-shaped Yanbaru Rail Observatory (ヤンバルクイナ展望台; 973-5 Hedo) in the north.

Within the cape is **Daisekirinzan** (大石林山; 1241 Ginama; ☎ 0980 41 8117; w sekirinzan.com/en; ⌚ 09.30–17.30 daily; adult/child ¥1,200/600), a phenomenal park of unusual karst landscapes formed some 200 million years ago. Daisekirinzan also houses a sensational gajumaru tree, forest walks, an observation deck and a sotetsu palm grove.

Oku (奥) is Okinawa-hontō's northernmost community and home to many an Okinawa rail. Cut through by the clear waters of the Oku River, and surrounded by emerald-green and blue seas, it's a lovely village to drive through. If you're passing by, check out Oku Beach (奥海岸) in the village's north – so isolated it's basically your own private beach. The rest of Yanbaru, the eastern flank, is home to a few beaches and isolated viewpoints, and the **Okinawa Rail Learning Centre** (ヤンバルクイナ生態展示学習施設; 1477-35 Ada; 0980 41 7788; w kuinapark.com/kuina; 09.00–17.00 Thu–Tue) where you can gain in-depth knowledge about the endemic flightless birds and see them too.

Round to the eastern side of Kunigami is the **Kunigami Village Environmental Education Centre** and **Yanbaru Discovery Forest** (国頭村環境教育センター やんばる学びの森; 1301-7 Aha, Kunigami; 0980 41 7979; w yanbaru-manabi.com; adult/child ¥300/100–200). This excellent family-friendly outdoor museum has guided trails with animal, nature, canoe and birdwatching tours and canopy walks.

IEJIMA

Iejima (伊江島), 9km west of Okinawa-hontō's northwest coast, could be called a surprise. Despite being a 22.75km^2 flung-off fragment of the main island, it's a trove of history and horticulture.

Ie has been occupied for millennia, with human bones found in Gohezu Cave dating back 20,000 years. This has long been a fertile land: it was the biggest wheat producer in the Ryūkyū Kingdom, likely thanks to its almost entirely flat expanse. Today Iejima produces sugarcane, beef and peanuts – occasionally earning it the moniker Peanut Island, based on its shape and supply. These peanuts pop up in a variety of local dishes, including sweet-salty *misopi* snacks and peanut ice. Local sugarcane is also put to unique use: unlike the rest of the archipelago, which makes awamori with it, Ie's distillery turns it into rum.

More fragrantly, Ie is renowned for its April–May Lily Festival, the earliest of its kind in Japan, which sees a million lilies bloom along its coast. Ie is also the centre of Japan's Hibiscus Association, with research and cross-breeding at its Hibiscus Gardens resulting in entirely new species. Over 1,000 species bloom during the Hibiscus Festival in December, so it's little wonder Ie has also been nicknamed Flower Island.

HISTORY The island's sweet branding rather belies its more recent history. Iejima was one of the islands that suffered most during World War II. In 1942, Ie's farmlands made way for two of the largest runways in Asia, making it a base for the Japanese army – and in turn a major target of the US military. Children and the elderly were evacuated out of the prefecture as Ie's villages and buildings were destroyed by airstrikes.

When the war made landfall, the US approached Ie with 1,000 troops. Remaining residents either hid in caves or were forced to fight – women and youths included – often with rudimentary weapons. Imperial Army soldiers gathered families together and assigned each group a hand grenade. The expectation was that no-one would surrender: those who did were shot by the Imperial Army themselves.

In the end, many died in acts of group suicide, including 150 villagers who blew themselves up in Ahasha Cave. Some 20 people survived but the explosion buried

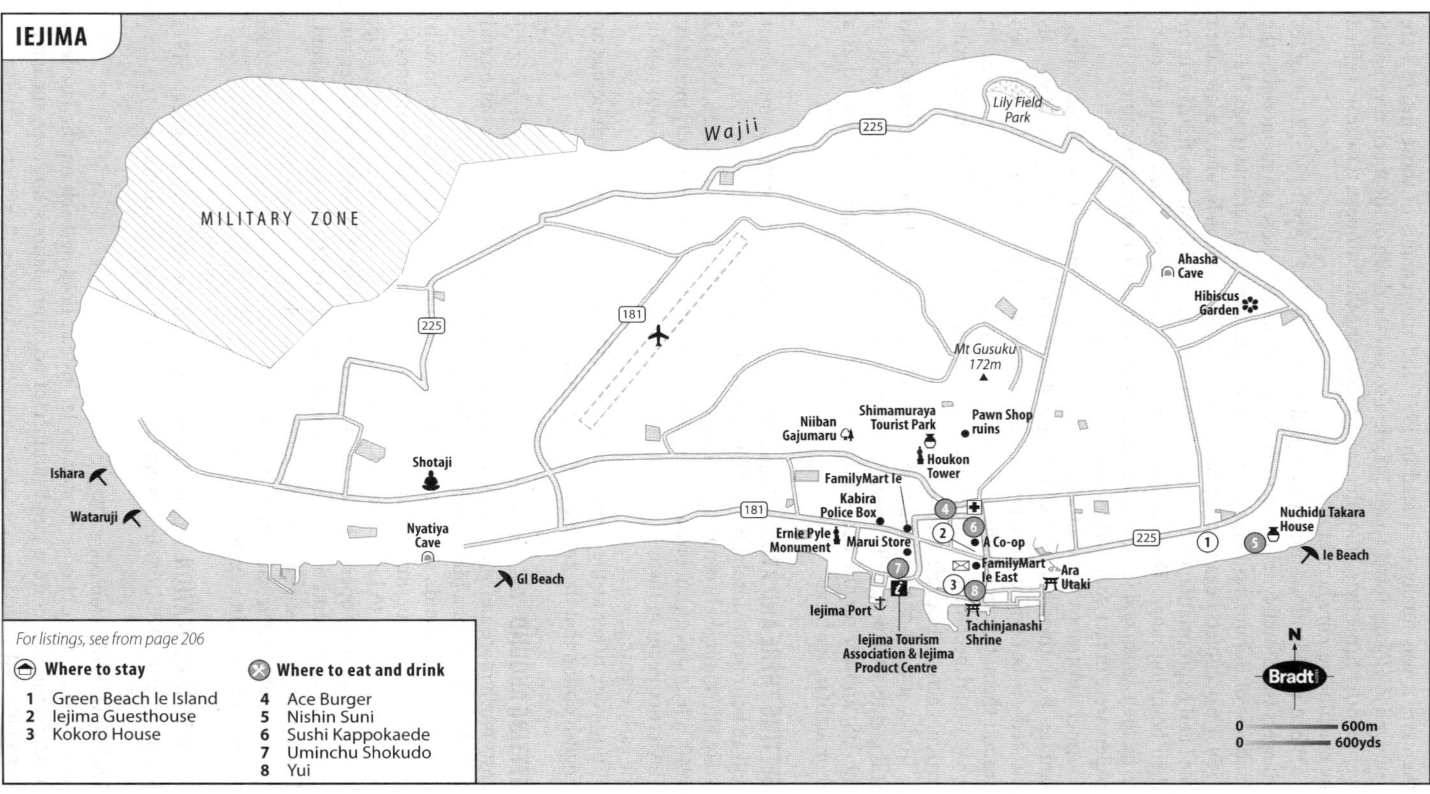
IEJIMA
MILITARY ZONE
Wajii
Lily Field Park
225
181
Ahasha Cave
Hibiscus Garden
Mt Gusuku 172m
Shimamuraya Tourist Park
Pawn Shop ruins
Niiban Gajumaru
Houkon Tower
FamilyMart Ie
Kabira Police Box
Ernie Pyle Monument
Marui Store
A Co-op
FamilyMart Ie East
Ara Utaki
Tachinjanashi Shrine
Iejima Port
Iejima Tourism Association & Iejima Product Centre
Nuchidu Takara House
Ie Beach
Shotaji
Ishara
Wataruji
Nyatiya Cave
GI Beach
N
Bradt
0 600m
0 600yds
For listings, see from page 206
Where to stay
1 Green Beach Ie Island
2 Iejima Guesthouse
3 Kokoro House
Where to eat and drink
4 Ace Burger
5 Nishin Suni
6 Sushi Kappokaede
7 Uminchu Shokudo
8 Yui

the cave; it was finally excavated in 1971 and the remains of those inside were removed to Hōkon Tower (page 208). Ie also saw the death of the much revered US war reporter Ernie Pyle, who after years of covering the European theatre was killed by machine gun fire here in April 1945.

When the island was finally occupied by the US on 22 April 1945, 2,000 of Ie's villagers were forcibly relocated to the Kerama Islands – there is a memorial to the kindness of Kerama residents who made way for them on Geruma (page 253). In 1954, US occupiers began a campaign to seize farmers' land on Ie, under a law called the Land Expropriation Ordinance. Their aim was to requisition two-thirds of Ie for their bombing range. They began by conducting land surveys and asking farmers to fix their *hanko* seal (essentially a signature) to the English survey documents: the papers were in fact voluntary evacuation orders.

American troops came in and destroyed huge amounts of the island, turfing families from their homes, bulldozing buildings and burning crops. Many locals insisted on farming on the remaining pockets of land, even as test bombs fell around them, but most who tried ended up arrested. The islanders embarked on what would become a 50-year-long campaign against the bombing range, with marches across the prefecture.

Today, a third of the island remains under the control of the US military, who still conduct training drills there. The three runways built still exist; one used by the US, another for the occasional charter flight and the middle one used as a thoroughfare for locals.

GETTING THERE AND AWAY Iejima Port is on the south side of the island, about half an hour from Motobu Port on Okinawa's northwest coast. There are four ferries a day, alternating between Ferry Ishima and Ferry Gusuku (☎0980 49 2255, 0980 47 3940; w iejima.org), but on national holidays and festival days this usually increases. The ferries begin in the morning from Ie and the final journey from Motobu is in the early evening.

Buy your ticket at the ferry counter or ticket machine – the machine has an English option that the counter staff won't have.

GETTING AROUND You can take your car to Ie from Okinawa-hontō by ferry, but it costs much more and you have to book well in advance. If you have the option and will, it's best to rent a **bike** or simply **walk** the island.

Many of the island's sights are in the east. It would take around 4 hours to walk the island's entire perimeter, minus the airbase region, but is about 50 minutes by foot from the port to Lily Field Park. Iejima Kankō (478-9 Kabira; ☎0980 49 2053; w iejima-bus.com) operate **buses**, **taxis** and **car rental** on the island. The buses run from the port around the north of the village and across to the west of the island. During the Lily Festival, they also operate to the field.

For an alternative car option, Tama Car Rental (520-2 Kabira; ☎0980 49 5208; w tmp.co.jp) is right next to the port.

TOURIST INFORMATION Iejima Tourism Association (伊江島観光協会; 519-3 Kabira; ☎0980 49 3519; w iejima.okinawa) resides by the port terminal.

WHERE TO STAY *Map, page 205*

Most visitors don't choose to stay on Ie, instead heading back on the last ferry to Okinawa. There are a good number of accommodations however, including minshuku and resorts.

Green Beach Ie Island (whole villa) グリーンビーチ伊江島; 1894 Higashiemae; 0906 868 0543; w ieisland.com. Handsome luxury beach house rental with stunning tatami-meets-Western rooms, garden, kitchen-living room, BBQ, laundry & bathrooms. Accommodates up to 14. **$$$$$**

Kokoro House (23 rooms) こころハウス; 641-1 Higashiemae; 0980 49 5005; w kokoro-house.com. Charming self-contained wooden 'cottages' with bath en suites, & upper terrace with views to Mt Gusuku. HB options. **$$$**

Iejima Guesthouse (9 rooms) 伊江島ゲストハウス; 193-6 Kabira; 0907 461 8726; w haisaiieshima.wixsite.com/ieshima-guest-house. Beyond basic & dated but the cheapest accommodation on Ie, with remarkable prices for mini private rooms. Kitchen in garage, shared bathrooms, free laundry & bike rental, occasional sanshin shindigs at night. **$$**

WHERE TO EAT AND DRINK *Map, page 205*

Nishin Suni にしんすに; 2438 Higashiemae; w nishinsuni.com; 09.00–22.00 daily. Brilliant beach option that puts on BBQ dinners, shaved ice & lunches. $$

Sushi Kappokaede 寿司割烹楓; 144 Kabira; 0980 49 5333; 18.00–23.00 daily. Handsome & traditional sushi spot with local catch. $$

Uminchu Shokudo 海人食堂; 519-3 Kabira; 11.00–13.30 daily. Run by a local fisherman, Uminchu does a fab sashimi lunch set with tempura, rice & seaweed soup. $$

Yui 古民家味処結; 639 Higashiemae; 0980 49 5455; w japanese-restaurant-6056.business.site; 11.00–14.00 & 17.00–22.00 Wed–Mon. Pretty restaurant in old renovated house serving elegant set meals for good price. $$

Ace Burger エースバーガー; 136 Kabira; 0980 49 2052; 11.00–19.30 Thu–Mon. Friendly fast-food joint offering more than just burgers. $

SHOPPING Ie's main village Kabira has two supermarkets and two FamilyMarts for picking up food. For souvenirs, the best (rather only) place is Iejima Product Centre (伊江島物産センター; 519-3 Kabira; 0980 49 5555; 07.00–16.00 daily), which sells island food, drink and souvenirs. These include Ie speciality products like peanut sweets and 100% sugarcane rum called Yeram Santa Maria. It also sells soda water pumped from the well at Wajii in the north.

SPORTS AND ACTIVITIES

Iejima Beach Horseriding 伊江島のビーチで乗馬体験; 2525 Higashiemae; 0980 49 2337; w ie-horse.wixsite.com/ieuma; 09.00–17.00 daily. Horseriding tours.

Iishima Uminchu Yuugaku い〜しま海人遊学; 498 Kabira; 0980 49 2772; w uminchu-yu-gaku.jp. Fishing & traditional rowboat experiences.

Marine House Ie Island マリンハウスIEアイランド; 1947-1 Higashiemae; 0980 49 2569; w ie-island.com. Fun, experience & licence diving with port pick-up service.

Seamonkey's シーモンキーズ; 655 Higashiemae; 0980 49 2375; w seamonkeys.client.jp. Diving school & snorkelling with 30 years' experience.

OTHER PRACTICALITIES There are FamilyMarts for ATMs but otherwise Ie has one of everything: Ie Post Office (伊江郵便局; 196-2 Kabira; 0980 49 2322; 09.00–17.00 Mon–Fri, ATM: 08.45–18.00 Mon–Fri, 09.00–17.00 Sat–Sun) for money withdrawal, Kabira Police Box (川平駐在所; 437-2 Kabira; 0980 49 2313) and a small clinic (伊江村立診療所; 459 Higashiemae; 0980 49 5161; 09.00–noon & 14.00–17.00 Mon–Fri).

WHAT TO SEE AND DO

Ie Village Ie's ferry drops you straight on to the island's only real settlement, where you'll find a good number of sites. The closest to the port is the small

MYTHS AND FOLKTALES: THE GHOST OF HANDUU-GWA

In the 18th century, a prince from Iejima visited Hentona village on Okinawa-hontō and fell in love with a stunning girl with glorious long, black hair called Handuu-gwa. They spent every moment possible together, until one day the prince had to visit Japan on royal business. He promised to return to Handuu-gwa as soon as he could.

A long time passed, but the prince didn't return. Handuu-gwa decided to hire a boat to go to Iejima to find out what was happening. The captain warned her against visiting the royal family residence but she was determined. At the court, she discovered her charming prince had a charming family – a wife and child. In her anguish, Handuu-gwa climbed up Shiroyama hill and hung herself using her long hair.

Shortly after, disaster struck the royal family: the king and the wayward prince both died mysteriously, and the family fell into poverty. But Handuu-gwa's vengeful ghost wasn't finished. She looked for the homes of the prince's descendants: if she appeared at the birth of a child, the baby would be stillborn with black marks about its neck. Ie has a statue of the betrayed Handuu-gwa in Shimamuraya-kankō, near Shiroyama hill.

Tachinjanashi Shrine (タチンジャナシ宮), just beside the port building that's dedicated to the god of the sea. To the east is **Ara Utaki** (阿良御嶽), built on Ara Beach, which from the mid 1600s was the entry point to Ie for centuries. Ara Utaki enshrines the gods Tatsuganashi, who sees off those leaving, and Sarameganashi, who ensures ships run smoothly.

West of the port leads straight to Ie's dark modern history: the **Ernie Pyle Monument** (アニー・パイル記念碑). Ernie Pyle was a US military journalist who reported from the Battle of Okinawa's front line. On 18 April 1945 he was killed while interviewing soldiers on the battlefield. To the monument's north is the **Niiban Gajumaru** (ニーバンガズィマール), a large banyan tree that became the temporary home of two Japanese soldiers after World War II. The pair hadn't heard of Japan's surrender, so stayed hidden in this tree in occupied US territory for two whole years.

Further north is **Hōkon Tower** (芳魂之塔), which enshrines some 3,500 people who died on Iejima, approximately 1,500 villagers and 2,000 soldiers. Nearby is **Shimamuraya Tourist Park** (島村屋観光公園; 17 Nishiegami; 0980 49 2422; 09.00–17.00 daily; adult/child ¥400/200–300), which has a folk museum showing aspects of Iejima life and exhibits on habu. The park is built on the site of the Shimamuraya residence, where the tragic story of Handuu-gwa took place (see above).

The shrapnel-riddled **Pawn Shop ruins** (公益質屋跡; 75 Higashiekami) are a leftover of the war, one of the few remaining buildings after the village burned down.

At the top of the village is the symbol of Ie, **Mount Gusuku** (城山). The highest spot on the island, this sacred mountain dotted with shrines has a brilliant panoramic viewpoint at its top, well worth the short but steep 25-minute hike. Known locally as Tacchu, the mountain erupts seemingly out of nowhere, soaring 172m up like a conical hat.

The coast The south coast is home to **GI Beach** (GIビーチ), so named because it was exclusively set aside for US military when Okinawa was under their occupation.

It's not designated a swimming beach but it's a white-sand stunner, with views back towards the mainland.

Just beside it is **Nyatiya Cave** (ニャティヤ洞), one of Ie's most sacred places, where the god of child-giving dwells. Lifting the stone here is said to grant childless women wishes and predict your child's sex: if it feels heavy, it's a boy, if light a girl. During the war, the cave was used as an air raid shelter which gave it its other name, Sennin-gama (1,000 People Cave). North of the cave and beach is **Shotaiji** (照太寺), a Zen temple founded in 1554 by King Shō Sei and restored after the war. Ie is a deeply religious island, so shrines like the banyan-bowered Shotaiji and its Gongendō (hall) have flourished under villagers' care.

A huge chunk of Ie's west is given over to military airfields, but there are a couple of almost abandoned beaches on the very west coast: **Ishara** (イシャラ浜) and **Wataruuji** (ワタルージ浜). On the very northwest coast is **Wajii** (湧出), an area lined with 60m-high cliffs with an unusual freshwater spring at their briny base. For a long time this was a valuable water source for Ie. The observation deck shows off the roiling waves and sharp rocks, which made collecting water here far from simple. Today the spring's water is made into soda, which you can buy at the port souvenir shop.

Ie's northeast has **Lily Field Park** (リリーフィールド公園), which becomes a bright white carpet at the end of April when 1 million Easter Teppō lilies bloom and spread their perfume along the coast during the much-awaited Iejima Lily Festival. There's an observation deck, picnic area, fern clusters and the Kadahara Cave, too.

On Iejima Country Club's perimeter is **Ahasha Cave** (アハシャガマ), where 150 villagers hid from the final battles on Ie and blew themselves up with grenades. To the club's south is Iejima's **Hibiscus Garden** (伊江島ハイビスカス園; 0980 49 5850; 09.00–17.00 daily; free, charge for Hibiscus Exhibition Hall only), home to over 1,000 hibiscus varieties.

The southeast is the location of the eponymous **Ie Beach** (伊江ビーチ), technically the only swimming beach on the island. Life-guarded from May to November, it also has an array of facilities: jellyfish nets, toilets and showers, barbecues, a shop, beach volleyball and camping. It's also a great place to go horseback riding. Behind the beach is a small war museum at the **Nuchidu Takara House** (ヌチドゥタカラの家; 2300-4 Higashiemae; 0980 49 3047; 09.00–18.00 daily; adult/child ¥300/200). Though all in Japanese and often unmanned, its cluttered walls hold artefacts from daily life and military weapons.

IZENAJIMA

Found about 30km off Okinawa's Cape Hendo, culturally rich Izena is made up of four islands: the main inhabited island Izenajima (伊是名島), plus the three uninhabited islands of Yanaha (屋那覇島), Gushikawa (具志川島) and tiny Urugami (降神島).

Izena, along with northern neighbour Iheya (page 213), is a historical big hitter and land of legends. The island's Aza Shomi district is where Ryūkyūan King Shō En, the farmer who became the first king of the Second Shō Dynasty, was born. Originally called Kanemaru, he was known to be remarkably skilled at farming and his enviable crops led neighbours to accuse him of theft. He ended up fleeing Izena, going to Okinawa and finding a position in the king's court that would eventually result in his coronation.

The Second Shō Dynasty lasted 409 years until the islands were subsumed into Japan, so Izena was long considered the birthplace of the royals, and in turn the

Ryūkyū Kingdom. In addition, the lord of Izena Castle was the grandfather of a First Shō Dynasty king, Shō Hashi, who unified the three Okinawan kingdoms into one (page 11). The island has leaned into its royal history: it hosts a King Shō En Festival in August and a King Shō En Marathon in February.

Royal connections aside, Izena is a peaceful, remote idyll of coral reefs, hills and historical ruins. There are several archaeological sites on the island, and on Gushikawa human bones with a tortoiseshell bracelet – the first of its kind in the prefecture – have been found. There are a few small mountains across Izena, with a carpet of farmland and Ryūkyū pines between. The main agriculture is sugarcane and rice, as well as fishing and mozuku seaweed farming. The small villages feature

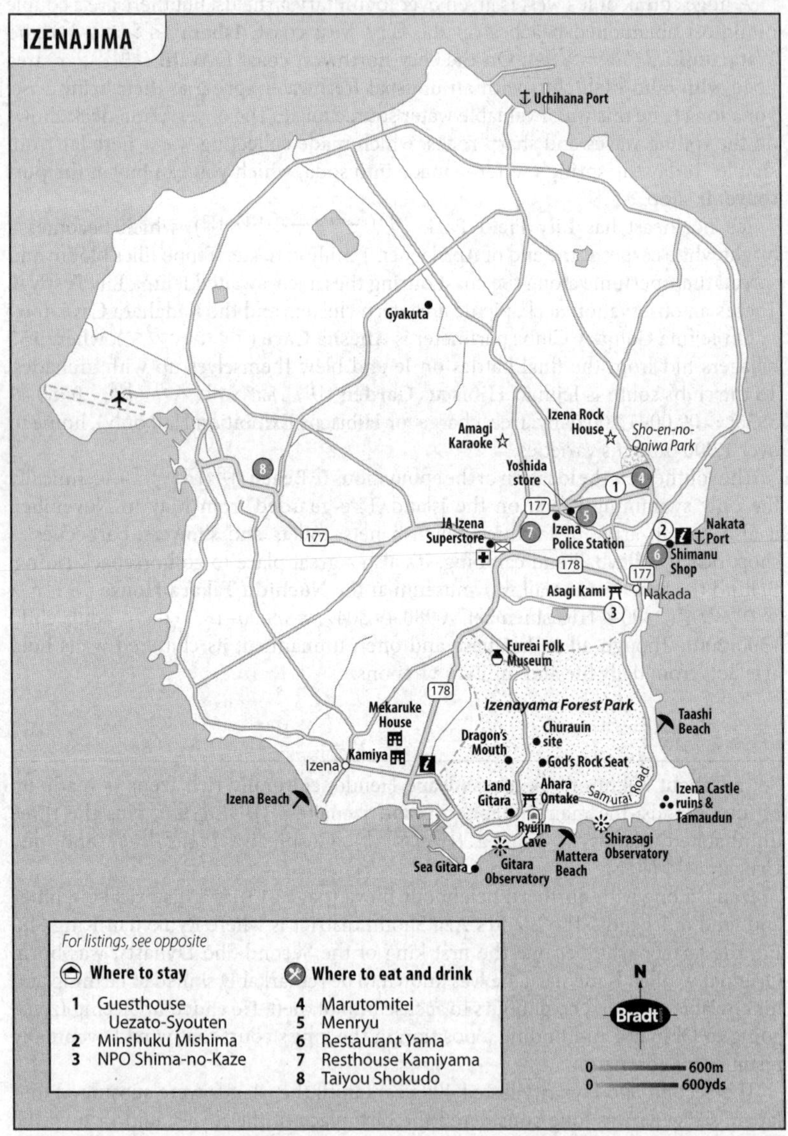

traditional red-roofed houses and narrow paths lined with limestone walls and fukugi trees. Locals here are known for their friendliness, as there is a tradition of sharing harvests and catches with everyone.

GETTING THERE AND AWAY The ferry for Izena leaves from Nakajin Unten Port twice daily, once in the morning and once in the afternoon, taking 55 minutes to arrive at Nakada Port. To take a car, you need to reserve in advance and arrive 30 minutes before departure. Reservations are made through both Nakijin Village Unten Port Office (0980 56 5084) and Nakada Port (0980 45 2002). Return tickets are valid for 14 days, and you will need to pay a ¥100 environmental tax too.

GETTING AROUND There are no buses on Izena so you will need to rent transportation. With a circumference of just 16.7km, the island is easy to **cycle**, but **mopeds** are also a good way to get around. Izena Rent-a-Car (伊是名レンタカー; 177-6 Nakada; 0980 45 2394; w izenarental.ti-da.net) offers all forms of transport.

If you are looking to travel between Iheya and Izena, it's often cheaper to take a **marine taxi** than go back via Okinawa-hontō. These can be chartered with HY Marin (0703 995 8051; w peraichi.com/landing_pages/view/hymarineizena), who also run glass-boat, fishing and cruising tours, Miu Marine (0901 942 5160; e miu.marine2021@gmail.com), and Iheiya Island Tourism Association AMATERAS (0980 46 2526).

TOURIST INFORMATION Izena has an excellent tourist map available at the port and the Izenajima Sightseeing Information Centre (いぜな島観光協会; 177–7 Nakada; 0980 45 2435; w izena-kanko.jp), but the latter is only open weekdays. There's a new tourist office in Izena village (伊是名村体験交流観光連携施設; 795-2 Izena; 0980 45 2103; 10.00–16.00 Mon–Fri).

WHERE TO STAY *Map, opposite*

Map, opposite

✷ **NPO Shima-no-Kaze** (4 houses) NPO法人島の風; 1542 Serikyaku; 0980 50 7330; w shimanokaze2.com/stay. A non-profit organisation dedicated to revitalising traditional old houses across Izena into accommodation. Multiple addresses; all modernised with verandas, kitchens & bathrooms, gorgeous wooden interiors. Dinner delivery service, cooking classes & shamisen performance available. 2 night min. **$$$$**

Guesthouse Uezato-Syouten (3 rooms) ゲストハウス上里商店; 5066 Shomi; 0901 081 5628; w uezatoshowten.com. Shared living space & bathrooms in small guesthouse. Basic twin bedrooms, clean but small. Laundry available. **$$$**

Minshuku Mishima (12 rooms) 民宿美島; 177-8 Nakada; 0980 50 7111; w mishima-izena.com. 1-star hotel with clean bright rooms in Western & Japanese style. Home-cooked HB option using seasonal ingredients & home-grown vegetables. **$$$**

WHERE TO EAT AND DRINK *Map, opposite*

Marutomitei まるとみ亭; 137 Shomi; 0980 45 2666; 17.00–23.00 Mon–Sat. Welcoming lantern-lit izakaya selling drinks, teishoku & yakitori. $$

Restaurant Yama 食事処やま; 177-44 Nakada; 0980 45 2990; 11.30–midnight Mon–Sat. Set meal restaurant turned izakaya in later hours. If available, try the limited special Izena *menheechi donburi*, featuring mozuku, fish & veg. $$

Resthouse Kamiyama レストハウスかみやま; 764 Nakada; 0980 45 2363; 17.30–22.00 Tue–Sat, plus 11.00–14.00 Thu. Large diner serving bountiful set meals that are both cheap & delicious. The Island of Sweets cake shop is on the same site. $$

Taiyou Shokudo 太陽食堂; 1542 Serikyaku; w shimanogenki.net; ⌚ 11.00–16.00 Wed–Mon. Set meals on the west side made with original homemade rice flour noodles, using leftover rice from milling. Also has shop on site. $$

Menryu 麺龍; W423-1 Nakada; ☎ 0980 43 5142; ⌚ 11.00–14.00 & 17.00–21.00 Mon–Tue & Thu–Fri, 11.00–14.00 & 17.30–22.00 Sat–Sun. Bentō box lunches on w/days, big ramen selection at dinner & at w/ends. $

ENTERTAINMENT AND NIGHTLIFE Aside from a few izakaya, Izena's nightlife consists of Izena Rock House (イゼナ ロック ハウス; 4750 Shomi; ☎ 0806 496 9435; w izena-rock-house.com; ⌚ 19.00–late), which plays live music and serves a large range of drinks, and Amagi Karaoke (カラオケ酒場天城; 3872-1 Shomi; ⌚ 18.00–midnight).

SHOPPING There are a handful of shops in Nakada and the south, plus one in the north for food supplies. The largest and most useful is the JA Izena Superstore (ＪＡおきなわ農協スーパー伊是名店; 1165 Nakada; ☎ 0980 45 2722; ⌚ 09.00–19.00 Mon–Sat), but the smaller Yoshida store (吉田ストアー; 417-1 Nakada; ☎ 0980 45 2608; ⌚ 10.00–21.30 daily) is open later and on Sundays too.

For souvenirs, you can pick up trinkets at the port's Shimanu Shop (しまぬ売店; 177-7 Nakada; ☎ 0980 45 2781; ⌚ 08.00–13.30 daily).

SPORTS AND ACTIVITIES

Izena Marine Service Guin イゼナマリンサービス グイン; 813 Izena; ☎ 0980 43 9984; w izenaguin.com. Diving & snorkelling.

Luana Paddle Sports ルアナパドルスポーツ; 3432-24 Izena; ☎ 0902 249 2783; w izena-luana.okinawa. SUP & snorkelling.

Right Stuff ライトスタッフ; 126 Nakada; ☎ 0980 45 2463; w dive301.wixsite.com/rightstuff. Dive shop.

OTHER PRACTICALITIES Izena has a single post office (伊是名郵便局; 1166 Nakada; ☎ 0980 45 2015; ⌚ 08.00–16.00 Mon–Fri, ATM: 08.00–17.00 daily), a police station (伊是名駐在所; 914-1 Nakada; ☎ 0980 45 2034) and a small clinic (伊是名診療所; 1198 Nakada; ☎ 0980 45 2017; w ritoushien.net/izena; ⌚ 09.00–noon & 14.00–17.00 Mon–Fri).

WHAT TO SEE AND DO **Nakada** (仲田) isn't replete with sites: the majority are in the south. But the village's north has **Shō En-no-Oniwa Park** (尚円王御庭公園), built to commemorate the 580th birthday of King Shō En. There's a statue to the king, and the park also incorporates **Mihosodokoro** (みほそ所), his legendary birthplace. This is where his umbilical cord is said to be buried, and it has become a sacred place on Izena.

To the south is **Kami Asagi** (神アサギ), a thatched building where rituals and prayers for fertility, harvest and fishing are performed. Also used for festivals, the building is purposefully low so that it forces people to bow upon entering. On your way out of the village is the **Fureai Folk Museum** (ふれあい民俗館; 196-129 Izena; ☎ 0980 45 2165; ⌚ 09.00–17.00 Tue–Fri; adult/child ¥200/100). Here you can learn about Izena's cultural heritage and see royal gifts and lacquerware.

The coastline towards the south has the pretty **Taashi Beach** (ターシの浜), but the main draw here is the historical ruins and forest. The **Samurai Road** (サムレー道) leads round to the **Izena Castle ruins** (伊是名城跡), which were built by the grandfather of King Shō Hashi. The castle was believed impregnable due to its high sea-cliffs, though there's little left to see now. You can climb up to the promontory; the trail is usually overgrown but there are thankfully no habu. The only real tangible site here is the **Tamaudun** (伊是名玉御殿), which sits at the foot of the castle ruins. It's a sacred tomb built by Shō En for his family. Nearby is **Ryūjin Cave** (龍神洞), a natural holy site where a dragon god is enshrined.

One of the better observatories is **Shirasagi** (シラサギ展望台), which looks back to the castle promontory. To its west, the white-sand stretch of Futamigaura, which includes **Mattera Beach** (マッテラの浜), was previously selected as one of the 100 best beaches in Japan. This gorgeous area is awash with *gitara*, meaning 'sheer rock'. The **Gitara Observatory** (ギタラ展望台) overlooks the so-called Sea Gitara (海ギタラ), a stone eruption off the beach, while behind it is Land Gitara (陸ギタラ), a huge stone monolith with viewpoints up to it, including a perfectly placed swing. To its side is the **Ahara Ontake** (アハラ御嶽), which offers simultaneous views of both sea and land gitara.

North of here is **Izenayama Forest Park** (伊是名山森林公園), a beautiful wild landscape with a walking path and 360-degree views of Izena across natural observatories like the **Dragon's Mouth or Wind Rock** (龍の口・風の岩) and **God's Rock Seat** (神の岩座). It's also home to the **Churauin site** (美織所), linked to the tale of longing about when Shō En was a farmer and fell in love with a woman from Ie. They couldn't see each other often, so she came to Izena but for unexplained reasons was unable to live with him. So she stayed on the mountain and wove beautiful cloth.

The southerly **Izena village** (伊是名村) is the prettiest part of island life. Its coral walls and winding lanes are home to the **Mekaruke House** (銘苅家住宅; 902 Izena; 0980 45 2318; 09.00–17.00 daily), belonging to an uncle of Shō En. This family served as the head of Izena and Iheya for many generations and their home is a well-preserved monument of traditional Ryūkyū warrior housing. This village has rows of fukugi trees, another thatched prayer building known as **Kamiya** (神屋) and **Izena Beach** (伊是名ビーチ).

From here, Izena's coast snakes round in an assortment of small beaches, cliffs and the northwest settlement. It's a pleasant cycle, but the only historic site of note in the north is **Gyakuta** (逆田), the fields said to belong to Shō En when he was a farmer. These fields never ran dry and always had good harvest.

IHEYAJIMA

Iheyajima (伊平屋島), the northernmost inhabited island of the prefecture, is one of the most popular tourist spots on Okinawa and it doesn't take long to see why. Some 23km off Okinawa-hontō, this stretch of green mountains and rice paddies, surrounded by coastline of coral and sandy beaches, is known for its seafood, stars and some of the clearest waters in the prefecture.

More importantly, Iheya is an island of old Okinawa, of legends and gods. Revered in Ryūkyūan folklore, it is the home of the sun goddess Amaterasu. The story states that after a fight with her troublesome brother, Amaterasu hid in the large Amano-Iwato cave (now shrine; 天岩戸神社). Her disappearance plunged the world into terrifying darkness. The gods did what they could to encourage her out, and after the goddess of the dawn did a dance to make them all laugh, Amaterasu came out to join in, bringing light back to the world. On the Japanese mainland this cave is associated with the Ise shrine, but on the islands it is believed to be a deep seaside cavern on the eastern shore of Iheya. This cave, Kumaya, is still considered sacred by locals.

Iheya began paying taxes and tribute to Okinawa during the reign of Eiso in the 13th century. When King Shō En – born in Izena (page 209), which is historically linked to Iheya – was crowned, he appointed his sister the chief noro priestess in Iheya, called Iheya no Amaganashi. She was ranked second in the kingdom and was the first in a long line of priestesses who governed the island until the 19th century – longer than all other districts in the archipelago.

Locals also believe that the first Japanese emperor Jimmu launched his conquest of Japan from Iheyajima. There's little evidence for such a tale, but the island does have its more tangible history. Iheya's oldest archaeological site is the Kurihara shell mound, an early Jōmon period (3520–5000BCE) site that shows humans have been living on the island continuously since that time.

Despite this long history of habitation, Iheya's nature has been left delightfully untouched. Only 3km in width but 14km in length, the island is dominated by hills: 80% of it is mountainous, with dark green peaks of up to 200m rolling dramatically down the coastline. The night sky here is so remarkably clear and bright that the island hosted Japan's first official night marathon, known as the Iheya Moonlight Marathon.

Iheya's bright cyan seas are transparent up to 50m and filled with coral, flora and fauna, while the coast is a geological smorgasbord of rocks and caves. Water clarity is at its best between January and March, but even at its 'worst' in summer, transparency is around 30m. Iheya's table of coral reef is a whopping 3km;

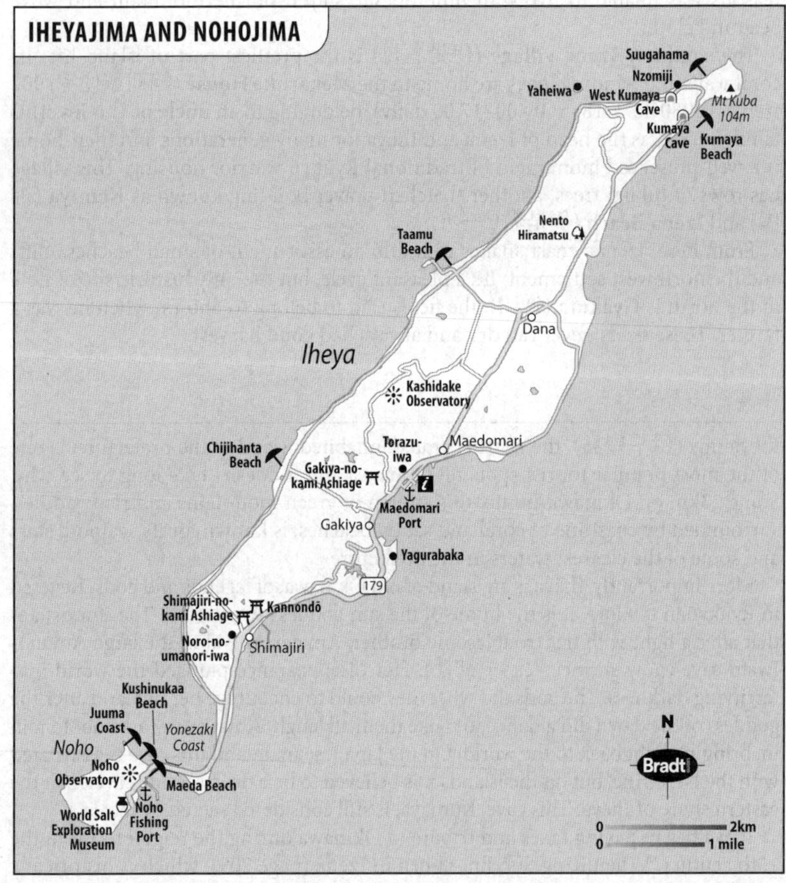

IHEYA FESTIVALS

As well as fish and shellfish, the island relies heavily on its own rice, which is harvested biannually and has been proudly cultivated here for centuries. Many of the ancient festivals here are linked to rice or harvest, including Gamiya's summer tug-of-war. There's also a unique scarecrow festival in April, where residents cover the fields in homemade scarecrows, as well as the August Unjami sea god festival that prays for a good catch. Multiple dance festivals include the colourful Ushideeku dance that prays for women's good health in September. Welcoming and hosting people has been at the heart of Iheya's culture for centuries. In fact, locals are so known for their hospitality that there's a phrase encapsulating 'hospitality beyond one's means': *Iheya jūtē*.

it includes scarlet fingers of isobana coral, stretching for 1km. With such clarity, coral, plentiful colourful fish and green turtles in summer, Iheya is a sensational diving and snorkelling destination, particularly off the north coast. Even on land, you can enjoy the marine life: from winter to spring, pods of humpback whales can be spotted near the fishing port, joined in the spring months by pilot whales and dolphins.

Iheya is connected to Noho Island, a tiny 1km^2 island to its south, by the Noho Bridge.

GETTING THERE AND AWAY Iheya's ferry leaves from Nakajin Unten Port twice a day, in the morning and afternoon, taking 1 hour 20 minutes to arrive at Maedomari Port. There is parking at Unten Port for ¥500 a day if you don't want to bring your car. With only two services a day, it's worth spending a night on Iheya to get the best of the island. You can also get to Iheya's Noho Fishing Port (野甫漁港) from Izena Uchihana Port (内花港) by chartering a boat. Though prices can change depending on the number of passengers, it's usually cheaper to do this than return to Okinawa-hontō (page 173).

GETTING AROUND At 34km around, you really need more than a bicycle to explore – even if it's an electric one. There are **rental cars**, **mopeds**, very limited **taxis** (Hub Taxi; ☎ 0980 46 2373) and a village **bus** (☎ 0980 46 2001), which runs from Nohojima along the east coast to Maedomari Port and up to Dana Gajina. You can bring a rental car over from Okinawa but you'll likely find it far more expensive than renting on Iheya.

Vehicle rental

Rental Iheya レンタル伊平屋; 217-32 Agiya; ☎ 0901 949 2090; w rental-iheya.jp. Car, moped & bike rental.

Soyokaze Rent-a-Car 伊平屋島 そよかぜレンタカー; 217-27 Agiya; ☎ 0806 499 0566; w r.goope.jp/sanshalenta. Mini cars, electric vehicles, mopeds & electric bicycles.

TOURIST INFORMATION There's a single tourist centre on the island by the port: the **Issha Iheyajima Sightseeing Information Centre** (一社 伊平屋島観光協会; 217-27 Gakiya; ☎ 0980 46 2526; w iheyazima-kankou.jp; ⏲ 08.30–17.00 Mon–Fri). It seems a remarkably big building for a relatively small office, but does the job.

WHERE TO STAY

Iheya Traditional House (whole house) 伊平屋島古民家; 448 Maedomari; 0909 780 4614; w airbnb.jp/rooms/14560921. Unique Airbnb rental of entire traditional 2-bed house with tatami & Western rooms, beautiful old interiors with big kitchen-diner, lounge & washroom. Surrounded by coral walls & garden. **$$$$**

Matsugane Hotel (17 rooms) 松金ホテル; 2135-27 Gakiya; 0980 46 2282; w matugane.com. A more updated hotel in Gakiya, Matsugane has tidy Western & Japanese en-suite rooms, & bright shared spaces including laundry, rooftop & tatami lounge. HB options. **$$$**

Miraisō (9 rooms) みらい荘; 724-1 Shimajiri; w mirai-sou.com. A little out the way in Shimajiri but a pretty, remote little minshuku run by a couple. Japanese en-suite rooms & HB Okinawan meals. **$$**

Yonezaki Campsite (camping) 米崎キャンプ場; 1982 Shimajiri; 0980 46 2570; w iheya-island-yonezaki.net. Well-lit forested campground with clean hot showers, beside beautiful beaches and coastline. Cooking facilities, tent rental, auto camping & tours. **$**

WHERE TO EAT AND DRINK

Kaigyo 海漁; 217-30 Gakiya; 0980 46 2544; 11.30–13.00 & 18.00–23.00 Mon–Fri, 18.00–23.00 Sat–Sun. Café-cum-izakaya near port specialising in cheap delicious seafood. Try the squid ink dumplings. $$

Café Harumaai はるま～い; 96 Shimajiri; 0507 115 8282; 10.00–15.00 Fri–Mon. Local café serving an excellent cheap lunch menu of island favourites, juices & coffees. $

Kura 蔵; 199 Maedomari; 0902 398 2832; 10.00–14.00 Sat–Thu. Unique restaurant in private home offering 3 lunch options for a brilliant price. $

Satoe 里江; 62 Noho; 0980 46 2428; 11.00–14.00 Mon–Tue & Thu–Fri. Tiny store in Noho offering bentō boxes & Okinawa soba. $

Village ヴィラージュ; Port Terminal 1F, 217-27 Gakiya; 0980 46 2027; 11.30–13.00 daily. Coffee shop at port terminal operated by Iheya's Fishery Co-operative. Amazing fresh seafood, unique mozuku soba. $

SHOPPING For picking up supplies, Gakiya and Maedomari have plenty of shops, including the large JA Okinawa Haisai supermarket (JAおきなわ ハイサイスーパー; 257 Gakiya; 0980 46 2349; 10.00–18.30 Mon–Fri). The closest to the port terminal, however, and the more regularly open is the smaller Super Zenchan (スーパー・ゼンチャン; 217-49 Gakiya; 0980 43 5859; 07.00–22.00 daily). There are further shops in Dana and Shimajiri if you need to stock up while sightseeing. Souvenirs are incredibly thin on the ground on Iheya, but you can always pick up some local salt at Noho's salt factory (page 218).

SPORTS AND ACTIVITIES

Diving shop JIN ダイビングショップJIN; 345 Shimajiri; 0901 179 1803; w divingshopjin.jimdofree.com. Diving, boat snorkelling & skin diving.

Mermaid Reef 1601 Dana; 0909 586 7571; e m.reef0212@gmail.com; w mreef0212.wixsite.com/mermaidreef. Snorkelling, skin diving & kayak tours.

Shumidoka 2135-63 Gakiya; 0901 944 6702; w syumidoka.com. Popular folk craft gallery & workshop running crafting experiences.

OTHER PRACTICALITIES Iheya has two main ATM points: the post office near the port (伊平屋郵便局; 256-1 Gakiya; 0980 46 2101; 08.00–16.00 Mon–Fri, ATM: 08.00–17.00 daily) and the JA Okinawa Haisai supermarket (see above). The Police Station Iheya (伊平屋駐在所; 316-1 Gakiya; 0980 46 2130) is very close to the port, while there is a single clinic in Gakiya village (伊平屋診療所; 217-3 Gakiya; 0980 46 2116; reception hours: 08.30–11.30 Mon–Fri). For emergency medical assistance, contact the Iheya Village Office (0980 46 2001).

WHAT TO SEE AND DO The first thing you see from the ferry is **Torazu-iwa** (虎頭岩), a huge rock that's said to look like a tiger lying down. You can drive most of the way up, before walking the last 5 minutes on foot to enjoy a full panorama of Iheya. In front of this is the **Iheya Village History and Folklore Museum** (伊平屋村歴史民俗資料館; 217-27 Gakiya; 0980 46 2384; 10.00–17.00 Tue–Sun; adult/child ¥200/80–160), covering the island's origins, history and culture.

Gakiya-no-kami Ashiage (我喜屋の神アシアゲ) to the south is where the noro priestesses both rested and performed rituals. These palm-roofed *asagi* are built low to make people purposefully bow into them. Further up the road into the island's centre is **Katakuma Shrine** (片隈神社), a small, somewhat standard shrine – until Taiwan cherries pepper it with magenta come February.

Passing through the coral-walled village of **Gakiya** (我喜屋) towards the east coast, you meet **Yagurabaka** (屋蔵墓). The tomb of an ancestor to the First Shō Dynasty, it's not one to go out your way for, but the coast here is scintillatingly blue and beautiful. **Shimajiri** (島尻) village has a handful of little sites: the Kannondō (観音堂), where people prayed for safe fishing voyages; Shimajiri's own thatched *ashiage* (島尻の神アシアゲ), used as a rest place for visiting Shuri noro; and the Noro-no-umanori-iwa (ノロの馬乗り岩), a rock used by noro to mount horses.

Iheya's southern tip ends in the **Yonezaki Coast** (米崎海岸): a stunning shoreline of dark hills, shallow waves and powdery shores. It's the ultimate sunrise/sunset spot, with the thin isthmus ideally placed to catch both – the best way to witness the spectacle is to camp at the nearby campsite. From here, Iheya connects to Nohojima via the Noho Bridge (page 218).

The majority of the island's historic and religious sites understandably face towards Okinawa, so Iheya's western coast is far less visited. It does, however, host **Chiijihanta Beach** (チーヂハンタの浜) and the great carpeted forest views from **Koshidake Observatory** (腰岳展望台), though this viewpoint can only be accessed via the road in the east.

The northwest of the island has a gorgeous beachy coast beloved by fishermen, with the curve of **Taamu Beach** (タームの浜) and two large shiisaa (伊平屋のシーサー) along the roadside. Eventually this coast comes to **Yaheiwa** (ヤヘ岩), a towering rock that emerges from the surf some 50m offshore. Yahe was actually an old fortress, from where locals corresponded with the Ryūkyū army, but today it is a popular diving and fishing spot. This north coast then takes you past the picturesque but wee **West Kumaya Cave** (西くまや洞窟) to **Nzomiji** (無蔵水). Nzomiji is the name of a shallow pool atop a boulder that's believed to never dry up. Connected with the legend of Majiru (page 218), it's said any woman who leaves her husband should have this water poured over them.

Cape Dana (田名岬), the island's very northern tip, is home to both **Suugahama** (潮下浜), a beautiful sunset spot, and **Mount Kuba** (久葉山), a sacred mountain covered in primeval kuba palm forest. The kuba tree is said to be visited by gods so is often found in areas of worship. At Mount Kuba's apex is the northernmost lighthouse in Okinawa prefecture.

Down Iheya's eastern flank from Cape Dana is **Kumaya** (クマヤ洞窟): the cave of sun goddess Amaterasu. Formed of quartzite some 280 million years ago, Kumaya is entered through a narrow gap, whereupon it opens into a large 600m^2 hollow, appropriately bathed in sunlight. Out front is **Kumaya Beach** (クマヤ海水浴場), a favourite local fishing point. The coast south is a brilliantly pretty spread of blue shallows and white sands, sprinkled with deserted beaches and rock formations.

The north of Dana village (田名) is shaded by the great **Nentō Hiramatsu** (念頭平松), a stunning Ryūkyū pine estimated to be around 300 years old. The symbol

MYTHS AND FOLKTALES: MAJIRU

Long ago, a beautiful and kind young woman named Majiru lived in Dana. Everyone on Iheya and Izena knew her name, and many wanted to marry her. But Majiru fell in love with Taru-hi, a man from her village, and chose to marry him. One day, Taru-hi went fishing and a strong wind blew him and his boat out to sea. In her anguish, Majiru went to the beach and stood crying, refusing to move until her husband returned.

Months passed. While her family and friends worried for her, men began to come up to the mourning Majiru and propose. This included the richest, most powerful man in Dana. Wanting to refuse but worried about the vengeance he could wreak on her family, she tried to run away – but the young men of the village followed her. She ran again, ending up at Nzomiji (page 217): a pool halfway up a huge rock on the beach. This pool never dried up, leaving her with fish and water to live on. She sat and weaved and prayed for Taru-hi.

A few years later, a small boat appeared far out on the horizon. Majiru saw the man and couldn't believe her eyes – it was Taru-hi. Taru-hi was astonished she had waited for him so faithfully for so long. They lived happily ever after and Ryūkyūan songs were written about Majiru's unwavering loyalty.

of Iheyajima, it was selected as one of the 100 best trees in Japan for it's perfectly domed shape. The long beloved tree has spread out its heavy branches so far in its dotage that it now requires multiple supports to prop them up.

Nohojima Connected to Iheya's southern tip by the 320m-long curve of Noho Ōhashi (野甫大橋), Noho (野甫島) is an almost untouched island of wildlife, farmland and quietude. From the bridge you can see the **Noho Observatory** (野甫島展望台), which offers views over Iheya's mountainous stretch, the seas and villages about Noho, and even neighbouring Izena.

Noho is a very small, local fishing island, sprinkled with a few stone wall hamlets and interesting sites. One such is the rather astonishing **World Salt Exploration Museum** (世界塩の探検館; 396-1 Noho; 0980 46 2180; w nohonoshio.okinawa; 13.00–18.00 Mon & Thu–Sat, 08.00–13.00 Sun). The couple who own it, the Matsumiyas, travelled to over 30 countries to explore the world of salt, and settled upon Noho as the ultimate place to make it. Today they produce salt – once a big problem for Noho drinking water – and run the museum, which has colourful salt crystals from around the world.

Elsewhere, Noho's coast has a few beaches and observatories – the brilliant white sands of the **Juuma Coast** (ジューマ海岸) and **Kushinukaa Beach** (クシヌカーの浜) to the north, and the ombré sea of **Maeda Beach** (前田の浜) by the bridge. However, Noho's best is below the waves. Its sea has stunning transparency and some of Okinawa's largest and densest table coral colonies, making it an increasingly popular but still relatively undiscovered diving spot.

Aside from the obvious and easy drive, you can reach Noho by chartered boat, which drops you at the small port.

AGUNIJIMA

Agunijima (粟国島) comes far down the tourist list when it comes to Okinawa. Quiet, remote, with no neighbours but gulls and waves, Aguni is known as the island of cycads and wild birds. Some 60km northwest of Naha, measuring just 12km around, it doesn't have a huge number of sights and activities. What it does have, however, is untouched local life, history and some cool topography.

Unlike most other Okinawan islands, created by uplifted coral, Aguni was made through volcanic activity. The result is a unique coastline of dramatic and colourful cliffs in the south, as well as a limestone cave considered a sacred temple. Unsurprisingly, this island created by fire is said to be home to a fire god, who is often enshrined in people's houses.

The rest of the island is largely agricultural. Alongside plentiful cows, Aguni has swathes of cycads (sotetsu) lining its landscape. These have a rather darker past than at first appears: they are a leftover from years of famine. Hardy cycads were planted where other crops wouldn't grow, for desperate islanders to eat in times of famine and during the war, despite their poisonous nature. The islanders also made them into miso, which is still produced, eaten and bought today.

What Aguni is best known for, however, is its villages. The island exudes simplicity, with rustic old settlements full of red-tiled houses, coral walls and the sound of the sea. It's one of the reasons it was chosen as a filming location for the movies *Navi's Love* (1999) and *Bonewashing* (2019). *Navi's Love* was an incredibly popular film about a grandmother's love story and parts of the set still exist around town, while *Bonewashing* is a family drama depicting the funerary and ancestral rituals on Aguni.

Recently, the island has also become known for its birdwatching. Some 15 or so bird species naturally inhabit Aguni, but over the years it has seen the arrival of

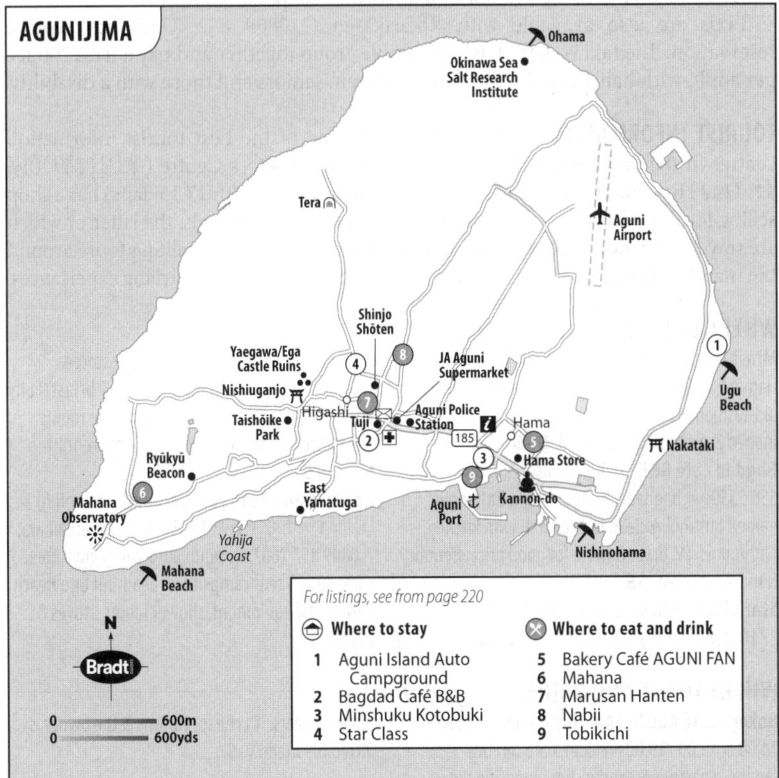

over 150 species of migratory birds. These appear throughout the year and across Aguni's multiple habitats – villages, fields, grasslands, ponds, waterways, forests and tidal flats – and include songbirds, water and ground birds and birds of prey. Aguni is now trying to plant coastal forest areas to encourage birds and increase their habitat, and it's expected that birdwatching tours will start to run.

GETTING THERE AND AWAY Aguni is accessed from Naha's Tomari Port. The **New Ferry Aguni** (0988 62 5553; w vill.aguni.okinawa.jp) leaves Naha in the morning and returns from Aguni in early afternoon, taking 2 hours 10 minutes. With adult round trips costing over ¥6,500, it's one of the more expensive ferries in the Okinawa group.

Flights, operated by **Daiichi Aviation** (0988 59 5531; w dai1air.com/okinawa), take 25 minutes from Naha Airport. There's only one round trip every Monday, Wednesday and Saturday, with both outbound and return leaving the same morning.

GETTING AROUND You can rent an electric **car** at the Agunimura Sightseeing Visitors Centre (see below). The flat charge is ¥2,000 for 3 hours, with a ¥50 surcharge for every kilometre covered. Given Aguni's size, this tariff isn't as bad as one might imagine.

There is, however, a cheap community **bus** called 'Annie' on Aguni, which travels from the port, around the island's two villages of Hama and Higashi, to the airport. The timetable and route can be found at the port and Japanese-language website (0989 88 2016; w vill.aguni.okinawa.jp/soshiki/senpaku/32.html).

Taxis are also available with Rikarika-go (0809 852 7362) but require reservation. The taxi is shared, where people group together and pay a flat ¥200 fee per adult, with half-price discounts for children, seniors and those with a disability.

TOURIST INFORMATION Aguni strangely has one of the best tourist information centres in the archipelago. Agunimura Sightseeing Visitors Centre (粟国村観光協会; 1142 Higashi; 0988 96 5151; w aguni-kankou.jp; 08.30–17.15 daily) has a shop selling local products and the island's only car and bicycle rentals, the latter of which are traveller-friendly electric-assist models. They also organise walking tours around the island and villages, as well as stargazing, crafting, cooking and dyeing experiences.

WHERE TO STAY *Map, page 219*

Minshuku Kotobuki (5 rooms) 民宿寿; 407 Hama; 0989 88 2407. Sweet little minshuku with old-fashioned feel, homemade Okinawan food, moped & motorbike rental. HB. **$$$**

Bagdad Café B&B (whole house) 0805 556 5559; w bagdadcafe-aguni.com. Bafflingly named but cool & clean house for 4, with kitchen, bathrooms, TV, dryer & more for good price. Rental & tours available. **$$**

Star Class (whole house) 星のクラス; 87 Higashi; 0903 795 8591; w reserva.be/hoshinoclass/about. Beautiful restored traditional house with BBQ, garden & b/fast. Fully kitted kitchen & bathroom, 2 Japanese rooms & 1 Western. Laundry, TVs & optional rental bikes. **$$**

Aguni Island Auto Campground (camping) 粟国島オートキャンプ場; 3220-1 Hamarukihara; 0809 853 7607; w aguniauto-camp.jimdofree.com. Auto & tent campsite on beautiful Ugu Beach with rental equipment, shower rooms, stoves & toilets. **$**

WHERE TO EAT AND DRINK *Map, page 219*

Bakery Café AGUNI FAN 109 Hama; noon–14.00 & 15.00–19.00 Fri–Sun. Café serving Japanese pastries & sandwiches alongside hot drinks & beers. It's cheap, yummy & the owner is incredibly friendly. **$**

AGUNI SALT

Salt has long been part of Aguni's culture, with the island suffering from regular droughts but surrounded by seawater. The salt here is made in a special way: seawater is dribbled down hundreds of suspended bamboo poles, evaporating in the gaps as it goes. The process is repeated until the concentration is incredibly high. This water is then either slowly boiled in a flat pan or evaporated in a greenhouse using sunlight. The resulting salt, which is still produced here at a large research centre, has a prized high ion content and excellent flavour.

Salt has even retained a place in island festivals. On Aguni, lunar New Year is celebrated with the *maasuyaa*, or salt-selling festival. Locals gather together to deliver salt to every home on the island, while praying, singing and dancing for health, fertility and good harvest.

Mahana まはな; 1548 Nishi; ⌚ 09.00–15.00 Mon–Fri, 09.00–17.00 Sat–Sun. Lunch spot out of the village offering coffee & incredibly cheap meals of curry, ramen, *cha-han* & desserts. $

Marusan Hanten 丸三飯店; 21 Higashi; ☎0989 88 2186; ⌚ 11.00–14.00 & 17.30–22.00 daily. Hearty bowls & set meals with Okinawan & Chinese influence. A popular eatery that's great for the belly & wallet. $

Nabii なびぃー; 2004-1 Higashi; ☎0989 88 2992; ⌚ 11.30–14.00 & 18.00–21.00 Mon–Sat. Teishoku restaurant serving all the greatest hits at good prices. $

Tobikichi とび吉; 431-1 Hama; ☎0989 88 2611; ⌚ 10.30–18.00 Thu–Mon. Beloved restaurant serving sushi & Aguni special *mochikibi* noodles. Try them with citrus shiikwaasaa flavour. $

SHOPPING There's a single food store in Hama, Hama Shōten (浜売店; 145 Hama; ☎0989 88 2360; ⌚ 07.30–21.00 daily), which has a few fresh meals and supplies. The larger Higashi village has more: the JA Aguni Supermarket (JA粟国支店購買店舗; 463 Higashi; ☎0989 88 2261; ⌚ 09.00–18.00 Mon–Fri) and small Shinjo Shōten (新城商店; 51 Higashi; ☎0989 88 2043; ⌚ 08.00–21.30 Mon–Fri, 08.30–21.00 Sat–Sun). The best souvenirs you can buy are locally made salt, brown sugar and sotetsu miso, which are sold at most stores.

SPORTS AND ACTIVITIES

Aguni Sea Base Diving 粟国島Sea-Baseダイビング; 249 Hama; ☎0989 88 2366; w seabaseaguni.com. Beach & boat diving.

Bagdad Café 宮里 粟国; 354 Higashi; ☎0805 556 5559; w bagdadcafe-aguni.com. SUP, kayak, snorkel & kickboard scooter rental.

Diving House Aguni ダイビングハウスアグニ; 399 Hama; ☎0988 96 5001; w agunijima.com. Rentals & experience & fun dives.

Minankai Diving Club 美南海ダイビングクラブ; 48 Hama; ☎0806 493 1789; w minami373.biz. Fun & night dives.

OTHER PRACTICALITIES There's a single post office in Higashi (粟国郵便局; 369-1 Higashi; ☎0989 88 2004; ⌚ 09.00–17.00 Mon–Fri, ATM: 08.45–17.30 Mon–Fri, 09.00–17.00 Sat), a clinic (粟国診療所; 573 Higashi; ☎0989 88 2003; w ritoushien.net/aguni; ⌚ 09.00–noon Mon–Fri) and a police station (粟国駐在所; 453 Higashi; ☎0989 88 2010).

WHAT TO SEE AND DO The majority of Aguni's sites – such as they are – reside in the south. Arriving into the southeast port, the first (very quick) stop is **Nishinohama** (西の浜), a small beach between two rocks that featured in the film *Navi's Love* (page

219). Unless you're a fan of the obscure film, the outlying Nishinohama is entirely skippable: instead start at **Kannondō** (観音堂). This small temple overlooking the port has a single stone engraved with Sanskrit; islanders worship here when leaving from and returning to Aguni, and when a local child born off the island comes here for the first time.

The two settlements – the former Higashi and Nishi villages, which now form one main settlement in the central south, and the former Hama village, a smaller settlement by the port – are arguably the main sights of Aguni. The red-tile houses, coral stone walls and protective fukugi trees hearken back to old Okinawa. Nothing has much moved on on Aguni, with farmers wandering the lanes carrying hand tools or driving old tractors, so there's a real rural, rustic charm. In the main settlement, by the town hall, you can see the **Tuuji** (トゥージ) – large stone tanks used for storing rainwater for daily use when water was scarce on Aguni. Some of these tubs, made from hollowed rock from Yahija coast, reached a tonne in weight and had to be transported by ships and huge numbers of men.

In the settlement's west, past yet more *Navi*-related sites, is a collection of small sacred sites and protected plant communities. **Nishiuganjo** (西御願所) is a forested shrine still used for worship by locals (which means it's sometimes inaccessible). Eegaa (エーガー) nearby is a cave-like utaki; next to it is the site of **Yaegawa, or Eegaa Castle** (八重川城). The castle is long gone, now a few scraps of stone wall, but the top of the hill gives you a view over the east.

Taishōike Park (大正池公園) is the first real sight of Aguni, outside of village life. Built to commemorate the Emperor Taishō's enthronement, the park has some incredible flowers and other flora, as well as the Taisho Pond where migrating and local birds come to rest. The wooden Taishō Observatory still exists but is no longer in use.

The southern coast is geologically fascinating. **East Yamatugaa** (東ヤマトゥガー) is a sacred, naturally split rock where visitors can descend into a 1m-wide crack to reach the beach. On this beach is a natural well and the remains of a water facility. East Yamatuga forms part of the **Yahija Coast** (ヤヒジャ海岸), a colourful paint pot of rock strata and formations. The upper parts of the beach are black basalt lava, the grey and white parts tuff (rock made of compacted volcanic ash). Some of this tuff has oxidised due to the lava's heat and turned a vibrant rust colour, which blends into the yellowing beach.

The coast then slides into Fudenzaki, a cape that features **Mahana Beach** (マハナの浜) and **observatory** (マハナ展望台). An excellent sunset point and birdwatching spot, the observatory sits 90m above sea level and overlooks remote Kume, Tonaki and the Kerama Islands. Mahana Beach is relatively rocky, but has dramatic cliffs that loom above it. On the road above the observatory is the small **Ryūkyū beacon** (番屋跡遠見台).

Heading north takes you through Aguni's agricultural pastures, filled with cows, goats and ranches. These bring you to **Tera** (洞寺), the kanji for which fully reads as 'cave temple'. This limestone cave takes its name from an exiled monk who lived out his days here 200 years ago. Beyond the castle-like entrance gate lie a monument to the Aguni-born Ryūkyū folk song 'Munjuru-bushi' and the uplit cave of stalactites. Tera has a maintained path but retains its aura of mystery and sacredness.

The very north of the island has **Ōhama** (大浜), a rather rocky and justifiably overlooked beach, and the **Okinawa Sea Salt Research Institute** (沖縄海塩研究所; 8316 Higashi; 0989 88 2160; 09.00–18.00 daily). Aguni's salt is well known, so this factory offers tours – though they are entirely in Japanese.

The east of Aguni is given over to **Uugu Beach** (ウーグの浜), also called Nagahama Beach, a phenomenal 1km stretch of white sand surrounded by a community of *monpa* bushes, creating a gradient of emerald, ivory and cyan. The sea is full of coral and creatures, making it ideal for swimming and snorkelling, and if you decide to camp on the beach you'll see an excellent sunrise. Further down along the road, marked by a small white post, is a small forest shrine called **Nakataki** (ナカタキ), hidden away in the forest and ethereally overgrown with banyans.

TONAKIJIMA

Tonaki (渡名喜島) is about as un-touristed as the Okinawa group gets. Only a rare handful of Japanese visitors come to the island's near-silent shores, where fukugi trees tower over carefully stacked walls hiding traditional houses from the wind and wandering eyes. This is Okinawa of the past; people come here to soak up the centuries on white-sand paths, to relax with sea turtle beaches and starlight.

Around 58km northwest of Naha, Tonaki lies between Okinawa-hontō, the Kerama, Kumejima and Aguni. It is the second smallest municipality in Japan, with an area of 3.84km^2 and a circumference of 12.5km. In 2000, it was selected as an Important Preservation District thanks to its untouched Ryūkyū village architecture and way of life. In the morning, schoolchildren sweep the white-sand paths as part of the near-century-old tradition of *asaokikai*, or 'morning wake up gathering'. At night, the island lights up from below with delicate footlights and from above with a carpet of unsullied stars.

Though known for its settlement, Tonaki is blanketed with mountains and greenery, its coast awash with turquoise. While the north has rather more gentle hills, the south explodes with dynamic scenery and towering strata cliffs – it's said that Tonaki was once two islands, but gradually became connected by sandbars. The landscape here is home to habu, and folktales of the deadly snake are rife, but you can also find the magnificent coconut crab, the world's largest terrestrial crustacean, along its quiet coast.

Tonaki's seas are alive with teeming corals and large numbers of green sea turtles. There are snorkelling spots and a few dive points around the island, but no dive shop; instead, a couple of companies on Kerama (page 240) take tours to Tonaki. Off the northwest coast is Irisuna, a small uninhabited island with a sizeable sandy atoll. Once a sacred isle with four ontake and three gods, where Tonaki locals would farm, Irisuna was confiscated by the US military after the war and designated a bombing practice site. Today it is still a no-go zone, but Tonaki locals are allowed to harvest the prolific aosa seaweed growing there on Sundays.

GETTING THERE AND AROUND Unless you fancy chartering a ¥176,000 helicopter, you'll be taking the ferry. Tonaki's ferries are the same as those to Kume (page 228), leaving from Naha's Tomari Port and taking 1 hour 55 minutes. The journey on to Kume takes 80 minutes. Only one of Kume's two daily ferries to Naha stops at Tonaki. This changes on Fridays in the April–October high season, when both stop, making this the only time you can take a day trip to Tonaki.

On the island, there are no rental cars, motorbikes, taxis or buses: **bicycles** are the only vehicle. You can rent these from the Tonaki Village Information Centre (page 224) but note there are limited numbers. The other option is, of course, **walking**. Luckily Tonaki is all about slow travel, and the island itself isn't large: a full circuit takes less than 3 hours to walk.

TONAKI FESTIVALS

The islanders hold a Sea God (Kaijin) Festival each year in lunar May, where there is fishing, haarii boat races and boat parades. June sees the Tonaki festival, full of events, stalls, crafts and fireworks, followed the next day by the Kashiki tug-of-war. This tug-of-war prays for young people and good harvest, and in the evening both adults and children are encouraged to act up, being silly into the night. The most unique occasion, however, is the Shimanooshi – a centuries-old five-day event held every three years for island prosperity. Women gather at the noro's house in the morning and when the tide rises, they worship as a group, praying for good harvest, fishing, voyages and health.

TOURIST INFORMATION Tonaki Village Information Centre (渡名喜村観光案内所; 1917-3 Tonaki; ☎ 0989 96 3758; w tonaki-kanko.com) is right by the port and has coin lockers, luggage storage and a shop selling souvenirs.

WHERE TO STAY If you decide to stay overnight on Tonaki you will need to make a reservation: you cannot simply rock up on the day. There are minimal minshuku on Tonaki but all come with half-board options – pricing below includes two meals. Phone lines are the only way to book but beware they're rather ropey on Tonaki, and you may have to try several times to get through.

Minshuku Muranaka (6 rooms) 民宿ムラナカ; 1866 Tonaki; ☎ 098 989 2626. The closest inn to the port. Each tatami room has its own toilet but the showers are shared. Laundry, fridge & bike rental available. Meals are simple but home cooked. Reservations a month in advance. No meals makes it a budget stay. **$$$$**

Red Roof Inn Fukugiya (6 houses) 赤瓦の宿 ふくぎ屋; 1909 Tonaki; ☎ 0904 350 9299. An inn spread across 6 traditional houses in the village with meals served in the Fukugi Shokudō. Buildings are, unsurprisingly, a little weathered, but the old-world ambience in clean tatami rooms is wonderful & the food good. Port pick-up & laundry available. **$$$$**

WHERE TO EAT AND DRINK There are very few restaurants on Tonaki and those that are here usually require a reservation in advance. This is why most minshuku provide meals but there are a few spots to eat at (all of them cheap) if you want, and of course village stores to stock up in.

Atoa Shokudo あとあ食堂; 1846 Tonaki; ☎ 0903 792 5134; ⏲ 11.30–13.30 daily, izakaya on reservation. A tatami izakaya drinking & dinner spot that recently began lunchtime service. Menu changes daily but stays cheap. Reservation required. **$**

Coffee Nuyahakushu コーヒーヌヤーハクシュ; 2F 1917-3 Tonaki; ⏲ 11.00–13.00 & 14.10–15.30 Mon, Wed & Fri–Sat, 10.00–13.30 Sun. Newly opened at the tourist centre, this café does proper coffee, snacks & sweets. **$**

Fukugi Shokudō ふくぎ食堂; 1876 Tonaki; ☎ 0989 89 2990; ⏲ 11.30–13.00 & 17.30–23.00 Mon–Fri, 11.30–13.00 & 17.30–22.00 Sat. Tonaki's best-known eating spot, Fukugi also runs the best minshuku too. Set meals are delightfully cheap & ideal for powering you around the island. **$**

Ikoisho Iriijo 憩い処西門; 1843 Tonaki; ☎ 0901 230 9049; ⏲ 19.00–23.30 Fri–Wed (winter 18.00–23.30). An izakaya in an old house popular with locals. The menu changes every day but the sushi is a highlight. **$**

SHOPPING There are two small shops for food in Tonaki: **Matayoshi** (又吉商店; 1966-2 Tonaki; 🕘 08.00–20.00 daily) and **Touhara** (桃原商店; 1838 Tonaki; 🕘 08.00–20.00 daily). The port also has a **shop** (1917 Tonaki; ☎ 0989 96 3758; 🕘 09.30–10.30 daily, high season also 14.30–15.30 Fri) selling a few nibbles and lunch bits.

The island is known for its mochikibi millet and its large carrots, the latter harvested between December and March. Both are used to make local *tonakki* cookies, popular little souvenirs that are available at the port.

OTHER PRACTICALITIES Tonaki has a post office (渡名喜郵便局; 1977 Tonaki; ☎ 0989 89 2004; 🕘 09.00–17.00 Mon–Fri, ATM 08.45–17.30 Mon–Fri, 09.00–17.00 Sat), as well as a small clinic (渡名喜診療所; 1916-1 Tonaki; ☎ 0989 89 2003; 🕘 09.00–noon & 13.30–17.00 Mon & Wed–Fri) and a police station (渡名喜駐在所; 1919 Tonaki; ☎ 0989 89 2019).

WHAT TO SEE AND DO Exploring Tonaki begins and ends with the village. Admire this historical settlement of shiisaa-topped old houses, fukugi windbreaks and white-sand paths. You'll inevitably bump into locals – take care not to invade their privacy when admiring their homes.

The **Tonaki Village History and Folklore Museum** (渡名喜村歴史民俗資料館; 1935 Tonaki; ☎ 0989 89 2015; 🕘 09.30–17.00 Tue–Wed & Fri–Sun; adult/child ¥300/free) has little English information but shows off displays of local tools, equipment and other aspects of life. Outside it is a legendary row of fukugi trees said to be 300 years old.

At night, road 1 through the village is lit up by soft footlights, painting the paths with a gentle glow designed to avoid polluting the myriad stars. These pretty, empyreal lights are one of Tonaki's most photographed features.

The east side of the village ends in **Agarihama** (あがり浜), a shallow beach with transparent seas and wide sands, flanked by rich green mountains. Ideal for swimming and picnics, Agari has showers, benches and tables. A walk to the very north of this beach brings you to Megane Rock (めがね岩), or 'glasses rock' – a double window in a rock that looks like eyeholes.

The road up from Agarihama arrives first at **Kaminote Observatory** (上ノ手展望台), which has wonderful views over the beach, and then at **Satoiseki** (里御嶽). This scenic utaki atop a small hill is a sacred place for the islanders, where excavations unearthed pottery and nails indicating it had been used from the 14th century. From here, Tonaki's undulating green is laid out before you.

The north of the island is given over to the 1,602ha **Nishimori Park** (西森園地). A road north out of the village leads to the **Sakashi Walking Path** (サカシ散策道), which explores the park and cape. The 20-minute walk up gentle hills offers views across the open sea and back to the village. A staircase of 643 steps off this path takes you to the **Nishimorienchi Observatory** (西森園地展望台), a deck with a brilliant view of Tonaki, Irisuna Island, Kume and Aguni.

The road down Tonaki's east coast is home to the old road **Amanjaki** (アマンジャキ), the 200m-long rugged rocks of **Shunza cliff** (シュンザ), and finally **Angeela Beach** (アンジェーラ浜), where sea turtles gather close to the shore either side of high tide.

The south of Tonaki rises up into an astonishingly dramatic cliffside; thankfully walking up it isn't too taxing. In the centre of this coast is the **Shimajiri Walking Path** (島尻毛散策道) and observatory. Completed in 2006, the well-maintained path passes through seasonal flora such as easter lilies, pink dianthus and plentiful adan to reach a view of the wild, rocky coast.

MYTHS AND FOLKTALES: THE MONKEYS' RED BUTTOCKS

Two brothers on Tonaki were neighbours: one wealthy, the other poor. One New Year's Day, an old beggar visited the wealthy house asking for a night's shelter. The rich brother turned him away, calling him bad luck. The beggar called at the poor house next door, where the brother and his wife welcomed him in, apologising for their poverty. The old man said, 'If you have nothing to eat, prepare two pots – leave one empty'. The wife did as she was told, cooking plain rice in one pot. But when she finished, she discovered a hearty feast in the empty pot: the three enjoyed a magical New Year meal.

The next morning the beggar said, 'Boil water in the pot then drink it'. They did so, and the poor old couple immediately became youthful again. When the rich brother saw this, he asked the beggar for rejuvenation too. The old man told his family to repeat the steps but bathe in the water: when they did his family turned to monkeys.

All his wealth was passed to the poor brother, but every day the monkeys came demanding the property back. The poor brother turned to the beggar again, who said: 'Burn stones and leave them outside.' That day, the monkeys came to harass the couple: when they sat down on the stones, they burned their behinds and ran back to the mountains, never to be seen again. To this day, the monkeys' buttocks remain red.

Winding round the south you reach **Ufunda Observatory** (大本田展望台) atop the mountain of the same name (165m). From the viewpoint you can see much of the emerald island's mountainous terrain, but also Aguni, Kume and the Kerama rising out of the azure sea. Moving north and towards the ocean, the road comes to **Yobukohama** (呼子浜), a peaceful and rarely visited white-sand beach where turtles lay their eggs. At its southern point, a rock emerges from the sea, said to be the home of a god.

KUMEJIMA

Kume (久米島) is an unexpected delight; a far-off outpost that delivers not just local life but sites, cuisine and history too. It's by no means overflowing with tourist favourites, but it's hard not to like this quiet island of rather shy people.

In the 17th century, trade ships between China and Satsuma-controlled Ryūkyū would often stop at Kume, the westernmost of the Okinawa group, for repairs or to wait for better weather. More often than not, Shuri sailors would offload goods on Kume to later smuggle on to Okinawa-hontō for their own benefit. Kume flourished, but when Satsuma found out, they set up a beacon system across the islands so that ships couldn't stop at Kume without their knowledge. There was occasional unrest on the island, but largely it was considered a beautiful, if unsophisticated, backwater. During the Ryūkyū Dynasty it was known as 'Kumi no Shima' (久美の島) – the changed '*mi*' meaning 'beautiful' – for its pretty coral reefs, green fields and landscape dotted with camellias and, come spring, cherry blossoms.

Indeed, the waters around Kumejima are home to over 260 corals and 2,000 marine species. Today the island is a hotspot for scuba tourism, with divers getting to explore a 35m-deep submarine limestone cave, manta cleaning stations, coral crowds and even on occasion glimpse whale and hammerhead sharks. Kume's beaches are also used for sea turtle laying and spawning, though turtle numbers are sadly decreasing (likely due to the bright hotel lights lining their shore). The top tourist spot is Hatenohama, an unearthly swirl of sand that floats out in the blue 7km offshore.

On land, the island's biggest natural draw – and success story – is the Kumejima firefly, an aquatic firefly species discovered in 1993. Only found on Kume, it turns up in April–May and has a larger light than other fireflies. The species was expected to go extinct 30 years ago, but the Kume Firefly Association brought it back from the brink in just seven years. The island is also home to the *kikuzatosawa*, a rare endemic snake that lives in Kume's mountain streams.

Nowadays the island's income is from fishing, farming and tourism – though with the island mostly self-sufficient, Kume locals aren't especially PR-conscious when it comes to the latter. They are, however, big foodies: Kume is also known as the gourmet island of Okinawa. It's famed for its extraordinary large prawns, farmed by the shoreline, and its oceans are the source of Kume deep-sea water. Taken from some 600m down, this highly pure, mineral-rich water is used across much of Kume's cuisine – in its beer, soups, noodles and seaweed farming.

The island is also renowned for its tsumugi cloth (page 27), the techniques of which travelled from Kume over to Okinawa and up to Amami Ōshima and the mainland. Historically it was used as tribute to Shuri, and the oldest known piece made on Kume is silk underwear dating back to the 1470s, believed to have been worn by a chieftain's daughter.

Culturally, Kume has a rich religious history: the *chinbee* priestess based on Kume was traditionally the oldest sister of the Ryūkyū king and one of the few priestesses allowed to visit Shuri Castle for events. (Today the final priestess is over 80 and there is no-one in the Shuri religion to take over.) Legend has it that one of the Kume chinbees used religious witchcraft to fight an Ishigaki priest, helping to defeat the Ishigaki lord Oyake Akahachi in 1500 (page 11).

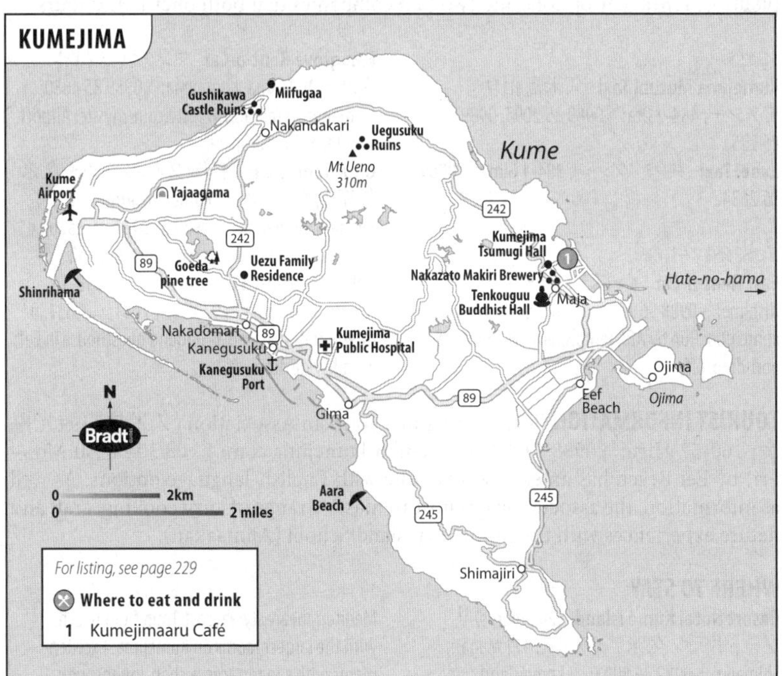

The Okinawa Islands KUMEJIMA

5

GETTING THERE AND AWAY Kumejima is usually accessed via the **Kume Line ferry** (☎ 0988 68 2686 (head office), 0989 85 3057 (Kume office); w kumeline.com) from Naha Tomari Port. This ferry operates each way twice a day, morning and afternoon, excepting Mondays which only has a morning ferry. The ferries take two routes: one direct between Naha and Kanegusuku Port on Kume's central southwest coast, the other via Tonaki Island. The direct takes around 3 hours, the Tonaki stop 3½ hours. In the high season (1 April–31 October), an extra one-way ferry runs on Fridays, only from Kume to Tonaki to Naha. Tickets, which at over ¥6,500 return are among the more expensive in the group, can be bought at the Tomari terminal office.

You can also fly to Kume from Tokyo Haneda and Naha. Both routes are operated by **JAL** (☎ 0570 02 5071 (charged); w jal.co.jp/jp/en). Naha flights take 30 minutes, while the Haneda service only runs in the summer season and takes 2 hours 35 minutes. Naturally flights are far more expensive than the ferries, with Naha–Kume costing twice the ferry price, but more reliable in bad weather.

GETTING AROUND Kume is a large, trapezoidal island with towns down its southwest and southeast coastlines; its north is the most remote part. The majority of the population lives around Eef Beach on the east coast and Kanegusuku where the ferries dock. For an outlying island, Kume is wonderfully connected. If you are only going between the main town and Eef Beach, you could get away with **bicycle** rental, but by and large you need more than that – the 23km ring road has a fair number of hills.

There is a **bus** service (☎ 0989 85 8260; w town.kumejima.okinawa.jp) with five lines; together they connect the airport, Shimajiri, and the west to the main towns, as well as completing a full loop. Buses are reliable if a little sporadic. There are plenty of **rental car** options and two **taxi** companies that both offer island tours.

Taxis

Kumejima Mutual Taxi 久米島相互タクシー; 484-2 Ota; ☎ 0989 85 2095, 0989 85 2251

Kyoei Taxi 共栄タクシー; 384-1 Gima; ☎ 0989 85 2634

Vehicle rental

East Rent-a-Car イーストレンタカー; 1346 Nishime; ☎ 0988 96 7766; w abc-car.net/plan_kume.php. Run by ABC rentals, airport counter & port drop-off.

Mangrove Rent-a-Car マングローブレンタカー; 164 Gima, Kumejima; ☎ 0989 85 4680; w mangroverentacar.wixsite.com/mysite. Airport counter & ferry drop-off.

ORIX Rent-a-Car オリックスレンタカー久米島空港カウンター; Kumejima Airport, 603-1 Kitahara, Kumejima; ☎ 0989 85 5151; w car.orix.co.jp. Airport counter, hotel & port drop-off.

Shima Rent-a-Car 島レンタカー; 548-16 Janado, Kumejima; ☎ 0705 271 7631; w 7631.jp/free/rentalcar. Based at Dugong guesthouse in Eef; island-wide drop-off.

TOURIST INFORMATION Kumejima Town Tourism Association (久米島町観光協会; 160-57 Higa; ☎ 0988 51 7973; w kanko-kumejima.com; ⏲ 08.30–17.30 Mon–Fri) by Eef Beach has an excellent website with English-language options. As well as information, the association organises a massive range of local cooking, craft and nature experiences with the Kumejima Island School (Ajimaakan).

WHERE TO STAY

Resort Hotel Kume Island (201 rooms) リゾートホテル 久米アイランド; 411 Magari, Shimajiri; ☎ 0989 85 8001; w kumeisland.com. Mediterranean-style resort 1min from beach with the largest rooms on Kumejima. Excellent rooms with sun terraces, a shop, lounge with welcome drinks, tours, rentals, outdoor pool, spa & laundry. **$$$$**

Bears Stay Kumejima Ifu Beach (12 apts) ベアーズステイ久米島イーフビーチ; 582 Janado, Eef Beach; 0120 43 8952; w bears-stay.com. Unmanned apt hotel with large balcony rooms complete with washing machine, small kitchen & en suites. Short walk from Eef Beach. **$$$**

EN Resort Kumejima Eef Beach Hotel (78 rooms) ENリゾート 久米島イーフビーチホテル; 548 Janado, Eef Beach; 0989 85 7111; w courthotels.co.jp/kumejima. Beautiful resort with tennis courts, outdoor pool, gym, games room, shop, café & restaurant. En-suite rooms. **$$$**

Minshuku Kuroshio (6 rooms) 民宿黒潮; 548-24 Shamedo, Eef Beach; 0989 85 7355. Next to the beach, Kuroshio is a long-standing minshuku with clean basic rooms, known for its home-cooked cuisine using plentiful local seafood. HB option. **$$**

Resort House Minami (9 rooms) リゾートハウスみなみ; 548-14 Janado, Eef Beach; 0988 51 7254. Incredibly affordable guesthouse near beach with en-suite rooms, warm, friendly communal areas, outdoor seating & excellent meals (HB option). **$$**

Oujima Camp Ground (camping) おうじまキャンプ場; 170-1 Ou, Oujima; 0989 85 8600; w kume-ou-camp.com. Campground on Ou Island beside sea, forest & lawn. Rental equipment & BBQ available, guest lounge & co-working space too. **$**

WHERE TO EAT AND DRINK Unsurprisingly for Okinawa's 'gourmet island', there are an amazing number of restaurants on Kume. The area around Kanegusuku Port has a proliferation of cafés and eating spots, while Eef Beach has an entire stretch of them – there's no end of choice. The season for Kume's famed succulent, sweet giant Kuruma prawns is December–May; other beloved local products include umibudō (sea grapes that are grown in Kume's deep waters), as well as goat, miso and watermelon. Make sure to grab a bottle of Kumejima 612 beer – brewed on Okinawa-hontō using Kume deep-sea water.

Backshore Ranch バックショアランチ; 169-54 Shimajiri, Shimajiri; 0989 87 4627; w backshoreranch.shopinfo.jp; 10.00–20.00 Wed–Sun. Backshore is the only real option for eating in Shimajiri. Pasta, pizza & rice bowls. $$

✷ **Restaurant Washima** ゆくい処 笑島; 1372-1 Nishime, Nakadomari; 0903 790 4518; 11.00–14.00 Fri–Wed. Roaring trade in Kume soba noodles, best topped with exquisite Kuruma prawns. Unique & one of the best on Kume. $$

Yangwa そば処やん小; 509 Nakadomari, Nakadomari; 0803 226 3130; noon–14.30 Mon–Sat. Beansprouts crop up a lot on Kume & Yangwa's *sokei miso moyashi* soba are a big hit. All local, the noodles are made from Kumejima deep-sea water. $$

Yunami Factory ユナミファクトリー; 1146-1 Kanegusuku, Nakadomari; 0989 96 5087; w yunami-factory.business.site; 11.00–17.00 Thu–Tue. American-owned eatery, but their garlic prawns made with Kume shiikwaasaa citrus & garlic oil is a local staple. $$

Kumejimaaru Café [map, page 227] くめじまーるカフェ; 500–7 Maja; 0989 87 1108; w kumejimarl.com; 11.00–16.00 Thu–Tue. Coastal café serving ice cream, waffles, pancakes, original lemon squash & Kumejima 612 beer. $

Yuki ゆき; 298 Torishima, Nakadomari; 0989 85 3919; 11.00–21.00 Thu–Tue. Fun eatery specialising in homemade sooki soba with Kume noodles. $

ENTERTAINMENT AND NIGHTLIFE Kume has no shortage of bars. Few open really late, but there are some excellent drinking spots in Eef Beach in particular, including Shima-Monkey (島の猿; 160-56 Higa; 0989 85 8585; 17.30–22.00 Tue–Sun), Kiyose (きよせ; 160-40 Higa, Eef Beach; 0989 85 7473; 18.00–23.00 Mon–Tue & Thu–Sat) and Umibozu (海坊主; 150-31 Higa, Eef Beach; 0989 85 7887; 17.00–23.00 Thu–Tue).

SHOPPING There are plenty of supermarkets across Kume, with large ones in each village. Nearest the port is **Tamaki Super** (玉寄スーパー; 1186 Nakadomari; 0989 85 2104; 08.30–21.00 daily) in Nakadomari and in Eef Beach there's **A Co-op** (Aコープ久米島店; 905-15 Janado; 0989 85 7788; 09.00–22.00 daily).

Kumejima Gift Centre 久米島ギフトセンター; 835 Nakadomari, Nakadomari; 0989 85 3260; w kumejima-shirushi.com; 11.00–16.00 Wed–Mon. Kume special products with another store at the airport.

Kumejima Tsumugi Studio 久米島紬工房; 501 Ota, Nakadomari; 0989 85 2153; 08.30–17.30 Tue–Sat. Workshop for tsumugi items like bags & cloth, at cheaper prices.

Kumi's Island Souvenir Store 球美の島おみやげ品店; 298-1F Torishima, Nakadomari; 0989 85 5514; 09.00–19.00 daily. T-shirts, souvenirs & food.

Sachi Souvenir Store 祥おみやげ品店; 548 Ota, Nakadomari; 0989 85 2262; 08.30–20.30 daily. Miscellaneous goods including crafts, food & awamori.

SPORTS AND ACTIVITIES In addition to those listed below, there are so many dive shops in Eef Beach it's hard to go wrong.

Craft workshops

Ajimaakan あじまー館; 966-33 Nakadomari, Kumejima; 0988 96 7010; w shimanogakkou.com. Run by island *anma* (mothers) who offer craft, cooking & more.

Ryūkyū Glass Studio 琉球ガラス王国工房; Ruri Hotaru 944–11 Nakadomari, Kumejima; 0989 85 2738. Glass workshops re-using old awamori bottles. Japanese only.

Tsumugi Weaving Pavilion 久米島紬事業協同組合; 1878-1 Masaki, Kumejima; 0989 85 8333; w kume-tumugi.com. Museum for tsumugi weaving with crafting experiences.

Outdoor activities

Diving Shirahama ダイビングセンターSHIRAHAMA; 548-17 Janado, Kumejima; 0988 96 8787; w shirahama-marine.com. Women-owned dive shop.

Island Expert Kumejima アイランドエキスパート久米島; 411 Resort Hotel, Kumejima; 0989 85 7746; e info@ie-kumejima.com; w ie-kumejima.com. Marine sports shop.

Kumejima Firefly Hall 久米島町 久米島ホタル館; 420 Ota, Kumejima; 0806 490 3850; w kumejimahotaru.jimdo.com. Tours across Kume, including night walks, Yajaagama & river clean-up.

Kumejima Horse Ranch 久米島馬牧場; w kumejimaumabokujyo.com. Massive selection of beach/nature rides on native Ryūkyū horses.

Kumejima Marine Sports Club 久米島マリンスポーツクラブ; 939-1 Janado, Kumejima; 0989 85 8648; e kumejima.marin@gmail.com; w kumejimamarine.server-shared.com. Boats to Hate-no-hama.

Yuumimaru 優美丸; 602 Nakadomari, Kumejima; 0806 496 3321. Fishing experiences.

OTHER PRACTICALITIES Kume has three post offices with ATMs, four police boxes and the Kumejima Public Hospital (公立久米島病院; 572-3 Kadekaru; 0989 85 5555; w kumejima.jadecom.or.jp; 09.00–noon & 14.00–17.00 Tue–Sat).

Police

Gima Police Substation 儀間駐在所; 171 Gima, Gima; 0989 85 2216

Janado Police Substation 謝名堂駐在所; 906-31 Janado, Eef Beach; 0989 85 8311

Kumejima Police Box 久米島交番; 484-2 Ota, Nakadomari

Nakandakari Police Substation 仲村渠駐在所; 57 Nakandakari, Nakandakari; 0989 85 2211

Post offices

Kumejima Post Office 久米島郵便局; 171-3 Gima, Gima; 0989 85 2022; 09.00–17.00 Mon–Fri, ATM: 08.45–17.30 Mon–Fri, 09.00–12.30 Sat

Nakazato Post Office 仲里郵便局; 906-12 Janado, Eef Beach; 0989 85 8010; 08.30–16.30 Mon–Fri, ATM: 08.30–17.30 Mon–Fri, 09.00–12.30 Sat

Ota Post Office 大田郵便局; 580-1 Nakadomari, Nakadomari; 0989 85 2008; 08.30–16.30 Mon–Fri, ATM: 08.30–19.00 Mon–Fri, 09.00–18.00 Sat, 09.00–17.00 Sun

WHAT TO SEE AND DO The ferry comes into **Kanegusuku** (兼城), one of the northwest villages. On the left of the port is a rock called Garasaa (ガラサー), a little-known site of Kume said to represent a phallus. It is the male counterpart to the much more famous female rock, Miifugaa (page 232), in the north.

Kanegusuku is home to the **Kumejima Firefly Hall** (久米島ホタル館; 420 Ota; 0988 96 7100; w kumejimahotaru.jimdo.com; 09.30–17.00 Wed–Sun). This museum has natural displays inside but better still the outside has been turned into a gorgeous habitat for fireflies and visitors alike. To its south is the **Kumejima Museum** (久米島博物館; 542 Kadekari; 0988 96 7181; w sizenbunka.ti-da.net; 09.00–17.00 Tue–Sun), a densely packed exhibition space showing off Kume's nature and culture. Even if there isn't much in English, the displays are worth the visit, and there are castle wall ruins just outside.

Towards the coast is **Aara Beach** (アーラ浜), a very quiet beach good for sea turtles, sunsets and corals. Ara leads to **Shimajiri** (島尻) in Kume's south, which has dramatic cliff and ocean scenery. The Tori-no-kuchi (鳥の口) – literally 'bird's mouth' – trail around it is named for the shape of the rocks you can see off the coast. Shimajiri village itself is an old, quiet, often-overlooked place.

Coming round the coastline brings you to **Eef Beach** (イーフビーチ), a built-up seaside village with plentiful shops, hotels and restaurants. The 2km-long stretch of sand here has been chosen as one of Japan's top 100 beaches, and is ideal for high-tide swimming. At night, the Milky Way stretches above it, but you'll need to find a darker point away from the ever-growing resorts to fully appreciate the celestial display.

A walk north brings you to the bridge to **Ōjima** (奥武島) – keep an eye out for locals farming in the ombré sea shallows as you cross it. The beach stretching around the south shore of this quiet little island opens on to a strange geological phenomenon known as the **Tatami Stones** (畳石). A natural patchwork of over 1,000 hexagonal rocks, the stones spread for some 50m out into the sea and 250m across the sandy beach, resembling a tortoise shell when they emerge at low tide. They're formed when andesite lava cools, cracks and forms columnar joints that are then eroded flat by the sea – and made slippy in the process.

Ōjima also has the **Sea Turtle Museum** (久米島ウミガメ館; 170 Ou; 0989 85 7513; w kumejimataro.okinawa; 09.00–16.00 Wed–Mon; adult/child ¥300/200), a facility dedicated to the endangered creatures, but it is unfortunately mostly Japanese language. Directly east of Ōjima is **Hatenohama** (ハテの浜), a floating sandbar in the azure sea. Slim and stunning, Hate (pronounced ha-tey) is 20 minutes by hired boat or tour; you can swim, snorkel and sunbathe in total peace. Back on Kume, the village of **Maja** (真謝) has a wonderful row of fukugi trees along the road, planted 200 years ago.

The northern coast is home to **Tsumugi Weaving Pavilion** (see opposite), where you can learn about and craft with Kume's famed material; the ruins of the mid 1700s **Nakazato Makiri Brewery** (旧仲里間切蔵元跡; 122 Masa); and the **Tenkouguu Buddhist hall** (天后宮), built in 1756 to enshrine a Chinese goddess of navigation.

Hiyajō Banta (比屋定バンタ; *banta* meaning 'cliff' in the dialect) forms the middle of this coast. The cliffside rises a sharp 200m above sea level, giving you great views of Hatenohama and outlying islands on a clear day. Hiyajō Banta is also popular with hang gliders. With a small rest stop comprising a restaurant, shop and observatory, from where you can view the Kumejima Shrimp Farm pools below, it's an ideal place to take a break from driving. This forested area is also the site of a cool abandoned village, which you can visit on a horseback tour (page 230).

Driving up the winding Mount Ueno road reveals **Uegusuku Ruins** (宇江城城跡), an old fort built on the highest point of Okinawa Prefecture, Mount Ueno, at 310m. Constructed around the 15th century before becoming part of the Ryūkyū, these ruins overlook the entirety of Kumejima – when the weather plays fair. On cloudy days it's hard to see your own feet.

Back down on the coast is **Miifugaa** (ミーフガー), a sacred rock from ancient times where women would pray for pregnancy. The rock has a split in the middle, eroded by wind and sea, giving it the labial shape that makes Miifugaa a 'female' rock. Nearby is a small, somewhat slippery stream walk to a little waterfall: at night this area is a good place for spotting fireflies.

Up the hill from Miifugaa are the impressive **Gushikawa Castle Ruins** (具志川城跡). Although only walls remain, it's easy to see the outlook this stronghold would have enjoyed across the sea during the Ryūkyū trading era. The castle is still a site for religious worship: just up the stairs is a stone where Kume priestesses perform the Umachi ritual in thanks for a good rice harvest.

Kume's inland west holds arguably its most inspiring and beautiful site. This is **Yajaagama** (ヤジャーガマ洞窟), an 800m cave system where funerals and burials for the poor local populace took place. Descending into Yajaa, down stairs into a pit of jungled leaves, vines and dappled light, you can see remains of some of these people: bones in the cave to the left. Traditionally the bones were placed into urns (after washing), but many have been broken over the centuries. Mysterious Yajaa has a full cave system too – a must when visiting Kume.

Underneath the airport, which takes over Kume's westernmost point, is **Shinrihama** (シンリ浜). The sheltered lagoon here is nearly always calm, thanks to the atoll just off the coast, and sea creatures abound. You can walk near the atoll at low tide, making it a great shallow spot for young kids. There are showers, shops and a campsite too, from where you can watch the planes take off and land.

South of Yajaagama and back towards the port is Kume's **Goeda pine tree** (久米の五枝の松), a massive Ryūkyū pine shaped like a giant bonsai. Measuring 6m up and 4.3m around, the branches spread and sprawl a sensational $250m^2$ across the ground. Mesmerisingly beautiful, and voted one of Japan's most beautiful pines, the tree was planted at the start of the 18th century and enshrined as a god of agriculture.

Nearby is the **Uezu Family Residence** (上江洲家住宅; 816 Nishime), said to be the oldest private house in Okinawa, built around 1754. The home of a Ryūkyū warrior clan, Uezu is surrounded by stone walls, hinpun and fukugi trees. The interior is currently closed to the public, but the ancient house is visible from the outside.

6

The Kerama Islands

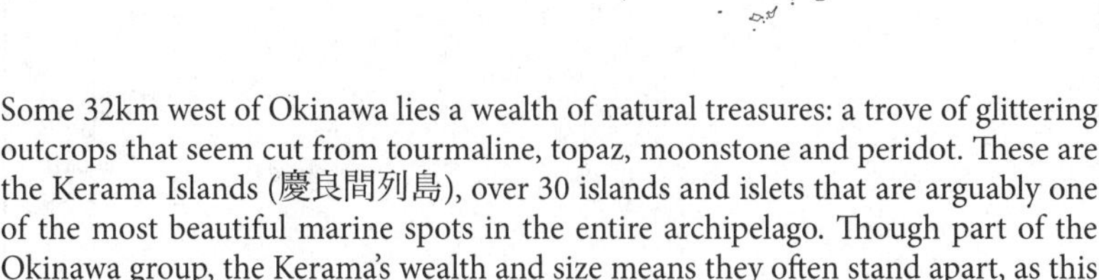

Some 32km west of Okinawa lies a wealth of natural treasures: a trove of glittering outcrops that seem cut from tourmaline, topaz, moonstone and peridot. These are the Kerama Islands (慶良間列島), over 30 islands and islets that are arguably one of the most beautiful marine spots in the entire archipelago. Though part of the Okinawa group, the Kerama's wealth and size means they often stand apart, as this chapter does.

They're popular for that very reason. Being only a short 35- or 50-minute ferry journey from Okinawa-hontō means the Kerama are an easy day trip or multi-day destination. Only four of the Kerama are inhabited: Tokashiki, Zamami, Aka and Geruma. Together they make up the Kerama-shotō National Park, encompassing 3,520ha of land and 90,475ha of marine environment, renowned for world-class diving, exquisite beaches and local wildlife.

The shallow waters surrounding these islands are astonishingly transparent and rich with marine life. Some 250 species of reef-building corals have been found on the Kerama: a whopping 62% of the building species found in Japan.

These reefs began life 400,000 years ago and are vital to the Kerama ecosystem, providing food and shelter for 360 species of fish, 1,400 invertebrate species and both green and hawksbill turtles (which have been known to lay on shore during summer), as well as protecting the islands from coastal erosion. Today, the corals are vital to tourism too, with visitors coming to snorkel and dive the glassy 'Kerama Blue' waters – so named for their electric colour – at over 50 dive sites around the islands.

The Kerama also provide a migratory home for humpback whales, which come to the group every January–March to breed and raise their young (page 235). Alongside the humpbacks, divers can also see other big migratory creatures like manta rays and whale sharks.

It's no surprise, then, that life on the Kerama has always been connected with the ocean. The islands have many traditional customs based around the sea, with the date for April's Hamauri Festival (a ritual for the health and happiness of Zamami's women) decided by the tide, the June–July *sabani* boat race to placate sea gods and pray for safety and abundance in the sea, and September's Umiugan, when women wade into the sea to give thanks. The islands are also said to be where Okinawan bonito fishing began: it became a popular form of income in the late 19th century and Kerama became famed for high-quality katsuoboshi (page 56).

While the national park is mainly marine, the land is important for wildlife too. Originally the Kerama were part of the mountains of northern Okinawa-hontō, before tectonic folding and faulting created the islands we see today. Though small, they're awash with a mix of peaks, deeply indented and dramatic coastline reaching up to 200m high, soft-white sand beaches and forests of Chinese fan palms (*kuba*)

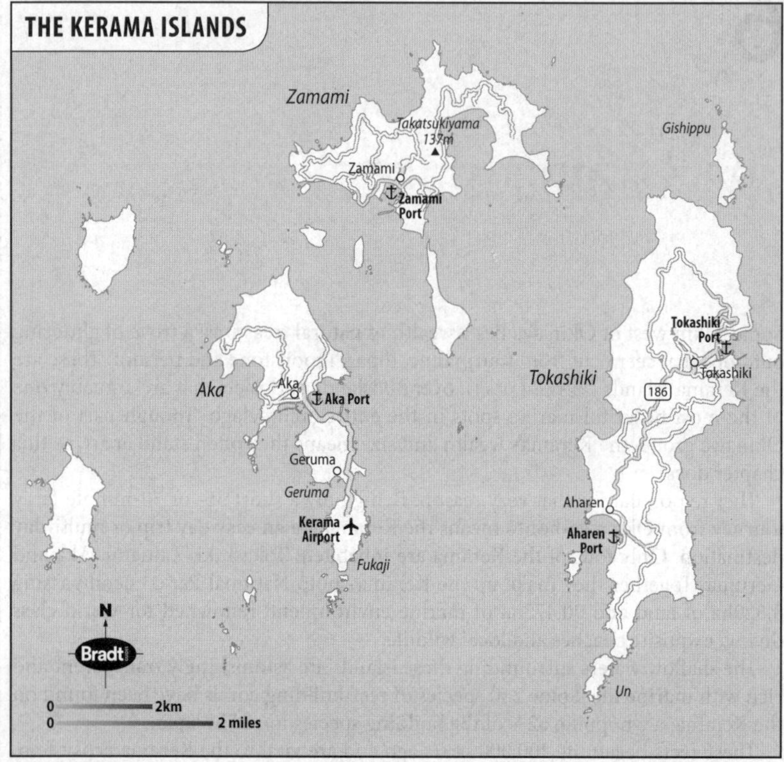

and Ryūkyū pine. Over 620 native plants are found on the Kerama, replenished by the summer rains and winter monsoons, and kept relatively low-lying by typhoons.

The big draw when it comes to terrestrial animals is the *keramajika*, a small species of endemic deer that are found on Aka, Geruma and Yakabi. Recognised as a national treasure, these deer have small heads and antlers and tend to hide in the forests during the day. They're best spotted at twilight and night, when they roam closer to the villages.

As well as the deer, there are threatened and rare species like the Ryūkyū flying fox, Ryūkyū robin, Japanese black-breasted leaf turtle and the spotted ground gecko. Yakabi Island is a Japanese wood pigeon habitat while the Keise Islands, the easternmost point of the Kerama, are a protected area for the common tern.

HISTORY

The Kerama were historically a stop-off point for Chinese and Ryūkyūan trade. In 1264, the islanders began paying tribute and tax to the Ryūkyū Kingdom, and for 600 years after were employed as trade navigators.

Despite their relatively tiny size, the Kerama became a vital stake in the Pacific War. Their proximity to Okinawa-hontō made them strategically useful to the Allies as a reinforcement base. The US plan was to take the Kerama with a comparatively small number of troops just days before the Okinawa-hontō invasion. Luckily for them, Japan hadn't predicted the Kerama takeover, and had moved the majority of troops stationed there to Okinawa-hontō. Nonetheless, Japan planned to use the

Kerama as a shinyō suicide boat station (page 126), so 975 men remained – as well as the population of over 6,000 islanders.

The invasion force arrived off the Kerama in the early morning of 25 March. The attack began on Fukaji, taking Japanese troops by surprise, who retreated en masse into tunnels and caves with the civilian population. Many islanders – long told tales of American cruelty – decided to enact 'self-determination': the Japanese phrase for suicide.

Akajima was defended by Japanese soldiers as well as 200 Korean forced labourers. Come evening, most of Aka had been taken but there were still 300 troops holding out, with 400 civilians in uncaptured territory. The majority of the islands were taken easily (Zamami less so), until only Tokashiki remained. It was here that the worst incident of the Kerama invasion occurred. As US troops rested

WHALE WATCHING

Every winter, the Kerama Islands are host to around 150 migrating humpback whales. These great whales travel extraordinary distances around the Pacific over the course of the year, taking in Alaska, Hawaii, the Ogasawara Islands and the Kerama. They arrive in the warmer waters of the Kerama around December and leave in April, though the height of the season is January–March. The humpbacks breed here then return the following year for birth. They leave for the north once the calves are strong enough; adult humpbacks weigh some 25–40 tonnes and are about 12–15m in length.

The waters here see a lot of whale activity, which is generally related to mating. Pods of males will often do battle with each other, vying for the females. The males also sing songs which can last anywhere from 5 minutes to several hours, with the sound travelling for 30km.

Despite their popularity today, these whales were once hunted on the Kerama and were threatened to the point of extinction. However, in the 1980s, after more than 20 years with no sightings, a Kerama fisherman spotted a humpback in Zamami waters. In 1991, Zamami set up a protection association that offered rules for whale-watching boats to follow to help protect the whales and their habitat. Individual animals have been identified and logged ever since, with over 1,600 catalogued by the end of 2017. Thankfully it's believed the whales' numbers are increasing each year.

The islanders here are veterans at finding these animals, and form an information network with other captains and land lookouts. It means spotting the whales is highly likely, with an 80% chance of seeing them. The guides are also trained in protecting the whales and are required to keep 50–100m away from them. Humpbacks are a particularly human-friendly species, and will tend to draw close to whale-watching boats. Better still, they will often put on a show of breaching, blowing and slapping. Visitors will commonly spot mothers with their calves too.

Whale-watching tours (page 240) depart twice a day, for 2 hours, with the schedule designed so day trippers from Okinawa-hontō can join. Some tour companies also put on lectures, forums, festivals and parties during the season. Make sure to call in advance on the day to check your trip is going ahead, just in case of weather changes, and take warmer clothes. The animals are extraordinary to see, especially the babies, so book on to a tour to make sure you catch a glimpse of these huge, remarkable animals.

for the night outside the northern town Tokashiki, the darkness was ripped by the thud of explosions and screams from inland. The next morning, the battalion looked for the source and found a small valley filled with an estimated 329 dead and dying islanders who had committed mass murder-suicide. Tokashiki was fully taken on 28 March, though a holdout of Japanese soldiers hid in the hills until the end of the war. Over the three days, around 155 American and 530 Japanese troops were killed, while over 500 civilians lost their lives.

By 29 March, the Kerama were already an active base. The Japanese bombarded US ships between Okinawa-hontō and Kerama with kamikaze, and conducted small air raids on the Kerama. Japanese soldiers holding out on the islands would occasionally conduct 'suicide swims' with explosives attached to them, to US ships. The Kerama would remain under US occupation until being returned to Japan in 1972.

TOKASHIKIJIMA

The largest of the Kerama, Tokashikijima (渡嘉敷島) is mostly given over to nature – just 0.78% of its 15.31km² is residential. This long, narrow island stretches north to south, hiding the other Kerama from Naha's gaze with its steep sandstone cliffs and undulating mountains. These hills, reaching up to 227.3m at their highest, also act as a natural light block, making the stars shine brightly along its secluded coastline.

Tokashiki's three settlements sit in coastal lowlands: Tokashiki, a third of the way down the east, Tokashiku, in the central west, and Aharen, two thirds down the west. Both Aharen and Tokashiki serve as ports – Tokashiki to Okinawa-hontō's Tomari Port and Aharen to Zamami. As the closest settlement to Naha, Tokashiki has become the gateway to the Kerama.

Like many other islands, Tokashiki has seen population decline, but its natural attractions have been steadily bringing young people here to live. Diving and snorkelling are huge, with waters known for their 50–60m transparency. The majority of dive points are very close to the island, making them easy to reach for day trippers. In particular, Tokashiki is a paradise for turtles, with healthy populations of both green and hawksbill turtles in Tokashiku Beach, the north and on Gishippu, an island off the north coast. The seas are also known for whales and great fishing.

With much of the main island covered in forest and shrubland, Tokashiki is also an excellent habitat for flora and fauna. This includes a selection of reptiles and amphibians, such as the Ryūkyū black-breasted leaf turtle, spotted ground gecko, Holst's frog, dagger frog, sword-tail newt and Anderson's crocodile newt. The island is also known for its colourful flowers, including azaleas, cherry blossoms, bougainvillea, leopard plants and Easter lilies; the latter are indigenous to the Ryūkyū and pepper Tokashiki with white blooms and scent come spring.

HISTORY The island has a long history: the second oldest pottery found in Okinawa Prefecture, dated to around 7,000 years old, was unearthed near southerly Unjima. Since ancient times, Tokashiki has been a place for rice cultivation, a rarity on these smaller islands that often face difficulties retaining water.

Bonito fishing has been carried out on Tokashiki since 1901; before this locals lived in poverty, their income made through line fishing and selling firewood. When larger bonito fishing took off, the village became richer, but fishing was far from easy. From March to October, fishermen would wake in the middle of the night to catch Japanese sand eels and scorpionfish as bait, then head to the waters

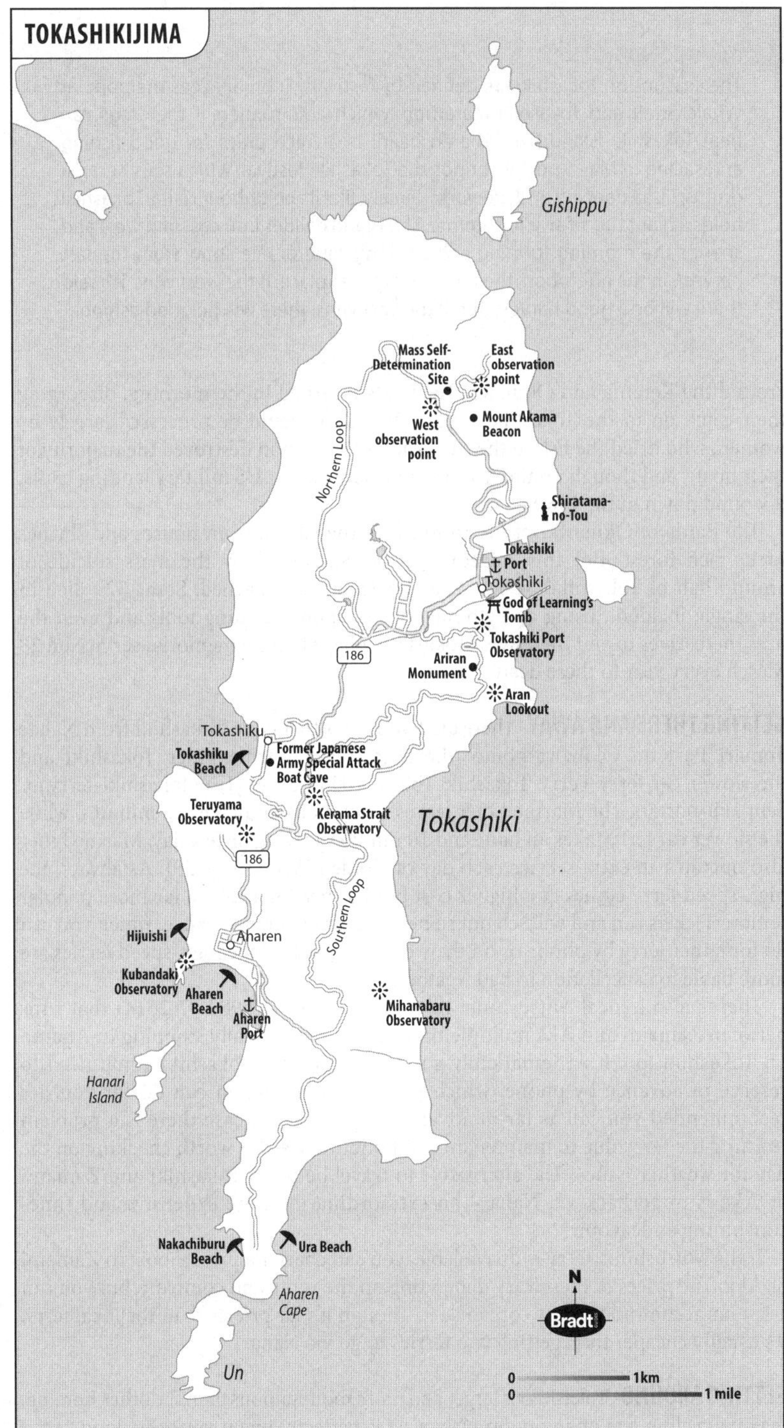
TOKASHIKIJIMA
Gishippu
Mass Self-Determination Site
East observation point
West observation point
Mount Akama Beacon
Northern Loop
Shiratama-no-Tou
Tokashiki Port
Tokashiki
God of Learning's Tomb
Tokashiki Port Observatory
186
Ariran Monument
Aran Lookout
Tokashiku
Tokashiku Beach
Former Japanese Army Special Attack Boat Cave
Teruyama Observatory
Kerama Strait Observatory
Tokashiki
186
Southern Loop
Hijuishi
Aharen
Kubandaki Observatory
Aharen Beach
Aharen Port
Mihanabaru Observatory
Hanari Island
Nakachiburu Beach
Ura Beach
Aharen Cape
Un
N
Bradt
0
1km
0
1 mile

TOKASHIKI FESTIVALS

The seasons on Tokashiki are defined by festivals. February sees the popular Whale Strait and Tokashiki marathon, which asks runners if their legs can beat Tokashiki Island. The Aharen haarii boat race prays for good fishing and sailing in May, and July brings the Tokashiki festival, which sees Kerama drums, Eisaa dancing and fireworks. Finally, like its neighbour Naha, Tokashiki holds a giant tug-of-war in summer. The island divides into east and west and spends the morning forming a 200m-long rope of rice straw from the last harvest. In the afternoon, the tug-of-war takes place: if the west wins, it's said there will be a good harvest and if the east wins, there will be good fishing.

around the Kerama and Okinawa. The boats returned in the morning, disgorging their catch on to the Tokashiki sands. Here they would be processed largely by women, who dried the fish in the sun. The 1945 invasion destroyed the majority of their boats, and though bonito fishing did resume using US military landing crafts, it wound down in the 1960s.

The Battle of Okinawa set fire to much of the island, from houses and shrines to its rich forest. But this tragedy was overshadowed by the mass suicide of around half of Tokashiki's residents as US troops approached. Some 329 died in the single incident, using everything from weapons, farming tools and even the fires themselves to end their lives. Tokashiki village holds a memorial service on 28 March every year to these dead.

GETTING THERE AND AWAY There are two ferries that go to Tokashiki from Naha's Tomari Port on Okinawa-hontō: the high-speed Marine Liner Tokashiki and the slower car ferry Ferry Tokashiki (both ☎ 0988 68 7541; w tokashiki-ferry.jp/Senpaku/portal). The Marine Liner leaves twice a day and takes 40 minutes, while the slower car ferry takes an hour and 10 minutes leaving once a day. Marine Liner also operates an extra service each day of Golden Week (page 59). As always, the high-speed ferry comes at a higher cost but its speed makes it a far more popular option. Tickets can and will sell out so best to grab them in advance, which you can do for either ferry by phone or on the website. Note that the high-speed ferries are more liable to cancellation in bad weather.

There's also a local Mitsushima inter-island ferry (☎ 0989 87 2614) that runs between Zamami and Aka multiple times a day, occasionally stopping in Aharen on Tokashiki too. It's a remarkably good price, but for Tokashiki you'll need to reserve in advance by phone, which your accommodation can do for you. It's recommended you call as far in advance as possible, in case there is a problem running the ferry due to maintenance or holidays. It's also worth checking on the day for weather issues. The alternative to travel between Tokashiki and Zamami or Aka is to go back via Naha – an extraordinarily more expensive and time-consuming endeavour.

If the Mitsushima ferry is unavailable, you can charter a private boat to Zamami or Aka. The prices of these vary depending on the route and company, but you can ask your accommodation to organise it. Though it's far pricier than the local ferry, it's usually cheaper than getting two ferries to go via Naha.

GETTING AROUND Tokashiki is larger and more mountainous than the other Kerama, making **cycling** less of an option. A bicycle is perfectly fine if you're sticking to the villages, but can be pretty hard going for exploring the island's further flung points. A better way to get about is by **moped**; you get the breeze, sunlight and avoid the hills.

There are **buses** run by Tokashiki Kanko (0989 87 2232) between the two main villages of Aharen and Tokashiki, but they are, as usual, few and far between. They also don't go to Tokashiku Beach, so you will need to take a taxi or rent a vehicle to visit there.

Aloha Rental Kikaku (0989 87 2272), Kujira Rent-a-Car (0989 87 2836), Kariyushi Rental Service Tokashikijima (0989 87 3311) and Yonehara Kotsu (0903 078 5895) all offer **rental cars and motorbikes**, while Yonehara also operates **taxis**.

TOURIST INFORMATION Both Tomari and Tokashiki ports have information on the island, with the latter housing the Tokashiki Tourist Information Centre (渡嘉敷村観光案内所; 0989 87 2332; w tokashiki.info; 09.00–17.00 daily). Tokashiki village has a sightseeing information app called Tokashiki Navi (公式とか式ナビ); though only in Japanese, it allows users to easily copy to translation apps and contains maps and ferry schedules too.

WHERE TO STAY

Kerama Terrace (8 rooms) ケラマテラス; 130 Aharen; 0989 87 3477; w keramaterrace.jp. The more luxe accommodation in Aharen, Kerama Terrace has wonderful en-suite Western rooms with jacuzzi baths, aroma lights & plush amenities. Its restaurant offers the closest thing to haute cuisine on Tokashiki. Marine tours available. **$$$$$**

✷ **Tokashiki Guest House** (2 cabins) トカシキゲストハウス; 572 Fusato, Aharen; 0908 292 2696; w tokashiki-guesthouse.com. 6-person log cabins in the trees on Mt Teru, offering spacious Japanese-style sleeping downstairs & on a mezzanine. Decent kitchen with fridge & cooking facilities, bathroom & separate toilet. Excellent stargazing, habu-protective fencing, palm-lined veranda & ferry transfers. **$$$$$**

Sea Friend (14 rooms) シーフレンド; 155 Aharen; 0989 87 2836; w seafriend.jp/en. A couple of mins from Aharen Beach, Sea Friend has log-house & minshuku accommodations with tidy, en-suite Western rooms. Restaurant, marine tours, BBQ & car rental. B/fast inc. **$$$$**

Marine House Aharen (8 rooms) マリンハウス阿波連; 106 Aharen; 0989 87 2335; w aharen.com. Bright inn decked with colourful bougainvillea, with simple Japanese & Western rooms, garden & marine dive shop. Night star & firefly tours for guests, laundry, BBQ evenings, restaurant & free transfers. **$$$**

Kerama Backpackers (dorms) ケラマバックパッカーズ; 40 Tokashiki; 0705 277 4522; w kerama-backpackers.com. The only dormitory guesthouse on Tokashiki. Delightfully cheap, comfy common room, shared kitchen, laundry, clean mixed & separate gender dorms. Free transfers to Aharen Beach & Tokashiku Beach. **$**

WHERE TO EAT AND DRINK

Café Shimamun+ Cafe島むん+; 152 Aharen; 0806 497 1392; 18.00–22.00 Fri–Wed. Very popular garden café serving pizzas, salads & wonderful Okinawan dishes like squid ink cha-han. $$

✷ **Half Time** ハーフタイム; 122 Aharen; 0989 87 2021; w azhoop.com; 19.00–midnight daily. Colourful junkyard oasis in north Aharen. Unassuming outside, but step through the door into a neon garden with multiple bars & American diner-style menu. Jackie Chan bar's Aharen burger, a beer & 60s tunes are a perfect mix. $$

Masa's Shop まーさーの店; 70 Aharen; 0989 87 2911; 11.30–15.30 (to 14.00 winter) & 18.00–22.00 Thu–Tue. Often-crowded restaurant with classic set meals & tuna bowls made with locally caught tuna. $$

Hauoli 海の家ハウオリ; 170-6 Aharen; 0989 87 2335; 10.00–16.30 daily. One of the many little eateries around the beach. Classics like kara-age & curry. $

Izakya Maruni 居酒屋丸二; 86 Aharen; ◷ 17.00–22.00 Wed–Sun. Cheap plates of Tokashiki & Okinawan food in warm atmosphere. Red pepper dumplings, soba, grilled squid, fries & fish. $

Seaside Café Gakiya シーサイドカフェガキヤ; 1923 Tokashiki; ☎ 0988 96 4566; ◷ noon–14.00 & 17.00–23.00 daily. The only café & marine shop near Tokashiku Beach. Snacks & meals like taco rice & fresh pineapple juice. Drinks available 14.00–17.00. $

ENTERTAINMENT AND NIGHTLIFE Aharen's nightlife revolves around the few restaurants open late. Izakaya Maruni is a local favourite while Half Time (page 239) attracts a younger crowd and a lot of domestic tourists.

Bar Ni-Bui Bar にーぶい; 37 Aharen; ☎ 0909 592 2456; ◷ 19.00–midnight daily. Great little izakaya on Aharen's outskirts with impromptu karaoke & friendly crowd.

Izakya Maruni 居酒屋丸二; 86 Aharen; ◷ 17.00–22.00 Wed–Sun. Popular wood izakaya with hearty menu & good drinks selection.

Karaoke Izakaya Marine Box 島人ダイニング まりんぼっくす; 1779-2 Tokashiki; ☎ 0989 87 2570; ◷ 18.00–22.30 Mon, 11.30–13.30 & 18.00–22.30 Tue–Wed & Fri. Essentially the only Tokashiki town bar. Seafood focus but karaoke & live sanshin music too.

Summer Snow Bar & Eatery 民謡居酒屋サマースノー; 37 Aharen; ◷ 18.00–midnight daily. Very local bar: plastic chairs, tiny space & brilliant drinking buddies.

SHOPPING There's one small supermarket in Aharen: Arakaki Shōten Convenience Store (新垣商店; ☎ 0989 87 2347; w arakaki-s.com/index.html; ◷ 07.00–20.00 daily). It's pretty well stocked with fresh vegetables, baked goods, ramen, rice, drinks, alcohol, snacks and the occasional bentō box. It also covers toiletries, household goods and even some DIY and fishing equipment. The biggest food store, JA Shop (JAショップとかしき; 222 Tokashiki; ☎ 0989 87 2150; ◷ 09.00–18.30 Mon–Wed & Fri–Sat), is in Tokashiki. There are a couple of convenience stores operating on the days JA is closed, like Shinhamaya (新浜屋; 331 Tokashiki; ☎ 0988 96 4455; ◷ 08.30–21.00 daily).

Chip Chip Tokashiki チップチップとかしき港店; 346 Tokashiki; ☎ 0989 87 2652; ◷ 08.00–17.30 daily. Original T-shirts with Tokashiki Island motifs, as well as sandals & souvenirs. There's a second shop in Aharen (170 Aharen).

Viel Spaß 128 Aharen; ☎ 0802 696 2020; ◷ 09.00–17.00 daily. Shop selling small number of bags, sandals & accessories.

SPORTS AND ACTIVITIES The island has a few marine tour operators who can help you explore all that its clear oceans have to offer.

Acoustic Life Tokashiki アコースティックライフ; 1923 Tokashiki; ☎ 0802 795 9967; w acousticlife-tokashiki.com. SUP tours at Tokashiku Beach where you can meet sea turtles & snorkel.

Hauli 海の家ハウオリ; 170-6 Aharen; ☎ 0989 87 2335; w aharen.com. English-language friendly dive shop (owned by Marine House) offering intro dives, tubing, snorkelling to uninhabited islands & jet skis.

K's Marine Club K'sマリンクラブ; 111 Aharen; ☎ 0988 96 4756; w ksmarineclub.com. Beach snorkel tours at Aharen.

Prism Dive プリズムダイブ; 116-1 Aharen; ☎ 0806 413 8050; w prismdive.com. Licence, fun & experience dives & snorkel tours.

Retreat Dive リトリートダイブ; 108 Tokashiki; ☎ 0806 483 6240; w retreatdive.jp. Tokashiki-based dive school with numerous diving options included private couples/family tours.

Waterkids 178 Aharen; 0989 87 2206; w kerama-tokashiki.jp. Operated by Reef Inn, Waterkids offer snorkelling & diving with English-speaking guides.

OTHER PRACTICALITIES Tokashiki village has a single clinic (沖縄県立南部医療センター; 277 Tokashiki; 0989 87 2028) that can handle minor issues like jellyfish stings, but the main hospitals are on Okinawa-hontō. It also has a police station (渡嘉敷駐在所; 1728 Tokashiki; 0989 87 2039) and post office with ATM (渡嘉敷郵便局; 209-3 Tokashiki; 0989 87 2131; 09.00–17.00 Mon–Fri, ATM: 08.45–17.30 Mon–Fri, 09.00–17.00 Sat). If there's an emergency, you can also contact the Tokashiki Village Office (0989 87 2321).

WHAT TO SEE AND DO

Tokashiki Ferries from Okinawa largely stop in **Tokashiki village** (渡嘉敷村) on the northeast coast. This is the smaller of the two main villages, a port town which had long ties to bonito fishing and processing. Look out for the old bonito factory chimney on the northbound road, which still stands despite the shrapnel blasts in its brick. The village is home to a few minor sites, like the intricately stacked old stone walls of the **Nemoto Family House** (根元家の石垣), the concrete **Tokashiki Shrine** (渡嘉敷神社) that traditionally enshrines noro priestesses, and the **Tokashiki Village History and Folklore Museum** (渡嘉敷村歴史民宿資料館; 2F 346 Tokashiki; 0989 87 2120; 09.00–17.00 daily, reservation desk Mon–Fri). This museum on the second floor of the port building requires a reservation to visit, but you can learn about Tokashiki nature, history and culture, as well as see a baby humpback whale skeleton.

Shiratama-no-Tou (白玉之塔) is a northerly memorial to those who died on the island during the war. This area of Tokashiki has a grim history: here, the cornered islanders committed mass suicide as US troops invaded. The site of the tragedy is atop the northernmost mountain, known as the **Mass Self-Determination Site** (集団自決跡地) or Mass Suicide Site, and is marked by a stone monument.

This hilltop also has a monument to the **Mount Akama beacon** (赤間山立火所跡), which was used to notify Shuri's royal palace of ships approaching the kingdom. Even after the kingdom's takeover, the islanders used this point to wave off those leaving the island with bonfires. On either side of the hill are the **east and west observatories** (東・西展望台) overlooking the sea and Tokashiki's green scenery. The road from the village up to the mountain does loop entirely round, but you will have to open and close the protective wooden habu gates.

The road southeast takes you across the river to **Tokashiki Port Observatory** (港の見える丘展望台), a fine enough outlook across the village and bay, and the **God of Learning's Tomb** (学問の神様). This commemorates an exiled monk who came to the island, bringing with him Japanese writing – previously the Ryūkyū had used Chinese characters to write.

Further round the road is the **Ariran Monument** (アリラン慰霊のモニュメント), which commemorates more than 1,000 Korean women and 10,000 Korean men taken as military or sex slaves ('comfort women') by the Japanese army on Okinawa. On the Kerama, there were 1,000 slave soldiers and 21 comfort women, many of whom died in the self-determination. Just past this is the **Aran Lookout** (アラン展望台), with views over Maejima.

From here, the road can take you south or to the wee hamlet of Tokashiku (渡嘉志久). This is home to **Tokashiku Beach** (渡嘉志久ビーチ), arguably the island's best, with a Kerama-blue sea and light sand where turtles come to feast during high tide. Snorkelling in the shallows here is a must, with waters up to

MYTHS AND FOLKTALES: TOKASHIKI HANARI

Long ago people on the Kerama and Kume travelled in Yanbaru sailing boats, which relied on good winds. When the wind direction was unfavourable, boats could be stuck for months. One year, a Kume ship became anchored in the waters off Aharen, beside the small, remote island of Hanari, because there were no winds to Kume.

On board was an important noro priestess from Kumejima called Kimihae-Kanashi, who was forced to live on Hanari with her companions while they waited for a change in the weather. In an effort to cheer up Kimihae-Kanashi, local women and priestesses from Aharen prepared a great feast and went to Hanari on 3 March to entertain her.

Hanari had never had a priestess or deity, but now there is a tradition to go to Hanari on 3 March to fish. There is also a small shrine there, said to be where Kimihae-Kanashi stayed.

50m transparency – just don't go too close to the turtles, as they are protected and endangered. Being in the centre of Tokashiki's west coast, the beach has excellent sunsets, but no bus service and few restaurants – although it does have amenities like snorkel rental and toilets. Behind these is the **Former Japanese Army Special Attack Boat Cave** (旧日本軍特攻艇秘匿壕), where so-called suicide boats were stashed.

Aharen The road between Tokashiki and Aharen is home to two observatories with views of the extraordinary colours of the Kerama Strait. On sunny days, the **Kerama Straits Observatory** (慶良間海峡展望所) and azalea-strewn **Teruyama Observatory** (照山展望台) offer up neon-blue seas and islets of lush green.

Aharen (阿波連) is the more built-up of Tokashiki's two villages; here you'll find lots of accommodation, restaurants, dive shops and cafés. This makes it the most touristed place in Tokashiki, which has had an effect on its beloved, cat-filled beach. Indeed the coral at **Aharen Beach** (阿波連ビーチ) has been so damaged by clumsy tourists that it's now mandatory to wear a life vest in designated swimming areas.

The beach's west side develops into a rocky playground of caves, tunnels, rock holes, pools and islets, which are great fun to explore whether adult or child – **tunnel rock** (トンネル岩) is a particular favourite. Above this is **Kubandaki Observatory** (クバンダキ展望台), which overlooks Aharen, the beach and the cape, and is reached through a rare kuba palm community by the campsite.

North of here is Aharen's western beach, **Hijuishi** (ヒジュイシビーチ), a comparatively unfrequented beach without snorkelling restrictions. Hijuishi can be accessed across the rocky coastline or from Aharen, via an unmarked path in the northwest.

Hanari Island (ハナリ島), occasionally known as Shibugakijima, is an uninhabited island off Aharen Beach with waters of phenomenal transparency. You can reach it by sea kayak, either rented independently or as part of a guided tour. It's also a great diving point with a great amount of sea life, particularly clownfish.

East of Aharen is the **Mihanabaru Promenade** (見花原遊歩道), a 1km trail that immerses you in Tokashiki shrubland. The wind here is too strong for larger trees to grow (the short Ryūkyū pines here were once farmed for bonsai) so you get far-reaching views across the ocean. The trail leads down to **Mihanabaru Observatory** (見花原展望所).

The very south of Tokashiki is given over to **Aharen Cape** (阿波連岬), an undulating landscape of sandstone, palms and emerald-coloured sea overlooked by observatories. Known locally as Hinakushi, the cape has boardwalks, picnic sites and sprawling lawns too. If you can face the lonely journey back (should you not have a rental car), the cape is a brilliant sunset and stargazing spot as there are no lights.

On the cape's east is **Ura Beach** (浦のビーチ). Well away from Aharen's tourists, it's a peaceful spot where you can enjoy the sands as you wish. It's deemed a non-swimming beach because of strong currents further out so take care. On the west is **Nakachiburu Beach** (中頭の浜), another deserted stretch of sand accessed via the Aharen Cape Garden. The bottom of this beach leads to **Unjima** (ウン島), an uninhabited island that you can walk to in low tide.

ZAMAMIJIMA

Zamami (座間見島) is *the* day-trip destination from Okinawa-hontō for good reason: its bucolic communities and steep forested hills, which trail down to tranquil sands, feel light-years away from the bustle of Naha.

The island's 16.7km² is a mishmash of bays and promontories – its north coast a great, sharp cliffside, while the softer south is home to the main Zamami village and port. The majority of the island's 600 people live in the central village, a relaxed little community with shops, restaurants, izakaya, minshuku and dive shops. (Confusingly, the larger municipality covering some 20 islands – including Zamami, Aka and Geruma – is also named Zamami Village.) The rest of Zamami's viewpoints and beaches spread out from the central village, including two other hamlets, Ama in the west and Asa to the east.

Zamami has long been a fishing heartland in Okinawa – in the late 1880s it became the prefecture's first bonito fishing ground. Like the rest of the Kerama, Zamami suffered during the war; it lost 234 residents to murder-suicide among families. Ama was the first place in Zamami Village municipality to be reconstructed after the war.

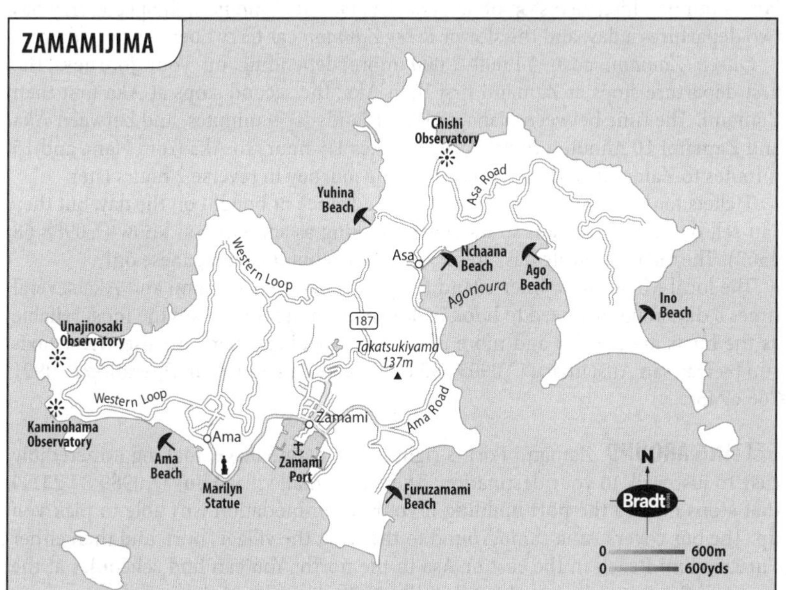

ZAMAMI FESTIVALS

Though Zamami and the Kerama as a whole are not big destinations for cultural experiences, Zamami's annual yacht race in early July is one of the biggest events in Okinawan sailing. International competitors come for this 28-mile race that begins in Ginowan on Okinawa-hontō, zips round the Kerama, and ends at Zamami Port. The village then hosts a festival of music, dancing, food and drink for competitors, visitors and locals. There's also a smaller, traditional sabani boat race between Zamami and Naha in late June.

The island also holds a Whale Music Festival in March, meant to send the whales back to the north with songs of the islands, and the summer Zamami Island Festival on the fourth Saturday of August, which features traditional performing arts and foods.

Since the 1970s, Zamami has been recognised internationally as a leading dive destination, with whales, sea turtles and remarkable reefs offering the Okinawa group's best diving and snorkelling. Today, most visitors come to Zamami for the award-winning white beaches and laid-back atmosphere, without exploring much further.

Springtime is when the island is at its best, when the humpback whales raise their young in the surrounding waters. Joining a whale-watching tour is a must, but you can also spot these graceful giants from afar, at some of the island's observatories (page 248). Elsewhere on land, most of the rugged landscape is given over to forests, largely made up of kuba palms, where native Kerama deer roam. Zamami is also home to the Ypthima masakii butterfly, endemic to the Ryūkyū, and the sword-tailed newt.

GETTING THERE AND AWAY Zamami is serviced by two ferries from Naha Tomari Port, both of which also stop off at Aka. The *Queen Zamami* high-speed ferry has two departures a day, and the slower *Ferry Zamami* car ferry operates once daily.

Queen Zamami costs ¥1,000–2,000 more depending on your journey. The first departure stops at Zamami first then Aka, the second stops at Aka first then Zamami. The time between Naha and the islands is 50 minutes, and between Aka and Zamami 10 minutes. *Ferry Zamami* takes 1½ hours to Aka from Naha and 15 minutes to Zamami, and then does the same journey in reverse 2 hours later.

Tickets for both ships can be reserved in advance or bought on the day, but they can sell out in high season so it's worth booking as soon as you know (☎0988 68 4567). The village website has a reservation form but it is in Japanese only.

The local Mitsushima inter-island ferry runs between Zamami and Aka several times a day. You don't need to book in advance, but it's not always the most reliable as the boats are smaller and more affected by weather. There are also water taxis run by Dai-san Anseimaru (☎0903 795 8467) and Zamami Tour Operation (☎0901 766 6745).

GETTING AROUND Zamami Port is right in the main village, making it incredibly easy to just walk to your destination. There is a small village **bus** (☎0989 87 2311) that stops next to the port building if your accommodation isn't able to pick you up. The bus covers Ama campground to the west, the village, port, and then either Furuzamami Beach in the east or Asa in the north. You can find schedules at the port and tickets can be bought at the village office vending machine.

Though the island looks large compared to nearby Geruma, it has few roads, all of which are navigable by moped. **Cycling** round the island is possible if your legs are up to it – there are some seriously steep hills that may make you regret the decision. The route to Ama Beach is flat and walkable in 20 minutes, but beaches like Yuhina are further afield and over steep hills. You can rent a **moped** from any of the local companies in Zamami village; it's quick to walk between them for price and vehicle comparisons. Some may stock higher CC bikes, others two-seaters and some plain old bicycles. There are also **car hire** options.

Vehicle rental

Charinko Bike Rental Ishikawa レンタルちゃりんこバイク石川; 83 Zamami; 0989 87 2202
Oceana Rental オセアナレンタル; 1945-2 Zamami; 0989 62 1999
Rental Bike Kaniku レンタルかにく; 1909 Zamami; 0989 87 2334; w kaniku.info
Rental Miyamura レンタルみやむら; 156 Zamami; 0905 129 6749
Zamami Rent-a-Car ざまみレンタカー; 13 Zamami; 0989 87 3250

TOURIST INFORMATION Zamami's tourism association has an excellent website, as well as a centre by the port terminal (座間味村観光協会; 95 Zamami; 0989 87 2277; w visit-zamami.com; 09.00–17.00 daily). They have maps, leaflets and paid-for baggage storage.

WHERE TO STAY

✷ **Kanusuba Zamami** (5 rooms) カーヌスバザマミ; 851-2 Zamami; 0989 96 3383; w kanusuba.jp. Zamami's only small luxury accommodation, Kanusuba is a stunning, relaxing space with brilliant restaurant, kind staff & large tasteful rooms full of sunlight. Free beach transport, marine equipment rental, tours with DRIFTER, bingata & shiisaa making, & more. B/fast inc. **$$$$**

Minshuku Yadokari (6 rooms) 民宿やどかり; 142 Ama; 0989 87 2231; w zamami-yadokari.com. Bright, breezy guesthouse with futon & Western rooms, majority shared showers. Hammocks, garden, cycle rental & free drinks. HB options available. **$$$**

✷ **Homestay Kucha** (3 rooms) 23 Asa; 0989 96 4781; w zamami-homestay.shopinfo.jp. One of Asa's only accommodation options, this sweet homestay is near the beach. Ideal for experiencing local culture, Kucha's tatami rooms are run by a local mum. Homemade meals, laundry & snorkel rental available. **$$**

Zamamia International Guesthouse (2 rooms, 2 dorms) 座間味インターナショナルゲストハウス; 126 Zamami; 0989 87 3626; w zamamia-guesthouse.com. Cheapest non-camping option on the island given its shoestring dormitories. Also has clean private rooms & is foreign-owned so English-friendly. **$$**

Ama Beach Campsite (campsite, 7 lodges) 阿真海岸キャンプ場; 697 Ama; 0989 87 3259; w vill.zamami.okinawa.jp. All-year camping at fully equipped campsite next to Ama Beach. Cold showers, no electronic equipment allowed & quiet time from 21.00, but shared kitchen, BBQ tables & cooking field. Book through village website. Closed during typhoons. Tents available. **$**

WHERE TO EAT AND DRINK

Kanusuba カーヌスバ; 851-2 Zamami; 0989 96 3383; w kanusuba.jp; 11.00–15.00 & 17.30–22.00 daily. The fanciest restaurant on Zamami is attached to a resort. B/fast bowls, BBQ lunches with island ingredients & *omakase* fine dining dinners. **$$$$$**

COCO Kitchen 128 Zamami; 0702 637 5065; 10.00–22.00 daily. Snack bar overlooking the beach, specialising in keema curries & local marlin. **$$**

Izakaya Ao-no-umi 南島酒楽青の海; 32 Zamami; 0989 96 2820; 18.00–22.00 Tue–Sun. Classic island dishes including sushi & modern takes like rafutee pork pizza. **$$**

Little Kitchen リトルキッチン; 29 Zamami; 0989 87 3070; 11.30–14.00 Fri–Mon, 18.00–

23.00 Thu–Tue. Very popular restaurant serving a much-needed mix of Western & Okinawan dishes. Daily specials like penne gorgonzola, steak with bourbon, & Zamami fish & chips. $$

Restaurant Marumiya レストランまるみ屋; 432-2 Zamami; 0989 87 3166; 11.00–14.30 & 18.00–22.30 Thu–Tue. Okinawan cuisine with local ingredients, including mozuku, Okinawa soba, juushii rice and chanpuruu in a handy English menu. $$

Healthy Dining Tanpopo ヘルシー食彩たんぽぽ; 76 Zamami; 0906 890 5727; 11.30–16.00 daily. Much-loved healthy dining restaurant using seasonal ingredients to make fresh onigiri, croquettes, saataa andagii & bentō. $

Wayama Mozuku 和山海雲ワヤマモズク; 9 Zamami; 0989 87 2069; w wayamamozuku.jp; 11.00–14.00 Wed–Mon. Lunchtime spot serving Zamami speciality mozuku noodles. $

✷ **Zamami Village Fisheries Co-operative** 座間味村漁業協同組合; 94 Zamami; 0989 87 2015; 08.30–17.30 (until sold out) daily. Arguably the best place for lunch on Zamami. Local fishermen bring their catch here in the wee hours, which is turned into deliciously cheap & incredibly fresh sashimi, tempura & donburi bowls ready for lunch. Tempura can be bought by the piece & plain rice on its own too. $

ENTERTAINMENT AND NIGHTLIFE

amulet zamami アミュレットザマミ; 153 Zamami; 0989 87 2861; w amulet.tokyo; 18.00–23.00 Wed–Mon. Modern(ish) bar serving cheap yakitori & drinks.

BAR303 125 Zamami; w bar303-japanese-izakaya-restaurant.business.site; 11.00–15.00 & 18.00–midnight daily. Charming izakaya with terrace that opens for lunch too.

La Toque ラ・トゥーク; 105 Zamami; 0989 87 3558; 18.00–22.00 Tue–Sun. Arguably the most popular bar on the island with excellent dinners & drinks. May need to book ahead.

✷ **Torajirou** 寅次郎; 382-1 Zamami; 0989 87 2388; 18.00–23.00 daily. Delightfully friendly ramshackle izakaya: think picnic benches in a welcoming, warm-lit shack. Takoyaki, fried cutlets, seafood & buzzing, drinking locals.

SHOPPING The main village has the 105 Store (105ストアー; 106 Zamami; 0989 87 2656; 07.00–21.00 daily), the island's largest shop where you can pick up food, alcohol, souvenirs and general goods. 105 is the only place to buy Zamami's own mountain peach sake, Zamami-no-Yamatoshū alcohol. There's also the smaller Komine Store (小嶺商店; 164 Zamami; 0989 87 2151; 07.00–20.00 daily) which is near the port, selling bentō, barbecue meat, vegetables and necessities. There are a fair few options for souvenir shopping, whether T-shirts, foodstuffs or photography.

KIRARI 82 Zamami; 0904 142 7213. Beautiful products from illustrator Yui Oe, depicting aspects of Zamami on T-shirts, postcards & phone cases.

Nagisa なぎさ; 94 Zamami; 0989 87 2233; 10.00–18.00 daily. A café & souvenir store by the port selling T-shirts, swimwear & snorkelling sets.

Petit Gallery Umimaru プチギャラリーうみまーる; 150 Ama; 0906 869 4213; w umima-ru.com/shop.html. Gallery shop of nature photographers, offering photos, postcards, calendars & more.

Zamami-Mun Market ざまみむん市場; 1-1 Zamami; 0705 536 3934; w zamamun.com; 09.00–17.00 daily. Ferry terminal shop selling Zamami products like mozuku seaweed, fruit jams & T-shirts.

Zamami Village Whale Watching Association 座間味村ホエールウォッチング協会; 1 Zamami; 0988 96 4141; w zwwa.okinawa; Dec–Apr 08.00–17.00 daily. Original goods, T-shirts, bags, postcards, foods.

SPORTS AND ACTIVITIES

Coral Divers コーラルダイバーズ; 421 Zamami; 0989 87 2930; w coraldivers.la.coocan.jp. Diving company with 30 years' experience offering fun, experience & licence dives.

Daikoku-maru 大黒丸; 88 Zamami; ☎0802 736 6320; w hoshizuna.sakura.ne.jp. Fishing tours operated by Pension Hoshizuna, with sashimi & grilled fish made on board from your catch.

Dive Centre NO-Y ダイブセンターノーイ; 878 Zamami; ☎0989 87 3262; w kerama-zamami.com. Snorkelling, diving & whale-watching tours.

Diving Anata-no-kiyoshi あなたの清; 167-1 Zamami; ☎0989 87 3023; w anatano-kiyoshi.okinawa. Diving & whale watching with dive photographer.

Diving Team Ushio 潮; 143 Zamami; ☎0989 87 3533; w divingteam-ushio.jp. Fun diving, diving licensing, snorkelling, & whale-watching tours.

GOODDAYS STANDUP 512-1 Ama; ☎0704 453 0135; w gooddaysstandup.com. Ama-based SUP, skin diving, snorkelling & whale-watching tours.

Kerama Kayak Centre ケラマカヤックセンター; 125-2 Zamami; ☎0988 96 4677; w keramakayak.jp. Sea kayaking, snorkelling & uninhabited island camping tours.

Marine Shop Heartland マリンショップハートランド; 105 Zamami; ☎0989 87 2978; w heartland105.com. Diving tours on 40-seat cruiser with kayak & whale-watching tours too.

NatureLand Kayak ネイチャーランド カヤックス; 434-3 Zamami; ☎0989 87 2187; w okinawakayak.jp. Sea kayaking tours with snorkelling included.

Noah ノア; 30 Zamami; ☎0906 859 5544; w noah-zamami.jp. Small group SUP, kayak & snorkel tours.

Zamami Sailing ザマミセーリング; 36 Zamami; ☎0989 87 2633; w zamami.net. Sailing on large catamaran with scuba, snorkel & sunset cruises.

Zamami Whale Watching Association 座間味村ホエールウォッチング協会; 1 Zamami; ☎0988 96 4141; w zwwa.okinawa. The definitive whale-watching tours on Zamami with sunset cruise opportunities. Operates during whale season only.

OTHER PRACTICALITIES Zamami has a single police box (座間味駐在所; 66 Zamami; ☎0988 36 0110), the Zamami clinic (沖縄県立南部医療センター; 441-1 Zamami; ☎0989 87 2024; w nanbuweb.hosp.pref.okinawa.jp), and a post office with ATM (座間味郵便局; 371-1 Zamami; ☎0989 87 2221; ⏲ 09.00–17.00 Mon–Fri, ATM: 08.45–17.30 Mon–Fri, 09.00–17.00 Sat–Sun).

WHAT TO SEE AND DO Coming into port you may clock the first of Zamami's sights before you've even arrived. **Takarakujira** (宝鯨) is a whale sculpture that leaps out of the harbour's western side, though is arguably better seen from land.

The ferry brings you to the heart of the island, the main village of **Zamami** (座間見). It's very much a lived-in village, not a tourist one, but you'll find all the shops, hotels, restaurants, rentals and hangouts you could want. At the very top of the village, which begins to quickly slope upwards into the wilderness, you'll find the **Peace Tower** (平和之塔) – a memorial to those who lost their lives in the Pacific War. It's also an excellent lookout over the village and bay, when foliage hasn't taken over.

Heading west out of the village, you'll first meet **Marilyn** (マリリンの像), Zamami's famous dog (page 252), immortalised in a statue. This cape is also a great place to see the sunset. Further along brings you to **Ama** (阿真), a small settlement around **Ama Beach** (阿真ビーチ). Ama is a beautifully shallow beach with turtles that come remarkably close to shore in high tide – it's one of the closest encounters you can get in the archipelago. The coral reef here is rich, plentiful and calm, though close to the surface at low tide so be careful, especially with young children. Furthermore, it has excellent facilities, and nearby recreation grounds and camping.

From here, Zamami is largely given over to trees and viewing spots. The road from Ama starts to steeply rise towards **Kaminohama Observatory** (神の浜展望台), a deck in Zamami's southwest with panoramic views of Ama Beach, the morphing sea and forest-green islands erupting from it. This section of water between Aka and Zamami is listed as a Wetland of International Importance. Being on the west with few tall trees around it, Kaminohama has become a famous sunset

MYTHS AND FOLKTALES: THE WHALES

There are a few island legends about how whales came to be, often involving cattle (page 336). The Kerama locals have one such tale.

The water buffalo on the islands were so lazy that, in the hopes of escaping working the fields, they begged to become whales. They thought a life in the oceans would be easier. However, as soon as their wish was granted, the god of the sea used them as beasts of burden at his palace. Hating this new position equally, the cow-whales escaped again.

This made the god of the sea very angry, so he sent orca whales after them. Now, when people hear the 'mooing' whale song as the animals migrate, they say it is the buffalo fearing that the orcas are coming to eat them.

spot. Similarly, **Unajinosaki Observatory** (女瀬の崎展望台) just north of it has excellent sunsets.

Heading around Zamami's ring road brings you to the small **Nita Observatory** (ニタ展望台) and then to **Inazaki Observatory** (稲崎展望台), a site that shows off the northern sea of Zamami where humpbacks are regularly observed during the December–April season. When there aren't frolicking whales to watch, you can also see Aguni, Tonaki and Kume islands on clear days.

The road from here splits, the right turn heading back to Ama, the left to the north of the main village. On this second road you can reach **Takatsukiyama** (高月山), a mountain reaching 137m that has views across the entire Kerama Strait, the archipelago and beaches. The observatories here are the highest on the island and are used for spotting whales. The first overlooks Zamami's Agono Bay, Tokashiki and even Okinawa-hontō on the horizon, while the second shows off Furuzamami Beach and uninhabited Amuro Island. During March–April the rhodedendrons on Takatsukiyama are in full, brilliant bloom, making for a glorious rest stop.

Back at the village, the eastern road brings you to **Furuzamami Beach** (古座間味ビーチ) and its observatory. This elegant 800m white stretch along the south coast is an award-winning beach and excellent snorkelling point for getting close to the tropical fish as the coral is so close to shore. There are showers, toilets and, in the high season, a small marine shop called Sunny Side (サニーサイド; 1743 Zamami; 0803 834 7565; w sunnyside-furuzamami.com; 08.30–17.00 daily) offers rentals.

The road from here runs around **Agonoura** (安護の浦), a stunning quiet bay, and the village of **Asa** (阿佐)– a supremely quiet place of fukugi trees and a few family households. This is said to be where Chinese trade ships stopped off before heading to Okinawa-hontō during the Ryūkyū era. Here is also the peaceful, pretty **Nchaana Beach** (ンチャーナの浜).

The road once again splits at this point, the left turn heading over to the other coast and little **Yuhina Beach** (ユヒナ浜). This beach has a big rock in its middle, which is said to bring blessings to any couple swearing their love on it. The right turn leads to **Chishi Observatory** (チシ展望台), which has views of rough, cliff-edged bays and blue seas.

From here, Zamami peters out into little-visited beaches, often because the road isn't always open or recommended for mopeds. If you do make it out to this peninsula, the collection of **Uhama** (大浜), **Ago Beach** (安護の浜) and **Inoo Beach** (イノー浜) are some of the most secluded and pristine sands you can find this close to Okinawa.

AKAJIMA

Aka (阿嘉島) sits sandwiched between Zamami to the north, Geruma to the south and Tokashiki to its east. Once a prosperous transit port during the Ryūkyū Kingdom's trading era, Aka, like its little sister Geruma, is today known for nature and diving. Its transparent seas and the excellent Nishi Beach attract day trippers, snorkellers and swathes of divers hoping to glimpse sea turtles. With over 50 dive sites around Aka, all 5–20 minutes by boat, it's ideal for those looking to pack quality and quantity in a short time.

One of the most unusual sites is Tomumooya Reef, off the south of Aka, which is home to strange stone structures including the so-called 'centre circle', said

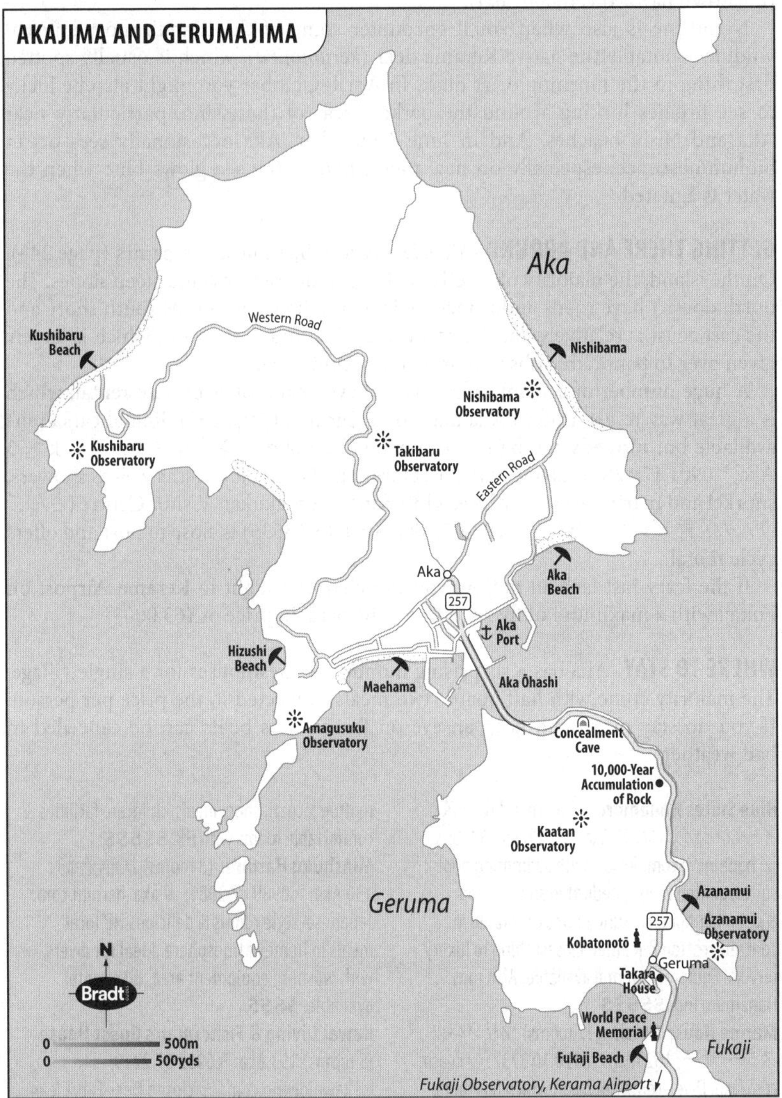

to be human-made, the Gusuku (Castle) rock with stair-like notches, and the small 'shrine', named after its resemblance to a place of worship. These unique formations have attracted attention from the local Akajima Marine Science Laboratory, which also studies coral reproduction and looks into restoration of the reef.

Although the Kerama are usually fitted in as a day trip, it's well worth incorporating an overnight stay on Aka into your schedule. This chilled, pretty island of around 200 people is undoubtedly small, but it's surprisingly lively thanks to its plethora of dive shops. The island comes alive at night, with vibrant local restaurants and bars and skies that light up with the Milky Way; stargazing is spectacular here, with shooting stars dashing across the darkness to the sound of the brown hawk-owl (*aobazuku*).

Nighttime is also when you'll encounter some of the island's most unusual wildlife – notably the native Kerama deer (*keramajika*), which is usually spotted first thing in the morning or at dusk. In April–October you might also be lucky to see fireflies lurking around the darker areas of the island, particularly near Aka and Nishi beaches. And in June–November, Aka occasionally sees ocean bioluminescence: especially on new moon nights, the sea glows blue when the water is agitated.

GETTING THERE AND AROUND Aka's ferries are the same as Zamami's (page 244). On the island, the majority of land is made up of dense forest and steep slopes. The north doesn't have roads and is inaccessible, but the village on its south shore and the east coast is relatively flat. There are a few inclines to the west, which is largely given over to panoramic observatories and secluded beaches.

A huge number of accommodations and even cafés offer **bicycle** rental, which is a great way to get around Aka and on to Geruma (page 253). Rental cars aren't available but **mopeds** can be found. Rental Shop Sho (レンタルショップしょう; 3 Aka; 0901 179 2839) is one of the best for mopeds and bicycles, as well as showers, snorkel and marine accessory hire, while Sango Yuntakukan Visitor Centre (さんごゆんたく館ビジターセンター; 936-2 Aka; 0989 87 3535) is close to port and offers cycle rental.

If the ferry just isn't an option, you can charter a flight to Kerama Airport on Fukaji with a maximum of five people for the bargain price of ¥63,000.

WHERE TO STAY Aka has a surprising number of guesthouses for a single village. The majority come with half board (two meals), reflected in the price per person. If you do stay overnight, keep an eye on forecasts as boats can be cancelled in bad weather.

Blue Suites Hanamuro (3 rooms) ブルースイーツ・ハナムロ; 91 Aka; 0906 857 5430; w hanamuro.com. Resort with swimming pool suites, garden rooms, dedicated spa, rooftop & open bar hour. En-suite rooms decorated in concrete, cotton & leather; closest thing to luxury on Aka. Equipment rental available. Also runs Hanamuro Inn. **$$$$$**

Marine House Seasir (17 rooms) マリンハウスシーサー; 162 Aka; 0120 10 2737; w seasir.com/aka. Diver-centric pension which has tours, rooftop jacuzzi, shop, meals, childcare facilities & comfortable rooms with HB. **$$$$$**

Minshuku Harumi (8 rooms) 民宿春海; 130 Aka; 0989 87 2081; w aka-harumi.com. Japanese-style rooms & delicious HB local meals in homey atmosphere. Ideal for divers, with washing equipment area. Bike rental available. **$$$$**

Kawai Diving & Fisherman's Guest House (5 rooms) 153 Aka; 0989 87 2219; w kawaidiving.com; closed Dec–Feb. Clean single, couple & family Japanese rooms or larger options with sea view & excellent fish meals. HB. **$$$**

Minshuku Suehiro (4 rooms) 民宿末広; 94 Aka; 0989 87 3170; w eonet.ne.jp/~kasumi-suehiro. Quiet & welcoming, this is Aka's cheapest accommodation option (no meals) so is popular for budget-friendly travellers. Landlady is full of knowledge too. **$$**

WHERE TO EAT AND DRINK There are lots of little eateries around the village, all of which are local and serving up fresh fish and cheap meals.

Akajima Café Guu Guu あかじまのカフェとごはんguu guu; 53 Aka; 11.00–18.00 Fri–Tue, 11.00–14.30 Wed. Cute, wooden-décor, 10-seat café serving prettily presented food & drinks on Okinawan pottery. $$

Haana Café はぁなカフェ; 61 Aka; 0989 87 2104; 09.00–18.00 daily. Outdoor terrace & indoor café serving pizza & pasta meals. Also cheap bike rental. $$

Yonamine House ヨナミネハウス; 144 Aka; 0988 96 4786; summer 19.00–midnight Wed–Mon. Bar in a remodelled 100-year-old house serving beers, shots, cocktails & snacks. Occasionally irregular hours outside summer months. $$

✷ **Zamami Village Fishery Co-operative** 座間味村漁協; 60-4 Aka; 10.00–16.00 daily. Similar to its compatriot on Zamami (page 246), Aka's fishermen bring their morning's catch to this humble co-operative where it's quickly made into exquisitely fresh donburi sushi bowls, tempura, onigiri & more for an extraordinarily good-value price. $

SHOPPING Aka has a few shops for picking up ingredients and take-away if you don't have meals included in your accommodation. The east of the village has Kakihana Shōten (垣花商店; 256 Aka; 0989 87 2089; summer 08.00–21.00, winter 08.30–20.00 daily) while the west has Nakamura Shōten (中村商店; 159 Aka; 0989 87 2018; 08.00–22.00 daily). Neither has a huge selection, but enough to get you through a day or two. For souvenirs, the island has an entirely online gallery, the Kerama Museum of Art (w keramabi.thebase.in), where you can find a small selection of items to buy.

SPORTS AND ACTIVITIES Aka has a huge number of dive shops, but Kawai and Marine House Seasir stand out for English-language accessibility. However, if you are a more experienced diver who doesn't need hefty instruction, the rest should suffice.

Diving Blue Planet ブループラネット; 137 Aka; 0989 87 3965; w blueplanet-aka.com. Offering more unusual dive spots like Kuba, Yakabi & Ou islands.

Earthship Kerama アースシップ慶良間; 1239 Aka; 0909 050 2584; w peraichi.com/landing_pages/view/eskerama/. Snorkelling, sea kayak & cycle rentals which can be delivered to port.

Kawai Diving 153 Aka; 0989 87 2219; w kawaidiving.com. The best of the dive shops for English-language accessibility & accommodation inclusivity.

Marine House Seasir マリンハウスシーサー; 162 Aka; 0120 10 2737; w seasir.com/aka. English-friendly dive shop with on-site store for diving, snorkelling & souvenirs.

OTHER PRACTICALITIES Aka has no police box but has a clinic (沖縄県立南部医療センター; 441-1 Zamami; 0989 87 2002; 09.00–11.30 & 14.00–16:30 Mon–Wed & Fri, 09.00–11.30 Thu). There's also the Aka post office with ATM (阿嘉郵便局; 68 Aka; 0989 87 2101; 09.00–17.00 Mon–Fri, ATM: 08.45–17.30 Mon–Fri, 09.00–17.00 Sat).

SHIRO AND MARILYN

One morning in 1986, Aka residents the Nakamuras realised their dog Shiro was missing. All day they looked for him, until he returned late at night and soaking wet. This started to happen regularly, so the Nakamuras decided to follow him and find out where he was going. Shiro headed to the beach, jumped into the water and started swimming. Mr Nakamura followed in his boat and after 3 hours and 2 miles, Shiro reached Zamami Island. He walked up to a house – their old neighbour's house – and waited. A beautiful dog, Marilyn, appeared and the two pranced off playing.

The Nakamuras had moved from Zamami to Aka that summer and Shiro had missed his girlfriend so much that he swam back throughout the week to see her. The pair became known to locals and eventually throughout Japan, even inspiring a film. Decades after both dogs died, their statues stand waiting on each island: Shiro on Aka and Marilyn on Zamami.

WHAT TO SEE AND DO Coming into Aka by ferry, the first thing you'll see is **Aka Ōhashi** (阿嘉大橋), the big bridge connecting Aka and Geruma. This bridge has great views of the seas around the Kerama, which are so clear you can sometimes spot turtles in the water. In the square by Aka's ferry terminal you'll find the **Shiro Statue** (シロの像). This dog from Aka became famous for swimming to Zamami to meet his girlfriend, a dog called Marilyn (see above). Nearby is the **Sango Yuntakukan National Park Visitor Centre** (さんごゆんたく館慶良間諸島国立公園ビジターセンター; 936-2 Aka; ☎ 0989 87 3535; e sango@yuntaku-kan.jp; ⏲ 09.00–17.00 daily), where you can learn about the ecology of Kerama's coral and ocean. It also acts as Aka's tourist centre, offering luggage storage, coffees, ice creams and maps.

Heading west, you come to **Maehama** (前浜), a beach flanked by Aka's village, restaurants, accommodations and cafés. It's not a swimming beach (though you'll see locals use it) as there are stonefish lurking near the shore. It's also under the watchful eye of concrete bridges and ports, but is a great place for lunch. The village itself is full of narrow sand paths, old red-roof houses and stone fences. It's a peaceful place to meander, but 10 minutes is more than enough to see it all. While walking, look out for **Urunnoki** (御殿の木), a massive tree opposite the school. It has been on Aka for over 400 years, reaching 13m high and a spread that's 17m at its widest, and has been a protected place of worship for centuries.

Continuing past Maehama brings you to a steep slope that leads to **Amagusuku Observatory** (天城展望台) which shows off Tokashiki and Keruma, as well as the bridges connecting them. North of this is **Hizushi Beach** (ヒズシビーチ) on the west coast. Walkable from port, the beach is in a calm bay with Kumajima in front of you. Hizushi is not an official swimming beach because you quickly move past the coral reef into strong currents, but it is a quiet, picturesque stop ideal for sunset.

In Aka's centre is **Takibaru Observatory** (タキバル展望台), which gives a 360-degree view of the green island and its neighbours. It's surrounded by Kerama deer habitat and mountain paths full of Kerama azalea (*tsutsuji*), which blooms beautifully come spring. **Kushibaru Observatory** (後原展望台) is Aka's westernmost observatory and is known for its remarkable sunsets. Near the deck is **Kushibaru Beach** (クシバルビーチ).

The north of the island isn't traversable. To get to the east, you have to travel back via the port. The east coast itself is largely given over to **Nishibama** (北浜),

the only swimming beach on the island. A brilliant 1km arc of white and cyan, with a horizon flecked by uninhabited islands, Nishibama is a great snorkel, scuba and skin diving point for seeing colourful corals and fish. It's only 10 minutes' cycle from the port, making it ideal for day trippers. Swimming season technically runs April–November, 08.30–17.30, as there are guards, shops and bathroom facilities during this time. You can get a wider view of the beach and islands at nearby **Nishibama Observatory** (北浜展望台). Back towards port is the smaller **Aka Beach** (阿嘉ビーチ), another non-swimming, sunbathing spot; look out for *murasaki* (purple) hermit crabs under the nearby adan tree.

GERUMAJIMA

Connected to Aka by a bridge, Geruma (慶留間島, occasionally and confusingly called Keruma) is the smallest inhabited island within the Kerama. Just 5km around, it's a sleepy little spot that a handful of people call home. Once a 17th-century transit area for trade ships, Geruma became a boatman's village and hasn't much changed since.

The tranquil village in the south features fukugi trees, traditional coral walls and red-roofed houses that are typical of Okinawa. One of these is the well-preserved **Takara House** (高良家住宅; ⌚ 09.00–17.00 Tue–Sun; adult/child ¥300/160), which is a nationally designated important cultural property. Originally thatched but now tiled, it's a 19th-century residence said to be built by a chief boatman of the local trade routes. The village here suffered little damage in the war, leaving it to posterity, and the lifestyle here remains slow and peaceful, with tourism based on embracing laid-back mindfulness.

Fittingly, then, the rest of Geruma is given over to nature. Its fan palm forest is one of only a few protected areas for *keramajika* deer, which were originally brought over from Kagoshima (then Satsuma). Over the centuries, the deer have become a separate species, adapting to their island home with larger eyes, darker fur and a smaller size than their mainland cousins. The kuba palms that form the deer's habitat have also carved out their own niche, being used in a variety of ways by the locals: the plant's young buds are edible, while the leaves are turned into thatch or sabani boat sails. During the Ryūkyū era, Geruma was a source of many kuba products, sent as tribute to the king.

Geruma has just one proper road, which only arcs round the right-hand side of the island – the left is inaccessible forest. On the north of this road just after the bridge, you can find **Concealment Cave** (秘匿壕), a suicide boat hideaway left over from the war. Geruma has some surprisingly dramatic mountains, steep sea cliffs and strata. One such is the lengthily named **10,000-Year Accumulation of Rock** (万年累積の岩石), a colourful geological formation where a great chunk of grey cliffside on the northeast road is shot through with slabs of intrusive orange rock.

In the centre, at the end of a slim and very steep road, is **Kaatan Observatory** (カータン展望台), a small outlook that takes in some of the typically stunning sea, its coral-laden cobalt dotted with peaked islets. Geruma has a smattering of white beaches – **Azanamui** (アザナムイの浜) in the south by the town is the largest, with **Azanamui Observatory** (アザナムイ展望台) overlooking it and Fukaji Island. Just south of here is the village, where you'll find the Takara House and a small elementary and junior high school, whose entire register can often be counted on two hands.

There's also a monument on its northwest side, up a hilly side street, called **Kobatonotō** (小鳩の塔). This is dedicated to the 53 Kerama locals killed in the US seizure of the island. Some 33 children, including 13 from Geruma, died alongside their families in mass suicides. Geruma also has a historic connection to Ie Island (page 204) from this time; 450 Ie residents were sent to Geruma to live with the remaining locals while reconstruction efforts began after the war's close.

Geruma is connected by bridge to **Fukaji** (外地島), a southern uninhabited island home to the Kerama Airport. It's incredibly rare to use this airport (the cheaper ferries being favoured) but it's worth heading to Fukaji to see its panoramic observation deck and beaches. **Fukaji Observatory** (外地展望台) is sometimes used by whale-watching companies for spotting humpbacks in the water, while **Fukaji Beach** (外地の浜) is used by sea turtles for laying eggs. By the Fukaji side of the bridge is the austere **World Peace Memorial** (世界平和祈念碑), which marks the landing point of US forces on 26 March 1945 and commemorates the lives lost. The islet to Fukaji's south, **Mokaraku** (モカラク島), is a great diving spot too.

PRACTICALITIES Getting to Geruma is as simple as crossing the bridge from Aka, which affords views over both islands and Sakubaru Kigan (さくばる奇岩) – a tail of rocky isles that puncture the ocean off Aka, surrounded by fishing and dive spots. Bicycles are the easiest way to get around (page 250; with just one road, there's not much use for a car) but you can also walk it.

Few people stay on Geruma, choosing instead to stay on Aka, but there's a single accommodation on the island, Marine Service & Lodge Geruma (マリンサービス ペンションゲルマ; 60 Geruma; ☎ 0989 87 2976; **w** geruma.com; HB inc; **$$**). This budget pension has twin rooms with half board and, as the name suggests, also offers diving tours. There's also a single restaurant, Trattoria Geruma Niyon (Torattoria 慶留間Gnon ゲルマニヨン; 54 Geruma; ⏰ 12.00–15.00 & 19.00–late, reservation required; **$$$$$**), serving up Italian-inspired dishes made with local fish and ingredients.

7

The Miyako Islands

In the middle of Okinawa and Yaeyama, between Iriomote's rain-dripped grit and Naha's debatable glitz, lies the sparkling Miyako group (宮古列島): the archipelago's mellow bunch of surf spots and shining white sands. It's known for its marine scene, whether that's award-winning beaches, unique and unbeatable dive spots, or free-diving caves. There's excellent fishing and aquaculture, with Irabu seeing year-round bonito catch. The islands' indigenous creature is also sea-based: the Miyakosawagani crab.

About 290km from Okinawa-hontō, Miyako not only has its own rich history, but has also helped reconstruct the history and culture of the entire Nansei-shotō. Unlike Okinawa, Miyako and its southern neighbours were relatively undamaged by World War II, leaving them as better monuments to the archipelago's past. What has been found archaeologically and architecturally on the Miyako (and also the Yaeyama; page 291) dates to around two centuries later than Okinawan finds: a result of later introduction on to the southern islands.

Evidence suggests that trading vessels have used the Sakishima Islands (Miyako and Yaeyama) as reference points and stop-offs along sea routes since the 13th century. Traditional stories tell of heroes coming to the island and bringing with them culture and sophistication to reform the Miyako natives, and conversely of locals travelling abroad to gain wealth and glory. Often Okinawans play the hero in these tales and the southerly Yaeyama natives play the villains. These prescribed roles were likely influenced by the Ryūkyū Kingdom and Okinawans themselves. The Sakishima have always lagged behind Okinawa in terms of development and ideas thanks to their outlying geography, which resulted in the Okinawans viewing those in the south as simple and rusticated. This sense of inferiority shows up in Sakishima arts, where themes of isolation from the capital on Okinawa-hontō abound. Miyako songs and poems often feature tragedy, abandonment, revenge, poverty and cruelty.

Miyakojima is the main island, the biggest by far, and the poster boy of the group. It has thriving agriculture, producing sugarcane, tobacco, beef, tropical fruits and vegetables. Of the seven other inhabited islands, Ōjima in the northeast and Taramajima and its tiny neighbour Minna way out west are unconnected to Miyakojima by road. The rest are joined through architecturally astonishing (and indeed record-breaking) bridges. This makes Miyako one of the easiest groups to fully explore, popping from beach to beach to beach along the endless coastline.

HISTORY

It's thought the Miyako Islands were united as a group in the 14th century. In the 15th century, Miyakojima-born Nakasone Tuyumya (Toyomiya in Japanese) fought and won against the Yaeyama rebel Oyake Akahachi on behalf of the Ryūkyū king Shō Shin. Nakasone was rewarded with leadership of the Sakishima, making

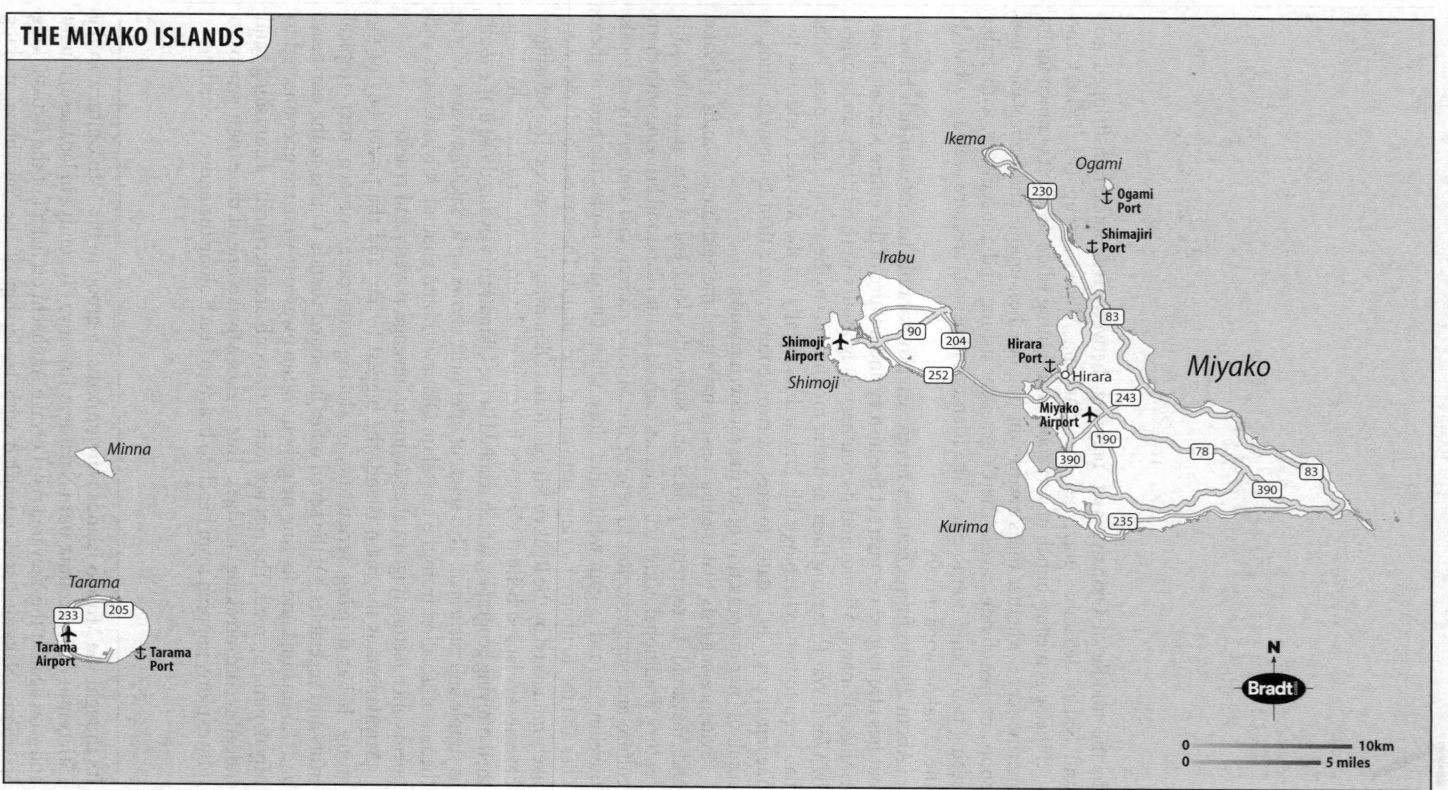
THE MIYAKO ISLANDS
Ikema
Ogami
230
Ogami Port
Shimajiri Port
Irabu
83
90
204
Shimoji Airport
Hirara Port
Hirara
Miyako
252
Shimoji
243
Miyako Airport
190
Minna
78
390
83
390
235
Kurima
Tarama
205
233
Tarama Airport
Tarama Port
N
Bradt
0
10km
0
5 miles

him the first Miyako ruler under the Ryūkyū Kingdom. The disparity between Miyako and Okinawa began to shrink under Shō Shin, who increased inter-island communication, but even today Miyako tends to lag behind Okinawa.

After the head tax was introduced in 1637 under Shimazu rule (page 11) – which Miyako islanders were forced to pay in crops for men and traditional Miyako jōfu woven cloth (page 27) for women – Miyako experienced several centuries of hardships, like the Yaeyama in the south. The head tax had islanders and farmers protesting regularly, an earthquake in 1667 sank parts of Miyakojima by 90cm, there were regular food shortages and smallpox spread through the island. (Miyako introduced a very early form of smallpox vaccine in the 1760s.) Then came the 1771 Great Meiwa Tsunami, with 5–10m waves that washed away four villages, killing an estimated 2,548 in the Miyako group. In the 20th century, Miyakojima also suffered badly during World War II (page 12).

MIYAKOJIMA

Miyakojima epitomises the Japanese term *nonbiri*, best translated as 'carefree' or 'leisurely': islanders live for the time when they can ditch the workwear and zip up the wetsuits, grab the golf clubs or head to their favourite bar for beer and a chunky

MIYAKO FESTIVALS

Miyako is full of festivals: there are multiple lion dance celebrations, a tug-of-war held at Bon, and the Kawamitsu bo-odori, a stick dance originating in a 1686 plague designed to get rid of evil. There's also the Kagisuma Music Convention in May, an annual event held across the island.

The most exciting (and arguably fun) festival is the Paantu. This UNESCO-recognised local event happens annually in September or October and involves a masked, mangrove-dwelling spirit called Paantu. This supernatural spirit descends on the village dressed in leaves, grasses and mud from a sacred well, and brings luck to inhabitants with their evil-banishing mud. Paantu were once celebrated throughout the islands but they are now limited to Miyakojima and a few small southerly islands, with a large two-day festival each year.

It is believed that anyone or anything splashed or swiped with Paantu mud will be spiritually cleansed and blessed with good luck. Nothing is spared; cars, buildings, old people, policemen and tourists all get the sacred mud treatment. In recent years, the latter have caused problems; some tourists have caused overcrowding, while others haven't got into the muddy spirit at all (cameras aren't guaranteed safety) and have complained. The dates of the festival are therefore kept secret until a few days before the celebration.

Noro priestesses from Miyako villages also join in, dressing up with sugar palms and carrying camphor sticks. They join the dressed-up Paantu and perform good luck rituals alongside them. Unfortunately the festival seems to be slowly fading out as people are less inclined to be involved, the number of noro priestesses dwindles, and the population ages and fewer children are born.

The Miyakojima City Museum has exhibits about the Paantu and the guides there will often know the exact dates of the upcoming festival. If you miss the festival, you can see signs of the Paantu dotted around Miyakojima – decorating shops in town and on the Batarazu Bridge in the Shimajiri mangroves.

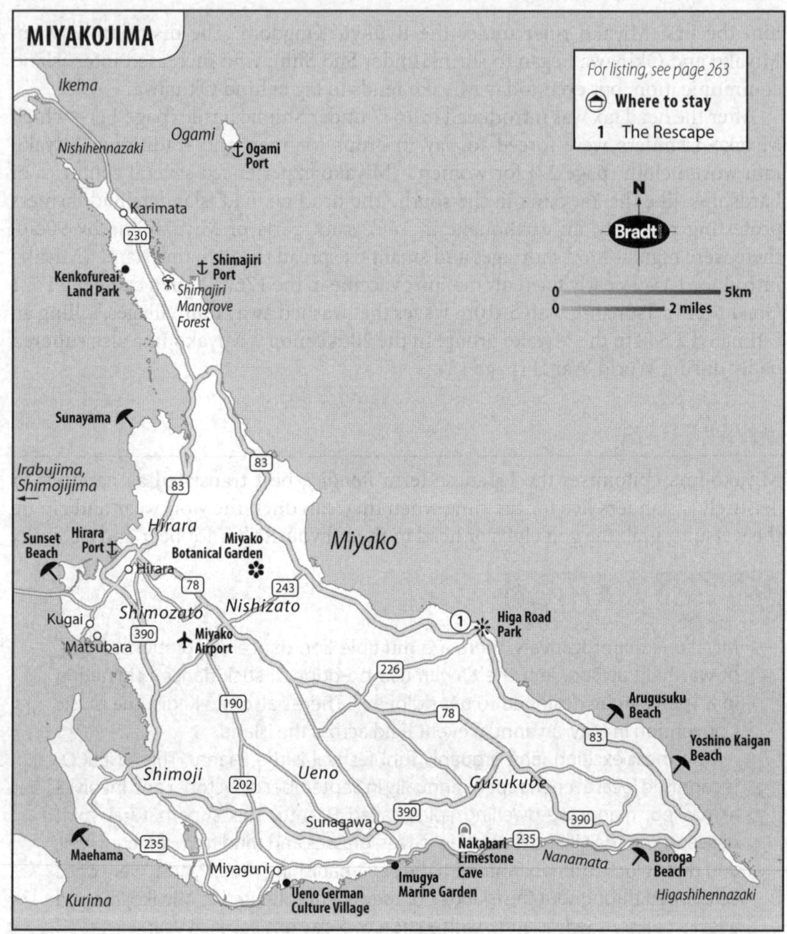

satapanbin doughnut (pages 278 and 281). It's about as far from Tokyo salaryman life as you can get.

And who can blame them? Miyako is home to the best beaches in Japan. Stretches of white seem to drift on the blue horizon, where kite-surfers kick over the waves and free-divers plunge below them. All throughout the waters are colourful coral, turtles, caves and critters. Though most tourists come for the beaches and sea, Miyako has many traditional sacred and natural sites, such as caves, wells, springs and tombs.

HISTORY The earliest written recognition of Miyakojima came in the 1300s, when clans across the island were in constant battle for domination. At this time, islanders lived a very simple life with primitive agriculture, tools and travel, but little else is known of them. The mythic stories that chart the introduction of modernised equipment and life always come from elsewhere: Okinawa, China and Japan.

During the late 1700s to 1800s, two British ships and one German came to Miyakojima, one of each nationality running aground. The islanders helped the hapless foreigners, earning accolades and distinctions in Europe as a great and kind people. Another famous maritime feat occurred in 1905, during a critical stage of the Russo-Japanese war. Japan had been unable to find Russia's naval fleet, but Miyakojima islanders sighted ships heading for the war zone. Their discovery would be crucial to Japanese success, but there was no way of telegraphing from Miyakojima – the closest transmitter was on Ishigaki. Five fishermen from Hisamatsu in Hirara were selected to row their small vessel the 100 miles to Ishigaki. They arrived the next day to discover that patrol cruises had also spotted and reported the fleet just hours before their arrival. Still, their efforts were considered essential to the resulting victory and they were lauded throughout Japan – the incident was turned into a tale called 'The Five Brave Warriors of Hisamatsu', told volubly at the time to rouse nationalistic pride.

THE MUDAN INCIDENT

In 1871, Miyako locals were victims of a brutal incident that set off global repercussions. Four tribute ships returning from Shuri, two from Miyako and two from Yaeyama, were hit by a typhoon and blown off course. One Yaeyama ship was lost, while the other landed on the west coast of Taiwan. Here they found help from Qing Dynasty officials who delivered them back home. Of the two Miyako ships, one made it home but the other shipwrecked off southeastern Taiwan, just north of today's Nanren Nature Reserve.

What occurred to the latter was pieced together by survivor accounts, but details are hazy – especially as the parties involved did not have their own writing systems and were therefore reliant on Japanese interpreters who would later use the incident to their own ends. It seems, however, that three of the ship's 69 passengers drowned, but the remaining 66 made it to shore and encountered two Chinese men who warned them against the Paiwan indigenous tribe. These Chinese men then robbed the Miyako survivors and left.

The Miyako people headed west and met the Paiwan people, who brought them to Kuskus village and provided them with food, water and shelter. It's said offering water was a symbol of protection. However, the survivors claimed that they were robbed in the night and in the morning were told to remain while armed hunters left to find food. Fearing the hunters and rumours of head hunting, the Miyako people left and sheltered at the house of a nearby Chinese serviceman. The Paiwan tribe found them; they dragged them from the house and slaughtered 54 of them. The survivors stayed hidden in the serviceman's home, before being moved, ransomed and sheltered in a Hakka settlement. They were taken back to Naha (via Fuzhou) in July 1872.

It's uncertain why the tribe attacked, but it has been suggested that the Miyako people accidentally offended them by taking protection then disappearing. Originally Japan was seemingly uninterested in the massacre, and the still independent Ryūkyū Kingdom did not ask Japan for help or vengeance – in fact the kingdom thanked the Qing government for the survivors' return. However, the kingdom was subsumed into Japan months later and Japan began demanding the Qing government take responsibility. They refused, citing they had no jurisdiction over the indigenous people.

The Mudan Incident was then used as an excuse for Japan's invasion of Taiwan in 1874 – the first deployment of the Imperial Japanese army and navy. The invasion resulted in the Peking Agreement, which cemented Japan's rule over Ryūkyū, but also showed Qing's weaknesses. This influenced the French invasion of Taiwan in 1884 and arguably Japan's later reoccupation in 1895.

In around 1944, in the closing chapter of World War II, some 30,000 Japanese troops were stationed across Miyakojima. However, the seas around Miyakojima were controlled by British and US forces, cutting off food, transport and mainland supplies. The island's 53,000 residents were required to share food and crops, resulting in both famine and forced relocations: some 10,000 were sent to Taiwan and Kyūshū. Those who remained (including soldiers) faced not only warfare but malaria too.

In 1945, a British fleet bombarded Miyakojima and most of Hirara was burned to the ground. Miyakojima was also the departure site of several kamikaze fighters, who sank the destroyer *Callaghan* in 1945. The result is some 66 war sites left on the island, including dugouts and bunkers.

GETTING THERE AND AWAY Miyakojima is only accessible by plane, with short regular hops to Miyako Airport (☎ 0980 72 1212; w miyakoap.co.jp) from Okinawa-hontō (45mins), Ishigaki (25mins) and across the mainland.

The airport is roughly 6km from the main town and port, locally called Hirara (it was uselessly renamed Miyakojima). Buses to and from the airport are few and far between, so you will likely find yourself with time to kill on departure or arrival; there's a great JA Atarasu Farmers' Market (あたらす市場; 1440-1 Nishizato; ☎ 0980 72 2972; w ja-okinawa.or.jp; ⏲ 09.00–18.00 daily) less than 10 minutes' walk away for grabbing snacks and last-minute souvenirs. Timetables are available at the airport tourist information counter, bus and inter-island port terminals. If you prefer to take a taxi, you can pick one up from the stand at the airport or book with Kyoei Taxi (協栄タクシー; ☎ 0980 72 3091), who also run the bus company.

GETTING AROUND Miyako island is a splat: a sand-scattered egg dropped between the Yaeyama and Okinawa. It's surrounded by six islands, four of which are connected by impressive bridges – the sizeable Irabu and Shimoji to the northwest, Ikema on the northeast tip and Kurima in the southwest.

The main town of Hirara is on the north coast, with the airport to its south. There is a much smaller port in the north, Shimajiri, that services Ōgamijima Island. The big beaches are Sunayama on the north coast and Maehama (also Maepama or Maebama) on the west; the south is mostly given over to agriculture and golf resorts.

Bus lines do cover the majority of Miyako but are scarce. The lines take in Maehama, the German Village, Kurima, and Yonahama, but stop an hour's walk short of Higashihennazaki and don't go towards Sunayama. They're operated by Kyoei Bus (協栄バス; ☎ 0980 72 3091; w 385kyoei.com/route) and you can find maps and timetables online.

Given the painful public transport, the best way to see Miyako is to get yourself a hire **car**, or **motorbike** if you prefer. Apart from Tarama and Minna, all the islands are connected by bridges, making it the most easily accessible group by car. If using a motorbike – or indeed bicycle – take care on the bridges as they can experience high winds.

If you only have a few days on Miyako and don't fancy going further afield, you can **cycle** around town and to the beaches of Maehama and Sunayama. It's a longer trek to Maehama, but doable if you have the energy. Most accommodations offer cycle rental.

Vehicle rental

BIGJOY Miyakojima 宮古島; 827-2 Higashinakasone, Hirara; ☎ 0903 796 4336; w miyakojiman.com. Motorbike, scooter & cycle rental.

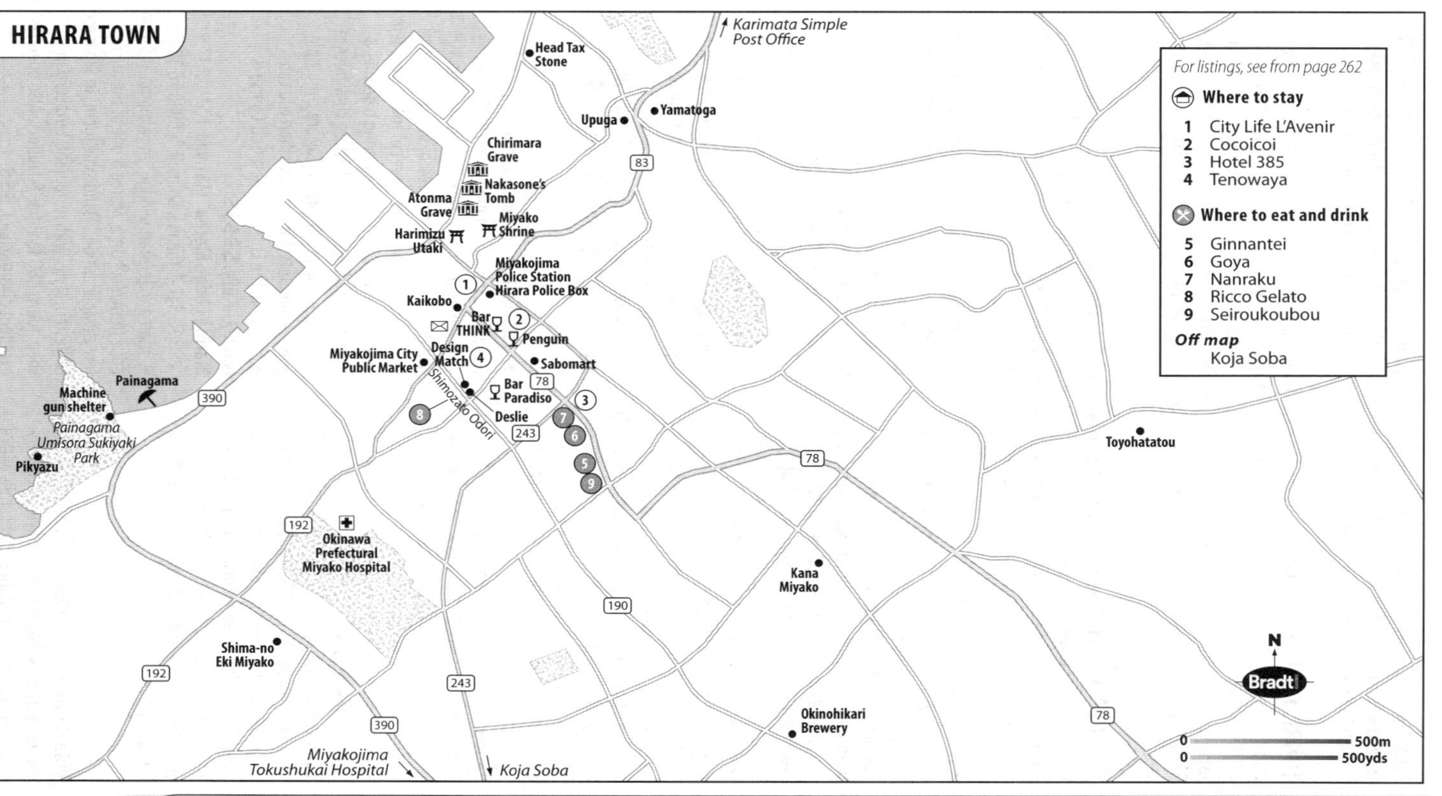
HIRARA TOWN
For listings, see from page 262
Where to stay
1 City Life L'Avenir
2 Cocoicoi
3 Hotel 385
4 Tenowaya
Where to eat and drink
5 Ginnantei
6 Goya
7 Nanraku
8 Ricco Gelato
9 Seiroukoubou
Off map
Koja Soba
Karimata Simple Post Office
Head Tax Stone
Upuga
Yamatoga
Chirimara Grave
Nakasone's Tomb
Atonma Grave
Miyako Shrine
Harimizu Utaki
Miyakojima Police Station
Hirara Police Box
Kaikobo
Bar THINK
Penguin
Sabomart
Miyakojima City Public Market
Design Match
Bar Paradiso
Deslie
Shimozato Odori
Painagama
Machine gun shelter
Painagama Umisora Sukiyaki Park
Pikyazu
Okinawa Prefectural Miyako Hospital
Shima-no Eki Miyako
Kana Miyako
Okinohikari Brewery
Toyohatatou
Miyakojima Tokushukai Hospital
Koja Soba
83
78
390
243
192
190
N
Bradt
0 500m
0 500yds

ORIX Rental Car オリックスレンタカー; Miyako Airport, 1657-128 Shimozato, Hirara; 0980 73 5500; w car.orix.co.jp/eng

Times Rental Car タイムズカー 宮古空港店; Miyako Airport, 2203-1 Shimozato, Hirara; 0980 73 0515; w rental.timescar.jp

TOURIST INFORMATION Tourist information is thin on the ground here, despite there being plenty to do. The Miyako Airport Tourist Information Centre (観光案内所; 0980 79 6611; 07.30–20.00 daily) is unmanned, but has plenty of English-language leaflets and information to go on. You can also call the Miyakojima Tourist Association direct (0980 73 1881). Your best bet for information is via your accommodation.

WHERE TO STAY The majority of people stay in Hirara, but if you're looking to be closer to beaches or golf courses, you'll want to head further north or down south. Many of the hotels in Hirara are your standard high-rise options with business-like rooms – clean but a little lacking in character.

Hirara *Map, page 261*

Hotel 385 (37 rooms) ホテル 385; 561 Nishizato; 0980 79 0998; w hotel-385.com. Stylish 3-star hotel in the heart of Hirara with handsome, welcoming wood-finished rooms. Balconies provide city views & all rooms are en suite with kitchenettes. Spacious, clean & modern throughout, 385 also includes Asian b/fasts, complimentary laundry & optional rentals. Free parking. **$$$$$**

City Life L'Avenir (9 apts) シティライフ宮古ラヴニール; 176-2 Nishizato; 0980 72 2620; w resortlife.co.jp/lavenir. Pristine, broad & modern apts with both Western & Japanese-style rooms. Terraces with sea or city views, dining areas, fitted kitchens (dishwasher, microwave, toaster, kettle) & en suites. Hotel has restaurant & wellness centre & offers car rental. **$$$**

Tenowaya (2 rooms & dorm) てのわや; 2F 263-2 Nishizato; 0807 986 5159; w tenowaya.link. A beautifully kept & decorated guesthouse; minimalist wood décor, big kitchen, communal spaces & laundry. Dorms, private rooms & entire house available. **$$**

Cocoicoi (6 rooms) ゲストハウスココイコイ; 218-3 Nishizato; 0980 79 7122; w cocoikoi.com. Cocoicoi is a small guesthouse with a range of minimalist but clean rooms, including dorms, twin & dbl. Communal areas of fully kitted kitchen, small lounge, covered roof terrace, laundry & bathrooms. **$**

North

Villa Rikyu (3 rooms) Villa 離宮; 676-7 Nikadori, Hirara; 0120 60 5888; w villa-rikyu.jp. Entirely private luxury accommodation that comes with a free rental car (taxi needed for airport). A variety of rooms close to Sunayama Beach, with private pools, ocean/sunset views, huge lounge & kitchen spaces, terrace, BBQ & multiple Japanese or Western bedrooms. **$$$$$**

✱ **Guesthouse Koa** (9 rooms) 宮古島ゲストハウスコア; 504-1 Nikadori, Hirara; 0980 79 9768; w guesthousekoa.okinawa. A walk from Sunayama Beach, this pretty, clean, beach-themed guesthouse is remarkably friendly, with impromptu BBQ, drink & games get-togethers in the garden & communal rooms including kitchen. Excellent hosts & a change from Hirara. Offers marine tours & equipment & car rental. **$$$**

South

✱ **Miyakojima Tokyu** (242 rooms) 宮古島東急; 914 Yonaha, Shimoji; 0980 76 2109; w tokyuhotels.co.jp/miyakojima-h. Next to world-famous Maehama Beach, Tokyu is an oasis in an otherwise unexciting part of town. Decadent rooms are fully kitted out, featuring balconies & en suites. Facilities include shuttles, convenience store, laundromat, children's play area, multiple good restaurants & more tours than you can possibly do. The Emerald Coast Golf Course is handily nearby. **$$$$$**

Marine Lodge Marea (46 rooms) マリンロッジマレア; 847-3 Yonaha, Shimoji; 0980 76 3850; w marea.co.jp/marinelodge_miyakojima. A 5-min drive from Maehama, Marea is one of the area's few cheaper options. Handsome rooms in Japanese & Western style, with restaurant, terrace, garden, shop, tours, BBQ facilities & laundry. Also operates excellent diving school. **$$$**

East

✷ **The Rescape** [map, page 258] (38 rooms) ザ・リスケープ; 1901-1 Nagama; 0980 74 4120; w okinawa-uds.co.jp/hotels/the-rescape_en. One of the only Western accommodations & the most luxurious resort on the island. Gorgeously decorated in calm, dark colours, villas have soft beds, terrace, living space, private outdoor bath & pool. Resort contains private beach access, shop, bar & restaurant. Free rentals are copious. **$$$$$**

WHERE TO EAT AND DRINK

Shimozato Ōdori is the central street running through Hirara and plays host to a range of restaurants, cafés and boutiques. It's a great place to head for dinner; rock up and see what takes your fancy. Otherwise, the island is smattered with places to eat, offering local fare, international cuisine and pubs.

Miyako is known for fresh fruit, melt-in-the-mouth beef and Miyako soba, which is a thinner and rounder noodle than the Okinawa type. The best fruit season is June–August, when Miyako's mangoes are in their prime. You'll also be able to find unusual fruit species, like apple mangoes, peach pineapple and pineapple sugar apple. July is also when the spiny lobster fishing season begins. Called *ise-ebi*, the meaty lobster is caught the night before and served up in soup, roasted or as sashimi.

Hirara *Map, page 261*

Seiroukoubou 島中華 蒸籠工房; 607–3 Nishizato; 0120 18 6688; w seiroukoubou.com; noon–14.30 & 17.30–23.00 Tue–Sun. Chinese-style restaurant doing a roaring trade in dim sum, as well as fresh fish, Chinese & local mains. $$$

✷ **Ginnantei** 吟なん亭; 605-1 Nishizato; 0980 72 6993; 18.00–23.00 daily. Brilliant spot owned by a friendly couple with slap-up local fare at excellent prices. $$

Goya 郷家; 570-2 Nishizato; 0980 74 2358; w zumi-goya.com; 17.30–22.00 Fri–Wed. A bar-restaurant that has sanshin concerts daily, traditional food & an astonishing selection of awamori. $$

Koja Soba 古謝そば屋; 1517-1 Shimozato; 0980 72 8304; w kojasoba.com; 11.00–16.00 Thu–Tue. Wood-panelled lunch spot serving good value set meals. Make sure to try their most popular dish, stewed pork soba soup. $$

Nanraku 南楽; 568 Nishizato; 0980 73 1855; 18.00–23.30 daily. A colourful local drinking spot that serves up decent donburi, hearty fish & beef dishes in a welcoming, relaxed atmosphere. $$

✷ **Ricco Gelato** リッコジェラート; 550 Shimozato; 0980 73 8513; w ricco-gelato.com; 11.00–17.45 Thu–Mon. Exquisite gelato, much needed in the heat, that makes use of Miyako ingredients. Make sure to try the tropical fruit options. $

Elsewhere

Shigira Resort Restaurants シギラ; 1405 Arazato; 0980 74 7240; w shigira.com. Shigira Resort has 20 restaurants spread out across the south, from Imgyaa Marine Garden to Ueno German Village. All of them are worth the journey, but particularly the onsen café Morinoizumi (カフェ森の泉) for lunch & the Chinese hotpot restaurant Xiao-Fei-Yang (薬膳火鍋 小肥羊) for dinner. $$$$

Hirochan Shokudo ひろちゃん食堂; 746-9 Miyaguni; 0980 76 3565; 11.00–20.30 Thu–Tue. Deep-fried deliciousness & noodle bowls for a reasonable price: make sure to try the seasonal mozuku tempura. $$

Mayuroshi Shokudo 丸吉食堂; 975-1 Sunagawa; 0980 77 4211; 10.30–14.00 Wed–Thu & Sat–Mon. Cheap, though with a less than cheerful exterior, this unassuming local café on the 390 Rd does amazing soba noodle soups & succulent pork ribs in teishoku set meals. $$

Shima Café Tounkaraya とぅんからや; 1214 Ueno; 0980 76 2674; w nangokutida.com; 11.00–17.00 Tue–Wed & Fri–Sun. A gorgeous dark-wood café overlooking the ocean just above Shigira's golf club. It serves up island ingredients in meals like taco rice & sooki curry, as well as ice cream, beers & – if booked in advance – BBQ. Come early as locals love it & it sells out. $$

Shiro Farm Goat Café しろう農園合同会社; 214-1 Miyaguni Ueno; 0803 982 0460; w goatcafe.jp; 11.00–17.00 Mon–Tue & Fri, 10.00–17.00 Sat–Sun. Adorable, colourful café that's entirely rough & ready. Sit with ice drinks & cheap bagels while simultaneously feeding the baby goats. $

ENTERTAINMENT AND NIGHTLIFE Miyako has more recognisable nightlife than most islands, though that isn't difficult. Hirara has a healthy number of bars, with plenty of options to choose from, but few stay open until the wee hours.

✷ **Bar Paradiso** Barぱらでぃそ; 575 Shimozato; 0980 72 6747; w paradiso-miyako.com; 20.00–late Mon–Sat. A small, chic bar with jazz music, homemade chocolate, good drinks & a calm atmosphere.

Bar THINK 221 Nishizato; 0980 73 6009; w barthink.web.fc2.com; 18.00–23.30 daily. A slightly more sophisticated watering hole with wood décor & dickie-bowed bartender. Amazing selection of international & local drinks & a barman who knows exactly what to do with them.

Penguin Bar BARペンギン; 2F 221 Nishizato; 0980 79 0204; 21.00–06.00 daily. Best place for games like billiards, darts & board games. Good fun & one of the latest closing spots on Miyako.

SHOPPING Though it doesn't have the same number of shops as Okinawa-hontō, Miyako has a whole swathe of beautiful, unique boutiques, particularly in Hirara. For more general souvenirs, beauty products and food, try the Miyakojima City Public Market (宮古島市公設市場; 1 Shimozato; 0980 73 2690; 08.00–20.00 daily).

Arts and crafts

Kaikōbō 海工房; 160 Nishizato; 0980 73 0849; w kaikobo.net; 11.00–19.00 daily. Handmade Miyako accessories & goods, including jewellery, figurines & natural materials.

Kana Miyako 宮古島の工芸品 叶; 985-6 Nishizato; 0980 75 3818; w kana-miyako.net; 11.00–18.00 Thu–Tue. High-end shop selling beautiful & traditional Ryūkyū glass, lacquerware, yachimun pottery, Miyako jōfu, bingata & more.

Shiisaa Monogatari Gallery シーサーモノガタリ; Gallery 1135-6 Matsubara; 0980 75 0660; w seasah.net; 10.00–18.00 daily. Alongside pottery workshops, this gallery displays & sells ceramics in a range of prices.

Clothing

Design Match デザインマッチ; 572-3 Shimozato; 0980 79 0239; w designmatch.ciao.jp; 10.00–19.00 daily. Gorgeous clothing, tenugui, accessories & baby clothes made by relocated Tokyoite.

Sabomart サボマート; 2F 303-4 Nishizato; 0980 73 0407; w sabo-t.com; 11.00–18.30 daily. Cool Miyako Island-based T-shirts; sold online & on the 2nd floor of Guesthouse Saboten (サボテン).

Food and drink

Miyakojima no Yukishio 雪塩製塩所・雪塩ミュージアム; 191 Karimata; 0980 72 5667; w museum.yukishio.com; 09.00–18.00 daily. Home of Miyako's salt. There's a great selection of foods – try the peanut miso.

Okinohikari Brewery 沖之光酒造; 1174 Shimozato; 0980 72 2245; w okinohikari.com; 08.00–19.00 Mon–Sat. Awamori brewery that sells new & aged spirits. They ship outside the prefecture for those with limited baggage.

Shima-no-Eki Miyako 島の駅みやこ; 870-1 Kugai; 0980 79 5151; w shimanoeki-miyako.com; Jun–Sep 09.00–19.00 daily, Oct–May 09.00–18.00 daily. Supermarket that sells authentic, island-based food products including alcohols & seasonings. Ideal for self-catering.

SPORTS AND ACTIVITIES

Watersports Miyako is synonymous with marine sports, so it's no surprise that plentiful tours operate here. First and foremost is scuba-diving and snorkelling; the Miyako blue seas are filled with corals and critters, from large turtles to tiny clownfish. There's also wreck diving, arches, caves, grottoes, pond-to-pond diving, lakes and channels: in short, enough to spend a whole week just diving.

The majority of sites are concentrated in the south. Turtles frequent Shigira and Waiwai beaches, while Imgyaa has gentle coral gardens. The area between Maehama and Kurima offers shore and boat diving, full of colourful reef fish, and possible rays, turtles and trevally. The very south is filled with interesting topography, like the luminescent Nanamata arches, Gao and Thanks Cow caves. Yabiji (八重干瀬) is a rich coral reef area north of Ikema, with a huge amount of sea life.

Finding English-speaking instructors isn't always easy; your best bet is to look to resort hotels who offer a wide range of activities, rentals and tours. If you're just looking for rental items away from your accommodation, you can usually find shops at major beaches.

Carte Marine カルトマリーヌ; 118-1 Ikema, Hirara; ☎ 0904 708 9575; w cartemarine.net/english. Ikema Island English-speaking diving instructor, operating fun day, dive courses, snorkelling & charter ships. Their prime area of expertise is Yabiji, a rich coral reef area north of Ikema.

GRAT!S!SUP グラッツサップ宮古島; 746-9 Miyaguni; ☎ 0980 79 7724; w gratssup.jp. SUP, snorkelling & yoga tours with a friendly team.

Marine Lodge Marea マリンロッジマレア宮古島; 847-3 Yonaha, Shimoji; ☎ 0980 76 3850; w marea.co.jp/marinelodge_miyakojima. Attached to a resort by Maehama Beach, Marea offers licences, fun dives & dive opportunities across multiple islands.

Miyako Diving Aquatic Adventure アクアティックアドベンチャー; 543-1 Shimozato; ☎ 0980 79 5009; w miyako-aquaticadventure.com/en. Hirara-based, operates in English with vast selection of diving sites & courses across Miyako's islands.

Miyakojima Tokyu Hotel 宮古島東急ホテル; 914 Yonaha, Shimoji; ☎ 0980 76 2109; w tokyuhotels.co.jp/miyakojima-h. Operates a huge number of marine tours for guests & non-guests, including snorkelling, diving, yacht & motorboat cruises, glass boats, jet skis & banana boats, as well as rental cycles & electric bikes.

Swell 664 Kugai; ☎ 0980 79 9900; w swell.shopinfo.jp. Hirara company running SUP & surf lessons & fun experience days.

Golf Golfers couldn't ask for a better getaway than Miyako. Blessed with three big golf courses – Emerald Coast, owned by the Tokyu resort (see above), Shigira Bay Country Club (w shigira.com/en), and Ocean Links Miyakojima (w ocean-links.co.jp) – the island attracts domestic and international golfers. The courses are all on the coast, so the backdrop to your bunker is a beauteous stretch of coral-crusted blue-green sea.

OTHER PRACTICALITIES Miyako has enough post offices and convenience stores to make finding an ATM comparatively easy. There are two major hospitals in Hirara and police boxes and stations across the island. Those provided are spread across the island in tourist areas.

Medical

Miyakojima Tokushukai Hospital 宮古島徳洲会病院; Matsubara-552-1, Hirara; ☎ 0980 73 1100; w miyatoku.jp

Okinawa Prefectural Miyako Hospital 沖縄県立宮古病院; 427-1 Shimozato, Hirara; ☎ 0980 72 3151; w miyakoweb.hosp.pref.okinawa.jp

Police

Gusukube Higashi Police Box 警察署城辺東; 1094 Fukuzato, Gusukube; ☎ 0980 77 4516

Karimata Police Box 警察署狩俣; 1234-1 Karimata, Hirara; ☎ 0980 72 5331

Miyakojima Police Station Hirara Police Box 警察署平良交番; 184 Nishizato, Hirara; ☎ 0980 72 0110

Shimoji Police Box 警察署下地; 513 Uechi, Shimoji; ☎ 0980 76 6010

Post offices

Hirara Nishizato Post Office 平良西里郵便局; 142 Nishizato, Hirara; ☎ 0980 72 1617; ⌚ 09.00–17.00 Mon–Fri, ATM: 08.00–19.00 Mon–Fri, 09.00–18.00 Sat, 09.00–17.00 Sun

Karimata Simple Post Office 狩俣簡易郵便局; 1435 Karimata, Hirara; ☎ 0980 72 5702; ⌚ 09.00–16.00 Mon–Fri

Shimoji Post Office 下地郵便局; 545-12 Uechi; 0980 76 6004; 09.00–17.00 Mon–Fri, ATM: 09.00–17.30 Mon–Fri, 09.00–17.00 Sat–Sun

WHAT TO SEE AND DO

Hirara Hirara (平良) is everyone's first stop on Miyako as it's the best place to base yourself. There's a good number of shops and a handful of restaurants and tour companies, but the low-rise 'capital' of Miyako is pretty lacking in sights.

Hirara's top spots are largely related to Nakasone Tuyumya, who crushed the Yaeyama rebellion and helped to unite the islands under the Ryūkyū Kingdom – to both the happiness and horror of archipelago residents. **Harimizu Utaki** (漲水御嶽) is a pretty little red-roofed shrine in northern Hirara now dedicated to Tuyumya in commemoration of his victory. Before this, however, Harimizu enshrined Koitsuno and Koitama, the male and female gods of Miyakojima's creation myth.

Also near Hirara Port is **Nakasone's Tomb** (仲宗根豊見親の墓), a large grave unique to Tuyumya that's designated a national cultural asset. Tombs on Miyako come in many forms, but traditionally the general populace had wind burials; bodies were exposed to the elements by leaving them in caves. Higher ranking islanders were buried in *myaaka* – graves of stacked stones. Nakasone Tuyumya's grand tomb combines elements of both caves and myaaka, resulting in a large stepped tomb resembling the beginnings of an Incan pyramid. To the tomb's north is **Chirimara Grave** (知利真良豊見親の墓), belonging to Nakasone's third son, and to its south the **Atonma Grave** (あとんま墓), a beautiful tomb for Nakasone's concubines. While in the area, pop to the **Head Tax Stone** (人頭税石; 90 Nikadori) along the port road for a glimpse at harsh life under Japanese rule. In a small green garden, signified only by a small sign, this 143cm-high stone was supposedly used to determine if someone was old enough (or indeed tall enough) to pay tax.

Nearby is **Miyako Shrine** (宮古神社; 5-1 Nishizato; 0980 72 6137; w miyako-jinja.com), a large handsome shrine flanked with shiisaa, instead of the traditional mainland komainu (lion dogs), which holds a yearly festival.

Should your passion for old stone constructions remain unsated, check out the **Yamatogaa** (大和井・やまとがー), a well dating from around 1720. Mustering excitement over a spring may sound a big ask, but the old stonework is sunk into the ground and delightfully overgrown with roots and moss. Beside Yamatogaa is the commoners' well, beneath a long, draped banyan tree. It's across the road from **Upugaa** (大川・ウプガー), another jungly ruin of a spring, originally used for watering livestock.

On the opposite side of Hirara's small coastline there's a petite beach called **Painagama** (パイナガマ), with toilet and shower facilities and a jellyfish net. A sweet spot for brief bouts of swimming and tanning, it's favoured by locals for catching up on the sands. The beach is hugged by a small peninsula, **Painagama Umisora Sukoyaka Park** (パイナガマ海空すこやか公園), which has some playground equipment, a picnic area and a coastline of caves. You'll also find a stunning, cenote-like pool in its north called **Pikyazu** (ピキャズ) and a somewhat underwhelming **wartime machine gun dugout** (機関銃壕) – a letterbox in some overgrown scrub – by the beach's west side.

To the south of Hirara, somewhat in the middle of nowhere, you'll find the memorials to Japanese war dead at **Toyohatatō** (豊旗塔), where the remains of 2,569 soldiers are interred.

Northeast **Sunayama** (砂山ビーチ) is arguably the most picturesque beach on Miyako – or it is, as long as its famous raised coral archway hasn't been cordoned off for safety with rather unattractive metal barriers, which occasionally happens. Previously a swimming beach, it's now semi-retired after a shark attack on a surfer, and left for paddling and picnics. The beach is accessed by a small path over a steep sand dune – getting down is a doddle, but getting back is a bit of an uphill trek. Go early to avoid crowds and have a blissful moment of serenity with just the sounds of the shore. Toilets and showers are available.

Zooming up the peninsula towards Ikema Island brings you to **Shimajiri Mangrove Forest** (島尻のマングローブ林). Small but beautiful, Miyako's mangroves are a natural monument crisscrossed with boardwalks, from where you can watch mangrove crabs and other critters skitter along. You can get a nice view across the waters and islets from **Batarazu Bridge** (ばたらず橋).

On the opposite coast is **Miyakojima Underwater Park** (宮古島海中公園; 2511-1 Karimata; 0980 74 6335; w miyakojima-kaichukoen.com; 09.00–17.00 daily; adult/child ¥1,000/500–800), a tiny submarine aquarium with viewing windows into the reef. On good days you'll be able to see a host of animals in the clear waters – on bad days you get a discount but not much else. The park isn't much more than a single large room with café and crafts to boot, but it's ideal for young children and for anyone unable to enjoy snorkelling or diving with the sea life. The aquarium is situated in **Kenkō Fureai Land Park** (健康ふれあいランド公園), a large coastal park which has remnants of a **Japanese Special Attack Force facility** (海軍特攻艇格納秘匿壕跡) used for storing suicide boats.

At Miyako's northern end is **Nishihennazaki** (西平安名崎), not as picturesque as its southern sibling but a fine stroll with a shrimp food truck and nearby **Miyakojima no Yukishio** salt museum café and shop selling edible souvenirs to Miyako's salt production (page 264). To its east is the 1.4km **Ikema Bridge** (池間大橋), a sleek humped stretch across Miyako's sea.

Central Heading southeast out of Hirara, you'll first hit the **Miyako Botanical Garden** (宮古島市熱帯植物園; 1166-286 Higashinakasonezoe; 0980 73 4111; 10.00–18.00 daily). This large park covering 120,000m² has a collection of over 1,600 plants, trees, flowers and bushes from across the archipelago, southeast Asia and further afield. Well-kept walking paths and courses cobweb the blooming, buzz-filled area and strolling them is a lovely way to spend a sunny afternoon. The **Miyako Taiken Craft Village** (宮古島市体験工芸村) that sits within the garden has child-friendly workshops keeping traditional Miyako crafts alive.

A little further south is **Miyako City Museum** (宮古島市総合博物館; 1166–287 Higashinakasonezoe; 0980 73 0567; 09.00–16.30 Tue–Sun; adult/child ¥300/100–200), which hosts exhibits on the culture, history and nature of Miyakojima. Family-friendly learning takes you through festivals and traditional performing arts, and you'll also find the second oldest human remains ever found in Japan, some 26,000 years old.

On the drive past the airport, in front of the Japanese Self-Defence Force base, is the **Miyako Centre for Traditional Crafts** (宮古島市伝統工芸品センター; 1190-188 Nobaru; 0980 74 7480; w miyako-kougei.com; 09.00–18.00 daily; free). Home to Miyako jōfu, the island's 600-year-old cloth (page 27), the centre shows off the history and process of growing, dyeing and weaving the material. Naturally you can buy the cloth at the centre's shop.

East There are viewpoints and small beaches all the way down the northeast coastal road, particularly **Higa Road Park** (比嘉ロードパーク). This scenic spot is one of the highest points on the island, showing off the coral reef, cliffs and colourful sea.

MYTHS AND FOLKTALES: MAMUYA

On the cliffside of Higashihennazaki lies a gravestone belonging to Mamuya, an incredibly beautiful Miyako woman who is said to have died and been buried there.

Legend has it that Mamuya was so beautiful, the village's people would form a wall around her trying to glimpse her face. An army general called Nugusuku-Aji, who already had a wife and children, met Mamuya and fell in love with her. They began a relationship and he boasted to all of her beauty. When telling his uncle about his lover, Nugusuku-Aji exclaimed that while his uncle's wife smelled like urine, Mamuya smelled like sweet herbs and perfume. His uncle replied that Mamuya might smell nice now, but as the years went by he would realise his wife and mother of his children was better and more valuable to the general.

In some versions, Nugusuku-Aji leaves Mamuya and she kills herself by throwing herself from Higashihennazaki. In others, Mamuya hears this and goes to the cape where she lives out her days in a cave on the cliffside, alone with her weaving, while her lover wanders every day in search of her.

It is said that Mamuya cursed the beauty that brought her heartbreak and placed a curse on the women of her village, Hora, that none of its daughters would ever be beautiful again. The only way to counteract this curse is if a pregnant woman goes to Higashihennazaki and drinks from a puddle that reflects the light of a full moon.

While Sunayama and Maehama have the fame, they also get the crowds. Easterly **Arugusuku Beach** (新城海岸) is enough off the beaten track that only those with determination – and a car – visit. This makes it an incredibly quiet, local beach with great snorkelling and coral. Further down the same coast sits **Yoshino Kaigan Beach** (吉野海岸), arguably the best place on the island for snorkelling. Yoshino's protected reef is full of tropical fish and is known as a nesting ground for sea turtles. You'll also find gentle waves, changing rooms, showers and toilets.

The southeast culminates in a thin trail of land known as **Higashihennazaki** (東平安名崎). Considered one of Japan's 100 most beautiful views, this cape ends in a handsome white lighthouse used to protect ships from the scattered reef. Wander the trail and stop for an ice cream while spotting islets in the great green-blue. In spring, the area is daubed with white Easter lilies. You can climb the 97 steps of **Hennazaki Lighthouse** (平安名埼灯台; 0908 294 4010; 09.00–16.00 daily; ¥200) for a 360-degree panorama from the observation deck. On the way into the cape on the eastern side you will come across **Mamuya's grave** (マムヤの墓), the resting place of a legendary woman (see above). To get to the cape, it's about 35 minutes by car from the airport, or you can get a bus to the Bora bus stop, followed by a 90-minute walk to the lighthouse.

To the cape's west is **Boragaa Beach** (保良泉ビーチ), a gorgeous marine sports park for surfing, swimming, snorkelling and cave exploration. Surfers have to head further out for waves and will need to keep an eye on the wind direction, while snorkellers need to watch out for rocks and tides. Boroga is famous for its cliff-side limestone cave, colloquially known as the **Pumpkin Hall** (パンプキンホール), accessible at certain tides and wave conditions. Believed to be the home for a Ryūkyū god, the small entrance through the sea hides a gigantic cave that holds a pumpkin-like rock. Many locals swim to the cave entrance at low tide and go climbing inside, but it's recommended you take a tour as it can be incredibly dangerous and confusing for those unfamiliar with the area. Umiinooto kayak tours (0980 77 7577; w uminooto.com; 08.00–18.00 daily, to 17.00 winter) leave from the beach.

South Tracing the island south takes you along **Nanamata** (七又海岸), a dramatic coastline that has plentiful viewpoints and an old spring called **Muigaa** (ムイガー). Just north of Muiga is **Nakabari Limestone Cave** (仲原鍾乳洞; 1114 Tomori; 10.30–16.30 Fri–Wed; adult/child ¥600/400), which feels rather in the middle of nowhere, its entrance concealed by fields and trees, but it's a cool little trip. Pay your fee at the somewhat ramshackle reception (it's run by local farmers who own the land) and descend to some small but impressive caves, which sink 15m into Miyako's limestone.

Imgyaa Marine Garden (イムギャーマリンガーデン) is a free and pretty park built around a natural cove, which is used for scuba and snorkelling classes. There are boarded promenades, an observatory and views over the lagoon, all ideal for children.

Just north of Imgyaa is a collection of archaeological ruins, the most interesting of which are the **Amagaa** (あま井), a dramatic limestone spring cave ripe for exploration, and the three houses of **Uibyaayamiseki** (比屋山遺跡), which have been excellently preserved from the 14th and 15th century.

One of Miyako's strangest collections of sites sits in the centre of the southern coast, west of **Shigira Beach** (シギラビーチ). The **Ueno German Culture Village** (うえのドイツ文化村; 775-1 Miyaguni; 0980 76 3771; w hakuaiueno.com; 09.30–17.30 Wed & Fri–Mon; adult/child ¥750/400 not inc Kinderhouse) was erected in memory of the German boat shipwrecked off Miyako's coast and saved by locals. This frankly bizarre theme park has a replica castle, German exhibits and a chunk of the Berlin Wall. Alongside the village is another baffling structure – an abandoned palace hotel, which overlooks the sea and **Heart Rock** (ハートロック), that's now used for storage. You can take 45-minute **glass-bottom boat tours** (0980 76 6336; adult/child ¥2,000/1,000) from the village's SeaSky dock, leaving seven times a day depending on weather.

West The southwest brings you to another of Miyako's outer bridges: **Kurima** (来間島). Sleek and shiny under the sun, this 1.7km bridge connects with little Kurima and has great views over Miyako's best tourist spot: **Maehama** (前浜). Voted the most beautiful beach on Okinawa – and one of the most beautiful in the world – Maehama has quite the acclaim. However, this 7km strip, also known as Yonaha-maehama, has had a hard time recently, being battered by typhoons and losing some of its extensive pristine sands. Its wildlife and activities are still vibrant though. Snorkel tours – such as the one run by Miyakojima Tokyu (page 265) – will get you up close and personal with frolicking clownfish, an array of pufferfish and seaweed-munching turtles just offshore. There's also windsurfing and kiteboarding, depending on the weather, and, of course, lots of kicking back and relaxing on award-winning sands. **Yonaha Bay** (与那覇湾), just above Maehama, is home to a small selection of mangroves.

Behind Maehama is **Maipari Miyakojima Tropical Orchards** (まいぱり宮古島熱帯果樹園; 1210 Yonaha; 0980 74 7830; w maipari.jp; 10.00–17.00 daily; adult/child ¥700/350), a truly excellent jaunt from the beach that takes families and friends through some of Miyako's tropical crops and animals. Golf-cart tours (adult/child ¥1,400/700) pass untold species of pineapples, bananas, starfruit, papaya, mangoes and more, as well as Miyakojima horses (page 270), which kids can ride. Best yet, the café on site makes incredible smoothies and ice creams with their own produce – make sure to try the peach pineapple or the atemoya, aka pineapple sugar apple.

MIYAKO HORSES

The island has its own indigenous pony, the Miyako horse (Miyakouma). Its origins are unknown, but theories suggest that it was introduced from China or Korea, or arrived through a shipwreck. The ponies are only about 110cm tall, but are very strong, stable-footed and obedient. They were prized by the Ryūkyū Dynasty and ridden by the king, and in the Meiji period were used for agriculture. The horses were also sent as gifts and tribute to China and Edo.

In 1935, Japan's imperial crown prince – then only 20 months old – was given three Miyako horses to learn how to ride. Some 40 years later, in 1975, the crown prince visited the International Ocean Expo on Okinawa and met the man who raised one of his beloved Miyako horses.

As agriculture became mechanised, the breeding of the horses slowed and numbers dropped from around 10,000 in 1955 to just seven in 1983. Now the horses have been proclaimed a natural monument of the prefecture, and the island's preservation society is working to increase the number. In 2024 their population had risen to 49, with the first foal born in two years.

Near Maipari is the **Grave of Kawamitsu Ōtodo** (川満大殿の古墓; 576 Sugama), a fine example of Miyako's traditional myaaka graves (page 266). Kawamitsu was a great and unprecedented chief of this region, as he was formerly a commoner. He was buried here with his wife, covered by huge stones. Taken over by nature, this air burial site dates to the 1500s.

The final bridge, **Irabu Ōhashi** (伊良部大橋), is Miyako's truly special feat of engineering. Connecting Miyako and Irabujima since 2015, this is the longest toll-free bridge in Japan. The clean undulating lines of the 3,540m bridge span deep blue waters where Tarama ferries pass below. The wind on the bridge can be quite overpowering – take care when cycling. For good photos, the view is best from **Sunset Beach** (サンセットビーチ) and the **Tu River Seaside Park** (トゥリバー海浜公園), which looks out over the entire bridge.

ŌGAMIJIMA

It may only take 15 minutes to get to Ōgamijima (大神島) off the northeast coast, but it's almost a world away from tourist-friendly Miyako. Literally meaning 'Big God Island', Ōgamijima is considered a sacred place, particularly to the handful of people who live there.

Ancient belief says that Ōgamijima is home to two incredibly holy sites in Japanese mythology: **Amanoiwato** (天岩戸), a cave where the sun god hid the light of the world, and **Takamagahara** (高天原), the god's home. Rituals and prayers have been performed on Ōgamijima for centuries, the holiest of which is the Uyagan. This incredibly secretive ceremony, conducted by women, happens up to five times annually, usually in the latter part of the year. During these rituals, parts of the island will be off-limits. The rest of the year, Japanese people visit to pray and make wishes at this 'power spot' (page 24).

All of this means Ōgamijima is covered in prohibited utaki shrines, and therefore much of the island is restricted access. It's not advised to visit Ōgamijima without a guide or a strict idea of where you are allowed to go; don't simply go wandering, as you may inadvertently stroll into unassuming holy grounds and cause deep offence.

The tiny island is certainly beautiful, but there's admittedly little here that you cannot find elsewhere without the restrictions and etiquette concerns. Tourism is very limited; there's a grandfather on the island who gives 90-minute **guided tours** (Ōgamijima Grandfather Guide; 0980 72 5350; 09.00–18.00 daily) – but only in Japanese. There's also **Ōgamijima Marine Club** (大神島マリンクラブ; 0904 075 0428; 09.00–17.00 daily), which runs twice-daily 3-hour snorkelling tours, needing at least two adults booked for it to go.

If you do visit, you can see a minuscule, quiet village of old houses just up from the port. The top of the village has a steep set of stairs up to the centre of the island and its highest point, **Tōmidai** (遠見台). The 10-minute hike brings you panoramic views of Ōgami, Miyako, Ikema and the surrounding shallows.

Just outside the port is the island's only diner, **Opuyuu Teishoku** (おぷゆう食堂; 130 Ogami; 10.00–17.00 daily). Here you can try some of Ōgamijima's specialities including *kakidako* smoked octopus, oyster octopus bowls, mībai coral trout soup, aosa seaweed soup and smoked grilled fish. Some of Ōgamijima's speciality products, like mozuku seaweed, are popular on Miyako and can be bought in its shops.

The road around Ōgamijima doesn't circumnavigate its entirety; there are dead ends in the north and southeast. Largely the walk along it takes in the coastline and the beautiful, empty Ōgamijima beaches. In the north are the mushroom-shaped **Nocchi** (ノッチ) or 'notch' rocks, unbalanced-looking stacks with thin bases formed through erosion. Ōgamijima is a geologically interesting site, where you can see some of the Miyako group's oldest geological strata in its rock formations.

The island also has coral reefs for snorkelling, but since there is no clinic, beware of venomous sea snakes and deadly conches. Locals recommend caution and equipment such as long-sleeve rash guards and leggings, gloves, boots and even life jackets for the seriously prepared.

The Ōgami Kaiun ferry (大神海運; 0980 72 5477; w oogamikaiun.com) from Miyako's Shimajiri fisherman's wharf is cheap and runs five times a day in high season, four in low. Tickets can be bought at the port office.

IKEMAJIMA

Ikema (池間島) is an interesting island with a surprising amount to offer for such a small, 2.83km^2 blip. It has the largest wetland in Okinawa, a whole host of picturesque beaches and wildlife, and one of the strongest festival and religious cultures on the Miyako. Touring round the island is an enjoyable way to spend half a day or more, especially combined with seeing Miyako's northern mangroves.

At 1.5km northwest of Miyako and a 40-minute drive from the airport, Ikema is the northernmost point of the island group, attached to the main island by the 1,425m Ikema Bridge. Built in 1992, this bridge was once the longest in Okinawa, before being usurped by the Kurima Bridge.

The village in the south centres on fishing, with drying nets and buoys scattered around and the ever-present sea peeking out between the houses. Before the introduction of bonito (skipjack tuna) line fishing, bonito were traditionally worshipped as messengers to the gods, and would be neither caught nor eaten. Though eventually becoming a food source, bonito retained an important place in Ikemajima, spiritually, economically and socially. For a century, Ikema was renowned for its bonito fishing. The catch was so successful that they sometimes used excess bonito as field fertiliser, and locals would joke about having too much money. These local experts were even sent to Borneo during World War II, to help

IKEMA FESTIVALS

Ikema has strong indigenous beliefs and holds many annual religious ceremonies. There's the haarii boat race in lunar May, and Myaakuzutsu and Yuukui in lunar September. Yuukui is a fertility festival that also takes place on Irabu, introduced by Ikema islanders who emigrated across. Here it is conducted by women between the ages of 51 and 55, with divine songs and prayers.

The Myaakuzutsu is the island's biggest ritual: a three-day event with four rituals at four shrines called *mutu*. Each mutu ritual is done by an age-tiered group, overseen by the *mutunuuya* – a group of men over 55. During the festival, which prays for good fishing and harvest, the mutunuuya gather together in the early morning to drink and chat. On the second day of the festival, families come to register children born since the previous Myaakuzutsu, men and women visit the shrine and there's dancing in the evening. Milk sake, a drink made of awamori and condensed milk that's incredibly popular on Ikema, is drunk as part of the festival.

fish bonito for troops there. However, fluctuating prices and falling fish stock meant the industry declined around 1965.

Today the village is home to the island's 680 residents, and has dive shops, a few restaurants, a limited information centre and a shrine. The bridge opening changed Ikema significantly, bringing a natural increase in visitors, but life here remains pretty rural, with older residents still speaking a variation of the Miyakoan language called Ikema or Ikima.

Nature is quite literally at the heart of Ikema: the entire island is designated as a national wildlife refuge and the largest wetland in Okinawa Prefecture sits in the centre. Multiple white-sand beaches line the coast, their entrances often hidden from the road, earning them a level of seclusion. Ikema also sees mass crab spawning, which takes place a week before and after the full moon in the lunar calendar months of May–July. Crabs march across the island and its roads to make their way to the sea to release their eggs.

Ikemajima is famously home to the Yabiji Reef, which consists of over 100 coral reef formations spanning a 25km² area off Irabu's northeast tip. The largest coral reef in Japan, Yabiji surfaces several times a year in the spring tide, earning it the nickname 'the phantom continent'. Designated a national treasure in 2013, it's an excellent snorkel and dive site.

WHERE TO STAY

Island Terrace Neera (5 rooms) アイランドテラスニーラ; 317-1 Maezato; 0980 74 4678; w neela.jp. Beachfront, Western-style spacious villas with private hot tub, balcony, lounge, kitchenette & free shuttle. Pool, spa, snorkel rental, BBQs & restaurant attached. **$$$$$**

Alohana (1 villa) アロハナ; 156 Maezato; 0902 776 8773; w alohana.hp.peraichi.com. Stunning 2-bed self-catering villa with living room, garden, kitchen, terrace & shower bathroom. **$$$**

Aitai Nagahama (5 rooms) あいたい長浜; 151 Ikema; 0908 762 0051. Incredibly friendly minshuku with communal spaces including kitchen, Japanese rooms & shared bathrooms, plus fishing equipment rental. **$$**

WHERE TO EAT AND DRINK

Ikema Shokudou 池間食堂; 0980 75 2505; w restaurant-64123.business.site; 11.00–15.00 daily. Lunch place doing excellent value, hearty set meals. **$$$**

Doug's Burger ダグズバーガー池間島店; 76-1 Hirara; 0980 79 6888; w dougsburger.com; 11.00–17.30 daily. Chain outlet offering burger meals made with local ingredients. $$

Ohama terrace OHAMAテラス; 1059 Hirara; 0980 79 5696; w rest-ohama.com; 10.00–16.30 daily. Basic terrace café doing drinks, sweets & limited set meals. $$

Kaimirai 海未来; 1173-7 Hirara; 0980 75 2121; 09.30–20.00 daily. Famous road station eatery offering Miyako soba & island classics. $

OTHER PRACTICALITIES There is an ATM at the Ikema Post Office (池間郵便局; 186-2 Ikema; 0980 75 2014; 09.00–17.00 Mon–Fri, ATM: 09.00–17.30 Mon–Fri, 09.00–17.00 Sat). Tourist information is available on Miyako (page 262).

WHAT TO SEE AND DO Heading over **Ikema Ōhashi** (池間大橋) you come to the bridge viewpoint, a rest stop of souvenir shops, restaurants and toilet facilities. It's a great place to get a good view of the bridge and cyan sea, and is also an excellent sunset spot. The rest stop is also the entrance to eastern **Ohama Beach** (オハマビーチ). From here the road splits, heading north to the beaches or west to the village.

The best beaches are in the north arc of the island. The first you come to is **Funakusu** (フナクス), also known as Block (ブロック) – an odd, one could say unimaginative, nickname from the block that marked its concealed entrance from the road. Nowadays it's more obvious thanks to the car park. The small beach has very pretty crystal-clear waters and fine sand: there aren't reefs here but plentiful little fish.

Further north, the naming theme continues at **Kaginmi** (カギンミビーチ), aka Rope Beach (ロープ). Ropes mark the narrow entrance to the beach, a large white curve flecked by adan trees, with good snorkelling spots. The outer road heads then to **Ikema Lighthouse** (池間島灯台), the tallest building on Ikema, dating back to the 1940s.

Below Kaginmi are the **Ikema Wetlands** (池間湿原), a peaceful little spot with bird huts and observation decks. It's home to migratory birds like ducks and herons and a huge number of dragonfly species and insects, as well as the spawning crabs. Originally connected to the sea, the mouth of the wetlands was reclaimed from the sea for the fishing port, and the water became desalinated.

Ikema's western coast is speckled by hidden little beaches ripe for exploration and is a great place to watch sunset. Here you'll find **Ikizuu Beach** (イキヅービーチ), a small beach surrounded by overgrown adan and monpa trees, and **Heart Rock** (ハート岩), Ikema's best-loved sight. Raised coral reef has gradually been eroded into the shape of a heart – a claim that should be treated with the usual recommended sprinkle of cynicism. Heart-ish, it's become a location for TV dramas and tourist couples. The heart itself is best seen at low tide, but otherwise it's still a pretty beach, though far more crowded than anywhere else on Ikema.

Next comes **Arashissuhida Beach** (アラシッスヒダビーチ), a mouthful of a private beach beside the Island Terrace Neela hotel. It's relatively shallow and easy to swim here, and there are shower facilities too. The beach gives way to Ikema's only town, where you'll find restaurants, plenty of dive shops and guesthouses.

The small peninsula jutting out in the island's southwest contains Ikema's biggest shrine, the **Daishu Shrine** (大主神社), which is only visitable with permission from the village, but it has a nice sea view. There's also the remains of the old **Sakishima Beacon Tower** (池間島遠見台跡) nearby, which overlooks the sea between Ikema and Miyako.

KURIMAJIMA

Kurima (来間島) is a small island off the southwest of Miyako. Sleepy and sweet, it hasn't much to its name – a single small settlement, a couple of good beaches, fields of sugarcane and some viewpoints. Though in recent years that's been added to with a selection of cool shops and cafés, as well as some incongruous large resorts. Overall, Kurima is better as a day trip than somewhere to actually stay, unless you are looking for solitude and nothing more.

The island was connected to the Miyako mainland in 1995 by a 1,690m bridge at the south end of Maehama Beach. The bridge allowed much more flow between Miyako and Kurima, livening up the island little by little. Kurima's only village, still with traditional red roofs, is on this east side. Its small population of around 165 people, who rely largely on fishing and farming leaf tobacco, sugarcane and fruits, has been growing as the island has become popular with Miyako locals wanting to relocate from the 'mainland'.

PRACTICALITIES The village houses two cute souvenir shops: Hakoniwa Namima (370-5 Kurima; 0980 79 0208; w hakoniwa-namima.com; 10.00–18.00 daily) and Utatane (105-9 Kurima; 0980 76 3725; 10.00–noon & 13.00–17.00 Fri–Wed). Meanwhile, you'll find local eco crafts and workshops at MAHINA Island Naturals (8 Shimojikoma; 0803 018 0532; w tidamahina.com; summer 09.00–18.00 daily, winter 10.00–17.00 daily).

The village also has plentiful cafés, like the popular Aosora Parlour (104-1 Kurima; 0980 76 3900; w aosoragr.com; 10.00–noon & 13.00–17.00 daily) and nearby YakkaYakka (ヤッカヤッカ; 126-3 Kurima; 0980 74 7205; w cafe.miyakojimacity.jp; 11.30–sold out daily), a quiet spot serving traditional Miyako food at reasonable prices. There are noodle shops and bars as well, making Kurima an unlikely food hotspot.

WHAT TO SEE AND DO Aside from shops and eateries, the village is home to the sacred **Rain-begging Deigo Tree** (雨乞座のデイゴ), beside the Kurima Elementary and Junior School. Every September, the *masumori* dance is held under this tree to celebrate children born since the previous year. There are in fact two deigo trees here (though there is suspicion that one is dying), which are the remains of a trio representing the three brothers who founded Kurima. These brothers are also celebrated in the island's October Yaamasu Punaka festival, which prays for the prosperity of descendants.

There's also **Pacha Beach** (パチャビーチ・浜辺のサウナ; 98-1 Kurima; 0806 497 8369; w coubic.com/pachabeach/4821643; 14.00–18.00 Thu–Tue), a place that offers tent saunas on the beach among gajumaru trees, plus barbecues and catamaran cruises.

Kurima's **Ryūgu Castle Observatory** (竜宮城展望台; 476 Kurima) is on the steep coast by the village and can be seen from Maehama Beach on Miyako. It's built to look like an old castle, with its three storeys overlooking the bridge to its right and the strait between Kurima and Maehama. On the left you can see Irabujima and Shimojijima; on the opposite side, the entirety of Kurima's 2.84km^2 is laid out before you. Beside the observatory are the piled stone ruins of the **Kurima Tomibansho** (来間島通見番所), another of the old Sakishima beacons. There's also another viewpoint closer to the bridge, **Matsunoki Observatory** (松の木展望台), which lies at the bottom of some steep steps where you'll find a shady tree sculpture to sit under.

It only takes 20 minutes to drive around Kurima's 9km circumference. The main reason to head out of the village is to visit the beaches. **Nagama Beach** (長間浜) forms almost the entirety of Kurima's west coast. It's a long, wide white-sand beach with coral reefs, abundant hermit crabs and relatively few tourists. It looks like all beach access is through the resort café at its northern tip, but there is a small, rocky road flanked by monpa trees further south that leads to a parking area. Its place on the west coast means it has excellent sunsets, but the open ocean means there can be big waves on the beach.

Just south are **Musunun Beach** (ムスヌン浜) and **Nagasaki Beach** (長崎浜), both quieter and smaller than Nagamahama but incredibly picturesque. The southeast holds **Tako Park** (タコ公園), a coastal park inexplicably dedicated to a large octopus statue. Its wholly secluded area has beautiful views, boardwalks and some small beaches that come and go with the tides.

There are also lots of old wells on the island. Like many Miyako Islands, Kurima suffered over water access. With no mountains or rivers, wells offered the only available water. **Kurimagaa** (来間ガー), near the fishing port, was the site of three wells for the village. The first well was for consumption, the second for washing and the third for laundry.

In the centre of Kurima is an ancient tomb called **Sumuryaamyaaka** (スムリャーミャーカ). It's somewhat hard to imagine when faced with a pile of rock, but this is the burial place of an old Kurima family. The tomb was built into the ground and covered with a coral limestone slab; inside are three chambers, where pieces of 15th-century Chinese celadon were found.

IRABUJIMA AND SHIMOJIJIMA

The histories of Irabu (伊良部島) and Shimoji (下地島) are scraped from the same legacy as Miyako's. Relatively small at 29km^2 and 9.6km^2 respectively, the two coral islands are separated only by a narrow, mangrove-flecked inlet measuring just 40–100m and spanned by six bridges. Both Shimoji and Irabu to its east are remarkably flat; the highest natural point is Mount Maki at 89m.

In a group known for watersports, Irabu and Shimoji pip most to the post. Riddled with caves on land and sea, they share one of the best scuba and free-diving playgrounds in the archipelago, with clear waters featuring arches, a shipwreck and reefs. The exceptional visibility makes them ideal snorkelling spots, too, with uncrowded beaches and warm, easy-to-swim waters.

The first village on Irabu was established in 1310, when people made their way across from Kugai on Miyako, and there's evidence to suggest that Irabu was involved in trade on the islands. Just like Miyako, Irabu and Shimoji were affected by the head tax and subsequent protests, as well as the Meiwa earthquake and

IRABU FESTIVALS

Immigrants from Ikema brought multiple festivals and rituals to Irabu. These were traditionally led by three women called Dachinma and mainly took place at Dainushi Utaki (also known as Nanamui) on the east coast overlooking the sea. Events that still take place today include the Yuukui harvest festival, where women between the ages of 47 and 57 spend two days praying for a bountiful harvest, and August's Myaakuzutsu, which began as a celebration for paying off head tax.

tsunami. In 1940, the island saw disaster when the *Irabu Maru* ferry sank off the Irabu coast, killing some 73 people. During the war, Irabu and Shimoji saw little action, though 4,000 troops were stationed on Irabu in 1944 – equal to half the island's population at the time.

Today the islands' core industries are agriculture and fishing. The hub of agriculture is to the south, where the main crop is brown sugar. Fishing has long been a major industry for Irabu in particular. Sarahama, a fishing port on its east coast first settled by Ikema migrants in 1720, became the centre for catching bonito using traditional pole methods. Even today, the bonito fishing here comprises almost 80% of Okinawa Prefecture's bonito catch.

Irabu is known for grey-faced buzzards called *sashiba*, one of many migratory birds that come to Irabu in the colder season. This elegant, sickle-beaked bird of prey became Irabu's natural mascot: the island even erected a sashiba-shaped observatory, which unfortunately was destroyed. Shimoji, like Ikema, sees crab spawning events in lunar May–July, when crabs cross the road at night to lay eggs in the sea.

Archaeologically, Irabu excavations have discovered a range of fossils dating back tens of thousands of years. In Nagayama, in the island's south, a cave revealed human bones aged around 20,000 years old, and the remains of roe deer and Miyako horseshoe bats. Further roe deer bones, some 20,000–30,000 years old, were excavated in northern Sawada at Ubutakinaka Cave. There are utaki shrines across the island, but few are particularly beautiful or accessible.

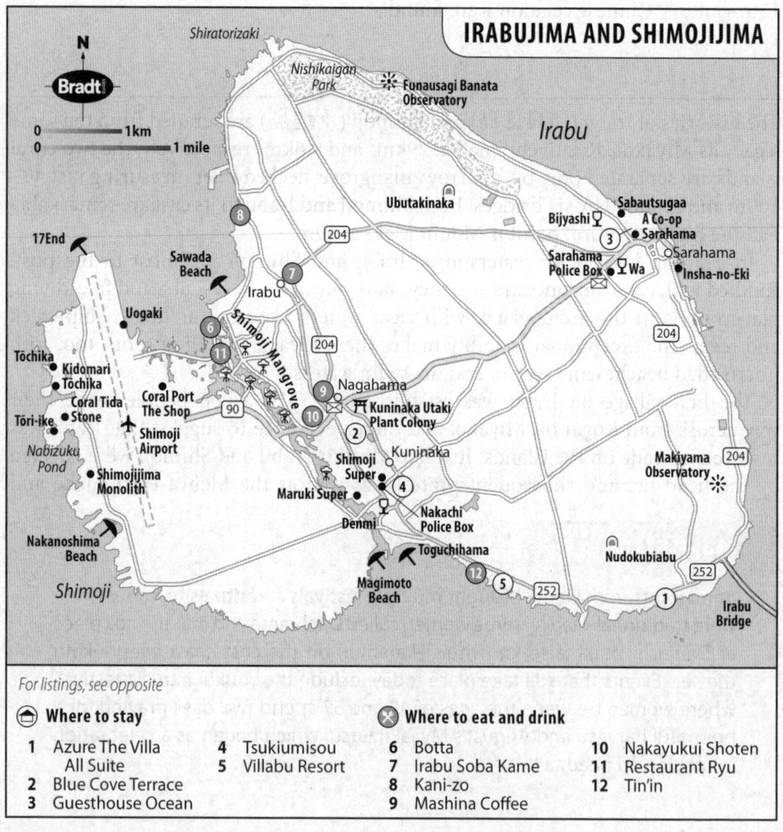

Despite their size, the islands have four language variants, including a version called Sarahama, a variant of Ikema's language brought over by the 18th-century migrants.

GETTING THERE AND AWAY Irabu was finally connected to Miyako main island in January 2015 by the Irabu Bridge, which is how most access the two. Somewhat surprisingly, Shimojishima has an airport, with regular flights between Tokyo Narita, Osaka and Hong Kong operated by Jetstar (w jetstar.com/jp/en) and Skymark (w skymark.co.jp). However, you'll likely find the flights to and from Miyako cheaper.

The airport is accessed by two buses. The No 9 Resort Line run by Miyako Kyoei (0980 72 2414; w 385kyoei.com) goes from Shimojishima Airport to Miyako, through Hirara to the Tokyu Hotel at Maehama, hitting the majority of resorts. The Miyako Shimojishima Airport Liner operated by Chūō Kotsu (0980 79 5540; w ck-okinawa.com) takes a similar route, but includes Miyako Airport and continues on to Shigira Resort further south.

Taxis to Hirara take just under half an hour and are more expensive than the buses, but are at least regular. Four car rental companies operate at Shimoji – Orix (w orac-miyakojima.com), OTS (w otsinternational.jp), Toyota (w rent.toyota.co.jp/eng) and Pine (w pine-rentacar.jp).

GETTING AROUND **Driving** and **cycling** are the best ways to explore these flat islands, and make it easy to access the more off-the-beaten-track bits. Bike rentals are available from most hotels and Shimojishima Airport, which has electric and folding bikes and baggage storage. The two airport **buses** (page 260) pass some sites, and the small Kyowa Bus (共和バス; w kyowabus.studio.site) hops a few times a day between the villages in Irabu's west, Sawada in the east, and Miyakojima.

For **taxis**, try Irabu Credit Taxi (0980 78 3093) or Nikko Taxi (0980 78 3007).

TOURIST INFORMATION Though there's little tourist information on the island, you can call the Irabu Tourist Association direct (0980 78 6250).

WHERE TO STAY *Map, opposite*

Accommodation on little Shimoji is very limited, so most people stay on the mainland or on Irabu. Irabu overflows with luxury coastal resorts; you will be hard pressed to choose one as they are largely excellent and relatively secluded. There are a handful of more budget-conscious hostels and minshuku, but Miyako has more options for cheaper digs (page 262).

Azure The Villa All Suite (8 villas) 紺碧ザ・ヴィラオールスイート; 119-1 Ikemagoe, Irabu; 0980 78 6000; w konpeki.okinawa. Gorgeous sand-tone, ocean-view luxury villas on the south coast. Private gazebos & pools, wine bars in each room, plush living space & botanical bath products. On-site French restaurant uses island ingredients. **$$$$$**

Villabu Resort (6 villas) ヴィラブリゾート; 817 Irabu, Irabu; 0980 78 6777; w villabu.jp. Stunning Bali-style houses with private pools, gazebos, private beach & spa treatments. Restaurant serves Irabu produce with Ryūkyūan & Italian cuisine, omakase & tasting menus. Cycle, fishing & snorkel rental & tours available. **$$$$$**

Blue Cove Terrace (24 rooms) ブルーコーブテラス; 183-8 Kuninaka, Irabu; 0980 79 7411; w bluecove.jp. Handsome 3-star rooms with mini kitchens, washing machine & dryer, TV & speakers, at one of the cheapest prices. B/fast inc. **$$$**

PINK GENMEI

A vibrant, near-neon magenta drink found in shops and cafés around the island, Irabu's pink *genmei* is difficult to ignore. Genmei – which strangely enough, actually means 'brown rice', even though the drink is usually white – has been drunk for a long time on Miyako, believed to be good for energy and cooling off. It's a mix of glutinous mochi flour, water and sugar – but on Irabu it's been laced with a fluorescent food dye. The texture is certainly unique; it's thick and gloopy. You can try it in Irabu's A Co-op (see opposite), Irabu Ōhashi service station, and other stores.

Guesthouse Ocean (2 rooms) ゲストハウスオーシャン; 554-1 Maezatozoe, Irabu; 0907 862 0479; w guesthouseocean.com. Bright, cheap guesthouse with large rooms that can convert from dorms to private. Shared spaces, snorkel & car rental. HB available & English-speaking. **$$$**

Tsukiumisou (4 rooms) つきうみ荘・月海荘; 158 Irabu, Irabu; 0806 492 6969; w tukiumisou.com. Local house with Western & Japanese rooms, living space, hammock, garden, bar & chicken that lays eggs for b/fast. Can be rented as whole house or individual rooms. Wheelchair access possible. **$$$**

WHERE TO EAT AND DRINK *Map, page 276*

Irabu

Tin'in てぃんいん; 818-5 Irabu; 0980 74 5511; w suihotels.com; 07.00–10.30, 11.30–15.30 & 17.30–21.00 daily. Utterly gorgeous restaurant at Iraph Sui Hotel. Window walls that overlook the sea & French-inspired takes on island ingredients. **$$$$$**

Botta ボッタ; 1726-4 Sawada; 0980 78 5010; w botta-irabujima.jimdofree.com; 11.30–16.00 Wed–Mon. Open-air pizza joint overlooking Sawada Beach. Italian-style, stone-baked, handmade dough; sweet options available. **$$**

Kani-zo 蟹蔵; 1181-6 Sawada; 0980 78 4737; w kani-zo.com; 10.00–18.00 Mon–Sat. A lovely seaside restaurant serving noodles, mangrove crab, tempura & desserts. Offers large multi-course (more expensive) seafood dinners too. **$$**

Irabu Soba Kame 伊良部そばかめ; 251 Nagahama; 0980 78 5477; 11.00–16.00 & 18.00–21.00 daily. Incredibly popular vending machine shop with succulent meat & soft noodles. The most popular, *kame soba* (かめそば) and *Irabu soba* (伊良部そば), are numbered 1 & 2. **$**

Mashina Coffee ましな珈琲; 431-1 Kuninaka; 0980 74 5056; 10.00–15.30 Mon–Fri. A fish processing factory with café serving coffee, juice & the freshest tempura. **$**

✷ **Nakayukui Shoten** なかゆくい商店; 573 Kuninaka; 0909 476 3215; 09.30–noon & 13.30–16.00 Tue–Wed & Fri–Sun, 13.30–16.00 Mon. Famous family shop selling special satapanbin doughnuts: huge crispy balls flavoured with beni-imo sweet potato, turning the inside a fantastic lilac. Also sells tempura for ¥80 a piece. Closes early when sold out. **$**

Shimoji

Restaurant Ryu 島野彩カフェ龍; 2F 1647-3 Nagahama; 0980 78 5252; w tidanosato.com; 07.00–21.00 Fri–Wed. Also known as Island Vegetable Café, this café on the 2nd floor of Hotel Tidanosato serves organic 'medicinal' cuisine. Sizeable set meals overlooking the gorgeous channel between Irabu & Shimoji. **$$**

ENTERTAINMENT AND NIGHTLIFE Irabu has a fair number of traditional izakaya options. The best way to approach a nightcap is to simply find a bar that calls to you; the drinks and fare are often much of a muchness, so it's hard to go wrong.

Bijyashi びじゃし; 588-98 Maezatozo, Irabu; 0980 78 3444; 18.00–23.00 Mon–Wed & Fri–Sat. Out-of-the-way izakaya serving delicious bar food in a surprisingly pretty setting. Wood-crammed diner gives way to Japanese tatami & windows overlooking Irabu fields.

Denmi 居酒屋でんみ; 1394 Irabu, Irabu; 0980 78 3535; w izakayadenmi.wixsite.com/denmi; 18.00–23.00 Tue–Sat, 18.00–22.00 Sun. Local favourite in Irabu town with chilled atmosphere, friendly staff & cheap prices.

Wa お食事処居酒屋和; 624-1 Maezatozoe, Irabu; 0980 78 6338; 09.00–22.00 Mon–Sat. Sarahama izakaya with bar-style food that's equally good for family meals & having a drink.

SHOPPING

Food and drink

A Co-op Sarahama Aコープ さらはま店; 471-1 Maezatozoe, Irabu; 0980 78 4103; w ja-okinawa.or.jp; 09.00–20.00 daily
Maruki Super まるきスーパー; 1493-1 Irabu, Irabu; 0980 78 3638; 08.00–20.00 daily
Shimoji Super シモジスーパー; 22 Irabu, Irabu; 0980 78 3693; w shimoji-super.com; 07.30–20.00 daily

Souvenirs

Coral Port The Shop Shimoji Airport, Shimoji; 0980 78 6602; w store.shopping.yahoo.co.jp/shimojishima; 09.00–19.00 daily. Airport shop with foodstuffs, clothing & souvenirs.
Coral Tida Stone コーラルティダストーン; Tori-ike Car Park, Shimoji; 0803 282 3323; w painagama.thebase.in; 10.30–15.00 daily. Jewellery & accessories, handmade & sold from van stall at the Tori-ike parking.
Insha-no-Eki いんしゃの駅・佐良浜; 689-5 Ikemazoe, Irabu; 09.00–17.30 daily. Trinkets, postcards & souvenirs, with café on site.

SPORTS AND ACTIVITIES Despite being the home of Miyako marine sports, Irabu and Shimoji are limited on local, English-speaking dive schools. Snorkel rental is best done from your accommodation, and while there are some tours available from Irabu, the majority of dive schools operate from Miyakojima (page 264). Both islands offer dives for a range of abilities, making them perfect for mixed groups and families.

Irabu's dive sites include the jaw-dropping sun-dappled Blue Cave on the west coast, which is perfect for introductory dives at just 3m. This westerly spot is rather out on its own, however; the rest of the topographical features are generally around the north and northeast of the island. There you'll find the Snake Hole, a bright blue cave pool where you can come to the surface; the dynamic L-shaped Arch, which dives down to 35m and features a cave; the heart-shaped Double Arch; the Z-shaped Arch; the Overhang Rock; and Cross Hole, one of Irabu's most ethereal underwater spots.

Coral reefs include Saba, a largely shallow reef full of big and small fish including sharks, dogtooth tuna and the occasional turtle. There's also Surgeon Reef, which has a stronger current but is ideal for larger fish including sharks, turtles and occasional rays and mantas. Shiratorizaki is covered in whip corals and has a sunlit rock hole, while Shiratori Kindergarten is a haven for macro life like nudibranchs and pygmy seahorses.

One of Irabu's best sites is the Wreck Ship, between the island and Miyako. Previously a car ferry, this ship was purposefully sunk and left to the reef. There are plentiful fish about, but the wreck is known for its cool internal exploration.

Shimoji is even more mottled with dive sites, covering the west from top to bottom. It holds three of Miyako's most popular dive spots: Tōri-ike, the Devil's Palace and Antonio Gaudi. Tōri-ike comprises two ponds connected below by an underwater tunnel (page 282); the Devil's Palace contains three illuminated rooms; and Gaudi's multiple rock windows glow with neon-blue sunlight.

Shimoji is additionally home to Panata; strong currents mean it's not for the faint of heart, but it has tornadoes of bigeye trevally, as well as dogtooth tuna,

Napoleonfish and big sea turtles. There are also big drops at Hon Drop and Wall Cave, where you see massive schools of fish.

Irabu Kicks 85-2 Kuninaka; w irabukicks-g.com. Fun buggy/quad bike tours around the islands; also sells Irabu-based clothing.
Kani-zo 蟹蔵; 1181-6 Sawada; ☎0980 78 4737; w kani-zo.com. Traditional sabani boat or mangrove tours by a local crab farmer & restaurant owner, served up alongside mangrove crab meals.
Miyako Diving Reef 宮古島ダイビングREEF; 1F 1493-1 Irabu; ☎0909 695 7781; w reefmiyako.com. Snorkelling & PADI licence course based at Hotel South Island Irabujima. Lunches for day tours put on at the hotel's Restaurant Irie.
Miyakojima Sea Breeze 1391-1 Irabu; ☎0902 887 1218; w miyakojima-seabreeze.com. Jet-ski tours & 3-wheeled motorbike tours, based at Toguchi Beach.
✷ **OneBreath Irabu** ワンブレス イラブ; 97 Kuninaka; ☎0806 485 7663; w onebreath-irabu.sakura.ne.jp. Free-dive instructor who (importantly) speaks English. Tours include boat & skin diving, licence & training courses, & rental.
Waterman SUP ウォーターマンサップ; 925 Kuninaka; ☎0904 542 8945; w watermansup.com. A wealth of SUP tours provided by Ryo, including sunset & cave options.

OTHER PRACTICALITIES Irabu has minimal services. ATMs can be found at Irabu Post Office (伊良部郵便局; 8 6-16 Kuninaka, Irabu; ☎0980 78 4965; ⏲ 09.00–17.00 Mon–Fri, ATM: 08.45–17.30 Mon–Fri, 09.00–17.00 Sat–Sun) and the Sarahama Post Office (佐良浜郵便局; 646-1 Maezatozoe, Irabu; ☎0980 78 4966; ⏲ 09.00–17.00 Mon–Fri, ATM: 09.00–17.30 Mon–Fri, 09.00–17.00 Sat).

There are two police boxes: Sarahama (佐良浜駐在所; 643-2 Maezatotzoe, Irabu; ☎0980 78 4110) and Nakachi (仲地駐在所; 24 Irabu, Irabu; ☎0980 78 4842; ⏲ 07.30–16.15 Mon–Fri, 09.30–18.15 Sat–Sun) in the southeast. For medical emergencies and issues, look to the main hospitals on Miyakojima (page 265).

WHAT TO SEE AND DO

Irabu The most likely entry point for Irabu and Shimoji is from Miyako over the Irabu Bridge, where it's worth stopping at **Uminoeki** (いらぶ大橋 海の駅), the roadside shop and information point, to pick up souvenirs or a refreshing pink genmei.

The southwest of Irabu is filled with concealed caves called *abu*, but many people – including some locals – don't even know they exist. You'll need grippy shoes to explore them and make sure to mark them on a map in advance as they're often hard to locate. One of the more accessible caves is **Nudokubiabu** (ヌドクビアブ), hidden in an unsuspecting copse in the middle of a field; the northwest corner of the copse has a plaque and narrow path between the trees and a low wall. The path is muddy and undulating, but soon becomes stairs. Descend 22m into this fantastical cave, where tendrils of the trees above plunge into the cavern. It's a phenomenal photo spot, though the lighting conditions aren't easy to work with.

To the bridge's east is **Makiyama Observatory** (牧山展望台), the highest point on Irabu. This observation deck is built like a sashiba – the grey-faced buzzard that's Irabu's symbolic bird. From here you can see Irabu, Ikema, Kurima, Miyako and the exquisite sea. You can also walk through the primeval forest surrounding the observatory.

The coastline to **Sarahama** (佐良浜) is filled with small beaches, old wells and caves, but these are largely difficult to get to, being unmarked, without paths and through thick foliage. Above Sarahama, where you can find great cafés, restaurants and local life, there's **Sabautsugaa** (サバウツガー). Set in a dramatic coastline area of azure sea and crags, this well supplied the people of Sarahama for over 240 years.

LOCAL RECIPE: SATAPANBIN

Better known as saataa andagii in the rest of the archipelago, on the Miyako these just-sweet doughnuts are called satapanbin. Though they come in a variety of sizes, the famous lilac Irabu ones are nearing a tennis ball. The bigger ones tend to be less dry, but are harder to form with the soft batter. If you don't have access to the archipelago's purple potato, sweet potato and pumpkin work just fine.

150g sweet potato
1 egg
60g sugar
2 tbsp milk
1 tbsp vegetable oil, extra for hands
150g plain flour
1 tsp baking powder
Oil for deep frying

1. Steam the sweet potato till soft, then make into a smooth paste using a sieve or potato ricer.
2. Mix the egg, sugar, milk, and oil together until well combined.
3. Add the sweet potato paste and mix well.
4. Sift the flour and baking powder in and stir. This will form a very sticky batter.
5. Heat oil in a deep pan to 150°C. To make the balls, coat hands or an ice cream scoop/large spoon in oil and form a rough ball – somewhat larger than a golf ball – with the batter. This will be messy, it will stick to your fingers, but it's part of the fun.
6. Gently drop the ball into the oil (it won't be perfectly round – in fact, the knobblier, the crunchier). It should fizz gently. Fry low and slow until a very deep golden brown, the colour of hazelnuts. The ball should flip over on its own, which helps you know how long each side takes – roughly 10 minutes depending on heat.
7. Before making another, re-oil your hands/utensil. Remove balls when ready and rest on kitchen towel to remove excess oil.

Its name comes from the word for 'shark': when seen from Ikema, this area was said to resemble a shark's mouth.

Just up and inland from here is **Ubutakinaka** (大竹中洞穴), a valuable archaeological cave where ancient fossils of humans and deer were found. You can find it off an agricultural road, marked by a sign. Back on the coast, you'll find the once bird-topped **Funausagi Banata Observatory** (フナウサギバナタ), which has had its wings clipped: the bird no longer exists but the views remain. People once prayed here for the safety of those leaving the island.

Irabu's northernmost part is **Nishikaigan Park** (西海岸公園), a beautiful coast full of inlets, promenades and rest areas with views of Ikema and Nishihennazaki. In winter, clear waters may well reveal mantas migrating, even from clifftop viewpoints. Next door is **Shiratorizaki** (白鳥崎), a weathered limestone cape of emerald and cyan with an eroded atoll-like reef and a seaside boardwalk. Walking off the path is a test of ankles – the heavily eroded limestone is incredibly ragged and sharp enough to pierce flip-flops. Losing your balance here will hurt. The sea around Shiratorizaki Head has famed diving spots with complex topography like underwater arches and caves.

On Irabu's northwest is **Sawada Beach** (佐和田の浜), one of the island's best fishing grounds and voted one of Japan's 100 most beautiful beaches. Its lagoon is littered with some 300 large and small rocks, likely deposited from the Meiwa tsunami. Sitting between Shimoji and Irabu, the waters are filled with colourful fish and coral reefs. The beach is safe for swimming and snorkelling, though that's occasionally debated by the local government as there are shallow, sharp rocks and occasional currents and fast-rising tides. There are camping, shower and barbecue facilities, and Sawada is one of the best places for sunset too.

The west of the island is largely given over to beautiful views over the mangroves towards Shimoji. The towns of **Nagahama** (長浜), **Kuninaka** (国中) and **Irabu** (伊良部) are all on this side, rather blending into each other, and are ideal for picking up lunch or dinner to enjoy along the waterfront. In Kuninaka, you'll also find the **Kuninaka Utaki Plant Colony** (国仲御嶽の植物群落), just east of Irabu Junior High School. This small shrine is a protected place of worship, so the forest surrounding it has been allowed to grow. It's now an excellent representation of the natural Miyako/Irabu forest with 60 different plant species.

The southwest coast is home to **Toguchihama** (渡口の浜), a beautiful and pristine white-sand beach that curves up towards Shimoji. From the 800m beach, you can see Kurima Island and Miyako's western coast. It's a popular beach, particularly for the resort hotels that line its cliffs, but is by no means overcrowded. The waters here are incredibly clear and cobalt and excellent for swimming, but note that when the wind blows up from the south, the waves can get choppy and occasionally bring in jellyfish. Barbecues, parasols and snorkels can be rented from nearby.

Shimoji Between the islands is a channel of mangroves, which are a haven for animals and migratory birds. Travelling from Irabu to Shimoji by the northernmost bridge brings you to Shimoji Airport, which takes up a large amount of the island.

A tarmac path leads around the runway along the coast, for bicycles or walking only. It's worth exploring (there's dedicated parking on the west entrance), specifically at low tide. This is when you'll see ***katsu*** (魚垣), traditional fishing walls in **Karabaruinau** (カタバルイナウ), a lagoon on the east side of the runway. These underwater walls made of piled rocks rely on the tide to trap fish; fish enter at high tide and are unable to escape as waters recede.

At Shimoji's northernmost point is an oddly named low-tide beach, **17End** (17ENDビーチ). Stunning shallow waters lead away from the runway and its guiding lights stretching out into the sea. The name (one seven end) comes from the 3,000m-long runway on Shimoji, where aircrafts land at a 170-degree angle to the tip of the island. Despite its beauty, 17End is not for swimming, but it's nonetheless a wonderful place to cycle alongside luminescent turquoise and watch planes come and go.

The end of the runway path brings you to the west of the island, which is a topographical playground of karst and limestone, renowned for snorkelling and free diving. The first sites you come to are on land: two machine gun nests, **Toochika** (トーチカ跡) and **Kidomari Toochika** (キドマリのトーチカ跡), which are carved into rock near the beach above **Tōri-ike** (通り池).

Tōri-ike itself is arguably these islands' best tourist site. It's formed of two eroded limestone sinkholes that look separate from above, but are connected by an underwater channel, with another channel on the south side connecting them to the ocean. The ponds are popular with divers, who swim through their tunnels to enjoy drastic thermocline temperature changes and various marine life. As the

MYTHS AND FOLKTALES: TŌRI-IKE

A Shimoji fisherman lived with his wife and son, but often went out overnight on his small boat to fish. His wife, angry at his nightly absence, left him. He remarried and had a second son, but though the children grew up as brothers, his second wife hated his first son and wanted him dead.

One night, when her husband went fishing, the stepmother took the children to Tōri-ike, telling them they would await their father there, and settled them around the pond edge to sleep. The wife fell asleep quickly, but the first son at the outer edge couldn't thanks to the sharp rocks. He asked his half-brother to switch places as the mother slept on.

When the mother woke in the night, she initiated her plan: she pretended to roll over and accidentally push the outermost child into the deep pond. When she realised she had murdered her own beloved son, she threw her stepchild in too, before fleeing and going mad with grief. The father returned, calling for his children, but to no avail.

Even now, there is supposedly a rocky area near the southern pond called Mamakodai (ママ子台), literally 'the pedestal of the mother and the children'.

tides change, the colours of the ponds do, too. Their unusual formation and scenic location have not only led to them being designated a natural monument by the government, but have also given rise to multiple local legends and made them a spiritual spot of worship. The ponds are 75m and 55m across, and at a depth of 45m and 25m. This area has boardwalks, but to get closer to some parts, like the **Nabizuku Pond** (ナビズク・鍋底) further south, you'll have to walk on harsh, eroded rock: wear good shoes.

Further south is the **Shimojijima Monolith** (下地島巨石・帯石), a massive rock fronted by a torii gate. With a diameter of 59.9m and a height of 12.5m, it weighs some 20,000 tonnes and is said to have been launched on to Shimoji by the Meiwa tsunami. It has become a revered place of worship for fishing and family.

Nakanoshima Beach (中の島海岸), also known locally as Kayaffa (カヤッファ), is one of the best places on the Miyako for shore snorkelling and diving. It has a huge sprawling reef close to shore, protected calm waters and plenty of fish and coral, as well as the occasional turtle and octopus. It's without facilities, however. Shimoji's south is sprinkled with small pretty beaches hidden from the road, culminating in **Magimoto Beach** (曲元の浜).

TARAMAJIMA

Tarama (多良間島) is a Miyako afterthought – a somewhat forgotten blob way out west that most travellers clock on the flight to Ishigaki and never think of again. This forgotten feeling is very much part of Tarama's charm: you can safely assume you're the only foreign tourist on the island most of the time.

Tarama is a 19.75 km^2 near-perfect circle and incredibly flat: the highest point on the island is a 34m-tall observation tower. A quick climb up here shows exactly how levelled this place is, as the entire island pans out before you. This makes getting around by bike incredibly easy, but does mean Tarama is a little lacking in dramatic scenery.

Despite being part of the Miyako group, Tarama is some 67km away from its fellow islands but only 35km from Ishigaki. This made it a strategic stop-off in

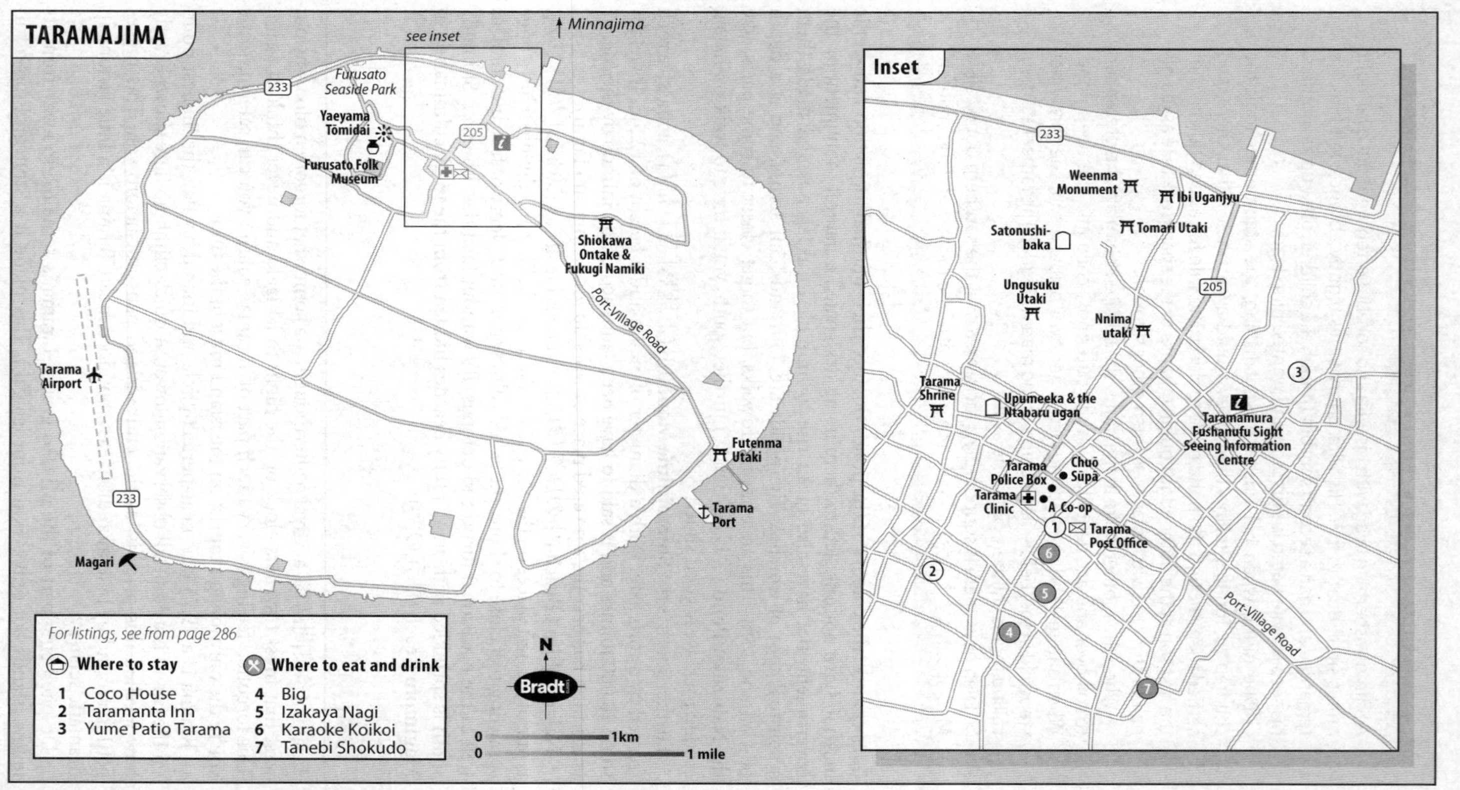
TARAMAJIMA
see inset
Minnajima
Furusato Seaside Park
233
Yaeyama Tōmidai
Furusato Folk Museum
205
Shiokawa Ontake & Fukugi Namiki
Port-Village Road
Tarama Airport
Futenma Utaki
Tarama Port
Magari
For listings, see from page 286
Where to stay
1 Coco House
2 Taramanta Inn
3 Yume Patio Tarama
Where to eat and drink
4 Big
5 Izakaya Nagi
6 Karaoke Koikoi
7 Tanebi Shokudo
N
Bradt
0 1km
0 1 mile
Inset
Weenma Monument
Ibi Uganjyu
Tomari Utaki
Satonushi-baka
Ungusuku Utaki
Nnima utaki
Tarama Shrine
Upumeeka & the Ntabaru ugan
Taramamura Fushanufu Sight Seeing Information Centre
Tarama Police Box
Chuō Sūpā
Tarama Clinic
A Co-op
Tarama Post Office

TARAMA FESTIVALS

Tarama's big cultural event is the August festival, which takes place over three days from the 8th to the 10th. Seeming to have originated as an event to pray for a good harvest year and celebrate the payment of the harsh poll tax (which took place in July), its highlight is a 400-year-old folk dance. It's a great time to visit if you can get accommodation and ferries booked well in advance. There's also the Sutsuupunaka, a harvest and prosperity festival that takes place around June across four sites with chants and feasts.

A more secular festival is the Pinda Aasu – the goat fighting festival. It's an unusual take on bullfighting, capitalising on goats' tendency to head-butt and lock horns. Held to promote goat production and farming, it takes place in May and October, with local goats and goats from outside the island. Naturally goat dishes are served too.

the Middle Ages for the voyage between Okinawa, Miyako and Yaeyama. It isn't known when Tarama was first inhabited, but archaeological finds here and on tiny, neighbouring Minna suggest the pair have been settled for a long time, with trade and exchange outside of the island.

Tarama's history is unsurprisingly vague, but its 15th-century chief Ntabaru Tuyumya was famed for unifying the island and helping to fight Akahachi on the Yaeyama. He was rewarded by being made lord of Tarama by King Shō Shin. The island first appears in literature in 1479, in Korean chronicles of sailors who ended up on Tarama after getting lost. Indeed, Tarama's history is littered with people washing up on its shores, including those forced there by exile.

Tarama locals have – or perhaps once had – a strong connection to nature. They prize the Taramabana, or safflower: a thistle-like plant of orange and yellow. It's seen as a herald of springtime and its delicate fragrance and medicinal and dyeing properties meant the flowers were once sent as Tarama's tribute to Shuri. The island's symbolic bird is the Japanese quail, known as *uzura* – a rotund bird popular in fairy tales and love songs – though the population on Tarama is unfortunately in decline and in need of protection. The island also hosts plenty of butterflies too.

The island's village, where the majority of its 1,068 inhabitants live, is rather special – it even joined the 'Union of the Most Beautiful Villages in Japan' in 2010. Built with Ryūkyūan feng shui principles in mind, it is filled with narrow streets that radiate out from the main village and head to the sea. These ocean-bound roads are known as *tuburi*, and Tarama has 47 of them. It also has rows of handsome fukugi trees, which have been planted to protect houses and agriculture from strong winds and typhoons. Thanks to the village's small size, there's little light pollution, making Tarama a great stargazing island.

In general, Tarama isn't an island of sights and spectacle. Tranquil and understated, this is a place to come for extraordinary snorkelling, deserted beaches, and being so off the beaten track that the bus is basically a private taxi service. One of the best aspects to the island is its wilderness, left to grow over old shrines, graves, monuments and paths. These sections of flat jungle are brief but dense; the tree roots have a life of their own, and you're almost guaranteed solitude when exploring.

GETTING THERE AND AWAY Tarama is accessed by ferry and plane, though the ferry is the most cost-effective option. The *Ferry Tarama III* leaves from Hirara and is run by Tarama Kaiun (多良間海運; 108-11 Shimozato; 0980 72 9209;

w taramakaiun.com); there's one return trip every day except Sunday, taking 2 hours 5 minutes each way.

The office is in the main Hirara Port building but you buy tickets at the ferry dock. Staff at the main office can direct you, but simply turn right when coming out of the building (facing the harbour), walk down the road, across another, and keep going until you see a small, square, peach-coloured building. This office opens about an hour before the ferries depart and closes again when they leave.

Although the ferry is cost-effective, it comes with another price: cancellations. Being so far out from any other islands, Tarama's commute is a long stretch of water easily affected by bad weather. Tarama itself is best explored in sunshine, so wait for a bank of clear days to go, lest you find yourself stuck.

If you decide to fly, the route is covered by Ryūkyū Air Commuter (w rac-okinawa.com). Tickets are hard to come by online and usually require a phone call, which your accommodation can handle for you. Flights are twice a day, take 20 minutes and seat 50 people.

GETTING AROUND Tarama is small and best traversed by **bicycle** or **motorbike**. There's a **bus** (☏ 0980 79 2619) that runs between the three access points – the ferry terminal in the south where Miyako ferries operate, the north port where private boats to Minna depart (page 290), and the airport in the southwest. The bus is timed to meet the ferries and flights and that's it; you'll find bus times on arrival at the ferry terminal.

Unless your accommodation is picking you up, take the bus to the village where you can rent a bicycle from your minshuku. If you prefer to rent a **car**, look to minshuku such as Coco House and Taramanta (see below); just don't expect a shiny clean model. Tarama Concierge (TARAMA観光コンシェルジュ; 397 Nakasuji; ☏ 0906 858 6268; w taramaconcierge.com; ⏰ 09.00–17.00 daily) offers **electric kickboard scooter** rental. Bafflingly these are considered a 'motorised bike', so you'll need a driving licence, to wear a helmet and to use roads.

TOURIST INFORMATION There's a tourist information centre in the northeast of the village, Taramamura Fushanufu Sightseeing Information Centre (多良間村ふしゃぬふ観光協会; 445-1 Shiokawa; ☏ 0980 79 2828; w kyodomarine.wixsite.com/tarama2; ⏰ 10.00–18.00 Thu–Tue), which has a workspace, information, rental services and a shop. The ferry company also has a comprehensive and incredibly useful map to Taramajima in English.

WHERE TO STAY *Map, page 284*

Tarama has a surprisingly healthy selection of hotels for such a tiny out-of-the-way place. None is high end, but they're clean and comfortable and perfect if you're staying overnight or a couple of days. Most of these are cash only, so be prepared.

Taramanta Inn (5 rooms) たらまんたINN; 139 Nakasuji; ☏ 0908 294 0121; w taramantainn.studio.site. Bright cyan building with basic small dbl & family rooms. Scooter, car, cycle & BBQ rental. Snorkelling, water scooter, jet-ski & Minnajima tours. **$$$**

Yume Patio Tarama (12 rooms, 2 dorms) 夢パティオたらま; 18 Shiokawa; ☏ 0980 79 2988; w vill.tarama.okinawa.jp/夢パティオたらま. A village-run accommodation with private room & tatami shared rooms; HB available. Lounge, kitchen, communal bath, laundry, ideal for groups/long-term stays. **$$$**

✷ **Coco House** (18 rooms) ココハウス; 153 Shiokawa; ☏ 0980 79 2133; w www2.miyako-ma.jp/cocohaus. Seriously cheap accommodation in village centre. Luminous yellow building & very basic rooms – comfy & clean, kitchen, shared room, gym & HB option. Rental car & cycle available. **$$**

TARAMA AGRICULTURE

Agriculture is important here – in fact the whole island is pretty much given over to it. The main crops are vegetables, leaf tobacco and sugarcane, but beef is also an increasingly important market and has become a popular ingredient in Tarama cuisine, with dishes like Tarama beef soup. Kokutō brown sugar remains the island's major export – this is Japan's largest brown sugar production area – and Tarama's brown sugar is lauded as the best in the entire Nansei-shotō. Though many other islands would fight such a claim, Tarama has set itself apart by having 200 farmers certified as eco-farmers for sugarcane; it's the first of the islands to receive such a certification. These farmers are working to reduce pesticides and chemical fertilisers by 30%.

WHERE TO EAT AND DRINK *Map, page 284*

Proper restaurants are essentially non-existent, but there are izakaya and cafés. If you stumble across an open bar, don't expect to be out late.

There are a few shops and supermarkets in the village (see below) but things do tend to sell out early. It's worth grabbing lunch or dinner early on in the day. Foods to look out for on Tarama include *panapanbin*, a fried curl of pastry originally made for celebrations and memorials. Its gently salted flavour is surprisingly moreish. Tarama's high-quality brown sugar features in a lot of its sweets: brown-sugar cookies, *uuyakigasu* fired dough, rustic *taramanbo* sticks, and Tarama gelato. Local gelato flavours also include pumpkin and black bean.

At restaurants, look for goat soup, making use of Tarama's beloved, grass-rich goat meat, and black beans, known as *sasage*. *Noni* juice is a Tarama speciality – better known as moringa, this 100% organic juice is aged for half a year and is known for its health benefits and rich minerals.

Big ビッグ; 527 Shiokawa; 0980 79 2118; 19.00–midnight daily. Standard izakaya fare with Okinawa soba & the like. $$

Izakaya Nagi 居酒屋凪; 187 Shiokawa; 0980 79 2750; 18.30–22.30 Mon–Sat. Cheap tempura, fried foods, Miyako beef gyoza, sōmen & chanpuruu in a small, very local setting. Beers, highballs, awamori. $

Karaoke Koikoi カラオケこいこい; 170-2 Shiokawa; 0980 79 2090; 18.00–midnight daily. Not a place to go for food – nor, arguably, if you're imagining a Tokyo karaoke night – but locals go to town on the mike at this izakaya. $

Tanebi Shokudo たねび食堂; 539 Shiokawa; 11.30–14.00 Mon–Sat. Japanese-only menu that heavily focuses on soba, but is excellent value & hearty. $

SHOPPING Tarama has two main village stores opposite each other, as well as a few small satellite shops, which have a good selection of nibbles and supplies between them. You'll not be able to make a four-course feast, but you won't go hungry if you find yourself stranded. There's the A Co-op Tarama (Aコープ たらま店; 158 Shiokawa; 0980 79 2339; w ja-okinawa.or.jp; 09.00–19.00 Mon–Sun) and Chūō Sūpā (中央スーパー; 113 Shiokawa; 0980 79 2850; 09.30–20.00 Mon–Sun).

Tongue-twisting souvenir shop Sumamunutarama (すまむぬたらま; 445-1 Shiokawa; 0980 79 2828; w kyodomarine.wixsite.com/tarama2; 10.00–18.00 Thu–Tue) is part of the information centre (see opposite). Tarama mementoes include *shichimi* spice, flower teas and Tarama *beni-tsumugi* – a local cloth dyed by the symbolic taramabana flower that's been cultivated on the island for five centuries.

SPORTS AND ACTIVITIES Of course, the seas surrounding Tarama are great dive sites. The water is incredibly transparent, with far-reaching, unspoilt coral reefs. These reefs are home to fish, sea turtles, and even dolphins. To the north are coral fields and giant coral clusters, the east dynamic terrain, the west migratory fish and the south macro life and interesting topography.

Kyodo Marine Service JAWS II 郷土マリンサービス; 514-1 Shiokawa; 0980 79 2452; w divehousejaws2.web.fc2.com; 08.00–19.00 daily. Recommended by the Tarama Tourist Association, this diving service offers fun dives, free diving, snorkelling, experience diving & equipment rental.

OTHER PRACTICALITIES Tarama has the single Tarama Police Box (警察署多良間; 161 Shiokawa; 0980 79 2010), the Tarama Clinic (多良間診療所; 162-3 Shiokawa; 0980 79 2101; 08.30–11.30 & 14.00–16.30 Mon–Fri), and the Tarama Post Office (多良間郵便局; 152 Shiokawa; 0980 79 2104; 09.00–17.00 Mon–Fri, ATM: 08.45–17.30 Mon–Fri, 09.00–17.00 Sat). Tarama is not the place to come for medical treatments.

WHAT TO SEE AND DO If you're not heading straight to the beach to surf, swim or snorkel, Tarama's big attractions can be counted on one hand. The village is very much for local life, not tourists, but you can find a few interesting oddities as you make your way round.

The central **Tarama Shrine** (多良間神社), built in 1902, is dedicated to Ntabaru Tuyumya, the 15th-century hero of Tarama who unified the scattered villages (page 285). There's also an annual festival here.

The **Yaeyama Tōmidai** (八重山遠見台) is a 37m-high observatory in the west of the village and is a useful landmark when navigating the island. It's a short climb to the top, where you can see every compass point of the island. On clear days, you may be able to see the northern tip of the Yaeyama too. Next to it is a **Sakishima beacon** (八重山遠見台), built in the 17th century to watch out for incoming ships.

A short walk south of the observation tower is the **Furusato Folk Museum** (多良間村 ふるさと民俗学習館; 1098-1 Nakasuji; 0980 79 2223; 09.00–17.00 Tue–Sun; ¥200). The folk museum is quite impressive given the island's size, but it's unsurprisingly all in Japanese. However, the man running it is desperately friendly and will set you up with an English-speaking video of the island's festival. Explore excavated oddments, ceramics, agricultural tools, marine paraphernalia and costumes from the annual matsuri.

Furusato Seaside Park (ふる里海浜公園) sits on the north of the island, not far from the observatory. It's a park fronted by a lovely sandy beach with clear shallow seas and a massive tsunami rock that's revealed to be balancing on two legs at low tide. It has toilet and shower facilities and a rest area with picnic table.

In the north of the village you'll find **Upumeeka and the Ntabaru ugan** (ウプメーカ・土原ウガン) – a grave built to honour Ntabaru Tuyumya. Despite its age, the stone sarcophagus is excellently preserved and impressively made.

The area between the village and the north port is covered in utaki. One of these, read as **Nnima Utaki** (嶺間御嶽), has a spring behind it, where a now extinct Shintō festival was once held. It's fronted by an impressively large *akagi* tree which is revered as sacred. The utaki is also home to a valuable plant community.

Tucked away in an ancient fukugi forest, **Ungusuku Utaki** (運城御嶽) was supposedly founded by Ntabaru Tuyumya in the 1500s and it enshrines the

MYTHS AND FOLKTALES: THE YAMATO TOMBS OF TARAMA

Tarama has multiple types of cemetery, one of which is Yamato graves, which came later than the traditional Miyako myaaka air burial sites (page 266).

A long time ago, a small boat containing a group of young men believed to be from mainland Japan ran ashore at Tarama. They had been drifting for some time; by the time they made it to Tarama, they were exhausted and starving and couldn't make it to the village. A few villagers found them, and awaited permission to intervene and rescue them.

At the time, Tarama was under the tyranny of the Taramayakara – a band of seven brothers who decided punishments and rules as they saw fit. The Taramayakara gathered the islanders together and forbade them from saving the mainland foreigners. Anyone caught helping them would be punished. The islanders, fearing for their lives, left the shipwreck survivors to perish. One by one, they all died out.

An old woman on the island felt sorry for the dead and their unmourned spirits. She brought incense, flowers, water and rice cakes to their bodies so that they were properly mourned. However, one of the mainlanders had survived, and he was kept alive by the old woman's offerings of water and rice cakes.

Eventually this man became one of the islanders, but he never forgot his friends who had died. He made a grave where he could bury their bones, in the style of the mainland. Legend has it that this was Tarama's first Yamato grave, which eventually inspired others throughout the island.

guardian deity of the island. Festivals celebrating the crop harvest are regularly celebrated here.

As you explore, make sure to investigate some of Tarama's habu-free jungle – the land not used for agriculture has been left to the wilds, with gloriously photogenic results. Though it's not advised to go tramping willy-nilly through the forests, there are a few shrines and cemeteries dotted throughout, with grey stone torii gates emerging from the twisted vines and ruins subsumed into roots. One such example is northward of Ungusuku, where an old building has been taken over by tree roots. Behind this incredible structure, into the woods, is the **Satonushi-baka** (里之子墓): an old gravesite sunk into the leaf litter. It's eerily beautiful; just make sure to explore with respect.

Further on towards the coast you reach **Tomari Utaki** (泊御嶽), which enshrines the god of boatmen. The red-tiled shrine looks after the safety of sailors and ship owners. Finally the road ends at the **Ibi Uganju** (イビの拝所), a place of worship for safe voyage. It's said that an official's wife would see her husband off on a voyage and pray here for his return. Nearby, there's a statue of a wife and child called the **Weenma Monument** (ウェーンマの碑), which commemorates the legend of a doomed love between a local woman and a Shuri official, who left her and their son behind when he was called back to the capital.

One of the prettiest spots on Tarama is the **Shiokawa Ontake and Fukugi Namiki** (塩川御嶽とフクギ並木), which sits on the east of the village. The ontake has long been a religious site for islanders; legend says that two sacred stones flew and landed here, marking out the shrine. The red-tile shrine is at the end of a 650m row of fukugi trees, which were planted to protect the ontake from the strong winds that blow across flat Tarama and have been designated a natural monument of Okinawa Prefecture.

In the southeastern forest you'll find **Futenma Utaki** (普天間御嶽). The gods of this utaki are worshipped for safeguarding ships and sailors, especially those just leaving the island. It's host to a festival believed to be over 200 years old; legend has it that there was a local man who worshipped here faithfully and died on a difficult sea journey, but his body came back to this spot on the tide. The villagers believed this was because of his devotion and began to pray here too.

There is exceptionally little in the south of the island. Other than a pleasant circumnavigation of Tarama, beaches are the only reason to head that way. The most important is **Magari** (マガリ), a long and entirely empty beach on the southwest coast which is also a green turtle nesting site – take care.

Untouched beaches stretch all the way around the island's perimeter (which means no jellyfish nets or lifeguards). An enjoyable Tarama day involves jumping in and out of the coastline on your way round by bike, discovering all the different coves, sandy inlets and big beaches the island has to offer.

Minnajima A small island just off the north coast of Tarama, Minna (水納島) is touted as the best snorkelling spot in the entire archipelago. This may be in part due to its entirely untouched nature – getting to Minnajima is a bit of a mission. There's no ferry, so you need to charter a boat or join a tour. Few tour companies on Tarama go there, however, as they tend to promote diving, which is better done away from Minna's shallows. You also won't be able to visit outside of the summer season as the waves are too big for little boats to navigate and there isn't enough demand to operate anyway. The best option is to ask around – you'll need to stay on Tarama overnight in order to fit in a Minnajima visit, so check with your accommodation if they know of any tours or locals going out that way. Minna certainly isn't a guarantee when visiting Tarama, but if you're lucky, you can see the Nansei-shotō's most spectacular reefs, corals and marine wildlife.

8

The Yaeyama Islands

Standing on the Yaeyama Islands (八重山列島) today, the glittering clear seas speckled with great crags of deep, unexplored jungle, it's hard to imagine they were once a forgotten outpost of disease and exile, where disasters regularly crippled the supposedly savage population. Now they're a world-renowned nature sanctuary, where breathtaking landscapes of lagoons and tropical forests hide remarkable sea life and endangered species.

Far closer to Taiwan than Okinawa-hontō, and much nearer the Philippines than mainland Japan, the Yaeyama – often referred to locally as Yaima – formed a small trading hub, with immigration from Asia and even Oceania influencing the quiet, indigenous cultures. There's evidence of prehistoric trade and exchange with Taiwan, the Philippines and mainland Asia, as well as trade with Shuri and the archipelago, from around 1500.

Each of the 12 inhabited islands are wonderfully rich and individual, with their own legends, gods, utaki and traditions, where accepted history is formed of fact and folklore. Their close communities embody nonbiri – the archipelago's phrase for a laid-back, chilled-out lifestyle. Although the official language is Japanese, the Yaeyama language is still spoken in homes across the group, with each island developing its own mutually unintelligible dialect. Now with around 7,000–10,000 speakers (primarily over-70s), Yaeyama is considered 'severely endangered' by UNESCO. The language has been invaluable for linguistic study, as it has retained more aspects of original proto-Japonic than modern Japanese. For centuries, the Yaima were persecuted by Satsuma and Shuri, for decades neglected and sacrificed by Japan. It's easy to see why locals often separate themselves from the rest of the archipelago and mainland. Despite being part of the same kingdom and prefecture since the 16th century, Yaima people still refer to Okinawans as Uchinaanchu and themselves as Yaamaanchu. Years on, there's still a little rebelliousness left on the Yaeyama.

Forming the southwestern tip of Japan's near 3,000km stretch, the 23 total islands are gathered around one of the largest coral reefs in Asia, the Sekisei Lagoon. Once a shelter for trade ships, this reef has shaped and supported Yaeyama life for centuries. It's now the main reason why tourists make the trek from Tokyo, hoping for a glimpse of migrating mantas and to snorkel with sea turtles.

Nature doesn't just shimmer under the blue surface. It erupts across the islands in great peaks, green valleys and twisted mangroves, culminating in the Yaeyama's crowning glory: Iriomote, an untouched jungle island ripe for adventure. Iriomote is the largest of the group, but its wilderness is far from Yaeyama's central hub. Instead, easternmost Ishigaki is the most populated and most accessible, easily reached by direct flights from the mainland and other islands.

It would be hard not to claim the Yaeyama as the Nansei-shotō's best, meaning itineraries benefit from an extra day or two compared with other groups. For a

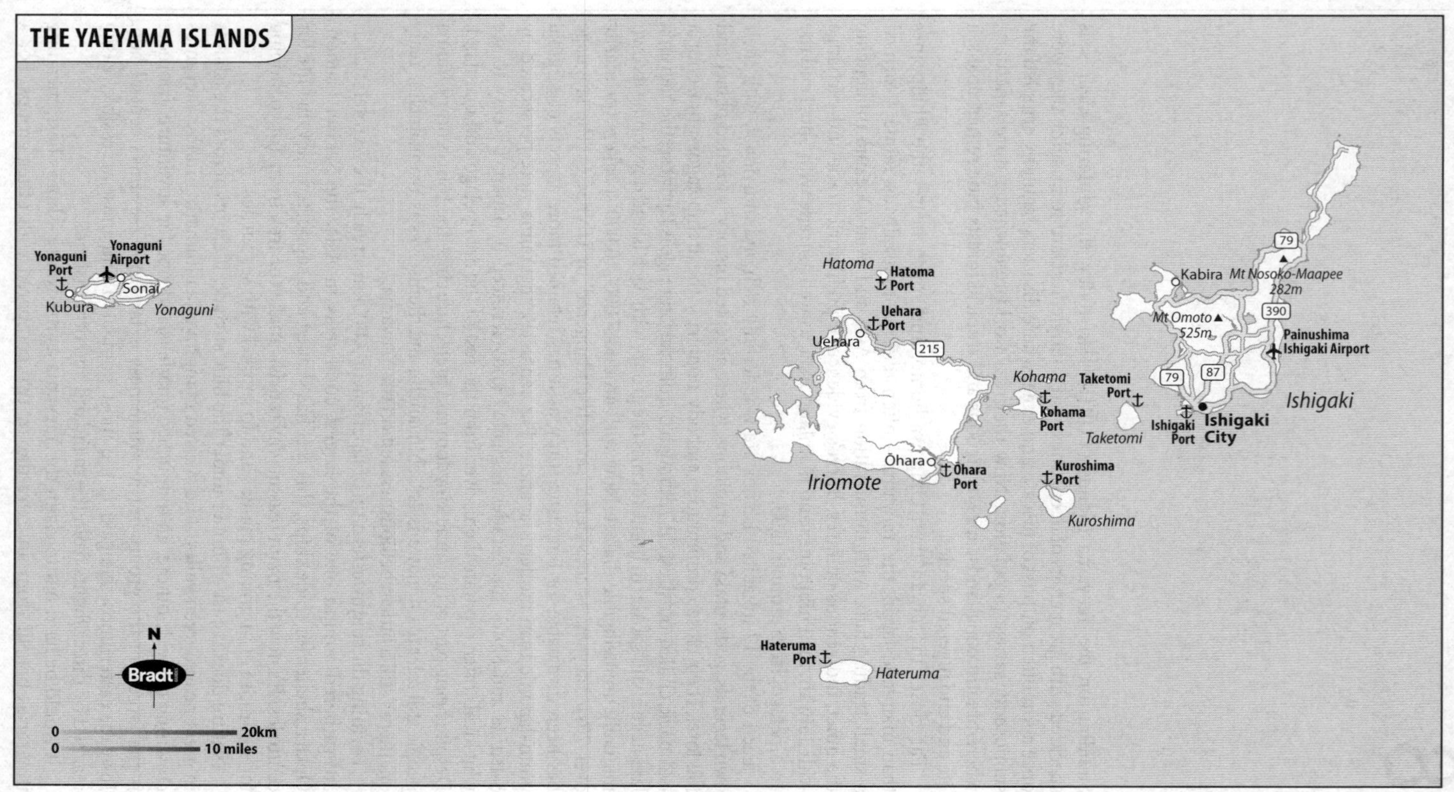
THE YAEYAMA ISLANDS
Yonaguni Port
Yonaguni Airport
Kubura
Sonai
Yonaguni
Hatoma
Hatoma Port
Uehara Port
Uehara
215
Iriomote
Ōhara
Ōhara Port
Kohama
Kohama Port
Taketomi Port
Taketomi
Kuroshima Port
Kuroshima
Hateruma Port
Hateruma
Kabira
Mt Nosoko-Maapee 282m
Mt Omoto 525m
79
390
87
Painushima Ishigaki Airport
Ishigaki Port
Ishigaki City
Ishigaki
N
Bradt
0 20km
0 10 miles

taster, you could pop to Ishigaki for a couple of days and do a day trip to traditional Taketomi – but missing Iriomote would be a mistake. Opt instead for a week minimum here.

HISTORY

The Yaeyama's early history has been pieced together through broken pottery and burials. Human remains found on Ishigaki in 2011, while building the new airport, date to around 24,000 years old. They're some of Japan's oldest human remains and conclusively prove Ishigaki's prehistoric habitation. Archaeological finds on Yaeyama and Miyako are culturally distinct from Okinawa and the northern Kagoshima islands. While the north shows Jōmon and Yayoi influence from mainland Kyūshū, Miyako and the Yaeyama exchanged more with Taiwan and the Philippines.

For centuries the Yaeyama lived quietly, with local lords (aji) trading (and occasionally smuggling) with Asia. However, cracks appeared in the peace in the 1500s, as Shuri began to spread its fingers and forces out across the archipelago.

For a while, chieftains from Miyako had sent tribute to the Ryūkyū Kingdom and at the close of the 15th century they encouraged the Yaeyama to do the same. While some saw prudence and protection in bowing to Shuri, others saw subjugation. In the early 1500s, the Akahachi Rebellion was the group's last independent stand. It split the Yaeyama: rebel leader Oyake Akahachi was backed by Ishigaki chiefs, while his pro-Shuri counterpart and former playmate Naata Ufushu was supported by Iriomote's aji. Naata also had the might of Miyako behind him, meaning Akahachi didn't stand a chance. His defeat brought the Yaeyama under the Ryūkyū Kingdom and, from then on, things went swiftly downhill.

As battle raged, something more deadly swept towards Yaeyama shores. Malaria arrived in around 1530, believed to be brought to Iriomote by a Dutch ship carrying Chinese people, and it wasn't eradicated until 1961. Alongside smallpox and cholera, malaria brought society and economy on forested Ishigaki and Iriomote to a halt. Tens of thousands died, resulting in loss of settlements, culture and history. The consequent gap in the workforce was filled through forced relocation. Populous little islands were wrenched apart and their people spread across the group, doing untold cultural damage. To outsiders, the Yaeyama became a place of exile and punishment: being sent here was a death sentence.

After Ryūkyū's invasion came the Satsuma one in 1609; the Shimazu barrelled through Okinawa, all the way to Yaeyama. Satsuma introduced the deadly poll tax, also known as the head tax (page 11). Levied only on Miyako and Yaeyama, it took two years to be implemented as far as Yonaguni and it crippled the disease-riddled group. Paid through agricultural goods and crafts, the tax was per capita, calculated early on and never readjusted. While Iriomote and Ishigaki had plenty of land, they were losing whole villages of people to disease, leaving the taxes high and the workforce low. The smaller islands had booming populations that required feeding and clothing, taking away from precious taxes. In Yonaguni, this prompted horrific population-control measures.

Drought, typhoons and famine were old foes here, but the biggest disasters rolled in off the turquoise seas. The Great Meiwa Tsunami of 1771 devastated the struggling Yaeyama. Multiple waves reached heights of 33m as they hit the islands, centred on Ishigaki where people were gathered to bring annual tribute. Some 9,500 people died in the disaster – 32% of the Yaeyama population. Ishigaki suffered most immediately, with 40% of the land flooded and 48% of its population

WAR MALARIA

For more than 400 years, malaria plagued the Yaeyama, with Iriomote's virgin jungle as its epicentre. Known as Yaeyama fever, the disease and its aftermath fractured society and stifled economy in a way that is still felt today. It was so rife that outsiders once called the region Yakiinushima – 'the islands of malaria'.

Before the outbreak of the Pacific War, malaria had actually been in decline, but as residents were forced into known malaria-riddled areas and military camps, it exploded across the group, infecting islands that had never before seen the disease.

This was war malaria, spread through troop dispersal, evacuation and battle-related incidents. It's a little-known aspect of warfare, which dealt far more death and damage to the Yaeyama than any air raids. As battle crept ever nearer, locals from smaller islands were forcibly evacuated to Iriomote and Ishigaki (supposedly for their safety) with little to no protection, supplies or even shelter in the height of summer.

Makeshift rural huts were often communal and thatched, rendering mosquito nets useless. Malnutrition had already set in, weakening immune systems, while poor sanitation resulted in standing water and more mosquitoes. They were the perfect conditions for causing large-scale death, and the forced evacuation has been called criminal by many.

After surrender, the evacuation order was reversed, but poor communication (in some cases purposeful withholding of information) meant many stayed in deadly conditions. When people were allowed to return to their own islands a few months later, they took malaria with them. In 1945 alone, 3,647 people died and over half the Yaima population was infected. The disease continued to spread after the war, with a 1947 epidemic infecting 12,131 people. Malaria was eventually eradicated in 1961.

gone, leaving great gaps in infrastructure, agriculture and the economy. (This wasn't a one-off; research has found that major tsunamis big enough to kill and damage structures hit Miyako and Yaeyama every 150–400 years, with the 1771 tsunami the most recent.)

The fallout of the tsunami was unfathomable. Crops and livestock were destroyed and land rendered unusable from saltwater. The ensuing famine lasted for 80 years, diseases ran amok and, even a century later, the Yaeyama population was just a third of what it had been. This was the beginning of a terrible century for the main island, followed by a list of biblical-level plagues: famine, epidemics, typhoons and droughts. None of which helped change mainland Japan's image of Yaeyama as a place of disease, savagery and danger. Efforts to encourage people to the islands failed and Ishigaki was repopulated at the expense of its Yaeyama neighbours.

When the Ryūkyū Kingdom became fully subsumed into Japan in 1879, territorial disputes over the islands broke out between Japan and China. Although Japan suggested ceding the Yaeyama and Miyako to the Qing dynasty, the islands rebelled against the idea – the treaty was abandoned, which led to the Sino-Japanese War and resulted in the group being under Japanese rule in time for the Pacific War.

World War II brought troops, bombings and shore fire to Yaeyama. Ishigaki had over 10,000 troops stationed from 1944, at a time when the local population numbered 32,000. Locals had their houses requisitioned and were expected to share their already meagre food supply. Ishigaki also suffered from air raids, with regular bombings from October 1944 until the war's end, and shore gunfire from Allied ships.

Still, the death toll from active battle was minimal compared with those from war malaria (see opposite). Islanders were made to split rations with troops and sent away to the malaria-riddled jungle for their 'safety', and once again the Yaeyama was left to rebuild from the ground up.

Malaria's eradication in Yaeyama wouldn't come until the 1960s. Similarly, both water and electricity supplies wouldn't be instated until the 50s and 60s, starting with Ishigaki. The final island to get regular electricity, Aragusuku, was connected by submarine cable in 1988. The result has left the Yaeyama far behind mainland modernisation and progression, but not entirely to their detriment. Though services and infrastructure limp along, traditional culture and island life have been better preserved.

ISHIGAKIJIMA

Despite not being the biggest Yaeyama island, Ishigaki (石垣島) has always been its heart, where people from the other islands come to gather, trade, work and be educated. This makes Ishigaki sound touristically boring, but it's much more than a jumping-off point for the Yaeyama.

The most populous of the Yaeyama, Ishigaki is an easy-going place of chilled locals, late-night hotspots and lively restaurants. Just under 50,000 people live across the 223km² island, the majority of which is covered in dense vegetation, with wild forest and winding mangroves. Ishigaki's shape rather defies description, with endless bluffs and bumps and beautiful bays shaping the cuspate coastline. Its flat south is home to the majority of the population and the main town, handily named Ishigaki. Here you'll find dining, drinking and shopping options aplenty, but these quickly dwindle outside its environs. The road network is extensive and well kept, but concentrated around the south and the island perimeter. You'll find the airport is on the island's east side.

Head north and the island erupts into mountains that spread up and out from the corners, with the highest point, Omotodake, in the middle. Kabira Bay, Ishigaki's picturesque poster child, is in the northwest, where you'll find extraordinary natural beauty and the world's first black pearl farming (page 300). The northeast's long Hirakubo Peninsula is largely overlooked, but is home to quiet beaches, undulant coastline and is perfect for exploring by car.

Ishigaki is known for its sporting events. Annual highlights include the Ishigaki Marathon (w ishigakijima-marathon.jp) and the Great Earth's 55–100km cycle (w great-earth.jp), but the most awaited tournament of the Ishigaki calendar happens on four legs rather than two. Bullfights (page 33) are incredibly popular, being held several times a year across the island.

Of course, cows are more than just athletes here. The island is home to Ishigaki wagyū beef. Only 600–800 of these cows are bred each year, making their marbled meat rare and highly prized.

One of the most culturally fascinating and unique aspects of Ishigaki is found in the way its dialect uses directions. Locals often use compass points to direct each other, saying 'the cup is on your north'. Speakers innately know the cardinal directions of a place, even if they've never stood there before.

GETTING THERE AND AWAY There are regular direct international flights from Hong Kong and Taipei Taoyuan to Painushima Ishigaki Airport (also known

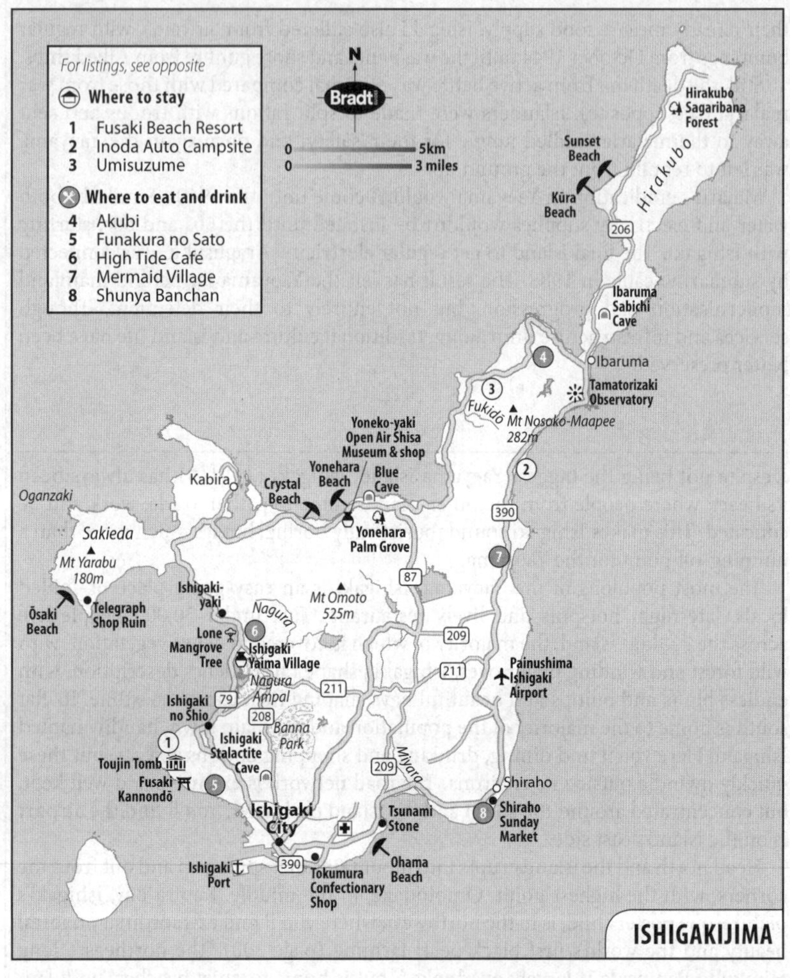

as Shin-Ishigaki Airport; ☎ 0980 87 0032; w ishigaki-airport.co.jp/en). Regular domestic flights to Ishigaki leave from mainland Japan, Okinawa-hontō and Miyako. The airport is 12km and a 25-minute drive from the city centre; if hiring a car, book in advance if possible. The fixed-rate Karry Kankō bus and slow local buses service the airport; timetables are available at the information counter, bus and port terminals. Otherwise, there are taxis into town; try Kyōdō Musen Taxi (共同無線タクシー; ☎ 0980 83 3355) or Ishigakijima Taxi Call Centre (石垣島タクシーコールセンター; ☎ 0980 82 4649).

GETTING AROUND Ishigaki **buses** are slow, sporadic and confusing at best. Run by Azuma Bus (w azumabus.co.jp) there are around one to two buses daily to each area. Buses here require planning so you're not left high and dry – or indeed humid. One-day and five-day passes are available, as well as a twice-daily sightseeing bus.

Hire vehicles are the easiest way to access Ishigaki, especially the furthest corners of the island. Vehicles can be rented by the hour or day, and most companies drop cars at the airport, city or port for pick-up.

Vehicle rental

Futaba Rent-a-Car フタバレンタカー; 1351-3 Ohama, Ishigaki; 0980 87 6280; w futaba-ishigaki.com

GO SHARE Anei Kankō Ferry Terminal, 1 Misakicho, Ishigaki; 0980 87 5562; w ridegoshare.jp. Electric mopeds with batteries lasting 80km, quickly replaced around the island.

Kumanomi Rental くまのみれんた; 504-5 Ishigaki; 0906 862 0755; w yaeyamaocean.com/kumanomi

Smile Rent-a-Car スマイルレンタカー; 53 Maezato, Ishigaki; 0808 951 7125; w smile-rentacar.jp

TOURIST INFORMATION There are no dedicated tourist information centres on the island except a general information counter at the airport (0980 87 0468; 07.30–21.00 daily). Tour companies such as those in the port or hotels are your best bet for information.

WHERE TO STAY The city and Kabira are the main accommodation areas, though Kabira is generally more expensive.

Ishigaki City *Map, page 298*

Art Hotel Ishigaki (245 rooms) アートホテル石垣島; 559 Okawa; 0980 83 3311; w art-ishigakijima.com. Facilities-packed 3-star hotel, 10mins' walk from centre's noisy nightlife. Rooms & bath en suites are bright, spacious & modern, with TV, fridge & hot drinks. On-site pool, spa, shop, launderette & wonderful onsen. There are multiple restaurants & a scenic bar. Art Hotel supports Yaeyama arts with a gallery & shop. Tours & rentals available. **$$$$$**

Hotel Patina (23 rooms) ホテルパティーナ石垣島; 1-8-5 Yashimacho; 0980 87 7400; w patina.in. Straightforward friendly hotel southwest of the harbour with an eco-point system: keeping towels & linens unchanged earns points to spend at the shop. En-suite rooms are a good size with nice décor & very well-equipped. Restaurant & free launderette on site. Free portable chargers & bike rental. **$$$**

Ishigaki Guesthouse HIVE (24 beds) 石垣ゲストハウスハイブ; 3F 12-7 Misakichō; 0980 87 9432; w ishigaki-guesthouse-hive.com/en. Cheerful backpacker option with mixed & female dorms. Its questionable entrance (down a side street & up fire-escape-style stairs) hides a fun MDF capsule-style hostel. Beds are large & comfy with private lockers, shared bathrooms & free earplugs. Features a rooftop terrace, washing machine & well-stocked large kitchen with free hot drinks. Family-feel HIVE also organises cheap meal nights. **$**

Kabira

Ishigaki Seaside Hotel (108 rooms, 19 villas) 石垣シーサイドホテル; 154–12 Kabira; 0980 88 2421; w ishigaki-seasidehotel.com. On the quiet coast overlooking Sukuji Beach, this resort has private garden villas or big & bright ocean-view rooms with fully kitted en suites & balconies. The only hotel on this bay (it isn't subtle about it), the beach is yours. There's a restaurant & bar, BBQs, swimming pool, onsen, vending machines, laundromat & shop. Offers tours, bicycle & fishing gear rental. Wheelchair accessible. B/fast extra; HB options. **$$$$$**

Lulaliya (8 rooms, 1 suite) るらりや; 921–1 Kabira; 0980 87 0059; w lulaliya.com. Lovely husband-&-wife-run guesthouse. Dbl rooms are basic with en suite & a balcony; sgls share bathrooms. The 6-person suite is a fully kitted apartment with deck. There's a rooftop veranda, kitchen & restaurant (b/fast). Kitchen is staff-only but you can use basics (inc fridge). The lounge is comfy & welcoming with free hot drinks, TV, DVDs & library. BBQ eves available. **$$$$**

Iriwa Guesthouse (3 rooms, 2 dorms) ゲストハウスイリワ; 599 Kabira; 0980 88 2563; w iriwa.org. Palm-flanked guesthouse & dormitory with beautiful pastel décor & large gardens. Gendered dorms sleep 6 with shared bathroom. Rooms have wide windows & fridges; welcoming communal spaces have free hot drinks, microwave, stove & rice cooker. A 13min walk to Kabira Beach; outdoor options include hammocks & BBQ. Car, cycle, snorkel, mask & towel rentals. **$$**

Elsewhere on the island

Map, opposite

Fusaki Beach Resort (260 rooms, 138 villas) フサキビーチリゾート; Arakawa; w fusaki.com/

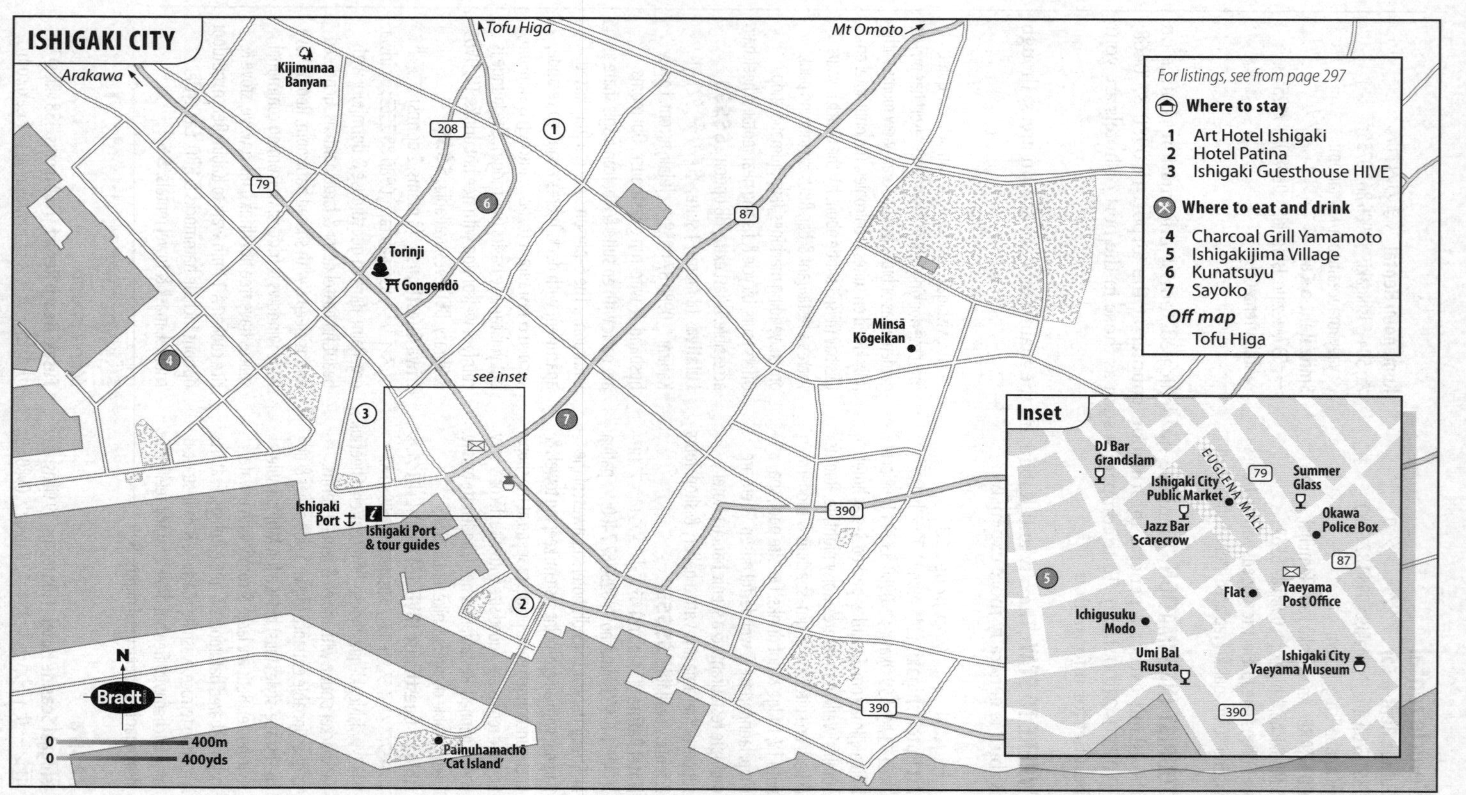
ISHIGAKI CITY
Arakawa
Kijimunaa Banyan
Tofu Higa
Mt Omoto
208
79
87
390
Torinji
Gongendō
Minsā Kōgeikan
see inset
Ishigaki Port
Ishigaki Port & tour guides
Painuhamachō 'Cat Island'
N
Bradt
0 400m
0 400yds
For listings, see from page 297
Where to stay
1 Art Hotel Ishigaki
2 Hotel Patina
3 Ishigaki Guesthouse HIVE
Where to eat and drink
4 Charcoal Grill Yamamoto
5 Ishigakijima Village
6 Kunatsuyu
7 Sayoko
Off map
Tofu Higa
Inset
DJ Bar Grandslam
EUGLENA MALL
Ishigaki City Public Market
Jazz Bar Scarecrow
Summer Glass
Okawa Police Box
Flat
Yaeyama Post Office
Ichigusuku Modo
Umi Bal Rusuta
Ishigaki City Yaeyama Museum

eng. Sprawled 1km across a sunset beachfront, this resort is far from amenities but provides everything on site: crêche, BBQ pavilion, live music, spas, tour desk, beach shop, market & Ishigaki's largest pool. Extensive restaurants & bars, which will cook fish you catch on the pier. Room options are plentiful, from large dbls to 4-person garden cottages, & all come with big en suites & fridges. **$$$$$**

Umisuzume (5 rooms) 海すずめ; 1086-14 Nosoko; 0980 84 5066; w umisuzume.org. Umisuzume is a simple guesthouse perfectly placed for Ibaruma stopovers. The rooms are clean & basic with futon beds & shared bathrooms. There are free hot drinks, free washing machine & meal options available. **$$$**

Inoda Auto Campsite (11 cars, 3 campers) 伊野田キャンプ場; 201-1 Tozato; 0980 83 4373. A lovely beach-side place to park up, pitch & camp just 10mins from Nosokodake. The site has individual power & water supplies, paid hot showers, BBQs & coin laundry. There's also ridiculously cheap tent space for those without a vehicle. **$**

WHERE TO EAT AND DRINK

Ishigaki City *Map, page 298*

Charcoal Grill Yamamoto 炭火焼肉やまもと; 2-5–18 Hamasakicho; 0980 83 5641; 17.00–21.00 Thu–Tue. Is Yamamoto the best place for Ishigaki beef? Definitely not, but it is the most popular. Always busy, don't expect fine dining or a calm atmosphere: this casual *yakiniku* (grilled meat) joint means grill smoke, noise & full bellies. $$$$

Ishigakijima Village 石垣島ヴィレッジ; 8–9 Misakicho; 0980 87 0708; 11.00–22.00 daily (individual shops vary). 3 storeys of *yatai* food-stall restaurants filled to the brim with local specialities & modern crowd-pleasers. Perfect place to mix palates; groups can order from different restaurants & enjoy together. It's no traditional sanshin-serenaded tōfuyō, but it's good fun & plentiful. $$

✷ **Kunatsuyu** 来夏世; 203 Ishigaki; 0980 82 7646; 10.00–14.00 Mon–Sat. Half-hidden behind a huge hibiscus bush, Kunatsuyu is an Okinawa soba oasis away from the port's hubbub. Slurp back steaming bowls inside or in the small garden. $

Sayoko さよこの店; 170 Tonoshiro; 0980 83 6088; 10.00–14.00 (or until sold out) Mon–Sat. The go-to for traditional saataa andagii doughnuts in a variety of flavours. Soft but crispy, it's deep-fried divinity. $

✷ **Tofu Higa** とうふの比嘉; 570 Ishigaki; 0980 82 4806; 06.30–15.00 Mon–Sat. On the outskirts of the city in a sugarcane field, this popular spot makes tofu from scratch. Its cheap & delicious fresh b/fast is so popular they often sell out before morning is up. $

Kabira

✷ **Sushi Jinbei** 味屋じんべい; 906 Kabira; 0980 84 4819; noon–14.00 & 18.00–22.00 Mon–Sat. Superb menu, in English, with huge set meals for a great price. The atmosphere is lively, the shop cosy & staff incredibly helpful. If you don't fancy locally caught sashimi, try the kara-age or spare ribs. $$$

Pina Colada Bakery ベーカリーピナコラーダ; 836–4 Kabira; 0980 88 2501; w pclkabira.exblog.jp; 09.00–13.00 Thu–Sun. Perfect stop for bread, cakes & doughnuts. So popular, it's worth arriving early & staking your claim. $

Elsewhere on the island

Map, page 296

Funakura no Sato 舟蔵の里; 2468–1 Arakawa; 0980 82 8108; w funakuranosato.com; 11.00–22.00 daily. Traditional restaurant in a private residence serving local-cuisine set menus. Ingredients are grown locally & the house speciality is eel. Sanshin performances take place every evening & staff speak English. $$$$$

Akubi あくび; 635–2 Nosoko; 0980 87 7843; f; 07.30–16.00 Tue–Wed & Fri–Sun. Cute vegetarian restaurant serving up small plates of pesticide-free locally farmed produce. Meals are cheap, healthy & wholesome. The café is small so does set meal times: reservation essential. $$$

Shunya Banchan 旬家ばんちゃん; 13–1 Shiraho; 0980 87 0813; w shun-ya-banchan.com; 08.30–15.00 (or until sold out) daily. Beloved by domestic tourists, Shunya's b/fast set is famed for its ridiculously large rolled omelette, but their daily lunches are mouthwatering & equally massive. $$$

High Tide Café ハイタイドカフェ; 982–51 Nagura; 0980 83 5029; 11.30–17.00 Fri–Wed. This marine-themed, glass-fronted café has titanic portions that are great value. Try their curry soups or the rich beef bowl with meat sauce. If you have room, High Tide is cake heaven. $$

Mermaid Village 人魚の里; 165–1005 Tozato; 0909 781 8393; 11.00–18.00 daily. If you're driving up the east coast to Ibaruma, stop at this pink house where the owner serves his own Ishigaki-grown coffee, harvested against the typhoon odds. $$

ENTERTAINMENT AND NIGHTLIFE Ishigaki is one of the few islands in the archipelago with a bit of nightlife. The clubs, bars and hostess bars are concentrated in Misakichō, the area around the port. None of the clubs is anything to write home about, but there are some real gems hidden about town, from jazz joints to kerbside cocktails.

DJ Bar Grandslam 261–2F Okawa, Ishigaki; 0980 87 0442; 22.00–05.00 Mon–Sat. This dimly lit bar & DJ goes on until morning. It has basic English menus that make life much easier, especially when drinking.

Jazz Bar Scarecrow JAZZ すけあくろ; 213–1 B1 Okawa, Ishigaki; 0980 87 7696; w scarecrow-ishigaki.com; noon–16.00 & 17.00–21.00 Tue–Sat. This inviting, family-owned venue has been putting on live jazz & a great range of whiskies at reasonable prices for 20 years.

Summer Glass サマーグラス; 198–7 Okawa, Ishigaki; 0980 83 3274; w shotbarsummerglass.wixsite.com/summerglass; 19.00–01.00 Mon–Sat. A cocktail powerhouse with cool dark interiors & extensive alcohol collection, particularly whisky. Knowledgeable bartenders, late openings & great atmosphere.

Umi Bal Rusuta 海BALるすた; 2 Misakicho, Ishigaki; 0980 87 6290; w asovinbar.com/rusuta_bal; 11.30–23.00 Thu–Tue. Great little wine bar that's lively, cosy & usually teeming.

SHOPPING If you've come to the Yaeyama to shop, you've already made a grave miscalculation, but if you're looking to browse boutiques, Ishigaki is the only place to do it. The biggest shopping areas are Euglena Mall (ユーグレナモール) and Ishigaki City Public Market (石垣市公設市場), but they're aimed at tourists looking for tatty trinkets.

If you need to shop for ingredients, go to JA Yuratiku farmers' market (ゆらてぃく市場; w ja-yurathiku-ichiba.com) or roadside stalls, where the produce is freshest. Shiraho Sunday Market (白保日曜市; 118 Shiraho Coral Village; 10.00–13.00 Sun) sells fresh produce and meals alongside music.

Arts and crafts

Yoneko-yaki 米子焼; 447–1 Yonehara; 0980 88 2559; w yonekoyaki.com; 09.00–17.00 daily. Fun & colourful pottery largely dedicated to shiisaa guardians.

Clothing

Gruppo グルッポ; 0702 017 9780; w gruppo.jp. This island-wide chain sells colourful bags & wallets made of *minsaa* & bingata patterns. There's also an outlet at the airport.

BLACK PEARLS

Kabira Bay, Ishigaki's postcard spot, is the home of black pearls. Although black pearls are now associated with Tahiti, pearl cultivation was actually first developed in Japan – and Kabira Bay was the first place in the world to cultivate and mass-produce the black version. Kabira and Iriomote are the only places in Japan to cultivate these iridescent black-blue pearls, which are formed by the black-lip oyster. If you want to find out about the process, there is a pearl jewellery shop with English information, just along the bay walkway. Because of the pearl cultivation, swimming is no longer allowed in Kabira Bay.

Ichigusuku Mode イチグスクモード; 3 Misakicho; 0980 87 5282; w ichigusukumode.com; 09.00–18.00 Mon–Fri. Ishigaki-born, Ishigaki-designed, Ishigaki-made. Designs are fun & ingenious: T-shirts with pocket square face masks are a highlight.

Food and drink

Takeda Coffee 武田珈琲; 0503 393 9158; w takedacoffee.com. Now only available online, it's worth pre-ordering a bag of Ishigaki-grown coffee beans to your hotel.

Tokumura Confectionary Shop 徳村菓子; 230–10 Maezato; 0980 83 1177; 09.00–19.00 Mon–Sat, 10.00–19.00 Sun. Hold on to your kids: this huge sweet shop has aisle upon aisle of chocolate & Japanese candy.

Jewellery

Ryukyu Pearl Kabira Main Store 琉球真珠本店; 934 Kabira; 0980 88 2288; w ryukyu-shinju.co.jp; 09.00–18.00 daily. Known for being first in the world to cultivate them, Ishigaki is the place to buy black pearls. Kabira's main store is a good place to start pearl shopping, with English information about the cultivation process.

Souvenirs

Flat 1F 777 Bldg, 1–11 Okawa; 0980 87 5836; w flatishigakijima.com; 10.00–19.00 Mon–Sat. A little shop in the heart of the city that sells quality souvenirs of all kinds, from food & coffee to clothing & trinkets.

SPORTS AND ACTIVITIES

Blue Coral ブルーコーラル; w bluecoral73.okinawa. Offers tours of Shiraho Reef, though this can be snorkelled solo.

Field Nature Ishigakijima フィールドネイチャー石垣島; 972 Miyara; 0980 86 7150; w fieldnature.com. A mix of kayak & canoe courses with jungle exploration, night & sunset tours.

Hirata Kankō 平田観光; w hirata-group.co.jp/english. Offers Sekisei Lagoon snorkelling tours.

Ishigaki Adventure PiPi 144-1 Ishigaki; 0980 87 5722; w ishigaki-pipi.com/en. Offers multiple tours including SUP in Kabira Bay.

Ishigaki-yaki 石垣焼; 1356–71 Nagura; 0980 88 8722; w ishigaki-yaki.com. English-speaking owner guides 1hr bowl-making or 90min shiisaa courses.

Minsaa Kōgeikan みんさー工芸館; 909 Tonoshiro; 0980 82 3473; w minsah.co.jp. Traditional textile workshop where you can try weaving; reservations recommended for the class.

Prime Scuba Ishigaki 345–9 Maezato; 0980 87 5980; w primescuba-isg.com; 08.30–18.00 daily. English-speaking, friendly staff who go above & beyond, especially trying to ensure manta sightings. The boat is well equipped & lunch plentiful. PADI-certification courses, gear rental & boat chartering available.

Sky Adventure Woomacoo スカイアドベンチャーうーまくぅ; 249–42 Ibaruma; w woomacoo.com/english-site. Paragliding is a breathtaking way to see the island; English-speaking guides. Flights weather-dependent.

OTHER PRACTICALITIES There are ATMs at post offices across the island and in larger big-name convenience stores like FamilyMart in the south. The island has at least one police box in each town, open 24 hours, and the lone Yaeyama Hospital (八重山病院; 584–1 Maezato; 0980 87 5557; w yaeyamaweb.hosp.pref.okinawa.jp/en; reception: 08.00–11.00 Mon–Fri).

Police

Ibaruma Police Box 八重山警察署 伊原間駐在所; 40–4 Ibaruma; 0980 89 2110

Kabira Police Box 八重山警察署 川平駐在所; 907 Kabira; 0980 88 2110

Okawa Police Box 八重山警察署 大川交番; 13–1 Okawa; 0980 82 0110

Post offices

Ibaruma Post Office 伊原間郵便局; 26–9 Ibaruma; 0980 89 2140; ATM: 08.45–17.30 Mon–Fri, 09.00–12.30 Sat

Kabira Post Office 川平郵便局; 1033–70 Kabira; 0980 88 2140; ATM: 08.45–17.30 Mon–Fri, 09.00–12.30 Sat

Yaeyama Post Office 八重山郵便局; 12 Okawa; 0570 94 3300; ATM: 08.00–21.00 Mon–Sat

WHAT TO SEE AND DO

Ishigaki City The Yaeyama travel hub, Ishigaki City (石垣市) is unavoidable, but it's a great little city worth exploring for a day or so in its own right. You'll find sunlit neighbourhoods, a handful of cultural experiences and some charming coast too. In the city's northwest are **Tōrinji** (桃林寺; 285 Ishigaki; 0980 82 2142; 07.00–19.00 daily) and **Gongendō** (権現堂; 285 Ishigaki; 24hrs; free). These neighbours are a Buddhist temple and a Shintō shrine respectively, both built in 1614. Only the Tōrinji temple survived the 1771 tsunami – the Gongen shrine was rebuilt in 1787. Tōrinji also survived the war, making it the oldest wooden house in Okinawa.

A short walk north, a block away from Smiling Car Rental, you'll find **Kijimunaa Banyan** (キジムナーの宿る森). Supposedly home to the islands' mischievous kijimunaa imps, this colossal tree makes for a cool photo, with great orange beard-like roots draping down from its branches. Starry or sunny blue skies make the best backdrop, as long as cars aren't parked beneath.

Head south from here to **Ishigaki City Yaeyama Museum** (石垣市立八重山博物館; 4–1 Tonoshiro; 0980 82 4712; 09.00–17.00 Tue–Sun; adult ¥200), a museum housing cultural and historic items from the island group alongside English explanations. There are traditional wooden canoes, clothing, pottery and exhibits on festivals and events.

Nearby **Painuhamachō 'Cat Island'** (南ぬ浜町; 24hrs), a reclaimed island near the port, is used by locals for fishing, barbecues, events and watching sunset from the newly formed beach – all under the watchful eye of the island's plentiful feline residents. The southern shore has a memorial park dedicated to the ten kamikaze who set off on their final flight from Shiraho on 26 March 1945, as well as other special attack forces who took off from Ishigaki.

Ōhama Coast (大浜海岸) in the southeast is off the city's main drag but has wonderfully alien sandstone formations great for family exploration, as well as the **Tsunami Stone** (津波大石・ツナミウフイシ; 182 Ōhama). This 700–1,000-tonne rock in Sakibaru Park (崎原公園), now entirely subsumed by a tree, was thrown ashore by a tsunami some 2,000 years ago.

Geologic gems continue at **Ishigaki Stalactite Cave** (石垣島鍾乳洞; 1666 Ishigaki; 0980 83 1550; w ishigaki-cave.com/en; 09.00–18.30 daily; adult ¥1,200) in the city's north. Of its 3.2km, only 660m are open to the public, taking some 30 minutes to explore. The cave has illuminations, fossils and a genuinely convincing Totoro stalagmite, as well as an on-site restaurant, souvenir shop and tropical garden with butterflies, goats, coconut crabs and fruit trees. The shop has shiisaa painting: a perfect rainy-day option for kids (¥1,100; 30min).

Outside the city's northern limits sits **Banna Park** (バンナ公園; 0980 82 6993; 09.00–21.00 daily), a great place to see wilderness without having to trek. Less a park and more a massive mountainous jungle with sensational views, Banna is home to many species of butterflies, birds and tropical plants. The Crested Serpent Observatory gets you an incredible view of the suspension bridge rising out of the forest. You'll need a vehicle, or at least a bike and some willpower, to get round it.

Kabira With its transparent waters and dark, tree-covered islets breaking out from the blue, **Kabira Bay**'s (川平湾) beauty has single-handedly put Ishigaki on the tourist map. You can't actually swim in the bay, as it's protected for black pearl farming, but you can kayak, SUP or join a glass-bottomed boat tour to see the marine life. There's a chance of spotting manta rays come July–October, when they visit Kabira in full force, as well as sea turtles, clownfish and replete coral gardens.

Kabira's northwest is home to a manta scramble, where mantas (*Mobula alfredi*) collect en masse. High season is July–November, when there's an extraordinarily high chance of seeing them while diving.

On land, you'll find bay views at the **Kabira Park Observatory** (川平公園展望台), while the stunning **Ishigakijima Science Garden** (石垣島サイエンスガーデン; Kabira; ☎0980 88 2475; w passion-jp.com/sciencegardern; ⌚ 10.00–17.00 Mon–Tue & Thu–Sat; ¥200) in the bay's south is filled with water lilies, tropical fruit trees, showy flowers, mangroves and animals such as the crested serpent eagle and the oogomadara, the rice paper butterfly, with eye-catching caterpillars and golden pupae.

The lagoon is home to several gorgeous **beaches**, particularly on the eastern side by the island Kojima (小島). West of Kabira are Tabagaa (タバガー) and Sukuji (底地ビーチ) beaches, both ideal for swimming; the latter is also a great sunset spot and has changing rooms, showers and toilets.

Kabira village itself is actually very small, making it easy to explore on foot. It's worth seeking out the small, family-run **Takamine Distillery** (高嶺酒造所; 930–2 Kabira; ☎0980 88 2201; w omoto-takamine.com; ⌚ 09.00–17.00 daily; free), which sells fantastic island awamori and alcohol products, many of which you can sample. The building has a glass wall allowing you to see the working distillery from where those delicious fermentation smells emanate.

Sakieda Usually forgotten in favour of Kabira, Sakieda (崎枝) is a peninsula on Ishigaki's westernmost point, an unexpectedly rich photography spot with unique sights easily explored on a day trip from the bay. Buses don't cover the majority of the area, so you'll want a vehicle or bike to explore fully. The coastal road is relatively flat, but central **Yarabudake** (やらぶだけ) involves a 150m climb over 3km. It's definitely worth the effort, with extraordinary panoramic views over the cape, forest, reefs and brilliant blue bays. The road goes practically all the way to the 180m top, making it a quick and easy viewpoint. Yarabu also has its own 'pride rock' that juts out at its summit.

Known as the **Kabira Terrace mountain trail**, the track to Sakieda's southwest heads up to Buzamadake (ぶづま岳) over 1 hour, giving a brilliant view of the UNESCO bay. You can see buttress roots and tropical plants along the clearly marked, if overgrown, path. The trailhead is at the end of a road perpendicular to the Sakieda bus stop (2, 3, 7 & 9 buses); buses are infrequent but handy if timed well.

Sakieda's southern tip is home to the historic **Telegraph Shop Ruin** (電信屋), a concrete shack that became used for military communications in the war, making it a target for the US. It now stands moody and bullet-riddled from Allied naval fire. To find it, follow the coastal road west from the deserted southern beach until you reach a crossways with a farm ahead. The road to the left has a sign for 'Densinya': go down here to reach the relic.

Continuing around the headland from the ruin, you'll come to **Ōsaki Beach** (大崎ビーチ). Also known as Tachiihama, it has a reef some 200m from the shore and at low tide you can walk to its edge and swim from there – though best only for strong swimmers. A little-known but awesome natural event is the aggregation of broadclub cuttlefish (*Sepia latimanus*), which gather around Ishigaki's west coast in early March. Join a diving tour to see the colour-changing creatures en masse.

In the northwest is **Oganzaki** (御神崎), a dramatic cape and lighthouse with dynamic coastal scenes. It's at its finest in the spring when wild lilies bloom on the rugged cape. There's a monument here to the *Yaeyama Maru*, a ship that got lost in bad weather in 1952 with a full cargo of passengers, killing 35.

Shiraho Village The beautifully preserved Shiraho Village (白保村), a community of around 1,500 people in Ishigaki's southeast, is home to traditional wooden houses, red-tile roofs and stone walls. Pretty fukugi trees are used as protection from the winds, making it a green and peaceful place to wander. Folk art is prolific here, and you'll often hear the sound of sanshin and singing around the place.

Offshore, Shiraho's reef is the northern hemisphere's largest blue coral colony and fantastic for snorkelling; glass-bottom boat tours are organised by **Shiraho Tourism Service** (白保観光サービス; w shirahokankou.com). This southern coast also sees manta from December to April.

Arakawa On Ishigaki's southwest coast sits Arakawa's (新川) clutch of hotels and handful of sites. The ornate **Tōjin Tomb** (唐人墓; w ishigaki-pr.com/toujinhaka; ⏲ 24hrs) is a 1971 grave commemorating the Chinese people who were murdered in an 1852 incident in which an American slave ship took 400 prisoners from China and began torturing them on board. The prisoners mutinied and ran the ship aground on Ishigaki. Yaeyama officials set up a camp at Fusaki for them, but US and British armed soldiers came back for the captives, hanging and shooting many. Afterwards, more died from illness, went missing or committed suicide.

To the tomb's east is the handsome hilltop shrine **Fusaki Kannondō** (冨崎観音堂; 1607 Arakawa; ⏲ 24hrs). Built in 1742, it's dedicated to safe sea voyages and protection from disease; a much-needed shrine in these parts. The quiet sprawling grounds are delightful: wild forest, lantern-lit pathways and scenic views over Ishigaki.

Arakawa was also known for its salt production, which is believed to have begun in 1717. You can try your hand at making your own salt or bath bomb at **Ishigaki-no-Shio** (石垣の塩; 1145–57 Arakawa; ☎ 0980 83 8711; w ishigakinoshio.com; ⏲ 09.00–18.00 daily). There are English-speaking specialists and the shop also offers floating salt-water therapy.

Yonehara This small section of northern coastline is a little treasure trove and an easy trip from Kabira. Despite its lack of crowds, **Yonehara Beach** (米原ビーチ; 644 Fukai) is one of the nicest on the island with some of the best snorkelling too. Hemmed in by dark trees and palms, the sandy stretch has a public shower and toilet facilities and a campsite where you can rent snorkels. To its west, **Crystal Beach** (クリスタルビーチ) is a secret cove and another stand-out snorkel spot, though the best views are further from the shore.

In Yonehara's east is **Blue Cave** (青の洞窟; 527 Fukai), a gorgeous white and blue grotto accessed by SUP and kayak at high tide and walkable at low tide. The snorkelling here is brilliant, with plentiful coral and colourful fish. Blue Cave is also popular with divers as it's filled with macro life.

A short hop inland you'll find **Yoneko-yaki Open Air Shiisaa Museum** (米子焼工房 シーサー農園; 656-1 Fukai; ☎ 0980 88 2559; w yonekoyaki.com; ⏲ 09.00–17.00 daily). This brilliant, bizarre park is dedicated to big, bold, brightly coloured shiisaa statues (page 23). Great fun to wander for young and old, it's attached to the Yoneko-yaki pottery shop (page 300), where you can buy souvenirs and refreshments. Further east, **Yonehara Palm Grove** (米原のヤエヤマヤシ群落; 546 Fukai), is a forest filled with endemic, protected satake palms with a short boardwalk section for easy access.

Just south of Yonehara is **Mount Omoto** (於茂登岳), Ishigaki's top hiking spot. The 1½-hour walk up 525m Omoto isn't easy: the trail isn't maintained and is slippery enough on sunny days. After a bout of rain, consider Omoto closed. The trail heads through forest alongside a small river that you always hear but rarely see, excepting a small waterfall stop. The mountaintop itself is covered in ungovernable bamboo, which forms a 1.5m-high tunnel you'll need to duck (or just plough) through. A brief bamboo break provides a false sense of security as the attack continues to the top, where you'll reach a clearing past the radio tower with rocks just big enough to give you a panoramic view. Always keep an eye out for habu, even when said eye is full of bamboo. You can drive to the trailhead or take the number 11 bus to a stop 30 minutes' walk away.

Nagura Stop off in Nagura (名蔵) on the drive between Arakawa and Kabira to see **Ishigaki Yaima Village** (石垣やいま村; 967–1 Nagura; ☎ 0980 82 8798; w yaimamura.com; ⏱ 09.00–17.30 daily; adult ¥1,000). This village of relocated Yaeyama-style houses from the archipelago is a fascinating must for architecture and history buffs. There are also traditional song and dance performances, a squirrel monkey park, mangrove, restaurant and souvenir shop.

There's also the **Nagura Ampal** (名蔵アンパル), a wetland perfect for a birdwatching picnic as it's home to the crested serpent eagle and ruddy kingfisher, as well as Chinese box turtles and plentiful fiddler crabs. It also has a cool little quirk: old cart tracks appear at low tide, reaching into the receding waters – you'll see them looking east from the bridge. Up the coast is the striking singular **Lone Mangrove Tree** (一番マングローブ), best photographed at high tide.

Ibaruma and the Hirakubo Peninsula At its thinnest, this 19km-long mountainous northeast peninsula is just 300m wide. In the old days it was quicker to dock, cross the land and pick up another ship than it was to sail around. In the 1771 tsunami, low-lying Funakoshi, the squeezed section of Ibaruma, lost every single one of its settlements and was repopulated by Kuroshima locals. The area is split between Ibaruma (伊原間) in the south and Hirakubo (平久保) to the north. Ibaruma is as far as most tourists go, but Hirakubo has gorgeous coastlines smothered in secluded beaches and makes for an ideal driving tour.

Ibaruma's 282m **Mount Nosoko-Maapee** is a quick 20-minute climb with incredibly rewarding views. You can drive straight to the trailhead, but if using buses you'll want an early start as the stop is an hour's walk away. The buses are also rare, so you'll be in the area a while. It's tradition to climb the mountain and think of your loved one. Legend tells of Maapee, a Kuroshima woman divided from her sweetheart through forced relocation. She succumbed to malaria atop Nosoko, hoping to catch a glimpse of her homeland.

East coast lookout **Tamatorizaki Observatory** (玉取崎展望台; Ibaruma; ☎ 0980 83 8439) is surrounded by flowering hibiscus in spring and has sweeping views of Ibaruma Bay, Cape Tamatori, the deep emerald hills of Hirakubo and the sparkling aqua reef.

Missing Iriomote would be a mistake, but Ibaruma's **Fukidō River Mangrove** (吹通川; Nosoko) is a great alternative for those unable to make it. Take a kayak tour through the mangrove, spotting river residents and floating under clouds of green trees.

It's believed the limestone **Ibaruma Sabichi Cave** (伊原間サビチ洞; 185–44 Ibaruma; ☎ 0980 89 2121; w ishigaki-ibaruma.com; ⏱ 09.00–18.00 daily; adult ¥700) was formed 370 million years before Ishigaki Island even existed. The main cave is 237m long, with an additional 85m branch, which connects through to a brilliantly secluded beach. Sabichi is full of stalactites and interesting little things to discover.

MYTHS AND FOLKTALES: THE MERMAID AND THE WARNING

An old fisherman from Nohara Village could hear singing out at sea, and as he reeled in his nets, he found a beautiful mermaid caught up in them, crying. She begged the old man to release her, as she'd die outside the sea. She had come to warn him of a terrible tsunami that was on its way to the island. The fisherman thanked her and quickly freed her. He ran back to Nohara and warned the locals, who fled to higher ground. They told the neighbouring village, but no-one believed the tale and they refused to evacuate. The very next morning, a great tsunami came and Nohara villagers watched as the waves hit Ishigaki and wiped out all the villages below.

Sheltered by a cove on the west coast, **Sunset Beach** (サンセットビーチ; 234-323 Hirakubo; w i-sb.jp; ⌚ May–mid-Oct 09.30–18.00 daily; adult/child ¥500/300) offers snorkelling and swimming even at low tide. It has a net to protect swimmers from jellyfish, free showers and toilets. Parking is an extra ¥500. Snorkels, wetsuits, chairs and umbrellas are available for rent.

If you want to see what the fuss is about but resent forking out for a beach, the south side of Sunset is actually free. This part is **Kūra Beach** (久宇良の浜), which is accessed from a different road. The main difference between the two is Sunset's all-important jellyfish net.

Hirakubo Sagaribana Forest (平久保サガリバナ群落; Hirakubo; ☎ 0980 82 9911) holds 300 sagaribana (*Barringtonia racemosa*), a fantastic flowering tree specifically found in coastal swamp forests. Sagaribana bloom for a single night, though luckily not all at the same time, in June–July. The flowers themselves are remarkable: they split open into puffs of white and pink stamens. A tree of many names, its less pretty moniker is the Fish Killer Tree, thanks to its poisonous properties.

TAKETOMIJIMA

Taketomi's (竹富島) 6.3km² is packed with heritage, culture and beauty and is a standout for preserved Okinawan housing (page 31). There aren't big sights or adventurous activities: simply wander the vehicle-free walkways of white crushed stone, peeking at shiisaa-topped red roofs and bright pink bougainvillea tumbling over dark, igneous walls.

Technically there are three settlements – eastern Ainota, western Innota and central-south Naaji – on Taketomijima but they all rather blend into one in the centre, with the only port on the northeast coast. Taketomi's sights are in the village or on the west coast, where the beaches are. The south is entirely given over to the Hoshinoya Taketomi resort, kept well away from the protected village. The outer road runs around the north and west, connecting the port and beaches. Aside from this and the village streets, the only other road of note heads to Hoshinoya and Aiyaru Beach. A somewhat confusing aspect of the Yaeyama is that Taketomi is the name of both this island and a district covering half the islands. Called Taketomi-chō, you'll often see it crop up in addresses for other islands.

The island itself is known as Teedun to locals and Taketomi to Japan. A baffling blip in Taketomi's history is that its name is spelled with the kanji for 'lucky bamboo', though this was briefly changed in 1729 when the Ryūkyū government banned the word for 'bamboo'.

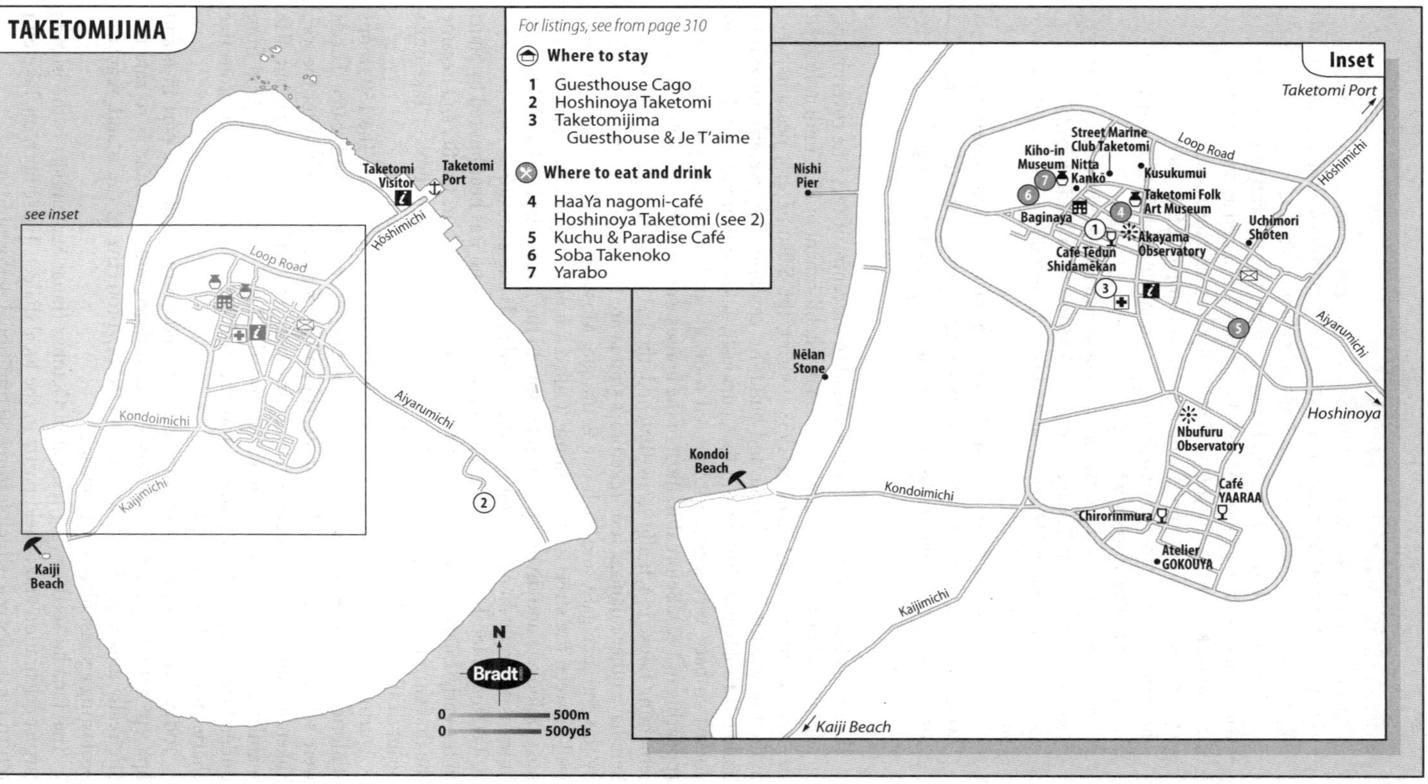
TAKETOMIJIMA
For listings, see from page 310
Where to stay
1 Guesthouse Cago
2 Hoshinoya Taketomi
3 Taketomijima Guesthouse & Je T'aime
Where to eat and drink
4 HaaYa nagomi-café
Hoshinoya Taketomi (see 2)
5 Kuchu & Paradise Café
6 Soba Takenoko
7 Yarabo
see inset
Taketomi Visitor
Taketomi Port
Hoshimichi
Loop Road
Aiyarumichi
Kondoimichi
Kaijimichi
Kaiji Beach
N
Bradt
0 500m
0 500yds
Inset
Taketomi Port
Hoshinoya
Kaiji Beach
Nishi Pier
Nēlan Stone
Kondoi Beach
Street Marine Club Taketomi
Kiho-in Museum
Nitta Kankō
Kusukumui
Taketomi Folk Art Museum
Baginaya
Akayama Observatory
Café Tedun Shidamēkan
Uchimori Shōten
Nbufuru Observatory
Café YAARAA
Chirorinmura
Atelier GOKOUYA

HOW YAEYAMA EARNED ITS NAME

Legend has it that Taketomi was formed by the god of island creation who, along with the god of mountain creation, went on to make the rest of the Yaeyama. Both are worshipped at Taketomi's Mainu-on shrine.

Taketomi's villages were founded by six men who divided the island to avoid conflicts over cultivable land. The six were enshrined as deities in their own utaki, known as *on* or *yama* in Taketomi dialect, and they became known as 'the gods of the six mountains'. The 'mountain' part of the name comes from this *yama*: in Japanese it translates as 'mountain' but in Taketomi dialect it means 'place overgrown with trees'.

Together, these six mountain shrines are known as Mūyama. Add to them two more important Taketomi shrines, Finaa-on (enshrining the deity of peace) and the original Mainu-on and you get the so-called eight mountains: literally Yaeyama (八重山).

You'll find many *on* shrines hidden around the island, but visitors aren't welcome in most. They often have small (and entirely ineffectual) wooden barricades to signal they're off-limits – remain respectful of the signs.

Taketomi's booming population once made it the centre of Yaeyama government; an administration office existed there from its establishment in 1524 until its limited size saw it moved to Ishigaki in 1938. During the Satsuma era, peasants were limited in what they could wear and build: for centuries they weren't allowed to build red-roof houses. This means that, curiously, Taketomi's architectural tradition doesn't go back very far. The iconic red roofs are in fact relatively modern, first appearing in 1903. Before this, most of the houses were thatched: Taketomi's oldest remaining house is actually straw-thatched, the last of its kind. The idyllic houses here have other nuances, too. Taketomi's shiisaa are found on the roof, rather than by the entrance gate, and each one is unique. Most houses have a free-standing wall between the street and the house. Called a *himpun,* it provides privacy from nosy onlookers and divides the entranceway to the house: the left-hand side is for humans, the right-hand side for the household gods and ancestors.

Taketomi's local hero is Nishitoo, a brilliant man who was headhunted by Shuri in the early 1500s. He became an architect, built parts of Shuri Castle, and became the first Governor of the Yaeyama. Nishitoo urged his people to protect Taketomi's beauty, calling the island 'a tray served in front of a royal guest'.

During World War II, air raids risked Taketomi's preservation. The 150 troops stationed here in 1944 made it even more of a target and made food scarce. Locals were sent to malaria-riddled Iriomote, supposedly for their benefit. After the war, Taketomi suffered from depopulation, droughts and typhoon damage, but also mainland investors who saw the island's worth. They began buying up land from under locals, until island leaders protested and the official Taketomi protective charter was established in 1987.

Today over 340 people live on Taketomi and everyone plays a part in island upkeep: not a single neighbour lets the team down and the island is so safe no-one really uses keys. Locals are also incredibly protective of the island, regularly protesting against planning proposals.

The Tanadui seed-sowing festival in October (lunar September) is the island's largest celebration and is held partly in the local dialect. Those born on Taketomi return for the festival, which features 80 traditional performing arts.

Though the island isn't known for its wildlife, it has coconut crabs, Chinese box turtles, plentiful butterflies and a rather unexpected booming feline population. You'll come across a few cats here and there but the biggest gang hangs out at Kondoi Beach, hoping for food and attention.

Taketomi is *not* a hidden gem. Its proximity to Ishigaki makes it the most popular day trip on the Yaeyama, seeing 500,000 visitors annually. Tourists pour from the 10-minute ferries to paddle Taketomi's postcard-perfect beaches, search for star sand and cycle around the iconic village.

Do hordes of tourists and a somewhat deceptively belated heritage mean you shouldn't visit? Absolutely not. Taketomijma remains a delightful day trip for very good reason, but definitely consider staying overnight. Once the day droves disappear, the stunning minshuku, friendly locals and fabled glistering stars emerge: at night, Taketomi gets even better.

GETTING THERE AND AWAY Ishigaki has many daily returns taking just 10–15 minutes. Two ferries a day from Iriomote Ōhara stop at Taketomi, taking 75 minutes. Kohama also has two daily ferries that stop at Taketomi. There are also lockers at the port for day-trip convenience. Since 2019, Taketomi has asked for a small entrance fee, payable at the ticket vending machines at both Ishigaki and Taketomi ports. The fee is optional, but goes towards upkeep and protection of the island. Yaeyama Kankō (八重山観光フェリー; 0980 82 5010; w yaeyama.co.jp) offers one-day packages which include a round-trip ferry from Ishigaki and the buffalo tour. You will need to reserve this in advance.

GETTING AROUND There are no rental cars or mopeds on the island. **Bicycles** are the nicest way to experience Taketomi; the island is flat and takes 2–3 hours to cycle around slowly. There are plentiful bike hire places, all charging roughly the same price. Most rental shops operate a free shuttle by the port, which drops you at their store, no reservation required. Shops will also hold baggage.

If you are taking a buffalo cart ride and renting a bike, use Taketomi Tourist Centre (see below). Remember your bike number as most of them don't lock, and they look the same.

It's entirely possible to explore Taketomi **on foot**. From port to town is just 10 minutes and the village and beaches are easy to wander.

Taketomi Kotsu (0980 85 2154; w taketomijimakotsu.business.site) operate **minibuses** from the port, as well as shuttles to the beach and village. If you want to board somewhere other than the port, you'll need to reserve via phone. You can also book a short bus tour of Taketomi at Ishigaki Port before leaving for Taketomi.

The Hoshinoya resort operates three buses and other accommodations will usually provide port shuttles. There are also a handful of **taxis** run by Tomori Kankō (0802 751 3229) but no taxi stands.

TOURIST INFORMATION Taketomi has hands-down the best Yaeyama tourist office. The **Taketomi Visitor Centre** (竹富島ゆがふ館・竹富島ビジターセンター; 2350 Taketomi; 0980 85 2488; w taketomijima.jp; 08.00–17.00 daily) by the port has comprehensive information, exhibits and souvenirs. It's also a much nicer place to wait for your ferry than the port. The **Taketomi Tourist Centre** (竹富観光センター; 441 Taketomi; 0980 85 2998; w suigyu.net; 09.00–17.00 daily) in the village offers tours and information, and has the cheapest buffalo tour (page 311) ticket when combined with bike rental.

WHERE TO STAY *Map, page 307*

✷ **Guesthouse Cago** (3 rooms) ちいさい島宿cago; 362 Taketomi; 0980 85 2855; w taketomi-cago.com/english. A locally run oasis with small plunge pool, 2 individual villas & 1 room. One of the most beautiful stays in Taketomi, bath en suites come with all the expected amenities, & rooms have a fridge. Dinner is optional but highly recommended: the owner cooks up an elegant storm of local food with island-grown ingredients. **$$$$$**

✷ **Hoshinoya Taketomi** (48 rooms) 星のや竹富島; 0570 07 3066; w hoshinoya.com/taketomijima. Hoshinoya has worked wonders keeping with Taketomi traditions. Its local-built villas are sensational: a tatami lounge & wall of windows on to the stone garden, plush futon beds, bath en suite, walk-in closet, refrigerator & hot drinks. Rooms are only outdone by the food: a 9-course dinner worth every penny (see below). Tours, shuttles, free craft & food experiences, an outdoor pool & spa. **$$$$$**

Taketomijima Guesthouse & Je T'aime (2 rooms, 2 dorms) 竹富ゲストハウス&ジュテーム; 321–2 Taketomi; 0980 85 2555. Basic but well-decorated hostel with gender-segregated dormitory bunk bed accommodations & private twin rooms. Rooms have fans; bathrooms & toilets are shared. The communal area has a fridge, microwave, kitchen & coin laundrette. Bike rentals are free & tours available. **$**

WHERE TO EAT AND DRINK *Map, page 307*

Restaurants aren't large and fill up quickly at lunch, so you're advised to go early as you may have to wait for a table. If possible, opt for accommodation with dinner as it's excellently done and part of the experience.

✷ **Hoshinoya Taketomi** 星のや竹富島; 0570 07 3066; w hoshinoya.com/taketomijima; 17.30–late daily. Hoshinoya's 9-course island terroir dinner is the stuff of food-critic dreams, & is more than worth making the trek for. A combination of spectacle & flavour with incredible service & an eye-watering bill. **$$$$$**

Soba Takenoko そば処竹乃子; 0980 85 2009; w soba.takenoko-taketomi.com; 10.30–16.00 & 19.00–21.00 daily. A famous Yaeyama soba spot that's been running 40 years. Sit in the garden & sprinkle your fresh soba with *piyaashi* island pepper. In the evening, pop in for several drinks. You can buy the pepper sauce as a spicy memento. **$$**

Yarabo 事処 やらぼ; 107 Taketomi; 0980 85 2268; 11.00–16.00 Tue–Sun. Cosy & famous among locals, the menu is full of freshly caught fish & seafood. The vegetable soba with tiger prawns are a must: sweet, plump & absolutely massive. **$$**

HaaYa nagomi-café 379 Taketomi; 0980 85 2253; 10.30–17.00 daily. Although this café does set meals, come here for the *teedun* (てーどぅん) sweets set: proper handmade island sweets best enjoyed from the 2nd floor overlooking the village. **$**

Kuchu & Paradise Café くちゅ&パラダイスカフェ; 531 Taketomi; 0908 035 6152; noon–17.00 Fri–Tue. Big pizzas, chilli, frozen cocktails & icy smoothies under the canopy of a gorgeous Taketomi garden, out the way of the tourist thoroughfare. **$**

ENTERTAINMENT AND NIGHTLIFE Nightlife on Taketomi mostly involves stargazing but a few local cafés turn into izakaya after dark, where you can enjoy a cool pint of Orion or an awamori with constellations and locals to keep you company. It's a rare side of Taketomi life that day trippers don't get to see. These izakaya also open at lunchtime for food, with Café YAARAA particularly pretty in the sunshine.

Café Teedun Shidameekan カフェテードゥンしだめー館; 361 Taketomi; 0980 85 2239; w sidame-kan.com; 11.00–14.30 & 18.30–20.00 daily

Café YAARAA 637 Taketomi; 0980 85 2040; f 南潮庵nan-chou-ann; 11.00–22.00 daily

Chirorinmura ちろりん村; 653 Taketomi; 0980 85 2007; w taketomichirorin.jp; 10.00–midnight daily.

SHOPPING There are enough souvenir shops in the east and west settlements that it's best just to abandon your bike and go on foot. If you're interested in buying more than typical tourist stuff, there are a few pottery workshops, generally in the south, where you can see tiles, shiisaa dogs and crockery being made and buy some to take home. Make sure to pop into places like **Atelier GOKOUYA** (アトリエ五香屋; 1478 Taketomi; 0980 85 2833; w atelier-gokouya.com; 10.00–17.00 daily) to check out their beautifully simple earthenware crafts, many drying in the sun.

If you need to pick up food the best general store is **Uchimori Shōten** (内盛商店; 490 Taketomi; 0980 85 2210; 10.00–18.00 Fri–Wed, 13.30–18.00 Thu), at the village entrance.

SPORTS AND ACTIVITIES

Glass-bottom Boats 0903 797 7881; w taketomijima.com. The platform for these boats is at Taketomi Port, to the right as you disembark the ferry. Tours go every 30mins between 08.15 & 16.15 & take 25mins. You can reserve in advance but also see availability on arrival.

Hoshinoya Taketomi 星のや竹富島; 0503 786 1144; w hoshinoya.com/taketomijima. Half-day snorkel tours, beginner diving, experience diving & full equipment rental.

Nitta Kankō 新田観光; 97 Taketomi; 0980 85 2103; w nitta-k.net; 08.30–17.00 Thu–Tue. Traditional buffalo tours, the cheapest option if not hiring a bike.

Street Marine Club Taketomi ストリートマリンクラブ竹富島; 393 Taketomi; 0901 943 3765; w taketomijima-street.com/tour; 08.00–21.00 daily. 2hr snorkel tours & 3hr Hamashima & Seabird Rock tour; also offer accommodation.

OTHER PRACTICALITIES There are no police on Taketomi. Taketomi Clinic (竹富町立竹富診療所; 324 Taketomi; 0980 85 2132; w taketomi.jadecom.or.jp; 09.00–noon & 13.00–16.00 Mon–Fri) near the school operates infrequently, with an Ishigaki doctor coming in every now and again. Taketomi Post Office (竹富郵便局; 500 Taketomi; 0980 85 2342; 08.45–17.30 Mon–Fri, 09.00–17.00 Sat) has the only ATM.

WHAT TO SEE AND DO Taketomi doesn't take a lot of time to scoot through. The sights are small and easily navigable by cycle. The best way to start is heading into the village for a **Water Buffalo Tour**, the must-do Taketomi activity. The buffalo cart ride ambles about the slim village roads to the sound of sanshin. There's a certain awkwardness to being serenaded in a different language at the slowest pace possible; 5 minutes into the 30-minute tour, you've got the gist, but it's great for kids and a tick-list experience. No need to reserve: just get in the buffalo tour shuttle for one of the two operators, Nitta (see above) or Taketomi Tourist Centre (page 309), at the port.

Once you've completed the ride, grab a bike or walk the beautiful village, where you'll find multiple photo ops. The myriad shiisaa guarding the roofs with orange at their feet and deep blue sky as their backdrop are beautiful shots. There are also great macro flower opportunities, with entire streets painted bright pink with bougainvillea and hibiscus. On these bougainvillea roads, the bright flowers tumble over the village's volcanic walls much of the year but are at their best in February and March. The flowers were used to decorate Yaeyama graves and altars but are now a kind of show-stopping competition between locals.

Opposite Nitta Kankō's buffalo cart area is Taketomi's oldest house, **Baginaya** (馬儀納屋; 372 Taketomi), built in 1866. It's the only one with a *kaya* thatched roof and is what the more traditional houses would have looked like before the red-tile revolution. In the central north of the village you'll find **Kusukumui** (小城盛), one of the Sakishima watchtower beacons used to send signals to other islands. There's also the nearby **Akayama Observatory** (あかやま展望台; 379 Taketomi; ⌚ 24hrs; ¥100). This observation deck overlooking the village has become the replacement for nearby Nagominotō (なごみの塔), which is now unsafe. Pop ¥100 in the box as you go.

When travelling between the two towers, keep an eye out for the **Request Shiisaa** (お願いシーサー). We can't say any more, as you're not allowed to know where it is – if you look it up, ask someone, or get told its location, your wish won't come true. You have to come upon it naturally. It's a dark brown shiisaa, standing with its paws together and donations in front, carefully camouflaged against rock. Good luck.

The south of the village has a few cafés and restaurants and **Nbufuru Observatory** (ンブフル展望台; 648 Taketomi; ⌚ 24hrs; ¥100). This southern observatory is Taketomi's highest and on good days you can see Ishigaki and Iriomote. Its unusual name has a bewildering origin: it's apparently the triumphant noise made by the cows who secretly built this hill at night using their horns. Again, put your ¥100 donation in the tin as you go.

To jump into Taketomi culture, visit the **Kihōin Museum** (喜宝院蒐集館; 108 Taketomi; ☎ 0980 85 2202; ⌚ 09.00–17.00 daily; adult ¥300). While the displays aren't in English, this museum's 4,000 artefacts speak for themselves. There's a traditional boat, uniforms from World War II, festival costumes, crafts, farm tools and more. It's also got an example of *warazan*, the method of tying knots in straw as an alphabet. Afterwards, head to the **Taketomi Folk Art Museum** (竹富民芸館; ☎ 0980 85 2302; ⌚ 09.00–17.00 daily), where displays are a mix of material-making processes and locals hunched over looms creating pieces of original minsaa material. It's amazing to see Taketomi's craft heritage being kept alive by men and women, young and old. The museum is free and you can even have a go.

When you're done soaking up the island life, head to the sea and enjoy Taketomi's truly impressive beaches. **Kaiji Beach** (カイジ浜), better known as *hoshizuna* (star sand) beach, has sand made from the exoskeletons of tiny sea-dwelling organisms called *foraminifera* (*Baculogypsina sphaerulata*). A Taketomi highlight is sifting

MYTHS AND FOLKTALES: THE STORY OF STAR SAND

A long time ago, the North Star and Southern Cross decided to bring life to earth. When the Southern Cross was ready to give birth, she asked the heavenly god where she should have her children. The god showed her Taketomijima and told her to give birth where the current is warm and slow.

The Southern Cross gave birth many times into the ocean, but the Dragon God of the sea got angry; the Southern Cross had not asked *his* permission to use his waters. He sent his giant serpent to get rid of the babies – the snake swallowed and killed them all. He spit out their skeletons, which floated to Higashimisaki on Taketomi's southern shore.

A kind village goddess there saw the dead star children and wept. She gathered them up and put them in her incense burner, telling them 'when the villagers worship me at the festival, you can follow the smoke back to your mother star in the sky'.

The goddess was right; the baby stars were returned to their mother. Now, every year, the villagers put star sand in their incense burner at Higashimisaki. If you look up at the Southern Cross, you can see many baby stars circling around their mother.

through the sand to find them. Few people realise how ancient they are: evidence suggests they may be hundreds of millions of years old. There's a souvenir shop for anyone wanting to take star sand home – don't remove it from the beach. Walk north from Kaiji and you'll reach **Kondoi Beach** (コンドイ浜). Kondoi is the only swimming beach, though that's a trickier endeavour than it sounds. The waters are so shallow that you can walk far from the shore and still be only ankle deep. Just watch out for the sea cucumbers, which are prolific. Kondoi has facilities, guarded by a bevy of cats. Sunset at Kaiji Beach is an unhindered ombré of pinks, oranges and blues mirrored in the sea, while Kondoi's exceptional extensive low tide shallows allow photographers to walk out into the sea's midst.

Keep walking northwards and you'll bump into the unassuming **Neelan Stone** (ニーラン石). This stone stands like a big shark's tooth on the shore between Kondoi and Nishi Pier. Neelan is another word for Nirai Kanai, the home of the gods across the sea. This marker welcomes gods to Taketomi, who use it for tying up their boats. The 'world welcoming' ceremony is held here, beckoning the gods from Nirai Kanai.

Eventually you'll come to **Nishi Pier** (西桟橋), an old, disused jetty that was once a commuting point for farmers heading to Iriomote. The beach to its north side was where traditional bashōfu material (page 27) was exposed to seawater as part of the dyeing process. Now it's a wonderful spot for stargazing and fishing.

Though Taketomi isn't known for its diving or marine sports, it has plentiful coral and fish, an offshore sandy crescent that disappears with the tide, and a submarine hot spring.

KOHAMAJIMA

Kohama (小浜島) is a stunning day-trip island with blindingly pretty beaches. Sharing the manta way with Iriomote, Kohama's waters are remarkably clear, making it a beautiful dive and snorkel spot. Outside tourism, Kohama is a 7.84km^2 agricultural island for sugarcane, home to a sizeable 614 people. Much of it feels untouched, but large luxury resorts take over some of its eastern coast.

Kohama is famed in Japan for its paradisiacal scenery and as the setting for a famous NHK TV drama, *Chūrasan*, which brought domestic tourists flocking to its shores. If you're looking for island luxury, Kohama is the place to put down some money and stay in superb style.

As an island of resorts, Kohama's culture is little-heard and even less seen. The local dialect has been kept alive through Kohama's secret Akamata Kuromata festival. Known locally as *pōru,* the festival doesn't allow photography, recording or sketches. Kohama's dialect also travelled to Ishigaki, when Kohama locals were forced to repopulate Miyara village after the tsunami. Kohama and Miyara dialects have now diverged, but they share festivals and customs. In Miyaran, the word for Kohama is *ujaziima* – 'parent island'.

GETTING THERE AND AROUND Kohama is accessed by **boat** from Ishigaki, Iriomote and Taketomi. The 25-minute Ishigaki route has regular daily ferries, one of which returns via Taketomi. The Taketomi–Kohama service goes once a day and Iriomote Ōhara has a daily return service, both requiring reservations. As a popular day-trip island, the final ferry can get very busy. If full, another service will be arranged for stragglers but it can take another hour.

Resort **transfers** will pick guests up from the port at the northeast tip of the island, as will some minshuku in the village in the centre. The small, flat island is best travelled by **bike**. There aren't many sights outside the beaches, so it's quick to travel.

TOURIST INFORMATION The **Kohamajima Total Information Centre** (小浜島総合案内所/小浜島レンタカー; 3400-38 Kohama; 0980 85 3571; w kohama-marine.com/rent; 07.00–19.00 daily) next to the port can organise your trip if you don't have a hotel to help you. They offer transport rentals and tours.

WHERE TO STAY

Haimurubushi (148 rooms) はいむるぶし; 2930 Kohama; 0980 85 3111; w haimurubushi.co.jp. Haimurubushi luxury resort occupies Kohama's southeast. Big enough to need golf-cart transfers, its stunning accommodation has plush rooms & restaurants manned by helpful staff. Beachfront suites have wide patio views, hammock & even the bathtub. Loungewear, espresso machine, minibar & fridge. Best of all, an onsen with extraordinary stargazing at night. Extensive tours, services & entertainments. HB. **$$$$$**

Ufudakisō (6 rooms) うふだき荘; 52 Higashiomote; 0980 85 3243; w kohama52.ti-da.net. This budget central minshuku is a charming place with a friendly owner, who adds homely touches with baking & sanshin playing. Rooms are simple, with sharing & private options. The 5 Japanese & 1 Western rooms have fridges & there's a washing machine. HB available. **$$**

WHERE TO EAT AND DRINK

Saltyeed 736-1-3-150 Kohama; 0805 914 9661; 11.00–16.00 & 18.00–23.00 Tue–Wed & Fri–Sun. This casual café's cool eco-décor made of reclaimed materials would turn heads in a city, but it's happy lazing away on Kohama's west coast, serving rice bowls, ramen & waffles. **$$**

BOB's Café 3400–38 Kohama; 0980 85 3970; 11.00–17.00 Mon, 11.00–23.00 Wed–Sun. A Kohama legend, this brilliantly cheap burger joint at the tourist office is popular with visitors & locals. Pop in for the signature teriyaki burger with Kohama brown sugar before your ferry. **$**

WHAT TO SEE AND DO Kohama can be seen in short order with only a bicycle to hand. Heading west from the port, start at **Ufudaki** (ウフダキ・大岳), Kohama's highest point at just 99m. Ufudaki's observation tower provides a 360-degree view of Kohama, as well as neighbouring islands across the sea. Kohama's westernmost tip is **Uminchu Park** (海人公園), next to the manta waterway. It's home to a ray-shaped observation deck and is good for picnicking. Nearby **Kubazaki Beach** (細崎海岸) fronts the manta strait and is a gorgeous place to paddle. One of the better beaches is on Kohama's southeast. Visit via the straight stretch of Sugar Road, between the village and the southeast resorts. This road is a favourite Kohama site for domestic tourists as it featured in the *Chūrasan* drama.

Young tourists love the beachside swing at **Haimurubushi Beach** (はいむるぶしビーチ), which overlooks the bright blue waters. Connected to the eponymous resort but not private, this is the best beach on Kohama. The café has a nice menu and loungers on the sand. The swimming section of beach is to the left. The hotel (see above) organises tours here, including banana boats and jet skis.

Off Kohama's northeast is **Kayama Island** (嘉弥真島), which is accessible by tour from April to September. A 2.5km-around island where the beach is all yours, here you can spend the day snorkelling with tropical fish in the shallows and lazing on ivory sands. Inexplicably, Kayama is also home to 500 rabbits. It's one of the coolest places to camp, year-round, where you can barbecue under the stars and look for star sand in the morning light. Book with a travel agency or tour from Kohama, available via resorts and Kohamajima Total Information Centre (see above).

KUROSHIMA

Kuroshima (黒島) means one thing: cows. Kuro rears many of Japan's world-famous wagyū beef cows through infancy, selling the calves on at auction. Cows outnumber Kuro's 230 humans 13 to 1.

If cattle isn't high on your hit list, you might reasonably overlook Kuroshima. Many people do; its 10km² of uninspiring flatness has few attractions to recommend itself. But what Kuro does have is remote charm by the bucketload. It's untouched, unvisited and delightfully quaint. It has the beaches of Kohama without the resort hotels; the local welcome and stars of Hateruma without the questionable sea voyage. Kuro also has the best turtle spawning grounds in the area, giant coconut crabs and, of course, its February cow festival, which is entirely, uniquely and spectacularly Kuro.

Before cows, Kuro had the sea: its culture has been tied to the ocean since ancient times. Many of its shrines are to seafaring safety and there's even a legend that Kuroshima is the start of all journeys.

It was once a shipbuilding island, with new vessels prayed for at Miyazato's boat shrine (船浦御嶽), though production moved to Iriomote in 1738, with craftsmen commuting over. Kuroshima turned to cattle in the 1600s and hasn't looked back.

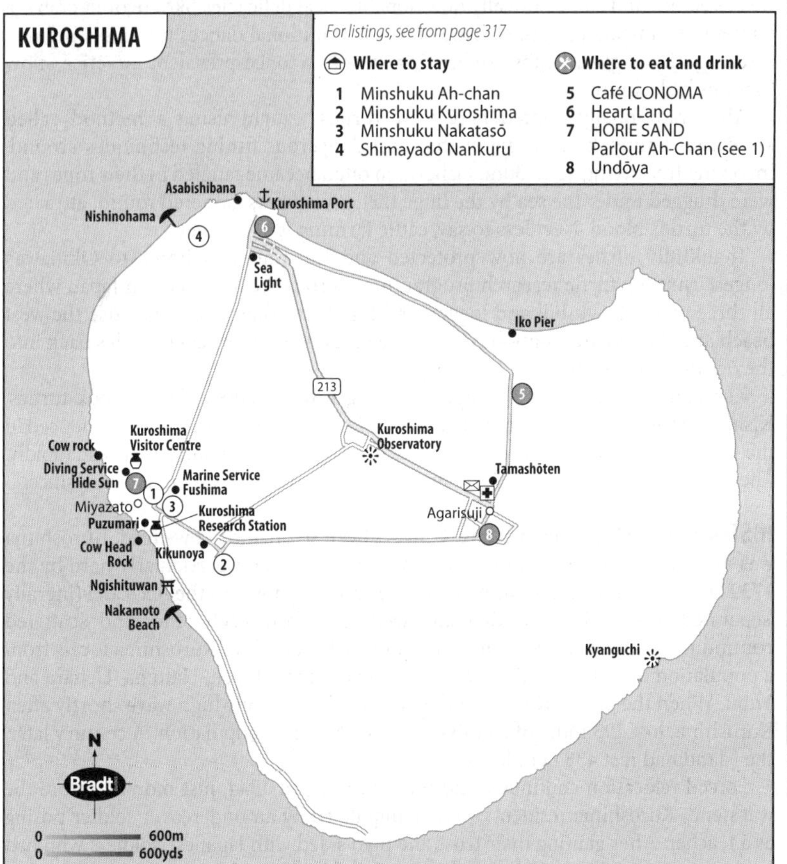

KUROSHIMA FESTIVALS

The cow festival, or Ushimatsuri, is *the* event in Kuroshima's calendar. Taking place on the final Sunday in February, the festival has live music, plentiful food stands of sizzling beef, traditional arm-wrestling and sports-day races that include hay-bale rolling and literal wheelbarrows. A riotous day of truly local activities, its highlight is the lottery: visitors have a chance to win their very own cow.

Other annual celebrations include dragon-boat racing at Hōnensai in July, and the New Year's north vs south tug-of-war, which prays for good harvest. Conveniently the harvest will be good whichever side wins. Kuroshima's utaki shrines, known as *wan,* are forbidden to tourists, so admire their overgrown façades from afar.

With sea and livestock comes food. Despite severely lacking restaurants, Kuro offers a soupçon of surprising gastronomy. The beef is some of the best in the world, with cafés producing rice bowls topped with velvety soft meat, grilled smoky skewers and umami-filled broths. Seafood shines in rich creamy soups, fresh sashimi and some ethically questionable local delicacies like coconut crab – a vulnerable indigenous species. One of Kuro's traditional dances mimics fishermen catching these giant crabs, suggesting it was a once-prevalent practice, now thankfully declining.

Also traditionally hunted here were turtles, caught using a method called *kamikake.* Kamikake was one of the most dangerous fishing techniques around, involving free diving up to 30m. Fishermen often became tangled in their ropes and were dragged under the sea by the huge turtles as sharks gathered round, attracted by the turtle's blood. Needless to say, cattle farming is a lot safer.

Thankfully turtles are now protected and Kuroshima is home to Okinawa's longest-running turtle research programme. Kuro is the only place in Japan where all three green, hawksbill and loggerhead turtles lay their eggs. They use the west beach and the research station regularly releases new and rescued turtles back into the ocean during summer.

Kuroshima is also home to Ryūkyū flying foxes, fireflies, Chinese box turtles, Kishinōe lizards and, oddly enough, the occasional peacock. These were introduced in the 1980s for ornamental purposes, but escaped during a typhoon and spread rapidly. They've decimated Kuroshima's endemic wildlife and have been hunted ever since.

HISTORY The island's history hasn't always been so quaintly cow-filled. Kuroshima was once one of the more populated Yaeyama, so was hit particularly hard by the 1732 law that enforced migration across the group, known as the *michikiri* (literally 'separated way'). Michikiri divided loved ones from each other and scattered communities, and over the course of centuries, hundreds of Kuroshima locals from a population of just over 1,000 were sent to Hirakubo, Fukai, Hatoma, Uehara and Yubu. When the 1771 tsunami hit the flat island with a 5m-high wave shortly after, Kuroshima lost 293 more of its inhabitants – 25% of its population. A century later, the island had just 438 people left.

Forced relocation continued into the war. In April 1944, just months before the war's end, Kuroshima residents were manipulated by an undercover soldier posing as a teacher. After gaining their trust, the man sided with Japanese soldiers who had landed on Kuro, telling residents to evacuate and forcibly relocating them to Iriomote and Ishigaki's malaria-prone jungles. Villagers were also ordered to slaughter their precious 1,600 cows to avoid them falling into enemy hands – or more likely to feed the Japanese military. Remnants of the war are still uncovered today on Kuroshima: as recently as 2016, an unexploded US military ordnance was found on the island.

GETTING THERE AND AWAY Kuroshima is accessed by regular 20–30-minute daily ferries from Ishigaki, with an increased service during Ushimatsuri. Kuroshima's small port building on the northwest coast has a waiting area and a tiny souvenir shop. Yaeyama Kankō Ferry (八重山観光フェリー; Ishigaki Port Terminal Building, Misakicho; 0980 82 5010; w yaeyama.co.jp) do a package deal for ferry tickets and all-day bike rentals.

GETTING AROUND Kuroshima is famously heart-shaped, though you may need an active imagination to see it. This floating heart is 10km² with five small villages grouped into two main settlements. The central settlement, Agarisuji, has the one small shop and post office. Miyazato on the west coast has the few tourist sites, most accommodation and beaches. Just 13km around and entirely flat to boot (its highest point is an impressive 15m), Kuroshima is easily travelled by **bicycle**, taking 4–5 hours to see its attractions. You can also walk to the villages and Iko Pier in 20–30 minutes, but it's hot work.

Accommodations will have port shuttles and bicycles to rent. For day trippers, there are three rental shops. You'll find shuttles at the port on arrival, which take you to shops with no reservation required – a touch lazy given they're 2–4 minutes' walk away. The cheapest hourly option is Kuroshima Rental Bicycle.

Vehicle rental

Heart Land ハートらんど; 466 Kuroshima; 0980 85 4007; w heartland96.com/rentalcycle; with 1st & final ferries

Kuroshima Car Rental 黒島レンタカー; 1024–1 Kuroshima; 0980 85 4211; 08.00–20.00 daily

Kuroshima Rental Bicycle 黒島レンタサイクル; 488–1 Kuroshima; 0904 996 2512; 08.30–17.30 daily

Macchan Obaa's Rental Cycle & Moped まっちゃんおばー レンタサイクル; 449 Kuroshima; 0806 497 2323; 08.30–17.30 daily. Car & moped rentals will either pick you up from the port or drop the vehicle there (sometimes just leaving it with the keys ready to go). The only petrol station is in Agarisuji.

TOURIST INFORMATION In a now familiar pattern, tourist information is limited and you're best off collecting it before you go. Don't be fooled by the name of Kuroshima Visitor Centre: it's a small museum entirely in Japanese.

There are also no bins as Kuroshima's crows are both active and bold: don't leave food unattended. Keep swimwear to the beaches and be careful of habu and sunstroke, as there's very little shade.

WHERE TO STAY *Map, page 315*

All accommodations are local minshuku, many of them half board. As there's absolutely no nightlife on the island, where you stay has a large effect on your evening's entertainment.

Minshuku Nakatasō (8 rooms) なかた荘; 31-1 Kuroshima; 0980 84 6811; w kuroshima.net. The closest thing to a hotel, lovely Nakatasō has beautiful gardens & great rooftop stargazing. Japanese-style rooms are airy & light (AC coin operated) with private & shared bathroom options.

The home-cooked meals are brilliant with multiple board options. Port shuttle. **$$**

✷ **Shimayado Nankuru** (6 rooms) しま宿南来; 412 Kuroshima; 0980 85 4304; w nankuru.biz. Nankuru's newer building is roomy & welcoming. Simple tatami rooms with shared bathrooms (old annexe has cold showers), terrace, BBQ & laundry. Nankuru hosts occasional *yuntaku*: spontaneous nights of food, free alcohol & chatting. Owner Kugai-san is a sanshin master & provides music. HB optional. **$$**

Minshuku Ah-chan (11 rooms) 民宿あーちゃん; 83 Kuroshima; 0980 85 4936; w ah-chan.com. Ever-friendly Ah-chan will take you fishing & creates the most local dishes you can possibly find at Parlour Ah-chan (see below). Rooms are both Japanese & Western & are incredibly basic, with shared & private bathroom options; HB option too. **$**

Minshuku Kuroshima (11 rooms) 民宿くろしま; 1948 Kuroshima; 0980 85 4280; w peacefulyogaya.com. A typical small-island guesthouse: a little run-down on the outside but perfectly clean & welcoming inside. Tatami rooms are simple with shared bathrooms. Common areas have TV, free hot drinks, garden & roof terrace. It operates diving, yoga, snorkel & SUP tours & free bike rental. HB options. **$**

WHERE TO EAT AND DRINK *Map, page 315*

Heart Land ハートらんど; 466 Kuroshima; 0980 85 4007; w heartland96.com; 11.00–18.00 daily. Heart Land serves sea lettuce (aosa) & Yaeyama soba, lunch sets & its iconic ice cream tempura. **$$**

Parlour Ah-chan パーラーあーちゃん; 83 Kuroshima; 0980 85 4936; w ah-chan.com; 11.00–14.00 daily. Parlour Ah-chan's speciality is *yashigani soba* – coconut crab noodles (advance order). For something less troubling but equally local, try the porcupine fish soup. **$$**

Café ICONOMA イコノマ; 1409–1 Kuroshima; 0901 179 3204; noon–17.00 Thu–Tue. This sweet art café near Iko Pier serves drinks, cakes & light lunches. The papaya curry & fruit shakes are particularly good. **$**

HORIE SAND ホリエサンド; 10.00–14.00 daily. This sandwich truck sits outside the research institute. Sandwiches are supremely cheap & are best eaten overlooking Nakamoto Beach. **$**

Undōya うんどうや; 1552 Kuroshima; 0980 85 4660; 11.00–14.00 daily. This Agarisuji noodle shop has an incredibly pretty garden sheltered by flowering vines, where they serve hearty beef soba, curry, shaved ice & drinks. **$**

SHOPPING Kuroshima's one store is in Agarisuji: Tama Shōten (たま商店; 0980 85 4223; 10.30–20.00 daily) stocks a variety of basics, fresh produce, meat and drinks. It has a tendency to shut for an unofficial lunch break at noon. Miyazato's kiosk shop Kikunoya (きくのや; 1832 Kuroshima) sells snacks and beers, but has no specified opening hours.

If you're looking for souvenirs (cow-shaped, naturally) you may find minimal selections at cafés, accommodations, the port, and the visitor and research centres. Realistically, your best hope for a proper Kuro memento is winning the Ushimatsuri cow.

SPORTS AND ACTIVITIES The seas around Kuroshima are some of the clearest in the archipelago, where you'll find turtles, nudibranchs, clownfish, corals and amazing macro life. In winter, manta rays migrate off Kuro's reef.

There are four dive shops including Minshuku Kuroshima (see above).

Diving Service Hide Sun ダイビングサービスひでsun; 117 Kuroshima; 0980 85 4777; w hidesun.jp; 08.00–19.00 daily. Fun dives, experience dives & certification courses.

Marine Service Fushima マリンサービスふしま; 62 Kuroshima; 0901 870 4550; w fushima.net; 08.00–20.00 daily. Fun dive, experience dive & snorkelling.

Sea Light シーライト; 1825 Kuroshima; 0907 885 6123; w ishigaki-snorkel.jp; 09.00–18.00 daily. Single dives & experience dives.

LOCAL RECIPE: GYŪDON

Although a national rather than local recipe, *gyūdon* is one of the best rice bowl (donburi) meals available at Kuroshima's cow festival. Serves two.

1 medium onion, thinly sliced
450g beef, thinly sliced
240ml dashi (fish stock)
6 tbsp soy sauce
4 tbsp sake
4 tbsp mirin
2 tbsp sugar
200g Japanese rice, cooked as per packet instructions
2 spring onions, sliced diagonally, and pickled red ginger to serve

1. In a large pan add the dashi, soy, sake, mirin and sugar. Mix to combine.
2. Cover the bottom of the pan in the onion slices, then cover them with a layer of beef.
3. Cover the pan and start to cook over a medium heat, skimming off scum from the broth as it appears. Turn down to a simmer and cook covered for 3-4 minutes.
4. Fill a bowl with rice and top with the beef and sauce. Sprinkle with spring onions and ginger and serve.

OTHER PRACTICALITIES Agarisuji has an ATM at the post office and a small clinic open three days a week. There are no police on Kuroshima.

Kuroshima Post Office 黒島郵便局; 1032–1 Kuroshima; 0980 85 4342; 09.00–17.00 Mon–Fri, ATM: 08.45–17.30 Mon–Fri, 09.00–17.00 Sat

Taketomi Municipal Clinic 竹富町立黒島診療所; 1474 Kuroshima; 0980 85 4114; 09.00–noon & 13.00–16.00 Tue–Wed & Fri

WHAT TO SEE AND DO Kuroshima is remarkably easy to get round – all you need is a bike. You can walk if you don't care to see the further reaches, but be aware the flat landscape is uninspiring and unshaded. Start out at **Nishinohama** (西の浜; 412 Kuroshima) to the west of the port. This stunningly empty, 2km white-sand beach isn't really for people but turtles: Nishinohama is their nesting ground, so don't dig here and give eggs and turtles a wide berth. Access to Nishinohama is easiest via **Asabishibana** (アサビシバナ), a narrow gap between two rocks. Known as 'Play Rock', it was once a place where islanders gathered, sang and danced.

Head south to the **Kuroshima Visitor Centre** (西表国立公園黒島ビジターセンター; 1 Kuroshima; 0980 85 4149; 09.00–17.30 Tue–Sun, closes 17.00 in winter), a museum which has lots of Japanese information and little English. It's free though, so you can wander the exhibits of photos, festival outfits and old boats without feeling too hard done by. Its highlight is a cow cut-out with a screen attached – stand on the footprints and find out how many Kuroshima heifers you weigh. Behind the centre sits **Puzumari** (プズマリ), a mound that formed Kuroshima's 17th-century beacon and lookout tower. It's now too dangerous to climb: attempting it could also collapse the structure.

MYTHS AND FOLKTALES: THE OLD CROW'S WISDOM

Long ago there lived an old crow on Kuroshima. He flew very slowly, and the young crows would taunt and look down on him. One day, a young crow came from Hateruma with news that a large cow had died and was just lying there, ready to be eaten. The crows were ready to leave immediately, but the old, slow crow told the youngsters he would catch them up, and begged for a favour. He asked them to leave the cow's horn for him as it was the tastiest part.

The young crows had never heard this, but wanted it for themselves. They sped to Hateruma, found the cow and pecked at its horns, injuring their beaks. It was simply too hard. Perhaps it was the *inside* that was so tasty. As they wasted time trying to figure it out, the old crow arrived and found the eyes – the true tastiest part of the cow – untouched, and ate them all to himself.

Cow Island wouldn't be complete without a bonny basalt bovine or two. Wander southwest to the coast to find **Cow Head Rock** (牛頭岩) or Ushitōiwa, the first 'cow' made from a table of rock jutting out on the right-hand side of the beach by Puzumari. While here, check out the picturesque **Ngishituwan** (迎里御獄), a coastal utaki that is off-limits but has a beautiful entrance with a stone torii gate that opens up into a tunnel of twisted, leaning tree trunks.

Nearby **Nakamoto Beach** (仲本ビーチ) has crystal waters and a full reef that's home to everyone's favourite clownfish. Great for snorkelling, it's a playground of deep rock pools at low tide, some big enough to swim in. You can rent free life jackets at the hut, and there are toilets and showers. You don't need a guide to snorkel Kuroshima, but you do need caution as beaches are tidal and covered in sharp coral. There have been increasing accidents (some lethal) – if the signboard by the stairs is red, don't swim. Some of the better snorkelling spots towards Panari (Aragusku Island) require a tour. All dive shops offer snorkelling, though the 6-hour tour with Marine Service Fushima (page 318) is highly recommended. Many minshuku have snorkel tours and hire too.

Towards the western side is the **Kuroshima Research Station** (黒島研究所; 136 Kuroshima; ☎ 0980 85 4341; w kuroshima.org; ⌚ Apr–Sep 09.00–18.00 daily, Oct–Mar 09.00–17.00 daily; ¥500): a museum, aquarium and science centre studying and breeding turtles and other animals. Through the year you can feed turtles and see coconut crabs, habu, and Yaeyama exhibits. The summer turtle release is a remarkable must-see and they also offer night tours in laying season. Loggerhead, green and hawksbill turtle spawning happens sporadically during May–August: these night tours are the best opportunity to spot them. Land crab spawning happens June–September, peaking during the full moon in June–July. You should be able to watch the juveniles scuttle over any sandy beach. Just up from the research station on the **Hokei Coast** (保慶海岸) is the second cow rock: a vague cow-shaped outline between the mushroom rocks.

From there you can return back to the port or carry on south to explore the photography spot of **Kyanguchi** (キャングチ): a delightfully desolate view of boat rails disappearing into the waves beside the ruins of a wall topped with a colourfully glazed shiisaa.

The north's only real sight is **Iko Pier** (伊古桟橋), a disused 350m jetty where locals fish and tourists come for a near-360-degree panorama. Iko stretches far into the clear waters, which spread out before you in blue and gold waves of shallow, sandy sea, and at high tide, the water laps the pier making it look like you're floating on the ocean.

Similarly barren is the island's centre, where you'll find the **Kuroshima Observatory** (黒島展望台; 1463 Kuroshima). The 10m-high view over pastures isn't much to write home about, but you may see other islands on clear days. The road it's on was once bewilderingly designated one of Japan's 100 characteristic roads: in the past it was bright white and unpaved.

IRIOMOTEJIMA

If you visit only one of the Yaeyama Islands, make it Iriomote (西表島). This is where the wild things roam: a cloaked land of cloudy canopies, fantastical creatures and dense, unexplored jungle. At 289km², it is the Yaeyama's largest island and almost entirely mountainous, with 90% of its land covered in subtropical forest. Cleaving these trees are winding, twisted waterways, mangroves and falls that pour out towards the coast.

The island is regularly referred to as 'the Galapagos of the East' – a name that seems to be generously bestowed around these parts. Though Amami and Tokunoshima have been called the same, Iriomote feels wilder; its jungles are that bit more tropical, its nature more ever-present, making the majority of Iriomote impenetrable.

Settlements are perched around the edge of the big island, backed by the ever-reaching tendrils of mangroves, myrtles and sugar palms. Villages start in the southeast with Haemi and Ōhara, which hosts one of the two major ports. A 50-minute drive anticlockwise up and over the island's north brings you to Uehara, the other primary village and port. This well-kept road continues round a little further, finishing at Shirahama in the west. Below Shirahama sits Funauki, the last of the island's villages, accessible only by boat. There are no settlements or even roads on the southern and southwest coastlines.

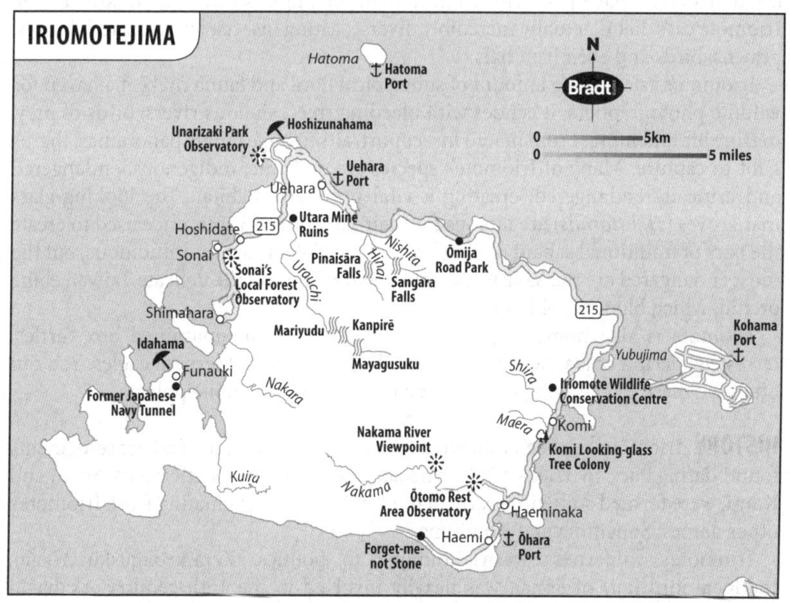

Most of Iriomote is uninhabited, untouched jungle. Rivers form not only a huge part of the landscape, but a large part of your trip, with activities and sights centred around them. There are over 25 rivers, but the two major ones are Urauchigawa (浦内川) in the west and Nakamagawa (仲間川) in the east, both leading towards the centre. The majority of hikes and sights are to the north of these two rivers. The area below them is largely unexplored, even by locals.

Nature runs the island's calendar, with each season bringing a different side to the island. Manta rays turn up in the south and east in January. Come spring, endemic Yaeyama fireflies emerge after dark, painting the forests in flickering lights. In May, the coral reefs start to spawn and June brings sagaribana flowers. The wet season here is May–June, with another large splash in October. Rain falls in big bucketing squalls that average 2,200mm a year. This keeps the rivers full, the greenery happy and the tourists damp: wet weather gear is a must.

The island's greatest resident, the Iriomote cat (*P. bengalensis iriomotensis*) was officially discovered in Funauki in 1967. Many islanders had sworn to the presence of the cats, but none had ever been photographed or captured. The cat gained international notoriety, earning fans such as the UK's late Prince Philip, and it was designated a special natural monument of Japan in 1977. It also gained a scroll of names, from the commonly used Japanese *yamaneko,* to the local trio of *yamamayaa, yamapikaryaa* and *meepisukaryaa.* The last translates as 'that which has flashing eyes'.

A faunal and photographic prize, the perpetually grumpy-looking yamaneko is often mistaken for a normal tabby cat. Weighing just 3–5kg, this endemic wild feline is distinguished by its rounded ears, fat tail, flat nose and white furry eyeliner around its big, yellow eyes. Rarely seen, it's in danger of becoming entirely extinct, with the last official count in 2008 around 100. Since then, the numbers have only diminished further. Busy in the twilight hours, you might see one on a night tour or by the roadside, but glimpses are miraculous.

The cats are solitary and crepuscular, living in the lowlands between coast and mountain – exactly where the villages and roads are. Yamaneko suffer from road accidents and village pets which injure them or diminish their food source. The Iriomote cat's diet is actually incredibly diverse, eating insects, frogs, lizards, snakes, prawns, birds and even fruit bats.

Iriomote's astonishing amount of subtropical flora and fauna make it a haven for wildlife photographers; it echoes with bleeding trees, sinuous rivers, birds of prey, marine life and more. From macro insect portraits to huge jungle panoramas, there's a lot to capture. Many of Iriomote's species are endemic, indigenous, endangered and critically endangered, creating a vital protective habitat. The looking-glass mangroves (*H. littoralis*) are famous for their tall buttress roots, once used to create the oars of traditional sabani rowing boats. Jungle plants are multitudinous, but the most endangered are the Sakishima-habukazura vine and the delicate Taiwan ebine orchid, which blooms gold in October.

Iriomote is also home to giant coconut crabs, yellow-margined box turtles, terrestrial hermit crabs, Atlas moths, jewel bugs and crested serpent eagles. You can often see these eagles along the roadside in trees and telephone poles.

HISTORY Iriomote has been inhabited for a long time, with the earliest settlements found dating back to 3,500–4,000 years ago. Two of today's settlements, Sonai and Komi, were formed sometime early in the 15th century, originating from Iriomote's other names: Sonaijima and Komijima.

Iriomote's wilderness wasn't immune to politics. Keraikedagusku Yōcho, the local lord (aji*)* of Sonai, was heavily involved in the 15th-century Akahachi rebellion, aligning with Shuri and Miyako against the rebels. Miyako soon turned to Keraikedagusku Yōcho for help subduing Yonaguni, and he was instrumental in that island's defeat and the completion of the Ryūkyū Kingdom.

Iriomote was also no stranger to tragedy. The Yaeyama island most affected by malaria, it lost all but one of its villages to disease and disaster: Sonai is the only remaining village with unbroken occupancy. Though the 1771 tsunami's immediate death toll was comparatively low on Iriomote (290), it suffered above all others in the famine and fallout, losing 80% of its population.

Coal was discovered on the island in the late 1800s, and the first mine opened in 1886 using prison labour and workers brought from Japan, Okinawa and Taiwan. Within three years, half the prisoners had died from malaria and the mine closed. Despite this, the Utara and Marusan mines opened in the 1930s, filled with workers lured by money and prospects. They met instead harsh labour, poor conditions and a salary paid in vouchers to stop them escaping. Many still tried to flee; those who were caught were tortured, and those who weren't often died in the forests.

In 1941, the Japanese army set up a fortress in Funauki for anti-aircraft guns and suicide boats. Funauki residents were forcibly removed to Shirahama where a 'comfort station' (an offensively benign phrase for a slave brothel) was set up. As the crisis deepened, more military facilities popped up on Iriomote.

Though locals knew which malaria-riddled areas to avoid, it didn't much matter. The Japanese army forced them and other Yaeyama evacuees into the jungle, known for malignant malaria, at the height of the rainy season: thousands died. Even as malaria disappeared, inhospitable weather remained problematic.

As multiple generations of islanders died in crises across the centuries and settlements were abandoned, huge swathes of Iriomote's indigenous heritage was lost, including its own dialect. Even Iriomote's nature, which remains relatively unscathed from the disasters, didn't escape entirely. Yubujima, an island off its northeast coast, was devastated by a 1969 typhoon, forcing residents to abandon it. A husband-and-wife team eventually returned and spent nine years creating today's botanical gardens.

The 1970s brought bridges around the island, finally connecting the east and west by land. The Shirahama tunnel was completed in 1993, leaving only Funauki – which only got stable 24-hour electricity in 1985 – unconnected by road.

GETTING THERE AND AWAY Iriomote is only accessible by ferry. All ferries are from Ishigaki, occasionally stopping at one of the neighbouring islands of Taketomi, Hatoma, Hateruma or Kohama. There are multiple ferries daily run by Yaeyama Kankō (八重山観光フェリー; Ishigaki Port Terminal Building, Misakicho; ☎0980 82 5010; w yaeyama.co.jp) and Anei Kankō (安栄観光; Ishigaki Port Terminal Building, Misakicho; ☎0980 83 0055; w aneikankou.co.jp), servicing both Uehara Port in the northwest and Ōhara in the southeast. Journeys to Ōhara are about 5 minutes shorter, taking 40–45 minutes.

Uehara is more often affected by bad weather, but in case of cancellations you will be provided with a free bus ticket from Ōhara to Uehara. Day trippers commonly head to Ōhara for a Nakama River tour and a visit to Yubujima, while those interested in hiking venture to Uehara.

Ferry schedules are updated every six months, so check company websites, which have the timetable and prices in English. Ōhara is the bigger port with more destinations: one daily ferry stops at Kohama and Taketomi on its way to Ishigaki, and there's a daily inbound and outbound ferry servicing Hateruma. Uehara has two daily ferries calling at Hatoma. Tickets can be bought in advance, where you may get a discount, or on the day at the ferry terminals.

IRIOMOTE FESTIVALS

Religious events on Iriomote are like its jungle: plentiful, with an air of mystery. Celebrations and rituals have travelled over the island as the population has moved, and many are limited to residents only.

The largest traditional event is the 500-year-old combined Shichi festivals of Sonai and Hoshidate. Taking place in October, they celebrate the end of the harvest. The festivals last three days, the second being the most visited by tourists. The beginning is calculated by the high tide and the day includes boat rowing, parades and a male islander acting as the yellow-robed god Miruku. Sonai also has a black-robed female called Fudachimi, said to be even older than Miruku, while Hoshidate has Ohoho, a laughing god that gives out money.

Komi's Akamata, Kuromata and Shiromata festival happens in lunar May–June. It's designated a 'secret festival', where all recordings, photos and even drawings are strictly prohibited. Some even say speaking of it to outsiders is forbidden, though there are some broadly known elements to the festival. It involves three gods, covered head to toe in grasses and wearing coloured masks, who emerge from the forest depths at night to visit houses. The three aren't allowed to meet in the street and villagers shouldn't look directly at them. At the end, Kuromata leaves his costume at the nearby utaki: a sign of a good harvest.

This festival has spread to Kohama, Aragusuku and Ishigaki, though it lost the third god Shiromata along the way. The festivals are so protected that when a journalist tried to sneak in in 1969, he was assaulted by enraged locals: if you're lucky enough to witness it, leave phones and cameras elsewhere.

GETTING AROUND Iriomote is the largest of the Yaeyama Islands. If you're used to the quick circumnavigation of Taketomi or Kuroshima, you'll be in for an unpleasant surprise trying to tackle Iriomote without an engine. There's a single main road traversing one side of the island, between Shirahama in the northwest over and down to Haemi in the southeast. **Rental cars** and **scooters** are easily the best way of getting around Iriomote, but they're not mandatory. You can find rental companies by both of the ports, as well as **taxi** services. Sightseeing taxis are also available, with both standard and larger vehicles, though few of the drivers speak English.

A **bus** service run by Iriomote Kōtsu goes from Shirahama to Toyohara (Haemi), via both ports. It's slow-going and sporadic: a one-way stretch takes 2 hours. This usually means staying in an area for a good few hours. With activities aplenty, this isn't necessarily troublesome, but affects day trippers and planning. One-day and three-day passes save huge amounts. A one-day pass is cheaper than a single between the ports. Buy these as you get on the bus. Prices and timetables change regularly, so look them up online (w iriomote.com/top/routebus) or pick up a timetable from a port.

To access Funauki, you'll need a **boat**. Get the 20-minute Funauki Kaiun ferry (☎0980 85 6552) from Shimahara. This departs four times daily and you buy the ticket on board. Alternatively charter a marine taxi service from Yarashōten (屋良商店; ☎0980 85 6126).

Taxis

Iriomote Kankō Taxi Ōhara; ☎0980 85 5333; w iriomote-kanko.jp; ⌚ 08.00–17.00 daily

Iriomotejima Kotsu Yamaneko Taxi Uehara; ☎0980 85 5303; w iriomotejima-koutsu.com/#taxi; ⌚ 08.00–18.00 daily

Vehicle rental

Hoshizuna Rent-a-Car 星砂レンタカー; 339–6 Uehara; w hosizunarentacar.amebaownd.com; 08.00–22.00 daily

Iriomote Rent-a-Car 西表レンタカー; 36–11 Haeminaka; 0980 85 5950, 0980 85 5440; w iriomote-rentcar.jp; 08.00–18.00 daily

Yamaneko Rent-a-Car やまねこレンタカー; 201–109 Haemi/337–1 Uehara; 0980 85 5111 (Ōhara), 0980 85 6111 (Uehara); w iriomote.com/top/rentacar-2; 08.00–18.00 daily

TOURIST INFORMATION The ports have some information, but very little in English. Your best option for information is your accommodation or Ishigaki Port before departure. You can also use the somewhat limited but ever-useful 12 Taketomi-chō free Wi-Fi spots around the island.

WHERE TO STAY

Ōhara

Takemori Inn (10 rooms) 竹盛旅館; 36-5 Haeminaka; 0980 85 5357; w takemori-inn.net. A 2min drive from Ōhara Port, Takemori was apparently Iriomote's first inn. Japanese-style rooms have AC, TV, fridge & shared bathroom. Family room has a veranda & en suite. Optional meals are traditional & delicious. Rental cars available. Historical with a homely feel. HB. **$$$**

✷ **Guesthouse Shimaotoya** (4 rooms, 2 dorms) ゲストハウスしまおとや; Haeminaka; 0980 85 5078; w shimaoto.com. Superbly equipped hostel with dorms, private dbls & trpl bunks. Shared bathrooms & washing machines. There's a large lounge, reading area, dining room & a restaurant-worthy kitchen with free hot drinks. Yaeko-san is incredibly helpful & speaks English. Port shuttle available. **$$**

Haimida Campsite (campsite) 南風見田キャンプ場; 508–33 Haemi; 0909 781 0940; w haimidakyanpu.com. The cheapest accommodation on Iriomote. Located on Haemida Beach, there's no electricity, toilet paper, shops or restaurants. Reserve at least 1 day in advance. Tent & sleeping bag rental must be booked. **$**

Uehara

Nilaina Resort (3 rooms) ニライナリゾート; 10–425 Uehara; 0980 85 6400; w nilaina.com. Set in stunning jungle scenery, Nilaina's 3 large Western-style villa-like rooms come with a private balcony, en suite, seating area, fridge, tea set & more. There's a free washing machine too. Meals are served on the terrace or in the restaurant. HB options available. A luxury stay without a resort hotel feel. **$$$$$**

Minshuku Sawayakasō (11 rooms) さわやか荘; 10–448 Uehara; 0980 85 6752; w sawayakasou.com. Owner Aki-san is chef, tour guide & manager, with adequate English. Enjoyably old-fashioned Western & Japanese rooms with en suite, & cheaper options with shared bathrooms. All clean & cheerful. Meals made with local ingredients & served in the cosy dining room. Rental cars, HB & b/fast options available. **$$$**

Elsewhere on the island

Irunti Futademura (9 cottages) イルンティフタデムラ; 973–3 Hoshidate; 0980 84 8484; w hpdsp.jp/hutademura. Lodge accommodation run by Hoshidate townspeople, with profits going back into the town. Cabins feel cosy but are a good size, with 2 types: 7-person family cabins & twin-room cabins with office space. Both have a fully stocked kitchen, laundry & nearby shop. Oddly, the TV has to be rented. Tour options & bike rental available. **$$$$**

Kamadoma-sō (4 rooms) かまどま荘; 2462 Funauki; 0980 85 6165. Older minshuku has HB & self-catering. Rooms are pleasant & large. Common room has TV, book nook, sanshin & coffee. Snorkelling & fishing rental. **$**

WHERE TO EAT AND DRINK Iriomote cuisine is influenced by nature and is a fantastic aspect to the island. Spring brings winged beans, pineapple, aosa and mozuku seaweeds. Summer has gourds, mango and dragonfruit. With autumn comes purple sweet potatoes, while winter is the season of wild boar, known as kamai locally or inoshishi. Boar hunting is limited to 15 November–15 February and is eagerly anticipated. Their meat is delicious and highly prized, grown fat on large acorns in the forests.

Offshore, there's such a range of seasonal seafood that even locals don't know what half the fish on the menu are. One of the most popular fish here is *irabuchaa*, a type of parrotfish that's often served raw or simmered in salt. Squid ink soup is also much loved on the island, as are scylla mangrove crabs.

Iriomote is awash with great restaurants, the majority of which teeter between rock-bottom and mid-range prices, offering proper island cooking made with locally caught, locally farmed ingredients.

Ōhara

✷ **Hateruma** 泡波と島の味 はてるま; 201–73 Haemi; 0980 85 5623; 18.00–23.00 Mon–Sat. Hateruma serves Okinawan kaiseki in a pretty wooden house, with multiple courses reflecting the season & speciality seafood of the day. This feast is so fresh that if the sea is rough, dinner may well be cancelled. Using foraged & locally grown ingredients, Hateruma is Iriomote fine dining on the lower end of the expensive range. Reservations essential. $$$$$

Kajiya Shokudo かじやー食堂; 36-20 Haeminaka; 0903 795 8792; 11.45–14.00 & 18.00–20.00 Mon–Sat. This marine-themed izakaya restaurant, bedecked in netting, is often packed with people clamouring for its massive drink & food menu. Set meals & small plates that are brilliantly cheap, as well as massive sashimi & sushi platters. $

Maya Rock Café まやろっく; 29-7 Haeminaka; 0903 792 5808; 11.30–13.30 daily. This adorable wooden shack does simple things well: hamburgers, hot dogs, Yaeyama soba & stunning cakes. A great lunch spot with terrace, Wi-Fi & cats. It's run by a bouldering gym, should you feel like working off the calories. $

Uehara

✷ **Hatsue** 初枝; 195 Uehara; 0980 85 6023; Mar–Dec 17.00–22.30 Wed–Mon. Iriomote's only sushi restaurant, the menu here is full of unusual (indecipherable) island fish but the chef is incredibly patient & staff speak English. Alongside gorgeously presented sashimi, there are specialities like papaya kimchi, umibudo & island tempura. Comparatively expensive but very reasonable for sushi. $$$$$

Island Feast Irumutiya 肉処 いりおもて家; 10–625 Uehara; 0980 85 6878; Apr–Dec 11.30–16.00 & 18.00–21.00 Sat–Thu. A lovely drinking & dining spot with ocean views managed by pineapple farmers. At lunchtime, it's dedicated to tropical fruit ice creams, juices & cakes. At night it becomes a yakiniku restaurant. It isn't just customers eating pineapple: the rare Iriomote beef served here feeds on pineapple, creating a sweet & incredibly soft meat. A foodie must. $$$

Ichitaka 一隼; 10–720 Uehara; 0980 85 7833; 17.00–23.00 Thu–Tue. Popular for its stone-baked pizzas, Okinawan cuisine, awamori & tropical fruit sours. This place gets packed, so worth booking. Try the deep-fried sooki pork spare ribs, *ahijo* fish with Yaeyama soba, crispy fried adan, rafutee pork belly fried rice, wild boar tataki (just-seared thin slices) or the daily assorted sashimi. $$

Kitchen Inaba キッチンイナバ; 742–6 Uehara; 0980 84 8164; w teisan-shima-life.com/kitchen-inaba; 11.30–14.30 & 18.00–22.30 Tue–Sun. Stylish family-friendly kitchen & bar serving island specialities: wild boar sashimi, *irabu-jiru* (snake soup), *gazami* (swimming crab) & green papaya salads. Also Western, Japanese & Okinawan dishes, & the awamori ice cream is a must. Live sanshin Jul–Oct. Some English & wheelchair friendly. $$

✷ **Pari's Rice** 巴里のごはんや; 331 Uehara; 0980 85 6137; 18.00–23.00 Thu–Mon. This ramshackle, uninspiring building hides a wholesome menu. Island & Western food with a touch of Hokkaidō, where the owners hail from. Drinks menu is vast, including shiso leaf shōchū. Try the mussels in cream & oddly named black meat pasta, dyed with squid ink. For a lighter option, try seasonal mozuku seaweed porridge. Cash only. $$

Tohenboku 唐変木; 749 Uehara; 0980 85 6050; 11.30–17.00 Thu–Mon. This knick-knack covered eatery is the place to try *ikasumi-jiru* – squid ink soup. It also serves boar, mangrove crab & freshly baked sweet *taimo* (also *taanmu*: taro) pies. Cash only. $$

Pocket House ぽけっとはうす; 870 Uehara; ☎ 0980 85 6571; ⏲ 16.00–01.00 Tue–Sun. Local izakaya serving a wealth of island dishes & ingredients such as inoshishi, mangrove crab, octopus & other seafood. The roasted wild boar & gyoza are particularly good. This becomes a late-night watering hole thanks to its closing time. $

Funauki

Buu no Ie ぶーの家; 2462 Iriomote; w sites.google.com/view/yarabunokokage; ⏲ 09.00–17.00 daily. Café that serves wild boar curry & soba set meals, with rental showers available. Simple hearty fare on a wooden deck surrounded by banana trees & chickens. Also operates a beautiful private cottage, Yarabu no kokage. $$

Yamaneko Terrace 山猫のテラス; 2461 Iriomote; ☎ 0904 470 5966; w funauki.com/restraurant/food.html; ⏲ 11.00–22.00 daily. This sizeable wooden building by the port serves alcohol, sooki soba, fried potato, grilled sausages, papaya salads. $

SHOPPING Uehara and Ōhara have gift shops in and around the ports, and Sonai has a souvenir shop with a great range. For more interesting souvenirs, buy your own mangrove tree at Yubujima (page 329) or Iriomote salt from Kitchen Inaba (page 326).

Markets are small but well stocked, selling bentō, fresh ingredients, snacks, toiletries, simple medications and miscellaneous goods. You'll also find unmanned roadside stores, mujinbaiten or mujinhanbai, which rely on honest customers to leave the right change.

Kawamitsu Super 川満スーパー; 547–1 Uehara; ☎ 0980 85 6157; ⏲ 07.00–21.00 daily

Ōtomi Co-op Store 大富共同売店; 29–52 Haemi; ☎ 0980 85 5410; ⏲ 07.00–21.00 daily

Super Hoshizuna スーパー星砂; 659 Iriomote (Sonai); ☎ 0980 85 6265; ⏲ 07.00–21.00 daily

Tamamori Supermarket 玉盛スーパー; 201–73 Haemi; ☎ 0980 85 5320; ⏲ 07.15–21.00 daily

SPORTS AND ACTIVITIES Of all the islands in the Nansei-shotō, Iriomote is the place for adventuring. The island is a playground for jungle trekking (page 330), canoeing, kayaking, diving and snorkelling. The majority of these are covered by single tour companies. Local tour operators Nonpura and Duck Tours (page 328) are excellent and speak English.

Iriomote has the largest and best mangroves in Japan. Vast but easily navigated by canoe, kayaks and boat tours, the mangroves support a huge amount of the island's wildlife and are unmissable for anyone visiting. **Kayaking** is the most idyllic way of exploring: you can hire one and make your own way or join a tour. **SUP** are also available. For those looking for a little bit more laid-back exploration, **river cruises** are an easy day-trip activity, with the Nakama River in the south being the most popular.

There are a few things to watch out for when exploring. Habu live on Iriomote; it's arguably the most likely place you will encounter one. Waterfalls can be slippery and accidents have occurred so use good shoes and good sense. You'll also likely encounter leeches in rivers, so take precautions. Endangered wild animals often cross the roads – the number one cause of Iriomote cat deaths is vehicles – so drive slow and watch out as you travel round.

There's also plentiful **diving and snorkelling**: Iriomote's most unique underwater experience is the coral spawning, seen on night dives after the full moon from May to September. You can also find manta for the majority of the year. In January to early summer, they stay near cleaning stations in the south and east, while July to September is when you might see manta mating trains in the Yonara Channel.

Dive sites here are also home to pelagics: thousands of bluefin trevallies and sharks, including whale and the occasional hammerhead. Turtles, dogfish tuna and barracuda are also common, as well as macro life and reef fish. Many accommodations have dive shops, offering deals to guests. The best snorkelling requires a boat. Barasu (バラス島) is the most popular spot: a rare coral-fragment island to the north of Uehara Port, where the sea has well-developed coral and great transparency.

Iriomote Duck Tours 552 Uehara; ☎ 0909 786 9987; w ducktours.jp. Canoeing, kayaking & trekking tours, with night canoe tours particularly good for fireflies, stars & potential Iriomote cat. Though his website is Japanese, Takahashi-san has good English & offers pick-ups. The base has hot showers (& a few goats).

Nakama River Mangrove Cruise 仲間川マングローブクルーズ; 201 Haemi; ☎ 0980 85 5304. 70-min river cruise on the Nakama, with tickets available at the Jugon Shop, left of Ōhara Port.

Nonpura のんぷら; 339–3 Uehara; ☎ 0980 85 7840; w npura.com. Mangrove kayaking, Yubujima & Pinaisaara hikes. Run by Shūichi-san who speaks reasonable English & offers a host of tours. Lunch is made fresh on your trek & hotel/port pick-up is available.

Smile Fish スマイルフィッシュ; 10–662 Uehara; ☎ 0980 85 6413; w smile-fish.com; ⏲ 08.00–21.00 daily. English-speaking instructors offer snorkelling, introductory & experienced dives.

Urauchigawa Kankō 浦内川観光; 870–3 Uehara; ☎ 0980 85 6154; w urauchigawa.com. Jungle cruises, canoeing & trekking. The 1hr Urauchi tour takes you up the wide river to the hiking trail base, with free shuttle from Uehara Port.

OTHER PRACTICALITIES There are two clinics and three police stations on the island. Two post offices with ATMs are the only way of getting cash out; larger places usually accept cards, but cash is expected for shops and most restaurants.

Medical

Iriomote Ōhara Clinic 西表東部大原診療所; 201–131 Haemi; ☎ 0980 85 5516; ⏲ 08.30–11.30 & 13.30–16.30 Mon–Fri (closed Thu afternoon)

Iriomote Seibu Clinic Sonai 西表西部診療所; 694 Iriomote (Sonai); ☎ 0980 85 6268; ⏲ 08.30–11.30 & 13.30–16.30 Mon–Fri (closed Tue & Thu afternoon)

Police

Ōhara 大原駐在所; 201 Haemi; ☎ 0980 85 5110

Shirahama Police Box 白浜駐在所; 1499-8 Iriomote; ☎ 0980 85 6110

Uehara 上原駐在所; Uehara; ☎ 0980 85 6510

Post offices

Iriomotejima 西表島郵便局; 628 Iriomote (Sonai); ☎ 0980 85 6342; ⏲ ATM: 08.45–19.00 Mon–Fri, 09.00–17.00 Sat–Sun

Ōhara 大原郵便局; 201-117 Haemi; ☎ 0980 85 5342; ⏲ ATM: 08.45–18.00 Mon–Fri, 09.00–17.00 Sat–Sun

WHAT TO SEE AND DO What Iriomote offers is natural activities (page 327), with few indoor activities. There are lots of sights around the main road, such as viewpoint observatories, so adventuring into the interior isn't mandatory – but it is seriously good fun and highly recommended.

Iriomote is covered in swimming beaches but beware of tides and jellyfish. Sadly, many of its beaches now suffer from increasing levels of rubbish from the East China Sea. The difference over the last ten years is vast: locals are trying to fix it, but the problem lies elsewhere.

Uehara The northern port of Iriomote, Uehara (上原) has some of the prettier sites and the majority of the beaches. At its northwest tip are the western observatories. **Unarizaki Park Observatory** (うなりざき公園展望台) is a brilliant place to watch wild waves crash into the coast and great for sunset and stargazing, while **Sonai's**

Local Forest Observatory (祖納ふるさとの森) to the south overlooks the bay's many shades of blue and is great for seeing fireflies.

The biggest attraction lies just south of the town. The **Urauchi River** (浦内川) is the longest, widest and deepest river in Okinawa. A rich olive-green treasure trove for plants and animals, its 19km banks are flanked with mangroves and filled with hikes. It's wonderful to kayak, but sightseeing boats also travel to the trail's starting point. If you're incredibly lucky, you may even see an Iriomote cat swimming across the river.

Hikes along the Urauchi include the three waterfalls of Mariyudu, Kanpiree and Mayagusuku (page 331) and the Utara Coal Mine Ruins (page 331).

There are plenty of beaches to choose from in Uehara, but **Hoshizunahama** (星砂の浜) is the island's own star sand beach. Found on the northwest tip, this pretty beach (despite occasional rubbish) has green islets and interesting rock formations, as well as facilities like showers, toilets and vending machines. You can watch sunset over the western promontory.

To the south of Uehara is Iriomote's biggest attraction, **Pinaisaara Falls** (ピナイサーラの滝). This 54m-tall cascade is best explored by kayak tour followed by a walk up the mountain trail, but it can also be hiked (page 331). The best part of Pinaisaara isn't the fall but the view from its top, an extraordinary panorama of Iriomote from over the precipice. Its name comes from the words for 'beard' and 'down', a reference to its appearance and the fact it is said to be inhabited by a water god with a white beard.

Not to be overlooked, the **Sangara Falls** (サンガラの滝) to Pinaisaara's east are less busy but no less remarkable. A kayak trip and quick jungle hike leads to a short, split cascade that falls in sheets into a large pool. Sangara's surprise is that you can get behind the right-hand falls and sit on a hidden ledge, watching the water tumble over.

Moving away from Uehara to the area of Takana, you'll drive past **Ōmija Road Park** (大見謝ロードパーク), a promenade through the mangrove and tidal flats at the mouth of the Ōmija River. The section under the bridge is a popular place to swim and for kids to play and on clear days you can see Hatoma Island (page 330) from the observatory.

Yubujima This tiny, once-inhabited island off the east coast is now a glorious botanical garden created by former residents. To get to Yubujima (由布島), take a buffalo cart from Mihara: a journey based on the buffalo's mood, accompanied by sanshin and singing. If you had your fill of painfully slow buffalo on Taketomi, you can also walk across the water if you're willing to get your calves wet.

Alongside hundreds of plants, the garden is home to a butterfly house, mangrove, the occasional snake and a beach featuring a nightmarish manta sculpture. There's a gift shop, café and restaurant too.

Cart ride fares include garden admission but you can buy the garden ticket separately. Tickets are purchased from the desk or vending machine at the Yubu Traveller Station (旅人の駅; ⌚ 09.30–16.00 daily).

Komi The kind of place you'll likely drive through but never know the name of, Komi (古見) sits below Yubujima on Iriomote's east coast and has a couple of cool stops. The **Komi Looking-glass Tree Colony** (古見サキシマスオウノキ群落) at the south end of Maera Bridge has a boardwalk around a colony of looking-glass trees and their amazing sheet-like root systems. As the colony is beside a sacred utaki, please remain quiet and respectful while exploring. Take care too as typhoons have previously damaged the boardwalk. Further north, the **Iriomote Wildlife**

Conservation Centre (西表野生生物保護センター; ☎0980 85 5581; w iwcc.jp/english; ⌚10.00–16.00 Tue–Fri, 10.00–noon & 13.00–16.00 Sat–Sun) researches, promotes and protects Iriomote's rare wild animals and nature. It has specimens, a yamaneko exhibit, wildlife-viewing guides and information on culture, seasons and topography – plus the rare benefit of comprehensive English signs and website. The centre also treats injured cats. If there are any, you can view them through a live video feed. There's also the **Iriomote Tropical Tree Breeding Garden** (西表熱帯林育種技術園) just in front.

Ōhara and Haemi Ōhara (大原) is the southern entrance to Iriomote, and the site of the **Nakama River** (仲間川), one of Iriomote's best-loved sights. Designated a national natural monument, the river's conservation area has a 400-year-old looking-glass tree (the largest in Japan) which features on one of the sightseeing cruises (page 328). The Amazonian-like waterway twists and meanders through the dense jungle, offering some extraordinary views from the water and above. The Nakama has two **Eastern Observatories** (仲間川の展望台): the closest to town is a pagoda that surveys the jungle, but the better one is a basic platform a 50-minute walk northwest into the jungle. This gives one of the greatest views on Iriomote: sinuous river bends carving through trees and heading out into a horizon of deep blue sea. In the very south at Haemi (南風見), you'll find the **Forget-me-not Stone** (忘勿石) – a monument to Hateruma's war malaria victims. It sits on a beach filled with interesting geological sandstone formations, eroded by wind and sea to look like popped lava bubbles.

Funauki Funauki (船浮) village is just 4km away from Shirahama, but it feels worlds apart. Around 40 people live here, in somewhat dilapidated corrugated-roof houses. The declining population and low birthrate mean Funauki's days may be numbered. Today the bay is used for black pearl farming, but in the war it was used by the navy, who built a fortress here. Funauki is a short day trip, taking about 2 hours to sightsee.

A 15–20-minute walk north of Funauki, through a beautiful forest, brings you to **Idahama** (イダ浜): a white-sand snorkelling beach on the other side of the cape to the village. After exploring the main beach, head round the promontory to its right to an even more secluded spot with cool rock strata. There are no facilities. On the opposite side, to the south, is a **Former Japanese Navy Tunnel** (旧日本帝国海軍跡). These 80m tunnel ruins south of Funauki were once a secret suicide boat base and power station. The entrance is through the hand-dug air-raid shelter through the forest trees. These tunnels are old, crumbly and full of bats: be cautious.

Hatoma Hatoma (鳩間島) is a very small island, less than 1km^2, situated off Iriomote's north coast. It has a population of 60, a smattering of minshuku and restaurants and a coastline bursting with beaches. Surrounded by reefs, quiet Hatoma is frequented by a handful of day-tripping sunseekers. There is some shore snorkelling, but for the best reefs you'll need to venture into deeper waters with a tour from Iriomote. Hatoma is a 10-minute daily hop from Uehara Port or a twice-daily 45-minute Ishigaki ferry via Uehara. The island is lovely to walk around, taking an hour to complete a loop.

Hiking Hiking is the heart of Iriomote. Some trails are easy, others hard-going; treacherous treks should be registered with the town office or police. If you have internet, there are QR code signs on trails where you can register. It's advised that you don't go alone for safety and opt for a guide.

If a trek involves a waterfall, assume you'll be going through a stream at some point and ensure your gear is up to the task. All treks are marked with pink ribbons, though many of these are old or hidden. There are many more smaller, lesser known trails on the island – feel free to trust local recommendations.

Utara Mine Ruins Utara Mining Village offered a comparatively luxurious life of near-slavery in the 1930s, with a 400-person dorm, shop, projector room, clinic and communal bath. It was abandoned in 1943 and designated a modernised archaeological site in 2007.

The Utara Mine Ruins (ウタラ炭坑) are an easy 15-minute walk along a boardwalk surrounded with seasonally flowering trees. From Urauchi Bridge parking, follow signs to the boat landing, but instead of going down to the right, continue straight on and follow the Utara signs. The mine looms out of the forest that has reclaimed every brick and column. They're deliciously creepy, grown over and returned to nature. The entire site is a photography gem; look out for the banyan-smothered remnants of the blacksmith, the rail arches, old Utara Bridge and the cart rail tracks. You'll need to be careful though as bricks, scree, tree roots, everyday objects and, worst of all, habu lurk underfoot.

Mariyudu, Kanpiree and Mayagusuku falls To see the three falls, you'll first need to kayak or boat to the trailhead 8km upstream, known as Battleship Rock (Gunkan-iwa). If you're travelling out of season on the cruise, you may need to tell the boat driver what time you would like to be picked up.

From Gunkan-iwa it's a 40-minute, relatively uphill hike to the first Mariyudu Falls (マリユドゥ). These magnificent 20m-wide falls are Okinawa's largest and often considered its best. You can't actually go on to the rocks near the falls, after several accidents led to them being cordoned off, but there are viewpoints along the track.

Another 15 minutes' walk brings you to Kanpiree (カンピレー), a somewhat horizontal waterfall. Rather than Mariyudu's perfect tumbledown tiers, Kanpiree surges and sprawls across the stone plateau. Kanpiree comes from the local words for 'god' (*kan*) and 'sit' (*piree*), as it's considered a sacred place where Iriomote's 15 gods gather.

If you're quick, strong and willing you can carry on another 2½ hours to little-visited Mayagusuku Falls (マヤグスク), with its incredibly cool stone formations. This section is much harder and involves muddy tracks and scrambling over rocks. It's doable in 6 hours, but don't miss the last boat. Follow the pink ribbons but know there are other trails marked up here.

Pinaisaara Falls Pinaisaara, the highest waterfall in Okinawa-ken, is best reached by a combination tour of kayak and hike, but if you want to do the full hike it takes 2–3 hours. Starting from the canoe car park (カヌー業者向け駐車場), close to the Maare River Kayak landing, the easy trail is signposted with pink ribbons. Early on there will be a split with a boardwalk to the left: this takes you to the mangrove for kayaking, so stick to the ribbons and mud track on the right. There are signboards along the way too. Near the end, the trail splits – the left-hand track goes down to the base (about 45mins) and the right to the top (5mins).

Nakama River Viewpoint This very simple and easy-going introductory walk takes you on wide, jungle paths regularly frequented by crested serpent eagles. The view from the observatory is one of the best on the island, making it a worthwhile jaunt. Wild boar inhabit this area so be careful. For some of the way you can take a

MYTHS AND FOLKTALES: KUROMATA

One day, an old woman's son went into the Iriomote forest to hunt but never returned. She gave him up for dead and mourned his loss, but on a stormy night, she heard his voice coming from outside.

She spoke to the voice, only to find out that her son had become a god. He asked his mother to meet him on the first day of June, when he would be able to appear before her for a short time.

They met every year on that date, and the villagers noticed that when he was nearer the village, the harvest improved. When he went away, the harvest faltered. He was enshrined as the god of good harvest, known as Kuromata. Kuromata went on to have two children, the gods Akamata and Shiromata, who also appear during the secret festivals.

bike and there are signs where you can leave it and start the hike. The entrance to the trail starts to the right of the Ōtomo Rest Area Observatory, past the paddies.

Cross-island trail This hike crosses the island from Ōtomi to Uehara, taking you along the two great rivers and up into the jungled mountain. The 21km trail can be done in a single day, with good hikers taking around 8 hours, though mountain huts along the way mean you can stretch it over multiple days. To do the immense hike, it's recommended you take a guide (page 328) or go in a group, and you'll need to notify the forestry office and police.

HATERUMAJIMA

Looking at the map, Hateruma (波照間島) almost seems like an afterthought: a coral blip that broke off from Iriomote and floated 25km south, never to be seen again. Its 12.77km^2 technically has five settlements in the centre (though these blur into two), where the majority of its 480 people live. Here you'll find a fair number of traditional houses: Hateruma is a Taketomi left to everyday wear-and-tear. It has a days-gone-by feel and is charmingly dilapidated.

A flat oval splat, Hateruma doesn't overflow with activities: it's a small, quiet, local island known for its glass-like underwater visibility (50m), stargazing, 'phantom' awamori, and being Japan's southernmost inhabited point. This accolade is reflected in its name, which it's thought translates as 'coral reef at the end'. Islanders often call Hateruma 'Besuma' or 'Besima' translating rather sweetly as 'our island'.

The sea is what made Hateruma's name; a startling shade of teals and aquas that's been named 'Hateruma blue'. Its northwest is home to the port and the only swimming beach, Nishihama, while the island's west coast has gloriously secluded, non-swimming beaches too. Hateruma is very much an island of two seasons. In summer, its shores are laden with beach-goers kitted out in fins, snorkels and floats, hurling themselves into the ombré waters, while the fine sands are strewn with parasols. Outside of summer, you'd be forgiven for thinking no-one actually lives here.

At night, its coast becomes star-strewn. Iriomote-Ishigaki National Park was Japan's first location to receive the International Dark Sky Park accreditation, with 84 of the 88 constellations visible on Hateruma, including the Southern Cross in December–June. The south has a Japanese-language observatory beside the southernmost monument.

In spite of Hateruma's quiet history, it played a massive part in changing the archipelago forever. It's the birthplace of Yaeyama heroes Oyake Akahachi and Naata Ufushu, who grew up on the island together. Akahachi's legacy depends on who writes the history: in Shuri records he's a traitor, locally he's considered a freedom-fighter.

The island is also home to the legend of Paipatirooma. When islanders tried to escape Shuri's crippling taxation, they tried sailing to Paipatirooma – a mythical island to the south. Island records actually show 40–50 people went missing this way in 1648, and though multiple expeditions over the centuries have searched for Paipatirooma, nothing has been found. Many believe it to be Taiwan, Orchid Island or Luzon.

Islanders also believe that Nirai Kanai, the place of the gods, lies underground, not across the sea as the other Yaeyama. There are speaking spots on the ground made of stones where people can mutter their wishes into the earth – a unique ritual to the island. Each of the island's settlements has a place of worship (*uzinuwaa* or *ugan*) that corresponds to a natural utaki in the nearby forests (*pitenuwaa)* where the god resides. These pitenuwaa are also unique to Hateruma.

During the war, Hateruma residents were forced to Iriomote and were made to slaughter all their livestock by Japanese troops before they left. Soldiers claimed it was to avoid feeding invading US troops, but they were in dire need of food themselves: it's likely the evacuation and slaughter benefitted their bellies. A third of Hateruma's population perished on Iriomote, including 66 children, and only three of Hateruma's 1,590 people avoided catching malaria. When survivors

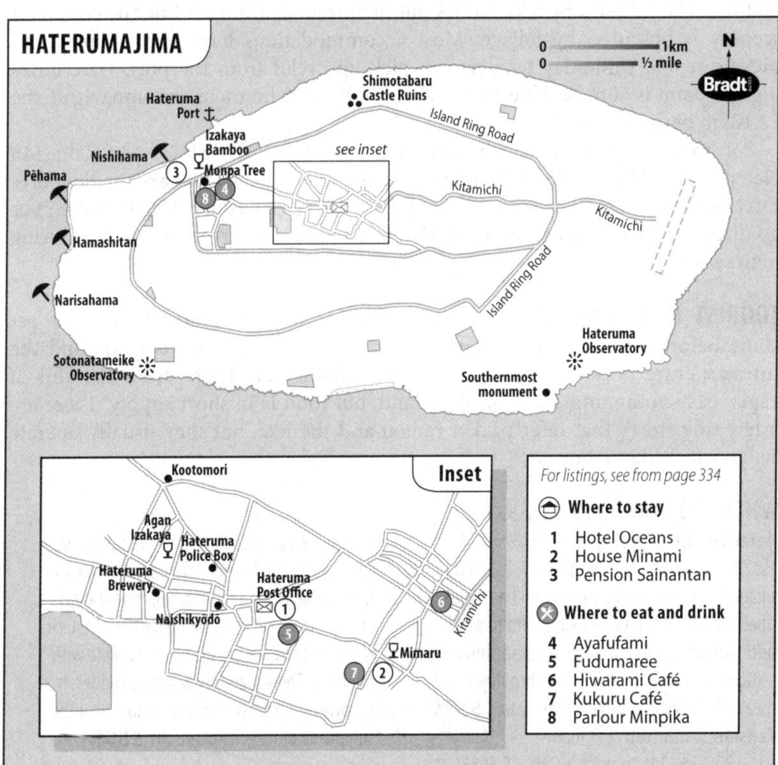

returned to Hateruma, taking malaria with them, livestock, land and crops were dead.

Today, alongside beaches, the island is famed in Japan for its alcohol. Hateruma's small brewery makes the rarest awamori of all: *awanami* (泡波). Its tiny batches and low export has earned it the moniker 'phantom awamori'. Hateruma also joins Yonaguni in having winds worth harnessing and its turbines are pretty cool: they're entirely collapsible so they can be quickly dismantled and protected from typhoons, which hit the island directly and can often render sea travel impossible.

GETTING THERE AND AWAY Since Hateruma closed its airport, the only way to reach the island is by ferry. Anei Kankō (0980 83 0055; w aneikankou.co.jp) runs 1½-hour high-speed ferries with a few daily trips. There's also a single daily Iriomote Ōhara ferry (page 323) that carries on its way to Ishigaki, which must be reserved. In summer, ferries fill up fast.

Being so isolated, Hateruma's sea journey is occasionally bone-shaking and there are regular cancellations (20% are cancelled each month, 50% in typhoon season). The little-advertised car ferry is a great alternative for those without sea legs or large budgets. It runs Ishigaki–Hateruma once a day, three days a week taking 2½ hours. Anei Kankō also offers 6-hour sightseeing minibus tours that include ferries, bus and lunch.

GETTING AROUND Hateruma is a small 15km-round island without taxis or buses. As well as a cobweb of roads and field-access tracks, there's also a 9km ring road that takes 50 minutes by bike but it's not picturesque: it doesn't hug the coast and scenery is obscured by foliage. Most accommodations have port shuttles and **bicycle** rental, while day trippers can pick up cycles from the port. Hateruma's highest point is 60m, so it's easy to cycle. It takes 2–3 hours to circumnavigate the 12.13km perimeter road.

For **mopeds**, head to Hoshi Rent-a-Car (星レンタカー・レンタサイクル; 148 Hateruma; 0806 482 5643) rental shop in the main village, for **cars** use the port's Oceans Rent-a-Car (オーシャンズレンタカー; 402-1 Hateruma; 0980 85 8387) or go direct to the Oceans accommodation (see below). Reservations are key during high season.

TOURIST INFORMATION The only option for tourist information is to get some before you leave. Hateruma is used as a day trip from Ishigaki and the infrastructure doesn't support much more than that. There are a handful of eager, easy-going minshuku on the island, but food is in short supply. There are a few tiny stores that offer packet ramen and the like, but they usually operate 'as-you-feel-like-it' hours.

WHERE TO STAY *Map, page 333*

Hotel Oceans (9 rooms) ホテル オーシャンズ; 78-2 Hateruma; 0980 85 8787; f. In the village centre the pension-like hotel has sweet, small Western & Japanese rooms with fridge & en suite. There's laundry facilities & Hama Shitan-tei restaurant. The owner is immensely obliging, but speaks no English. Vehicle & bike rentals. **$$$$**

Pension Sainantan (13 rooms) ペンション最南端; 886-1 Hateruma; 0980 85 8686; w pensionsainantan.wixsite.com/hateruma. Sainantan is 'high-end' Hateruma. Overlooking Nishihama, it has a rooftop bar, restaurant & often holds yuntaku drinking parties. Western & Japanese rooms are pleasant, sizeable with en suites. There's laundry & shared fridges. It is however furthest from the village, near the sugarcane processing plant. HB. **$$$$**

✷ **House Minami** (9 cottages) ハウス美波; 3138 Hateruma; 0908 437 3132; w minami85.sakura.ne.jp/index.html. Modest Minami is a 'cottage'-style guesthouse of pre-fab suites. Rooms range from A–D: larger As have en suites, Ds have shared bathrooms. Well-stocked kitchenette has hob, fridge & TV. Décor is typical outdated Yaeyama guesthouse (think chintz) but the welcome is incredibly warm, if entirely Japanese. Perfect for groups & budget stays. **$$**

WHERE TO EAT AND DRINK *Map, page 333*

Hateruma's restaurant scene relies almost entirely on izakaya & small cafés.

Ayafufami あやふふぁみ; 475 Hateruma; 0980 85 8187; w ayaffami.amebaownd.com; 11.30–15.00 daily. Casual wooden setting serves set lunches using Hateruma-grown rice, veggies & fish. Near Nishihama, it's incredibly popular & fills up in high season. English menu & small souvenir shop. $$

Fudumaree ぶどぅまれー; 2844 Hateruma; 0980 85 8271; noon–14.00 & 18.30–23.00 Wed–Mon. Soba shop offering a delicious range of stewed things – pork, daikon, cabbage & best of all, oden (stew). Cheap & cheerful, with outdoor seating. $

Hiwamari Café ひまわりcafé; 5227 Hateruma; 0980 85 8214; 07.30–10.00 & 11.30–16.00 Mon–Wed & Fri–Sat. Open early for b/fasts, Hiwamari does a roaring trade in homemade hamburgers, tempura & chanpuruu for lunch. The outside doesn't look much but inside is delightful. $

Kukuru Café 3146 Hateruma; 0980 85 8135; 10.00–15.00 daily. Kukuru sits in a jungle of plants & specialises in mango milks & shaved ices, but serves cheap lunches too. Beautiful, ramshackle & very Hateruma. $

Parlour Minpika パーラーみんぴか; 465 Hateruma; 11.00–13.00 & 14.30–16.30 daily. Sweet shaved ice bar & light lunch spot: try the black sugar special with *kinako* (toasted soy bean powder). $

ENTERTAINMENT AND NIGHTLIFE

The most nightlife Hateruma can boast is some izakaya, sprinkled around the settlements.

Agan Izakaya 居酒屋 あがん; 148 Hateruma; 0980 85 8088; w sites.google.com/view/hateruma-agan-kuromitsu; 17.00–20.00 Tue–Sat. Local watering hole with shimadōfu taco rice & sake-steamed clams.

Izakaya Bamboo 居酒屋バンブー; 439–2 Hateruma; 0980 85 8136; 11.30–14.30 & 18.00–22.00 Wed–Mon (closed mornings Sun). Squid-ink ramen, awanami, & a free, closing-time shuttle (reservation needed).

Mimaru 味〇; 3112 Hateruma; 0980 85 8070; 18.00–23.00 daily. Locally caught fish & sashimi in warm, wooden izakaya.

SHOPPING

General rule of thumb: bring what you need with you. Otherwise you'll be left shuffling through odds and ends at the four small local stores. The largest, Naishikyōdō (名石共同売店; 0980 85 8456; 07.30–13.00 & 15.00–20.30 daily), has some fresh produce, store-cupboard items, alcohol & sundries.

Hateruma Brewery 波照間酒造所; 156 Hateruma; 0980 85 8332; w awanami.net; 09.00–noon & 14.30–17.00 Mon–Sat. Phantom awamori is much cheaper straight from the brewery. It sells minis up to massive 1.8l bottles.

Monpa Tree モンパの木; 464–1 Hateruma; 0980 85 8354; 11.30–13.00 & 15.00–17.00 daily. Souvenir shack selling accessories & original T-shirts.

SPORTS AND ACTIVITIES

Hateruma isn't considered a diving destination, despite having the clearest waters (30–50m visibility) in the archipelago and plenty of things to see. Dive sites aren't far offshore, so operators return to shore between.

MYTHS AND FOLKTALES: THE COWS AND THE WHALES

A clever but lazy farmer realised he could plow his fields faster if he lashed eight cows together instead of using one. He began to work the field, but was so focused on getting home quickly that he didn't notice a tsunami approaching. His neighbours and their single cows quickly climbed to safety, but the lazy farmer and his cattle were washed out to sea.

The farmer drowned, but the gods turned his cattle into whales. This is why whales 'moo' like cattle: it's the sound of the cows trying to find their way home.

You can spot sharks, large migratory fish and macro creatures, while the eastern drop occasionally houses whale sharks, manta, and hammerheads. On night dives in May–June you may catch coral spawning.

Atlas Hateruma アトラス波照間; 131-1 Hateruma; 0980 85 8182; w hateruma.xsrv.jp; 09.00–19.00 daily. Fun dives, experience dives, & glass-bottom boat tours perfect for Hateruma's glassy waters.

Diving Service Ishino ダイビングサービスいしの; 231-1 Hateruma; 0980 85 8469; w www7b.biglobe.ne.jp/~ishino/index.html. Popular with regulars & veterans, Ishino offers fun dives, experience dives & PADI certification dives & guesthouse discount.

OTHER PRACTICALITIES Cash payment is common, with the only reliable ATM at Hateruma Post Office (波照間郵便局; 84-1 Hateruma; ATM: 08.45–17.30 Mon–Fri, 09.00–17.00 Sat–Sun). There's a single police box: Hateruma Police Box (八重山警察署波照間駐在所; 129 Hateruma; 0980 85 8110).

WHAT TO SEE AND DO Visitors come to Hateruma to swim, stargaze, sunbathe and snorkel. **Nishihama** (ニシ浜) is a long sweep of powdery white curves around Hateruma's northwest, near the port. The only swimming and snorkelling beach, its shallow green-blue waters are protected by a reef with turtles, fish and corals. It has facilities, lockers and a nearby snorkel rental shop. Confusingly, in Japanese *nishi* means 'west', but in Hateruma's dialect it means 'north': Nishihama is therefore 'North Beach'.

The west coast has more sandy spots that often need teasing out of the undergrowth. **Peehama** (ペー浜) and **Narisahama** (ナリサ浜) are sunset cove beaches so delightfully hidden that you'll likely get them to yourself. Picture-perfect Narisa is clambered to through a dark tunnel of palms with a white coral light at the end. Pee similarly appears from the undergrowth: down an overgrown path and through another tree tunnel. The backroads to them are overgrown but trust the track. **Hamashitan** (浜シタン群落), or Mōsaki Beach, is a deserted sunset stretch between Peehama and Narisa. Full of rocks, jungle backdrops, and 100-year-old trees, it's great for people-free beach photos.

There are a few things to explore outside of the beaches. Heading from the port to the village you'll immediately meet **Kootomori** (コート盛), a 4m-high platform of perfectly puzzled stone forming Hateruma's old Sakishima beacon. In the village seek out the **Shimotabaru Castle Ruins** (下田原城跡). All that remains of this 15th–16th century castle are some walls and steps, reclaimed by nature's tendrils.

Hateruma is a celestial spectacle: it's said to have the best **stargazing** in Japan. There's little light pollution and is one of the only places in Japan where the

Southern Cross shines bright. There used to be a working observatory, but it closed due to staff retirement; you can just sit on the beach and gaze or try **Sokonatameike Observatory** (底名溜池展望台) instead. This absolute mouthful is a southern viewing platform with a view of the sea and the night sky, accessed only by a track between farms.

Beside the seasonal observatory is the **Southernmost Monument** (日本最南端の碑). Hateruma is Japan's southernmost *inhabited* point, an accolade of interest to Japanese people and few others. Its monument isn't much, but it's impressive to know the horizon has nothing but open sea until you hit the Philippines. Cape Takanazaki, the cliffs around the monument, is a picturesque, wild area of asperous rocks and big waves. Wear sturdier shoes than flip-flops.

YONAGUNIJIMA

Forming Japan's westernmost edge is Yonagunijima (与那国島), a small frontier of rock and rust that's been entirely left to its own devices. It's hardly surprising: a 1,900km trek from Tokyo but a mere 111km hop from Taiwan, Yonaguni is as far from most people's idea of 'Japan' as it gets. The most telling thing about the island is just how many businesses don't have email but still use fax. While the world kept turning, Yonaguni became a time capsule. The intensely local feel is hammered home with the island alarms: tinny little jingles that mark the 1,700 islanders' daily schedule.

Yonaguni doesn't have a high school, meaning teens have to leave the island to continue mandatory education. The 4-hour ferry, expensive flights and minimal timetables make commuting impossible, so students simply move to another island. This has a huge effect on Yonaguni's demographic as many choose not to return, leaving the island with major depopulation problems. To keep the island alive, locals are encouraging tourists to visit and appreciate its traditions, culture, animals and throat-numbing awamori.

Few visit, but those that do dive. Yonaguni is a diving holy grail with a sea full of surprises. There's a mysterious underwater Atlantis and an immense swirl of migrating hammerheads brought on the strong Kuroshio current.

HISTORY Yonaguni's story is a spectacular haze of smuggling, South Asian influences and legendary women. The island's greatest figure is Sanai-Isoba, a

YONAGUNI FESTIVALS

The majority of Yonaguni's festivals happen across the farming season. During these events, the priest (*kabu*) connects islanders' prayers with the gods, asking for prosperity, peace, safety and good harvest.

The final festival of the harvest season is the Hōnensai, which happens around July (lunar June). Every couple of years, the festival involves a central tug-of-war between the east and west settlements. The celebration has specific food: seven dishes of fried tofu, barley tempura, mountain potato, kelp, mochi, *kamaboko* (fish cake) and *yōkan*, a kind of jelly made with red bean paste. The Kuburamachiri festival in autumn prays for the expulsion of foreigners and great powers from the island. In the olden days, this festival continued the supposed Sanai-Isoba idea of throwing giant sandals into the sea, to make foreigners fear the island.

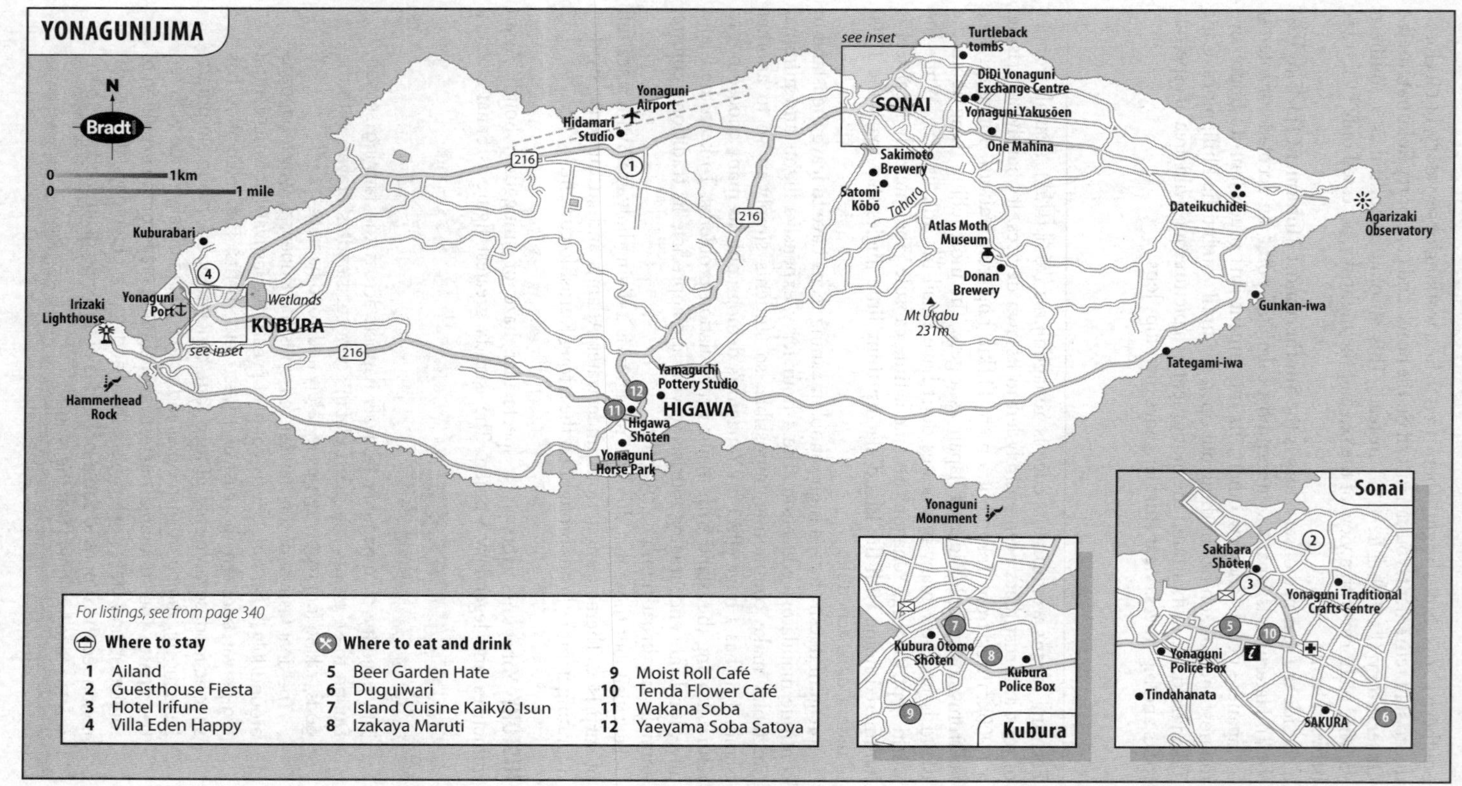
YONAGUNIJIMA
N
Bradt
0 1km
0 1 mile
Yonaguni Airport
Hidamari Studio
216
see inset
SONAI
Turtleback tombs
DiDi Yonaguni Exchange Centre
Yonaguni Yakusōen
One Mahina
Sakimoto Brewery
Satomi Kōbō
Tahara
Atlas Moth Museum
Donan Brewery
Mt Urabu 231m
Dateikuchidei
Agarizaki Observatory
Gunkan-iwa
Tategami-iwa
Kuburabari
Irizaki Lighthouse
Yonaguni Port
Wetlands
KUBURA
Hammerhead Rock
Yamaguchi Pottery Studio
HIGAWA
Higawa Shōten
Yonaguni Horse Park
Yonaguni Monument
For listings, see from page 340
Where to stay
1 Ailand
2 Guesthouse Fiesta
3 Hotel Irifune
4 Villa Eden Happy
Where to eat and drink
5 Beer Garden Hate
6 Duguiwari
7 Island Cuisine Kaikyō Isun
8 Izakaya Maruti
9 Moist Roll Café
10 Tenda Flower Café
11 Wakana Soba
12 Yaeyama Soba Satoya
Kubura Ōtomo Shōten
Kubura Police Box
Kubura
Sonai
Sakibara Shōten
Yonaguni Traditional Crafts Centre
Yonaguni Police Box
Tindahanata
SAKURA

MYTHS AND FOLKTALES: THE LEGEND OF SANAI-ISOBA

Many of the folktales from Yonaguni focus on women, the greatest being Sanai-Isoba, the warrior woman who became chieftain of the island. Her name comes from one of the villages on Yonaguni at the time of her birth, Isoba, while *sanai* is the Yonaguni word for the holy, spiritual banyan tree.

The legend goes that Sanai-Isoba was respected from a young age – at five, she was already bigger than all the other children in the village. While the other children mocked and shunned her, she turned to adults and learned all she could from them. At 13, she was given the same consideration as a man and was given a place on a village committee.

When her village joined another to become Sonai, Sanai-Isoba was made project leader of clearing the fields for farming rice. She was so successful that she earned the villagers' respect, and when the next chieftain was picked, everyone voted for Sanai-Isoba. At first she refused, but the ritual handing over of power was performed and Sanai-Isoba became the chieftain of Yonaguni.

At this point she was only 20, but it was said she had the physique of a man, was 2m tall, and was so strong nobody could beat her. However, she never used her strength to govern: she was a fair, hard-working, popular and welcoming leader to all. She was also clever and shrewd, using her wits to solve problems and outwit enemies.

During her rule, Miyako invaded Yonaguni, killing Sanai-Isoba's four brothers and burning down villages. Sanai-Isoba was inconsolable at the loss of her brothers and turned her wrath on the invaders. The Miyako army was no match for Sanai-Isoba – she defeated them all and repelled the invasion, saving Yonaguni from Ryūkyū control.

female chieftain of insurmountable strength, courage and cleverness (see above). Her legends are legion: she defeated Miyako's invading army and threw giant sandals into the sea, fooling outsiders that Yonaguni was a land of giants.

In the invasion of the early 1600s, Satsuma cruelly slaughtered Yonaguni's populace, freeing up more resources for taxes. At Kuburabari, pregnant women were forced to leap a 3–5m chasm, often falling to their deaths or miscarrying. Men were annually made to race to a central field: anyone who fell behind or couldn't fit in was beheaded. Little wonder there's a legend about islanders escaping hardships by sailing to a southern, mythical paradise called Hai Dunan (South Yonaguni).

Yonaguni has always been close with Taiwan, using it for shopping, work and school trips, even using Taiwanese currency for a period. At one time Yonaguni was a stopover for large passenger ships, resembling a bustling Hong Kong harbour: a far cry from today's near-deserted dock. This proximity to Taiwanese shipping lanes made Yonaguni a target during the war, despite only 45 stationed soldiers. Much of Sonai and all of Kubura were burned down, including a ship carrying 53 Korean comfort women whose deaths went unacknowledged. After the war, Yonaguni regained its piratical position as a black market for smuggling restricted goods and stolen US contraband.

After occupation ended, many residents hoped to join Taiwan or become independent. Yonaguni has, after all, a unique culture that they want to protect, including its own language: Dunan-munui. Now considered severely endangered as all 400 speakers are over 50, Dunan-munui once had its own pictorial writing system called *kaidaadi*.

GETTING THERE AND AWAY Yonaguni Airport has four flights a day with Ryūkyū Air Commuter (w rac-okinawa.com) and Japan Transocean Air (w jta-okinawa.com), between Ishigaki (30mins) and Okinawa-hontō (1hr 15mins). Flying is expensive but quick and regular. The airport is in the centre of the north coast, just outside Sonai.

The only ferry comes from Ishigaki, run by Fukuyama Kaikun (☎ 0980 87 2555; w fukuyamakaiun.ti-da.net). The ferries operate twice-weekly, leaving Ishigaki on the opposite side of the harbour to the main port building. The 4-hour journey can get pretty choppy.

GETTING AROUND Around two thirds of Yonaguni's 29km² is fields and forest, culminating in three jungle-covered peaks across its centre. There are three villages: western Kubura is home to the port and small wetland, northern Sonai is the largest settlement, and southern Higawa is a small, near-missable blip. Yonaguni Airport is west of Sonai.

One road loops the island, with another connecting Sonai to Higawa. It takes 35 minutes to drive the island, making **moped** rental the ideal choice. You'll find the largest rental services in Sonai – try Yonaguni Honda (与那国ホンダ; ☎ 0980 87 2376; w yonagunihonda.jp). A free **bus** also runs between the three villages, with roundabout routes and sporadic timings. Another great way to see the rugged coastline is by **bicycle**. It'll take 3–4 hours and some breathlessness: Yonaguni is steep in places. Accommodations will have bike rental. The south coast is particularly rugged, eroded into sheer cliffs and crags by strong winds and seas. There are two capes: Irizaki in the west and Agarizaki to the east. The east is uninhabited, left mostly to Yonaguni's horses. Eastern Mount Urabe (231m) is the highest peak. The Yonaguni Monument and Hammerhead Rock dive sites are in the southeast and west respectively. You can also walk the island road in about 4½ hours.

TOURIST INFORMATION No bank, no high school, no hospital: Yonaguni is true, off-the-beaten-track Japan. It does, however, have the small Yonagunichō Sightseeing Information Centre (与那国町観光協会; 437-17 Yonaguni; ☎ 0980 87 2402; w welcome-yonaguni.jp; ⏱ 08.00–17.00 Mon–Fri) in Sonai. Your chances of getting much English information are slim, but they will have maps and bus timetables.

WHERE TO STAY *Map, page 338*

Sonai

Ailand Hotel (77 rooms) アイランドホテル与那国; 4647-1 Yonaguni; ☎ 0980 87 2300; w ailand-resort.co.jp. As deluxe as Yonaguni gets, Western rooms are large with en suite & fridges. Just outside Sonai, meaning airport shuttles & semi-isolation. The restaurant serves Okinawan dishes & b/fast buffet. Dinner & rental car are extra. **$$$$$**

Hotel Irifune (11 rooms, 1 villa) ホテル入船; 59-6 Yonaguni; ☎ 0980 87 2311; w yonaguni.jp/index.html. Clean rooms in Western (en suite) & Japanese (shared bathroom) style. Multiple board options (HB, b/fast only) & dive school attached. There's also an annexe villa overlooking the sea with 6 twin rooms, spacious living area, open-air rooftop bath, garden & karaoke. **$$$**

Guesthouse Fiesta (3 private, 2 dorms) ゲストハウスフィエスタ; 1080 Yonaguni; ☎ 0980 87 2339; w fiesta09.jimdofree.com. Fiesta's run-down exterior hides a welcoming home with bare futon dormitories & private rooms. Large communal space has shared bathrooms, laundry, well-stocked kitchen, fridge-freezer & a kitty for coffee, sake & awamori. Roof terrace, bike & fishing rentals. After a successful catch, ever-friendly Shige-san whips up a fresh sashimi feast for offensively little. Unsophisticated, easy-going & fun. **$–$$**

Kubura

Villa Eden Happy (15 rooms) Villaエデンの幸; 4022-253 Yonaguni; 0980 87 2450. Large & comprehensive accommodation with restaurant (Wed–Mon) & dive shop. Comfortable, en-suite Western rooms, common area, rooftop terrace & airport shuttle. **$$$**

WHERE TO EAT AND DRINK *Map, page 338*

Casual izakaya are the local dinner choice with a couple of higher-end restaurants creating interesting courses with Yonaguni ingredients. Yonaguni food is utterly unpretentious, with a few unusual twists including coriander, kamaboko fish sticks and kuba palm mochi.

Sonai

Duguiwari づぐいわり; 564 Yonaguni; 0980 87 3739; w duguiwari.com; 11.30–14.00 & 18.30–23.00 Mon–Sat. Famous in Yonaguni terms, Duguiwari's food is creative & a cut above the rest. The menu is a good mix of local dishes & fresh ingredients with Western touches, with handmade tofu, marlin, swordfish, & pizzas. $$$$$

Beer Garden Hate ビヤガーデン国境; 3F 22–4 Yonaguni; 0980 87 3255; 11.30–13.30 & 18.00–22.30 daily. The most recommended izakaya, Hate (pronounced 'Ha-te') is a Sonai staple serving specialities of marlin kara-age & scallop & swordfish sashimi. Lunch is reasonable meal sets, night is time to rub elbows with locals. $$$$

Tenda Flower Café てんだ花; 76 Yonaguni; 0980 87 9770; 11.00–15.00 Sun–Tue & Thu–Fri. This flower-strewn building serves cake, coffee & set meals, & there's free Wi-Fi. $

Kubura

Island Cuisine Kaikyō Isun 島料理海響・いすん; 4022–6 Yonaguni; 0805 476 2230; 18.00–23.00 daily. Popular izakaya with traditional Yonaguni cooking & freshly caught fish. Bring your day's catch to Isun & they will cook it (given notice). $$$$

Moist Roll Café モイストロールカフェ; 4022-119 Yonaguni; 0980 87 3130; f; 11.30–17.00 daily. This warm wooden book-filled café serves delicious cakes & meal sets with fish carpaccio pasta & pizzas. $$

Izakaya Maruti 居酒屋まるてぃ; 4022–21 Yonaguni; 0980 87 2550; 11.00–14.00 & 18.00–midnight Mon–Sat. Izakaya Maruti gets fish straight from the Kubura port every morning. Dishes are cheap, simple but good: the squid ink rice particularly so. $

Higawa

Yaeyama Soba Satoya 八重山そば さとや; 3093 Yonaguni; 0905 294 4445; 11.00–14.30 Fri–Wed. Satoya's cute wooden counter is home to hearty bowls of broth & soba. The pork is gigantic, but you can't beat fresh tiger prawns farmed 100m away. $$

Wakana Soba わかなそば; 3083 Yonaguni; 0980 87 3338; 11.30–14.00 Wed–Mon. The husband looks after the pigs, the wife the soba: Wakana's cloudy soup of slow-cooked, hand-reared pork is cheap & sensational. Don't leave it late as Wakana shuts when the soba runs out. $

HANASHU

Yonaguni is home to *hanashu* (花酒), an awamori with the highest alcohol content in Japan. Only Yonaguni is allowed to brew at such levels and the result could knock your socks off but is much loved by locals. Also called the flower liquor (*hana* meaning 'flower' in Japanese), the name is misleading. It's not made with flowers; instead the flower part refers to the old method of measuring awamori strength by the foam produced in the pour. Hanashu has the highest amount of bubbles, said to look like flowers in full bloom.

SHOPPING Yonaguni has a few locally made products, though limited English can make souvenir shopping a Ryūkyū roulette. The island just about manages a minimarket in each of the villages.

Clothing and textiles

Hidamari Studio ひだまり工房; Yonaguni Airport, 4350 Yonaguni; 0907 884 2913; 08.30–18.30 daily. Local textile souvenirs (ties, wallets, bags), which are occasionally made on the shop-floor loom.

One Mahina オネマヒナ; 1000 Yonaguni; 0980 84 8880; w onemahina.com; 10.00–18.00 daily. Brilliant store selling T-shirts, bags, tea towels & more emblazoned with Yonaguni motifs: horses, Atlas moths & hammerheads.

Satomi Kōbō 徳美工房; 2329 Yonaguni; 0980 87 2091; w satomikoubou.com; 10.00–18.00 Mon–Sat. 4th-generation textile shop by Sakimoto Brewery, producing natural cloth from local plants, with traditional Yonaguni ori patterns.

Yonaguni Traditional Crafts Centre 与那国町伝統工芸館; 175-2 Yonaguni; 0980 87 2970; 08.30–17.30 Mon–Fri, 08.30–17.00 Sat. Excellent centre for Yonaguni ori, where you can buy fabric made by local craftsmen, weaving in front of you.

Food and drink

Donan Brewery 国泉泡盛; 2087 Yonaguni; 0980 87 2315; w donan-kokusenawamori.com, donan.thebase.in; 10.00–15.00 daily. Small shop well stocked with sake, awamori & unique drinks like malted & aged awamori. Famed for its Hanashu 60, the highest percent legally brewed in Japan.

Sakimoto Brewery 崎元酒造所; 2329 Yonaguni; 0980 87 2417; w sakimotoshuzo.com; 09.00–noon & 13.00–17.00 Mon–Fri, closed for festivals. Oldest brewery on the island. Shop & Japanese-only tour, but there's an informative English-language video on their website.

Minimarkets

Higawa Shōten 比川地域 共同売店; 9076-1 Yonaguni; 0980 87 2888; w hikawa.ti-da.net; 07.00–22.00 daily

Kubura Ōtomo Shōten 大朝商店; 4022–38 Yonaguni; 0980 87 2605; 06.00–20.00 daily

Sakibara Shōten 崎原商店; 203 Yonaguni; 0980 87 2434; 07.00–20.00 Mon–Sat, 07.00–18.00 Sun

LOCAL RECIPE: PAKUCHI SHIRAAE

Yonaguni is one of the only places in Japan that heavily uses coriander in its cuisine, an influence from its westerly neighbour Taiwan and southeast Asia. You'll often find salads of coriander as a side in izakaya and restaurants. Referred to as *pakuchi*, or sometimes *kushiti*, coriander is grown October–March. The simplest version of this side dish or light lunch recipe is just coriander, sesame oil and tuna – the rest is optional.

Large bunch of coriander, washed and shredded
1 tin of tuna, drained
1 tbsp sesame oil
1 tbsp white miso
Pinch of sugar
½ block of tofu, drained and mashed
1 tsp of peanut butter, or to your preference
3 tbsp roasted sesame seeds
Handful of peanuts to taste

Mix the tuna together with sesame oil, miso, sugar, tofu, and peanut butter, before drizzling it over chopped coriander and coating well. Season if preferred and sprinkle with sesame seeds and chopped peanuts.

Pottery

Yamaguchi Pottery Studio 山口陶工房; 3119 Yonaguni; 0980 87 2072; w yonagunipot.com; 09.00–17.00 daily. Simple & stunning handmade crockery, ornaments, boxes & teapots.

Souvenirs

SAKURA さくら; 397 Yonaguni; 0906 858 9239; w sakura-yonaguni.com; 13.00–18.00 daily. This pretty bits & bobs shop in Sonai sells a remarkable mix of sweet handmade souvenirs. It's also a minshuku.

Yonaguni Yakusōen 与那国薬草園; 1106–1 Yonaguni; 0980 87 3245; w yonaguniyakusouen.co.jp; 09.00–16.00 daily. Co-operative beside DiDi selling herbal products from local ingredients; known for its chilli sauce.

SPORTS AND ACTIVITIES **Diving** is where Yonaguni really shines. Offshore, far from the crumbling concrete of island life, is a world of diving with two incredibly cool sites that have gained international notoriety: the winter hammerhead gathering and the Yonaguni Monument.

Neither are easy. Yonaguni's coast is a whirlpool of rip tides and strong currents, making diving, snorkelling and swimming outside the protected beach areas incredibly dangerous if you don't know what you're doing.

Every year in September–March (Jan–Feb high season) at **Hammerhead Rock**, hammerhead sharks gather off Yonaguni's west coast in their hundreds. It's an extraordinary and exhilarating dive where you get to see these remarkable creatures en masse and up close, those tell-tale shadows surrounding you on all sides. Due to currents and depth, it's recommended divers have 100 dives under their belt. In the south, the **Yonaguni Monument** – an eerie stone structure discovered in 1986 – is a total mystery. No-one knows if its strange, pyramidal structure, flat terraces and sharp angles are natural or manmade, but it's incredibly old. It's been linked to the legend of Atlantis, though most scientists agree the 200x50m ziggurat formation *could* have been created naturally, but are far from conclusive. Either way, it's an unearthly sight to see looming out from the blue. Though the monument isn't as tough as Hammerhead, allowing for trial dives and even occasional snorkelling, the currents mean a solid dive history is expected.

The monument can also be viewed by **glass-bottom boat**. Run by Sou Wes Dive Shop (see below), the boats have a sunken viewing platform: a quite literal immersive experience. Rarely seen, much-coveted English audio guides are available.

For locals, **fishing** is next to religion in Yonaguni. You can rent basic equipment from minshuku and join the locals catching dinner off piers and sea walls, or you can go big. Kubura brings in the highest number of marlin (*kajiki*) in Japan and is home to an annual competition for hauling in the monsters. In marlin season (February–November) there are deep-sea fishing tours that will guide you in catching your own, usually involving first catching your bait. Fishing charters will likely include filleting and packing the fish in the price. If you are heading onwards, you can look into the cool *takuhaibin* courier service (page 62).

Katsumaru 勝丸; 4022 Yonaguni; 0909 781 6852; w katsu-maru.com. Fishing boat charters with captain who is Japanese only, but you get by. Offers experience course for beginners, to full-fledged marlin trawling for the well-initiated.

Sou Wes Dive Shop ダイビングサービスマリンクラブサーウェス; 59-6 Yonaguni; 0980 87 2271; w yonaguni.jp. Scuba-diving, snorkelling & glass-bottom boat tours. Founded by the man who discovered Yonaguni Monument, Sou Wes's English-speaking staff are experienced & knowledgable. Manager Shotaro-san can recommend dives from Yonaguni's 67 sites, such as the Stone Stage. Single dives, Monument fun dives, Monument snorkelling & free diving in high season. Attached to Hotel Irifune.

TURTLEBACK TOMBS

It may seem macabre to include graves in a guidebook, but tombs are a strangely prominent feature of Yonaguni's landscape and culture. It has some of the most prolific and conspicuous tombs in the Nansei-shotō, as well as the most famous indigenous burial ritual in the archipelago, if not Japan.

The island's mausoleum-like tombs feature humped backs and beckoning arms, giving them the name 'turtleback tombs'. Most of them are sprawled across the coast north of Sonai, while others erupt from foliage in the middle of the town.

This style of tomb originally came to the Ryūkyū Kingdom from China, where there are multiple theories for their shape, from feng shui to the turtle's longevity. The most accepted theory on the islands is that they resemble the womb. Ryūkyūans believe that while people age physically, they get more youthful mentally, hence their somewhat perplexing annual festival for the elderly featuring children's pinwheels. The womb-shaped tombs, complete with fallopian-like arms, represent the return to the womb at the end of life. The Ryūkyūan versions are larger than the original as they are designed to be family vaults, but those on Yonaguni are extraordinary in size – particularly those near Sonai school.

The tombs are part of a remarkable ancient Nansei custom that's sacred to locals – though Yonaguni is most famed for senkotsu or bone washing. In the first burial, bodies are placed in these tombs alongside gifts, offerings and two bottles of the island's precious hanashu awamori. The bodies are left for seven years, after which there is a ceremony where the bones are taken from the tomb to the sea to be washed, usually by young female family members.

One of the bottles of hanashu is then opened and used to wash the bones a second time, before they and the rest of the alcohol are put on a crematory fire. The ashes are placed in urns back inside the tombs. The other bottle is then opened and drunk by those gathered and remembering the deceased; if they do not drink, the hanashu can be massaged on to aches and pains to heal them.

OTHER PRACTICALITIES Kubura and Sonai both have post offices with ATMs, vital for relatively cashless Yonaguni, and police boxes. There's a single clinic in Sonai.

Kubura Police Box 八重山警察署 久部良駐在所; 4022-199 Yonaguni; ☎ 0980 87 2154

Kubura Post Office 久部良簡易郵便局; 4022-230 Yonaguni; ⌚ 09.00–17.00 Mon–Fri

Yonaguni Clinic 与那国町診療所; 125-1 Yonaguni; ☎ 0980 87 2250; w ritoushien.net/yonaguni.shtml; ⌚ 08.30–noon & 13.30–16.00 Mon–Fri (open w/ends for emergencies)

Yonaguni Police Box 八重山警察署 与那国駐在所; 4841 Yonaguni; ☎ 0980 87 2152

Yonaguni Post Office Sonai 与那国郵便局; 49-3 Yonaguni; ⌚ ATM: 08.00–19.00 Mon–Fri, 09.00–18.00 Sat–Sun

WHAT TO SEE AND DO To see the island, start from the port in Kubura (久部良) and do a loop. Heading clockwise, you'll come first to **Kuburabari** (クブラバリ), an innocuous but deceptively large crevice (15x3.5x7m) that pregnant women were made to jump over by greedy officials (page 339). Obviously it's disrespectful and dangerous to try yourself. It's marked by a small Japanese information board outside Kubura; if you reach the abandoned building, you've gone too far.

Before long you'll reach **Sonai** (祖納), the main village. It's overlooked by **Tindahanata** (ティンダハナタ), a 100m-high overhanging rock with good views of the coast and village. Also known as Tindabana, Tindahanata is where Sanai-Isoba lived, looking across the ocean for incoming threats. Sonai is also home to **DiDi Yonaguni Exchange Centre** (DiDi与那国交流館; 1107 Yonaguni; 0980 87 2166; 09.00–17.00 Tue–Sun; adult ¥200). DiDi – *di* meaning 'let's go' in Dunan-munui – is a hub to explore Yonaguni culture, history, food and crafts. A highlight is sampling local cuisine at its food lab. DiDi also puts on festivals and exchanges with Taiwan.

Towards the east you'll find **Dateikuchidei** (ダテイクチデイ), the walled remnants of the first of the Sakishima beacon, which is hidden near the wind farm. This is near **Agarizaki Observatory** (東崎展望台), Yonaguni's easternmost point which has a 100m-high cliff with a lighthouse and views over the coast and crystalline shores. When it's not windy, Agarizaki's an ideal picnic spot surrounded by horses, and an even better sunrise spot. Bundle up in the wee hours to welcome the day.

With powerful waves and kuba palms carpeting the cliffside, the southeast has great coastal scenery. No Japanese coastline is complete without interpretive rock formations. Yonaguni has two: **Gunkan-iwa** (軍艦岩) and **Tategami-iwa** (立神岩). Gunkan is shaped like a sinking battleship, while Tategami is a rather phallic 'standing god' rock. On the right days, photos of the jagged coastline with Gunkan-iwa and the churning waves are spectacular.

To the rocks' north, between them and Sonai, is the **Atlas Moth Museum** (アヤミハビル館; 2114 Yonaguni; 0980 87 2440; 10.00–16.00 Wed–Tue; adult ¥500). Yonaguni has its own subspecies of the remarkable Atlas moth, one of the world's largest moths. The hardest-won wildlife shot on Yonaguni, the Atlas moth hangs around **Mount Urabu** (宇良部岳) in the west around dusk. If you have no luck spotting one on Urabudake, you can see them at this mostly Japanese-language museum. There's an English video and butterfly cabinets, as well as snakes and terrapins in upsettingly small tanks.

If you don't pop to the museum, continue on along the southern coast, littered with Yonaguni horses. These tiny horses are a surprising creature to find on such a secluded rock, but the small indigenous breed originated here. The protected ponies shuffle their bulbous bellies about both the east and south, with a Hitchcockian ability to suddenly appear en masse and slowly eat the island bit by bit. Small but strong, they can be ridden by children and the short-statured. Rides are available at a few places on the island, but the best are found at the **Yonaguni Horse Park** (与那国馬風(う)牧場; 3500 Yonaguni; 0902 502 4792; w tanpoporyu.com; 08.00–19.00 daily), where long and short experiences are available. You can also just meet the horses if you're too lofty to ride the little beasts.

In the very west, the Land of the Rising Sun ends with a setting one. **Irizaki Lighthouse** (西埼灯台) has Japan's final sunset, and offers great photo opportunities. When the weather is at its clearest, Taiwan's coast looms remarkably close on the horizon.

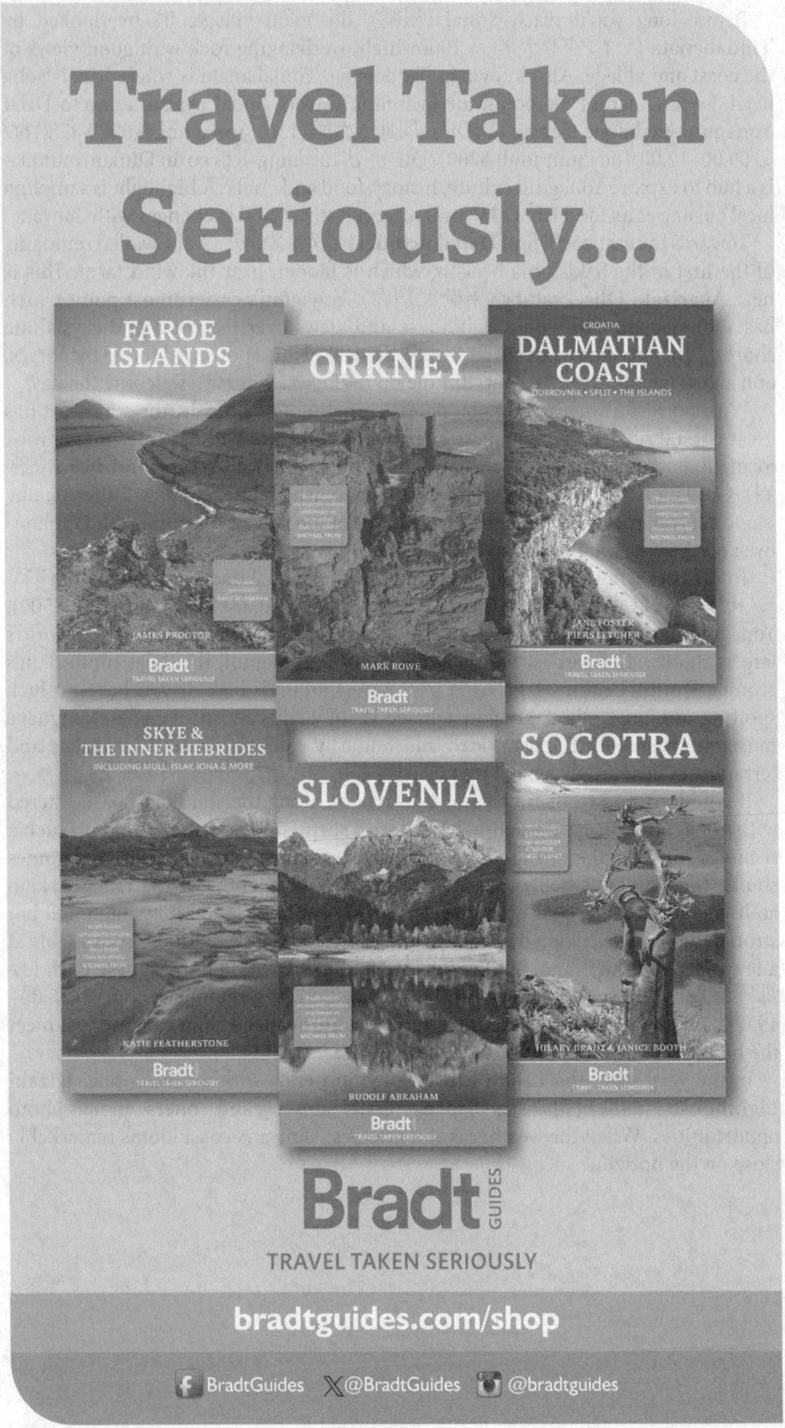
Travel Taken Seriously...
FAROE ISLANDS
JAMES PROCTOR
Bradt
TRAVEL TAKEN SERIOUSLY
ORKNEY
MARK ROWE
Bradt
TRAVEL TAKEN SERIOUSLY
CROATIA
DALMATIAN COAST
DUBROVNIK • SPLIT • THE ISLANDS
JANE FOSTER
PIERS LETCHER
Bradt
TRAVEL TAKEN SERIOUSLY
SKYE & THE INNER HEBRIDES
INCLUDING MULL, ISLAY, IONA & MORE
KATIE FEATHERSTONE
Bradt
TRAVEL TAKEN SERIOUSLY
SLOVENIA
RUDOLF ABRAHAM
Bradt
TRAVEL TAKEN SERIOUSLY
SOCOTRA
HILARY BRADT & JANICE BOOTH
Bradt
TRAVEL TAKEN SERIOUSLY
Bradt GUIDES
TRAVEL TAKEN SERIOUSLY
bradtguides.com/shop
BradtGuides
@BradtGuides
@bradtguides

Part Three

GATEWAY CITIES

9

Gateway Cities

TOKYO

With all direct flights from the UK landing in the capital, Tokyo (東京) is impossible to avoid – and why would you want to? Japan's capital is the largest city in the world; one of its safest, one of its most vibrant and far and away home to the best food on the planet.

The likelihood is, if you're visiting the islands you've been to Japan and Tokyo before. Very few simply skip the capital when coming to Japan. The wonder of Tokyo, however, is that even those who have lived in the city for years still stumble over new discoveries: tourists will never have a dull day in the city of neon.

GETTING THERE AND AWAY

By air Tokyo is serviced by two international airports: Haneda and Narita. If given the choice, Haneda in the south is a much more friendly entry point, being closer to the city and accessible by monorail or airport liner. Narita is east of the city, with the quickest transport options to central Tokyo taking just under an hour.

Airport transfers The monorail (w tokyo-monorail.co.jp/english) services all Haneda's terminals and connects to the handy JR Yamanote rail line – a national rail loop that circles Tokyo and takes you to many of the major sights – at Hamamatsucho in 15 minutes. The Keikyū airport liner (w haneda-tokyo-access.com/en) takes even less time to reach Shinagawa – also on the JR Yamanote line.

From Narita, the Keisei Skyliner train (w keisei.co.jp) is the simplest: 40 minutes to Ueno station where you can transfer to the JR Yamanote line or metro. The more expensive Narita Express (w jreast.co.jp/multi/en/nex) goes to Tokyo station in 53 minutes, with some carrying on to westerly stations like Shibuya and Shinjuku. All seats are reserved. The Keisei main line is the cheapest option – these are regular trains that go to Asakusa and Ueno in 80 minutes, or to Shinagawa in 1 hour 40 minutes. Some of the trains from Asakusa change from the underground straight into the Keisei main line. This line is half the price of the Skyliner, under a third of the Narita Express.

GETTING AROUND **Train** and **metro** are the way to do Tokyo. Sure there are other methods, but with the two being cheap, effective and all-encompassing, taxis, buses and self-driving are left in their comparative dust. Many of the stations have disabled access, but often have multiple access points so you'll need to find the right one for lifts.

The most useful line is arguably the JR Yamanote – a lime green rail loop that takes in major stations. This can often be simpler and quicker than metro lines, especially as you can transfer on to other JR lines. If you have a JR pass, you can utilise it on these lines, but whatever you do don't activate a pass just for Tokyo, unless you have days to spare on it.

The metro is divided into two companies, Tokyo Metro (w tokyometro.jp/en) and Toei (w kotsu.metro.tokyo.jp/eng), which have nine and four lines respectively. This can be incredibly confusing and annoying if using paper tickets – you won't be able to transfer between the two companies' lines. However, getting a rechargeable PASMO or SUICA card makes life much easier as you can beep in and out between all lines easily. You can buy and top these up at station machines, which have English-language menus.

Walking is also a great option – you won't be able to walk from one side to the other, but it's safe and you get to see so much more when you're not speeding underground.

WHERE TO STAY Tokyo has endless possibilities for accommodation. There are dorm rooms and capsule hotels for the truly budget-conscious, as well as some of the most luxurious hotels on the planet. As the city is so well covered by public transport, where you stay doesn't matter too much either – you're never very far from the centre of town, so stick to within short distance of a station and you'll be good to go. Take note, though, that the prices in Tokyo are naturally far more expensive overall than on the islands.

HOSHINOYA Tokyo (84 rooms) 星のや東京; 1-9-1 Otemachi; 0503 786 1144; w hoshinoyatokyo.com. Hoshinoya continues to combine modern luxury with traditional ideals in Tokyo. Award-winning hotel with tatami & traditional elements, each floor is designed as

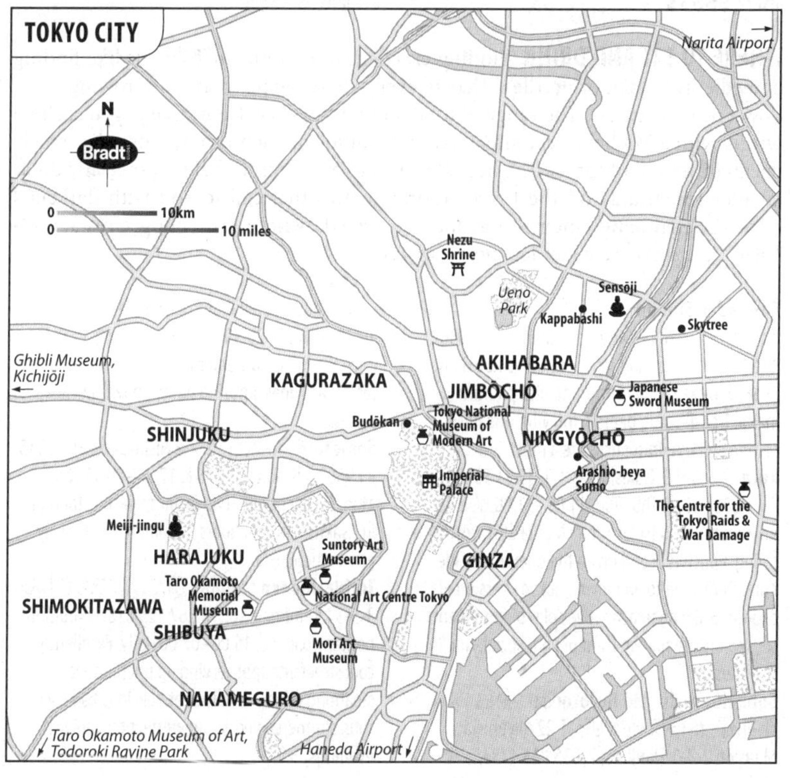

an individual ryōkan. The rooftop onsen is a scene-stealing highlight amid soft beds, stunning surroundings, guest-only restaurant & luxe living. **$$$$$**

Mandarin Oriental Tokyo (179 rooms) マンダリン オリエンタル東京; 2-1-1 Muromachi, Nihonbashi; 0332 70 8800; w mandarinoriental.com. The world-famous Mandarin Oriental is an elegant 5-star hotel with award-winning spa & arguably the best hotel dining in the city: multiple restaurants & a Michelin star. Rooms are huge, featuring stunning city views & chic, traditionally inspired aesthetics. **$$$$$**

TRUNK Hotel (15 rooms) 5-31 Jingumae, Shibuya; 0357 66 3210; w trunk-hotel.com. Ultra-trendy space near Shibuya, with garden & terrace, shop & handsome rooms. Options include private balconies/terraces, & outdoor dining area. TRUNK House is its new little sibling, a single-bedroom renovated Geisha house in Kagurazaka, a neighbourhood known as 'mini-Kyoto'. Contemporary décor, karaoke, butlers & private chef, TRUNK House is the ultimate in Tokyo luxury. **$$$$$**

Ryōkan Asakusa Shigetsu (18 rooms) 旅館浅草指月; 1-31-11 Asakusa; 0338 43 2345; e info@shigetsu.com; w shigetsu.com/en. 80-year-old ryōkan in heart of Asakusa with bright, neat traditional tatami interiors, variety of rooms, & a beautiful 6th-floor cypress-wood bath overlooking Skytree & Sensoji. **$$$$**

Nui. Hostel & Bar Lounge (18 rooms) 2-14-13 Kuramae, Asakusa; 0362 40 9854; w backpackersjapan.co.jp/nuihostel. Stylish hostel in an old toy factory, with industrial aesthetic that's popular with guests & residents. Piano bar & café, minimalist private & dorm rooms, right in Asakusa. **$$$**

Book & Bed Tokyo (dorms) 8F APM Bldg 1-27-5 Kabukicho; 0362 33 9511; w bookandbedtokyo.com/en. Décor of concrete, pipes, lanterns, ladders, wood &, above all, books. In this Shinjuku hostel-cum-café you sleep in a library of literature, with walls & beds of bookcases. The library is curated by a famed Tokyo independent bookstore. Homely, photogenic & ideal for bibliophiles & rainy days, with dbls, sgls, superiors & meal plans available. **$–$$$**

WHERE TO EAT AND DRINK Finding excellent restaurants in Tokyo is like finding a needle in a stack of needles. They're everywhere, which makes narrowing them down near-pointless. The range of food and budgets is extraordinary: you can't go wrong with a Michelin recommendation (w guide.michelin.com), nor a supremely cheap diner full of locals. The best idea is to explore everywhere – especially those smaller restaurants off the tourist thoroughfares that call to you with darkened doorways, enticing lanterns and muffled crowds within. The budget restaurants listed here serve excellent Japanese classics.

Dandadan Shinjuku 肉汁餃子のダンダダン新宿店; 1F 1-6-14 Kabukicho, Shinjuku; 0362 33 8343; w dandadan.jp; 15.00–04.00 daily. Gyoza & izakaya bar-restaurant with plentiful menu, free-flowing beers & fun vibe. The juicy stuffed chicken drumsticks are a must. **$$**

Kura 蔵; 3-9-9 Tsukishima; 0335 31 5020; 11.00–23.00 Thu–Tue, 11.00–21.00 Wed. Anywhere along Tsukishima's Monja St is worth trying, which is useful given the queues outside Kura. Dedicated to *monjayaki*, Tokyo's version of okonomiyaki: an unattractive splat of ingredients cooked on a teppan in front of you. Social, fun & delicious. **$$**

Soba House Konjiki Hototogisu 金色不如帰 新宿御苑本店; 1F 22 Miyaniwa Mansion 2-4-1 Shinjuku; 0353 15 4733; w sobahousekonjikihototogisu.com; 11.00–14.30 & 18.30–20.30 Mon–Fri. Earning a Michelin Bib Gourmand for its ramen, this counter restaurant does amazing noodle bowls at cheap prices. **$$**

Sometarō 染太郎; 2-2-2 Nishiasakusa; 0338 44 9502; noon–14.45 & 17.30–20.15 Thu–Mon. Excellent old-style okonomiyaki restaurant in Asakusa. Tatami floors, teppan tables & lively atmosphere. **$$**

Toridashioden Samon 鶏だしおでんさもん; 3-5-31 Kamimeguro; 0367 12 2818; w nomura-honten.co.jp; 16.00–02.00 daily. Excellently cool streetside spot serving up phenomenal steaming oden – a hotpot of delicious fish sticks, tofu, simmered veg & egg, perfect for cooler evenings. **$$**

Uogashi Nihon-Ichi Shibuya Dogenzaka 魚がし日本一渋谷道玄坂店; 2-9-1 Dogenzaka; ☎ 0354 28 4851; w uogashi-nihonichi.imachika.com; ⏲ 11.00–23.00 Mon–Fri, 11.00–22.00 Sat, 11.00–21.30 Sun. The extensive name is because Uogashi have standing sushi bars like this one all over Tokyo. If the Shibuya spot is too busy, head to one of the other branches. Cheap, delicious sushi, made in front of you. $$

ENTERTAINMENT AND NIGHTLIFE

Bacon 2F Tonchang Bldg, 1-17-5 Okubo; ☎ 0368 21 5193; ⏲ 18.00–midnight daily. Sitting in Tokyo's Koreatown, Bacon answers the question: 'What if Damien Hirst designed an Apple Store in a morgue?' White tiles, metal sheeting, neon lights – Bacon is a painfully cool young bar with w/end DJ events.

Benfiddich ベンフィディック; 9F Yamatoya Bldg, 1-13-7 Nishishinjuku; ☎ 0362 58 0309; ⏲ 17.00–midnight Tue–Sat. Ultimate Tokyo bar, with old glamour atmosphere thanks to white-tuxedoed mixologist Hiroyasu Kayama. Breathtaking drinks & prices, but well worth it.

Gen Yamamoto ゲンヤマモト; 1F Anniversary Bldg 1-6-4 Azabujuban; ☎ 0364 34 0652; w genyamamoto.jp; ⏲ 15.00–22.30 Tue–Sat. Calming sanctuary carved out near Roppongi, this eponymous cocktail bar is tiny & technically brilliant. The menu is omakase tasting flights, which Gen Yamamoto pioneered, with drinks using domestically sourced ingredients & measured by feel. ¥1,000 cover charge.

The Church 道玄坂教会; Central Kyoritsu Bldg, 2-16-5 Dogenzaka; ☎ 0364 33 7419; w dogenzaka-church.com; ⏲ 20.00–05.00 daily. Also called Dōgenzaka Church, this 2022 opening has an aisle, quieter chat-filled pews, an alternating DJ booth altar, and nun-themed staff. A delightfully mad, theological minefield.

Tír na nÓg ティル・ナ・ノーグ; B1F Chiazu Ginza, 5-9-5 Ginza; ☎ 0362 74 6416; w tirnanog-ginza.com; ⏲ 11.00–04.00 Mon–Sat, 11.00–23.00 Sun. An opulent cocktail cavern with a Celtic name. Fairytale fantasy meets steampunk, Tír na nÓg offers a book-sized menu with fun & phenomenally ornate drinks.

WHAT TO SEE AND DO If you're heading to the islands, the likelihood is you'll have already been to Tokyo: the archipelago is rarely anyone's first stop in Japan. Luckily there's never enough time to 'do' Tokyo – there's always more to see. When it comes to sights, Tokyo has few secrets: whether it's the Skytree, Shibuya crossing, Harajuku or the scarlet Sensōji, there's plenty of big hitters to go around (page 352). Tokyo has lots to discover underneath the vermilion veneer though, and even the well-known areas of Asakusa, Ueno, Ginza, Shibuya and Shinjuku have something a little different to offer. The following are some of Tokyo's lesser-known but no less brilliant sights, museums, parks and galleries.

Budōkan If you've come to the islands for karate, definitely book into the **Nippon Budōkan** (日本武道館; 2-3 Kitanomarukoen; w nipponbudokan.or.jp/english), Tokyo's centre for martial arts. This complex above the Imperial Palace has regular events, as well as weekend tournaments or championships that you can watch for free. Check out the website to find out more. The Budokan's hexagonal structure sits in the **Kitanomaru Park** (北の丸公園), which also features woodlands, sakura blossoms, a science museum and the **Tokyo National Museum of Modern Art** (東京国立近代美術館; 3-1 Kitanomarukoen; w momat.go.jp; ⏲ 10.00–17.00 Tue–Sun). The latter includes exquisite works from modern Japanese artists such as Taro Okamoto and Yayoi Kusama, as well as Westerners like Paul Cézanne, Oskar Kokoschka, Bridget Riley, Georgia O'Keefe, Francis Bacon, Gerhard Richter and Pablo Picasso.

Jimbōchō Just above the Budōkan is the neighbourhood of Jimbōchō (also Jinbōchō; 神保町). This old-world district is known for its warrens of secondhand

TOKYO'S TOP TEN FAMOUS SIGHTS

1. Ueno Park (上野公園) Sprawling park in the northeast that's home to some of Japan's best museums, galleries and cherry blossom viewings.
2. Sensōji (浅草寺) Asakusa's grand crimson temple, fronted by the busy tourist shopping thoroughfare Nakamise-dōri. Arguably best at night, when the crowds are gone and the lights are on.
3. Tokyo Skytree (東京スカイツリー) A 634m-high observatory tower east of Asakusa that's the tallest tower in the world.
4. Akihabara (秋葉原) Also known as Akiba or Electric Town, Akihabara is a geeky dream of electronic stores, video games and maid cafés.
5. Ginza (銀座) Tokyo's high-end shopping area, with huge numbers of stores, skyscrapers and cool architecture.
6. Imperial Palace (皇居) Taking up the centre of Tokyo is the Imperial Palace, with big parks that are free to roam.
7. Shibuya (渋谷) Famous for its busy crossroads, Shibuya is a glittering fun district full of restaurants and the new observatory, Shibuya Scramble Square.
8. Meiji-jingu (明治神宮) Glorious dark wood temple surrounded by tranquil forests, with sake barrels and a bridge entrance loved by cosplayers.
9. Harajuku (原宿) The ultimate Japanophile destination, Harajuku is best known for cosplay and the thronging Takeshita-dōri, a street of cutesie, cool and quirky shops.
10. Shinjuku (新宿) Home to the busiest station on the planet, Shinjuku is a district of nightlife, karaoke and restaurants, and where you'll see the biggest bright lights in the city.

bookshops, which may not sound wholly useful to those who don't read Japanese, but there are English-language books and tomes of photography, fashion, art and other visual subjects. These bookshops are also one of the best places to pick up old *ukiyo-e* artwork, which you can often find tucked away just inside. These woodblock prints, so decidedly Japanese, can cost a pretty penny to pick up elsewhere.

Nezu Shrine Further north is the **Nezu Shrine** (根津神社; 1-28-9 Nezu, Bunkyo; w nedujinja.or.jp; ⌚ 06.00–17.00 daily; adult/child ¥1,500/1,000), not often visited because it's a little out of the way of everything else in Tokyo, but it's a gorgeous spot. Known for its prolific azaleas that erupt with pink, white and red flowers each spring–summer, Nezu also has a short tunnel of red torii gates more commonly associated with the Fushimi-inari shrine in Kyoto. Spend some time exploring its exquisite grounds and traditional fine buildings, in a quiet neighbourhood away from it all.

Kappabashi Tucked between the great tourist spots of Ueno, with its bustling park and museums, and Asakusa's temples and Skytree, is Kappabashi Street (かっぱ橋道具街). This road is a chef's dream: a lengthy stretch of shops selling all kinds of kitchenware, from beautiful souvenirs like traditional ceramics, chopsticks and sake cups, to serious culinary purchases like Japanese knives, mousse cake moulds, eggroll pans, katsudon cookware and more.

Japanese Sword Museum On the banks of the Sumida is the **Japanese Sword Museum** (刀剣博物館; 1-12-9 Yokoami; w touken.or.jp/english; ⌚ 09.30–17.00 Tue–Sun; adult/child ¥1,500/500–800), which shows off the finest examples of

Japanese sword making, as well as armour and historical artefacts. Even if you're not a katana fan, the swords are both impressive and true works of art.

The Centre for the Tokyo Raids and War Damage Far into Tokyo's east but incredibly worth the short hop from Skytree, is the **Centre for the Tokyo Raids and War Damage** (東京大空襲・戦災資料センター; 1-5-4 Kitasuna, Koto; w tokyo-sensai.net; ◷ 10.30–16.00 Tue–Sun; ¥500). This little-known museum in an unassuming brick building is dedicated to the Tokyo firebombings. While the nuclear blasts in Japan's west held the global gaze for decades, the obliteration of Tokyo through napalm was one of the most deadly events in world history. Taking place on a single night, the raid destroyed 41km^2 of Tokyo and killed an estimated 100,000 civilians. This heartfelt museum feels hugely important and memorialises a vital, oft-overlooked piece of the Pacific War.

Ningyōchō A southeast stroll from Akiba's electric town is Ningyōchō (人形町), literally 'Doll Town', a neighbourhood known in the Edo period for its Kabuki theatres, puppet shows and doll makers. The area has survived earthquakes and bombings to retain a sense of Old Tokyo – many of the buildings and businesses, including traditional crafts and sweet shops, temples and original houses, have been here for years. There are even two clock towers that do an hourly puppet display during the daytime. Taste your way around the neighbourhood, particularly its main shopping street Amazakeyokochō and Kogiku-Dōri 'Geisha Alley', stopping at tea rooms, craft beer shops, traditional snack stands and more.

Arashio-beya Sumo If you're in town during Tokyo's January, May or September sumo tournaments, going to **Arashio-beya Sumo** (荒汐部屋; 2-47-2 Nihonbashihamacho; w arashio.net/tour_e.html) is non-negotiable. You can book in advance (and you will need to if you want guaranteed tickets and your choice of seats) or you can queue up in the morning for cheap, all-day tickets in the back rows – well worth the saving. If you visit outside the season, you can still see sumo wrestlers going about their practice: you can watch them from outside through Arashio-beya Sumo stable's big windows or organise a tour.

Roppongi Art Triangle Scooting past Ginza's shopping district, Tokyo Tower and the newly minted TeamLab home at Azabudai Hills, make sure to stop in at Roppongi (六本木). Perhaps better known for its nightlife, Roppongi is actually home to the so-called Art Triangle, a trio of excellent art museums. The **Mori Art Museum** (森美術館; 6-10-1 Roppongi; w mori.art.museum/en; ◷ 10.00–17.00 Tue, 10.00–22.00 Wed–Mon; adult/child ¥2,000/800–1,400), in the sleek Roppongi Hills mega-complex, is dedicated to contemporary art and regularly has brilliant exhibits of Western and Japanese artists. The **Suntory Art Museum** (サントリー美術館; 9-7-4 Akasaka; w suntory.com/sma; ◷ 10.00–18.00 Sun–Mon & Wed–Thu, 10.00–20.00 Fri–Sat; adult/child ¥1,600/1,000) in Tokyo Midtown mall houses traditional Japanese art (think Hokusai) and crafts. It often hosts exhibits from world-renowned galleries as well as having its own collections and shows. Finally, the **National Art Centre Tokyo** (国立新美術館; 7-22-2 Roppongi; w nact.jp/English; ◷ 10.00–18.00 Wed–Mon), one of Japan's biggest exhibition spaces, hosts regular exhibits of world-famous artists like Yayoi Kusama.

Nakameguro South of Shibuya's mad scramble is Nakameguro (中目黒), a serene and stylish section of Tokyo that's been coming up and up in recent years. Today its quiet, canal-split streets have chic stores, boutique cafés, artsy hangouts and cool bars. In springtime, Nakameguro has some of Tokyo's best sakura blossoms, which line the mirror-like canals and are lit up at night.

Shimokitazawa A little way from Shibuya and Shinjuku is Shimokitazawa (下北沢), a cool neighbourhood filled with vintage clothes shops, trendy cafés, bookshops, music stores and independent boutiques. If Harajuku was more spectacle than shopping, Shimokitazawa might be more up your street. The ultimate in secondhand and thrift shops, the neighbourhood can keep the eagle-eyed deal shopper busy for hours. It's also filled with great places to refuel before heading back into the racks.

Kagurazaka Not far from Shinjuku is Tokyo's 'Little Paris', a one-time geisha district that's now home to a little French community thanks to its two French schools. Here in Kagurazaka (神楽坂) you'll find fashionable shops, Michelin restaurants and chic cafés. Yet its surprisingly quiet cobbled streets also hark to its former life, with kimono shops and elegant high-class *ryōtei* restaurants. You can even see the occasional modern geisha, darting between shops. Visit the bright red Zenkokuji (善國寺; 5-36 Kagurazaka; w kagurazaka-bishamonten.com), revamped Akagi jinja (赤城神社; 1-10 Akagi Motomachi; w akagi-jinja.jp), Canal Café (1-9 Kagurazaka; w canalcafe.jp) and traditional alleyways.

Outside Tokyo In the capital's outskirts, particularly in its west, are some charming spots easily reached by train, which make a great addition to a second-time Tokyo itinerary.

Kichijōji and the Ghibli Museum Kichijōji (吉祥寺) consistently tops Tokyoites' list for most desirable place to live for good reason. A quiet neighbourhood with streets of little shops and eateries, it's easily accessed from Shibuya and Shinjuku, and home to the pretty **Inokashira Park** (井の頭恩賜公園). Inokashira is its main draw, a woodland-and-grass space that brings a bit of countryside to the city. It comes with cafés, a boating lake, a beautiful bright shrine, zoo, seasonal blossoms and red maples, but best of all the **Ghibli Museum** (三鷹の森ジブリ美術館; w ghibli-museum.jp; ⌚ 10.00–18.00 daily; adult/child ¥1,000/100–700). Recently moved and expanded, the museum is an interactive dreamscape for Studio Ghibli film fans, showing exhibits and activities related to *My Neighbour Totoro*, *Spirited Away* and more. When you've explored the park, head to **Harmonica Yokochō** (ハーモニカ横丁), an alley of bars and restaurants.

Taro Okamoto art museums Set among the big and beautiful Ikuta Ryokuchi Park (生田緑地), the **Taro Okamoto Museum of Art** (川崎市岡本太郎美術館; 7-1-5 Masugata, Tama; w taromuseum.jp; ⌚ 09.30–17.00 Tue–Sun) in Kawasaki, dedicated to Japan's beloved avant-garde artist Taro Okamoto, is brilliant. You can make a proper afternoon of exploring the kaleidoscopic artwork, forest trails, gardens, observation decks and further museums dedicated to science, culture and craft. If you're still hungry for more of Okamoto's work, there's also the **Taro Okamoto Memorial Museum** (岡本太郎記念館; w taro-okamoto.or.jp; ⌚ 10.00–18.00 Wed–Mon; adult/child ¥650/300) in Minami-aoyama, a great little gallery near the Nezu Art Museum that's far closer to Tokyo's centre.

Todoroki Ravine Park East of Ikuta Ryokuchi, Tokyo's only natural valley sees the Yazawa River swell into pretty Todoroki Ravine Park (等々力渓谷公園). Think bamboo groves and enveloping trees, bright red bridges that straddle the trundling river, tea houses and koi ponds, and seasonal pink blossoms. Todoroki is a place to escape Tokyo's bustle without really escaping Tokyo. Amble alongside the river, soaking up birdsong and breathing fresh air, passing little shrines until you reach the larger Todoroki Fudōson, a temple of scarlet that's especially beautiful among autumnal leaves.

KAGOSHIMA

Kagoshima (鹿児島) is the prefectural capital, one of the southernmost cities of both Kyūshū and the Japanese mainland, and a gateway to the northernmost islands. You can avoid Kagoshima should you want to – only the Mishima can't be accessed by flights and ferries from other areas – but the city is a fun, chilled-out place of southern cuisine, sights, and ever-spewing ash from its active volcano. Kagoshima (or Kagomma as locals call it) isn't huge: you can explore its best sites in a couple of days, making it a perfect base to return to when exploring the Ōsumi Islands.

GETTING THERE AND AWAY

By air Kagoshima has its own international airport served by multiple carriers. International airlines include ANA (w ana.co.jp/en), Japan Airlines (w jal.co.jp/uk/en), China Airlines (w china-airlines.com/uk/en), HK Express (w hkexpress.com/en-hk) and Korean Air (w koreanair.com), serving Tokyo Haneda, Osaka Itami, Taipei, Hong Kong and Seoul. Domestic low-cost carriers Solaseed (w solaseedair.jp/en), Skymark (w smart.skymark.co.jp/en), Peach (w flypeach.com/en), Jetstar (w jetstar.com/jp/en), Ibex (w ibexair.co.jp/en), Fuji Dream (w fujidream.co.jp/en) and Japan Air Commuter (w jac.co.jp) service mainland airports in Osaka (Itami and Kansai), Tokyo (Narita and Haneda), Fukuoka, Matsuyama, Nagoya, Kobe and Shizuoka. From Kagoshima to the islands, you can fly to Yakushima, Tanegashima, Amami Ōshima, Kikai, Tokunoshima, Okinoerabu, Yoron and Naha.

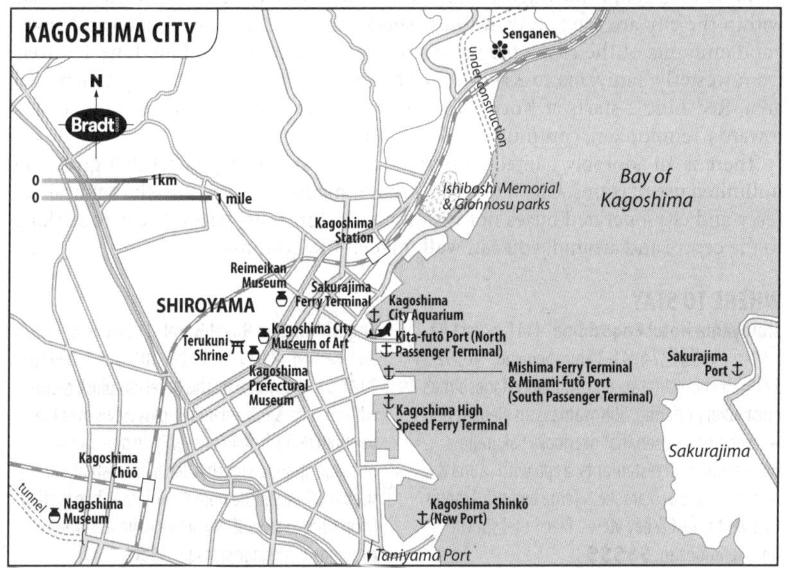

Airport transfers The airport is a way out from the city centre but is served by buses and rental cars. You won't need a rental car in the city, unless you want to travel further afield. The number 8 bus is the best for getting to the city, taking 45–60 minutes and stopping at multiple locations including Chūō Station and Tenmonkan.

In front of the terminal building is a natural hot spring footbath called Oyattosa – in Kagoshima dialect it means 'thank you for your hard work'. Make sure to take full advantage of it and the free Wi-Fi while waiting for your connection or flight.

By train You can travel to Kagoshima by train, including multiple *shinkansen* (bullet train) options. However, its southerly position in Kyūshū means this is a long trip. Tokyo to Kagoshima takes around 7 hours, with at least one transfer, usually in Osaka or Fukuoka. The Japan Rail Pass (w japanrailpass.net/en) covers the trip if taking Hikari or Sakura Shinkansen.

By ferry Islands as far south as Okinawa-hontō are connected to Kagoshima's multiple ports by ferry. These ferries are very long, often overnight, but are comparatively cheap and offer an aspect of adventure. The ports used are: Kita-futō Port (North Passenger Terminal); Minami-futō Port (South Passenger Terminal); Mishima Ferry Terminal; Kagoshima Shinkō (New Port) and Kagoshima Taniyama Port. See individual island sections for more information.

GETTING AROUND Kagoshima has extensive public transport (w kagoshima-kankou.com/for/access/movement), including a ridiculously complicated bus system, trains, and trams. There are so many **buses** that the names can get a little confusing, but once you've figured out which you need they're not difficult to use. The most useful are the two loop buses, City View and Machimeguri, which connect the main station and the ferry terminal to Sakurajima. Both buses offer day passes, costing ¥500–600.

The main **train** station in Kagoshima is central Kagoshima Chūō, which connects to the shinkansen, while Kagoshima Station sits in the city's east. Of much more use within the city are the two **tramlines**. These trams are fun, easy, cheap and cover good amounts of the city – they also surprisingly accept Visa. Blue Line 1 travels from westerly Taniyama to Kagoshima Station via Tenmonkan, the big downtown area. Red Line 2 starts at Korimoto, splitting north from the blue until it rejoins towards Tenmonkan, continuing to Kagoshima Station.

There is an adorably named **Cute Pass**, a one- or two-day ticket that gives you unlimited use of trams, City View bus, Sakurajima Island View Bus, the Sakurajima ferry and city-operated buses not including Machimeguri buses. If you're sticking to the centre and around, you can **walk** much of Kagoshima.

WHERE TO STAY

Shiroyama Hotel Kagoshima (141 rooms) 城山ホテル 鹿児島; 41-1 Shinshoincho; 0992 24 2211; w shiroyama-g.co.jp. Arguably Kagoshima's most luxury offering, Shiroyama is an elegant hotel with open-air onsen that overlooks Sakurajima. Huge number of restaurants, a spa with sauna & massages, shops, karaoke & large beautiful rooms. Excellent b/fast & bay views. Free hotel shuttle from Tenmonkan. **$$$$$**

Kagoshima Sun Royal Hotel (183 rooms) 鹿児島サンロイヤルホテル; 1-8-10 Yojiro; 0992 53 2020; w sunroyal.co.jp. This hotel has plush rooms with en suite & full amenities, plus views over the bay from its 13th-floor onsen. Cycle hire, sauna & massage options. French & Japanese restaurants, sky bar & free shuttle from Kagoshima Chūō Station. Rooms have views of city or Sakurajima. Currency exchange & luggage storage. **$$$$**

remm Kagoshima (250 rooms) レム鹿児島; 1-32 Higashisengokucho; 0992 24 0606; w hankyu-hotel.com. Handsome budget hotel in Tenmonkan area with smallish rooms but cosy atmosphere. Brilliant value for money, with en suite, fridge & usual amenities, on-site restaurant, laundry/dry clean & b/fast option. **$$**

Hostel Tomal (10 rooms inc dorms) ホステルトマル; 4F Tomaru Bldg, 1-8 Izumicho; 0505 436 0412. Cheap, excellent & centrally located hostel with dorm & private options. Shared kitchen, lounge & bathrooms with luggage storage. Friendly knowledgeable owner too. **$–$$**

WHERE TO EAT AND DRINK Kagoshima is known for Satsuma cuisine (*satsuma ryōri*) – not a menu of citrus but the name for the old Kagoshima region. The area's isolation meant it developed a distinct gastronomy from the mainland. Seek out regional dishes like kibinago (small herring served vinegared or as sashimi), *satsuma-age* fishcakes, kurobuta black pork, Kuroushi black beef, and one of Japan's most feared offerings, *torisashi*: chicken sashimi. Much more delicious than you'd ever imagine, the chicken is served as fresh as possible and has a delicate flavour not found in the cooked version. Kagoshima also has its own alcohol, *satsuma shōchū*, made from local sweet potatoes.

Coucou 洋食とワインの店; Coucou 6-11-205 Higashisengokucho; 0998 13 7798; 18.00–midnight Tue–Sun. Up the outer stairs on the 2nd floor is this French-inspired wine bar with exquisite dishes that change regularly based on season. Intimate, dim-lit & beautifully presented, Coucou is a family-run fine-dining secret. $$$$

Kagomma Furusato Yataimura Bus Chika かごっまふるさと屋台村 バスチカ; 1F 11 Chuo Terminal Bldg, Chuocho; 0992 04 0260; w kagoshima-yataimura.info; 11.30–14.00 & 17.00–23.30 daily. One of the saddest restaurant losses of Covid was Kagoshima's lively, open-air yatai street food market. It's now been moved indoors to 2 locations: they've lost some shine but they're still good fun. Make your way round different tiny stall restaurants, ordering bits & bobs as you go or picking one & staying put. This cosy one is in the Solaria Hotel basement. $$$

Kagomma Furusato Yataimura Li-Ka かごっまふるさと屋台村 ライカ; Li-Ka1920, 19-40 Chuocho; 0992 04 0260; w kagoshima-yataimura.info; 11.30–23.30 daily. Another Yataimura, this time in the Li-Ka – made to look like a street with lanterns, it's a little bigger than the Bus Chika yatai, but a little less buzzy because of it. The 2 offer different options, so it's worth going to both. $$$

ABDC エービーダーシー; 3-9 Meizanchō; 11.00–15.00 Thu–Mon. This is in a little-touristed area by Asahidori in the city's north that's brimful of cool little eateries. Squashed into a tiny traditional block, these restaurants can seat only a handful at a time & close when sold out. ABDC is a highlight, with kind owners serving some of the best ramen in town for great prices. $$

Kurobuta 黒福多; 1F Kamatsuki Bldg, 3-2 Sennichicho; 0992 24 8729; w satsumakurobuta.gorp.jp; 11.30–14.00 & 17.30–21.30 Tue–Sun. All of the Kuroshima black pork dishes you could ask for: hotpot, cutlets, donburi, set meals & more. $$

ENTERTAINMENT AND NIGHTLIFE

BAR 13 バーサーティーン; 1F Central Park Bldg, 15-1 Terukunicho; 0992 26 7523; 19.00–02.00 Tue–Thu, 19.00–03.00 Fri–Sat, 19.00–midnight Sun. Ultimately cool bar with ¥1,000 entrance, dark wood décor & high ceilings, backlit bar, mezzanine, excellent snacks, brilliant cocktails & dickie-bowed staff.

Bar Tsuki Bar 月; 3-11 Meizanchō; 0998 13 7488; noon–16.00 & 20.00–01.00 Mon-Sat. Found not far from ABDC in cool Meizanchō, this beautiful bar is a well-kept secret, with a single room & counter you must duck under to get into. Look for the crescent moon on the wall outside & let the done-up barman do his thing in the dark-lit atmosphere of cocktails, cognac & cigars.

Izakaya 017 Yokaban 居酒屋017 よか晩; 17-17 Higashisengokucho; 0992 27 1010; 18.00–midnight Mon–Sat, 18.00–23.00 Sun. One of the best places in the city to try every shōchū possible. Brilliant local snacks to keep you sober as you work your way through an amazing menu with the help of supremely friendly staff – you may even get to pour your own.

SHOPPING Kagoshima has a wealth of shopping areas. The best-known is Tenmonkan, which has old covered arcades filled with boutiques and cafés ripe for exploring. These arcades were built to protect people and stores from Sakurajima's falling ash. The area around Kagoshima Chūō Station was revamped in 2004, with a huge shopping complex complete with Ferris wheel. Along the bay, newly opened Dolphin Port has a load of restaurants and shops.

WHAT TO SEE AND DO

Sakurajima Funnily enough, the main activity in Kagoshima is to get on a boat and leave the city. Kagoshima's bay is home to Sakurajima (桜島), one of Japan's most active volcanoes. Spewing ash across the city most days, this volcano is always on the go but hasn't had a powerful eruption since 1914. Sakurajima has three main peaks, the largest of which is Kitadake (1,117m), with Minamidake its most active. You can't go closer than 2km to the craters but there are plenty of observatories from where you can watch the minor eruptions.

Sakurajima is best accessed by ferry. The island's ferry terminal has multiple attractions within walking distance. There's a small visitor centre; the Nagisa Park natural footbaths which are free of charge and have great bay views; Dinosaur Park, ideal for kids and springtime cherry blossoms; the 3km Nagisa Lava Trail walk; and the Magma Onsen, which has hot spring baths open to day visitors. For exploring further afield, you can bring a car or bicycle on the ferry, or take a loop bus. This opens up the Yunohira Observation Point, 2.5km from the crater; Kurokami Viewpoint, which regularly sees little eruptions; Arimura Observatory; and the Kurokami Shrine buried gate. This 3m-high torii demonstrates the power of the 1914 eruption: only its top is now visible, the rest buried in ash.

Terukuni Shrine The most popular shrine in the prefecture, Terukuni (照國神社) sits overlooking a massive torii gate and road intersection. Its deity is the 11th head of the Shimazu clan who helped industrialise the country. Built in 1863, Terukuni is famed for the *inumaki* pine tree at its entrance. This tree, named Saitaku, is trimmed to look like a crane with spread wings. There are a few little shrines within the complex and a museum that shows the Shimazu family genealogy. The area is particularly busy at New Year and during summer festivals.

Shiroyama Behind Terukuni is Shiroyama (城山), a cultural area with prolific history, museums, castle ruins and arts. Its park covers covers Shiroyama Hill (107m), where the old castle fortifications sat. Literally called 'Castle Mountain', this hill has an excellent observatory with views over the city, bay and Sakurajima, which are particularly good at night. There are also great views from Satsuma-no-Yu, an outdoor hot spring at the Shiroyama Hotel (城山ホテル; 41-1 Shinshoincho; **w** shiroyama-g.co.jp). The park was also the site of the Satsuma Rebellion's final battle, and the cave where Saigo Takamori (page 154) supposedly killed himself.

Reimeikan Museum (黎明館; 5-1 Shiroyamacho; **w** pref.kagoshima.jp/reimeikan; ⌚ 09.00–17.00 Tue–Sun; adult/child ¥300/120–190) The Reimeikan is an extensive museum dedicated to Kagoshima culture and history, covering ancient to modern eras. It's built on the site of the former Tsurumaru Castle, constructed by the 18th head of the Shimazu clan; you can still see the old moat and stone walls.

Kagoshima City Museum of Art (鹿児島市立美術館; 4-36 Shiroyamacho; w city.kagoshima.lg.jp/artmuseum; ⌚ 09.30–18.00 Tue–Sun; adult/child ¥300/150–200) Between Terukuni Shrine and the Reimeikan is the excellent Kagoshima City Museum of Art. The gallery has brilliant art displays with local, Japanese and Western artists including Claude Monet.

Kagoshima Prefectural Museum (鹿児島県立博物館; 1-1 Shiroyamacho; w pref.kagoshima.jp/hakubutsukan; ⌚ 09.00–17.00 Tue–Sun) One minute from Terukuni Shrine is the Kagoshima Prefectural Museum. Not everything here gets an English-language sign, but it's a free exhibit where you can explore culture, biology, geography and more, including aspects of the prefecture's islands too. Its large, colourful, often animal-based exhibits are great for children.

Kagoshima City Aquarium (いおワールドかごしま水族館; 3-1 Honkoshinmachi; w ioworld.jp; ⌚ 09.00–18.00 daily; adult/child ¥1,500/350–750) Just beside the ferry terminal to Sakurajima is Kagoshima City Aquarium. This seven-storey aquarium showcases the waters off Kagoshima Prefecture, rich with marine life brought in on the warm current of the Kuroshio. The aquarium has a massive Kuroshio tank with a whale shark, sea otters, electric eels, reefs and mangroves. There are feeding hours and dolphin shows, with dolphins that are allowed to run free in the canals outside the aquarium.

Nagashima Museum (長島美術館; 3-42-18 Take; w ngp.jp/nagashima-museum; ⌚ 09.00–17.00 Wed–Mon; adult/child ¥1,000/400–800) Sitting a 10-minute uphill walk behind Kagoshima Chūō Station, Nagashima Museum overlooks Kagoshima city and Sakurajima's cone. It's a fabulous gallery of myriad artworks, covering outdoor sculpture, pottery, ink drawings and paintings, from local artists to famous Japanese and Western artists including Aki Kuroda, Fujishima Takeji, Pablo Picasso, Auguste Rodin, Pierre-Auguste Renoir and Marc Chagall. There are also temporary exhibits through the year.

Senganen (9700-1 Yoshinocho; w senganen.jp; ⌚ 08.30–17.00 daily) This stunning, old Japanese landscape garden was built in 1658 by the Shimazu clan, who ruled Satsuma and the islands and were influential in popularising Western technology in Japan. Sitting in the city's north, Senganen (仙巌園) is also home to the elegant Iso residence, a former summer villa reconstructed in the 1880s. This was the Shimazu family main residence after the Meiji restoration and end of the feudal era. Well preserved and beautiful to walk through, it's worth adding the house to your ticket.

The garden frames Kagoshima Bay and Sakurajima, with viewpoints a worthwhile hike up into the garden. There are also streams, ponds, bridges, a bamboo grove, shrines and seasonal blossoms throughout the year. Senganen also has remnants and relics from the ages, such as furnace foundations, and a museum about the Shimazu industrialisation and more. A good 45-minute bayside walk from Kagoshima Station, the garden can also be accessed by the City View bus.

If you do walk to Senganen, stop at the two parks of Ishibashi Memorial (石橋記念公園) and Gionnosu (祇園之洲公園), which have three historical stone bridges. These bridges used to span the Kotsuki River in the city, along with two others. Those two were destroyed when Kagoshima flooded in 1998, so these other three were moved here.

Appendix 1

With Tom Fay

LANGUAGE

JAPANESE Though English is a core subject in schools, most Japanese people don't speak or understand the language well. On the islands, Okinawa-hontō has a comparatively large American influx but English still isn't guaranteed. Japanese people – well aware of their own language's endemism – are thrilled with any attempt by visitors at speaking and learning even just a few words of Japanese. On these islands, it makes your life much easier, particularly if it concerns food. Make sure to speak clearly and slowly (though you may not get this in return) and you can always try offering written Japanese phrases, or English as written English is often easier to understand than spoken.

Japanese alphabets Modern Japanese has a famously complex writing system comprised of three different alphabets. ***Kanji*** (漢字) is a script with Chinese origins. It has tens of thousands of characters (though you really need to know only the 3,000 or so most common ones to be considered fluent), and each one can have multiple pronunciations depending on context or the other characters it is paired with. Even Japanese people often have a hard time reading or writing the less frequently used kanji. ***Hiragana*** (ひらがな) is a phonetic syllabary (symbols representing syllables) and it has only 46 basic characters. Hiragana is usually attached to the end of kanji to form grammar conjugations, or sometimes represents words with no (or obsolete) kanji readings. ***Katakana*** (カタカナ) also has 46 basic phonetic characters which are more angular in appearance than the graceful curves of hiragana. It is mostly used to write foreign loan words (such as beer ビール; *biiru*), non-Japanese names, or is sometimes written to provide special emphasis.

If you are keen to learn a little Japanese before your trip, then both hiragana and katakana can be memorised fairly quickly, and they are quite useful for deciphering things like items on menus.

Grammar Japanese grammar can be quite confusing, with sentences structured back to front for English speakers, with seemingly key information such as pronouns often omitted entirely and no distinctions between singular and plural. There are multiple levels of polite and humble speech, plus the tendency to speak about subjects in an indirect manner.

A Course in Modern Japanese (University of Nagoya Press, 2002) is a good starting point for beginners.

Pronunciation Despite Japanese being a notoriously difficult language to master (especially reading and writing), Japanese pronunciation is relatively straightforward – however, if you don't pronounce words close to how a native would, then many Japanese people will struggle to understand what you are saying.

The words and phrases in this appendix have been written in a Romanised form called *romaji*. Vowels with a macron (small bar) over them (such as *ō*) are pronounced the same way as normal vowels, but the sound is held for twice as long. This can completely change the meaning of a word; for example, *kuki* refers to a plant's stem, while *kūki* means 'air'.

The five main **vowel sounds** are:

a as in 'art'
i as in 'ski'
u as in 'flu'
e as in 'bed'
o as in 'old'

'E' is of particular importance in Okinawan words, where double *ee* can be common. It's pronounced not as 'bee' but more an elongated 'beh'.

Consonants are pronounced almost the same as those in English, apart from:

g as in 'give' if at the start of a word, or a slightly nasal 'sing' if it appears mid-word.
f as in the 'wh' of 'who', made by pursing the lips and blowing gently.
r is closer to an 'l' than an 'r'.

Double consonants in words, such as the double *t* in *matte* (wait), should be pronounced with a slight pause between them.

Names In Japanese, the surname comes first, the forename after. Unless you know someone very well, you refer to them by their surname, followed by the unisex suffix *-san*. This is the equivalent to the English Mr or Ms. If you meet a Yamada Keiko, for example, you would refer to her as Yamada-san.

In place names, you'll notice the word *shima* crops up regularly, or its alternative form *jima*. Shima is Japanese for 'island', which is why you'll hear 'Miyakojima', or 'Miyako Island', but never 'Miyakojima Island'. There are many Japanese words that have a noun suffixed to the name like this. *Jinja* is the word for shrine, *dera/tera/ji* for temple, *jo* for castle and *mura* for village. One of the most common is *yama* or *san* for mountain, or on the islands *take/dake* for peak.

Useful vocabulary and phrases

	Japanese	Romaji
Basics		
Yes/No*	はい / いいえ	*Hai/iie*
Please	お願いします	*Onegaishimasu*
Thank you	ありがとうございます	*Arigatō gozaimasu*
Sorry	ごめんなさい	*Gomenasai*
You're welcome	こちらこそ	*Kochira koso*

*There are numerous ways to say 'yes' or 'no', and questions are often answered affirmatively simply by repeating the verb or adjective in question. For example, 'Are you hungry?' (お腹空いていますか; *onaka ga suiteimasu ka?*) can be answered with 'Hungry!' (お腹が空いている; *onaka ga suiteiru*).

Greetings and introductions The honorific suffix '*-san*' is often added to the end of people's names when speaking or referring to them, and unless very close, people generally refer to others by their family name, eg: *Takeda-san*.

Hello	こんにちは	*Konnichiwa*
Good morning	おはようございます	*Ohayō gozaimasu*
Good evening	こんばんは	*Konbanwa*
Goodnight	おやすみなさい	*Oyasuminasai*
Goodbye	さようなら	*Sayōnara*
See you again	またね	*Mata ne*
How are you?	お元気ですか？	*O-genki desu ka?*
I'm fine	元気です	*Genki desu*
What's your name?	お名前は何ですか？	*O-namae wa nan desu ka?*
My name is…	名前は…です	*Namae wa…desu*
Where are you from?	どこの出身ですか？	*Doko no shusshin desu ka?*
I'm from…	…の出身です	*…no shusshin desu*

Other useful phrases

Excuse me/I'm sorry	すみません	*Sumimasen*
Do you speak English?	英語が話せますか？	*Eigo ga hanasemasu ka?*
I don't understand	わかりません	*Wakarimasen*
It doesn't matter	気にしないで下さい	*Ki ni shinai de kudasai*
Can I come in?	はいっていいですか？	*Haitte ii desu ka?*
I want to go to…	…に行きたいです	*…ni ikitai desu*
Where's the…?	…はどこですか？	*…wa doko desu ka?*
Where's the toilet?	トイレはどこですか？	*Toire wa doko desu ka?*

Shopping

Do you have…?	~ありますか？	*…arimasu ka?*
This one please	これお願いします	*Kore onegaishimasu*
How much does this cost?	これはいくらですか？	*Kore wa ikura desu ka?*
Do you have a cheaper one?	もっと安いのありますか？	*Motto yasui no arimasu ka?*
Do you have a smaller size?	もっと小さいサイズありますか？	*Motto chisai saizu arimasu ka?*
Do you have a bigger size?	もっと大きいサイズありますか？	*Motto ōki saizu arimasu ka?*

Numbers

one	一	*ichi*	forty	四十	*yon jū*
two	二	*ni*	fifty	五十	*gojū*
three	三	*san*	sixty	六十	*roku jū*
four	四	*shi/yon*	seventy	七十	*nana jū*
five	五	*go*	eighty	八十	*hachi jū*
six	六	*roku*	ninety	九十	*kū jū*
seven	七	*nana/shichi*	one hundred	百	*hyaku*
eight	八	*hachi*	one thousand	千	*sen*
nine	九	*kū*	ten thousand	一万	*icchi-man*
ten	十	*jū*			
twenty	二十	*ni jū*			
thirty	三十	*san jū*			

Accommodation

Do you have any vacancies?	部屋はありますか?	*Heya wa arimasu ka?*
I have a reservation	予約があります	*Yoyaku ga arimasu*
single room	一人	*hitori no heya*
double room	二人の部屋	*futari no heya*
How much is it?	いくらですか?	*ikura desu ka?*
one night	一泊	*ippaku*
boarding only	素泊り	*sudomari*

Eating out

Do you have any tables (now)?	今は空いてますか?	*Ima aiteimasu ka?*
I'd like to make a reservation	予約したいです	*Yoyaku shitai desu*
How many people?	何名様ですか?	*Nan meisama desu ka?*
Do you have any recommendations?	何がおすすめですか?	*Nani ga osusume desu ka?*
May I order please?	注文していいですか?	*Chūmon shi te ii desu ka?*
Do you have any vegetarian dishes?	ベジタリアン料理がありますか?	*Bejitarian ryōri ga arimasu ka?*
I don't eat meat	肉は食べません	*Niku wa tabemasen*
May I have the bill please?	お会計下さい?	*O kaikei kudasai?*
Thank you for the meal	ごちそうさまでした	*Gochisōsama deshita*
Cheers!	かんぱい	*kanpai*
breakfast	朝ご飯 / 朝食	*asa-gohan/chōshoku*
lunch	ランチ / 昼食	*ranchi/chūshoku*
dinner	晩ごはん / 夕食	*ban-gohan/yūshoku*
all-you-can-eat	食べ放題	*tabehōdai*
all-you-can-drink	飲み放題	*nomihōdai*
set meal	定食 / セット	*teishoku/setto*
single item	単品	*tanpin*
small/medium/large	小 / 中 / 大	*shō/chū/dai*
chopsticks	はし	*hashi*

Food and drink

beef	牛肉	*gyū-niku*
black pepper	コショウ	*koshō*
bonito (dried)	かつおぶし/鰹節	*katsuobushi*
bread	パン	*pan*
cheese	チーズ	*chīzu*
chicken	鶏肉	*tori-niku*
chicken sashimi	鳥刺し	*tori-sashi*
crab	カニ	*kani*
eel	うなぎ	*unagi*
egg	卵	*tamago*
fish	魚	*sakana*
fruit	果物	*kudamono*
goat	やぎ肉	*yagi-niku*
ice cream	アイス / アイスクリーム	*aisu/aisu-kurīmu*
meat	肉	*niku*
noodles	麺	*men*

soba	そば	*soba*
udon	うどん	*udon*
octopus	タコ	*tako*
pork	豚肉	*buta-niku*
prawn	エビ	*ebi*
rice	ご飯	*gohan*
salmon	サケ	*sake*
salt	塩	*shio*
scallop	ホタテ	*hotate*
seaweed	海藻	*kaisō*
aosa	あおさ	*aosa*
mozuku	もずく	*mozuku*
sea urchin	ウニ	*uni*
shellfish	貝	*kai*
soy sauce	醤油	*shōyu*
squid	イカ	*ika*
squid ink	イカ墨	*ikasumi*
sugar	砂糖	*satō*
taco	タコ	*tako*
tofu	豆腐	*tōfu*
tuna	マグロ	*maguro*
vegetable(s)	野菜	*yasai*
awamori	泡盛	*awamori*
beer	ビール	*bīru*
coffee	コーヒー	*kōhī*
green tea	抹茶	*maccha*
juice	ジュース	*jūsu*
milk	牛乳	*gyūnyū*
red wine	赤ワイン	*aka-wain*
sake	酒	*sake*
tea	紅茶	*kōcha*
water	水	*mizu*
white wine	白ワイン	*shiro-wain*

Island-specific words

Welcome	めんそーれー	*Mensooree*
Person originating from Okinawa	ウチナンチュー	*Uchinanchu*
Okinawan language	ウチナーグチ	*Uchināguchi*
Ōsumi Islands	大隅諸島	*Ōsumi-shotō*
Amami Islands	奄美群島	*Amami-guntō*
Okinawa Islands	沖縄諸島	*Okinawa-shotō*
Kerama Islands	慶良間列島	*Kerama-rettō*
Miyako Islands	宮古列島	*Miyako-rettō*
Yaeyama Islands	八重山列島	*Yaeyama-rettō*
Kagoshima Prefecture	鹿児島県	*Kagoshima-ken*
Okinawa Prefecture	沖縄県	*Okinawa-ken*

Places (manmade) and infrastructure

aquarium	水族館	*suizokukan*
art gallery	美術館	*bijutsukan*

bank	銀行	*ginkō*
bar	バー	*bā*
bridge	橋	*hashi*
castle	城	*shiro*
cinema	映画館	*eigakan*
club	クラブ	*kurabu*
convenience store	コンビニ	*konbini*
dental clinic	デンタルクリニック	*dentaru-kuriniku*
department store	デパート	*depāto*
farm	農場	*nōjō*
hospital	病院	*byōin*
hotel	ホテル	*hoteru*
hot spring	温泉	*onsen*
market	市場	*ichiba*
museum	博物館	*hakubutsukan*
observation deck	展望台	*tenbōdai*
park	公園	*kōen*
pharmacy (drug store)	薬局 / ドラッグストア	*yakkyoku/doraggu-sutoa*
post office	郵便局	*yūbinkyoku*
restaurant	レストラン	*resutoran*
shopping street	商店街	*shōtengai*
shrine	神社	*jinja*
utaki/ontake	御嶽ウタキ	*utaki/ontake*
temple	寺	*tera*
toilet	トイレ / お手洗い	*toire/otearai*
men's	男	*otoko*
ladies'	女	*onna*
tourist information centre	観光情報センター	*kankō-jōhō-sentā*
unattended roadside stall	無人販売	*mujinhanbai*
vending machine	自動販売機	*jidōhanbaiki*
zoo	動物園	*dōbutsuen*

Transport

airport	空港	*kūkō*
bicycle	自転車	*jitensha*
bus	バス	*basu*
bus stop	バス停	*basu-tei*
bus terminal	バスターミナル	*basu-tāminaru*
car	車	*kuruma*
ferry terminal	フェリーターミナル	*ferī-tāminaru*
harbour/port	港	*minato*
motorbike	オートバイ/ バイク	*mōtobai/baiku*
road	道	*michi*
roadside service station	道の駅	*michi-no-eki*
subway	地下鉄	*chikatetsu*
train	電車	*densha*
train station	駅	*eki*
tunnel	トンネル	*toneru*

Geographical features

archipelago	列島/ 諸島/群島	*rettō/shotō/guntō*

beach	ビーチ / 浜	*bīchi/hama*
boulder	岩	*iwa*
cape	岬	*misaki*
cave	洞窟	*dōkutsu*
coast	海岸	*kaigan*
coral reef	珊瑚礁	*sango-shō*
field	畑	*hata*
forest	森	*mori*
hill	丘	*oka*
island	島	*shima*
lake	湖	*mizuumi*
marsh	沼	*numa*
mountain	山	*yama*
peninsula	半島	*hantō*
pond	池	*ike*
river	川	*kawa*
sea	海	*umi*
star sand	星砂	*hoshizuna*
summit	山頂	*sanchō*
valley	谷	*tani*
volcano	火山	*kazan*
waterfall	滝	*taki*

Nature

banyan tree	ガジュマル	*gajumaru*
bat	こうもり	*kōmori*
bird	鳥	*tori*
boar	イノシシ	*inoshishi*
butterfly	蝶	*chō*
cat	猫	*neko*
coral	サンゴ	*sango*
cow	牛	*ushi*
crab	カニ	*kani*
cycad	ソテツ	*sotetsu*
deer	シカ / 鹿	*shika*
dog	犬	*inu*
dolphin	イルカ	*iruka*
dugong	儒艮	*jyugon*
fern	しだ	*shida*
firefly	蛍	*hotaru*
fish	魚	*sakana*
flower	花	*hana*
frog	カエル	*kaeru*
horse	馬	*uma*
insect	虫	*mushi*
Iriomote cat	ヤマネコ	*yamaneko*
jellyfish	くらげ	*kurage*
leaf	葉	*ha*
lizard	蜥蜴	*tokage*
manta ray	マンタ	*manta*
monkey	猿	*saru*

pig	豚	*buta*
rail	くいな	*kuina*
rat	鼠	*nezumi*
ray	えい	*ei*
shark	サメ/ 鮫	*same*
sheep	羊	*hitsuji*
snake	蛇	*hebi*
spider	くも	*kumo*
starfish	ひとで	*hitode*
tree	木	*ki*
turtle	亀	*kame*
whale	クジラ	*kujira*

Miscellaneous

ambulance	救急車	*kyūkyūsha*
festival	祭	*matsuri*
flower	花	*hana*
foreigner	外国人	*gaikokujin*
Japanese person	日本人	*Nihonjin*
karaoke	カラオケ	*karaoke*
karate	空手	*karate*
police	警察	*keisatsu*
prefecture	県	*ken*

Appendix 2

GLOSSARY

aosa/aasa	あおさ・アーサ	green laver seaweed
asagi/ashage	アサギ・アシャゲ	a building where noro (priestesses) perform religious festivals
awamori	泡盛	alcoholic beverage unique to Okinawa Prefecture
bashōfu	芭蕉布	traditional material made from banana stalk fibres
bingata	紅型	traditional stencilled resist dyeing technique from Ryūkyū Kingdom
chanpuruu/chanpurū	チャンプルー	traditional dish similar to a stir-fry, the word means 'to mix'
Eisaa/Eisā	エイサー	folk dance popular at festivals
fukugi	福木	evergreen tree, also called the happiness tree, that was used in villages as a windbreak against typhoons
gajumaru	ガジュマル	banyan tree
gooya/gōyā	ゴーヤ	bitter melon popular in Okinawa-ken
habu	ハブ	deadly venomous snake found on many of the islands
izakaya	居酒屋	informal Japanese bar
Jōmon	縄文	earliest major culture of prehistoric Japan
juushii/jūshī	ジューシー	rice dish from Okinawa Prefecture
kaiseki	懐石	sophisticated traditional Japanese cuisine brought in multiple courses
kara-age	唐揚げ	deep-fried food, usually chicken, lightly coated in flour or starch
kokutō	黒糖	brown sugar, farmed extensively across the Nansei-shotō
kokutō shōchū	黒糖焼酎	shōchū made with brown sugar, famous on the Amami Islands
matsuri	祭り	festival
mimigaa/mimigā	ミミガー	traditional Okinawan dish of boiled or pickled pig's ear, dressed with vinegar and soy sauce and served thinly sliced
minshuku	民宿	bed-and-breakfast style accommodation
mozuku	もずく	type of edible algae

Nansei-shotō	南西諸島	the southwest islands; the entire archipelago chain
noro	ノロ	priestess of the Ryūkyū religion
omakase	お任せ	the act of leaving the choice of meal to the chef; as recommended menu
onsen	温泉	hot spring, often natural
rafutee/rafutē	ラフテー	pork belly stewed in brown sugar and soy
saataa andagii	サーターアンダギー	spherical doughnut
satapanbin	さたぱんびん	Miyako word for saataa andagii
sanshin	三振	stringed instrument native to the archipelago, also known as a *shamisen*
Satsuma	薩摩	historical southern domain, roughly correlating to modern Kagoshima Prefecture
sentō	銭湯	communal bathhouse, more local and basic than onsen
shiikwaasaa	シークヮーサー	type of sour citrus particular to the islands
shiisaa/shīsā	シーサー	mythical lion-dog figure, found in statues across the archipelago
Shimazu	島津	Samurai clan who ruled Satsuma domain
Shintō	神道	religion of Japan
shōchū	焼酎	distilled alcoholic beverage
shōgun	将軍	military ruler of Japan
shōten	商店	small shop
soba	そば	buckwheat noodles, of which there are unique varieties on the islands
sooki/sōki	ソーキ	stewed pork spare ribs
sotetsu	蘇鉄・ソテツ	cycad palm, poisonous to eat unless properly prepared
sugi	杉	Japanese cedar, prolific on Yakushima
Taira/Heike	平良	important family of feudal Japan
takoyaki	たこ焼き	deep-fried dough balls with octopus in the centre, covered in toppings and sauce
teishoku	定食	set meal that usually features main, soup, side and rice – often very good value and hearty
tsumugi	紬	traditional fabric made of short waste silk fibres
umibudō	海ぶどう	type of algae that pops in the mouth, translates as 'sea grapes'
utaki/ontake/ugan	御嶽	types of shrines found in the archipelago, often in natural spaces
yamaneko	ヤマネコ	endangered wildcat endemic to Iriomote
yuta	ユタ	female shamans or mediums from Ryūkyū religion

Appendix 3

FURTHER INFORMATION

BOOKS Books on the Battle of Okinawa are legion; only a handful are listed below, but many more are worth seeking out. English-language books on the nature, culture, geography and even fiction of the archipelago are much harder to come by. Those that do exist focus heavily on Okinawa-hontō, with areas like the Miyako, Amami and Yaeyama almost entirely forgotten.

History

David, Saul *Crucible of Hell: The Heroism and Tragedy of Okinawa, 1945* Hachette Books, 2020. Narrative from award-winning historian David, showing the battle from the side of US troops, drawing on archival research and survivor accounts.

Herndon, Booton *Redemption at Hacksaw Ridge* Remnant Publications, 2016. The story of army medic and conscientious objector Desmond Doss, made famous in the 2016 film *Hacksaw Ridge*, who went into the battle unarmed to save his comrades.

Higa, Tomiko *The Girl with the White Flag* Kodansha International, 2013. Memoir of seven-year-old Tomiko Higa's survival on the Okinawan battlefield – made famous by photos of her holding a white flag.

Kerr, George H *Okinawa: The History of an Island People* Tuttle Publishing, 2018. The definitive English-language history of Okinawa and the Ryūkyū Kingdom, from 1314 to the late 20th century.

Keyso, Ruth Ann *Women of Okinawa: Nine Voices from a Garrison Island* Cornell University Press, 2000. Nine Okinawan women across three generations tell their stories of invasion, occupation and life on the island today.

Kuwahara, Yasuo and Allred, Gordon T *Kamikaze: A Japanese Pilot's Own Spectacular Story of the Famous Suicide Squadrons* American Legacy Media, 2013. The story of being a kamikaze from one of their own.

Odachi, Kazuo *Memoirs of a Kamikaze: A World War II Pilot's Inspiring Story of Survival, Honor and Reconciliation* Tuttle Publishing, 2020. Another first-person kamikaze tale, this time from Kazuo Odachi, who signed up as a teen. Harrowing and heartfelt.

Ryukyu Shimpo (ed) *Descent into Hell: Civilian Memories of the Battle of Okinawa* MerwinAsia, 2014. Local newspaper *Ryūkyū Shimpo* carried out hundreds of interviews to tell the story of local experiences of the battle, collating them into a much-needed, if harrowing book.

Smits, Gregory *Visions of Ryukyu: Identity and Ideology in Early-Modern Thought and Politics* University of Hawaii Press, 2017. A book looking at the geopolitical side of the Ryūkyū Kingdom, its relationships with China and Japan and beyond.

Yahara, Hiromichi *The Battle for Okinawa* Trade Paper Press, 2002. The Battle of Okinawa as told by a Japanese colonel.

Fiction and creative non-fiction

Bird, Sarah *Above the East China Sea* Alfred A Knopf, 2014. Novel about the Battle of Okinawa and modern-day Okinawa, from the perspective of two teenage girls.

Brina, Elizabeth Miki *Speak, Okinawa* Vintage, 2022. Haunting and touching memoir – Brina reckons with her cultural heritage, belonging and the complex relationship between her parents, an Okinawan war bride and a Vietnam veteran.

Higa, Susumu *Okinawa* Fantagraphics, 2023. Two-volume manga by Okinawa's preeminent *mangaka*, intertwining stories of modern day life, US occupation and spirituality.

Higashi, Mineo and Ōshiro, Tatsuhiro *Okinawa: Two Postwar Novellas* University of California Berkley, 1989. Akutagawa Prize-winning novellas from two of Okinawa's most influential writers. Ōshiro's 'Cocktail Party' is the story of a father whose daughter is raped by a US soldier, while the narrator of Mineo's 'Child of Okinawa' is a boy growing up in a bar-brothel near a US base.

Medoruma, Shun *In the Woods of Memory* Stone Bridge Press, 2017. Powerful novel that tells of the sexual assault of a 17-year-old girl by four US soldiers during the Battle of Okinawa, and her friend's attempted revenge.

Rabson, Steve (ed) *Islands of Protest: Japanese Literature from Okinawa* University of Hawaii Press, 2016. Excellent anthology of stories, poetry and dramas on Okinawan culture and nature, written by locals and experts.

Culture

Bishop, Mark *Okinawan Karate: Teachers, Styles and Secret Techniques* Tuttle Publishing, 1999. Journeying from ancient China to modern day Okinawa, Bishop charts the teachers who evolved the sport, as well as styles and techniques.

Nelson, Christopher T *Dancing with the Dead: Memory, Performance, and Everyday Life in Postwar Okinawa* Duke University Press Books, 2008. Evocative book looking at the post-war transformation of Okinawan culture.

Takagi, Rin, Iwabuchi, Deborah and Enda, Kazuko *Traditional Cuisine of the Ryukyu Islands: A History of Health and Healing* Japan Publishing Industry Foundation for Culture, 2020. A rare book on Ryūkyū cuisine, this is a modern version of the Gozen honzō – a book charting court cuisine and its medicinal effects.

Tetsuhiro, Hokama *History and Traditions of Okinawan Karate* Masters Publishing, 2009. Hokama is a karate sensei and one of the most prolific writers on Okinawan martial art history, but few of his works are translated into English. This one covers history, pioneers, evolution and training guides of karate.

Willcox, Bradley J, Willcox, D Craig and Suzuki, Makoto *The Okinawa Diet Plan: Get Leaner, Live Longer, and Never Feel Hungry* Harmony/Rodale, 2005. A *New York Times* bestseller exploring the 'secrets' of the healthy Okinawan diet and lifestyle.

WEBSITES
Tourist information

w **kagoshima-kankou.com** Official travel website of Kagoshima Prefecture.

w **visitokinawajapan.com** Comprehensive website on Okinawa Prefecture tourism, with recommendations on sights, tours and regions.

Pre-travel information

w **fitfortravel.nhs.uk** NHS website for travel vaccination information.

w **mofa.go.jp** Visa and consular information from the Japan Ministry of Foreign Affairs.

Index

Page numbers in **bold** indicate major entries; those in *italics* indicate maps.

INDEX OF ADVERTISERS